ERRATA

STUDIES IN THE COGNITIVE BASIS OF LANGUAGE DEVELOPMENT
Harry Beilin with the collaboration
of Barbara Lust/Hinda G. Sack/Helen-Marie Natt

The sixth line in Footnote 5 on page 191 should read as follows:
"affirmation, e.g., the exclusion of A given $\overline{A}$. The other determines the affirmation of a"

The eighth line in Footnote 5 on page 191 should read as follows:
"complement of another set, e.g., $U - A = \overline{A}$. Psychological studies of negation usually"

The third line in the last text paragraph on page 192 should be preceded by:
"$(\overline{A \cap B}) \equiv (\overline{A} \cup \overline{B})$ and the complement of union is intersection"

The sixth line down in the third column across in Table 7–1 on page 221 should read as follows:
"B must be absent."

The last two entries at the right of the abscissa of Fig. 7–7 on page 246 should read as follows:
"$(\overline{A \vee B})$ $(\overline{A \vee B})$"

The twenty-fourth text line down from the top of page 256 should read as follows:
"other $(\overline{B})$ classes were given."

The third to last entry from the right in the table column heads in Table 8–7 on page 294 should read as follows:
"$\overline{A} \vee \overline{B}$"

The third text line down from the top on page 394 should read as follows:
"parts which must be related by the operation of inclusion to the whole B."

The column heads at the top of the text table on page 395 should read as follows:
"A_1 A_1'"

Studies in the Cognitive Basis of Language Development

THE CHILD PSYCHOLOGY SERIES
EXPERIMENTAL AND THEORETICAL ANALYSES OF CHILD BEHAVIOR

EDITOR
DAVID S. PALERMO
DEPARTMENT OF PSYCHOLOGY
THE PENNSYLVANIA STATE UNIVERSITY
UNIVERSITY PARK, PENNSYLVANIA

Studies in the Cognitive Basis of Language Development

Harry Beilin
Graduate School and University Center
The City University of New York
New York, New York

with the collaboration of

Barbara Lust

Hinda G. Sack

Helen-Marie Natt
Graduate School and University Center
The City University of New York
New York, New York

ACADEMIC PRESS   *New York San Francisco London*   *1975*

A Subsidiary of Harcourt Brace Jovanovich, Publishers

ACADEMIC PRESS, INC.
111 Fifth Avenue, New York, New York 10003

71221

United Kingdom Edition published by
ACADEMIC PRESS, INC. (LONDON) LTD.
24/28 Oval Road, London NW1

Library of Congress Cataloging in Publication Data

Beilin, Harry.
    Studies in the cognitive basis of language develop-
ment.

    (Child psychology series)
    Bibliography: p.
    Includes index.
    1.   Cognition (Child psychology)   2.   Children—Lan-
guage.   I.   Title.   [DNLM: 1.   Cognition—In infancy
and childhood.   2.   Language development.   3.   Psycholinguistics.   LB1139.L3 B422s]
BF723.C5B39   155.4'13   74-27515
ISBN 0−12−085650−6

PRINTED IN THE UNITED STATES OF AMERICA

Dedicated to the memory of Sarah Beilin

Contents

Preface

In this volume we first report on a series of studies that delineate the influence of cognition on language development. The results of these studies are then considered within the framework of findings obtained by others. Although that influence is shown to be great, there, nevertheless, exists considerable autonomy in the linguistic system that is not accounted for directly by the development of cognitive structure. The principal common denominator between language and cognitive development is logical structure that defines the fundamental properties of both systems. The evidence for this is detailed in the various chapters of this volume.

The aspects of development we selected to investigate were those most likely to show the presence of congruent, logical structures in language and cognition. They are: the passive construction, which is formally congruent with the reversibility feature of operational thought (discussed in Chapters 2 and 3); time and number conceptions, which are paralleled by time and number language (presented in Chapters 4 and 5); and finally, the logical operations of cognition, which, in part, find their parallels in the functions of the linguistic connectives (discussed in Chapters 6, 7, and 8). The final chapter (Chapter 9) summarizes our results and integrates them with those of others.

The influence of Piaget will be evident not only in our work but in that of others throughout this volume. The force of Piaget's recent influence with respect to language development has been to offset Chomsky's original thesis that the development of language structure is independent of extra-linguistic cognition. Nevertheless, Piaget's original view that language merely represents the content of cognition has also proven to be inadequate. What emerges now is the thesis that a common system that is structured in a logical form (whether described best by propositional, modal, or other logic is uncertain) determines the form of both cognitive and linguistic development. This volume reports the evidence in favor of this thesis and is its principal general contribution. Its specific contribution is to detail the relation between logic, cognition, and language development, and to specify cognitive processes that affect linguistic change particularly in the period from 2 to 7 years of age.

As with all research programs of this magnitude, many people have contributed to it with prodigious amounts of effort, technical skill, and ideas. Our thanks cannot be too generous to them, they are: Ann Marie Agnello, Sandra J. Dalton, Alice Finer, Irene S. Gillman, Jacob Kagan, Ruth Mechaneck, Ann-Marie Pictet, Rhea Rabinowitz, Ilana Reich, George Spontak, Joyce Weil, and Lenesa White. We are particularly grateful to Valerie B. Jordan whose contribution to the later phases of the work were important to its successful completion.

But above all we are indebted to the many children on whom all the data are based, who played our "games" with such good-will, and to the many public and private school personnel who made their facilities available to us. We are in debt to the Public School System of New York City for permitting us to collect data in a number of schools. Dr. Morris Pincus and Mr. Howard Frome are to be cited in particular for being especially helpful over a long period of time. The Nursery School of Temple Shaaray Tefila in New York City was cooperative in more than one of our studies, and we are grateful to the Directors, Mrs. Leah Leshefsky and Mrs. Minna Goldman for that. The Whitby School in Greenwich, Connecticut was a most important source of help and we thank the past-Director John Blessington for that assistance. The teachers and staff of all these schools were most helpful to us in all our work. Needless to say, neither the children nor the schools asked anything in return for the valuable resources they gave us. We hope that the product of our efforts recorded in this volume measures up to the value of theirs.

The Computer Center of the City University of New York Graduate School and University Center was generous in making its services available to us. In particular we thank Larry Jordan for valuable advice on statistical and computer analyses.

To the National Institutes of Health we owe a special debt for extensive research support through grants from the National Institute of Mental Health (MH 5681-01-02) and the National Institute of Child Health and Human Development (HD-00924-03-11).

Dr. D. Terence Langendoen was most helpful in his advice on a number of linguistic issues, although if any errors in fact or judgement have been committed, the fault is wholly our own.

Finally, we wish to acknowledge the aid given us by the City University of New York Graduate School and University Center and its President, Dr. Harold Proshansky, and the University Dean of Teacher Education, Dr. Max Weiner, in enabling us to complete this project.

Studies in the Cognitive Basis of Language Development

1

Linguistic Theory and Its Psychological Significance

The contemporary revolution within linguistics, which initially focused on Chomsky's theory, drew the attention of other outside disciplines. As a consequence, some social sciences including psychology considered linguistic theory as a possible conceptual model for their own disciplines. This initial enthusiasm has subsequently waned.

The changes in transformational theory that have occurred in the relatively short time span from 1957, when *Syntactic Structures* (Chomsky) appeared, to the present have been quite considerable. From all appearances the two most important developments, the introduction of a semantic component in 1965 and the introduction of surface structure into semantic interpretation in 1970–1972 (Chomsky, 1971; Chomsky, 1972), were changes ostensibly due to linguistic research. It would appear so if one judged solely from references cited in linguistic papers. However, this may not be entirely the case.

The reactions of psychologists to the implications of the 1957 version of Chomsky's grammar were almost immediate. Their first response was an attempt to establish the psychological reality of the transformational generative model. When it was discovered that there was no direct parallel between Chomsky's competence model and psychological performance, they began to look more closely at the competence model. The resulting examination led to dissatisfaction similar to that among linguists. Even before the 1965 version appeared, dissatisfaction was also evident concerning the effects of surface structure upon meaning, as well as with linguistic notions of language acquisition. The extent to which these psycholinguistic researches affected the insights of linguists is not documented.

Although the influence of psychological research upon linguists is not at all clear, there can be no question as to the reverse. Many linguistic

1

issues have engaged psychologists' attention. Here we will present some of the more general issues; in later chapters we will detail some of the specific ones.

The Creative Nature of Language

The implication in Chomskyan theory that language is produced and comprehended through a "creative" process has been particularly important in making the theory attractive to psychologists. In part, as Chomsky has implied, this inference is based upon a misconception of the theory. Some psychologists have taken the notion of "generative" to mean that the ability to produce an infinite number of novel and at the same time grammatical sentences is made possible by the possession of a finite set of rules of grammar possessed by the speaker. The hearer, in turn, comprehends the same set of sentences by possession of the same rules of grammar.

Psychologists could easily infer this from Chomsky's attack on Skinner (Chomsky, 1959), which contested the behaviorist notion that language was acquired through imitation, reinforcement, and generalization processes. The fact that the child's many "novel" utterances could not be accounted for by these processes suggested instead that more creative processes were required to account for them. Chomsky soon made it clear, however, that generative was to be understood in its mathematical sense, referring to the derivation of sentences based on a set of rules as a computer would that is programmed to produce all the possible combinations of a set of elements, or to realize all the possible derivations implicit in a mathematical formula. This creative capacity referred to the implicit ability or competence of the speaker–hearer and did not refer to the actual production or comprehension of sentences. The issue became important when actual language production and comprehension was tested in the expectation of providing psychological reality to the conception of the generative language user. What is increasingly evident is that no clear conception of what is meant psychologically by the creative or generative features of language is available. To many psychologists the competence–performance distinction appears to be increasingly ambiguous. With the more recent refinements in generative transformational theory, the competence–performance distinction has become more important to Chomsky, however, instead of less so, particularly in the debate with the generative semanticists over the nature of deep structure. Chomsky disputes assertions that a semantic component is *prior to* a syntactic component in sentence generation because this establishes *order* in a competence model that inherently requires no order as suggested above, Chomsky claims that only in a performance model is a specific order necessary.

Despite Chomsky's restriction of the linguistic meaning of generative, the explanatory value of the concept to psychologists has great appeal, and to some it appears to be necessary to an explanation of language behavior.

Linguistic Levels

The significance of the concept of levels in language structure that generative transformational grammar proposes has not been lost on psycholinguistics. The idea that the surface structure of a sentence is not determined by processes directly associated with the production of the sentence according to a theory of sequential ordering of lexical units but, instead, to syntactic processes operating at a *deeper* level whose structure is not in one-to-one correspondence with the surface structure has been a notion of considerable power for those psychologists who were dissatisfied with behaviorist explanations of language behavior. The notion of a covert system of linguistic rules and structures that determines surface behavior has had immediate appeal for cognitive theorists who were attempting to explain cognitive behavior by models that were similarly based on the operation of *mental* processes. It also has had appeal for information-processing theorists who were attempting to define cognition in terms of a model designed to specify the components of the processes that function between input (stimulus) and output (response) conditions.

A number of issues within linguistic theory are concerned with the nature of deep and surface structures and the transitions between them. The principal difference between generative semantics and generative transformational theory, in fact, is in their respective interpretations of the rule systems at each level. The psychological issues are of a similar nature. Immediately following the appearance of Chomskyan theory, George Miller and his students (G. A. Miller, 1962) attempted to provide psychological reality to the surface structure—deep structure distinction through their studies of the so-called derivation theory of complexity (DTC). These studies provided the impetus for an extensive examination of the transformational thesis. The psycholinguistic notion, as the linguistic, holds that the number of transformational operations applied to a base-produced phrase-marker (of a kernel sentence) determines the difficulty (or complexity) of producing or comprehending a surface structure sentence. The DTC, as will be indicated in Chapter 3, was given little support in a significant number of investigations, although more recently, the complexity thesis has been revitalized by information-processing theorists.

Despite differences, the notion of linguistic levels appears to be generally accepted among linguists and psycholinguists. The principal concern is over the nature of deep structure in that it is not at all clear that the deepest level is linguistic. Some psychologists (e.g., Piaget and Sinclair) contend that the ultimate level of linguistic control is an abstract cognitive structure that informs both linguistic and nonlinguistic cognition. This argument will be taken up in later chapters.

Meaning

Philosophers, linguists, and psycholinguists have pursued a satisfactory definition of meaning with only moderate success, and a number of definitions have varying degrees of acceptability. Despite the lack of a universally accepted conception of meaning, many linguistic and psycho-logical theories are constructed with one or another tentative concept. Chomsky's theory, for example, characterizes the grammar as the rule system that correlates meaning with a phonetic representation. This use of meaning can be differentiated into that which is associated with *thought* and that which is represented in language. Chomsky is principally con-cerned with the representation of meaning. Meaning appears in his theory in the only somewhat less-troublesome notions of "semantic representa-tion," "semantic reading," and "semantic interpretation," although he appears to accept two levels of meaning, propositional meaning for the sentence as a whole and referential meaning for the lexicon. The earlier version of generative theory implied that syntactic form (at the deep level) embodied or determined meaning and was the starting point for its transla-tion into surface form. The later, standard theory, which corrected the evident inadequacy of the notion of syntactic form embodying and deter-mining meaning, modified the theory to make the determination of meaning more definite by assigning one source of meaning in the lexicon, and provided a specific (semantic) component with a set of interpretive rules for introducing or extracting meaning—from deep structure. The extended standard theory (EST) goes one step further by recognizing that meaning is not solely determined by the base and the semantic component *but* is determined, in part, by processes in sentence surface structure. The generative semanticists (e.g., Fillmore, 1968; Fillmore, 1971; G. Lakoff, 1971; McCawley, 1971) hold that deep structure, if it exists at all, exists in the form of semantic representation that is acted on and transformed into surface structure by means of syntactic rules.

For psycholinguists, focus is principally on meaning and thought; linguistic issues involving syntactic structure, etc. are secondary—for most linguists the reverse is true. Thus, although the idea that linguistic structure embodies meaning had immediate appeal for cognitive psychol-ogists of a structuralist bent, a large number of investigations have shown the earlier conceptions to be incomplete, if not incorrect. Psycholinguistic studies almost immediately after the appearance of *Syntactic Structures* reported that semantic considerations associated with surface-structure processing played a role in sentence comprehension. They also detailed the various ways in which meaning enters into the processing of language so that it can now be said that some progress has been made in developing a linguistic processing model in which the representation of meaning plays a critical role. Where there is still little clarity is in the relation between nonlinguistic and linguistic "meaning."

Language Acquisition

When Chomsky attacked behavioristic approaches to language learning, he declared that language acquisition could not be accounted for by control from external stimulation or contingency management (Chomsky, 1968). He proposed, instead, that language competence was natively given, although he did not deny that, through maturation, language competence could be realized in a progressive fashion (Chomsky, 1968). Although basic linguistic structures were said to be universal, their realization could occur only within different linguistic communities of different languages. It was proposed that each child is endowed with a genetically given acquisition device (LAD) that abstracts syntactic rules from the limited language corpus experienced by the child in accord with the rules of an unexplained grammar (McNeill, 1970). The origin of linguistic systems, genetically controlled or stimulus controlled, has been a matter of debate among psychologists. Disagreements with the nativist position comes from Piagetians (e.g., Sinclair-de-Zwart, 1973) who argues that language, like other cognitive structure systems, is constructed and not innately programmed, and from neo-behaviorists (such as Osgood) who hold that language capacities are acquired through learning, at least in part, or that imitation and modeling play a greater role in language acquisition than Chomsky purports to be the case (Bandura, 1965).

Chomsky's recent proposals in the *extended standard theory* (Chomsky, 1971; Chomsky, 1972), which reflects a willingness to accept a place for semantic interpretation in surface structure, suggest a type of meaning representation that may differ from syntactically and lexically determined meaning. How much of a role Chomsky is now willing to assign to stimulus control or social experience in the development of language is difficult to say, but an accommodation to some such notions would be necessary to account for rule acquisition whose origin may be different from a natively given acquisition device.

These issues far from exhaust those with which contemporary research is concerned. In the chapters that follow a number of these general issues are provided greater specification. To varying degrees, the psycholinguistic investigations related to these questions are reviewed, and we present data from our own research that bear upon these same issues.

2

The Passive: Linguistic and Psychological Theory

Harry Beilin and Hinda G. Sack

The studies of the passive reported here and in Chapter 3 were undertaken in part to examine the applicability of linguistic theory to the explanation of language acquisition. It was assumed that psychological experimentation with the passive and other linguistic forms would provide a test of the applicability of such theory to psychological data. Our intent also was to test the alternative possibility that cognitive theory would provide a better explanatory model for at least some of the facts of linguistic acquisition than certain extant formulations.

The oft-cited passive was chosen for study because of its interest to linguists and psychologists as a model case for the test of alternative theories. In this chapter we review both the linguistic and psychological literature that bears on the passive to lay the groundwork for the report of the studies that appear in Chapter 3.

Linguistic Theory and the Passive

In *Syntactic Structures* (Chomsky, 1957), the relation of passive to active sentences provided one of the prime arguments for the superiority of transformational theory over phrase structure and other types of linguistic description. The consequent assignment of the active sentence to the kernel with the passive as a derivation from the kernel was part of the goal "to limit the kernel in such a way that the terminal strings underlying the kernel sentences are derived by a simple system of phrase structure and can provide the basis from which all sentences can be derived by simple transformations: obligatory transformations in the case of the kernel, obligatory *and* optional transformations in the case of non-kernel sentences [Chomsky, 1957, p. 61]."

The simple, active declarative strings to which the passive transformation was said to apply has the structure (1) *Mary hits John,* and the resulting passive sentence has the structure (2) *John is hit by Mary* or *John is being hit by Mary.*

$$(1) \quad NP_1 - Aux - V - NP_2$$
$$(2) \quad NP_2 - Aux + be + n - V - by + NP_1$$

The grammatical *subject* (NP_1) in the active (in 1) is the grammatical *object* in the passive (2), and the grammatical *subject* of the passive (NP_2) is the grammatical *object* of the active. At the phrase structure level the two constructions have the same representation, that is, NP_1 is the logical subject of both (1) and (2). In the active construction, the *logical* subject and object are congruent with the *grammatical* subject and object. In the passive, the *logical* subject is the *grammatical* object and the *logical* object is the *grammatical* subject. The mechanism that achieves this reversal is the passive transformation.

In the 1957 version of transformational theory, two properties were ascribed to transformations, in addition to the fact that they imposed structure on the sentence. First, transformations were applied in a defined order to ensure that certain grammatical features of a sentence, such as agreement in number between the grammatical subject and the verbal element, were established. Secondly, some transformations, as already indicated, were characterized as obligatory, others as optional. An obligatory transformation, negatively defined, was one that if not applied results in the generation of an ungrammatical string rather than a grammatical sentence. *"Kernel"* sentences were said to be produced when obligatory transformations were applied to the terminal strings of the phrase structure grammar. Transformations were applied to kernel sentences (or more precisely to the terminal strings that underlie kernel sentences), or to the products of earlier transformations. The passive transformation was an example of an optional transformation. That is, whether or not the transformation was applied, the result was still a sentence. The distinction between kernel and derived sentences was said to be required to make the rules of the grammar as simple as possible. For this reason the active sentence was in the kernel and not the passive, rather than the reverse. It also led to irreversibility; it was easier to carry out a transformation in one direction than the other, i.e., transform an active into a passive than vice versa.

The kernel sentences and sentences derived from the same terminal string through optional transformation were said to yield a "sentence family." Sentences in the same family differed according to their transformational histories in line with the number of transformations involved, and in line with their transformational complexity. Sentences differing by one transformation (such as an active and passive sentence) were more closely related than sentences differing by two transformations (such as passives and negatives, or actives and passive negatives).

In *Aspects* (Chomsky, 1965) with extensive changes in the theory, the place of transformations in the grammar was altered as were some features of the passive transformation itself. The restriction of the *base* to a system of phrase structure rules was now considered to be a "mistake," and the base component in *Aspects* was "enriched" by including transformational rules in it, although this was done under rather restricted conditions. In the standard theory the restrictions were associated with the subcategorizational rules of the base. By the strict subcategorization principle, certain elements are internal to the VP and others external to it. One of the internal elements is a marker for passivation associated with the presence of a **manner adverbial**. That is, a verb will appear in the frame: NP — Aux — V—NP—... by passive—... and "undergo the passive transformation only if it is positively specified, in the lexicon, for the strict subcategorization feature [— NP ∩ Manner], in which case it will also take Manner Adverbials freely [p. 104]."

In the *extended standard theory* (Chomsky, 1972, p. 41), the underlying structure of the passive is characterized as "roughly" NP—Aux—V— NP — by Δ, where "by Δ" is an agent phrase to means and manner adverbials. The passive operation is composed of two transformations: in the first, it is replaced by the subject NP; the second takes the NP to the right of the verb and inserts it into the position located by the subject. The first transformation is called **agent postposing**, and the second transformation is **NP preposing**. Both transformations are applied if the proposition is a full sentence.

Such transformations are said to map the base structures onto well-formed structures close to the surface structures. A set of rules generates items that become surface structures upon being applied to the product of the last cycle of transformation rules. As indicated, passivizibility is a property only of verbs, and V is the only lexical category that is mentioned in the "structure index" associated with the transformation.

In *Syntactic Structures* (Chomsky, 1957) the passive as well as other transforms were said to have different meanings from the kernel (active) or its underlying terminal string. The optional transformations, as distinct from the obligatory transformations of the kernel, were permitted to introduce meaning change. Part of Chomsky's argument, however, was that the ostensive lack of meaning equivalence (synonymy) of some active and passive sentences could not in itself to be taken as the basis of a formal grammar.

J. J. Katz and Postal (1964), however, argued that the active and passive could have the same meaning. They based their argument on the syntactic consideration that only those verbs that take manner adverbials could be passivized. The underlying structure of the passive has a manner adverb that, because the dummy marker has no semantic content, the semantic interpretation of the active and passive may be the same even though the underlying forms may be different. The passive is thus said to be derived from the underlying P marker indicated above and not from the P marker that underlies the corresponding active, as was true in *Syntactic Structures*.

In *Aspects*, Chomsky makes the claim that transformational facts account for (cognitive) synonymy, as in the active—passive pair *John is easy for us to please—It is easy for us to please John* He notes the exception to this generalization, however, in the pair *John strikes one as pompous—I regard John as pompous* in which the meaning relation between the two sentences cannot be accounted for in the same way. He recognized that some mechanism was needed to account for the latter relation, as neither lexical features nor deep structure were adequate to account for the meaning relation between the active and passive sentences.

In the *extended standard theory*, Chomsky (1972) accepts the fact that focus and presupposition, as well as comment, reference, and scope of logical elements are determined by other than deep structure. They appear to be due, in part, at least to the properties of surface structure as in the following sentences:

The sonata is easy to play on this violin
This violin is easy to play the sonata on

These sentences share the same grammatical relations; they are reasonable paraphrases of each other and have the same truth conditions. Nevertheless, they seem different in meaning in that the first makes an assertion about the sonata and the second about the violin. Chomsky does not believe that their deep structure can account for these differences in interpretation. In fact, the only way to account for them is in terms of some of their surface structure characteristics. This, of course, shows that the EST has come a long way from the 1957 version.

Psychological Reality of Linguistic Structure: The Derivational Theory of Complexity (DTC)

Not long after the appearance of *Syntactic Structures* (Chomsky, 1957), transformational relations were given a *psychological* interpretation in the proposal that a direct relation exists between "transformational complexity" and the "perception" and interpretation of sentences as complex (G. A. Miller, 1962; G. A. Miller & Chomsky, 1963). As a consequence, a surface structure sentence with a longer or more complex derivational (i.e., transformational) history was more likely to be judged or perceived as complex than a sentence with a shorter or less complex derivational history. This thesis, which has come to be known as the Derivational Theory of Complexity (DTC), led to considerable theoretical speculation and research because it was considered a critical test of generative transformational theory (Fodor & Garrett, 1966, 1967; Garrett & Fodor, 1968).

Fodor and Garrett (1966, 1967) in reviewing the early experiments that tested this thesis (McMahon, 1963; Mehler, 1963; G. A. Miller, 1962; Miller & McKean, 1964; McMahon, 1963; Savin & Perchonock, 1965) concluded that it was not supported. Fodor and Garrett (1966) made the strong claim, however, that, even though the evidence was negative, it was not sufficient to disconfirm the postulated theory of the grammar. As they put it, in an oft-quoted statement:

> A grammar is simply an axiomatic representation of an infinite set of structural descriptions, and the internal evidence in favor of the structural descriptions modern grammars generate is so strong that it is difficult to imagine their succumbing to any purely experimental disconfirmation. Rather, one would best interpret negative data as showing ... the relation between competence and performance models ... as abstract, the degree of abstractness being proportional to the failure of formal features of derivations to correspond to performance variables [1966, p. 152].

This assertion has been questioned on empirical grounds (e.g., Dingwall, 1971), but it also appears dubious on a priori grounds in light of Chomsky's (1968) claim that linguistic theories are also psychological theories. The force of Fodor and Garrett's assertion would obtain legitimacy only in a weaker version stating that an abstract theory is not easily disconfirmed by noncritical individual experiments. Abstract theory, however, can be disconfirmed by experiments that test a network of inferences or hypotheses drawn from the theory. If this were not so, generative transformational theory could make no claims to being scientific. It would not be empirically confirmable and at best could lay claim to the status of a logical theory, if not a metaphysical one. In any case, history has overtaken the claim in that many of the changes in generative transformational theory have come about through "empirical" evidence, even if defined loosely in terms of linguists' intuitions into the grammar.

Many of the studies undertaken as a test of the DTC were studies of sentence comprehension. A review of these studies reveals the following:

1. The psychological implications drawn from transformational theory (of the standard theory version) have not received consistent support. Sentence negativity (Gough, 1965; McMahon, 1963; Slobin, 1966), reversibility—whether an object can act as the subject of a sentence or not (Slobin, 1966), truth value—whether a pictorial representation verifies a sentence or not (Gough, 1965), and truncation—whether the passive to the sentence has an agent or not (Slobin, 1968b) all affect comprehension in ways not predicted by transformational theory. The principal alternative interpretations given these findings are that they conform to the influence of constraints of uncertain origin or are associated with surface structure constraints rather than to rules associated with deep structure.

2. The "kernelization" hypothesis that sentences are decoded by the hearer via a detransformation to an active declarative string, which is ostensibly easier to comprehend than the passive, receives weak support in some studies (McMahon, 1963; Morris, Rankine, & Reber, 1967) and is disconfirmed in others (Gough, 1966; Wright, 1969).

3. Whether a "kernelization" process operates or not, a number of studies point to other processes and effects that influence sentence comprehension. One is the **voice-match effect** (Wright, 1969), which

suggests that the match or mismatch of sentence constituents with questions affects comprehension. The **focal consistency effect** (proposed by K. H. Smith, Coriell, & McMahon, 1971 ; K. H. Smith & McMahon, 1970) suggests that the focus of attention created by sentence form is more critical to comprehension than the matching of constituents. The coordination of linguistic to perceived nonlinguistic events, in addition to syntactic complexity itself, also affects sentence understanding (Huttenlocher, Eisenberg, & Strauss, 1968).

Thus, although the DTC is not concerned with the passive transformation as such, many DTC studies utilized the passive, and Chomsky himself has used it in illustrating the virtues of transformational theory. Although interest in the DTC has declined, together with the view that syntactic structure is the critical determinant of psychological performance, the notion of complexity has been revived by psychologists interested in an information-processing approach to language comprehension. More will be said of this development later on.

Nature and Functions of the Passive

It seems necessary to consider (1) why most languages contain a passive form when it is a fairly rare occurrence in spoken and written language; (2) why, if an active sentence and its passive transform are usually considered to have the same meaning, at least in some sense, two forms are needed to express the same meaning; (3) if the two forms are needed, as they apparently are, what bearing their formal structural and semantic properties have upon comprehension and production.

Infrequency of Use

The passive form is used relatively little in speech and writing. In fact, the less spontaneous and more formal the speech, the greater the production of the passive (Goldman-Eisler & Cohen, 1970). About 70% of the passives that do appear in the works of English authors are in the agentless, or truncated (e.g., *The cup was broken*), passive form (Jespersen, 1964 ; Svartvik, 1966). It is difficult to assess, however, whether the difficulty of the passive is due to its infrequent use or whether its limited use results from the relative difficulty of the construction.

Derivational Complexity

The studies cited above sought to attribute the passive's relatively greater difficulty to its derivational complexity. Alternative explanations of processing difficulty have been offered, not necessarily to deny the psychological validity of transformational theory, but they have come to serve as examples of the limitations of such theory.

Change in Focus

Jesperson (1924) and Carroll (1958) propose, for example, that the difficulty of the passive stems from its shift of focus from logical subject to logical object. This interpretation implies that the SVO form (subject–verb–object) of the active is basic and psychologically simpler than the OVS form of the passive.

Jespersen's analysis of the passive, made on the basis of an examination of the way in which it is used in written texts, suggests that the passive voice is used in at least one of the following conditions:

1. The active subject is not easily known or stated.
2. The active subject is self-evident from the context.
3. There is a special reason for not mentioning the active subject.
4. When the active subject is mentioned, the passive may be chosen because at that moment one is more interested in the passive rather than the active subject.
5. Connection between one sentence and another is facilitated by the use of the passive, for example, *"He rose to speak and was listened to"* as against *"He rose to speak and the crowd listened to him"* [Jespersen, 1924, pp. 167–168]."

These instances reduce to the fact that instead of the theme, topic, or focus of attention falling on the logical subject, it falls on the logical object. (A number of studies have assessed this effect and will be discussed later in this chapter.)

Word Order

Although the difficulty of the passive may be due to its infrequency of use, or to a change in focus from subject to object, it also involves a change in word order. The effect of word-order change in the passive transformation may be part of the problem of the difficulty of the passive.

The subject of a sentence is defined by Chomsky (1965) as that noun phrase (NP) directly dominated by "S" in deep structure. He notes (Chomsky, 1965, p. 221) that there are sentences in which applying this definition results in ambiguity. A sentence such as *This book I really enjoyed* has two NPs directly dominated by S (*This book, I*). The order of constituents is significant in determining surface structure grammatical relations, in this instance whether *This book* precedes *I* or vice versa, although order plays no role in determining the relations in deep structure. Chomsky proposes that "topic–comment" is the fundamental grammatical relation of surface structure that corresponds roughly to the basic subject–predicate relation in deep structure. In this interpretation, the essential effect of the passive transformation is to separate topic from subject by reversing the subject–object order. This could be the source of the traditional difficulty of the passive. The cleft sentence does approximately the same thing and Bever (1970) reports that children have the same relative difficulty with *object-first* versus *subject-first* cleft sentences (e.g., *It's the car that the truck hit* versus *It's the truck that hit the car*) as they do with the passive–active relationship.

In a related vein, Bever (1970) holds that the "normal" word orders of English, which show a preponderance of NVN (noun–verb–noun) sequences, are correctly interpreted by children as actor–action–object (SVO). This order becomes overgeneralized, however, and some children tend to consistently misinterpret object-first focus in both passive and cleft sentences as they adopt this strategy in comprehending sentences.

Stylistic Device

Chomsky in *Aspects* (1965) makes a distinction between word-order devices that are stylistic and optional (e.g., *Him I like*), and those, like the passive, that involve transformations and are obligatory (*He is hit by Jane*). For Joos (1964, p. 94) the English passive form is one in which the subject does not designate the actor. He sees it simply as a word-order device that serves the same function as stylistic inversion. In this view, Chomsky's grammatical distinction between stylistic inversion and transformation results in little functional difference.

Logical Selection Device

Another conception of the passive is proposed by Langendoen (1969) in which for him the passive is neither a word-order device nor a true transformation. It is a device of lexical selection. In this formulation the deep structure order of categorical elements is Predicate—NP—NP. If the left-hand NP is interpreted as agent, then the predicate, identified as that which is required by the subject, is defined as verb and one generates the active form. If the left-hand NP is defined as patient, then the predicate is defined as adjective and one generates the Be + Past Participle form. The *by* is then inserted by syntactic rule and the passive sentence is generated. This formulation takes the semantic notions of topic and comment, or agent and patient, which Chomsky delegates to surface structure description, and introduces them into the base. There is no structural reason why passive sentences should be more difficult than "equivalent" active sentences in this description. The infrequency of the passive would have to be explained by a tendency for the verb and actor to be more closely associated than the verb and object. The truncated passive according to Langendoen which deletes the actor, seems to describe the state of the object, rather than what is occurring to the object. The passive not only emphasizes the subject, it also deemphasizes the action.

Grammatical Development

Langendoen's interpretation of the truncated passive, Chomsky's (1965, p. 228) proposal that postverbal adjectives are derived from underlying strings with sentence complements to the verbs, and the experimental evidence that truncated passives are easier to process than full passives (Slobin, 1968b), suggest the possibility that derivationally and developmentally the full passive arises from the truncated passive. In this view, the full passive would not develop directly as a true transformation but as an elaboration of the truncated passive, in which the *to get* form would be intermediate between transitive and intransitive sentences, between descriptions of state and descriptions of action. The truncated passive may, in turn, arise as a development from the predicate complement (*John is hit = John is human*), to which it is closer, according to Langendoen, than an active form. Given the added assumption of two separate derivations for the active and passive, it is possible to propose that the meanings of these two forms, represented by their respective deep structures, progressively converge over development until their full equivalence is established at a later age, about 7- to 8-years old.

Passive as Marked

Another interpretation of the passive is offered by Anisfeld and Klenbort (1973). Contrary to the standard theory thesis that deep structure captures the semantic commonality between the active and passive voice, the semantic difference between the voices is attributed primarily to the properties of the passive. The active voice is said to serve as a neutral base of reference because of its typical and normative status, and the passive is marked (in the Jakobsonian sense). The passive is identified as a marked form because it is longer, transformationally more complex, less frequently used, its formation is restricted, and its main function, that of reversing the noun phrases of a sentence, can be accomplished in some cases in the active voice. The passive is also more difficult to understand and remember. The function of the passive (following Jespersen) is to allow for emphasis on the logical object and provide discourse continuity.

In addition, Anisfeld holds the passive enables the speaker to build a presuppositional infrastructure into his statements. The passive sentence *The boy was bitten by the dog* presupposes that the boy was bitten by something and asserts that the something was the dog. The unmarked active form *The dog bit the boy* is said to be presuppositionally neutral although it too has assertive and presuppositional components. Experimental evidence suggests to Anisfeld that information presented on the presuppositional level is more readily accepted and less likely to be questioned than assertive information. The active thus offers the speaker a neutral form for conveying information when he does not wish to emphasize or presuppose anything in particular. A caveat is introduced by Anisfeld when he notes that the presuppositions of some sentential structures are less definite than others, so that the presuppositional message of some passive statements may be quite weak, particularly if the passive form is chosen by the speaker to serve the function of stylistic continuity and emphasis, rather than the purported presupposition function.

Synonymy of Active and Passive Sentences

It is generally considered that sentence pairs such as *Tony kisses Alice* and *Alice is kissed by Tony* have the same meaning. They appear to contain the same content, and, more importantly, the two sentences are identical with respect to their truth value. That is, if one is true the other is true, and if one is false the other is false.

However, as already indicated, the essential synonymy of the two voices has been questioned. In Chomsky's (1957) attempt to show that the fundamental linguistic relationship between the voices is not based on synonymy but on the syntactic relationship between them, a class of cases was cited in which actives and passives differ semantically (Chomsky, 1957, p. 94). These involve quantifiers—*Everyone in the room knows at least two languages.* This sentence, when true, has a correlative passive that is false as normally understood : *At least two languages are known by everyone in the room.*

Johnson Laird (1968b) studied these constructions to determine whether they do indeed lack a common semantic interpretation and, if they do, to account for the differences. In the pair of sentences *All philosophers have read some books* and *Some books have been read by all philosophers*, the quantifier *some* of the first sentence is usually interpreted as *some books or other*, whereas in the second sentence it is interpreted as *some books in particular*. Johnson-Laird systematically varied the effect of the quantifier in active–passive sentence pairs such as *Every man knows some woman* and *Some woman is known by every man*. The study was made on the assumption that when the existential quantifier (*some*) comes before the universal quantifier (*every*) it receives the emphasis usually accorded to that which comes first in a sentence, and its interpretation changes systematically from *some* to *some in particular*. The contradiction between the two possible interpretations of *some* should result in ambiguous sentences. The results did indeed show that subjects made interpretations based on *surface structure* differences, i.e., the actives and their correlated passives received different interpretations in accord with the authors' predictions. Johnson-Laird argued that the sentences Chomsky used to illustrate differences in interpretation of actives and passives fall within the grammar of quantified sentences as such, in which differences in meaning are a function of the surface order of the quantifiers and not due to the differences in sentence voice. However, other studies by Johnson-Laird (1968a) resulted in a different conclusion. The subject was given active and passive sentences of the form *Red follows blue* and *Blue is followed by red* with instructions to illustrate the sentences by coloring two rectangles red and blue with a vertical line to separate the colors. It was assumed that the relative size of the colored areas would provide an indication of emphasis. The prediction that grammatical subjects would be represented by larger areas than grammatical objects and the disparity would be greater for passive than active sentences was confirmed. Johnson-Laird concluded that when in the "real world" the object predominates, the passive voice is likely to be used; when the importance of the logical object and subject is more balanced, the active voice is more likely. In yet another study, Johnson-Laird (1968b) focused on the effect of word order as well as voice. Normal and inverted word orders were used: normal, *There is a blue area that precedes a red area;* inverted, *There is a red area that a blue area precedes.* Evidence was found for both a word-order and a sentence-voice effect. Voice determined the **levels** of emphasis the passive being used when the red and blue areas were asymmetrical, the larger area being mentioned first; word order determined **what** was being emphasized. The extent to which the choice of voice is governed by different referential events may thus be considered as evidence that actives and passives are not entirely synonymous.

Other studies have been concerned with an analysis of the surface structure of active and passive forms to determine whether a change in voice would be correlated with changes in the meaning. In H. H. Clark's (1965) view, the actor, verb, and object are functionally similar in the active and passive forms. Actors tend to be animate and create little uncertainty, and objects tend to be inanimate and create great uncertainty. Temporal order has similar effects. The beginnings of both active and passive sentences are on the whole more animate and certain; the ends of these sentences are more likely to be uncertain. H. H. Clark found a left-to-right increase in uncertainty in almost all fully and partially completed sentence forms, and he reasons that there is an interaction between syntactic and semantic structure. Support for the thesis that uncertainty increases from left-to-right in the sentence comes from Anderson (1963; also cited in H. H. Clark, 1965) and Prentice (1966) who reports that the first part of the sentence is most generally remembered in tests of sentence recall and is most instrumental in facilitating sentence learning. Wright (1969), however, found that subjects recalled the agent of the verb best, irrespective of whether it was on the left or right (i.e., in an active or passive construction). In her later study (Wright, 1972), however, agents were recalled more accurately for active sentences and patients (objects) for passive sentences, which argues for a surface structure effect rather than a derivational effect based upon identification of the logical subject or agent as do the H. H. Clark (1965), Anderson (1963), and Prentice (1966) studies.

Johnson (1967) was interested in whether the position of a word in a sentence affects the meaning of that word. He substituted nonsense syllables for words in the subject and object positions in active and passive sentence frames and asked subjects to rate these sentences on various semantic differential scales. Nonsense syllables in the active-subject position were rated more active and potent (animate) than those in the active-object position. Similar results were obtained by Gumenik and Dolinsky (1969), and Howe (1970). Johnson concludes that different sentence positions have different structural meanings, and these meanings are not the same in active and passive sentences even for functionally equivalent positions of logical subject and object. He suggests that this difference is a possible reason for the existence of voice.

These limited data on active–passive synonymy suggest that although active–passive sentence pairs are in most cases understood as equivalent in meaning, there are differences in both functional and structural features of the two voices that may be used to explain the existence and relative infrequency of the passive form. The synonymy of the voices depends on whether it is possible to capture the meaning of the sentence solely from its surface structure or whether that meaning has to be recovered from its underlying (deep) structure. The limited psycholinguistic data cited suggest that it is not possible to keep the two issues separate as Chomsky earlier wished. Because the meaning of active–passive sentence pairs is related to both its underlying syntactic structure and its surface structure, it is questionable whether the meaning of the sentence is fully captured by either the deep or surface structure alone.

Information-Processing Models of Sentence Comprehension

As already indicated, studies of sentence comprehension have exposed a series of effects that involve the match between sentence constituents and extralinguistic or other linguistic information. The mechanisms that mediate these effects have been explored in a series of studies. Many comprehension studies are based on judgments of **truth value** of a sentence. Truth value is usually judged by verifying that a sentence is in accord with a pictorial representation, or vice versa.

Trabasso, Rollins, and Shaughnessy (1971), consider the processing of active and passive sentences as one aspect of a more general information-processing examination of serial versus parallel processing and self-terminating versus exhaustive search procedures. An information-comparing model is proposed that is similar to the memory search model of Sternberg (1969). In the hypothesized comparison process, the object is first said to be encoded in an internal representation which is held in memory as a positive set for comparison against the individual constituents of the (test) stimulus. Items are taken from the stimulus, one at a time, and compared *exhaustively* against the items in the positive set. If a mismatch occurs, no more items are taken from the test set for comparison and the person responds *false*. If all items match, he responds *true*. The testing *self-terminates* after a mismatch, but the comparison process itself is *exhaustive*.

This information-processing model, Trabasso concedes, leaves open the question as to whether information is processed from the embedded representation "outward" to the outer embeddings; if it did this, it would by implication give psychological reality to deep structure. Also unexplored is the nature of the internal representation.

The assumption of the Clark model (Chase & Clark, 1972), which is different in some respects from that of Trabasso, is that the equivalence of active and passive sentences depends on the same underlying propositional structure but that they differ in their assertions. Basically, sentence comprehension is viewed as a set of psychological processes in which mental operations act on linguistic information from input to final response. Comprehension consists of two operations: *encoding* information into internal representations and *matching* these representations. Comprehension occurs when the internal representations match (Clark, 1973). Two models are proposed by Trabasso to account for the data of sentence verification experiments: (1) **the response change model** (Clark & Chase, 1972; Chase & Clark, 1972; Trabasso *et al.*, 1971) is based on sentence processing that does not go beyond the internal representation prior to matching, and (2) the **optional recoding model** in which transformations are made on constituents both prior to and during the matching stage.

The response change model posits four stages. (*Stage 1*) The person encodes a sentence (as in the verification studies) into an internal representation. For example, *The ball is not red* is represented in propositional terms as: [false (suppose *ball is red*)], which according to Chase and Clark (1972) is paraphrased as "It is false (for the listener) to suppose that the ball is red." An assumption of the model is that the preferred representation order is SVO. (*Stage 2*) In the same verification studies, the picture presented to the subject is encoded in similar form. (*Stage 3*) The two representations are compared to see if they match. A series of steps in this stage involves the monitoring of sentences and pictorial representations according to a "truth index," very similar to the truth-table decision function in Bourne's (1966) theory. (*Stage 4*) The result of the comparison and match process (including the truth decision) is converted into a response.

The general rejection of the DTC has resulted in reduced interest in sentence verification data. Trabasso considers the latter unfortunate in that information-processing analyses show merit in some form of a complexity thesis because the verification data are remarkably reliable and orderly. The model, for example, predicts the obtained order of verification times of various studies, from shortest to longest, to be: true affirmative (TA), false affirmative (FA), false negative (FN), true negative (TN) (Chase & Clark, 1971; H. H. Clark, 1970b).

The response change model assumes that verification starts first with the encoding of the sentence, then the picture, with no processing, of negation, for example, occurring beyond the internal representation. The only change said to occur at the comparison stage is in truth-index decisions. There is no transformation of the encoded information as in the derivational theory of complexity. Gough's (1966) data are cited by Trabasso in support of this model.

Other data, however, indicate that the response change model is inadequate, or is at best only an optional strategy. The contrary data come from studies by Wason (1961; Wason & Jones, 1963) who employed a procedure in which the subject verified sentences such as *7 is an odd number* and *7 is not an even number*. In an FN (false negative) sentence, two additional operations are required: recoding and response change. The optional recoding model, which assumes that transformations *are* made on constituents prior to and during the comparison stage, predicts TNs to be faster than FNs, whereas the response change model, which makes no such assumption, predicts an order from fast to slow of TA, FA, FN, TN. The TN processing-times were reported to be only slightly longer than FNs. Trabasso holds that if the (TA–FA) difference were added to the FN, the optional recoding model would underpredict the Wason (1961) results and overpredict the Wason and Jones (1963) results. He concludes that a mixture of optional processing strategies were used by subjects, and no single model could be said to fit the data.

Trabasso proposes that either the response change or optional recoding model operate, depending upon varying circumstances of an experiment, and upon the age of the subject. The study by Slobin (1966) is said to show that adults conform to the optional recoding model (they invert explicit negations), and children conform to the response change model (they do not invert explicit negations).

Olson (1971) proposes a model in many ways similar to Clark's and Trabasso's. His own studies (Olson & Filby, 1972) are based on a verification procedure in which subjects are shown a picture of an event, for example, *a car hitting a truck*. After a brief delay, a test sentence, *The truck was hit by the car*, is judged as true or false, and the subject's response time is recorded. Ambiguous pictures are presented that could be encoded with either active or passive sentences (i.e., *Car hit truck* or *Truck hit by car*). Olson's thesis is that the nature of picture encoding determines the ease of processing a subsequent sentence. If the subject codes the picture in terms of the actor an active sentence would be most easy to verify; if coded in terms of the recipient of the action, then the passive would be most easily verified. This proposal incorporates the focus effect into the processing model. Focus can be affected by the nature of the picture or by the verbal instructions. Passive codings were induced by presenting two pictures and asking the subject to attend to the second picture in terms of the patient. They found that it took longer for adult subjects to answer the question "What was hit?" than "What hit?" indicating that it is more difficult to extract information about the recipient of a specified action than about the actor.

Discovering longer response times to *false* sentences led Olson to add a processing step at the response phase that is not found in Clark's or Trabasso's models. He proposes a decision rule: Is index set at *true*? If true, response is output. If not, response is set to *false* (and so to reprocess).

Concerning his model, Olson observes that first the ease of sentence comprehension depends on the perceptual coding of the preceding event (reminiscent of Wright's [1969] findings on the influence of matching sentence and question voice). Second, comprehension or verification proceeds on the basis of the surface structure of sentences, contrary to the view proposed by Trabasso in which recoding resolves the passive into an SVO structure. If passive sentences take longer to process, but are resolved into an actor–action–object code prior to comparison, then FP (false positive or affirmative) passive sentences should take longer than TP passive sentences. In fact, however, TPs take longer than FPs from which Olson infers that the short-term memory representation of a passive sentence retains its surface grammatical form, and this surface form is involved in the verification process. Kernelization is thus not necessary for verification.

The use of information-processing models to explain sentence comprehension is designed to account for performance that is not fully or adequately explained by transformational theory. The Trabasso, Clark, and Olson models are based on matching and comparison processes; although these models are avowedly performance models, they differ in their assumptions concerning *base* structure. The Clark model assumes that processing entails a representational system common to perception and language. Pictures are coded into semantic representations similar to those of sentences. Clark's model is consistent with transformational theory in assuming in deep structure a propositional representation of meaning. Trabasso is more neutral about the nature of deep structure and the nature of representation, recognizing that there are other alternatives to the presumed role of presuppositions and assertions that are part of Clark's model. Olson, on the other hand, assumes that information may be extracted directly from surface structure.

The Clark and Trabasso models assume the operation of a truth index, i.e., the application of truth-table decision rules. The origin of the truth index is not explained, nor its relation to the semantic component of the grammar. These omissions leave a considerable gap in the theory. The Clark and Trabasso models, in addition, treat certain transformations, such as negation and the passive, as semantic notions. Although the negative may be represented syntactically, and sometimes lexically, it is the underlying semantic representation that is considered important for comprehension (H. H. Clark, 1970b). Olson's model emphasizes to a greater extent than the others the surface characteristics of sentences. In particular, it interprets voice difference as a difference in focus. The internal representation of the sentence is said to be in surface structure form with no kernelization or reduction to a proposition in an active affirmative form.

In general, studies of comprehension reveal a consistent tension between the desire to preserve linguistic integrity and the desire to demonstrate the dependence of language upon psychological processing. In a sense, this difference in view reduces to an acceptance or rejection of the competence–performance distinction and, if the distinction is to be retained, to a definition of the role assigned to performance factors.

The status of the kernelization hypothesis by which the surface structure sentence is reduced to an SVO form or other base form seems less clear, particularly in light of the contested status of deep structure. Nevertheless, there appears to be an unwillingness to throw out the baby with the bath water in that a hierarchy of sentence types based on complexity still appears to be a plausible conception, and the conception of transformations still provides explanatory power to a theory of derivations. What is no longer generally accepted is the idea that sentence comprehension is determined solely by syntactic structure. Where derivational rules are said to operate, they do so in the context of semantic considerations that are also associated with the surface structure of sentences, as well as through the control of psychological mechanisms that processes linguistic and nonlinguistic information. A gap results when the notion of base structure is eliminated or ignored. It leaves unspecified the origin of information, the source of meaning, and the source of the inherent logic of the sentence.

Children's Knowledge of the Passive

Studies of children's knowledge of the passive have been undertaken for the following reasons:

1. The earlier studies intended to test the DTC. It was reasoned that the age of acquisition of syntactic structure should parallel an order based on derivational complexity. Earlier acquisition was expected of forms less syntactically complex.
2. To determine the capacities that underlie linguistic knowledge, particularly syntactic and semantic competencies.
3. To determine whether linguistic abilities are dependent on or independent of other cognitive abilities.

Derivational Theory

The study by Fraser, Bellugi, and Brown (1963) set the pattern for a number of psycholinguistic studies with children. The relative effects of imitation, comprehension (identification), and production were tested with ten different grammatical contrasts, two of which involved the subject–object relation as expressed by the active–passive voices. Production was more difficult than comprehension, which, in turn, was more difficult than imitation. These results are consistent with the findings of a number of studies done prior to the contemporary era in developmental psycholinguistics (McCarthy, 1954). The interpretation of difficulty order, however, is different from that of past investigations. First, it is held that imitation is a "perceptual" skill that functions independently of the meaning system. This view is rejected in more recent studies which report that subjects distort sentences in imitation in the direction of the child's current linguistic knowledge. Second is the view that a common set of competences is shared in comprehension and production with observed performance differences accounted for by limitations imposed by the later-developing vocal ability required in language production.

For subjects 37–43 months of age, the subject–object contrast in active versus passive voice (with reversible sentences) was ninth in relative difficulty, with the direct–indirect object contrast the most difficult (tenth). Subject–object reversal difficulty was examined in greater detail in an analysis of subjects' errors. It was concluded that the sense of the passive construction is not guessed by children from knowledge of its constitutent elements. Instead, the child processes the passive as an active sentence with "odd appurtenances," i.e., *is ——ed by.* The child's response appears guided by the rule that the logical subject comes first in the sentence, with no differentiation between the logical and grammatical subject.

In a replication of the Fraser *et al.* study with normal and subnormal children, Lovell and Dixon (1967) found the same relationship among tasks and the same order of difficulty in grammatical contrasts for both groups.

Slobin's (1966) study of sentence comprehension with 6-, 8-, 10- and 12-year-old children and 20-year-old adults utilized a sentence verification procedure with pictures that represented reversible and nonreversible situations. Reversible situations are defined by Slobin as those in which the object of the action can also serve as subject, *The girl pushes the boy;* in nonreversible situations the objects cannot normally do so, *The boy washes the car.* The study was designed, in part, as a test of the DTC with the prediction that passives would take longer to verify than kernels (actives) and passive negatives longer than negatives. The order of difficulty for grammatical types from least to most difficult was K, P, N, and PN, contrary to the predicted DTC order of K, N, P, PN (which is based on the assumption that the passive is derivationally more complex than the kernel and negative). The "semantic" effect of negativity was said to outweigh the "syntactic" effect of passivity. For truth value judgments, the difficulty order, from easiest to hardest, was TK, TP, FP, FK, FPN, FN, TN, and TPN. There was thus greater difficulty in judging true negatives than false negatives. Slobin points out that transformational theory does not account for the interaction between truth value and affirmation–negation. At all ages, reaction time was faster for nonreversible sentences than reversible sentences. Nonreversibility largely eliminated the difference in syntactic complexity between active and passive sentences. Slobin concluded that the DTC correctly predicts that passives would take more time than kernels and passive negatives more time than negatives, but semantic and other factors account for the fact that simple negatives take more time to respond to than complex passives. Lastly, although there was a reduction with age in response time and errors, there were no performance differences in the ranking of sentence types with age.

The comprehension and production of different sentence forms (K, N, P, and Q) of different levels of complexity (single, center, and double embedding) was studied by Gaer (1969) with adults and children 3–6 years of age. Gaer predicted, consistent with the DTC, that the passive (P) would be the last acquired by the child, the active (K) earliest, and the N (Negative) and Q (Question) would be intermediate, with a slight priority to the N being acquired earlier. Comprehension was assessed through a picture verification procedure. Although at certain ages the N sentences were easier in the production task than Q and P sentences, they were most difficult in the comprehension task. Overall, as predicted, the passive construction was the most difficult, particularly in production. It was not until 6 years of age that subject showed above-chance comprehension of the passive.

Production of passive sentences was tested by Hayhurst (1967) in 5- to 9-year-old subjects. The child was presented with a picture, after which he was given a model of the sentence type he was to produce in describing the pictures that were to follow. Pictures were related to each of the following sentence types: truncated passive, reversible passive, passive negative without actor, passive-negative reversible, passive-negative nonreversible. There was an increase in correct responses with age, although the 5- and 6-year-old subjects did not reach 50% correct responses in any form of the passive. Truncated passive sentences were easier to produce than full passives, and there were no differences between reversible and nonreversible sentences. Error analysis showed that it was common for the subjects to produce the kernel form for various sentence types: the truncated kernel for P, and N for PN. Difficulty in comprehending the passive was attributed principally to the negative, which led younger children to make many false negative errors, i.e., they produced sentences in the negative that were inappropriate to the picture. Reversibility was not an important factor in comprehension and production—possibly because it was the only production study up to that time that reduced the effect of memory for previously presented sentences. The Turner and Rommetveit (1967a) study also reported little or no relation between reversibility and performance with the passive. Children were shown pictures and asked about the action in the picture, with particular reference to the subject or object. When the experimenter started the sentence for the child, for example, "The X (patient) is . . .," reversibility of the original sentence was unimportant. This result could be attributed, however, to the structure of the question, which may have identified the logical function of agent or patient and through its conceptual focus reduced the number of options for the hearer experimentally, thus mimicking the effect of nonreversibility.

In another study, Turner and Rommetveit (1967b) proposed that levels of sentence complexity are determined by both semantic and syntactic factors in active–passive and reversible–nonreversible sentences. With the content for the two voices controlled, response differences were expected to be due to (1) the total number of words in the sentence, (2) word order, or the relation between the semantic actor and acted upon elements, and syntactic subject–object constituents, (3) the form of the verb, and (4) transformational complexity. Using the Fraser et al. tasks with nursery through third-grade children, they found significant effects for age, task (imitation to production), reversibility, and sentence voice. Differences due to voice were stronger than the differences due to reversibility. The order of difficulty was: nonreversible active, reversible active, nonreversible passive, reversible passive. The latter finding differs from Slobin's (1966) in which nonreversibility eliminated the difficulty of the passive. They also found support for the Fraser et al. observation that children tend to process the passive in the active voice, treating the passive as a sign of "some uncommon tense." At all grade levels, but particularly with younger subjects, there was frequent use of the colloquial passive with the *to get* auxiliary, instead of the *to be* auxiliary in the imitation and production of passives. The authors claim that this was due to the unaccustomed use of the *to be* form prior to formal schooling.

Children apparently process passive–active sentences in verification tasks differently from adults. They cannot recode or transform negative sentences into affirmative as adults do (Trabasso, 1972, on Slobin's 1966 data) and furthermore, as already indicated, Olson holds that adults do *not* transform passives into actives for processing, otherwise they would find TA easier than FA, which they do not (based on Gough's and Slobin's data), even though most adults have the ability to do so. On the other hand, children 6–10 years of age find TA relatively easier than FA. Olson tentatively hypothesizes that in verification tasks young subjects recode the pictures; adult subjects give pictures a standard active-coding and then recode sentences relative to the pictures. Olson cites Beilin's data (Beilin & Spontak, 1969) as evidence to support both parts of this interpretation: Older subjects (children) process sentences better, while younger subjects process pictures better.

Olson draws two implications from these findings: (1) The surface structure of a passive sentence is not learned as a transformation of the base structure shared by the active sentence. Rather, it is learned as a new surface device appropriate for handling certain kinds of information. Only later is the equivalence to surface structure of actives learned. Thus, base structures should be considered as sets of invariants among sentences that are the end-product of development and not the beginning. (2) Active and passive sentences are verified against a common event by children. Because sentences cannot be recoded by children, pictures must be. Older children, on the other hand, can both see the equivalence between sentence and picture and recode the picture.

Olson refers to several experiments (with Robbie Case) that tested these hypotheses. They confirmed that young subjects could verify both active and passive sentences against a picture earlier than they could verify active and passive sentences against each other, as was found by Beilin (Beilin & Spontak, 1969). It was also shown that the more–less relation was verified against pictures before children could understand the (meaning) equivalence between these sentences.

In sum, the complexity thesis predicts fairly well the order of acquisition of active and passive sentences. The order of difficulty is consistent in imitation, comprehension, and production tasks. The complexity thesis does not predict equally well for the negative and other transformations.

Focus

Turner and Rommetveit (1967a, 1967b, 1968) were concerned with the focus of attention interpretation of the passive. Carroll's (1958) study, conducted with high school students, found that if the focus of attention was directed to the object of action, a subject's production tended to be in the passive; if focused on the agent, the subject tended to respond with active sentences. Turner and Rommetveit reasoned that the focus of attention during the storage and/or retrieval of sentences might likewise influence the choice of a subject of a sentence in recall. Subjects (nursery through third-grade) were presented with pictures of the agent, the patient, or total sentence content. Sentences were reversible or nonreversible. Pictures were presented in all combinations at the time of storage and at the time of sentence retrieval. It was predicted that (1) when the picture at the time of storage and retrieval was the same, recall would be facilitated, (2) when the picture on which the child focused was congruent with the subject of the sentence, recall would be facilitated, and (3) focus on the agent and total scene would facilitate recall of actives; focus on the patient would facilitate recall of passives. The results confirmed these predictions, although the picture at storage had less effect than the picture at the time of retrieval. In addition, more active and nonreversible sentences were recalled. At each age level reversible passive sentences were more difficult than nonreversible sentences. Twenty-nine percent of the passive sentences produced by subjects at all age levels were in the colloquial *get* form, with the proportion even greater at the kindergarten level.

Related to focus is the distinction between topic and comment. Topic refers to that part of the sentence the speaker is talking about; comment, the remainder. The topic–comment contrast is signaled in surface structure by temporal order (deGroot, 1957), contrastive stress (Chafe, 1970), and syntactic structure (Lyons, 1968). Sentence voice affects the topic–comment distinction principally through conceptual focus (Carroll, 1958; Tannenbaum & Williams, 1968a, 1968b; Turner & Rommetveit, 1968). Although Turner and Rommetveit's data show no clear developmental trend in the effects of attentional focus, those of Hornby and Hass (1970) indicate that children as young as age 4 are capable of marking the distinction by means of contrastive stress. Hornby, Hass, and Feldman (1970) also show a clear shift from age 5 to 7 in recognizing the topic–comment distinction. In response to questions asking for the identification of the most important word in a sentence, 5-year olds were equally likely to choose the subject as the predicate of the sentence. Seven-year olds, however, showed a definite shift toward the predicate as the most important segment of the sentence. In a further study, Hornby (1971) asked children 6-, 8- and 10-years old to select a picture to go with each of 30 sentences divided equally among various sentence types (active, passive, cleft, pseudo-cleft, and stressed). The subject's choice of picture was interpreted as indicating the part of the sentence to be the topic. The three ages tested were equally able to mark the topic–comment distinction in the sentences they produced, although various surface structure devices that marked the distinction were used differently at each age. Word order was not the only device to indicate the topic–comment distinction—both grammatical structure and stress were capable of doing so even for 6-year olds. Temporal order was the principal marker for 8-year olds for determining topic, but not for the 6-year olds. Sentence types, in which the comment preceded the topic (i.e., the cleft and the stressed sentences) and a word-order strategy that would hinder correct identification of the topic, did not show an increase in correct identification with age as when topic preceded comment (i.e., active, passive, and pseudo-cleft). In fact, the 8-year olds showed a decline in stress sentence identifications in which topic was stressed. The performance of the 10-year-old group showed a decline in the importance of word order. This was evident in the sharp decline in the production of actives when topic preceded comment; there was concomitant improvement in the sentences in which comment precedes topic. Following Berko (1958), McNeill (1970), and Bever (1970), Hornby explains the results as a consequence of a developmental pattern in which the child first develops rules for treating individual cases, then rules that tend to be overgeneralized, after which exceptions to the rules are differentiated.

Although word order is an important factor in the development of the topic–comment distinction, it is not the primary one. Contrastive stress (intonation) was shown with 4-year olds (Hornby & Hass, 1970) and both 6- and 10-year olds (Hornby ,1971) to be the principal device for marking this relationship. Lastly, the relatively late development in the production of the passive, cleft, and pseudocleft for marking the topic–comment distinction was ascribed to the greater syntactic complexity of these grammatical forms.

Synonymy

Very few studies with children have been concerned with judgments of the equivalence or nonequivalence in meaning of active and passive sentences. Novinski (1968) investigated the judgment of 5-year-old children on the equivalence and nonequivalence (same–different) of sentences in three different contexts: (1) in a so-called "recognition" task in which the children listened to a sentence pair and judged equivalence of the sentences; (2) in an "imitation" task in which they imitated the first sentence, then heard the second sentence, and finally judged the equivalence of the sentences; and (3) in a "comprehension" task in which the subject selected a picture that corresponded to the first sentence, then listened to the second sentence, and finally judged their equivalence. The first sentence was either an active, passive, or relative, and the instruction was to respond "same" only to identical sentences, that is, those that did not change in meaning or form. The relation of the first to the second sentence was (1) different in meaning, same in form, (2) same in meaning, different in form, or (3) identical in both meaning and form. Same–different judgments were most accurate in the imitation and least in the "recognition" task, with the comprehension task intermediate. Judgments were most correct for passives, least for the relative, and intermediate for the active sentences. Changes in meaning were detected more often than changes in form, and sentences identical in both meaning and form were judged correctly more often than those items that represented the single types of change. Novinski concluded that children pay more attention to syntactic information in imitation than in comprehension in which semantic factors receive focus, and that same–different judgments have more in common with processes involved in comprehension than in imitation. The imitation and comprehension tasks required correct sentence repetition or picture verification in addition to the equivalence judgment, so that Novinski's finding of greater accuracy in the comprehension than recognition task may be confounded with task variables (i.e., a picture may more readily hold the subject's attention and may be more easily held in memory for a subsequent same–different judgment), and not just reflect the nature of equivalence processing.

Olson (1971), in commenting on equivalence between sentences, points out that equivalence is established by the overlapping extension of compliance classes (Goodman, 1968, p. 144). That is, if two sentences correspond to some invariant in a particular situation they become equivalent to one another. The sentences *A is more than B* and *B is less than A* have the same extension and are thus regarded as equivalent. This applies also to lexical events. The semantic system, by sorting out the nature of reference or its extension or focusing on the "implicational relations" among terms, assumes the quasi-formal properties of superordination, inclusion, opposition, etc. that are said to characterize the intrinsic "meanings" of the subjective lexicon of adults. In other words, the features of the semantic system reflect the logical properties of the real world, and words that share such features may be said to be synonymous.

Olson (1971) develops the following points concerning the equivalence between sentences, based on the Beilin and Spontak (1969) findings as well as his own:

1. Recognition of equivalence between sentences is more complex than that involved in using language in ordinary communication.
2. Equivalence is developmentally late in appearing.
3. Recognition of equivalence provides a new basis for language use— a logical use for theorizing, justifying, and thinking.
4. Equivalence can be the basis *for a revised conception of base structures.* Base structures can now be seen as structural invariants, or the implicational relations among sentences. Olson points out that it was, by contrast, the posited *structural* equivalence of sentences that led Chomsky (1957) to propose the notion of base structure.

Principles of Linguistic Development

Slobin (1971) in a significant statement concerning the relation between language acquisition and cognition enumerates a set of principles designed to define that relation. These principles assert the primacy of cognitive development in relation to linguistic development, a view that contradicts McNeill (1970) and the generative transformational linguists and is more in accord with the Piagetian position. Slobin's main thesis is that language develops to enable the child to express his "intentions."

The first "universal" principle that Slobin proposes is that *"new forms express old functions and new functions are first expressed by old forms* [Slobin, 1971, p. 317]." The passive construction is cited as an example. Cognitive development gives rise to semantic intentions for which new means of expression must be found. Children's temporary idiosyncratic linguistic forms are often cues to the fact that development of a new notion has engendered a search for new means of expression.

Another "universal" principle states that *"sentences deviating from standard word order are integrated at early stages of development as if they were examples of standard word order* [Slobin, 1971, p. 350]." Fraser *et al.* [1963) report that preschoolers interpret passive sentences, such as *The girl is pushed by the boy,* as if the order of elements were SVO— in this example the children match it with a picture of a *Girl pushing a boy.* Children thus attempt to conform to known word order, and reverse meaning. This finding is in line with Bever's (1970) conception of a general strategy of English sentence interpretation in which the NVN sequence corresponds in the mind of the child to actor–action–object. (McNeill [1970] proposes a similar strategy.) Further evidence for Slobin's principle comes from the fact that conjoined sentences referring to temporally ordered events are first interpreted as though the order of mention matches the order of occurrence, even if the conjunction indicates otherwise (E. V. Clark, 1971 ; Cromer, 1968). Development of the passive occurs late in Indo-European languages, typically requiring several morphological changes and a change in word order. By contrast, the Arabic passive is learned early by Egyptian children (Omar, 1970) because it is marked no doubt by a single clear prefix with no required change in word order.

Slobin adds that children acquire a "working strategy" that says in effect : *Pay attention to the order of words and morphemes.* Slobin (1971) had suggested earlier, on the basis of limited data, that children adhere to fixed word order regardless of the degree of freedom of the input language. More recent data by Bowerman (1973) with Finnish-speaking and other children indicates considerable individual difference in this regard. Furthermore, American children tend to retain word order in sentence imitation (Brown & Fraser, 1963; Fraser *et al.,* 1963), yet Polish and Russian children frequently change word order in imitation.

Although Dingwall and Tuniks' study (1973) was specifically concerned with language comprehension in children, his more general intent was to challenge the view of Fodor and Garrett (1966) that transformational theory is of such generality, abstractness, and power that it is beyond validation by empirical means. Dingwall summarizes a variety of empirical studies which he says provide sufficient evidence to undermine confidence in some critical features of transformational theory. His own study of the acquisition of language in 30 Russian children of 1 year, 8 months to 8 years of age contributes to this conclusion. He found:

1. as in C. Chomsky's (1969) study of English-speaking children, acquiring Russian syntax is a protracted process. Children did not acquire syntax completely by 5 years of age as McNeill (1966, 1970) had asserted. Gvozdev's work with Russian children showed that some grammatical features were not acquired until 3 years of age; others not until age 7. This was confirmed by Dingwall.

2. C. Chomsky (1969) proposed that although the age of acquisition of particular syntactic features might vary among children, the order of acquisition did not. Dingwall questions the generality of this hypothesis because he found that the appearance of various, oblique case-markings was not ordered in the same manner among all children, although it was for most of them.

3. Gvozdev made the observation that categories of words learned later are placed after earlier-learned ones in sentences. When verbs begin to appear in NV constructions, for example, they are simply tacked onto the end of the sentences. Many of Dingwall's data supported this recency of learning or linear order hypothesis. Appearance of the sentence subject in final utterance position, however, did not. For these Russian subjects, a proclivity for topicalization appeared instead.

4. Contrary to the Brown and Hanlon (1970) and Slobin (1967) findings that mean utterance length (MLU) is a better index than age of grammatical development, Dingwall finds the reverse. The difference may be due to Dingwall's use of the *word* as the unit rather than the *morpheme* as used by Brown.

5. Slobin claims that semantic complexity determines the order of acquisition of various forms (concrete to abstract). Gvozdev's data show, however, that the conditional is learned quite late even though it is simple in form, yet grammatical categories with some abstract reference such as number are learned much earlier. The conditional may require logical capacities for comprehension beyond that of number alone. Furthermore, Dingwall found that the frequency of occurrence of a lexical item in adult speech was a better index of correct child usage than the character of the lexical entry. A common word such as *grandfather*, although masculine and requiring masculine concord (agreement), was declined as a feminine noun by children. On the other hand, *to call* (by telephone), which requires an object in the dative rather than the accusative, caused no difficulty for the children even though it would appear to be relatively complex.

6. Dingwall's study of gender distinctions and concord, which followed the design of an earlier study by Popova (1973), showed that the ability to assign informative lexical items to gender classes on the basis of their endings did not appreciably improve over the age range of the sample. The same was true for the development of numeral government (agreement in number); learning these was not complete by 5 years of age. At the same time, even the youngest children were aware of the constituent structure of the sentences used in the study.

On the basis of the Slobin and Dingwall proposals it would appear that principles concerning linguistic development, although helpful in ordering and explaining developmental data, are somewhat less than "universal". The generalizations that can be drawn suggest that linguistic development is affected by semantic and cognitive considerations equal to if not surpassing in significance those of the structural characteristics of language.

Genevan Studies of the Passive

H. Sinclair and Ferreiro's (1970) study of the passive bears directly on the investigations to be reported in Chapter 3. Because the original report appears in French, we will present its findings in some detail.

The Piagetian thesis that guides Sinclair's research is predicated on the purported parallel between the development of cognitive structures and the acquisition of language, with the implication that operative factors are critical in language acquisition, particularly in the development of syntactic structure.

Their main experiment, which was conducted with 174 Genevan public school children of ages 4.2–7.8, was in three phases: comprehension, production, and imitation (repetition of sentences). The Sinclair procedure for testing comprehension was to determine how the child, given a set of toys that he was able to identify by name, could act out a sentence read by the experimenter, e.g., "Show me with these toys what happens when I say 'The boy spills (renverser) the bottle.' " The introductory sentences were actives that were followed by passive test sentences. The sentences used varied in the verb (5 French verbs were used): 'to break' (casser), 'to spill' (or overturn) (renverser), 'to wash' (laver), 'to push' (pousser), and 'to follow' (suivre). They also varied in reversibility (in Slobin's sense) utilizing reversible, nonreversible, and intermediate sentences. The presentation of sentences was random.

In the production task, the experimenter carried out the action and said, "Tell me what is happening." This yielded a "free description." The experimenter then repeated the same actions and said, "Tell me again what is happening, but begin by saying the name of the patient." Half of the subjects received the comprehension questions first, half the production questions. The results for the two orders were reported to be completely similar.

In the imitation task the experimenter read the comprehension sentences one at a time; the subject was asked to repeat them and was then asked to demonstrate the action ("Show me what happens"). Although data are reported for the correctness of response, the emphasis in the analysis and in the interpretation was on the qualitative characteristics of the child's performance, on his errors, and upon the patterns or strategies indicated in his behavior.

The comprehension data indicated three types of child enactment:

1. *Inverse actions.* The subject acted out the inverse of the agent–patient order of the spoken sentence.

2. *Reciprocal action.* A passive sentence was translated into a reciprocal sentence and acted out as such. The sentence *The boy is knocked over* (renverser) *by the girl* led to an action in which the boy and girl pushed each other and fell together to the ground.
3. The *correct response.* The action corresponds to the order indicated in the sentence.

In the comprehension task, the 4- to 5-year-old age group gave 254 usable responses, 63.8% of which were correct; by age 7, 83.6% of the responses were correct. Although the proportions of correct response are undeniably high, Sinclair argues that the qualitative data show a different picture of the 4-year-old's competence (90% of the subjects at age 4 produced at least one inverse action, 42% at age 7 did; 23% of the 4-year olds produced at least one reciprocal action, none at age 7). Five- and six-year olds appeared to be the age at which the child began to really achieve "understanding of the passive," defined by Sinclair as an abstract structure. Understanding this abstrract structure was achieved, however, only when the child could comprehend the entire passive sentence and not simply parts of it. She implies that knowledge of nonreversible and truncated forms, which do not include the entire passive structure show less than full knowledge of the abstract structure that defines the passive. Nonreversible sentences are said to be comprehended uniquely on the basis of lexical entities without true comprehension of the passive voice.

Sinclair concludes that comprehension difficulty was due to at least three factors:

1. The nature of the verbs employed. Some verbs were comprehended very easily, e.g., *casser* "to break"; others were more difficult, e.g., *suivre* "to follow."
2. The nature of the grammatical subjects and objects, in particular the animate or inanimate character of nouns. In general, this distinction did not in itself influence the degree of difficulty, although in the context of reversibility it appeared to.
3. The reversibility or nonreversibility of the sentence. Sinclair points out that some words, by the nature of their defining characteristics, establish inviolable constraints upon the description of an event. In a sentence containing the words *Wash, car,* and *boy, boy* must be the agent and *car* the patient.

Different verbs affect comprehension of sentences differently:

1. Some, nonreversible verbs for example, suggest unambiguous and lasting effects upon objects, as in the case of "to break" (*casser*).
2. Others clearly express causal situations, such as direct action of the agent on the patient, usually with some forceful contract.
3. Some imply spatial order ("to break" does not ,"to follow" does—the latter is more difficult).

4. Verbs differ in the duration of action (some are very brief—"to break"; some long "to follow.")
5. For some verbs the result of the action is similar to the action itself (e.g., *push, follow*).
6. Then there is the reversibility or nonreversibility feature of the verb.
7. Finally, there are particular anomalies associated with some verbs. For "to follow" the agent changes his place in constant relation to the patient, but it is the patient who initiates the action.

Thus, the study reports a hierarchy in comprehension difficulty among sentences according to the verb employed, and the hierarchy was constant across the different age groups. The hierarchy was attributed to the changing nature of the relationship between the agent and the patient, and not to familiarity. These *semantic* characteristics of the sentence seemed to exercise an effect over and above that of the syntactic constraints.

Sinclair concludes that comprehension of the passive results from a gradual evolution in the capacity for understanding. It improves very markedly between the ages of 5 and 6, but the specific age of comprehension depends, again, upon the verb of the sentence.

The production data were derived from the "free descriptions" and the "induced descriptions." The free descriptions showed the following hierarchy:

1. Enumeration of objects. This was found only among 4-year olds.
2. A description of the action alone (*It rolls*) without any indication of whether the action was from the view of the patient or the agent.
3. Incomplete description. Only the *agent* and action was mentioned (*The dog jumps*).
4. Incomplete description. Only the *patient* and action was mentioned (*The match is broken*).
5. A complete active. The majority of sentences were of this type.
6. A complete passive. This was rarely given in a free description.

For "induced description" when the subject was asked to make his sentence begin with the patient, 160 subjects produced 1013 sentences. First, the proportion of complete sentences (expressing agent, patient, and action) increased with age (27% for age 4; 72% for age 7). The proportion of passive sentences with or without agents, however, was only 25% (at age 4) and 49.6% (at age 7). The passives that were complete descriptions ranged from 7.2% at age 4 to 25% at age 7. In all cases, there was gradual development with age.

Sinclair delineates six levels of production, each associated with a different age level.

1. The most primitive level is indicated by the *enumeration* of objects and the *denomination* of action. In this category no sentences in the proper sense were produced. The relation of agent–patient–action was not expressed and word order was of no significance.
2. There were two types of response at this level: (1) simple active

sentences were given, ignoring the request for the passive but appropriate to the action; and (2) simple utterances that permuted subject and object nouns. The subject responded to the passive command, but the response was not appropriate to reality. Although these sentences appeared at all ages, it was not clear whether these sentences represented the same psychological reality for children of different ages.

3. This level contains all the inverse-action types: object noun–verb. The patient (object) is the grammatical subject, followed by a verbal expression (predicate, interrogative verb, reflexive form, etc.), which does not admit of a grammatical object (*The boy runs*).

4. An infrequent type of response appears at this level in which the agent becomes the patient and vice versa, and the grammatical subject remains the logical subject. The permutation command was observed, and the action expressed was more or less compatible with the event acted out, but the relation between agent and patient was changed (*The dog follows the boy, The boy leads the dog, The car pushes the truck, The truck pulls the car*).

5. At this level are *compositions of two sentences*, either coordinate or subordinate, (*The girl fell down; the boy is standing*).

6. At the most sophisticated level is the correct application of the *passive* construction.

Imitation data were collected for only a portion of the sample (53 subjects). Associated with the 204 sentences imitated were 202 correct actions or inversions; there were no reciprocals.

The types of imitation response obtained were

1. correct repetition;
2. sentences different from the model but retaining the passive form; these begin with the patient and retain the meaning;
3. simple actives with the same meaning as the model;
4. simple actives with reverse meaning of the model;
5. sentences different from the model, having an uncertain meaning;
6. truncated passives.

At 4 years of age, 59% of the subjects gave correct repetitions of sentences, but only 32% followed the imitation with a correct enactment. By age 7, 95% correctly repeated the sentence and 82% followed it with a correct action. There were correct repetitions followed by false actions at all ages, although the latter occurred in reversible sentence contexts only. The types of imitation, as expected, changed with age:

1. The 4-year olds stayed close to the model. They did not introduce synonyms as was frequent among older children.
2. For 5-year olds, a great improvement took place, even in reversible contexts. *Parrot* repetitions, without understanding, decreased.
3. At age 6, there was considerable increase in correctly repeated sentences accompanied by correct enactments. Two novelties which

appeared among 5-year olds disappeared at this age : modifications of the passive and actives with correct meanings.

4. The 7-year olds were fully correct, except for parrot repetitions with *follow*.

Sinclair and Ferreiro find of particular interest the two "transformational types" of imitations: (1) the active sentence with correct meaning and (2) the modified passive. The first was seen as a type of detransformation (kernelization), resulting in a statement whose structure was closer to its deep structure representation than to the experimenter's model sentence. The second was interpreted as another type of transformation of the same deep structure contained in the model sentence.

Sinclair and Ferreiro conclude :

1. The attempt to apprehend the structure of a passive sentence is not based solely on correct lexical knowledge and knowledge of the reality to which sentences refer. Imitation requires from the start that the subject comprehend the deep structure of the heard sentence and successfully retransform the sentence in order to repeat it. For the young child, the limitations of his (linguistic) knowledge lead to imitations that are active sentences—with correct meaning. When he is more advanced, the subject not only retains the deep structure in order to transform it into a sentence, he also remembers and notes that the model (surface) sentence contains transformations. He is thus compelled to reconstruct the sentence in a creative manner according to his level of development, although this kind of creative response does not occur with all sentences. This suggests to Sinclair that two kinds of memory are necessary for imitative reconstruction. The first is "operative" memory, which leads to the creative reconstruction of the sentence; the second, the more "figurative" (perceptual) memory, which operates on the more superficial structure of the model. With "easy" sentences the two processes combine. In opposition, one mechanism assumes more importance than the other. Only the 5- to 6-year olds show the retransformations that come from a correctly understood deep structure —this is also the age at which the child begins to truly comprehend the passive. At age 4, it was figurative memory that dominated. At age 7, comprehension was no longer a problem and the two processes were no longer dissociated.

2. Sinclair implies that the true criterion for the achievement of the passive is not an understanding of truncated or nonreversible passives, as these may be achieved (particularly the former) on the basis of lexical knowledge alone. Rather, only knowledge of full reversible passive sentences indicates knowledge of the abstract structure of the passive.

3. Furthermore, production of the passive shows that development of this knowledge is dependent on the child's ability to see the action both from the perspective of the agent and that of the patient. This requires decentration on the part of the child.

a. At first, the child is unable to conceptualize the action from the view of the patient. Then, several types of description "announce" the group of operations necessary for the passive. These are indicated first by the expectation that reality will be in accord with the seen event, and then, that the event (or sentence) can be changed to make it in accord with the other.

b. The next level of development is characterized by three operations: (1) emphasis on the agent in the description of events, combined with (2) the operations of rearrangement which put the patient at the beginning of the sentence, and (3) an operation on the verb. Psychologically, the production command now induces a new centration—on the patient, which captures the result of the action. But the subject spontaneously makes another centration on the agent, without coordinating agent and patient. This is the beginning of decentration, however.

c. At the final level are complete descriptions. The three operations are now present. True decentration is apparent with the two different centrations coordinated. The relation between agent and patient is conserved and expressed in a single sentence.

There is a parallel, then, between language and cognitive "operativity," the critical characteristics of which are decentration and coordination. Operationally they permit the construction of a quantifiable invariant at the core of a system of transformations. With the passive, which involves the conservation of a semantic invariant, the meaning of an utterance is preserved within the context of a transformed syntactic structure.

Within the foregoing, Sinclair makes a number of strong claims. She says first, that only the full passive provides the basis for determining whether the child understands the structure of the passive. A significant aspect of this proposal is the claim that the passive represents an abstract structure that underlies the surface structure of passive sentences. The criterion for knowledge of the passive is a stringent one, because knowledge of the abstract structure is defined as understanding three operations that involve (1) the subject and the description of the event, (2) the patient and the permutation of its position in the sentence, and (3) the verb and its passivization—in addition to the ability to manipulate each independently and to coordinate them in a single sentence. The fact that subjects find nonreversible sentences easier to process and, thus, comprehend them earlier than reversible passives, and that truncated passives are easier than full passives, does not give adequate evidence of knowledge of the passive according to Sinclair. In our view it is too strong a claim to assert that the child does not have knowledge of the passive until he is 7-years old. It appears from the data of the studies we report in Chapter 3 that a substantial number of subjects perform quite adequately in a variety of comprehension tasks even with full passives.

Sinclair's second proposal is that upon hearing a passive sentence an apprehension of the deep structure is attempted. This is not a kernelization hypothesis, but it is like one, i.e., the passive is not reduced to an active kernel as such but to whatever form the representation of sentence-meaning takes. Apprehension of abstract sentence-meaning is processed in relation to the request for the surface representation in the passive form. Imitation requires both figurative and operative memory; comprehension demands operativity. If the child has at least partial knowledge of the abstract nature of the passive, but lacks knowledge of the appropriate surface structure elements upon which to map this knowledge, he attempts such a construction.

In addition to the foregoing study, which was conducted in French with French-speaking children, there were two studies (Caprez, Sinclair, & Studer, 1971; A. Sinclair, Sinclair & de Marcellus, 1971) with English-speaking subjects (in Geneva and the United States) and with German-speaking subjects. The same procedures were used with all three samples with only slight accommodations necessary to the uniqueness of sentence forms in each language. Although the method was comparative and designed to determine whether acquisition of a particular language depends upon general cognitive factors, it was recognized that the languages studied are in the same language family (Indo-European) and have many characteristics in common.

In none of the studies did success in the passive approach 100%. This was based on a criterion that defined success as knowledge of the full passive reversible form, as previously indicated. The lack of full success even at the older ages was due to the difficulty of the verb *follow*, although other verbs gave the oldest groups some difficulty too.

Deficiencies in comprehension were very similar for all three languages, i.e., sentences were understood correctly at the same age in each language. The same hierarchy of difficulty for verbs was found across groups for the three languages: *break*, *knock down*, *wash*, *push*, and *follow* (from least to most difficult).

Age development in the production of the passive was similar across studies. Grammatical errors were also similar.

Not one subject in any of the studies was capable of stating, without prompting, the three changes necessary to produce the passive from an active sentence: permutation of agent and patient, modification of the verb form, and addition of *by*. There was only one anomolous result. Only with the English sample was there no increase with age in the development of adult-like passives in production. Socially conditioned performance factors were offered to account for this result.

The 'unexpected' similarity in results in these cross-language studies was interpreted as lending plausibility to the hypothesis that a general cognitive factor influences the acquisition process. However, the possibility was not considered that the commonality might also be due to a common deep structure and to common transformation rules, so that a linguistic argument can just as readily "explain" the commonality in acquisition. It is further concluded that the evidence points to a slow process of acquisition that begins at least by age 3 (the age of the youngest English sample) and is not complete by 7 years of age.

The similarity in results for the three languages is also taken as support for the cognitive basis for acquisition of the passive because the passive was not fully mastered until the child was capable of considering an event from two points of view. Knowledge of some passive forms, such as the truncated passive, as already indicated, was not taken as evidence that the child had mastered the passive voice. The degree of difficulty associated with different verbs was said to be due to the different types of causal events expressed in sentences with these verbs. This results in a horizontal decalage similar to that reported in cognitive development.

Palermo and Molfese (1972), in a selected review of language acquisition studies conducted with children from age 5 onwards, conclude that the 5-year old is just beginning to fully comprehend the passive construction, but it is difficult to judge when the ability to produce the passive is fully developed. These observations are made within the context of a broader analysis in which it is concluded that (1) Language development is far from complete when the child reaches his fifth birthday. (2) A theory of language development must be embedded within the larger context of a theory of cognitive development, such as the kind provided by Piaget. Although cognitive development may precede its expression in language, the reverse is unlikely. (3) The age ranges of 5–7 and 12–14 may be important transition points in language development. These are the age ranges in which other more general cognitive changes are assumed to occur, at least within a Piagetian framework.

Summary of Studies with Children

1. The complexity thesis of G. A. Miller and Chomsky (G. A. Miller, 1962) predicts fairly well the order of acquisition of the active and passive. Fraser *et al.* (1963), Lovell and Dixon (1967), Gaer (1969), and Turner and Rommetveit (1967a, 1967b) show that the order of difficulty is consistent across imitation, comprehension, and production tasks. The complexity thesis, however, does not predict equally well for the negative and other transformations (Slobin, 1966).

2. Comprehension and production of the passive is sensitive to (a) focus of attention (Turner & Rommetveit, 1967a, 1967b, 1968), (b) reversibility (H. Sinclair de-Zwart, 1969; Slobin, 1966; Turner & Rommetveit, 1967a, 1967b, 1968), and (c) task difficulty (Hayhurst, 1967).

3. The passive is acquired progressively. Some forms of the passive are more primitive than others, e.g., the colloquial *got* form (Beilin & Spontak, 1969; Fraser *et al.*, 1963; Sinclair & Ferreiro, 1970; Turner & Rommetveit, 1967a). Furthermore, there is a developmental sequence in the production of the passive that reflects the development of different subject competences and strategies. Sinclair ascribes it to changes in the development of cognitive structures; Bever (1970) ascribes it to the learning of rules by which internal relations (SVO) are mapped onto external relations (NVN); Slobin (1971) ascribes it to the development of intentions.

4. The age at which the passive is acquired is unclear. Some argue it is about 5 years of age (Palermo & Molfese, 1972); others, about age 7 (Sinclair & Ferreiro, 1970); but the data are not consistent (Slobin, 1966).

5. Development of the passive and other transformations appears to be related to the development of more general cognitive functions (Beilin & Spontak, 1969; Olson, 1971; Palermo & Molfese, 1972; Sinclair & Ferreiro, 1970; Slobin, 1971).

6. The age period between 5 and 7 appears to be a time when a critical change in language occurs (Beilin & Spontak, 1969; Olson, 1971; Palermo & Molfese, 1972).

3

Experiments on the Passive

The studies we report in this chapter were designed to test the thesis that sentence forms, such as the passive and negative, which are ostensibly generated through the application of transformation rules, are related to the acquisition and development of specific cognitive processes. We assumed that linguistic rule systems are achieved progressively in development through constructive processes dependent upon the output of more general cognitive structures.

With the passive, specifically, the effect of the transformation is to produce a sentence that is equivalent in its logical relations to an active sentence, although a reversal of grammatical subject and object is achieved. The subject noun phrase that serves as the logical subject remains invariant whether in sentence-first position, as in the active sentence, or sentence-last position, as in the passive sentence. It serves as the agent of action whether it acts as grammatical subject or grammatical object. This type of linguistic reversal has many of the characteristics of reversibility described in conservation and related cognitive phenomena. In conservation, a quantitative property, such as number or length, is conceptualized as invariant even though related properties of the objects, such as location or configuration, are altered. Reversibility in thought, which becomes manifest at first in a primitive form in the behaviour of very young children ($1\frac{1}{2}$ to 2-years old), would appear to be necessary to the development of those linguistic functions that require some kind of logical reversal. Exploration of this relationship in the development of passive sentence construction is detailed in a series of experiments we report here.

We also report on the manner in which children come to recognize the equivalence in meaning between active and passive sentences. To Chomsky, the relationship between active and passive sentences is accounted for principally by formal structural relations rather than on the basis of their synonymy. As already indicated in Chapters 1 and 2, the nature of the meaning relation between the active and passive exposes some of the fundamental linguistic problems of their underlying linguistic structure. We were interested in how meaning equivalence judgments develop. Judged synonymy, we expected, would relate to the development of operational reversibility because reversibility in its *operational* sense provides the logical capacity to *intuit* the logical relations among sentences that involve reversal of phrase structure elements.

The first experiment undertaken produced results concerning reversibility and the meaning equivalence of active and passive sentences. Issues that arose in the first experiment were pursued more extensively in the second study.

Experiment 1: Logical Reversibility and the Judged Synonymy of Active and Passive Sentences[1]

Children at four age levels (5-, 6-, 7-, and 8-years old) were tested for their knowledge of active and passive sentences, presented singly and in pairs, and judged synonymy of these sentences. Their knowledge was assessed in the context of imitation, comprehension, and production procedures. The child's reversibility level was established with a set of cognitive tasks that focused on conservation, classification, and seriation abilities and was related to performance in the linguistic tasks.

Method

SUBJECTS

The subjects were middle-class white children who attended the same New York City schools as the subjects of the number language study to be reported later (Chapter 4), although these data were collected 2–3 years later. The youngest children in the sample attended private nursery schools in the same locale as the older children. The subjects were in the nursery ($\overline{X}$ CA = 4 years, 9 months), kindergarten (5 years, 10 months), first-grade (7 years, 1 month) and second-grade (7 years, 11 months). The number of subjects at each level were: nursery (21), kindergarten (22), first-grade (22) and second-grade (21).

MATERIALS

The linguistic and cognitive tasks were given to the subjects in counterbalanced order; subtasks within each set were randomized and presented in a fixed order.

Linguistic Tasks

The linguistic tasks assessed the child's ability to imitate, comprehend, and produce active and passive sentences singly and in pairs (see Appendix

---

[1] Experiment (1) was performed with the assistance of George Spontak and Sandra Dalton. An earlier report of a portion of the data was given in Beilin and Spontak (1969).

A for the specific sentences). A pretest was used to assess the ability to recognize, verbalize, and discriminate pictorial representations of actions—pictures of this type were used extensively in the language test.

Imitation

The imitation of single sentences and sentence pairs was designed:

1. to provide a test of syntactic and semantic processing—it has been proposed (Slobin, 1968a) that imitation can be an indicator of the child's knowledge of linguistic structure. Differential ability to imitate passive and active sentences could thus be indicative of different levels of linguistic knowledge.
2. to ensure that the child was able to store in memory the sentences he needed for the processing of information given him in the comprehension tasks.

Single Sentences: In sentence imitiation the child was asked to repeat:

1. *Simple active declarative sentences* (A) with direct and indirect objects (*Mark hits Susan,* and *Susan gives Mark the book*). The sentences were reversible in Slobin's (1966) sense of the term.
2. *Passive sentences* (P) with direct objects and indirect objects (*Susan is hit by Mark* and *Mark is given the book by Susan*).
3. *Nonreversible (active) sentences* (NRA). Sentences in which a subject—object reversal is not credible because of the nature of the subject, object and verb (following Slobin, 1966). A nonreversible sentence may be passivized, however, e.g., *Mark washes the car* (A)—**The car washes Mark* (NRA)—*The car is washed by Mark* (P).

Sentence Pairs: In addition to *single* sentences, children repeated *pairs* of sentences:

1. *Active–passive* (AP) : *Mark hits Susan* (A) ; *Susan is hit by Mark* (P). The passive sentence is the transform of the active. The active and passive have the same agent and patient although the grammatical subject in one is the grammatical object in the other. The active verb in the first is passivized in the second. The meaning of the two sentences, at least in the ordinary sense, was intended to be equivalent.
2. *Passivized subject–object reversal* (Psor): *Mark hits Susan* (A) ; *Mark is hit by Susan* (P). Two transformations are implicit in the second example sentence. The first, is a subject—object reversal *Mark hits Susan—Susan hits Mark*). The second transformation entails passivization of the reversed sentence (*Susan hits Mark—Mark is hit by Susan*). Considered in relation to one another (*Mark hits Susan* and *Mark is hit by Susan*), the latter is not the passivization of the former, but of another sentence. In this pair, the meaning of the two sentences was designed not to be equivalent. This pair was used as a control. An assertion of sentence equivalence for this pair would indicate that the subject was making his judgment on

the basis of word order (NVN or SVO) and not on the logic of the reversal involved in passivization.

3. *Subject–object reversal* (SOR) : *Mark hits Susan* (A) ; *Susan hits Mark* (A). The object of the first sentence is the subject of the second, and the subject of the first is the object of the second. The verb is unchanged so that the subject–object reversal results in a change in meaning.

Comprehension Tasks (Including Tests of Synonymy)

1. *Comprehension of single sentences* (A, P, NRA) was tested through the child's identification of equivalent pictorial representations. The child was asked to select from two pictures the one that corresponded to the sentence read to him, after the child had imitated (repeated) the sentence. He was asked to point to the picture that corresponded to the stimulus sentence. For example, the pictures placed before the subject, when asked to identify *Mark hits Susan*, showed **Mark hitting Susan** in one picture, and **Susan hitting Mark** in the other. The probability of correct identification by chance was .50.

2. *Synonymy Judgment.* (*a*) For this task the child was read two sentences (AP, SOR, and Psor). Instead of the two pictures used in the prior task, he had four from which to choose in making his identifications. Two of the pictures represented the active sentence (*Mark hits Susan*) ; the other two illustrated the agent–patient reversal of that sentence (**Susan hitting Mark**). Within each pair of pictures the actor was on the left in one and on the right in the other, in order to control for the tendency to scan from left to right. If the two sentences were understood to have the same meaning, the subject was expected to choose either one or two pictures that showed the same agent–patient relation (**Mark hitting Susan**). If the child understood the two sentences to have different meanings, he would choose pictures depicting **Mark hitting Susan** and **Susan hitting Mark**.

The child could thus choose one or two pictures to show equivalence (two, if he chose the actor on the left in one picture and on the right in the other). Again, the probability of being correct by chance was .50. Above-chance correct response to the sentence pairs was taken to indicate that the child conceived the sentences to be synonymous. Chance or below-chance responding was taken to suggest that the children could not equate meanings or equated them incorrectly.

A control pair consisted of an active sentence and a sentence that contained a subject–object reversal (SOR) of the active sentence *Mark hits Susan* and *Susan hits Mark*). The control pair was included to provide reference data against which to relate synonymy judgments of the (AP) pairs. SOR sentences were different in meaning; AP sentences had the same meaning. If a child could detect the nonsynonymy of the SOR pairs but not the synonymy of the AP pairs, one could assume that he lacked understanding of the equivalence relation between active and passive sentences.

(*b*) Knowledge of the meaning equivalence (synonymity) of transformed sentence pairs was also determined by direct questioning as to their equivalence. The child was asked if the sentences had the *same meaning* or *different meaning*. In the *pictorial* equivalence task (in *a*), the child invoked two systems of representation. A *perceptual* representation (coding of the picture) and a linguistic representation (coding of the sentence). The two codings could then be matched. The linguistic equivalence task required a match of two linguistic codings plus a decision related to the request for a judgment of meaning. In the pictorial task the equivalence decision was implicit in the procedures, (i.e., in the choice of pictures), in the latter it was made explicit through the verbal response.

3. *Enactment*. The child's comprehension of sentence forms was also determined from his ability to carry out actions with dolls in order to represent the meaning of both active and passive sentences (e.g., "Show me with the dolls what *Susan pushes Mark* would look like," and "What would *Mark is pushed by Susan* look like?").[2]

Production Task

The child's ability to produce the passive was determined from his description of what happened when the experimenter demonstrated an action between an agent doll and a patient (object) doll, (*Mark pushes Susan*). The child was instructed to start his description with the patient (or object)—"Tell me what is happening, but start your sentence with *Susan*."[3] The same procedure was carried out with a picture representing *Mark chases Susan*, but the results were uninterpretable, principally because the pictures were ambiguous in the action (verb) represented.

Cognitive Tasks

The cognitive tasks were tests of various types of thinking all of which embodied a reversibility operation, or a preoperational form of reversibility. In Piagetian theory, the reversibility operation is critical to the development of quantitative thinking, as well as to all logical thought. No process of logical thought is complete unless it embodies the negation or reversal of the operation it is designed to carry out.

The most elementary form of reversibility is evident in the actions of the child in the era of sensorimotor intelligence (up to $1\frac{1}{2}$ or 2 years of age). It is during this period that the child becomes capable of carrying out an action, such as displacing an object, and negating the action by returning the object to its original position, i.e., canceling the displacement. At a more advanced level (usually arrived at about 6–7 years of age), reversibility is a critical operation in the capacity to deal with conservation, seriation, and classification. In the logical rule structures of these tasks, reversibility is tied to the operations of compensation and negation. In intermediate stages these achievements are manifest in incomplete form: the operations are not fully reversible but involve what Piaget identifies as one-way mappings.

[2],[3] This follows the method used by Sinclair and Ferreiro (1970).

The child can comprehend functional relations between variables, but can carry out such operations in one direction only. They cannot negate or reverse them or concurrently consider the inverse of these relations. An example is the case in which A is understood to be bigger than B, but B is not understood *at the same time* to be less than A, although *independently* it might be understood to be (Inhelder & Piaget, 1964).

Five tasks were used to provide data for an evaluation of the reversibility level of the child.

1. *Sensorimotor reversibility:* The experimenter put two cards, one red and one green, in front of the subject approximately 12 inches apart. A toy car was then placed on the red card. The subject was asked to drive his car from the red card to the green card. Upon doing this, he was told to drive the car back to where it was before.

2. *Conservation of discontinuous quantity:* The subject was presented with two equal rows of M & M candies and asked whether or not dolls placed next to the rows had equal amounts to eat. If the subject said "No," he was asked which doll had more. The bottom row of M & Ms was then extended so that it covered a larger area than the top row, and the subject was again asked whether the dolls had the same amount to eat. If he replied "No," he was asked which had more. The subject was asked to anticipate whether they would be the same when moved back to their original position. The M & Ms were then moved back to their original position. The subject was asked whether the rows were equal or not.

3. *Conservation of continuous quantity:* Two containers of equal size were placed on the table, one in front of the child and one in front of the experimenter. The subject was asked if the two containers, which were filled with equal amounts of salt, had the same "amount" of salt. If the subject did not think them equal, the salt level was adjusted until he agreed that they were. The subject then anticipated what would happen if the salt was poured into a taller and narrower container than was placed in front of him. If he said there would be a different amount of salt in the new container as compared to the old, he was asked which would have more, and to point to the place on the new container where the salt would reach if it were poured from the old into the new one. The salt was then poured, and the child was asked whether they had the same amount. He was next asked to anticipate what would happen if the salt were poured back into its original container, both by pointing to the spot where it would reach and by stating whether the amounts would be the same or not.

4. *Seriation:* The subject was presented with 4 beds and 4 dolls. The sets consisted of corresponding ascending sizes. The beds were arranged in order, but the dolls were not. The subject was asked to put each doll in its bed. A set of sticks of ascending size, but disarranged in sequence, was then placed in front of the subject and he was asked to put them "in size place." The subject was then given a drawing of a series of upright lines ascending in size, as in a bar graph, with a double space between the third and fifth line. He was asked to draw in the missing line. A card with sticks

pasted on it with a double space between the third and fifth stick was next put before him. He was instructed to choose the missing stick from 4 remaining sticks of different size and put it into its proper place on the card.

5. *Classification:* A pile of toy horses and cows of different colors was placed in front of the subject, with a number of boxes next to it. The subject was asked "how many" boxes were needed to put the "same" toys together. Requests to classify the toys were repeated until the objects were grouped so that the horses were in one pile and the cows in another. The subject was asked further if he could reduce the pile yet again (i.e., as "animals"). If he did not spontaneously classify the toys either as horses and cows, or as animals, they were classified for him. The horses were put in one pile, and the subject asked what they were called: the cows were put in a second pile and the question repeated. Then he was asked if all the toys could be called by the same name. Finally, if he did not answer correctly, he was asked if they could be called "animals." (This series of classification questions was not scored.) The experimenter then placed the horses and cows together (the horses being more numerous than the cows), and asked, "What would happen if we took away all the cows? What would be left?" Then, "What would be left if we took all the horses away?" The cows were removed and the subject was asked what would be left if all the horses were taken away. The animals were grouped and the subject was asked whether "there were more horses or animals," and "if all the horses were taken away whether there would be any animals left." If the subject said "Yes" to the latter question, he was asked what would remain. He was asked further whether "there were any animals that were not horses," and, if so, what they were. He was also asked whether there were "any animals that were not cows" in the box, and if so what they were. These questions were designed to determine the ability to classify, add, and subtract classes, and deal with whole—part class relations.

Within each of these cognitive tasks the intent was to ensure not only that the subject had adequate understanding (e.g., of classification), but that he had knowledge of the reversible function (i.e., in regard to classification, that the class could be reversed by separating its component subclasses).

Results

KNOWLEDGE OF VOICE

The youngest children in the sample ($\bar{X} = 4$ years, 9 months) had no difficulty with active sentences. They repeated them perfectly, they enacted them to a high degree (84.5%), and were able to identify pictures portraying events referred to in them with skill (73.8%). The somewhat lower performance in picture identification was probably due to the nature of the task, which included the 2-dimensional depiction of objects and the pictorial representation of action. These elements alone created difficulty because it

TABLE 3-1

Imitation, Comprehension, and Production of Active and Passive Direct-Object Reversible Sentences (Percentage of Correct Responses)

| | Imitation | | Comprehension | | | | Production |
| | | | Enactment | | Picture identification | | |
	Active[a]	Passive[a]	Active[b]	Passive[b]	Active[a]	Passive[a]	Passive[b]
Nursery (n = 21)[c]	100.0	85.7	84.5	53.6	73.8	52.4	21.4
Kindergarten (n = 22)	95.5	88.6	90.9	59.1	74.9	50.4	39.8
First-grade (n = 22)	100.0	93.2	97.7	78.4	93.2	72.7	85.2
Second-grade (n = 21)	100.0	100.0	100.0	97.6	97.6	95.2	94.1

[a] Based on 2 responses per category.
[b] Based on 4 responses per category.
[c] n refers to number of subjects in this and all tables unless otherwise indicated.

was not until the first-grade that subjects were able to perform almost as well in the picture identification task as they did in *enacting* the same active sentences at nursery grade (Table 3-1).

Knowledge of the passive was not equal to that of the active in the same nursery school children. It was more poorly imitated (85 versus 100%) and more poorly enacted than active sentences (53 versus 84%). Picture identification and enactment showed the same relative proportions for actives and passives until the second-grade, at which point a large proportion of children performed correctly in both sentences. Although comprehension (measured by enactment and picture identification)[4] was evident in a fair number of subjects at nursery age, production showed the oft-reported lag relative to comprehension. Only 21.4% of nursery children produced the passive in the context of these experimentally eliciting conditions; and it was not until the first-grade (age 7) that a substantial number of subjects (85%) produced the passive. There was thus a decided difference in the performance of first-graders relative to the kindergarteners in both production and comprehension.

Although the foregoing data characterize response to direct–object reversible sentences (*Mark hits Susan*), response to indirect–object reversible sentences (*Mark gives the book to Susan*) was much poorer for the passive in both imitation and picture identification (Table 3-2). The discontinuity in performance level was again evident between first- and second grades

TABLE 3-2

Imitation and Comprehension (Picture Identification) of Indirect-Object Reversible Sentences (Percentage of Correct Responses)

	Imitation		Comprehension	
			Picture identification	
	Active[a]	Passive[a]	Active[a]	Passive[a]
Nursery (n = 21)	97.6	59.5	92.9	23.8
Kindergarten (n = 22)	95.5	68.2	79.5	11.4
First-grade (n = 22)	100.0	68.2	93.2	22.7
Second-grade (n = 21)	100.0	97.6	100.0	83.3

[a] Based on 4 responses per category.
[b] Based on 2 responses per category.

[4] Although picture identification performance is at chance level, the comparable levels of performance for enactment cannot be considered chance performance because of the nature of the response.

TABLE 3-3

Imitation and Comprehension of Active and Passive Direct-Object Non-reversible Sentences[a] (Percentage of Correct Responses)

| | Imitation | Comprehension | | | Picture identification |
| | | Enactment | | | |
	Active	Active	Active[b]	Passive	Active[b]
Nursery (n = 21)	100.0	100.0	61.9	47.6	14.3
Kindergarten (n = 22)	100.0	100.0	77.3	68.2	40.9
First-grade (n = 22)	100.0	100.0	100.0	72.7	77.3
Second-grade (n = 21)	100.0	100.0	100.0	95.2	100.0

[a] Based on responses to 1 item.
[b] Based on response to the nonreversible picture: *The car washes Mark*.

for passive sentences, although differences in correct response were proportionately less.

With direct–object nonreversible sentences (Table 3-3), including those that make no sense to an adult, (*The car washes Mark*), performance was about the same as with reversible sentences. There was an exception in the poorer performance of the nursery group in the picture identification of a nonsensible active sentence (14.3%). Children apparently treat such non-credible sentences as logical. Either the sentences were believable to them or else they were aware of its unbelievability but were willing to "play the game." A sentence like *The car washes Mark* may be perfectly acceptable to a young child whose life is filled with symbolic play. The dividing line for younger children between play and reality is much less important than it is for older children or adults. Although performing well in enacting the non-credible sentence (61.9% of nursery subjects), performance was nevertheless poorer than when enacting a credible, nonreversible active sentence, *Mark washes the car* (100%). This may indicate an unwillingness on the part of some nursery and kindergarten children to act out a sentence which is "silly," or, when they do act it out, it is as if it were a credible form to them.

PRODUCING THE PASSIVE

The sentences constructed by children to the indirect request that they describe the experimenter's enactment of *Mark pushes Susan*, starting their story with *Susan*, shows three levels of response (Table 3-4). The first level is one in which the child gives an active sentence. In one form, he gives the asked-for grammatical subject (*Susan*—the logical object), so that in context the statement is incorrect (he says, *Susan hits Mark*). This type of response suggests an attempt by the child to portray the correct meaning, but he lacks the linguistic resources to do it. In another case, the child ignores the experimenter's request for the passive and starts his sentence with *Mark*, the logical subject. He makes his statement consistent with the action, but opposes the subject and object (*Susan is here* and *Mark is here*). This strategy suggests that the child knows the critical relation is one between subject and object, or agent and patient, but he too lacks the grammatical resources to reflect this relation adequately.

At the most sophisticated level, the full passive is given in three forms: *Susan is pushed by Mark*, *Susan is being pushed by Mark*, and the so-called colloquial form *Susan is getting (or got) pushed by Mark*.

Between the active constructions and the full passives are a series of intermediate forms, which reflect the child's attempt to grasp the rules represented by the active–passive transformation. One strategy is to realize the intent of the passive by coordinating two active statements into a single sentence that conveys the meaning of the action, e.g., *Susan is running and Mark is pushing her down*. One active sentence with Mark as logical subject is attached to another active sentence in which Susan is the logical subject. Coordination by conjunction is an attempt to make Mark the logical subject and Susan the logical object. This is the meaning conveyed by the co-ordinate sentence. The attempt is even more successful when a causal connector such as *because* is used, as in *Susan is falling because Mark pushed Susan*.

Another intermediate form, which is rare in our data but which is reported by Sinclair and Ferriero (1970) as a significant development, is the sentence that shows **reciprocal action** (*The cars are bumping each other* in reference to *The car pushes the truck*). This construction indicates a strategy in which the child covertly constructs two active sentences, each with a logical subject, and in the reciprocal attempts to retain both logical subjects. There is a **coordinate** form of the reciprocal action sentence that demonstrates this more clearly, *Susan is pushing Mark and Mark is pushing Susan*.

Both the reciprocal action and coordinate forms indicate that the child is attempting to go beyond representing the meaning of the passive by the use of an active sentence. By taking two active sentences, each with a different logical and grammatical subject, and putting them together, an attempt is made to construct a single sentence that conveys the intent of the passive. The child is unable to liberate himself from the notion that the logical subject must be in the place of the grammatical subject, whereas in the full passive, the logical object becomes the grammatical subject. Thus, in the intermediate forms, the *logical* subject–object relationship is not fully articulated with the *grammatical* subject–object relationship. The reciprocal action form, as a technique for groping with the logical problem,

TABLE 3-4

Passive Production Sentence Types by Reversibility Level and Age (Percentage of Responses)[a,b]

Sentence type	Reversibility level			Grade			
	1 (n = 39)	2 (n = 10)	3 (n = 37)	Nursery (n = 21)	Kindergarten (n = 22)	First (n = 22)	Second (n = 21)
I. Active sentences							
1. Incorrect subject *Mark is pushing Susan*	13.5	—	—	21.4	2.3	1.1	0.0
2. Correct subject *Susan is pushing Mark*	9.0	—	.7	10.7	5.7	0.0	1.2
3. Subject description *Susan is on this side he's on that.*	18.6	—	.7	20.2	14.8	0.0	0.0
II. Intermediate forms							
1. Coordinate clauses							
a. **and** *Susan's going, and Mark pushed her.*	14.7	15.0	8.8	9.5	22.7	11.4	4.8
b. **because** *Susan is falling because Mark pushed her.*	3.2	5.0	—	0.0	5.7	2.3	0.0

2. Reciprocal action							
a. Alone *They're pushing each other.*	1.3	—	—	2.4	0.0	0.0	0.0
b. Coordinate *Susan is pushing Mark and Mark is pushing Susan.*	3.9	2.5	—	4.8	3.4	0.0	0.0
3. Syncretic *The car got bumped into the truck*	1.9	2.5	.7	1.2	3.4	0.0	1.1
4. Truncated passive *Susan's pushed*	7.1	—	2.0	7.1	7.9	1.1	0.0
5. Incomplete passive (No auxiliary)	.6	7.5	—	1.2	0.0	0.0	0.0
III. Passive							
a. *is (was)* verb *by*	5.1	45.0	46.6	4.8	7.9	37.5	60.7
b. *is being (has been)* verb	7.1	7.5	18.9	9.5	4.5	19.3	15.5
c. *is getting (got)* verb *by* *Susan got pushed by Mark.*	10.9	15.0	21.6	3.6	19.3	26.1	14.3
IV. Don't know	3.2	—	—	3.6	2.3	0.0	0.0

[a] Based upon 4 responses per category.
[b] Stimulus represents *Mark pushes Susan.* Correct response is *Susan is pushed by Mark.*

51

results in a poor solution. The coordinate sentence seems to be somewhat more successful in conveying the intended meaning.

There is a **syncretic** form in which an active sentence is incompletely integrated with a passive, and a poorly constructed ambiguous sentence results; *The car got bumped into the truck* results from joining *The car got bumped by the truck* with *The car bumped into the truck*. Other incomplete forms bring the child even closer to the use of the full complement of passive transformation rules. The truncated passive appears as one such attempt: although it is a form frequently used by adults, whether its use by children has the same significance as for adults is not clear. If the transformational theory interpretation is correct, the truncated form involves a deletion of the full passive and is thus an even more sophisticated form than the full passive. It should, in fact, be very late in development. Its use in the present sample suggests, however, that it represents an intermediate achievement in that it appears with greatest frequency in the younger rather than in the older age groups.

The level of passive sentence production was related to the reversibility level of the subject. As is evident in Table 3-4, there were relatively few reversibility third-level subjects (the highest operational level) who gave responses that are other than full passives (with the *is* verb *by* form most frequent). This was also true of intermediate second-level subjects. The first-level subjects, however, produced the largest proportion of *active sentence* responses, i.e., coordinate—*actives, reciprocals* and *syncretic*, giving support to the postulated relationship between reversibility level and linguistic performance. An age analysis shows the relationship between passive production and grade level to be in many respects similar to that of reversibility level. Because reversibility level was correlated with age, this would be expected. The colloquial *got* form of the passive, however, was more related to reversibility level than to age as will be pointed out shortly. Production of the syncretic form was also more closely related to reversibility level than to age. On the whole, although production of active forms declined with age and full passives increased, the intermediate forms showed a curvilinear relation with increase from nursery to kindergarten age and then a decline. This development was unrelated to the child's reversibility level.

SYNONYMY

The foregoing has dealt with the imitation, comprehension, and production of single sentences. One would expect the processing of pairs of sentences to be more difficult. The results are not straightforward, however. Some conditions led to greater difficulty than processing single sentences, but, over all, they did not. Our principal concern was with contrasts between active—passive pairs (AP), in which the passive sentence was the passivized version of the active sentence (*x* verb *y*: *y* passive verb *x*), and subject–object reversal pairs (SOR), in which the subject–object relation was reversed and the verb kept intact (*x* verb *y*: *y* verb *x*). The structural difference between the two sets was in the form of the verb because the grammatical subject–object reversal was the same in both pairs.

Imitation of active–passive pairs (AP) was poorer than when the sentences were presented singly. By contrast, for the SOR pairs, in which two active sentences were paired and subject–object were reversed, imitation of the pairs was high (Table 3-5).

The difference in judging the synonymy of active–passive pairs (AP) and subject–object reversal pairs (SOR) was quite large (Table 3-5). Correct *picture equivalence* of subject–object reversal pairs (SOR) was slightly above-chance (52.4%) at the nursery level, but was nearly perfect for kindergarteners (90.9%); however, for active–passive pairs (AP), it just about reached chance level (47.6%) at the second-grade with direct object sentences. Correct *linguistic equivalence* judgments were slightly above-chance at nursery level for the SOR pairs, and it increased progressively. A high correct performance level (90.5%) was reached at the second-grade. Likewise, linguistic equivalence judgments of (AP) pairs reached an above-chance and high level (81.0%) only in the second-grade. It is evident that picture equivalence for AP pairs was much more difficult than linguistic equivalence; for SOR pairs, picture equivalence was much easier until the second-grade when ceiling in performance was reached in both.

It was possible that incorrect judgments of equivalence were due to the inability to imitate the sentences (due to memory loss, for example). This was not likely, however, for even when correct imitation of both sentences of the pair was high, as in the first-grade, correct meaning equivalence of active–passive pairs was still low.

The relative difficulty of imitation versus linguistic equivalence judgment is indicated further in Table 3-6, in which AP pairs are broken down by whether the passive sentences were given first (1 case), or the active (2 cases). Imitation was almost perfect in the (SOR) condition (20 of 21 subjects were correct in both) at the nursery grade level; it was poorest for the passivized subject–object reversal (Psor) condition (an indirect object sentence).

What occurred with the Psor pairs is instructive. A very substantial proportion of even nursery subjects (14 of 21 subjects) understood correctly the nonequivalence of the two sentences (*Susan is given the book by Mark* and *Susan gives the book to Mark*). At the same time, only about *half* of the second-grade subjects could imitate both sentences correctly and *none* of the nursery subjects. It is possible that the length of the sentence could have affected the ability to imitate these sentences correctly. At the same time, the entire content of the sentence need not have been stored in memory in order to make an adequate meaning equivalence judgment. Conceptual coding apparently occurred that preserved the meaning of the sentence even though the actual constituents were not fully stored.

Further data concerning the functional dependence of judgment upon

TABLE 3-5

Imitation, Comprehension (Picture Identification), and Synonymy Judgments of Active–Passive Pairs (AP) and Subject–Object Reversal Pairs (SOR)—Percentage of Correct Responses[a]

	Active–Passive pairs				Subject–Object Reversal Pairs			
	Imitation		Comprehension	Synonymy judgment	Imitation		Comprehension	Synonymy judgment
	Active	Passive	Picture identification	Linguistic equivalence	Active	Passive	Picture identification	Linguistic equivalence
Nursery (n = 21)	66.7	71.4	9.5	42.9	95.2	100	52.4	57.1
Kindergarten (n = 22)	72.7	72.7	13.6	36.4	100.0	95.5	90.9	63.6
First-grade (n = 22)	81.8	86.4	18.2	45.5	100.0	100.0	100.0	59.1
Second-grade (n = 21)	90.5	90.5	47.6	81.0	100.0	100.0	95.2	90.5

[a] Direct-object reversible sentences: *Mark hits Susan, Susan is hit by Mark and Mark hits Susan, Susan hits Mark.*

TABLE 3-6

Imitation, Comprehension, and Synonymy Judgments of Active–Passive Pairs (AP), Subject–Object Reversal Pairs (SOR), and Passivized Subject–Object Reversal Pairs (Psor) (Subjects Correct)

| | Imitation (Both sentences correct) | | | | | | Comprehension | | | | | | Synonymy judgment Linguistic equivalence | | | | | |
| | A*–P[a] (Indirect object) | Psor[b] | SOR[c] | A–P[d] | A–P[e] | A–P[f] | Picture identification | | | | Enactment | | A–P[a] (Indirect object) | Psor[b] | SOR[c] | A–P[d] | A–P[e] | A–P[f] |
							A–P[a]	Psor[b]	SOR[c]	A–P[d]	A–P[e]	A–P[f]						
Nursery (n = 21)	0	0	20	13	7	2	3	14	11	2	6	3	8	12	12	9	10	15
Kindergarten (n = 22)	0	1	21	12	12	4	0	15	20	3	8	6	5	14	15	8	12	10
First-grade (n = 22)	0	2	22	16	16	11	2	15	22	4	12	3	8	13	13	10	12	13
Second-grade (n = 21)	10	11	21	18	18	17	16	12	20	10	15	12	19	12	19	17	17	17

* Italic letter indicates whether active or passive sentences was given first.

a (A) Susan gives the book to Mark; (P) Mark is given the book by Susan.

b (P) Susan is given the book by Mark; (A) Susan gives the book to Mark.

c (A) Mark hits Susan; (A) Susan hits Mark.

d (P) Susan is hit by Mark; (A) Mark hits Susan.

e (A) Mark pushes Susan; (P) Susan is pushed by Mark.

f (A) The truck bumps the car; (P) The car is bumped by the truck.

TABLE 3-7

Relation of Active–Passive and Subject–Object Reversal Pair Imitation to Linguistic Equivalence Judgments (Subjects Correct)

Imitation	Active–Passive pairs (indirect object; active first) Linguistic equivalence		Passivized subject–object reversal pairs (indirect object; passive first) Linguistic equivalence		Subject–Object reversal Linguistic equivalence		Imitation	Active–Passive pairs (passive first; direct object)		Active–Passive pairs (active first; direct object)		Active–Passive pairs (active first; direct object)	
	−	+	−	+	−	+		−	+	−	+	−	+
Nursery (n = 21)													
0	7	2	7	11	0	0	0	3	2	2	5	3	7
½	6	6	2	1	0	1	½	2	1	5	2	2	7
1	0	0	0	0	9	11	1	7	6	4	3	1	1
Kindergarten (n = 22)													
0	6	3	5	11	0	0	0	2	0	2	1	3	4
½	11	2	2	3	0	1	½	4	4	3	4	6	5
1	1	0	1	0	7	14	1	8	4	5	7	3	1
First-grade (n = 22)													
0	3	4	3	5	0	0	1	0	1	0	0	2	2
½	11	4	6	6	0	0	½	2	3	5	1	3	4
1	0	0	0	2	9	13	1	10	6	5	11	4	7
Second-grade (n = 21)													
0	1	3	3	1	0	0	0	0	1	2	1	1	3
½	0	7	3	3	0	0	½	1	1	0	0	0	0
1	1	9	3	8	2	19	1	3	15	2	16	3	14
	(A) Susan gives the book to Mark. (P) Mark is given the book by Susan.		(P) Susan is given the book by Mark. (A) Susan gives the book to Mark.		(A) Mark hits Susan. (A) Susan hits Mark.			(P) Susan is hit by Mark. (A) Mark hits Susan.		(A) Mark pushes Susan. (P) Susan is pushed by Mark.		(A) The truck bumps the car. (P) The car is bumped by the truck.	

imitation are indicated by contingency tables in Table 3-7.[5] The AP indirect object condition showed a shift at the second-grade level from little imitation to significant imitation (the score was based on both sentences being imitated correctly); concurrently, there was an increase in correct equivalence judgment. The AP (direct object) pairs, particularly at the early grades, showed that there could be correct equivalence judgment *without* correct imitation. In this condition, a significant improvement in imitation occurred about the first grade. A concomitant shift in correct equivalence judgments did not occur at the same time except in one of the test pairs. This suggests that a process other than imitation affected the shift in equivalence judgments. When the passive was presented first to nursery school children, the pair was imitated better (13 of 21 subjects) than when it came second (7 of 21, and 2 of 21). By kindergarten, however, the advantage changed (as in the active-first condition with the verb *push*). Whether this was a function of the particular verb used is not clear.

RELATION OF REVERSIBILITY LEVEL TO LANGUAGE PERFORMANCE

Subjects were classified in one of three reversibility levels. Reversibility for Level 1 indicated that the subject performed perfectly at the level of sensorimotor reversibility. Level 3 indicated that the child demonstrated *operational* reversibility in the context of the conservation, classification, and seriation tasks. Level 2 indicated transitional state performance in which the child's knowledge was at the level of one-way mappings, i.e., knowledge of an inverse or compensatory operation could not be demonstrated.

The relation between language performance and the child's reversibility level is shown in Tables 3-8–3-10 in which language scores are dichotomized into two levels (3–4 and 0–2 items correct). The data in Table 3-8, which relates reversibility level to the comprehension and production of the passive, shows that for both comprehension and production the nursery and kindergarten children were characterized by low level reversibility and poor language performance; high level reversibility and superior language performance characterized the second-grade subjects. An upward shift in reversibility level occurred between kindergarten and first-grade, and in comprehension of the passive in the second-grade. The relation between reversibility level and equivalence judgments of AP pairs is indicated in Table 3-9. The relationship is evident only with linguistic equivalence judgments and not with picture equivalence. Correct picture choice was not achieved to a high degree by even the oldest children who had already reached the highest reversibility level. Again, first-grade reversibility level

[5] The data within each set indicate the numbers of subjects classified as high or low on imitation and linguistic equivalence. Vertical shifts indicate change in imitation performance; horizontal shifts indicate linguistic performance change. Concurrent change suggests an interrelation.

TABLE 3-8

Relation between Reversibility Level and Language Response (Subjects Correct)

	Reversibility level	Passive[a] (comprehension)		Passive[b] (production)	
		Items correct		*Items correct*	
		3–4	*0–2*	*3–4*	*0–2*
Nursery	3	0	1	1	0
(n = 21)	2	0	0	0	0
	1	3	17	2	17
Kindergarten	3	0	3	2	1
(n = 22)	2	1	2	1	2
	1	0	16	3	13
First grade	3	4	12	14	2
(n = 22)	2	0	3	2	1
	1	0	3	2	1
Second grade	3	16	1	15	2
n = (21)	2	3	1	4	0
	1	0	0	0	0

[a] Direct- and indirect-object reversible sentences combined.
[b] Direct-object reversible sentences.

distributions changed, and superior linguistic judgment was achieved only at the second-grade.

Equivalence judgments of SOR pairs (Table 3-10) show a different pattern. Correct linguistic and picture equivalence judgments of SOR pairs improved significantly at the kindergarten level. The same was less true for the passivized subject–object reversal pairs (Psor). In fact, a substantial number of subjects already did well at the nursery level with these forms.

Reversibility level was also related to the type of passive sentence produced (Table 3-4). Children at the highest reversibility level (third) produced the most advanced passive forms. Generally, younger children produced primitive passive-attempting responses, and older children produced the full passive. There was an interesting exception to the age relationship which shows that production of the passive was more related to reversibility level than to age. It is in the production of the colloquial *got* form of the passive mentioned previously, which is the most frequent production form for children at the lowest reversibility level (10.9%). Although its absolute frequency increased in relation to reversibility level (to 21.6%), its frequency fell relative to the production of the *is* (V) *by* form.

TABLE 3-9

Relation between Reversibility Level and Synonymy Judgments of Active–Passive Sentence Pairs (Subjects Correct)

Reversibility level	Linguistic equivalence[a]		Picture equivalence[b]		Combined[c]		
	Items correct		Items correct		Items correct		
	3–4	0–2	2	0–1	5–6	3–4	0–2
Nursery							
3	0	1	0	1	0	1	0
2	0	0	0	0	0	0	0
(n = 21) 1	7	13	0	2	0	8	12
Kindergarten							
3	0	3	0	3	0	0	3
2	2	1	0	3	0	2	1
(n = 22) 1	7	9	0	16	0	7	9
First grade							
3	8	8	1	15	2	6	8
2	1	2	0	3	0	1	2
(n = 22) 1	1	2	0	3	0	1	2
Second-grade							
3	14	3	4	13	9	6	2
2	3	1	0	4	1	2	1
(n = 21) 1	0	0	0	0	0	0	0

[a] Direct– and indirect–object reversible sentence (combined picture and toy reference).

[b] Direct– and indirect–object reversible sentences combined.

[c] Linguistic equivalence judgments and picture identification, combined (direct– and indirect–reversible sentences: picture and toy reference).

TABLE 3-10

Synonymy Judgments of Subject–Object Reversal Pairs as a Function of Reversibility Level (Subjects Correct)

	Subject–Object reversal pairs		Passivized subject–object reversal pairs		Combined subject–object reversal pairs and passivized subject–object reversal pairs	
	Linguistic and picture equivalence		Linguistic and picture equivalence		Linguistic and picture equivalence	
	Items correct		Items correct		Items correct	
Reversibility level	2	0–1	2	0–1	3–4	0–2
Nursery (n = 21)						
3	0	1	0	0	1	0
2	0	0	0	0	0	0
1	4	16	8	13	7	13
Kindergarten (n = 22)						
3	2	1	1	2	2	1
2	1	2	1	2	1	2
1	9	7	7	9	11	5
First-grade (n = 22)						
3	10	6	6	10	11	5
2	2	1	1	2	2	1
1	0	3	1	2	1	2
Second-grade (n = 21)						
3	15	2	8	9	13	4
2	3	1	0	4	2	2
1	0	0	0	0	0	0

Production of the *got* form showed a different pattern in relation to age. It was among the least frequently used forms by the youngest children (3.6%). Its production rose to a peak at the first-grade (26.1%), and declined to 14.3% at the second-grade.

Discussion

Comprehension and production of passive and active sentences were achieved at different ages, although by first-grade (6-years old) these differences disappeared. This finding is consistent with the majority of studies that report a lag in the age of acquisition of the passive, although there is no consistency in the age at which knowledge of the passive is said to be attained. As expected, sentences with indirect subjects were comprehended less-well than sentences with direct objects.

Although differences in the comprehension of active and passive sentences was expected, the considerable delay in the ability to judge the equivalence in meaning of active and passive sentences was unexpected. Comprehension of the synonymity of active–passive pairs was not achieved until about the second-grade (7-years old). At that, adequate performance was evident only in linguistically expressed judgments; pictorial equivalence was never adequately achieved in this sample, due no doubt to the difficulty of matching pictorial and linguistic representations. On the other hand, sentence pairs with only a subject–object reversal (SOR) and no compensating change in the verb were understood by younger children to differ in meaning, as was seen in the kindergartener's picture selection performance.

A number of possibilities can account for the difference between judgments of subject–object reversals that change meaning (SOR) and those reversals that preserve meaning (AP). These will be discussed in connection with the experiments to follow that further explored this finding. Suffice it to say that these data raise doubt as to what is understood about children's intuitions of the grammar. If the data are reliable, they indicate that the child is able to produce and comprehend sentences, such as the passive, years before he is able to make judgments about such sentences. His "reflection" upon his language, which may be said to be one aspect of his intuitions into the grammar, must be separated from his functioning in accordance with the linguistic rule system. The origin of this reflective capacity appears to be related to the concomitant development of the child's knowledge of logical reversibility.

The data show further that possession of a low reversibility level is associated with poor passive sentence comprehension; although a high reversibility level does not necessarily ensure a high level of comprehension (in the first-grade, 12 of 16 operational level reversibility subjects had low passive comprehension). At the second-grade, however, the correlation between the two types of performance was much nearer to unity. The same pattern was evident for production of the passive, except that at the point where there was a substantial increase in reversibility level (first-grade) there was also substantial improvement in production of the passive. Low reversibility was also related to poor active–passive synonymy judgment, but this did not exclude some children from performing well in the linguistic task. Again, at the point where reversibility level improved (first-grade), there was improvement in correct equivalence judgment; by the second-grade, the improvement was substantial.

Reversibility level was also related to the type of passives produced by the subjects. Relatively few operational reversibility level subjects gave responses other than the full passive form. The least sophisticated reversibility subjects, on the other hand, produced the largest proportion of active sentence responses, including coordinate active, reciprocal, and syncretic forms.

The data of this experiment, then, show late development of the passive relative to the active, and an even later development of understanding of active–passive sentence synonymy. In general, they support a contingent relationship between the development of linguistic competence (of the passive) and development of operational reversibility. The grammatical and semantic properties of the child's attempts to construct the passive offers evidence of the constructive nature of language development. The underlying source of sentence construction, as the reversibility data suggest, is some logical representation of meaning. Knowledge of the transformation rules necessary to the construction of passive sentences is not achieved abruptly or spontaneously, but results from a progressive construction or reconstruction of what the child abstracts from his linguistic environment, which, in turn, is related to the underlying logical representation of meaning. In the intermediate stages, both incomplete and complete forms appear— sometimes in the same child. The incomplete forms are utilized, with less and less frequency as development proceeds.

Experiment 2: Synonymy Judgments of Active, Passive, and Cleft Sentences[6]

The results of Experiment 1 showed that children were able to comprehend the passive before they were able to judge the synonymy of active and passive sentences. In that study, the child's understanding of the meaning equivalence of actives and passives was tested in two ways. In the first task, the child was read two sentences and was asked whether the sentences had the same meaning. His response was verbal. In the second task, the child was read two sentences, after which he imitated them and selected the appropriate picture or pictures that represented the meaning of the sentences. In both tasks, the sentences were either synonymous, as ordinarily understood (as in the case of an active and its corresponding passive;

---

[6] In collaboration with Hinda G. Sack. A portion of this study was reported in Sack, H. G. and Beilin, H. Meaning equivalence of active–passive and subject–object first cleft sentences. Presented at the Developmental Psycholinguistics Conference, State University of New York at Buffalo, New York, 1971.

The boy hits the girl and *The girl is hit by the boy*), or, the meaning of the sentences differed because of the reversal of agent and patient (*The boy hits the girl* and *The girl hits the boy*). In the *linguistic equivalence* task, response was random up to the second-grade, at which point it was correct to a high degree. In the *picture equivalence* task, children consistently selected *different-meaning* pictures for synonymous active–passive pairs until the second-grade, at which point response became random.

There are two possible explanations of these results. One is that the active and passive do indeed mean different things to the child because he is particularly sensitive to the topic (or word-order) shift between the two constructions and bases his judgment of their meaning on this criterion. The usual tests of sentence comprehension such as picture selection and enactment do not capture this distinction. The other possibility is that the active and passive have the same meaning to the child, but, because of the memory load required by the two sentences, he is incapable of making the correct judgment. The child may also falter because he does not understand that the task requirement of comparing meanings requires judgments based on underlying rather than surface relations.

The basis for establishing the synonymity of sentences is a philosophical and linguistic question as we have already indicated, and over this question there is considerable controversy (see Quine, 1972), but the basis on which sentences are *judged* as synonymous is also a matter of dispute. One interpretation is based on equivalence of reference, another on factual equivalence or truth value, yet another on the equivalence of "underlying propositions." These criteria are considerations associated with deep structure relations. Other criteria such as equivalence of topic or theme are associated with surface structure relations. Although some linguists and philosophers contend that behavioral data are not particularly germane to establishing criteria for synonymy, this is apparently not Quine's position who holds that such data may be necessary. Furthermore, the fact that Chomsky depends on linguists' intuitions in judgments of sentence synonymy is paradoxical when contrasted with his efforts to divorce linguistic criteria from psychological criteria for the construction of a grammar.

Leaving aside whether psychological considerations are necessary to the criteria of linguistic synonymity and whether synonymity can be used as the basis for construction of a grammar, so little is known of the nature of synonymy judgments that we undertook a further study to extend the analysis of Experiment 1. In this second study, we assessed the child's judgment of subject-first cleft and object-first cleft sentences, in addition to actives and passives. Examples of subject-first cleft and object-first cleft sentences, which clearly parallel the active–passive contrast, are, respectively, *It's the boy that pushes the girl* and *It's the girl that the boy pushes*.

Three different techniques for assessing the understanding of synonymy relations were employed in order to explore in greater depth the nature of the child's intuition of synonymy. Two techniques were indirect; sentence recognition and sentence recall. The third was the direct judgment of synonymy used in the first study.

Method

SUBJECTS

The Ss were predominantly white middle-class children from nursery school through second-grade (4- to 7-years old) who were individually tested. English was the dominant language for the Ss, and none had a language disability. The mean ages for each grade were: nursery (4 years, 5 months), kindergarten (5 years, 2.7 months), first-grade (6 years, 6.7 months) and second-grade (7 years, 5.6 months). There were 16 Ss in each age group.

DESIGN

An outline of the design and the sentences used is presented in Table 3-11. Each child was seen twice with at least a week intervening between experimental sessions.

1. In each session, the subject was first tested for his *comprehension* of four sentences.
2. *Recognition* of these sentences was then determined from a longer list in which the comprehension sentences were embedded.
3. Recognition was followed by *recall* of the same comprehension sentences.
4. Finally, the child was presented with pairs of sentences, one member of the pair from the original *comprehension* set (of four) joined with another sentence selected from the *recognition* list. In this synonymy judgment task, the subject was asked to judge whether the sentences were equivalent in meaning (meant the same thing).

In each testing session, the sentences were either actives and passives (*voice condition*), or subject-first and object-first clefts (*cleft condition*). Each subject received both sets. Order was counterbalanced within each age group so that half the subjects received the voice condition first, with the cleft condition following a week later, and the other half, the reverse. Sentences were synonymous between conditions.

Comprehension Procedure and Results

COMPREHENSION PROCEDURE

The child was read a set of four sentences (two actives and two passives) and was questioned about the sentences (Table 3-11). The four sentences were read twice. In the first reading of a sentence, the child was either asked, "Who is doing the Xing?" or "Who is getting Xd?" In the second reading, the alternative question was asked.

TABLE 3-11

Experimental Sentences Classified by Task: Experiment 2

A. Comprehension (original list)

Voice condition	Cleft Condition

a. *The boy pushes the girl.*   a. *It's the boy that pushes the girl.*
b. *The cat gets chased by the dog.*   b. *It's the cat that the dog chases.*
c. *The donkey kicks the horse.*   c. *It's the donkey that kicks the horse.*
d. *The mommy gets helped by the daddy.* d. *It's the mommy that the daddy helps.*
Comprehension questions: "Who is doing the Xing?" "Who is getting X'd?"

B. Recognition

Voice Condition   Relation to Original List

1. a. *The boy pushes the girl.*   1. Identity (original list): same
   b. *The cat gets chased by the dog.*   meaning.
   c. *The donkey kicks the horse.*
   d. *The mommy gets helped by the daddy.*
2. a. *The girl gets pushed by the boy.*   2. Change of form: synonymous.
   b. *The dog chases the cat.*
   c. *The horse gets kicked by the donkey.*
   d. *The daddy helps the mommy.*
3. a. *The boy gets pushed by the girl.*   3. Change of form: agent–patient
   b. *The cat chases the dog.*   reversed; same content word
   c. *The donkey gets kicked by the horse.*   order; different meaning.
   d. *The mommy helps the daddy.*
4. a. *The baby gets pushed by the boy.*   4. Change of form: new patient;
   b. *The dog chases the squirrel.*   different meaning.
   c. *The cow gets kicked by the donkey.*
   d. *The daddy helps the grandma.*
5. a. *The girl gets pushed by the man.*   5. Change of form: new agent;
   b. *The kitten chases the cat.*   different meaning.
   c. *The horse gets kicked by the bull.*
   d. *The child helps the mommy.*
6. a. *The girl pushes the boy.*   6. Same form: agent–patient re-
   b. *The dog gets chased by the cat.*   versed; reversed content word
   c. *The horse kicks the donkey.*   order; different meaning.
   d. *The daddy gets helped by the mommy.*

C. Recall

"Tell me back those old sentences, the ones I asked you to remember, the ones I asked
you questions about."
Prompt: "Was there a story about *push*?"

D. Same-Different Judgments

1. a. *The boy pushes the girl.*   4. a. *The boy pushes the girl.*
   a. *The boy pushes the girl.*   a. *The baby gets pushed by the boy.*
2. a. *The boy pushes the girl.*   5. a. *The boy pushes the girl.*
   a. *The girl gets pushed by the boy.*   a. *The girl gets pushed by the man.*
3. a. *The boy pushes the girl.*   6. a. *The boy pushes the girl.*
   a. *The boy gets pushed by the girl.*   a. *The girl pushes the boy.*

TABLE 3-12

Sentence Comprehension as a Function of Syntactic Form: Experiment 2 (Percentage of Correct Responses)[a]

Grade	Active	Cleft: Subject-First	Passive	Cleft: Object-First
Nursery	70	75	70	70
Kindergarten	84	88	84	72
First	92	91	86	66
Second	100	98	89	47

[a] Percentage of 64 responses per cell: $n = 16 \times 2$ sentences of each syntactic type × 2 comprehension questions per sentence.

COMPREHENSION RESULTS

The results are presented in Table 3-12. In an analysis of variance with Grade and Syntactic type as main effects, the overall effect of Grade upon comprehension was not significant. Improvement in performance from nursery to second-grade was confined to active, passive, and subject-first cleft sentences. Nursery level performance, however, was significantly poorer than the older grades (indicated by Newman–Keuls tests: $p < .01$), although the older grades were not significantly different from each other.

The object-first cleft presented a different response pattern with age from the other three syntactic forms, and was generally more difficult than all other experimental tasks. Although the object-first cleft was no more difficult to comprehend than other syntactic forms at the nursery level, comprehension became progressively *poorer* up to the second-grade, while others improved.

The effect of Syntactic form was significant ($p < .01$), as was the interaction between Grade and Syntactic form ($p < .01$). The decline in object-first cleft performance accounted for both the significant Grade × Syntactic form interaction and the nonsignificant Grade effect.

The interaction between Syntactic form and Grade can be better understood through an examination of Table 3-13. This table reports the percentage of sentences comprehended correctly on one, both, and on neither of the comprehension questions. The most common pattern across grade levels and syntactic forms was for one or both questions to be answered correctly. Only infrequently were both questions miscomprehended. There was a major deviation from this pattern in the second-grade for the object-first sentence form. At that level, children were incorrect on both questions more often than they were correct. The data provide few indications to account for the poorer performance at the second-grade when performance on the other syntactic forms significantly improved. It would appear that a major confusion occurred. A partial clue to the reason for this is given by the fact that nursery school children, when incorrect, provided the same

TABLE 3-13

Comprehension of the Two Comprehension Questions as a Function of Syntactic Form: Experiment 2 (Percentage of Correct Responses)[a]

Grade	Active			Cleft: subject first			Passive			Cleft: object first		
	(0)[b]	(1)	(2)	(0)	(1)	(2)	(0)	(1)	(2)	(0)	(1)	(2)
Nursery	6	47	47	9	31	59	12	31	56	6	47	47
Kindergarten	13	6	81	0	25	75	3	25	72	6	44	50
First	0	16	84	0	19	81	3	22	75	9	50	41
Second	0	0	100	0	3	97	3	16	81	41	25	34

[a] Percentage of 32 responses per syntactic form at each grade level: $n = 16 \times 2$ sentences of each syntactic type.
[b] 0 = correct on neither question; 1 = correct on one of the questions (response is the same to both questions); 2 = correct on both questions.

noun to both questions, fewer second-graders did this. The second-graders eschewed what appeared to be a guessing strategy. They knew that the two questions required different answers, but were unable to supply the correct ones when faced with the object-first cleft syntactic form.

We were interested to know whether the form of the question "Who is doing the Xing?" versus "Who is getting Xd?" with the stress in the former on the agent and the latter on the patient made a difference in successful performance. The type of question was a significant factor only for the nursery children. For these subjects, agent questions were significantly easier than patient questions ($p < .05$; one-tailed). In the nursery grade, when agent questions were matched with agent-first sentences, and patient-first sentences with patient questions, they were *more difficult* than the unmatched condition ($p < .05$). This suggests a bias among nursery school children toward giving the last mentioned noun in response to a comprehension question. An inspection of the data showed this strategy to be confined to the object-first forms when questioning the patient. It may be a guessing strategy for dealing with a more difficult syntactic form.

A comparison with the active–passive comprehension data of the first study shows that active sentence comprehension was about the same as in the first study, but poorer than the enactment data of that study. Comprehension of the passive (Table 3-12) was greater than in the first study for all grades (in both enactment and identification tasks). When the data were analyzed in terms of whether the subject comprehended both sentences correctly, one correctly, or neither correctly (Table 3-13), superior performance, particularly of the nursery children, was substantially reduced.

Recognition Procedure and Results

RECOGNITION PROCEDURE

After the comprehension test, the subject was instructed to listen carefully and try to remember the sentences. The experimenter reread the comprehension sentences again twice, followed by a test of sentence recognition. Two sets of four comprehension sentences comprised the original list of the recognition task. A randomized list of the sentences in Table 3-11 was then read aloud. The subjects were to reply "old" to the sentences they thought they had heard before, and "new" to the sentences they thought they had not heard.

In experiments with adults (e.g., Sachs, 1967), it was found that memory for syntactic information tends to fade more quickly than memory for semantic information. This fact provided the rationale for one of the tests of the meaning equivalence of active and passive sentences. We assumed that "memory" loss for syntactic information would diminish the effect of differences in surface structure and lead to the *false* recognition of sentences in which there was a change of syntactic form but meaning was preserved. Errors showing such a selective recognition pattern would be taken as evidence (albeit indirect) that active and passive sentences had the same meaning for the child. An added justification for using this task was to check the possibility that immediate memory load in the direct linguistic equivalence task was an important source of the difficulty younger children had in making correct judgments. The recognition task would minimize this effect through the prior overexposure to the original list sentences.

The recognition list was constructed so as to systematically vary the semantic and surface structure relations between the *original* list and the *recognition* list sentences. It is identified in categories as follows:

Category 1. *Identity*. The original list sentences. Two instances of the same sentence were paired and thus had the same meaning.

Category 2. *A change in form through passivization*. Meaning was preserved. The original list and recognition list sentences were synonymous (AP).

Category 3. *A change in form and agent-patient reversal*. Passivization and agent–patient reversal combined. Meaning was thus changed (Psor).

Category 4. *A change in form and substitution of a new patient noun*. Meaning was changed.

Category 5. *A change in form and substitution of a new agent noun*. Meaning was changed.

Category 6. *Form preserved with agent-patient reversed*. Meaning was changed (SOR).

Response to the variations represented in these categories was expected to furnish information about the knowledge underlying the child's performance. The letter (a, b, c, or d), preceding each sentence of the recognition list in Table 11, indicates the original list sentence (a, b, c, or d) to which it is related.

The data in Table 3-14 show the following. For Category 1 (identity) the percentages indicate the proportion of subjects who *correctly* identified the sentences as "old," that is, as having been heard before. For the remaining categories, the data indicate subjects who also reported "old," that is, who thought they had heard the sentences before, except that these identifications were *false*, because in each case some change was made in the original sentence. The false identifications imply that the subject considered them equivalent either on the basis of meaning or form.

RECOGNITION RESULTS

The recognition data appear in Table 3-14. A Grade × Voice-Cleft × Category analysis of variance (4 × 2 × 6) was performed on the number of "old" recognition responses. The main effects of Grade ($p < .01$) and Category ($p < .01$) were significant, as were the Grade × Category interaction ($p < .01$), the Voice-Cleft × Category interaction ($p < .01$), and the triple interaction of Grade × Voice-Cleft × Category ($p < .01$). The main

TABLE 3-14

Recognition List Response: Experiment 2 (Percentage of Correct Responses)[a]

	Categories					
Grade	1 Correct (identity)	2 Error (same meaning)	3 Error (different meaning)	4 Error (different meaning)	5 Error (different meaning)	6 Error (different meaning)
			Voice			
Nursery	86**	75**	63*	47	41	58
Kindergarten	86**	89**	59	9**	16**	58
First	89**	83**	45	0**	6**	36*
Second	92**	89**	27**	5**	0**	23**
	Boy pushes girl.[b] Cat chased by dog.	Girl pushed by boy. Dog chases cat.	Boy pushed by girl. Cat chases dog.	Baby Squirrel	Man Kitten	Girl pushes boy. Dog chased by cat.
			Cleft			
Nursery	81**	69**	55	38	36*	61
Kindergarten	94**	77**	73**	11**	14**	58
First	86**	75**	58	2**	11**	47
Second	88**	63**	64*	0**	0**	41
	It's boy pushes girl. It's cat dog chases.	It's girl boy pushes. It's dog chases cat.	It's boy girl pushes. It's cat chases dog.	Baby Squirrel	Man Kitten	It's girl pushes boy. It's dog cat chases.

[a] Percentage of 64 responses per cell. $n = 16 \times 4$ responses per subject.
[b] Actual sentences are abbreviated in this table.
* $p < .05$.
** $p < .01$.

effect of Voice-Cleft was not significant, nor was the Grade × Voice inter-action.

The nursery school children showed a distinct disposition to respond "old" or "yes" to all the sentences of the recognition list. With increasing age there was a decrease in the number of such recognition responses. The age at which the decrease occurred depended both upon the category and whether it was the voice or cleft condition.

In the nursery group, there were no important differences between the voice and cleft conditions. Recognition responses to the identity category (Category 1, the original list) were significantly greater than responses to the agent–patient reversals of Categories 3 and 6 and greater than the responses to the categories with a new noun substitution (Categories 4 and 5). Responses to the original list sentences were *not* significantly greater than responses to the Category 2 sentences, the category that preserved meaning even though the sentence was passivized. However, as responses to the synonymy category (2) were not significantly greater than responses to the agent–patient reversals (3 and 6), it appears that the pattern of responding in the 4-year-old group cannot be said to be clearly selective with respect to either the underlying proposition or the word-order rela-tions. By kindergarten, however, response to Category 2 sentences (the passivization change) increased sufficiently, and the others decreased enough so that both the identity category and Category 2 receive signifi-cantly more recognition responses than all others. The same pattern held for the first- and second grades. It thus appeared that by kindergarten age, children's recognition responses to active and passive sentences were selective; selective in accordance with the adult conception (deep structure aspects) of the meaning relations among the sentences. Children made distinctions when meaning changed but failed to make them when only the form changed.

False recognition (recognizing sentences not actually heard before) was most frequent to sentences that adults identify as having the same meaning as the original list sentences. This being the case, it appears that a sub-stantial number of kindergartners also interpreted the active and passive as having the same meaning.

In the cleft condition, the pattern was not as clear. Response to Category 1 was about the same as in the voice condition, but there were fewer re-sponses in Category 2 and more in Category 3, where there was an agent–patient reversal. There were thus fewer false sentence recognitions judged synonymous by adult standards (especially in the object-first clefts of that category) and more false recognitions of the agent–patient reversal with the same grammatical subject. Unfortunately, because of the comprehen-sion difficulties of the object-first cleft, it is difficult to say whether this was due to perceptual confusion between sentences in Categories 1 and 3—subjects might have thought they were hearing sentences of Category 1 again—or whether subjects gave "old" response to sentences of Category 3 because they actually were judging them synonymous on the basis of shared grammatical subjects.

Recall Procedure and Results

RECALL PROCEDURE

Sentence recall followed the recognition task. Children were asked to "tell back" the old sentences. If they could not remember the sentences, they were prompted with the *verb*; "Was there a story about *push*?" or "What about *push*?" As with the recognition task, this was considered an indirect test of synonymy. It provides insight into the child's meaning—preserving errors in his processing of active and passive sentences.

RECALL RESULTS

The recall results are presented in Table 3-15 and 3-16. The most notable feature of the data in Table 3-15 (recall of sentence meaning) is the limited number of recall responses with agent and patient reversed, even in the nursery school group. Another aspect of the data worth noting is the greater recall of agent–patient reversals in the cleft condition when that condition was presented first than when the cleft condition followed the voice condition. Because of the interaction between cleft-voice order and meaning recall, the analysis of the influence of syntactic form on meaning recall (in Table 3-16) was for the first session only. The data indicate that most

TABLE 3-15

Number of Sentences Recalled:Meaning-Preserving and Meaning-Changing:

Level and test order	Cleft sentences (agent-patient)			Voice sentences (agent-patient)		
	same	reversal	other[a]	same	reversal	other
Nursery						
Cleft—Voice	10	2	20	11	3	18
Voice—Cleft	22	3	7	18	1	13
Kindergarten						
Cleft—Voice	18	8	6	25	3	4
Voice—Cleft	26	4	2	26	3	3
First grade						
Cleft—Voice	18	8	6	25	3	4
Voice—Cleft	26	4	2	26	3	3
Second grade						
Cleft—Voice	21	9	2	28	2	2
Voice—Cleft	22	6	3	26	1	5

[a] Includes confabulations, changes of verb, and unscorable responses.
Note: There are 32 possible responses per cell: 8 × 4 sentences per subject.

TABLE 3-16

Meaning and Form Recall as a Function of Original List Sentence Form: Experiment 2 (Number of Responses)

	Cleft: Subject first		Cleft: Object first		Active		Passive	
	NT[a]	T[b]	NT	T	NT	T	NT	T
Nursery								
Meaning same	5	0	0	5	7	1	0	7
A–P reversed[c]	0	0	0	2	0	0	0	0
Kindergarten								
Meaning same	5	0	0	8	8	1	2	10
A–P reversed	2	0	1	4	2	0	0	1
First-grade								
Meaning same	9	1	1	7	11	2	1	12
A–P reversed	2	1	1	4	0	0	0	3
Second-grade								
Meaning same	13	1	2	5	5	7	5	9
A–P reversed	1	0	0	8	0	0	0	1

[a] Nontransformed sentences in recall: subject-first forms recalled as such and object-first forms recalled as such.
[b] Transformed sentences in recall: from subject-first form to object-first form or vice versa.
[c] Agent–patient reversed in recall.
Note: Maximum 16 responses for each 2 × 2 classification of responses: two original list sentences for each grammatical type × 8 subjects in each age group who received either the *voice* or the *cleft* condition first.

sentences were recalled as subject-first forms. Thus passives and object-first clefts were generally recalled in the transformed active form. The most important data in Table 3-16 are for recall of the passive. Children recalled passive sentences with the correct meaning, and they preserved sentence meaning even when they transformed the sentence form in recall. This was true even for the nursery group.

These data point to the conclusion that even the nursery school child understands to some degree that active sentences and their corresponding passives have the same meaning. This is evidenced by the fact that the sentences transformed in recall preserve their meaning more often than change it, even though the nursery school child did not restrict his recognition selectively to those sentences that preserved the meaning of the original list sentences. Although in the recognition task the nursery school child said "old" to the agent–patient reversals about as frequently as he gave the correct "new" response, he rarely offered agent–patient reversals in recall of the original list sentences. This was so even in those cases in which recall was not verbatim but voice was changed from passive to active or active to passive.

As part of the recall procedure, subjects were asked after recall whether their sentence was exactly like the way the experimenter had "told the story." The child's answer varied with age and with the correctness of his original production. Very few of the nursery school subjects answered "No" or "I don't know." The number who did increased greatly between nursery and second-grade. The number of response changes after giving a "no" or similar response also increased.

Sentence recall was also scored for overall correctness in meaning and form. There was no increase with age in the proportion of sentences recalled that were correct in meaning, or that were correct in form (25%). The latter result is not too surprising. The proportion correct in form recall across age groups was the proportion of active sentences. The overwhelming tendency, in fact, was to recall sentences as actives. When clefts were given they were apt to be an immature form, without "it's," or they were apt to be subject-first clefts in the recall of object-first clefts. When responses were passives, which might have increased the correct proportion of form recall, they were given just about as often in the recall of original list actives as in the recall of original list passives. Thus the average proportion correct in form recall remained equal to the proportion of active sentences in the original lists.

The lack of a developmental trend in correct meaning recall requires explanation. Although younger children, on the whole, recalled fewer sentences, their accuracy was the same as that of the older children. In the recall task, in which the subjects did not feel constrained to recall sentences in a given syntactic form (even though the instructions requested "exact" recall), nursery school children were no more inclined than second-graders to produce intrusions from the recognition list sentences. Nor were they more likely to give the agent–patient reversal in recall. It seems that what developed from nursery through second grade was either the ability to encode for long-term storage or the ability to retrieve the encoded sentence. The issue cannot be settled in this experiment—though the recognition data for the nursery children would perhaps favor the second interpretation. What did *not* appear to undergo change was the nature of the encoded information. It might be argued that the nature of the sentences used here, as well as the characteristics of the recognition list, seriously constrained the type of recall errors and thus the nature of the encoded information. However, even though the range of probable errors in recall was constricted, this did not seem sufficient to explain the flatness of correct meaning recall across age groups. Even with a restricted range of possible error types, the younger children might have been less accurate in recall, thus producing more of each error type. Nevertheless, they did not. It is possible to assume then that the nursery school child's code for semantic information in the sentences heard was not qualitatively different from the code used by the older children. The difference between the younger and older children was probably the amount of information (the number of sentences) stored, or more likely the ability to retrieve the stored information.

Synonymy Judgment—Procedure and Results

SYNONYMY JUDGMENT PROCEDURE

The child was given two sentences and was asked to judge whether they "meant the same thing." The two sentences were formed by pairing each of the four original (comprehension) list sentences with its related member in the recognition list. In each case, the original list sentence was the first member of the pair. Table 3-11 (Condition D) presents the pairings of the original list sentence; *The boy pushes the girl*, that were used in this task. The number preceding each pair of sentences represents the recognition list category of the second sentence.

SYNONYMY JUDGMENT RESULTS

The synonymy judgment data are found in Table 3-17. A Grade × Voice-Cleft × Category (4 × 2 × 6) analysis of variance was performed. Each main effect was significant; Grade ($p < .01$), Voice-Cleft ($p < .01$) and Category ($p < .01$). Only the Category × Voice-Cleft interaction was significant ($p < .01$). The Grade × Voice-Cleft × Category interaction was also significant ($p < .01$). A Tukey test of the Grade effect showed the first- and second-graders to be significantly better than the nursery and kindergartners ($p < .01$), although the two older and two younger groups were not different from each other.

The major difficulty in making correct synonymy judgments was in Categories 2, 3, and 6 for the cleft condition and Categories 2 and 3 for the voice condition. Referring back to the examples given in Section D of

TABLE 3-17
Same–Different Judgments: Experiment 2 (Percentage of Correct Responses)[a]

| | CATEGORIES | | | | | |
	1 (same)	2 (same)	3 (different)	4 (different)	5 (different)	6 (different)
				Voice		
Nursery	59	48	61	72**	62*	62*
Kindergarten	83**	48	56	89**	89**	78**
First-grade	97**	55	62*	100**	95**	88*
Second-grade	92**	88**	72**	98**	98**	88**
				Cleft		
Nursery	66**	39	59	69**	69**	61
Kindergarten	83**	48	45	78**	75**	52
First-grade	98**	53	59	98**	89**	58
Second-grade	100**	52	56	100**	100**	84**

[a] Percentage of 64 responses per cell. $n = 16 \times 4$ responses per subject.

*$p < .05$.

**$p < .01$.

Table 3–11, we can see that when *surface* structural relations were ambiguous, children's synonymy judgments were random.

In Category 2, in which the order of Noun 1 and Noun 2 changed through passivization and the lexical items remained the same, the younger subjects gave about an equal number of "same" and "different" responses. In Category 3, in which the lexical items and their order (N_1 and N_2) remained the same but an agent–patient reversal occurred through passivization of the verb, younger subjects' responses were also random. In Category 6, the lexical items and syntactic form were the same but there was a subject–object (N_1–N_2) reversal. By kindergarten level (voice condition), there were significantly more "different" responses in this category than in Category 3. A comparison between Categories 3 and 6 seems to indicate then that change in word order, in which subject–object were reversed but no change occurred in the verb, was a more powerful determiner in signaling a "different" response than change in syntactic form per se. However, this generalization is qualified by the fact that children gave about equal numbers of "different" responses to Categories 2 and 3: Category 2 changed both word order and syntactic form; while in Category 3, only syntactic form changed. If word order and form changes interacted or were additive in their effects, one would have predicted more "different" responses to Category 2 than to Category 3.

Put another way, if the order of N_1 and N_2 in the two sentences was by itself important, with everything else equal, then Categories 2 and 6 should have yielded the same results, which they did not. If verb relations, by virtue of passivization were alone critical, again with everything else equal, Categories 2 and 3 should have been the same but different from Category 6. However, the $N_1 N_2$ relations were not equal in Categories 2 and 3 and thus should have affected the responses differently. The two effects together, N_1 and N_2 order and the verb changes, contributed to the ambiguity of Categories 2 and 3. Category 6, which had the same verb (with no passivization) and only the N_1 and N_2 order change, did not share the ambiguity and was thus different from 2 and 3.

This interpretation is made mainly on the basis of the surface structure relations between the categories. However, the performance patterns (of Categories 2 and 3) and the linguistic facts suggest a different explanation. This explanation assumes that children, at least beyond nursery level, were attempting to respond to the sentence pairs in respect to their deep structure relations, but two processes interfered. First, surface structure characteristics interfered with correct understanding. Second, as other data in the study indicate, some young children considered sentences with agent–patient reversals to have the same meaning. In a practice session, prior to the synonymy judgment task, children were presented with a sample active–passive sentence pair and were asked whether these had the same meaning. They were also asked how they differed or how they were the same, depending on what their answer had been. The nursery school child rarely verbalized a reason for his answer. The kindergartener, however, gave two explanations. With the two sentences *Mary washes John* and *John gets washed by Mary*, subjects responded (1) "Same—because they're washing each other" or (2) "Different—because they're washing each other." Children who gave the (1) answer would have been scored correct during the testing session when no explanation was required. This could account for the data in Category 2 not differing significantly from the Category 3 data. In the first grade, the (2) response type became more frequent, and was joined by the response (3) "Same—because the same person is washing in both."

Finally, in the second-grade, the third-response type became dominant. Although the kindergartners and first-graders may have varied between Judgments 1 and 2, they were relatively consistent in their explanation that the sentence pair expressed the agent–patient reversal. Although it might be argued that this explanation was given because it was the easier to make, and that it was not an accurate reflection of the children's comprehension of the sentence pair, two sources of data make it appear more probably that children were really misperceiving the sentences. The first came from the pre-training session. Kindergartners and first-graders who had given Judgment 2 were sometimes asked to repeat the sentence pair *Mary washes John—John gets washed by Mary*. The most common type of imitation was *Mary washes John—John washes Mary*. The next most common type of imitation was *John gets washed by Mary—Mary gets washed by John*. It was relatively rare that the child who had given Judgment 2 imitated the pair correctly. More frequent was the spontaneous change to Judgment 3 and Explanation 3, following multiple repetition of the sentence pair and corrected imitation.

Another source of data came from the first study's imitation task. There too the most common error in the imitation of active–passive sentence pairs was the transformation of one sentence to the same syntactic form as the other, resulting in a pair with agent–patient reversed. Thus, even when adult criteria for "same meaning" were already operating to some extent, the processing strategies and/or capacities of the child interfered with making correct same–different meaning judgments. By the second-grade, however, it appears that adult-processing strategies or capacities had been achieved, or had become organized in such a way that the child no longer misperceived the relation between the two sentences and judged them correctly. Evidence from the second-grade data suggests the development of some form of organized knowledge that enabled the child to perform correctly. In the second-grade for the voice condition, Category 2 became easier than Category 3. The sentences of Category 2 would be expected to be central in an organized system of relations and those in Category 3 would be more derivative.

Another possibility is that the second-grade child develops a new type of sentence analysis based on an understanding of the formal relationship among sentences rather than on (semantic) match of sentence content. Such knowledge of formal syntactic relationship could ease the task of making equivalence judgments because it would no longer be necessary to decode sentences for meaning in order to establish semantic relationships.

Although the response patterns for the cleft condition paralleled those of the voice condition, performance was nevertheless inferior in the cleft condition. The object-first cleft form introduced problems in comprehension not found for example even with the passive. These data, then, do not confirm the findings of Bever (1970) on the early development of understanding of the cleft construction.

Discussion

The synonymy judgment data coupled with comprehension data replicate the findings of the first study and show that children can indeed comprehend the passive before they can make correct judgments of the semantic equivalence of corresponding active and passive sentences. The main contribution of the present experiment is in showing that the failure to correctly judge synonymy is not necessarily evidence that the child is ignorant of the meaning equivalence relationship, or that synonymous and nonsynonymous sentences stand in a different relationship for him. Although it was not until the second grade that children responded above-chance on the linguistic equivalence task, there was indirect evidence that children at earlier ages had some understanding of the correct semantic relationship. The data on sentence recall indicated that children as young as nursery school-age transformed passives to actives while preserving sentence meaning. The most reasonable explanation of these data is that the child knew at least in some sense that the two sentences (the original passive and the recalled active) meant the same thing and produced the easier of the two sentence forms. In the recognition task, the data showed the emergence of selective responding according to sentence meaning at the kindergarten level for the voice condition. Again, the most plausible explanation of the recognition response pattern is that the active and passive sentences had the same meaning for them and were thus most often confused.

The question remains as to why the direct test of semantic equivalence proved difficult for children. There are at least three possibilities. One is reflected in the decline in the number of children who judged reciprocal action as meaning the "same thing." That is, there appeared to be a change in the criteria for judging synonymy.

Another possibility was reflected in the child's improved capacity to judge the sentence pairs. We suggested that this could have been due to improved understanding of the structural relations among syntactic forms independent of their specific semantic content. Such understanding could help reduce the immediate memory load, and enable the child to be consistently correct in his judgments of semantic equivalence.

The third possibility is that the child at the second-grade level developed new cognitive functions relative to language use, which enabled him to reflect on his statements, to match their meanings and their logics, and to judge them by criteria that were not available prior to that age. Not only was there a criterion change but also a process change that involved a different type of match from that which occurred, for example, in the judgment of the truth or falsity of a statement.

A more recent study by Sack (1973) sheds further light on the developmental processes involved in the linguistic equivalence task. In consideration of the results reported above, she was concerned that some of the younger children may have been guided by the principle that any two sentences that sound different differ in meaning. To rule out this possibility, subjects (kindergartners through third-grade) were tested on their ability to judge the synonymy of sentences, such as *The puppy sleeps* or *The baby doggy sleeps*. She found that even kindergarteners had no trouble judging synonymy based on this type of lexical substitution.

She administered the linguistic equivalence task, and tested the comprehension of nonreversible sentences (*Boys watch kites*), and sentences formed by substituting nonsense syllables for the nouns in active and passive sentence forms (*Jybs watch lebs*). Although on the reversible and nonsense sentences the subjects performed at chance levels through the second-grade, even the kindergarteners judged the synonymy of nonreversible sentences in accordance with adult criteria. Sack concluded that the linguistic equivalence task per se was not the source of difficulty for the 5- to 7-year olds but that the interaction between task difficulty and syntactic forms was the cause. In judging synonymy, it would appear that children in this age range attempt to transform sentences so that they match on syntactic form and only then do they make a judgment as to their meaning (as in the Clark model). The transformation process is a complex one, particularly for reversible sentences in which semantic constraints are of no assistance, and it accounts for the difficulty of this type of sentence for children prior to the age of 7 or 8. A model based on the comparison of surface structures (such as Olson, 1971: Olson & Filby, 1972) does not fit the data of the linguistic equivalence judgments of children as well as it does for adults.

The shift in processing strategies at about age 7 or 8 in the Sack (1973) data are accounted for by the ostensive availability of new cognitive resources at these respective ages. Although the transformation to common syntactic form appears superficially to be more complex, in fact, it is the rule structure governing the matching of sentence elements and its relation to the response index (same–different judgment) that is more complex and requires the cognitive capability of formal operational structures that are available only to the older child and adult.

Two recent studies by C. S. Smith (1972, 1973) appearing in preliminary reports add to the little that is known of synonymy. The first study was with adults who produced paraphrases to sentences that varied in structure, including the active, passive, and cleft forms. (Paraphrases were defined as sentences with the same underlying grammatical relations and the same cognitive content.) The most frequent response to actives were passives (83%); to subject-first clefts, passives (72%), and to object-first clefts, actives (85%). In a recognition memory task similar to the one used here in Experiment 2, Smith found a very inconsistent pattern of recognition to actives, passives, and other sentence types that she classed as "activity" sentences. These contrasted with another group of "existential" sentences that showed by way of their "false" recognition responses that subjects considered all the sentences they heard as paraphrases of the original sentences. Smith concluded that sentences, in order to qualify as paraphrases, required not only the same underlying grammatical relations but possibly the same presuppositional structure. (Although the recognition patterns for actives and passives were not too clear, she nevertheless had characterized them as having the same presuppositional bases.) Smith also concluded that the topic of the sentence was of great importance in determining a paraphrase.

The adult study was followed with one of children's paraphrasing and judging of sentence pairs for their synonymy (C. S. Smith, 1973). Of the 26 subjects (5- to 7-years old), 69% correctly judged an active–passive pair to have the same meaning; other sentence structures that were paraphrases of each other showed more and less correct judgment. Children, on the other hand, had great difficulty in producing paraphrases of passives and actives (9 of 26 could paraphrase a passive; none could paraphrase an active), although they had little difficulty in paraphrasing cleft forms. Smith concludes that the 5- to 7-year olds lack "active control" over the passive form although they comprehend it.

Our data, as well as Sinclair's, show that 5- to 7-year olds have more "active" control of the passive in production, if they are instructed by the investigator to start their sentences with the object (or comment) as topic. Smith's data imply that the success of Sinclair's method may be because the instructions indicate to the subject that the object (the comment) should be made the topic of the sentence—much of the ability to paraphrase, particularly for adults and to some extent for children, is dependent upon the topic.

General Discussion

An understanding of the way synonymy judgments are made by both adults and children can serve a number of purposes. First, such data may provide the basis for choosing between alternative formulations concerning the place of synonymy in linguistic analysis, as the significance of synonymy in linguistic analysis is open to question. Linguists as diverse as Bloomfield and Chomsky have taken a stand on this issue (Harris, 1973). Bloomfield holds that "linguistic analysis is based upon a postulate that requires us to suppose that within a given natural language there are no synonymous expressions [Harris, 1973, p.6]." Chomsky (1957) advances the view that synonymy is not to be taken as the basis for linguistic analysis lest some important formal relations within language become obscured. The linguistic and philosophic issues within this controversy are complex, and, as Harris points out, there would be no issue at all if the problems associated with the concept of "linguistic meaning" were resolved [p.4]. Leaving the larger issues aside, if the diverse philosophic and linguistic characterizations of synonymy are correct, there is no reason why they should be inconsistent with the psychological characterization of synonymy. If the results of psychological study are not in accord with these theoretical formulations, it may very well be that either the linguistic or psychological formulations require reexamination.

Our findings in these studies show that the child prior to age 7 or 8 is unable to define or describe the rules that guide his language behavior or even provide a statement of the synonymy of sentences that adults judge as synonymous. At the same time, these children are *rule-governed* so that they are able to comprehend and produce synonymous sentences. Quine claims that Chomsky's notion of linguistic knowledge, which is ostensibly part of the speaker's competence and shows rule-guided behavior, cannot be correct because the speaker cannot define or identify these rules. Quine's claim is itself questionable. His view is similar to the behaviorist's position that only demonstrable behaviors are acceptable for assuming any guiding force behind behavior, and at best one can only assume the presence of "dispositional concepts" to account for behavior. The Chomskyan claim, which is shared by cognitive psychologists, that linguistic behavior is under the control of a covert rule-governing system and not merely "dispositions," is supported by the data.

Chomsky's (1957) earlier claim that synonymy was not to be taken as the basis for linguistic analysis because of the obscurities and ambiguities introduced by problems of meaning does not reappear in his later work. His present position implies that analysis of the formal structural relations within the grammar, although not based on the criterion of synonymy, may nevertheless consider it as an adjunct to such an analysis. The grammar, in fact, has to take cognizance of the synonymy of sentences—that relation creates problems of interpretation if the grammar is characterized solely in syntactic terms.

Our data appear, at first glance, to give greater support to the Chomskyan notion that synonymy is determined at the level of deep structure rather than surface structural relations, at least for children. On close examination, however, a deep structure explanation is not sufficient. At a *deep* level, linguistic structure is intimately associated with processes that monitor sentence meaning. These are cognitive processes that also operate independently of the linguistic system.

Meaning-monitoring, which enters into linguistic processing as the "truth index" or the "response index," is an assumed component of a number of information-processing theories. Its function is more than linguistic and is part of the developing cognitive structures of the child. Thus, the ability to judge the synonymy of sentences, which one can assume to be part of the meaning-monitoring process, is not available to the child when he begins to speak or comprehend speech at about 18 months, even though other logical and semilogical cognitive abilities are available. It is also clear that a child has a system of meaning available to him upon beginning to speak, else there would be no such experience. A meaning system must be more general than just linguistic meaning for the simple reason that the child "interprets" his world before he has language; in fact, he gives evidence quite early that objects have "meaning" to him. The later-appearing ability to judge the synonymy of sentences at about 7 years of age is indicative of a new set of meaning-related processes at work. At this point, the child develops criteria for judging meaning and has the specific capacity entailed in judging more than one element at a time. This ability is reflected in the recognition of conceptual invariants under conditions of change and decision-making relative to a set of criteria. In the case of active–passive sentence pair comparisons, prior knowledge of transformation rules may be needed before meaning judgments can be made, but these transformations are in the child's repertoire prior to the age of 7. It is at the age of 7 that the child begins to function in the way Quine wishes him to function. He now carries the criteria of synonymy with him and can judge active–passive sentences as synonymous. Prior to 7 years of age, it is nonetheless evident (Experiment 2) that the child has the formal apparatus for covertly processing sentence meaning, but this apparatus does not permit conscious comparison between sentence structure and meaning.

If adults and adolescents are more likely to judge sentence synonymy by surface structure characteristics, as Olson implies, this would be due to the later availability of other logical processes. Children, however, do not appear to make synonymy judgments on this basis. The developmental data, then, support some linguistic and philosophic proposals concerning synonymy but not others.

The synonymy data, in addition to bearing upon linguistic and philosophical issues, also relate to issues concerning the nature of cognition and language development. Our findings support the general Piagetian claim that language development occurs as a consequence of and in association with the development of cognitive structures and functions. Our data on the later-appearing ability to produce and comprehend passive sentences relative to active sentences is associated with the development of non-linguistic cognitive functions that have formal structural relation to the developing linguistic structures. Although it would be invalid to claim a one-to-one relationship between the development of reversibility, de-centration, and associated logical functions to the development of passive, there is a general correlation between these developments. This relationship is buttressed by the formal structural relations between the reversible features of full passive sentences and the reversible relations of concrete logical operations.

4

Temporal Reference and Development of the Conception of Time

Natural language has two types of temporal indication; time syntax and the time lexicon. The time lexicon includes words that are time denotative, such as those indicating time of day (*hours, minutes*), time of year (*seasons*), time of action (*now*), time of life (*age*), and duration (*decade, instant*). Other words make indeterminate time reference (*before, after*), and comparative terms are either determinate or indeterminate (*earlier than, 5 minutes earlier than*). Systems for classifying the time lexicon are not new. *Roget's Thesaurus*, for example, distinguishes between words that indicate "absolute time," "relative time," and "recurrent time," with further distinctions within each of these categories. The syntax of time includes indications of tense and those aspects of constituent order within sentences that indicate time relations.

Linguistic Theories

A semantic theory that accounts for time language within the framework of generative transformational theory is spelled out in detail in Katz's (1972) *Semantic Theory*. The sentence constituents, following Chomsky, that are critical for the expression of time relations are the verbs, the tense of the auxiliary, and the temporal adverbials. The syntactic structure underlying the expression of time, says Katz, forms a "tightly knit self-contained system [p. 310]." The base of the syntactic component contains phrase structure rules in which the verbal auxiliary of English has a tense constituent, an optional modal constituent, and also optionally, an aspect constituent. The verbal auxiliary is either past or present, the modal constituent is one of the elements "can," "will," "may," "must," etc., and aspect is either perfect or progressive. The temporal adverbials are identified as constituents of the predicate phrase.

Two grammatical relations are described, one for the auxiliary and the verb, and another for the predicate and its temporal adverbials. The former is the **inflexional relation**, the latter the **temporalization relation**. These relations supply the information for the projection rule (i.e., trans-formation) in Katz' grammar that renders the derived readings.

The underlying phrase-marker expressed as a tree diagram for the sen-tence; *Tom drank milk* would look as follows:

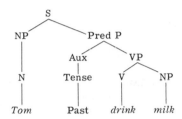

Katz proposes a series of rules, which indicate that the pastness or future-ness of prepositions in the clauses of sentences like

(1)   *Tom will kiss Pam before Dick (will) arrives.*
(2)   *Tom will kiss Pam after Harry (will) arrives.*

is fixed by their tense (*will kiss*), however, the events referred to in the main clause and the subordinate clause are temporally ordered with respect to each other by the time adverbial (*before–after*).

Katz introduces a system of sentence markers to designate time that are components of the lexical readings for the various temporal terms. This marking system employs notation derived from a spatial representation of time relations. A "time line" is conceived with time zero ($t^{[0]}$) at the origin of the time dimension covering the time span from the onset to the termin-ation of the utterance of a sentence. The sentence utterance is thus taken as the reference point for orienting time. Past tense is to the left of the origin ($t^{[-n]}$), the future to the right ($t^{[+n]}$). Both simple and complex tenses are placed on this spatial time dimension.

In the case of *before–after* sentences, in which *before* appears in the sentence, a fixed number of (positive) units of time are added to the value of the inflexional relation in the main clause (with concomitant reduction in the inflexional of the subordinate clause). Conversely, with the *after* relation, a negative quantity is added to the inflexional relation of the main clause. With adverbials like *at the same instant as* or *simultaneous with* the function is one of identity, and the value of the inflexional relation of the subordinate clause is replaced by the value of the inflexional relation in the main clause.

Semantically, time adverbials such as *in the last hours, for the last hour, yesterday, 3 minutes ago, an hour ago*, involve a number concept (that is not unique to time), a unit concept, and a direction concept. As the basic unit for time, Katz takes the "second"; the number concept serves as a coefficient of the unit concept, that is as a multiplier, as in "60 seconds." The direction concept indicates the direction from the origin, left in the case of past and right in the case of the future. The derived readings for temporal adverbials are thus constants representing a fixed number of basic units and a direction from the origin; they do not change the time relations represented by the tense constituent but make the time relation more determinate. In addition, a syntactic distinction is made between temporal adverbials and the adverbials of duration (*for 1 minute*) and frequency (*1 minute ago*).

Katz's theory is thus an attempt to introduce into syntactic theory a semantic basis for determining time relations within sentences. The semantic notions are very similar to those of cognitive theory that represent time in spatial terms.

A different kind of semantic interpretation is given temporal prepositions by MacDonald (1972). Time prepositions include *about, before, during, near, past, until, within*, etc. Membership in this set is determined both by syntactic and semantic considerations.

Syntactically, English prepositions are said to operate in the sentence within an object and a head. The role of the head (of the prepositional phrase) is filled most typically by a verb, adjective, noun, or a sentence. The prepositional structure thus functions as an adverbial.

Semantically, every preposition assigned a time designation must also have an object and a head to which either the rubric "time" or "event" is assigned. Time specifies reference to a point or period on a time scale (for such "signals" as *midnight, day, 1936*). Event specifies reference to anything which can be delimited by reference to time (*in World War II, died, promotion*, etc.).

The time rubric subdivides into the **punctual** and **durative** aspects of time. The punctual reference is to a point in time and ignores duration; the durative aspect regards time as if it were a continuum. The durative and punctual designation is given most clearly in verbs, nouns, and adjectives derived from verbs. The progressive form of the verb (the aspect verb *be* plus the present participle) specifies duration of an action, as in *I'm taking a shower. The earth revolves around the sun* has a durative verb; *She wrote a letter* has a punctual verb. Not only is the durative–punctual distinction given syntactically, it is a semantic distinction as well. The syntactic specification of duration may be redundant if duration is inherent in the meaning of the verb. On the other hand, there are some verbs that are semantically derivative and are not usually found in a syntactic durational form. One says, for example, *This perfume lasts* rather than *This perfume is lasting*.

Nouns and nominal constants, which serve as the object of a time preposition, are also distinguishable as durative or punctual, and prepositions themselves are classifiable as punctual or durative. Examples of the punctual are; *about, after, round, at, during*, etc. The durative prepositions are; *for, from, over, since, throughout*, etc.

MacDonald details eight theoretically possible combinations of durative and punctual sentence constituents (head, preposition, and object). Only four of these combinations are common: (1) all components punctual (*it went off at midnight*), (2) head and preposition punctual, object durative (*it went off within 3 hours*), (3) head and preposition durative, object punctual, (*it lasted until midnight*), and (4) all components durative (*it lasted for 3 hours*).

The punctual pattern ("all elements punctual") divides into three time segments: *Prior, Incident,* and *Subsequent.* The punctual prepositions and the time segments they represent are then detailed as *before* (prior), *toward* (prior), *at* (actual or incident), *after* (subsequent). Additional semantic distinctions are made for punctual prepositions for those that are precise and proximate. As an example, *before* is classified as prior, *toward* as prior, proximate, etc.

An analysis of the durative patterns yields the relations prior, incident, subsequent, and resultative. The durative prepositions can thus be characterized as follows: *till* (prior), *until* (prior), *throughout* (incident), *past* (prior, incident, subsequent), *from* (subsequent), *since* (subsequent, resultative).

MacDonald, less formally, analyzes the conjunctions of time. The similarity between adverbial conjunctions and prepositions is very marked. Many of the conjunctions are formally identical with time prepositions such as *after, before, since, till, until, when, whenever,* and *while.* The semantic features of conjunctions are said to be the same as those of prepositions.

Conjunctions, like prepositions, have similar time descriptions, such as *before* (prior), *when* (incident), *after* (subsequent). The conjunctions which call for a durative head and a punctual object are *since, till, until.*

Both the Katz and MacDonald proposals suggest a similar conceptual base for time reference, i.e., as a spatial continuum, with an additional distinction between reference and punctual reference. Although these conceptual distinctions are used within the framework of linguistic analysis, they are not analyzed as to their adequacy as conceptualizations of time. It is thus not clear as to whether the total richness of the conception of time is captured by the linguistic analyses. The psychological relevance of these linguistic theories is not spelled out in either proposal so that it is not apparent, for example, how these views can account for the asymmetry in the child's knowledge of the *before–after* relation.

An examination of the conception of time and the developmental sequence in which it is acquired may illuminate a number of questions concerning the relationship between language and cognition. The development of time language, for example, may or may not follow the orderly sequence in which the conception of time develops. More important is the question as to whether the mastery of time language is dependent upon the development of a conception of time.

Before presenting the studies that consider these questions, it is necessary to detail Piaget's analysis of the child's developing conception of time (Piaget, 1969).

Cognitive Theory: Piaget

Piaget holds that the conception of time results fundamentally from understanding the nature of the coordination of motions at different velocities—motions of external objects in the case of "physical time," and of the subject himself in the case of "psychological time." The development of this understanding occurs progressively, starting at a very early age and ending relatively late.

The most elementary forms of "knowing" time are found in the sensorimotor period, prior to the age of 2. The first experiences of *duration* come with "waiting time" as the infant cries with hunger, and the first experiences of *order of succession*, at least between means and ends, comes with attempts to reach distant objects with other objects close at hand. These events, however, merely involve the correlation of durations of action with the displacement of objects in space. (They are identified by Piaget as schemes of action.) At this age, each action is said to have "a time of its own," which makes the experience of events discontinuous, and there are as many temporal series experienced as there are schemes of action.

With the acquisition of language, temporal concepts enter into Piaget's Stage I ($1\frac{1}{2}$- to 4-years old). The first period is one in which the child reinterprets what he had previously learned on the "plane of action." His earlier "practical" anticipations of succession and awareness of duration are now reconstructed by substituting "virtual" for "real" actions, and signs and representations for purely perceptive qualities. At this stage, temporal succession coincides with spatial action, and durations with displacements. The child can say correctly that a walking man reached B after A, and C after B, and can say also that it took longer to go from A to C, than from A to B, but if the child were asked to compare the motion from A to C with another motion along the same AC path *but with a different velocity*, he would be unable to tell which of the two bodies would reach the destination first. Terms such as *before* and *after* lose all meaning to the child as soon as different velocities are introduced.

Temporal concepts at this stage are said to be "intuitive," as is the concept of velocity. (Velocity at this point is equivalent to the process of overtaking.) Thought at Stage I is characteristically egocentric, living is in the present and irreversible because each moment succeeds another without leading to the construction of *continuity*.

The next Stage (II), that of "articulated intuitions" (4- to $6\frac{1}{2}$-years old), marks the beginning of decentration and preparation for the development of operations. This is reflected in the gradual dissociation of temporal from spatial action: If B goes further than C, but C is still moving after B has stopped, the temporal *before* and *after* are no longer identified with the spatial, and the child is able to determine the correct sequence by trial and error alone. The child, however, is unable to do the same retrospectively, as in making drawings of past events.

In respect to durations, the child now appreciates that time is inversely proportional to velocity, and in respect to successions can anticipate and reconstruct motions themselves without attending solely to the end-points. Intuitive decentrations thus lead to a certain correlation between velocity and duration. This does not automatically result in the correct order of succession, or vice versa; only the interaction of operations in the next period permits that.

"Operational time," which comes with Stage III ($6\frac{1}{2}$- to 7-years old), is achieved very rapidly after the prior stage. Piaget (1969) considers operational time to be the very prototype of reversible thought [p. 260], and the clearest example of how rational operations, by their construction, take the form of logical "groupings."

Operational time is constructed as soon as the order of successions is deduced from the logical composition of durations and vice versa. The type of logical grouping involved in the idea of "order of succession," which in a formal sense is "an additive grouping of asymmetrical relations" (*before* and *after* in qualitative seriation), is not beyond the knowledge of $6\frac{1}{2}$- to 7-year-old children. In the context of *temporal* relations, it is difficult to achieve; however, in seriating sticks, it is not. The difficulty with time comes from basing one's notions of time on spatial transformations. In effect, simultaneous states need to be differentiated from successive states, which is particularly difficult to do with time. Parenthetically, the notion of simultaneity is identified by Piaget as a limited case of succession, which bears upon psycholinguistic studies of time prepositions (E. V. Clark, 1971).

Achievement of the qualitative operations of duration comes with the ability to correlate the seriation of asymmetrical relations (**successions**) with the addition of symmetrical relations (**intervals**). The correlation of both duration and succession groupings leads to the operational system of **qualitative time**.

The construction of qualitative time is cognitively related to the construction of number: The iteration of the unit of duration results from uniting durations (classes) with the seriation of successions (asymmetrical relations). In contrast to qualitative time where these are complementary, in **quantitative time** they are fused as operations.

The achievement of both qualitative and quantitative time leads to the construction of (continuous) **homogeneous time** that contrasts with the distinct, discontinuous segmentation of preoperational time. The operational child has a conception of time that frees him from the present and the constraints of space, and by the reversibility of his thought is able to retrace time in either direction. The young child, by contrast, with his empirical notion of time, is only able to follow time along a simple and irreversible course of events and thus has great difficulty with it.

This condensed statement of Piaget's discussion of the complex nature of time conceptualization suggests that if language is to represent this very complex system of operations its own structure would have to be equally complex. If not equally complex, the complexity would have to be reduced by a very powerful and necessarily abstract set of rules limited in number and capable of representing durations, order of successions, and simultaneity with units of equal and unequal magnitude and in the context of physical and personal or psychological time. Although linguistic theories such as Katz's (1972) do not seem to capture the richness and complexity of the system detailed by Piaget, Katz's spatial representation of time accords with many characteristics of that conception, particularly in respect to the parallels in the properties of temporal and spatial order. Whether linguistic theories can adequately account for the psychological aspects of the development of time language is a question to which the remainder of this chapter is addressed.

Empirical Studies

Piaget's description of cognitive development makes plain that the achievement of a conception of time is relatively difficult and takes place over a considerable age span. The conception of time, in fact, is accomplished later than other systems that embody analogous operational structures.

Casual observation suggests that time reference enters the child's verbal repertoire relatively late as well. There has been little evidence, until recently, of the way in which the child's conception of time influences the syntactic and lexical aspects of language that represent time. Studies by Weil, Cromer, and Sinclair and Ferreiro have done much to remedy this state of affairs.

Weil (1970)

Weil[1] (1970) studied the relationship of the child's knowledge of time concepts, following the Piagetian characterization of time development, with his time language based on the distinction between time syntax and the time lexicon. Two assertions were tested. The first was that the cognitive operations fundamental to the conception of time either anticipate or accompany linguistic development. It was posited specifically that before children could comprehend and use the tenses, and before they could properly use lexical items such as *before* and *after* in a sentence, children would have to have acquired related, reversible (cognitive) operations. The second assertion was that the possession of time language alone would not be a sufficient condition for an operational conception of time. That is, although the child might be able to demonstrate knowledge of both time vocabulary and time syntax, these would not be sufficient for a systematic conception of time embodying the ability to coordinate order and duration.

DESIGN AND TASKS

There were five groups of children in the study: 4-year olds, kindergarteners, first- and second-graders, and a group composed of 9- to 11-year-old children. The kindergarteners and first- and second-graders were

---

[1] Weil, J. The relationship between time conceptualization and time language in young children. Unpublished doctoral dissertation, City University of New York, 1970.

given both the language and time concept tasks in two testing sessions. The 4-year olds were only administered the language tasks because the concept tasks turned out to be too difficult for them, and the 9- to 11-year olds were only administered the concept tasks because the language tasks were too easy for them. Four testing sequences were used to counter-balance presentation order.

Time Language Tasks

Time Language Film

A film was made for use in the assessment of the child's time language. Presentation of the film was accompanied by a series of questions, response to which was made by choosing one of two cars in a film sequence. The film contained five *sequences* in which two toy cars were racing each other; accompanying each sequence was a block of four questions. The colors of the cars (black or white) and their position (top or bottom) were randomly assigned. In addition to the accompanying questions, the subjects were asked to explain the choices they made. A film sequence was replayed if a child was uncertain about a question or the scene represented. Each of the five film sequences (races) lasted about 6 sec. The films consisted also of two cue conditions that the child could use as a basis for responding to the questions: (I) in which both position and speed cues were present, and (II) in which only speed cues were available. The questions accompanying the films were either (time) syntax oriented or (time) lexically oriented questions.

A. The *time syntax* questions (there were nine), which were designed to test the child's understanding, embodied the following tenses: past, future, progressive, perfect, and conditional. Five of the nine questions could be answered correctly by relying on either position cues alone or both position and speed cues. Three of the items could be answered correctly by relying only on the speed cues.

The conditions indicated as (II) were distinguished from (I) by the fact that the (II) items required both linguistic and cognitive processing. For example, in the film for Future I, the question "Which car *will win?*" was asked. At the time it was asked, the car that won was already ahead. In the comparable film for Future II, when the same question was asked, both cars had stopped. In the latter case the child had to infer, as both cars had stopped, that the car that was going faster would win. To make this inference the child had to rely not only on comprehension of the sentence but also upon his knowledge of time.

B. There were seven, time, lexically oriented questions to assess comprehension of order (*first, last*), speed (*fast, slow*), and duration (*more* or *longer time* (I) and (II), *less* or *shorter time*). Again, *more time* (I) and (II) were distinguished by the fact that the car that took *more time* (I) was ahead of the other car when the question was asked, and for *more time* (II) the cars were at the same point.

C. Test of the child's comprehension of the time connectives *before* and *after* was not included in the film task because of the potential confounding of spatial and temporal cues—*before* and *after* can denote both spatial and temporal relations. Instead, testing was done with an enactment procedure utilizing a hand puppet and eight miniature toys.

The sentences were designed to focus on temporal order. The *before* or *after* connective indicated the time relation between two constituent actions. For example, in the sentence *I cut bait before I fish* (x *before* y) the arrangement of sentence constituents is in accord with the actual sequence of events. In "y *after* x" (*I fish after I cut bait*), the order of the constituents reverses actual event order. Two other sentence arrangements are possible: the event described may follow or precede the connective (*before* y, x— *Before I fish, I cut bait*). There are, then, four possible sentence constructions based on the two aforementioned variations: "*after* x, y," "x *before* y," "y *after* x," and "*before* y, x." In Weil's experiment, eight sentences were used (two for each sequence), presented in random order.

Time Concept Measures

Reversibility Tasks

This measure, consisting of two subtasks, tested the child's knowledge of reversibility in a time context. It was intended to determine whether a child could construct a time series in a particular order and could then reverse it.

A. The first reversibility task utilized four drawings of a tree. The drawings showed progressive stages of leaf growth. The instructions were to place the picture so that they showed the progression from spring (many leaves) to winter (no leaves).

B. The second task had five drawings depicting stages in the growth of a man, from babyhood to old age. All figures were of the same height. The procedure paralleled that of Task 1, starting first with one order (babyhood to old age) and then reversing it.

Time Concept Tasks

The time concept tasks were given to determine the child's understanding of the critical constituents of the notion of time (as characterized by Piaget): order of succession, simultaneity, and duration.

A. *Time concept film.* Another film was devised specifically to test for the child's understanding of order of succession, simultaneity, and duration. As in the language film, there were black and white cars that raced from left to right on a parallel (top versus bottom) course on the screen. Five situations were depicted, each course lasting about 6 sec. Time in these sequences was a function of distance covered and the speed of the moving car:

I. *Equality of times (equal distances and equal speeds).* Both cars started and stopped at the same time and traveled at the same speed. Questions were directed to whether the cars started at the same time, stopped at the same time, and traveled the same distance, or whether one traveled longer (more time) or went as far, or further than, the other.

II. *Equality of times (unequal distances and unequal speeds).* Both cars started and stopped *at the same time*, but the black car traveled faster and thus went further than the other. Simultaneity had to be deduced from the equality of the synchronous durations.

III. *Time inequality (more—unequal distances and equal speeds).* The cars started at the same time but the white stopped *first;* and the black car traveled *further* than the white. The same questions as before, but in addition, the subject was asked to identify the car that took more time, the car that stopped first, and the reason for choosing the car he did. *More* time was equivalent to more distance or further.

IV. *Time inequality (less—with unequal distances and equal speeds).* This situation paralleled that of Sequence III, except that the black car stopped first and covered less distance, with the speed of the two cars the same. The white car stopped last. The concept of *less* time was equivalent to less or shorter distance.

V. *Time inequality (equal distances and unequal speeds).* The black car started before the white and traveled faster than the white car. Both cars traveled the same distance. The inequality of durations was to be deduced from the speed of the cars, keeping the other variables constant. It was assumed that the subject's response would depend upon logical (cognitive) rather than linguistic processes.

According to Piaget, the predicted order of difficulty in these tasks would be I, III, IV, II, and V.

B. *Time concept attainment.* In the (concept) films it was assumed that performance would depend upon nonlinguistic processes. The extensive use of language in the instructions and questioning, however, could not preclude the intrusion of language into this processing. In many Genevan experiments that purportedly focus on the child's action, there is almost always an extensive use of language with the Genevan "clinical method."

Weil (1970), wished to obtain data that would be least contaminated by language. She utilized a nonverbal concept attainment procedure that had been used successfully in other Piagetian-type studies (Beilin, 1965; Beilin & Gillman, 1967; Beilin & Kagan, 1969). In Weil's task, time, speed, distance, and starting time were varied. It was comparable to a four-cue, simultaneous discrimination problem. A pilot study showed, however, that, even when training was continued for 60 trials, none of the subjects learned the relevant time concept. A verbal-training procedure was then introduced to examine the effects of introducing "appropriate" language on concept attainment.

Because Piaget has claimed that language is not a sufficient condition of logicomathematical thinking, verbal training was considered as a further test of that claim (cf. Beilin & Gillman 1967; Beilin & Kagan, 1969). The procedure consisted of three phases. Time concept attainment (test), verbal-concept training, and retesting.

In the attainment phase, there were 40 (4 blocks of 10) simultaneous discrimination problems involving the use of two toy cars which traveled across a screen. The "concepts" programmed for attainment were *more time* and *less time*; each was positive for half the subjects. In every block of 10 trials, starting time, speed, distance, color, and position of the correct car varied. The sequences were similar to those used in the time concept and time language films and were similarly on film. After each response (the selection of the black or white car by pointing), the subject was informed as to whether he was correct or not. At the end of the 40 trials, subjects were questioned about the basis for their choices. Criterion was reached with 18 correct responses in a 20-trial block. If the criterion was not reached in 40 trials, the subject was given verbal-concept training.

The *verbal-concept training* phase started with an identification by the experimenter of the correct car in a film sequence and an explanation of the rule governing the sequence (the black or white car took *more*, or *less*, *time* than the other, white or black). The experimenter next undertook a series of foot races around the room with the subject, in which the various trials presented on the films were repeated, with the experimenter and subject representing the black and white cars. At the end of each race the subject identified who took more time and why. The purpose of this procedure was to simulate through action the conceptual relationship between the cars.

Returning to a table, various trials were repeated, this time with miniature cars. The subject now observed the experimenter carrying out the actions with the cars. If correct identification did not occur, the subject was instructed to place his hands on the cars while the experimenter moved them concurrently, explaining the rule as the subject "felt" the action.

At this point there were 9 training trials: 3 with the experimenter and subject racing across the room, 3 with the subject watching the experimenter race miniature cars on a table, and 3 with the subjects' hands on the cars as they were raced.

Ten additional training trials followed with the first block of 10 trials of the concept attainment film. The subject received reinforcement for each correct trial, and, when incorrect, he was shown the correct choice and the verbal rule was reiterated. "No," the experimenter would say, "that's not right, it's the car that traveled for more time."

After this *verbal-rule feedback training*, there followed the retest phase. In the retest, the subject received the complete series of 20 concept-attainment film trials. Criterion was 18 of the 20 trials correct. If the subject had been correct within the last 10 trials of the *training* phase, he went on to the last block of 10 trials of the retest phase and could thus reach criterion without repeating the first 10-trial block.

SUBJECTS

The subjects were children from the kindergarten and first- and second-grade classes of a New York City elementary school located in a middle-class neighborhood in the Borough of Queens. All the subjects were white.

At the kindergarten level there were 29 subjects (15 boys and 14 girls) with a mean age of 5 years, 10 months. There were 29 first-graders (15 boys and 14 girls) with a mean age of 7 years, 1 month. For the 30 subjects of the second-grade (15 boys and 15 girls) the mean age was 8 years.

The Peabody Picture Vocabulary Test (PPVT), which is used as a measure of intelligence, was administered to the kindergarteners. The median percentile score was 81, well-above average. The nursery school sample consisted of 12 children (6 boys, 6 girls). The mean age for boys was 4 years and for girls 4 years, 6 months. The median PPVT score for boys was at the seventy-first percentile, and the seventy-fourth percentile for girls.

The oldest group of subjects consisted of 30 children (15 boys, 15 girls) equally distributed among 9-, 10-, and 11-year olds who attended a summer playground. The 9-year-old mean was 9 years, 5 months; 10-year-old mean was 10 years, 6 months; and the 11-year-old mean was 11 years, 4 months. The PPVT median percentiles for the three groups were 73, 81, and 90. All groups, then, from ages 4–11 were well-above average on intelligence measures and presented no obvious linguistic impairment.

RESULTS

Development of the Time Lexicon

There were three classes of time words (with seven specific terms) investigated in Weil's study, order (*first, last*), speed (*fast, slow*), and duration (*more time, longer time, shorter time*). The frequency with which subjects knew these terms at the ages tested from 4-years old (nursery) through 7-years old (second grade) is indicated in Table 4-1.

The total number of time words correctly known increased to the first-grade, and then declined slightly. In an analysis of variance the effect of Grade was significant ($p < .01$); Sex was not. Some terms were very well known by nursery-grade (speed terms), but those of order and duration were not. Knowledge of the latter increased, but even by second-grade, children were having difficulty, particularly with the duration terms.

Time Syntax

Knowledge of the simple tenses (present, past, and future), and the complex tenses (present, perfect, conditional, and past progressive) is indicated in Table 4-2. As already indicated, the (I) construction could be comprehended on the basis of speed and position cues, and the (II) constructions could be comprehended only on the basis of speed cues. Correct response means and proportions of subjects with knowledge of the tenses are given at each age.

The Grade effect was significant ($p < .01$) in an analysis of variance although only the difference between the nursery and second-grade scores was significant ($p < .05$).

The simple tenses were known by a substantial number of nursery school

TABLE 4-1

Comprehension of Time Vocabulary by Grade (Percentage of Subjects Correct)[a]

| | | TIME WORDS | | | | | | |
| | | Speed | | Order | | Duration | | |
Grade	Total Scores[b] $\bar{X}$ (SD)	Slower	Faster	First	Last	Shorter (less) Time	Longer (more) Time I	Longer (more) Time II
Nursery (n = 12)	3.92 (.90)	83.3	83.3	33.3	58.3	41.7	33.3	25.0
Kindergarten (n = 29)	4.48 (1.12)	96.5	96.5	51.7	65.5	75.9	27.6	34.5
First-grade (n = 29)	5.24 (1.15)	100.0	100.0	55.2	93.1	89.7	58.6	27.6
Second-grade (n = 30)	4.67 (1.06)	93.3	93.3	66.7	73.3	66.7	26.8	50.0

[a] Adapted from Weil (1970), Tables 1 and 2.
[b] Maximum score is 7.

TABLE 4-2

Comprehension of Tenses by Age (Percentage of Subjects Correct)[a]

| | GRADE | | | |
Tense	Nursery (n = 12)	Kindergarten (n = 29)	First (n = 29)	Second (n = 30)
Present progressive	100.0	93.1	96.5	100.0
Past	83.3	100.0	100.0	96.7
Past progressive	16.7	27.6	42.3	56.7
Future I	58.3	96.5	100.0	96.7
Future II	16.7	17.2	27.5	40.0
Conditional I	83.3	89.6	100.0	100.0
Conditional II	66.7	41.4	34.5	33.3
Present perfect I[b]	66.7	76.5	100.0	100.0
Present perfect II	8.3	41.4	34.5	50.0
Means of correct scores (SD)[c]	4.33 (1.37)	5.10 (1.52)	5.41 (0.97)	5.73 (1.58)

[a] Adapted from Weil (1970), Tables 4 and 5.
[b] 12 nursery, 17 kindergarteners, 22 first-graders, and 15 second-graders were given present perfect I.
[c] Maximum score is 9.

children. The present tense was almost perfectly known, the past only somewhat less so, and the future known to a lesser degree, although by kindergarten even that construction was almost perfectly comprehended. The complex tenses were less well known, except for the conditional. The test condition that permitted responses to be made on the basis of both position and speed cues (I) was responded to much more adequately than the condition in which only speed cues were available. Of these the future (II) and present perfect (III) showed increases with age. The past progressive also showed an age progression, although this test condition required the subject to remember two durations. The declining age trend of conditional (II) was difficult to explain. In general, differences in development were shown in tense knowledge, with the complex tenses acquired later than the simple, and the simple tense achieved in the order of present, past, and future. Correct tense performance was facilitated if position and motion (speed) cues were present in the test situation. When only motion (speed) cues were available, time judgments reflected by the tenses were more difficult. These data indicate that knowledge of the tenses is not solely a linguistic phenomenon but is affected by the manner in which information is extracted from observation and action.

Knowledge of the tenses and time vocabulary are correlated to only a fair degree ($r = .17, .22, .25$). The correlation between tense and time vocabulary performance was significant only for the second-grade ($r = .39$, $p < .05$). Syntactic and lexical knowledge appeared not to be dependent upon one another for their development or to develop concomitantly.

TABLE 4-3

Comprehension of Before and After by Grade
(Percentage of Subjects Correct)[a]

Grade	Sentence order congruent with event order		Sentence order noncongruent with event order	
	Before	After	Before	After
Nursery (n = 12)	75.0	66.8	33.3	33.3
Kindergarten (n = 29)	89.7 *	68.9 *b	72.4 *	37.9
First-grade (n = 29)	89.7	82.8	72.4	58.6
Second-grade (n = 29)	76.7	90.0	86.7	70.0

[a] Adapted from Weil (1970), Tables 6 and 7.
[b] Comparison is between *after* (=) versus (≠) condition.
* $p < .05$; X^2 value from McNemar test.

TABLE 4-4

Time Concept Responses by Grade and Film ($\bar{X}$ and SD)[a]

Grade	I		II		III		IV		V		Total	
	$\bar{X}$	SD	$\bar{X}$	SD	$\bar{X}$	SD	$\bar{X}$	SD	$\bar{X}$	SD	$\bar{X}$	SD
Kindergarten (n = 29)	3.59	.68	1.38	.62	2.84	.59	3.37	.75	2.38	.61	12.97	2.06
First-grade (n = 29)	3.76	.69	1.97	.91	3.24	.61	3.45	.51	2.97	.64	15.38	1.72
Second-grade (n = 30)	3.53	.86	2.03	.85	3.27	.81	3.37	.58	3.03	.74	15.23	2.36
Older (n = 30)	4.00	0	3.43	.73	3.82	.42	3.72	.47	3.33	.42	18.21	1.32

[a] Adapted from Weil (1970), Table 9.

98

Time Connectives (Before–After)

When the order of sentence constituents was congruent with event order, children had greater mastery of the *before–after* connectives than when sentence order was in reverse of event order (Table 4-3). In the nursery group, more than 65% of the subjects succeeded with the *before–after* connectives when sentence order accorded with event order, but only 33% succeeded when sentence order was not congruent with it. *After* was, on the whole, more difficult than *before*. The difference was particularly pronounced at the kindergarten level. There was a performance difference at all ages for the noncongruent condition, but for the congruent condition, the ceiling on performance with both connectives was approached at an earlier age. The differences, except for the kindergarten grade, were not large enough to be significant. The (point biserial) correlations between the *before–after* connective scores, time vocabulary, and tense scores showed no appreciable or significant relationships.

Time Concept Knowledge

The measure of time concepts consisted of five short films of two cars racing, in which elapsed time, speed, and distance varied. For each film, four questions were asked to make a total of 20 items.

Table 4-4 indicates the means (and SDs) of scores for each film by grade. The mean scores increased with age, with an increase at first between kindergarten and first-grade, then a plateau, and an increase again between the second and older grades. The Grade effect in an analysis of variance was significant ($p < .001$) except for the difference between the first- and second-grades. The subject criterion score also showed developmental

TABLE 4-5

Time Concept Responses by Grade and Film (Percentage of Subjects Correct According to Weak /W/ and Strong /S/ Criteria)[a]

| | Film | | | | | | | | | |
| | I | | II | | III | | IV | | V | |
Grade	W	S	W	S	W	S	W	S	W	S
Kindergarten (n = 29)	89.7	68.9	3.5	—	48.3	17.2	55.2	10.3	20.7	3.5
First (n = 29)	93.1	86.2	31.0	—	79.3	24.1	93.1	37.9	55.2	6.9
Second (n = 30)	90.0	73.3	33.0	—	70.0	40.0	80.0	43.3	70.0	13.3
Older (n = 30)	100.0	100.0	93.3	53.3	96.7	76.7	100.0	63.3	96.7	20.0

[a] Adapted from Weil (1970), Tables 10 and 11.

spurts in performance between kindergarten and first-grade, and between second-grade and the older group. Performance as expected was better with the weaker-scoring criterion.

There were performance differences for each film within each grade. They were significant (χ^2 test) for each of the tasks, except for Task I, in which performance for all ages was near ceiling. Significant grade differences using subject criterion scores paralleled those for the mean scores (detailed data may be found in Weil, 1970). Similar patterns appeared, using the strong criterion, with the exception that significant developmental differences appeared for Task I.

According to Piaget, the order of task difficulty (from least to most difficult) should have been (I), (III), and (IV) equally difficult, then (II). Task V, added by Weil, should have been equal in difficulty to (II) because it involved a coordination of time and speed. The obtained order, in relative overall performance (Tables 4-4 and 4-5), generally confirms the predicted order. Task (V) was somewhat less difficult than Task II even though it too required an inference about time from relative speeds. In the case of (V), however, the times were unequal, as were the speeds. It seems that when *inequality* of time is in accord with inequality of speed, correct judgments are more likely than when time *equality* has to be inferred.

Green's *Index of Consistency* was used to measure the scalability of these tasks according to the proposed order. With one scoring criterion, the reproducibility score was .94, with the other it was 95. The consistency score for the former scoring was .44, for the latter .46. These come close to, but do not exceed, the index of .50 suggested by Green as the criterion for scalability. Although the measures generally appear scaled, according to the proposed order, the nearly equal difficulty of levels (III) and (IV), and (II) and (V) had the effect of reducing scalability values.

Time-Concept Training

There were three training phases: attainment trials (test), verbal-training trials, and retest trials. Table 4-6 reports the mean correct scores for time concept attainment, verbal training, and retesting. The concept attained in the first phase was either *more time* or *less time*. There were 40 attainment trials. None of the subjects reached criterion (18 or 20 correct in the 20-trial block).

In a 2×4 analysis of variance of concept attainment scores, there was only a significant effect for Concept ($p < .001$). *Less time* was significantly more difficult to attain than *more time*. In a similar analysis of training-trials data, the only significant effect was Grade ($p < .001$). The significant grade differences occurred between kindergarten and first-grade, and between second-grade and the older group.

No kindergarteners reached criterion in the test trials, 17% of the first-graders did; 23% of the second-grade; and 80% of the older group. The difference between first- and second-grade was significant ($p < .01$), as was the difference between the second-grade and the older group ($p < .001$).

TABLE 4-6

Time-Concept Training by Grade and Concept (X and SD of Number of Correct Trials)[a]

Grade	Attainment trials[b]				Training trials[c]				Test trials[d]			
	More time		Less time		More time		Less time		More time		Less time	
	$\bar{X}$	SD	$\bar{X}$	SD	$\bar{X}$	SD	$\bar{X}$	SD	$\bar{X}$	SD	$\bar{X}$	SD
Kindergarten	28.1	3.5	21.3	5.5	5.8	1.6	5.4	1.4	4.0	4.1	2.3	2.6
First	28.2	3.6	24.3	4.5	6.7	1.5	6.6	1.4	9.2	6.4	6.9	6.6
Second	26.4	4.4	23.9	3.1	6.6	1.9	6.2	1.7	9.7	5.6	7.7	6.8
Older	25.4	3.9	22.6	4.5	9.0	1.2	8.6	1.2	18.6	2.2	14.6	6.4

[a] Adapted from Weil (1970), Table 12.
[b] Maximum = 40.
[c] Maximum = 10.
[d] Maximum = 20.

Time Reversibility

There were two reversibility tasks; the scores for these were combined and 3 levels differentiated. A combined score of 0 or 1 indicated *no* reversibility, 2 or 3 indicated *intermediate* reversibility, and 4 indicated *reversibility*. Table 4-7 shows the proportions of subjects at each reversibility level, by

TABLE 4-7

Reversibility Performance by Grade (in Percentage of Subjects)[a]

Grade	Reversibility level		
	No reversibility	Intermediate level	Reversibility
Nursery ($n = 12$)	100.0	—	—
Kindergarten ($n = 29$)	44.8	34.5	20.7
First ($n = 29$)	10.3	17.2	72.4
Second ($n = 30$)	.0	16.7	83.3
Older ($n = 30$)	—	—	100.0

[a] Adapted from Weil (1970), Table 13.

TABLE 4-8

Relation between Reversibility Level and Comprehension of Complex Tenses (in ns)[a]

Grade	Reversibility	Tense									
		Past progressive		Present perfect I		Present perfect II		Conditional I		Conditional II	
		−	+	−	+	−	+	−	+	−	+
Nursery	−	10	2	4	8	11	1	2	10	4	8
(n = 12)	+	0	0	0	0	0	0	0	0	0	0
Kindergarten	−	9	3	2	4	7	5	1	11	9	3
(n = 29)	+	12	5	1	9	12	5	2	15	8	9
First-grade	−	2	1	0	2	3	0	0	3	2	1
(n = 29)	+	14	12	0	20	12	10	0	26	17	9
Second	−	0	0	0	0	0	0	0	0	0	0
(n = 30)	+	13	17	0	15	14	16	0	30	20	10

[a] Adapted from Weil (1970), Table 18.

grade. At nursery level, no subjects showed any time reversibility and all subjects in the oldest group did. There were two critical discontinuities in development, one between the nursery and kindergarten grades, the other between first- and second-grade. These differences were statistically significant.

Relation between Time Language and Time Concepts

The correlation (Pearson) between the time concept scores (maximum = 20) and the combined language scores (vocabulary + syntax, maximum = 15) for kindergarten, first- and second-grades was .57 ($p < .01$), which indicates a substantial correlation over this age span. Within individual grades only the kindergarten correlation was significant ($r = .36$, $p < .05$).

The relationship between reversibility level and the tenses was tested on the assumption that the time conception implicit in the syntactic properties of tenses would require the development of time reversibility, as the child's ability to relate himself to objects in either the past or future would require the logical flexibility involved in reversibility. This was expected to be especially true for the simple tenses; but the assumption was not confirmed. The complex tenses, on the other hand, showed more of a contingent relationship.

Reversibility level was dichotomized, with 1 and 2 scores in the (+) reversibility category and 0 scores in the (−) category. The language scores were divided at the median value. The data in Table 4-8 indicate that reversibility was achieved about the kindergarten and first-grade levels. Superior performance in the complex tenses appears after that period, although the trends are not clear-cut.

The theoretical relation between reversibility level and knowledge of the *before–after* conjunctions is more direct, whereas in the tenses it is not. The tenses are more likely to indicate one-way relations, at least as Weil tested them. Reversal, however, is implicit in the construction of *before–after* sentences in which sentence order is noncongruent with event order. The contingent relation between performance on the reversibility and conjunction tasks is indicated in Table 4-9. Reversibility level, as before, was achieved principally at the kindergarten and first-grade levels, and few subjects showed correct *before–after* performance prior to that time. In general, correct language performance (time conjunctions and tenses) lagged behind the acquisition of reversibility although there were sufficient exceptions to weaken this generalization. There was no relation between language task performance and reaching criterion in the concept-training task.

Time-Processing Strategies

After each film the child was asked, "Which car took *more* (or *less*) *time?*" and/or "Did the two cars travel for the *same amount of time?*" After replying, the child was asked, "How do you know that car took *more*

TABLE 4-9

Relation between Reversibility Level and Before–After Conjunctions (Subjects)[a]

Grade		Sentence order noncongruent with event order			
		Before		After	
		−	+	−	+
	Reversibility				
Nursery	−	8	4	8	4
(n = 12)	+	0	0	0	0
Kindergarten	−	5	7	8	4
(n = 29)	+	13	14	11	6
First	−	1	2	1	2
(n = 29)	+	7	19	11	15
Second	−	0	0	0	0
(n = 30)	+	4	26	9	21

[a] Adapted from Weil (1970), Table 19.

time?" Responses were recorded and later classified. The first six categories describing the responses are those used by Piaget (1969):

1. *Perceptual*. The subject mentioned some perceptual property such as a positional relationship: *ahead, behind, further, as far as, under*. (This category indicates minimal use of cognition.)
2. *Spatial order*. Response indicated ordinal position, such as *first, second, last* in the comparison between the two racing-cars.
3. *Temporal order*. The cars were ordered, not spatially, but in a time relation, such as "This car stopped *first*." A punctual time relation had to be indicated in this category.
4. *Speed*. Some form of speed was mentioned. For example, "It went *fast (faster, slower, the same speed)*."
5. *Duration*. Reference was made to a time interval, such as *more time, less time, the same amount of time*. An extension in time, rather than a point in time, was indicated.
6. *Coordination of start and stop*. The subject dissociated spatial succession from temporal succession. For example, "When one car stopped, the other was still going."
7. *Combination*. A combination of the prior strategies.
8. *Don't know or guessing*.
9. *Ambiguous*. This category included responses that the raters could find unambiguous.

There were also other types of responses but they were too few to note, e.g., *alternation, hypothesis testing.* For the age analyses, grades were grouped so that kindergarteners and first- and second-grades were the younger subjects and children (ages 9, 10, and 11) were treated as the older.

The strategies used by subjects differed as a function of (1) the dimensions varied in the films, and (2) the age of the child. The dominant strategies (Table 4-10) were perceptual, temporal order, speed, and coordination of stop and start, as well as combinations of these.

Whether a strategy was used by a younger or older child seemed to be more a function of the specific task than his age. For example, temporal order was used predominantly by older children in Film III, and predominantly by younger children in Film V. The only exceptions were the coordination of start and stop strategy and the combination strategy, which were used predominantly by older subjects. When the data were analyzed as to whether particular strategies were associated with correct response, the results were not uniform. In some instances the use of a strategy was highly differentiating, as with the use of coordinated start and stop in Film I, or temporal order in Films I, III, and IV, but in other instances, as with the perceptual strategy, employing a strategy was not differentiating.

Subjects' explanations were also obtained after the attainment trials in the time-concept training experiment. The responses for the *more time* and *less time* groups were pooled, when no significant differences between them were found. The strategies used by younger and older subjects were quite different. Thirty-five percent of the younger subjects used the "perceptual" strategies, whereas only 6% of the older subjects did ($p < .01$). The older subjects, on the other hand, used a combination of strategies (47%) significantly more ($p < .05$) than the younger subjects (20%).

The younger subjects, who were trainable, were more likely to use the combination of strategies (50%) than if they were not trainable (18%) ($p < .05$). The older, trainable subjects were less likely to use the perceptual strategy than the untrainable subjects ($p < .05$); the older group was still more likely to use the combination of strategies (although the difference was not significant).

DISCUSSION

The data show that time language, represented by the time lexicon and time syntax (the tenses and time conjunctions), was achieved over a wide age span. Complex tense acquisition was particularly protracted, as was the development of the conception of time itself. The achievement of cognitive reversibility appeared to develop prior to or concomitant with the achievement of the complex tenses, but the relationship was not necessarily a contingent one. When the formal structural relation between reversibility and time language was more evident, as with the *before–after* conjunction, there was a greater performance relationship. Development of time concepts, however, did not appear to be critically related to simple

TABLE 4-10

Time-Concept Response Strategies by Age (in Percentage of Explanations)[a]

	Film							
	II		III		IV		V	
Strategies	Younger	Older	Younger	Older	Younger	Older	Younger	Older
Perceptual	37.2	20.0	53.4	40.0	55.7	63.0	29.5	43.3
Spatial order	1.2	0.0	1.1	0.0	4.5	0.0	1.1	0.0
Temporal order	8.1	13.3	5.7	36.7*	7.9	20.0	30.7	3.3*
Speed	27.9	10.0	12.5	3.3	13.6	0.0	9.1	13.3
Duration	3.5	0.0	5.7	3.3	0.0	0.0	1.1	0.0
Coordination of start and stop	0.0	30.0*	1.1	3.3	0.0	10.0*	3.4	0.0
Combination of strategies	8.1	16.7	4.5	6.7	4.5	0.0	10.2	30.3*
Don't know	15.1	3.3	14.8	6.7	13.6	3.3	10.2	3.3
Ambiguous	0.0	6.7	1.1	0.0	0.0	3.3	4.5	3.3

Note: number of subjects in younger group for Film II is 86; all other films: younger n = 88; older n = 30.
[a] Adapted from Weil (1970), Table 24.
* $p < .05$.

tense development, although this could have been a function of the tasks used. It is practically impossible to develop experimental time tasks that are wholly independent of language, and time language tasks that are wholly linguistic and independent of time conceptualization or cognition. Despite this, when Weil's film sequence included both position and speed cues, there was less dependence upon reversibility than when only speed cues were available. This was true when questions were in the future tense and in some of the complex tenses. Herriot (1969) also found that 4- to 6-year-old subjects' understanding of the future was influenced by the number of cues available in the test situation.

Despite these experimental difficulties, the reversibility tasks were mastered between the ages of 6 and 7; the complex tenses, such as the past progressive, were not mastered by 60% of the 8-year olds. Additionally, only 13% of the subjects who demonstrated knowledge of the *before* conjunction had not acquired reversibility, and only 10% for the *after* conjunction. Nevertheless, the relation between reversibility and the time conjunctions was not unequivocal.

The *sufficiency* of language for cognitive functioning was tested in the training experiment. Only 20% of the first- and second-graders profited from time language training whereas almost all of the 9- to 10-year olds were able to profit from it. These data support other findings (Beilin & Franklin, 1962; Beilin & Gillman, 1967) of the limited effectiveness of verbal training when the subjects lack an available operational structure. The data also show that younger trainable subjects used conceptual strategies common to older (trainable) subjects. Older subjects who were not trainable, likewise, employed cognitive strategies common to those used by the younger and nontrainable subjects.

Comprehension of the time lexicon and syntax was acquired over a broad age-range. Although the time lexicon appears on the whole to be independent of the achievement of time syntax, there is limited parallel development between the two over a broad age-span. Speed words are the easiest for children to acquire, although, paradoxically, the concept of speed is most difficult to incorporate into a conceptualization of time and is not done adequately until the age of 9. Logically the words *first* and *last* should be equally difficult to acquire, nevertheless, at every grade *last* was easier than *first*. The data show that speed, order, and duration words were acquired, generally, in that order.

The parallel syntax items also showed a clear development. Those items which could be answered on the basis of speed and/or position cues were answered correctly by 90% of kindergartners and first- and second-graders; speed cues appearing alone were more difficult for subjects and were used correctly by only 50%.

In the *after–before* conjunction tasks, *before* was consistently more easy than *after*. It was also the case that *more time* (longer time) was more easy to train than *less time* (shorter time). We will discuss these findings in detail later in this chapter.

Although there was a developmental trend in time conceptualization, no second-grade subject attained time operativity. This is contrary to the findings of Lovell and Slater (1960) who report that 13% of their 5-year olds, 17% of their 6-year olds, and 30% of their 8-year olds showed evidence of operativity. A variety of reasons may account for the difference between the Lovell and Slater and Weil results. The principal one relates to the criterion for operativity used in each study. The Weil criterion was based not only on the reply to the same type of questions used by Lovell and Slater, but was contingent also upon correct response to two prior questions to which that question was logically related. In other words, Weil used a more stringent criterion. Procedural differences may also have been involved.

Although operativity had not been attained by age 8 in Weil's sample, the general order of difficulty of the time concepts represented in the films was consistent with the proposed Piagetian order.

Other Studies

CROMER (1971)

Cromer (1968) studied the appearance of time reference in the language of two very young children and suggests that cognitive factors exercised constraint on the development of both grammatical form and the time lexicon. Although Cromer proposed that egocentrism, and the lack of ability to "decenter" (in Piagetian terms) affected time language development, no effort was made to test that effect. A later study (Cromer, 1971) was specifically designed to determine whether temporal reference, "apparently requiring an ability to decenter temporally [p. 354]," was associated with the more generally developing ability to decenter. To that purpose Cromer used two tasks that were designed as time analogues of Piaget's tests of spatial development. They paralleled the 3-mountain task in which a child is tested for his ability to see the "other side of the mountain" from the point of view of a doll placed on the far side. In the two Cromer tasks a picture series was used that told a story "in time." It involved a boy or girl. In the first task, after a picture series was laid out, the subject was asked to identify the picture in which the figures could make certain utterances spoken by the experimenter (Type I). In the second procedure (Type II), the subject was asked to take the point of view of the figure in one of the pictures and identify other points in time relative to that reference point. The subjects were provided with a warm-up (3-picture) series to familiarize them with the procedure and then a training-test series consisting of 7 pictures.

Two stories of the Type I series included questions posed in the present, present progressive, future, past (weak form -ed), past (strong form), future, present perfect, future perfect. The Type II stories had questions put in the indirect form, such as "What picture is he talking *about* when he says here...." The tenses of the statements embedded in this form were in the future, future embedded in past, past (work form), past embedded in future; past (strong form), present perfect, and future perfect. Responses were recorded as either "context coded" or "decentered." They were context coded ("I see birds") if the child pointed to a picture that encoded features pictured in the question. It was decentered if the subject said "I saw birds" or "I will see birds" in response to a picture that *preceded* or *followed* the one with birds in it.

Although there was a significant correlation between IQ (PPVT) and decentered response ($r = .45$), with IQ partialled out a significant correlation remained ($r = .38$). The youngest MAs (3:1–4:00) did not decenter at all, and very few (4%) of the MA 4:1–4:10 group did. Only the MA 4:11–5:99 groups (50%), and the group above MA 5:11 (84%) showed substantial decentration.

The Type II pictures showed less decentration and only the oldest MA group (over 5:11) showed above-chance responding. The children in the MA 4:11–5:9 and MA over 5:11 groups decentered, mostly with the weak past, strong past, past progressive, and perfect. The future was difficult for the younger children, but not the older, and the future perfect was difficult for both. For Type II, the embedded forms (the past in the future time, and the future in past time) were aids in decentering. In addition, sentence repetition (imitation) was not related to the ability to decenter.

Cromer concluded from these results that (1) the child's ability to decenter temporally occurred in stages (MA-related stages). The criterion for decentration used by Cromer was a weak one (2 or more correct responses of a maximum of 12). The actual distribution of correct responses were not reported, only the percentage of subjects with 2 or more decentrations. (2) Decentering occurred less often in the future and perfect form than the others. (3) Failures to decenter were not a function of misperception or lack of memory as the sentence imitation data showed. (4) In the Type II tasks, which involved the complicated embedded forms, children gave more correct answers than to simpler forms, but Cromer proposes that this may have been a consequence of the particular picture series used in which parts of the series required responses based on processes free of reversibility. The tasks could thus have been responded to on the basis of one-way mappings alone. (5) Cromer points out that although children of CA 7 or 8 can generally decenter, they are unable to coordinate spatial viewpoints in the 3-mountain problem. Younger MA children were able to decenter "without a coordination of viewpoints"; the oldest group (above MA 5:11) gave correct answers "approaching significant differences from chance levels" when such viewpoint coordination was required.

Again, Cromer's criterion for decentration was a weak one. The study also assumed that time representation is a proper analogue for space relations. Time, however, when represented spatially is usually two-dimensional. The 3-mountain problem, on the other hand, is three-dimensional. It is possible that this difference had an effect on Cromer's results. Further, the MA scores reported were not necessarily from average-age CA subjects, because the cut-off score was an IQ of 60. To further confound the results, a verbal intelligence test was used for classifying subjects, based upon lexical knowledge (the Peabody Picture Vocabulary Test); a nonverbal IQ measure would have been more appropriate.

Ferreiro and Sinclair (1971)

A Genevan study by Ferreiro (Ferreiro, 1971; Ferreiro & Sinclair, 1971) assessed the child's comprehension of sentences in which two events were described as taking place simultaneously or successively, without their being causally connected. The procedure to test comprehension was the one typically used by Sinclair, in which the child is asked to "act out" a sentence with toys made available to him by the experimenter. The sentences were of the form *The girl washed the bucket which the cat will knock over.*

A second procedure elicited the child's *production* of similar sentences by having him describe two events that the experimenter acted out with toys. After a free-choice description by the child, a second description was provoked by requesting the child to start his sentence with the description of the event that occurred *last* (inverse-order description). An interrogation often followed in which the experimenter drew the child's attention to the temporal relationship. A third procedure required repetition (imitation) of the sentences used in the comprehension test; it always preceded the comprehension task.

Ferreiro and Sinclair (1971) describe four response levels for subjects who ranged in age from 4- to 10-years old. (Ferreiro [1971] reports more detailed distinctions among the levels.) At the first level (about age 4–4½), the child's free-choice descriptions were in the form of two independently and weakly linked propositions, coordinated by either *and* or *then*. Both were in the same tense, and (for 80% of the cases) their sentence order corresponded to the event order of the experimenter's action (*She cleaned him and he went upstairs*). In the inverse-order task, these subjects always complied with the instruction to start their description with the name of the actor in the second event. They were incapable, however, of using the temporal indications needed to describe actual succession. At this stage they attempted various, partially successful, strategies for achieving a correct solution.

1. Simple inversion of the initial free-choice description, with the adverbial maintained in the same position it (correctly) occupied in direct-order description—*The boy went to the top of the stairs and afterwards the girl cleaned him.*
2. An inversion of the action performed by the actor of the second event— *He goes downstairs again and the girl washes his arms.*
3. An inversion concerning the actors of the two events; the action performed in the second event was attributed to the action of the first event and vice versa—*The boy goes and washes her face, and then it's her that goes upstairs.*
4. Attribution of a *neutral* action to the actor of the second event—*The boy came, she washed his face, and then he left.*

Those children who gave "curious" and always incorrect partial solutions in the inverse-order task had no trouble with the "when" questions. Their answers were correct both for syntax and temporal order of the two events.

From the second level onward, children seemed to process sentences on the basis of three hypotheses or strategies.

1. The order of enunciation of sentence constituents corresponds to the order of occurrence of events.
2. The conjunction *quand* "when" introduces the clause that refers to the prior event, when it is noticed that the two verb-tenses are not equal.
3. A temporal indicator (such as *before* or *after* as opposed to *when*) at the beginning of the whole sentence is a signal of inversion of order.

At the second level, the strategies did not constitute a system, and the first strategy appeared to dominate. The evidence for this was that direct-order sentences (those that follow event order) were perfectly comprehended. Sentences with *when* as a conjunction began to be understood as introducing a prior event, but if *when* introduced the subsequent event it systematically led to failure. *When* indicates a temporal relationship, but the verb tenses have to be analyzed to decide if the relationship is one of succession or simultaneity. *Before* and *after*, on the other hand, are *full* indicators that denote succession, and also indicate which event is prior or subsequent. These conjunctions nonetheless require comprehension of the syntactic structure of the sentence.

Some 69% of the children at this level understood the sentence form "*Before* q, p," which was comprehended better than the *after* form; findings which suggest that the third strategy (a temporal indicator with full value at the beginning of the whole sentence is a signal to inversion of order) should lead to an immediate re-translation which prevents further analysis of the signal. Ferreiro and Sinclair argue that the child would consider it "abnormal" that a sentence would begin with a strong temporal signal when the order alone could indicate the succession of events.

Requests for imitation of the sentence with *after* ("*After* p, q") at the second level, resulted in deletion of the conjunction ("*and* q, p") in the inverse order, or to a transformation into "*Before* p, q," which is congruent with the action "Q *is before* p." The sentence with *after* can be interpreted by the child using the first hypothesis, but at the price of deleting the conjunction, or with the third, but at the price of transforming the conjunction, which becomes a signal of inversion of order. At this level, verb-tense opposition did not seem to be understood. Sentences, in which only verb-tense opposition indicated succession, were imitated according to the order of enunciation. There was some indication, however, that the child recognized when two verb-tenses were different even if he did not fully appreciate their significance (the second strategy required this capability). So at this level, verb-tenses may be organized in functional couples (past perfect–present perfect), but the succession will only be interpreted one-way and in that precise order.

At the third level (ages 6–10), answers to all three types of production task were correct. Children were capable in their descriptions of using the opposition between future and future perfect tenses: *The boy will go upstairs when the girl has washed him.*

All inverse-order sentences (in which constituent order was noncongruent with the order of succession), whose comprehension depended on an analysis of the value of the conjunction inside a given syntactic structure, were now understood correctly. The new acquisitions of this level were of oppositions within the future and in context, "Q *when* p" and "Q *after* p."

Two types of sentence still resisted analysis: (1) inverse-order sentences with an opposition within the future, if the conjunction *when* introduced the subsequent event, and (2) inverse-order sentences in which only the verb-tense opposition indicated the succession.

Correct repetitions were always accompanied by correct actions, and there was no gap between production and comprehension. The sentence type "Q *after* p" was understood only when used in the inverse-order description. At this level, children were capable of "metalinguistic reflection," i.e., they could treat sentences in an objective fashion.

The fourth level (ages 6–10). Success in all tasks was complete. Only now were sentences that contained verb-tense oppositions understood; and, in production, a succession of events could be described with a verb-tense opposition as the only "indicator." Again, children had no difficulty with inverse-order descriptions; differing from the third stage only in that they did not hesitate, they could correct wrong answers, etc.

Ferreiro and Sinclair reveal that only when performance in Piagetian tasks (conservation of liquid, and the concept of time) was taken into account could clear age-distinctions be made among Categories 1–4. Category 1 grouped children 4–5 years of age. They were preoperational, that is, they had not even reached the preconservation level of *renversibilité*. In Category 2, children were still preoperational, and although they were of the same age as those in Category 2, they had reached the level of *renversibilité*, that is, they could both anticipate the correct height of liquid in a glass when it was poured back into its original glass, and could propose the return in order to establish the equality of the liquids. The children in Category 3 succeeded in the conservation of liquid task; they could take both height and width of the containers into account in judging the invariance of the liquid quantity. Level 4 children included those who had knowledge of liquid conservation and had an operational notion of time.

An example of the relation between operative level of the subject and his inverse-level descriptions is indicated in Table 4-11, in which inverse-order descriptions are classified according to level of operativity (according to the Ferreiro (1971) scheme). Incomplete descriptions, repetitions, and permutations were typical of the lower operative levels and decreased linearly. There was a linear increase in relevant and correct responses (opposition of tenses, use of relatives) with increasing operative level. Inversions, etc., showed a curvilineal relation, increasing at the intermediate levels, but leveling off at the higher operative levels.

TABLE 4-11

Inverse Order Description: Grouped Percentage of Responses[a]

Type of description	Operational level[b]					
	NR $\Sigma = 28$[c]	Int. 1 $\Sigma = 26$	R $\Sigma = 122$	Int. 2 $\Sigma = 122$	C $\Sigma = 209$	C/T $\Sigma = 35$
Repetition, incomplete description, permutation	67.7	76.7	44.2	37.1	22.6	2.8
Refusal	14.2	7.7	7.5	8.7	3.5	
Inversions of the relationship, of the actions, adjunctions, etc.	10.5	3.8	29.8	39.7	30.2	5.8
Others	7.1	11.6	4.5	3.7	0.9	
Relevant and correct answers (converses, opposition of tenses)			13.7	10.4	42.8	91.4

[a] Adapted from Ferreiro (1971), Table 2.
[b] NR = absence of renversibilité.
    Int.1 = intermediate level 1—beginning of renversibilité.
    R = renversibilité.
    Int.2 = intermediate level 2—beginning of conservation.
    C = conservation.
    C/T = conservation plus operative notion of time.
[c] Total number of responses.

Ferreiro and Sinclair propose that at the level below *renversibilité*, children regard the two events described in the sentence as separate entities, neither of which provides a reference point for the other. Although these children understood the "when" questions as referring to time, they nevertheless linked each event to the subjective view of the person who related it. This indicated egocentrism and the lack of cognitive decentration. At the more advanced preoperational level of *renversibilité* characterized by a semilogic of one-way mappings, the relationship of temporal order predominated but the dependency had only one direction. There was an absence of reversibility. This was indicated by the fact that children at this level established two separate temporal orders (a is *before* b; b is *after* a) but could not deduce one from the other. That is why inverse-order description, corresponding to the succession of events, was not possible. The construction of the full transformational syntax became possible only with the achievement of reversible operations.

In the context of production, comprehension, and imitation, the order in which the events were enunciated gave the primary indication of time to the young child. What was said first happened first. Later, adverbs and conjunctions were understood and correctly used. Only at a more advanced level were different tenses understood as indications of temporal relations.

Herriot (1969)

This study was an attempt to replicate the findings of Fraser *et al.* (1963) in regard to the comprehension of tenses. Fraser *et al.* found that the contrast between sentences in the *present* and *future* tense were better comprehended by children than the contrast between the *present* and *past*. Herriot used nonsense words and unusual referents, although the referents were real objects instead of the pictures used by Fraser. The tenses were the present, past, and future, and were presented in pairs. Each subject responded to only 3 sentence pairs; 6 sentences in all, out of 12 possible sequences. The referent was a toy with a woodpecker on a pole that descended in about 30 sec. With two such toys, as one woodpecker descended, a question was asked, "Which one is going to gling?", and after full descent, "Which one has glinged?" as a contrast between future and past. Of the 24 subjects, 36- to 48-months old, 5 made no adequate response at all. When the *future* and *past* were paired with each other, they were comprehended to a significant degree, although not when paired with the *present*. Herriot attributed the difference to attentional factors and tested this in another experiment with a wider age-range of subjects (3- to 6-years old) and with the number of woodpeckers increased. The change in procedure was made to permit questions in the singular and plural that was thought would foster greater distinctiveness and attention. The contrast was confined to the *future* and *present* tenses. The second experiment showed that the *future* tense utterance when paired with a *present* tense question was not comprehended until age 6, although in the first experiment it was comprehended at age 3 when paired with a *past* question. Additional grammatical and referential cues led to successful comprehension at 5, and in one case even earlier. The effect of sentence constituent order was significant in both experiments. That is, the *future* was always more difficult if presented first rather than second when paired with a *present* tense question, even for 6-year-old children. The change in verbal cues to direct attention did not affect the younger children, although it did the older. Herriot concluded that the ability to comprehend tense is a function of both grammatical form and the nature of the real-life situations to which reference is made. Comprehension was said to be a function not solely of derivational complexity, which was much at issue at the time, but of other factors in the extralinguistic context.

E. V. Clark (1970, 1971)

Eve Clark's (1970) account of temporal reference entails both surface structure and deep structure sentence elements. She defines three principles that dominate the development of children's descriptions of temporal sequence. The first is *order of mention:* It is simpler to talk about events in their order of occurrence (*We drove to the beach and then went swimming*) than in any other order. The second is *derivational complexity:* Sentences that are transformationally simpler are more easily produced than sentences that are transformationally less simple. A subordinate clause

embedded to the right of the matrix sentence in surface structure is transformationally simpler than the corresponding construction in which the
subordinate clause has been preposed to the first position in surface
structure (*Wc went swimming after we drove to the beach* is simpler than
After we drove to the beach, we went swimming). The third is *choice of
theme:* If the theme of the sentence is the first event to occur in time, then
the speaker may use a coordinate construction (*We drove to the beach and
went swimming*), or a construction with the subordinate clause first (*After
we drove to the beach, we went swimming*), and occasionally with the
subordinate clause second (*We drove to the beach before we went
swimming*). If the speaker wishes to introduce the second of two events as
the theme (as topic or first), which is less common in English, he has to use
before or *until* to introduce the second of the two events and uses a construction like *We went swimming after we drove to the beach* or *Before we
went swimming, we drove to the beach*.

The three principles are said to interact, and Clark predicted that the
developmental order for these constructions would be (1) coordinate
clause construction, (2) subordinate clause constructions with the subordinate clause in the second place, and (3) subordinate clause constructions in the first place. Clark maintains that the child begins to depend
upon *order of mention* first to convey a sequence of events, followed by
the realization that *theme* plays a particular role in speech and takes the
topic (first) position. The child then begins to use the subordinate clause
construction to replace the coordinate. Temporal conjunctions are finally
used that enable him to place the second event in the topic position.

Developmental order was tested through the analysis of spontaneous
speech samples collected each day over a period of 6 months, starting with
subjects 3-years old from 15 children attending an Edinburgh nursery
school. Only the temporal descriptions of children were analyzed, i.e.,
those constructions that contained at least two clauses. These constructions contained either two coordinate clauses (*We ate and then swam*)
or a main clause plus a subordinate clause (*We drove to the beach before
we went swimming*). The coordinate conjunctions used were *and, and
then*, and *and so;* the subordinate conjunctions were *when, because,
before, after, while, until,* and *unless*. The data confirmed Clark's predictions: *order of mention* was very important for children when they first
began to use compound sentence descriptions of time events. The principle of derivational complexity was also strongly supported: there was
not one instance of a first-construction subordinate clause appearing
before the appearance of a second-construction subordinate clause. The
results also indicated that children recognized the initial position as the
theme of the utterance. In addition, children began using *and* as their main
conjunction. The first of the main subordinating conjunctions were *when*
and *because*, followed by *if*, first for subordinating clauses in the second
position and then for the same clauses in the first position. Other conjunctions, such as *before* and *after*, appeared less frequently. Clark reports
"some evidence" that *before* and *after* appeared as "prepositions" before

they appeared as "conjunctions." In addition, *before* as a preposition and conjunction appeared to precede *after*.

The first purely temporal conjunction to appear was *when*, which Clark interprets as implying that the child understands *when* as "at the same time as," that is, to indicate simultaneity. It is characterized as equivalent to introducing clauses with the first temporal adverbs (*now, today*, etc.) that are used by children to indicate simultaneity. *Before* and *after* are held to develop analogously.

Clark concludes that the overall pattern of development, first at the level of the temporal adverb and later at the level of the subordinate clause, indicates a recognition of simultaneity, followed by the recognition of the first in a series and, finally, the recognition of the second or later event in a series.

A later study (E. V. Clark, 1971) predicted that children who did not understand either the *before* or *after* conjunction would rely on an *order of mention* strategy in sentences that used the conjunctions, and also that children would acquire the meaning of *before* prior to that of *after*. The latter prediction was based on the assumption that *before* is linguistically simpler than *after* because (a) constructions with the subordinate clause occurring second that also describe events in order are ordinarily constructions with *before*, as in *He jumped the gate before he patted the dog*, (b) *before* is considered linguistically marked as the positive member of the pair, which is closely related to the spatial preposition *in front of*, whereas its counterpart *behind* is marked negatively because it describes something out of sight. Combining the two predictions, she anticipated that in the first stage of acquisition children would use an order of mention strategy because they do not understand conjunctions. At the second stage, children would interpret the sentences with *before* correctly but not those with *after*, and in the third stage they would understand sentences with both conjunctions.

Her subjects were 40 nursery school children (at Stanford) of four age-levels from 3- to 5-years old. They were given production and comprehension tasks. In the (provoked) production task, the experimenter used two toys to carry out two successive actions (*The boy kicked the rock; The boy patted the dog*). This was followed by one of two *when* questions. *When did the boy kick the rock? When did the boy pat the dog?* For comprehension, the child was asked to carry out actions with toys from utterances containing the *before–after* conjunctions (*The boy kicked the rock after he patted the dog*). There were 32 sentences with two clauses. *Before* in Position 1 or 2 and the same with *after*. The results, as predicted, showed that children of the earliest stage (A), who come from the two youngest age groups, appeared to use an *order of mention* strategy in comprehension, indicated by errors in *before* (1) and *after* (2), but not *before* (2) and *after* (1). They also gave only nonrelational answers to the *when* questions in the production task. Although Stage B children interpreted *before* correctly, irrespective of the position of the subordinate clause, few gave evidence of understanding the meaning of *after*. Two-thirds of the children

(B1) treated *after* just as the younger (Stage A) children had: by naming an *order of mention* strategy to get *after* (1) correct and *after* (2) wrong. A few (B2), had learned something of the meaning of *after*. At Stage C, the children interpreted both *before* and *after* correctly, as adults do. The production task paralleled this development.

A theory of comprehension encompassing relational terms (such as *before* and *after*) was offered based on a linguistic analysis of meaning, in which it was assumed that the meaning of a word is made up of various semantic features. The components of meaning of *before*, *after*, and *when*, and similar lexical entries are said to be arranged hierarchically with *time* as the first feature. The next feature is *simultaneous* and has two values. +*Simultaneous* is found in words designating a punctual relation. −*Simultaneous* designates a serial relation. ±*Prior*, the next feature, occurs in words that are −simultaneous. *Before* is thus +time, −simultaneous, +prior; *after* is +time, −simultaneous, −prior; *when* is +time, +simultaneous.

This linguistic feature analysis is said to have psychological validity. The production data are taken to support the view that the superordinate features are learned first, from +time down. The sequence of acquisition is said to follow this order as well. Linguistically, +time is interpreted to be a combination of +*locative* and −*place* features. It is finally concluded that children learn the meanings of words component by component, that components are hierarchically organized, and the feature hierarchy is acquired in an order first beginning with the superordinate component.

The feature component explanation of the difficulty of *before* and *after* is challenged in a study by Amidon and Carey (1972). Their purpose was to show that with proper training, sentences with *before* and *after*, and sentences containing other words with the same semantic features, would show no differential response patterns in children 5.4- to 6.3-years old. There were five experimental and control groups. The experimental groups were given (1) corrective feedback, (2) intonational emphasis on the temporal marker, and (3) both. There were two control groups: (4) one lacking either feedback or intonational emphasis, and (5) another control which only received training with *first* and *last*. The latter control was to see if performance varied with another type of temporal marker. A post-test (there was no pretest) employed new materials. The training was organized around sentences of the form *"before x, y" (Before you move a red plane, move a blue plane)*, *"x, before y," "after x, y," "x after y."* Instructional sentences were on cards which the experimenter read.

An analysis of variance of post-test error scores indicated that feedback was effective, but intonational emphasis not. The authors report that few subjects trained with *before* or *after* could comprehend them before training (in the practice sessions), which varies from the E. V. Clark (1971) findings that 5-year olds had considerable knowledge of these relations, particularly in some conditions. Amidon and Carey report that sentences containing subordinate clauses were difficult (when *before* and *after* conjunctions were employed), but not when there were none (as when *first* and *last* were used). Because *first* shows the same semantic marking as *before* (+time, −simultaneity, +prior) it should give the same difficulty in comprehension, but it did not. The greater ease of *first* and *last* was accounted for by the salience of the first clause when the sentence contained two main clauses as it does with *first* and *last*. Another factor said to account for the difference was that the introduction of a subordinate clause led to a lack of attention, which feedback had the effect of negating. The lack of attention would also account for the effectiveness of feedback training because the child was assumed to have the underlying competence for temporal ordering. Feedback merely made it manifest. Why the "emphasizing training" did not do the same was not explained as it too was an attention-providing procedure.

Discussion

The child's early conception of time is composed of two undifferentiated components: (1) time identified with space and (2) time considered as a set of relations among states. The early identification of time with spatial transformations results in considerable conceptual difficulty for the child. Later in development, the distinctions become clear and a system of continuous time is more adequately comprehended. When this occurs, continuous time is differentiable into qualitative and quantitative time distinctions. The essential elements of the system of time conceptualization consist of notions of *order of succession* (from which the conception of simultaneity is differentiated) and *duration* (which itself combines the idea of succession and that of intervals).

Strategies of Ordering

Knowledge of time is associated developmentally with understanding of the motion of objects, particularly their velocity. Because motion takes place in space, notions of time have to be constructed from information derived from movement in space. The development of a spatial framework leads to particular expectations concerning natural events that lead, in turn, to the development of strategies for analyzing events in space. These strategies affect the conception of time, and result in a set of expectations that interrelate knowledge of space with the knowledge of time.

1. Events are ordered. That is, events are seen as occurring in a sequence.
2. Some type of system can be applied to this ordering. The child acquires and uses a set of linguistic algorithms to index these ordered relationships. Qualitative ordering occurs with such lexical distinctions as *before–after*, *first–last*, *this*, *then*, *that*, etc. Quantitative ordering occurs through the application of such lexical terms as *first*, *second*, *third*, etc., with the number system used to index events occurring in succession.
3. In spatial indexing, that is, in the attempt to keep track of physical events, ordering in most cultures occurs from left to right, and top to

bottom. The direction of these strategies appears for the most part to be conventional and arbitrary.

4. Time representation also tends to be ordered from left to right; *before* is associated with *left*, *after* with *right*.

5. At first, both spatial and temporal ordering are ambiguous in regard to the reference point. The person himself is later placed in the coordinate system and reference is indexed relative to himself.

6. The tendency to start with reference to an event on the left, and then to the right, becomes embodied in sentence reference. Events to the left, those that are enunciated first, are taken to have occurred first. Those on the right, uttered later, are considered to have occurred later. This primacy or scanning strategy leads to the expectation that elements in the first position are first in time and are also the most important. (It is also where the subject, agent, actor, is first.)

7. The child acquires the concept of succession, and the identification of the earlier event with *before* and the later event with *after*, concurrent with learning to produce simple sentences in which constituent order coincides with event order. These linguistic acquisitions exploit the child's use of the scanning hypothesis (left-to-right) and his event-ordering capability.

8. The (developmentally later) need to shift emphasis to the later of two events leads to the development of strategies for reordering the sentence so that, in referring to two events, the one to be focused on is placed in the first position. Thus the *after* event is placed first, and a linguistic form is constructed for making such reference.

The newer strategy, based on the need to transpose the order of events or to change focus, requires more operations than the earlier-acquired scanning-order strategy. As a consequence, the *after* preposition is more difficult to process than the *before* preposition, although in some contexts the reverse may be true. The difficulty of *after* may be due to the *after* clause: if found in other than the expected scanning order, it has to be transformed to its normal processing order. The comprehension of *after* in reversed order, as a more recently acquired strategy being less known and practiced, is thus processed more slower than the usual strategy. The Ferreiro (1971) and Amidon and Carey (1972) data support these possibilities.

Time Language and Space

Although the concepts of motion, space, and number are differentiated with age from the concept of time, linguistic time remains interchangeable in some contexts with reference to space, as in the case of *first–last* and *before–after*. The spatial notation for linguistic time relations, proposed by J. J. Katz (1972) embodies a common metric for both space and time reference. This system applies to the tenses as well as to the time and space lexicons. It has the virtue of coming quite close to Piaget's conception of time in some respects, although it does not fully embody the complexity of time representation. It may be, however, that natural language cannot adequately represent the full range of time relations and only special or formal language such as mathematics and logic can come closer to achieving such representation (as in the integral and differential calculi).

It is also possible that logically organized structures of the cognitive system are not fully needed for linguistic reference, and more simple and highly abstract conventional systems that embody only part of the complexity of a complete conception of time are needed, as for example in communication. The essential distinctions of time cognition would have to be represented with considerable parsimony to reflect the structure of time cognition. This is probably better accomplished linguistically in natural and constructed languages than in any other symbolic system.

A Piagetian analysis suggests that the time lexicon is structured according to the distinction between order of succession and duration. These categories, in turn, are subject to the logic of asymmetrical and symmetrical relations. Psychologically and developmentally it is to be expected that time language would be constructed parallel to and consistent with development of the conceptual structure of time. We would expect, for example, that reference to simultaneity would emerge as a differentiation of the language of event and time succession, of which it is a limiting case. This does not imply that language of order would necessarily precede development of the language of simultaneity or, contrarily, that simultaneity is the superordinate category or feature out of which nonsimultaneity differentiates. The relationship is more complex and is part of a set of logical structures in which simultaneous and successive relations are constructed into a single system. The idea (such as E. V. Clark's) that features become progressively differentiated is but half the story. That which is differentiated also requires integration, and a more appropriate conception of the developmental process is one in which both cognitive and linguistic meaning are achieved in a constructive process that is based on both the differentiation and integration of categories.

If natural language, as indicated before, does not fully embody the complexity of time cognition, linguistic rules nevertheless must be compatible with the nature of the cognitive representation of time—otherwise time reference would be consistently ambiguous. Although a linguistic theory of time reference would not have to be fully congruent with a theory of time cognition, it could not be seriously out of accord with it. From this point of view, the Katz and MacDonald conceptions are more fully in accord with the Piagetian view of time cognition than the Clark formulation. One reason is that the Clark formulation is based on feature differentiation in a binary system, i.e., dichotomized features are either present or absent. The Katz formulation based on semantic marking has conceptual dimensions that are neither binary nor limited by multiple classification schemes. For time reference, the conceptual dimensions although not treated by Katz as cognitions are nevertheless in greater accord with the scheme described by Piaget for the development of such cognitions. The Clark proposal, however, has the virtue of at least a limited psychological test of its suppositions.

The Time Lexicon

In respect to the development and knowledge of the time lexicon, the Clark and Amidon & Carey studies are limited to an intensive investigation of a few time prepositions, whereas the Cromer and Weil studies were concerned with a broader representation of the lexicon. From these data, it appears that the time lexicon develops in a progressive fashion. Time words related to motion and velocity (speed terms) appear to develop quite early, but time words related to order (*first, last*) and duration (*longer, shorter time*) are achieved in that order. This gross developmental pattern supports the Piagetian prediction that language acquisition occurs over a considerable period of time and is generally congruent with the development of the conception of time. The data at this point, however, are very limited.

Time Lexicon and the Tenses

Development of the time lexicon progresses in parallel with knowledge of the tenses, but there appears to be no causal connection between the two, which accords to some extent with intuition. The child can acquire the notions of *first* and *last*, for example, independent of knowledge of past, present, and future. Thus, the child could quite correctly comprehend and produce *The truck is first* without clear cut knowledge of the future–present contrast (*The truck will be first—The truck is first*). Whether a fully integrated conception of *first–last* or any time-word contrast can occur without articulating with the system of tenses at some higher level of integration is not apparent from available data.

Order of Tense Development

Development of knowledge of the tenses (Weil) progresses in the order of *present, past, future,* and the complex tenses in the order of the *conditional, present perfect, past progressive.*

Context Effects on Comprehension

Comprehension of sentences embodying the different tenses is affected by the nature of the referent situation (Weil, Herriot). It is possible, of course, to study comprehension through sentence contrasts with no reference to objects or events in the real world, but these conditions are usually difficult for young children. The study of comprehension, then, cannot be confined to linguistic "intuition," or to sentence-processing time. As the cited time-language experiments show (Amidon & Carey, 1972; E. V. Clark, 1970, 1971; Weil, 1970), the ability to understand the nature of external events interacts with knowledge of linguistic form in the use of time-representing language.

Temporal Connectives and Prepositions

The progressive comprehension of time relations also influences knowledge of temporal connectives and temporal prepositions. The child's development of strategies to deal with event order is reflected in his comprehension of such time connectives as *before–after* (Amidon & Carey, 1972; Ferreiro, 1971; Weil, 1970).

Although specific sentence constituents, tenses, temporal prepositions, and temporal connectives, develop in an order that parallels the development of time conceptualization, a higher-order cognitive control appears to determine the organized interaction of these constituents in a sentence. When, for example, a sentence consists of two clauses connected by a temporal preposition or connective, with each clause containing a time (tense) relationship, the capacity for comprehension requires the ability to relate the individual constituents in a time relationship to one another. The time relationship among constituents is concurrently a logical relation among them, and the evidence indicates (from the Weil, Ferreiro–Sinclair, and Cromer studies) that this capacity is dependent upon the child's operative (cognitive) level, that is, his ability to reverse, decenter, and otherwise transform the entities in a logical relation. Although this operative capacity exercises limited control over the development of the tenses, its control is more direct and greater in those cases in which sentence constituents are in a logical relation to one another, as when they involve temporal connectives.

5

Development of the Number
Lexicon and Number Agreement

Experiment 1: Development of the Number Lexicon[1]

Number Language: Linguistic Aspects

Mathematics is often characterized as *the language of science*. The superiority of mathematics as a language system derives from its ability to present abstract ideas with greater precision and clarity than other forms of representation. Mathematics also embodies abstract relations and operations that are useful for exposing meanings inherent in a wide variety of scientific concepts, even if these concepts have their origin in observation and are stated as empirical generalizations. Implicit meanings become explicit through operations performed upon numerically, algebraically, and figurally represented data. New knowledge is more readily created by this means than through the use of other forms of representation. The operations of arithmetic, for example, although expressible in natural language, could not have been discovered as easily, and possibly not at all, if there were no system of representation that could symbolize the number series

[1] A portion of this study was reported in Beilin, H. Development of the number lexicon in young children. Presented at the Developmental Psycholinguistics Conference, State University of New York at Buffalo, Buffalo, New York, 1971. An abstract of the study was reported at the First International Symposium of the Society for the Study of Behavioral Development, University of Nijmegen, Nijmegen, The Netherlands, 1971, and appears as Beilin, H. Development of the number lexicon in young children. In F. J. Monks, W. W. Hartup ,& J. de Wit (Eds.), *Determinants of behavioral development*. New York: Academic Press, 1972.

and express relations such as those indicated by fractions.[2] The application of the number system and arithmetic computation to the analysis of empirical data has made astronomy, physics, and the other sciences, as we presently know them, possible.

THE REPRESENTATIONAL FUNCTION OF LANGUAGE

In making explicit some of the reasons why mathematics is often the language of choice in the sciences, we have by implication also identified some of the properties that make it a language. The first of these is its representational function. In this sense, a language is a vehicle for expressing meaning that derives from sources other than language itself. If we wish to represent concepts of physical space and the relations that exist among such concepts, we can represent them in the language of Euclidean geometry as Galileo did. If we wish to express relations among the dimensions and properties of physical space, we can do so in the calculus as did Newton, even if it means creating the mathematical language to do it. With more contemporary conceptions of a relativistic or quantum physical universe, we can express these relations in non-Euclidean geometries, in statistical mathematics, and so on.

Mathematical languages are thus dependent for meaning upon the concepts of the system of science to which they refer. In this sense, mathematics provides abstract operators and quantifiers for concepts whose origin lie outside of mathematics. Although this may in part be true, it is not the only meaning of representation that applies to mathematics.

Arithmetic, geometry, and other mathematical systems have properties that are also independent of meanings associated with or derived from experience with the natural world. These properties express no physical reference as do statements and propositions of the physical sciences. The mathematical system constitutes a form of a priori knowledge that obtains significance from the nature of internal system relations themelves. Even though these abstract relations are a form of a priori knowledge, they nevertheless are employed in the study of physical systems because, in some instances at least, they are thought to have properties analogous to those of the real world. Put another way, the real world has properties that these relations are thought to represent in an abstract fashion. In deducing new properties and relations within mathematical systems that are treated as models of physical reality, one is able to explicate hitherto unknown relations and facts about the real world. In this sense, mathematical relations are representations of the logical relations (in a lawful or statistical sense) that define the dependences among physical entities.

In sum, mathematical language serves first to make precise what would otherwise be imprecise deduction. Secondly, through the process of

---

[2] Weyl (1949) makes the point that the construction of the mathematical number realm started with the sequence of natural numbers, 1, 2, 3, etc. The first step beyond this was the development of fractions, which owed their creation to the transition from counting to measuring.

abstracting essential meaning, it makes seemingly noncomparable data comparable. Thirdly, it supplies causal chains that are not evident when represented less abstractly or in other forms. Representation thus serves to facilitate thought.

THE COMMUNICATION FUNCTION

Mathematical language, in addition, makes communication of certain kinds of complex and abstract ideas possible with greater clarity, precision, and economy than other representational systems. The scientific enterprise is in one sense a social system whose participants require one or more languages to communicate the concepts and relations of their respective disciplines. Mathematics serves that communication function particularly well, although it does not serve all of its functions, not even all of its epistemological functions. The power of this communication system is evident in its comprehensibility and utility in every conceivable, natural language community.

STRUCTURAL RELATIONS AMONG LANGUAGES

Mathematics not only has representational and communication functions that are shared with natural language, it also has *structural* properties that parallel those of natural language. For one, each mathematical language has a lexicon composed of constants and variables. The terms in these lexicons, however, do not function strictly as words. In the case of constants, the meanings are fixed; for variables, different values (meanings) may be substituted. It is a language of abstractions for which particulars may be substituted. The lexical entries for the language of Euclidean geometry are different from those of algebra, although the terms of one are translatable into the terms of the other as are the terms of two natural languages.

Lexical terms in mathematical languages are related to one another by operations that parallel the manner in which natural language statements bind their lexical terms together. The lexical items are integrated by well-defined rules that constitute the syntax of the mathematical language. As Lenneberg (1971) argues, however, neither in natural language nor in mathematical systems such as arithmetic is there a clear-cut division between lexical functions and those of syntax. Lexical inflections, in some languages, for example, express relations that are expressed syntactively in other languages. Lenneberg's argument is based upon the reduction of linguistic functions to those of relation. Even the concept of *one* is seen as dependent upon the relation of *one* to *more than one*. Its conceptual status is intuitively dependent upon the recognition of this relation. Although Lenneberg's thesis indicates the difficulties in identifying or distinguishing the elements of a language and defining their properties, it would still appear that both natural and mathematical languages have differentiable elements that form a lexicon, each having a syntax or grammar.

Whatever the difficulties in identifying and defining their functions, they are at least shared by natural and constructed languages.

Mathematics is frequently characterized in natural language terms and, in turn, natural language is frequently analyzed for the properties that parallel those of mathematics. Dantzig, for example, points out that insofar as a natural language "is capable of precise statements, it is a system of symbols, a rhetorical algebra par excellence [Dantzig, 1954, p. 100]." In the nineteenth century, when comparative and historical linguistics developed into lively, scholarly pursuits, John Stuart Mill wrote of grammar, "the structure of every sentence is a lesson in logic [Jespersen, 1924, p. 47]." Mill's intent, which reflected a minority view at the time, was to show that the principles and rules of grammar were the "means by which the forms of language are made to correspond with the universal forms of thought [Jespersen, 1924, p. 47]." (As will be detailed in Chapter 6, the same goal was identified for logic by Boole.) Aspects of this conception appear in the views of linguists and philosophers since that time, but it was not until relatively recently that the logical status of language has received serious and extensive discussion.

Mill saw language as indicating the nature of thought. He considered that "the distinctions between various parts of speech, between cases of nouns, and the moods and tenses of verbs were distinctions of thought and not merely of words [Jespersen, 1924, p. 47]." Jespersen is less optimistic about being able to demonstrate the concordance between the distinctions in language and the distinctions in the outside world (as the mind conceives them). For him, logic apparently resides more in language itself than in the cognitive system.

Whether the "rules" (or the logic) of language are isomorphic to the "rules" or logic of thought is still an open question. Chomsky (1967) sees the problem of defining the relationship between language and cognition as one of considerable magnitude. He places the burden of difficulty mostly on cognition, asserting that there is practically no knowledge available of the laws of thought, at least in a form that can articulate with what is known of the rule system of language. Chomsky rejects Piaget's theory, for example, and all other theories of cognition as apt characterizations of the nature of thought. Piaget's position is that the structural characteristics of behavior, defined by regularities in action, have properties that are identical in many respects to the formal logical systems created by logicians. Piaget's delineation of the logical structure of the child's thought, although recognized as an abstract model, is nevertheless not considered by him to be simply a metaphor designed to serve a heuristic function. Piaget (1968b) sees this model as tied, however indirectly, to physical and psychological reality. It is Piaget's contention, furthermore, that both the developing logical system and the content of the child's thought provide the motive force for the development of language. Language, which is a symbolic system for the representation of thought, develops out of the more general capacity for symbolic functioning along with other types of symbolic representation such as imagery (Piaget, 1962). Until recently, few linguists or psychologists were ready to entertain, much less accept this proposal. The more usual view has been that thought is made possible by language, which expressed in its most extreme form is identified with the ideas of Whorf (Carroll, 1956). Another influential position is Vygotsky's (1962), which considers language and thought to have independent origins with thought becoming progressivley under the control of language.

NUMBER LANGUAGE

Mathematics is, in one view, synthetic and empirical, in accord with Kant's interpretation.[3] The more current view is that mathematical statements are a priori or analytic (Ayer, 1946), although the question as to whether mathematics represents the physical world still occasions debate. To hold that mathematics is an a priori construction does not put into doubt the suggestion that some mathematical ideas were developed from empirical data. The history of mathematics attests to this. Early forms of mathematics derived from natural experience and were only later fashioned into formal systems of representation and communication. Although this is not true for all mathematics, it is true for the number system. The evidence shows that number was constructed and represented in natural language long before it became formalized as a conceptual system. It is still to be found in natural language as well as in formal mathematical systems and theories.

In natural language, number is in both the lexicon and syntax. It appeared lexically in early language, in such collective terms as *flock, herd, bunch* and in *pair, couple, brace*, long before the appearance in the language of such words as *number, collection*, and *aggregate* (Dantzig, 1954). In syntax, number is evident in pluralization rules and in the rules that ensure agreement between individual lexical elements that embody number as part of their meaning.

Knowledge of how mathematical systems grew out of natural language or grew along with it is very limited. According to Menninger (1969), who provides the most extensive historical and cross-cultural linguistic analysis of number words and number symbols, the conceptual number sequence was not consciously created. It evolved slowly and in a stepwise fashion. Conscious elaboration of the number system occurred long after the foundations of number had been established in both natural language and in its graphic and linguistic representation.

Because number is part of a system of mathematical conceptualization and is at the same time part of the structure of natural language, it lends itself in a special way to exposing the nature of the relationship between language and cognition. The acquisition of number language and the developing conception of the number system provide the materials for an

---

[3] Mathematics (and physics), Kant argues, yield synthetic *a priori* knowledge as distinct from the analytic type of *a priori* knowledge that is derived from logic (Kemp, 1968).

analysis of the relation between the child's conceptual and linguistic structures. We now consider the development of the child's number lexicon and its relation to the child's developing, cognitive capacities; later in the chapter we report on one aspect of number within syntax.

THE NUMBER LEXICON

The number lexicon (natural language) divides into two major classes: **cardinal number-words** and **ordinal number-words.** Cardinal number-words refer to cardinal numbers. In the logicist tradition, cardinal number is defined in terms of classes and sets.[4] Ordinal number-words refer to ordinal numbers. They denote relative place, position, and order; that is, they describe positional and analogous relations among classes or entities.[5]

One class of cardinal number-words consists of terms in which number reference is definite as in "She has a *million* dollars." "He has *three* cats." There are other lexical contexts for cardinal terms that are more ambiguous such as; "What is *one* to do?" "We are as *one*." "On the *one* hand, . . ." "*One* day last month, . . ."

The contexts of these examples are ambiguous as to their number origin or reference. They have meaning only indirectly related to cardinal number. In some cases they imply unity (We are as *one*); in others, different relations are implied ("On the *one* hand" refers to a thing or event contrasted with another). Other cardinal numbers are, on the whole, free of this ambiguity except when used as prefixes, as in *two*-bits, *two*-faced, etc. Comparable unambiguous relations exist for ordinal numbers; "His is the *first* car in line." "Elvira ate the *millionth* hot dog." "Tom is the *third* smartest boy in the class."

These terms are ambiguous as to place, position, or rank: "*First* things first." "In the *first* place, I am not a tiger but a zebra." In these sentences, *first* has the meaning of "foremost." As a prefix, *first* has a variety of meanings all historically related to notions of position or rank such as *first*-class, *first*-estate, *first*-cousin, etc.

---

[4] How cardinal number is defined is the subject of some controversy (Weyl, 1949; Benacerraf & Putnam, 1964). Mathematical convention following the logicists' tradition holds that cardinal number is definable in terms of sets or classes in the manner of Russell and Whitehead. The relation of ordinal number to cardinal number is also disputed. Russell and Whitehead's view is that cardinal number is prior to ordinal; there is another view that ordinal number is prior (Weyl, 1949).

[5] Jespersen (1924) implies that ordinal words derive from cardinal number ". . . to indicate place in a series most [all?] languages have words derived from cardinal numerals; these are called ordinals [p. 211]." Although this appears to be a generalization from linguistic data, it parallels the Russell and Whitehead thesis that ordinal number derives from cardinal number.

A conception of number words limited to words that represent cardinal and ordinal numbers, even with remote and ambiguous reference of the kind referred to, would omit a large number of terms that entail some element of quantitative reference. Neglected would be an important class of relational terms including *more* and *less*. Even broadening the number categories to include relational terms would not be sufficient to encompass the domain of quantitative reference that exists in natural language.

The logicist definition of a cardinal number as the class of classes containing "couplets," "triplets," etc., is based upon the assumption that equivalence or nonequivalence of sets or classes is established by the method of one-to-one correspondence (i.e., pairing an individual in one set with an individual in another set until all possible pairs are exhausted). The inequality of sets, and thus the comparative identification of *more* and *less*, is established when a set has an excess or deficiency in individuals relative to another set. Once the concept of a set containing an aggregate of individuals is established, it can be identified or denoted by a number symbol, and the number itself utilized in place of the reference class. A counting procedure becomes possible because the numerals can be used independently for indexing purposes.

Closely related to counting in the conceptual realm of quantification is measuring (Weyl, 1949). In measuring a line, for example, length is most primitively determined by the iteration of a partitioned segment (call it a) along the length of the line. Iteration involves the notion of adding equivalent (i.e., congruent) segments $(a + a + a + a + \ldots)$ leading to (a, 1a, 2a, 3a, etc.). When combined, the operations of iteration and partitioning yield fractions, and one is led progressively into the arithmetic treatment (multiplication, etc.) of magnitudes. The physical domains to which these arithmetic operations are applied are irrelevent because the laws implicit in the arithmetic operations are independent of the nature of the magnitudes. It makes little difference whether one is dealing with temperatures or lengths if the arithmetic operations apply. For practically every physical and nonphysical description of the natural world it is possible to translate a qualitative into a quantitative measurement. A measuring scale can be applied or created in which every value can be indicated by a number (Weyl, 1949). There are natural language parallels in that many physical dimensions and their quantification or measurement are represented in the lexicon (e.g., *three o'clock* and *4:15* PM). The same is true for spatial dimensions that are represented cardinally, ordinally, and in various measurement terms. The intimate relation between counting (with numbers) and measurement (with numbers) is evident in the lexicon. Quantity in the number lexicon is represented by the cardinal–ordinal distinction, and quantitative measurement is indicated by determinacy. Number reference is made to classes whose members are determinable (countable), and to those that are not. It is made also to positional, order, and ranking relations that are precisely measurable, and those that are not. The cardinal–ordinal dimension and the derminate–indeterminate dimension multiply to yield a classification scheme with four classes of number words:

cardinal–determinate; *two, fifteen, one hundred and sixteen, million*, etc.
ordinal–determinate; *second, fifteenth, seventy-third, millionth*, etc.
cardinal–indeterminate; *odd, even, part, some*, etc.
ordinal–indeterminate; *more, less, fewer*, etc.

Some natural language terms are not unambiguously classifiable, however. In using this scheme, the first question to be asked is whether a word qualifies as a number word. *More* and *less*, as indicated, are terms that do refer to quantity and are thus number words, but not in all usages. They also have meanings that are not strictly quantitative, as illustrated in the sentences below, although even here they, in an indirect sense, make reference to arithmetic or measurement operations:—"Give them *more* cake"—additional; "There are a dozen martinis on the table, *more* or *less*"—approximately; "*More* and *more*, good chefs are disappearing"—to an increasing degree.

More and *less* derive their basic meaning from the fact they denote a quantitative relation, meaning "greater than" and "less than." But their relational reference is to "amount" (as the comparative of the term *much*) or to "number" (as the comparative of the word *many*). The fact that these terms refer to number and amount implies a cardinal number property. However, their salient relational property is more akin to the properties of *first* and *second* than to *one* and *two*, that is, they are inherently ordinal terms. The reason for this is that their reference is based on the logical properties of a series. First, they refer to asymmetrical relations. *More than* and *less than* refer to the relation of inequality in which one term of the relation is more and the other, by *necessity*, is less. Second, the relation is transitive. If the A is *more than* B (in amount or number) and B is *more than* C (in the same terms), then (necessarily) A is *more* than C. Some relational terms are not asymmetrical and transitive. *Father of*, for example, is asymmetrical but *not* transitive. If, "A is the *father of* B, B is **not** the *father of* A; further, if B is the *father of* C, A is **not** the *father of* C (he is his grandfather). The relation of *brother of* is transitive and symmetrical rather than asymmetrical (except in the case where A and B are of different sex).

The classification structure of cardinal number is such that it embodies the notions of inclusion rather than those of transitivity and symmetry. *Five* is a class that includes the class of *three* and the class of *two*. By partitioning the constituents of the class differently, *five* includes the classes *four* and *one*. Although the relation of *more than* can be applied to the relation between superordinate class (*five*) and a subordinate class (*three*), it is a relation which is secondary to the definition of a class relation, and not primary as it is in the definition of a series.

The terms *more* and *less* in a strict sense, then, apply to both series and classes. We choose to classify these terms as ordinal because the logical properties of the term are closer to and more generally applied to ordinal relations than to classes. The decision, although not arbitrary, still leaves the ambiguity inherent in these terms not completely resolved.

Thus, words in the number lexicon have a logical relationship to one another. The structure that defines this relationship is distinct from the purely linguistic relationship among these terms, that is, whether they are nouns, adjectives, etc. The logical structure is mathematical. Just as number is differentiable into cardinal and ordinal relations, so are the number words of natural language differentiated. Number is represented by a graphic symbol system (*1, 2, 3 . . ., 1st, 2nd, . . .*) independent of natural language, however, most if not all natural languages have words to represent the natural numbers. In addition, natural language embodies a grammar for generating well-formed number names, such as *fifteen-hundred and twenty* (1520), and not poorly formed names such as *twenty-hundred and fifteen* (van Katwijk, 1965). This grammar, according to van Katwijk, governs the position of the lexical items relative to each other, such that every existing integer is represented and every pair of synonyms is generated (for example, the pair *twenty-five hundred* and *two-thousand, five-hundred*— synonyms for *2500*). If one verbally presents a native speaker with *two-thousand, eighteen-hundred,* it sounds acceptable to most persons until it is called to their attention that it is not a number or until they attempt to record it. There are at least two reasons for accepting such an unacceptable number name. One, suggested by van Katwijk, is that the listener lacks some complicated rules that make such names unacceptable. Another possibility is associated with performance aspects of language in that the native speaker may lack a "perceptual" strategy for recognizing certain forms associated with the grammar even though he may have the basic competence that comes with knowledge of the rules of the grammar.

The grammar of number names, however, is not simply a linguistic rule system, it reflects the logic of the number system. The positions of generated lexical items and their combinations are critical because meaning changes with position. The positions of number words are determined by the relations between number domains (*million, thousand, hundred,* etc.) because natural language representation of number is designed to give the same information as *digital* number notation. That portion of the lexicon, then, that deals with number names (the names for cardinal and ordinal numbers) has its origin and reference in the system of natural numbers. The number system, which most logicians and mathematicians consider to be reducible to a system of logical relations (the logicist argument), is mapped onto the rules of the grammar that determine the positional relations among the names. Thus, there is a nearly complete isomorphism between the relative positions of number names and number digits.

Number names (determinate cardinal and ordinal numbers) do not exhaust the lexicon of number words. The dictionary of terms that makes quantitative reference is large. In approaching this dictionary, it is necessary to recognize a distinction between *quantity* and *number*. Number refers to a particular class (or set) relation among collections of delineated entities. The number system is a system of such class concepts, denoted by symbols called digits or numerals, that embodies relations between these classes, such as succession. Quantity is a general property of things to which a measure or number can be applied, or to which an indeterminate description can be given. Quantity, in other words, refers to attributes to which numbers can be applied to indicate magnitude. There is a class of quantitative attributes to which no numbers can be applied because the quantity is indeterminate. The number words that make reference to indeterminate quantity are considerable, although unequal to the cardinal and ordinal number-words which are infinite. Consider the range of the following, indeterminate quantity terms: *plural, several, some, numerous, multiple, profuse, assemblage, outnumber, various, manifold, fractional, part, nought*. And the comparative quantity terms, such as *equality, identity, balance, level, symmetrical, tantamount*, and so on. Finally, the large number of words that refer to other relations, to which ordinal numbers in theory apply: *next, follow, series, subsequent, later, earlier, position, size-place, precede, sequence, reverse*, and so on. In the latter examples, no specific ordinal or cardinal number is applicable. Even though clear reference is made in most cases to ideas of quantity, many of the terms have nonquantitative meanings as well. In the case of indeterminate number words, lexical meaning embodies the number or quantity feature, indeterminacy, and additional meanings that distinguish their special reference from words in the same category. *Next* and *follow*, for example, suggest common-order relations; their ordinal identifications are indeterminate because the specific positions to which they refer are not specifiable. Furthermore, the terms differ in properties that make their meanings in the most specific sense different (*follow* may mean later in time or in a series, but not necessarily next in a time sequence, or in a series). *Follow* also has a number of nonquantitative meanings such as pursue, engage in, etc. These indeterminate number of quantity references are not directly influenced by the logic of the number system in the same fashion as the natural number names.

Our study of number lexicon development was undertaken to determine whether the number lexicon is acquired in some logical order, particularly in an order that relates to the logical relations of number itself. It was a specific focus for the more general question as to whether the order in which language is acquired has some relationship to the order in which the conceptual and operative system is constructed by the child.

Method

The young child's knowledge of various components of the number lexicon was determined from his response to a series of questions in accord with (1) The four-fold classification of the number lexicon already referred to, and (2) A classification of definitional knowledge [Caws, 1959]. A test was devised consisting of a standard set of questions, and a set of materials to which some of the questions referred. The test is identified as the *Number Language Instrument* (NLI) and was administered to children at various age levels.[6]

The NLI was used in a study already reported (Beilin & Gillman, 1967). In that study the NLI yielded a series of composite scores related to performance in a number-reversal learning task and a cardinal–ordinal task (Piaget's staircase problem). A significant relationship was found between number language scores and staircase task performance, but not between language scores and number-reversal learning. The study we are now reporting focused on a descriptive analysis of the components of the number-language instrument rather than on the composite scores derived from that scale.

RATIONALE FOR NUMBER-LANGUAGE ASSESSMENT

It was assumed that number language embodies and represents the logical structure of the number system. It was on this assumption that number words were classified into the cardinal and ordinal number-words categories, and further differentiated into determinate and indeterminate number-word classes to reflect the representation of quantitative measurement. This characterization of the number lexicon can be said to underlie adult knowledge of number language; however, our interest was in developing a description of the steps taken by children in constructing that knowledge.

Knowledge of number words was assessed in the context of a classification scheme of "knowing" based on an analysis of definitional meaning in the development of scientific theory (Caws, 1959). The categories chosen from this scheme were as follows; (1) denotive meaning, (2) connotative meaning, (3) Symbolic representation of meaning, (4) operational meaning, and (5) theoretical meaning.

Although this selection assumes that definitional categories are hierarchically organized, it is not a necessary condition for using these criteria. Because number words quite naturally extend over this range of meanings, the ideal strategy would have been to apply the definitional criteria (utilizing all five types) to each of the four categories of number words. This was not possible, however, because there are no naturally occuring instances of some of the cells when a matrix, utilizing the definitional categories as one dimension and number-word categories as the other, is constructed. There are no instances, for example, of symbols that represent either cardinal or ordinal indeterminate number terms that a child of 3 is likely to know. (The symbols < or > for *less than* and *greater than* may be known by older children; but are not likely to be known by younger children.)

In addition to determining the child's understanding of these categories, we sought to differentiate between the comprehension of number words from the ability to produce these terms on request.

[6] Irene Gillman assisted in the development of the number-language instrument.

The way we employed the criteria was as follows:

1. *Denotation* as used here refers to a word's observational content. The denotative tests involved determination of the child's understanding of cardinal and ordinal number-terms in the ordering and evaluation of meaningful objects.   This test employed tasks requiring that the child correlate certain observational events with general number terms. In order to perform well, the child had to produce such terms as *number, quantity, order, size, place, before,* and *after* to the appropriate test conditions. The items refered to both numerosity and order (see Appendix B).

2. *Connotative meaning* referred to either explicit or implicit knowledge of the defining properties of a construct so that its common characteristics could be differentiated as a class from others. In the test of connotative meanings, we were interested in whether the child could implicity classify number words as cardinal or ordinal, and as determinate or indeterminate.

The productive aspect of this subtest utilized (1) a *word association test* in which a single response was required for each number-word stimulus, and (2) a *continuous word association test* in which the child was instructed to produce words that "seemed like" the stimulus word. The continuous word association item was intended to provide an indication of the size of the child's number or number-related vocabulary. The comprehension part of this subtest involved verbal meaning or a *forced-alternative type of word association.*

3. *The test of symbol knowledge* tested for recognition of the equivalence of number symbols to related numbers. The child was specifically tested for (1) the equivalence between spoken number words such as *two* and the written *2,* and (2) knowledge of *synonyms* of the same number constructs (*triple—three, dozen—twelve*).

4. *Operational meaning* referred to the application of an axiomatic system to a set of experienced events so that the axiomatic system is given empirical meaning. Operational meaning was determined from the child's ability to use number terms in the indexing of physical objects to determine their position or number. This test entailed correlating sense data with specific number constructs. When the child, for example, was shown five objects and asked, "what is the number of things on this card?" at least three capacities were required for successful response: (1) knowledge of the concept to which the word *number* refers, (2) knowledge of the number word, that is, the label for that concept, and (3) the ability to carry out an indexing operation correctly; that is, to determine by counting the amount or position of objects in an array.

5. *Theoretical meaning* was determined through the child's knowledge of additive and subtractive number operations. Each related question required the ability to deal with operations on numbers entailing, both relational (ordinal) and classification (cardinal) logics. Correct solutions of these tasks required that the composition of elements (either additive or subtractive) were carried out on an abstract level because physical objects were not available to the child. Each of the tasks was in theory, describable

by a propositional statement capable of being verified by eventual reference to sense data (Caws, 1959).

6. In the last subtest, the child's ability to count cardinally and ordinally without reference to particular objects was recorded. It was assumed that this ability could be acquired by a child through *rote* memory procedures.

PROCEDURE

The language instrument was given to children in the kindergarten and first- and second-grades as well as at nursery and prenursery levels. Each child was tested on an individual basis. The examination was posed in a game-like format in which various toys and other materials were presented to the child. Some of the questions related to the materials or to manipulations made with them; others not. The main portion of the NLI was preceded by a set of questions designed to ensure that the child understood the terms *same* and *different*. Object identification served as a warm-up for the main task.

After the administration of the number language instrument to 5- and 6-year-old children, it became clear that some items yielded no correct responses and others yielded very few. This led to the revision of a number of items to make them easier to administer to younger subjects. Other items were added to the test for younger subjects to provide maximum evidence of their number-language knowledge.

SUBJECTS

The subjects were white middle-class children. The younger children attended private nursery schools. The older children attended New York City public schools in residential areas to which the nursery school children ordinarily transferred. The first-grade children were also subjects in another study (Beilin & Gillman, 1967). The youngest age group ($\bar{X} = 2$ years, 9 months) of the sample ($n = 23$) is identified as the 2-year-old group. They were administered the revised NLI with items designed to facilitate comprehension. An older preschool group ($\bar{X} = 3$ year, 7 months) is identified as the 3-year-old subjects ($n = 27$). They were administered the regular form of the NLI. The remaining groups are designated as the 5-, 6-, and 7-year-old subjects. The study was based on a total of 387 individually tested subjects.

Results

ORDER AND QUANTITY TERMS

The emphasis of the present study is on number language although some aspects of the data provide evidence of the child's number conceptualization. In most instances, knowledge of number concepts and number language are so interrelated as to be undifferentiable.

Number theory, in the logicist tradition, reduces number to notions of class or sets with an accompanying emphasis on the operation of one-to-one correspondence in establishing the equivalence or nonequivalence of sets. One-to-one correspondence is thus a fundamental number operation and is also one of the early acquisitions in the child's conceptualization of number (Piaget, 1952).

The child's knowledge of one-to-one equivalence and the language associated with it was tested both in regard to the equivalence of objects and equivalence in the ordering of objects. We found that only a small number (9%) of the 2-year-old children recognized the equivalence of sets whose elements were identically ordered (Table 5-1).

The proportion of successful children increased rapidly however; 60% of the 5-year-old subjects could recognize the *lack* of correspondence between two ordered sets (trains), and could identify the lack linguistically. When objects were ordered according to size, the young child's response was minimal, indicating a lack of knowledge of positional order or a linguistic deficiency, or both. It was not until age 6 that 64% of the subjects responded correctly to the experimenter's use of the term *size place* in relation to variation in order of 3 objects of different size. When asked to judge whether the *size order* of houses was the same as that in corresponding and noncorresponding sticks, few, even among the 7-year-old subjects (16%) were correct in all 3 of the presented items, although 79% are correct on 2 of the items. Because a child could be correct by chance in 50% of the cases, 3 items were used as a response criterion to reduce the probability of correct chance response. By age 5, a substantial number (45%) were correct in at least 2 of the 3 arrangements shown. The considerable difficulty of this item was due either to the difficulty (or ambiguity) of the task itself or lack of knowledge of the term *order* uninterpreted by an adjective (e.g., size). Data from Piaget's studies, as well as others, show that 6- and 7-year-old children know these conceptual relationships, so either the task is ambiguous, or more likely, the linguistic terms are not known at this age. The same was probably true for two items that required subjects to identify positions *in front of, after, before* and *behind* which showed an age progression (4%, 30%, 46%, 40%, and 51% of subjects correct for ages 2, 3, 5, 6, and 7 respectively). Response was relatively low for the older part of the sample. This, again, may be a function of task difficulty or limitation of linguistic knowledge. It may also be that sentences in the form of "X *in front of* Y" or questions that ask " Is X *in front of* or *behind* Y"? are particularly difficult for young children.

When asked to judge the equivalence (same number) of two sets of *4 sticks* placed in a random array, as well as an unequal set of *5* and *4 sticks*, equivalence could be established by a one-to-one correspondence method, or by counting. Correct chance performance was 25% based on a "yes" or "no" response. Above-chance performance (45%) was achieved at age *5*. When the child was required to make a judgment of the equality of *amount*, with equal and unequal numbers of objects (*4* and *5*), it was not until age 6 that a chance level of performance was reached. Questions that

TABLE 5-1

Response to Cardinal, Ordinal, and Comparative Number-Words by 2- to 7-Year-Old Subjects (*in Percentages*)

Item description	Age group					
	2	3	4	5	6	7
Equivalence terms—cardinal						
Recognition of number equivalence (production of *number*)	0	0	—	0	0	1
Number equivalence (provoked *same amount*)	30	22	—	45	77	93
Equivalence of quantity	—	—	—	5	15	22
Equivalence of amount (*same amount*)	9	15	—	20	54	77
Equivalence terms—ordinal						
Recognition of nonequivalent order (production of *order*)	9	30	—	60	94	97
Size-place judgment	4	0	—	18	64	92
Size-order equivalence (2 items correct) 3 correct	(30) 8	(7) 7	—	(45) 13	(73) 9	(79) 16
Judgments cf *before, after, behind, in front of*	4	30	—	40	46	51
Recognition of order equivalence ("X in same order as Y"?)	39	41	—	—	—	—
Comparatives						
More–Less ("A's toys different from B's.")	9	33	—	—	—	—
More (Who has more marbles, A or B?")	70	96	—	—	—	—

137

asked whether the *quantity* in two arrays was the same (with 7 and 9 objects) showed that very few children responded properly even at age 7, although children well below these ages are able to count correctly. In the most difficult condition of all, in which the child was given the opportunity to produce the term *number* or its equivalent in identifying the common property of two identical arrays, no child younger than age 7 could.

The data of other studies that relate to these findings are not uniform. For a combined sample of 2- to 5-year-old subjects Griffiths, Shantz, and Sigel (1967) reported that 72% of their subjects identified 2 sets of *3 lollipops* as the same, in contrast to the much lower percentages here. The data in the present study, however, are based on arrays that were both equal and unequal. In comparing 6 objects with 6 others, 48% of Beilin's (1965) 5-year-old subjects were unable to identify them as the same; 56% of the subjects could duplicate the experimenter's array of 7 *chips*. Fifty-two percent of Brownell's (1941) 6-year-old subjects could match 7 objects in a drawing task. Holmes (1963) asked her subjects to compare 2 sets of *10 beads*. The percentages of successful subjects in the 3–6-year-old samples were 0, 11, 22, and 61 respectively. N. M. Russell (1936) asked subjects to identify two groups of blocks that were *alike, same* or *equal*. He concluded that *same* and *equal* were incomprehensible to 4-year olds and were unlikely to be fully comprehended even at 7- or 8-years old. Buswell and John (1931) found *same* especially difficult for 6-year-old children to define.

Earlier studies thus found children to be less knowledgeable of one-to-one correspondence than the more recent studies. Whether the difficulties of 2- to 5-year-old children in these studies were linguistic or conceptual or due to differences in methodology is not clear. In any event, some features of quantitative knowledge that involve one-to-one correspondence are known by one-third to one-half the children in the 2–5 age range, at least in middle-class samples.

The present study shows further that in comprehending and producing number terms related to the correspondence between seriated orders and quantities, the fifth to sixth year appears to be the critical age for developing the appropriate language terms associated with these concepts. This is also the age when the cognitive operations related to those number terms appear to develop, that is, when the child begins to have some notion of relative position even though he may not be able to construct a seriated order or have a full appreciation of transitivity (Piaget, 1952). When the same tasks are presented with terms of a more abstract nature (*quantity, number*), children do not respond correctly even in the seventh year, although they are then at an age when the intellectual operations necessary for the tasks are available to them. Again, this result may be a function of the difficulty of the task procedure, although it is more likely a function of the particular linguistic forms employed in the verbal exchange with the child. The data show further that nonequivalent orders are easier to identify correctly than equivalent orders.

COMPARATIVE TERMS

Comparative terms relate quantities rather than positions. To determine the number of children who could recognize quantitative inequality, we said, "Tell me how the men's toys are different from the women's toys?" Nine percent of 2-year-old subjects and 33% of 3-year-old subjects gave a relational response. To the question, "Who has more marbles, the man or the woman?" 70% of the 2-year olds, and 96% of the 3-year olds were correct, well above chance (50%). Interpreting the basis for this response is a complex matter which has received a good deal of attention of late (Beilin, 1968; Bever, Mehler, & Epstein, 1968; Bloom, 1970; E. V. Clark, 1970a; Donaldson, 1970; Donaldson & Balfour, 1968; Palermo, 1973).

In the Piagetian literature on conservation, there is considerable concern with the child's knowledge of the concepts of equality (represented linguistically by *same, like,* etc.) and inequality represented by the comparatives (*more, less, bigger, wider,* etc.), as the quantitative concepts (number, length, etc.) related to these terms are those that are conserved. Because conservation is dependent upon or associated with knowledge of concepts of quality and inequality, a lack of conservation may reflect either a lack of lexical knowledge or a cognitive deficiency. It has been shown that knowledge of the relevant comparative terms is known to the child well before his knowledge of conservation is acquired (Beilin, 1965), although knowledge of *more* is known better than *less* in this context (Beilin, 1964, 1965). Griffiths *et al.* (1967) emphasize that conservation tests may confound lack of conservation knowledge with lack of lexical knowledge.

Although conservation of equality is the more usual relation studied some investigators have focused on the conservation of inequality (Zimiles, 1966). Mehler and Bever (1967) and Bever *et al.* (1968) report on the development of the inequality relation in children from the age of 2 years on, which they originally characterized as conservation but later altered their view (Beilin, 1968; Bever *et al.,* 1968; Piaget, 1968). The developmental data they report were interpreted by Beilin (1968) as showing that a noncomparative use of the term *more,* 'addition,' is developmentally prior to knowledge of *more* as a comparative relation, which in turn is prior to *more* as a relation that is conserved (when the inequality relation is maintained despite contrary cues that suggest equality).

Bloom (1970) also proposes a developmental sequence for the acquisition of the comparative, in which a noncomparative understanding of *more* precedes understanding in the comparative sense. The first use of *more* appears in her data to signify "recurrence". Donaldson and Balfour (1968) and Donaldson (1970) also report the unequal knowledge of *more* and *less* in children, suggesting that *less* is at first understood as *more,* prior to being differentiated correctly. E. V. Clark (1970) offers a linguistic interpretation for the development of the comparative based upon the differentiation of lexical features. Donaldson's report of the child's understanding of the *more–less* terms is confirmed by Palermo (1973) and disconfirmed by

TABLE 5-2

Single, Continuous, and Forced-choice Associations to Number-Word Stimuli in 3- to 7-Year-Old Subjects (Percentages)

Item description	Age group				
	3	4	5	6	7
Word Association Items					
Single associates					
Less	(4) 0[a]	(6) 18	(3) 15	(6) 44	(22) 53
Eleventh	(11) 0	(49) 0	(43) 5	(51) 22	(65) 20
Position	—	—	(2) 2	(3) 8	(3) 14
Seventy-second	(4) 11	(12) 30	(30) 13	(29) 24	(42) 27
Next	(11) 0	(9) 9	(15) 15	(31) 17	(31) 18
First	(11) 0	(6) 12	(13) 23	(15) 48	(14) 58
None	(7) 4	(6) 6	(12) 12	(17) 36	(22) 47
Two	(0) 15	(3) 36	(10) 33	(13) 52	(22) 55
Billion	(0) 15	(3) 18	(7) 17	(13) 33	(17) 42
Amount	(11) 0	(3) 9	(13) 5	(25) 10	(28) 18
Fourteen	(4) 15	(9) 48	(12) 30	(14) 56	(26) 57
Number	(15) 0	(24) 0	(35) 5	(43) 6	(36) 15
Fewer	(11) 4	(12) 3	(8) 20	(4) 24	(7) 42
Any	(11) 4	(6) 15	(15) 2	(24) 1	(32) 2
Several	(15) 0	(18) 0	(15) 7	(24) 10	(28) 39
Fewest	(7) 0	(9) 6	(28) 0	(22) 4	(49) 8

[a] Numbers in parentheses indicate paradigmatic associations. The other value indicates nonparadigmatic association.

[b] Numbers in parentheses indicate percentage of subjects who gave 2 or more responses with at least 2 in the same category as the stimulus word. The other number indicates the percentage who gave 4 or more number associations with at least 4 in the same category as the stimulus word.

[c] Omitted due to an error in administration.

Weiner (1971, 1974). Weiner's data also show how unsystematic the young child's responses to *more–less* questions usually are.

These studies of *more* and *less* indicate that interpretation of the young child's response is fraught with problems. What the child understands by a question involving *more* is not easy to establish on the basis of a single question (or even two as in the present study), even when above-chance performance suggests comprehension of the terms. Although a variety of explanations have been offered for the meager and contradictory data, it would appear that the only statement that could be agreed on is that the sense in which these terms is understood undergoes change with age. Beilin (1968) and Bloom (1970) are at least in agreement that non-comparative senses of these terms precede understanding of the comparative sense.

TABLE 5-2—*cont.*

Item Description		3	4	5	6	7
				Age group		
Continuous word associations						
Seven	(7) 4[b]	(15) 0	(8) 8	(14) 19	(20) 23
All	—	—	(3) 0	(1) 0	(1) 0
Fifty	—	—	(8) 3	(18) 16	(21) 24
Hundred	(0) 4	(12) 3	(5) 8	(17) 13	(25) 23
Ninety-ninth	—	—	(2) 2	(14) 1	(24) 0
More	—	—	(0) 0	(7) 0	(13) 0
Fortieth	(0) 0	(9) 0	(8) 0	(18) 4	(28) 6
Eighth	—	—	(3) 2	(21) 12	(22) 16
Forced associations						
Third	26	15	23	25	37
Fourth	37	30	32	63	78
First	52	70	60	63	79
Primary	4	15	17	18	c
Eighteenth	30	58	51	63	83
Before	56	67	71	63	65
Single	22	18	22	55	77
All	67	76	55	44	28
Two	48	55	50	67	77
Twenty	41	70	43	71	83
Twelve	19	49	36	56	69
Two	—	—	10	36	51
End	67	52	75	65	74
Pair	48	79	67	69	75
Twelve	33	21	23	32	32
Fifteenth	33	30	26	37	28
Nineteenth	19	36	46	72	84
Ten	26	24	42	63	83
Most	11	42	46	65	79
Many	26	39	58	58	69

NUMBER-WORD ASSOCIATIONS

The word association subtest was administered to all subjects except the 2-year olds. For the *single-word* association questions, response was classified according to a scheme based on whether the response words were ordinal or cardinal, and determinate or indeterminate (the previously indicated fourfold classification scheme). Because the stimulus words were similarly classifiable, the subject's response was scored for whether it was in the same category as the stimulus word (e.g., cardinal-determinate) or whether it crossed categories (e.g., to cardinal indeterminate). Non-number words were not classified.

Associations in the same number category as the stimuli were considered as **paradigmatic** associations. Associations that crossed categories were considered **nonparadigmatic**. The remaining associations were considered nonrelevant.

The purpose of this analysis was to determine whether a child's response was rooted in a category scheme that embodied differentiation between cardinal–ordinal and determinate–indeterminate dimensions. We asked, in essence, whether the logical structure inherent in the number lexicon was implicitly known by the young child, based on the assumption that the logical properties of the number system play a part of the construction of the child's number lexicon.

Almost every stimulus word showed an increase in paradigmatic associations with age (in Table 5-2, paradigmatic associations are indicated by the percentages in parentheses). Nonparadigmatic associations, however, also increased with age. The paradigmatic and nonparadigmatic associations showed parallel increases as the total number of associations increased. Paradigmatic increase was not a function of nonparadigmatic decrease, at least during the ages studied. Increases in both categories occurred apparently because children were acquiring knowledge of number words at a rate too quickly to ensure complete differentiation of all the logical properties of the terms. This is consistent with the view that lexical acquisition is not an all-or-none affair but rather that word meaning is acquired in progressive fashion. A number word may not be known for its cardinal properties until other meanings have been acquired for the word. This knowledge comes as other meanings are not only differentiated but also integrated. A conception of lexical knowledge based on semantic features alone is inadequate if feature theory is based solely on the differentiation of features. Developmental progression in lexical knowledge involves not only differentiation of meaning as suggested by E. V. Clark's (1970, 1971) theory but involves integration of meaning elements into a more encompassing logical system. In addition, at least for those parts of the lexicon embodied in number, the underlying structure of the lexicon is part of a larger, logical framework that is cognitive and only secondarily linguistic.

Associations were not consistently greater to either cardinal or ordinal terms or to determinate as compared with indeterminate terms, although appropriate associations to cardinal terms (*two, billion, fourteen, hundred*) appeared somewhat earlier than they did to ordinal terms (except for *seventy-second*).

Abstract terms (*number* and *position*) were responded to less-well than less-abstract terms. Although the comparative terms *less* and *fewer* were associated paradigmatically to a reasonably high degree by the 7-year-old subjects, the same was not true for *fewest*, which was associated nonparadigmatically. Although *any* was increasingly associated as a number word, it was not associated paradigmatically.

The *continuous-word* associations gave the child the opportunity to respond to a stimulus word with as many words as he could produce.

Responses were scored for the total number of associations, and the proportion of these in the same number category as the stimulus. The figures, in parentheses (Table 5-2) indicate the proportions of subjects who gave two or more responses with a minimum of two in the same category as the stimulus. The other percentages are for the subjects who gave four or more number words with a minimum of four in the same category as the stimulus. There was a gradual increase in both figures with age. To some terms, however, there were very few number associations, which suggests that these terms were not understood as number words. Both *more* and *all* were in this class. These terms were responded to as adjectives (*more candies, all* the time). This is consistent with what was previously said of the early association of comparative terms with noncomparative meaning. (The same process appears to hold for such quantifiers as *all*.) Again, cardinal terms were responded to at an earlier age than ordinal terms. On the whole, the continuous-association task was not responded to well by the younger children, indicating a poverty of number terms in their repertoire.

As we already proposed, the word association test provides a means for obtaining data that can indicate the structural aspects of the subject's knowledge of number language. If, however, a subject fails to respond, misunderstands the intent of instructions, or understands the question but responds in a manner that addresses itself to unclassified aspects of the problem, then an incomplete picture of the child's capacity results. This is a general problem when one relies upon naturalistic observation and upon unprovoked or unstructured verbal production. To compensate for these potential limitations, a forced-choice association task was used that required choice between two possible responses to a stimulus word. The intent was to obtain an unequivocal response to the number-word stimuli. The subject was asked to choose the response word that "goes better" with the stimulus term (e.g., "Which goes better with *third: ninth* or *bird?*"). The decoy words that were included were *clang-associates*, as with *third–bird*, or adjectives, as with *most toys*. The "correct" choice was a number term in the same category, (*first–tenth, two–five, most–least*, etc). The probability of being correct by chance alone was 50%.

There was a steady increase from the 3- to 7-year-old level in the percentage of "appropriate" responses, although responses were not always above-chance. It is reasonable to infer from the levels of appropriate response that subjects were choosing according to some understanding of the logical relations among the terms. Some decoys appeared to exercise greater control over response than others to stimuli that were logically equivalent. Response to *third* (i.e., *ninth*) for example, was never above-chance nor ever reached a chance level, whereas response to *fourth* (i.e., *sixth*) was above-chance in the 6-year-old group. In the former instance, the decoy was *bird* (*third-bird*); in the latter, it was *path* (*fourth-path*). The clang-association exercises greater control than the adjective association. Again, with *two* as the stimulus, the decoy *arms* was the above-chance preferred response at age 6, but response to *two*, when *blue* was the decoy alternative, was never above chance.

Above-chance correct responding was evident for 4 of the 20 terms (20%) at the 3-year-old level, and 7 of the 20 terms (35%) at the 4-year-old level. It increased until the 7-year-old group, when 14 of the 20 items (70%) were responded to paradigmatically. There was thus a steady and large increase in paradigmatic association with age, which suggests that control over associations was increasingly exercised by knowledge of the logical system that structures the lexicon. Put another way, the logical category system that characterizes the conceptualization of number also increasingly characterized knowledge of the number lexicon.

In one instructively different case (*all: several–none*) subjects showed above-chance responding to the *none* alternative at the earliest age tested (3-years old), but by age 5, subjects were near chance-level for both alternatives, and by age 7 they were well-above chance on the *several* alternative, suggesting that subjects had changed to a completely different hypothesis. The term *several*, as other data in the study suggest, was equated by the child with the notion of *some*. *All*, which refers to a positive quantity, and *some*, which also refers to a positive quantity, were thus more closely associated in the mind of the 6 and 7 year old than the opposition term *none*, which denotes the absence of quantity. *All* and *some* may be closer in meaning in this sense, even though *all* implies determinacy and *some* implies indeterminacy. Another development that may contribute to this response shift is the transition from antonym to synonym association. Still another possibility is that the *some* (several)–*all* relation implies a part-to-whole relation, which would make the association paradigmatic but in a sense different from the determinate–indeterminate distinction we originally made. In any case, this atypical developmental pattern points to the potential effect of various types of word meaning upon number associations, in addition to the implicit category structure that derives from number and quantitative measurement.

NUMBER SYMBOLS

The extent to which children are familiar with numerals (number symbols) was tested by asking subjects to (1) produce verbal labels for written numerals, and (2) to identify the written symbol, given a verbal label. Half the identifications were of ordinal numbers, half of cardinal.

Many of the 2-year-old children (13–48%) could produce and correctly identify the printed cardinal numerals, however, it was not until the 7-year-old level that the same was true for ordinal numerals (Table 5-3). There was also a consistent difference within each age in correct identification as a function of the size of the number; the smallest number (*3*) was easiest, the largest (*12*) the most difficult. Although performance for ordinal numbers began to rise above zero at the 6-year-old level, there were no differences as a function of the size of the numbers. Pointing to the correct-printed numeral that corresponded to a spoken, number word showed a different picture, with a high level of performance for ordinal numbers and, surprisingly, a low level of performance for cardinal numeral

TABLE 5-3

Number Symbol (Numeral) Identification in 2- to 7-Year-Old Subjects (Percentages)

	Age group					
Item description	2	3	4	5	6	7
Numeral identification (production)						
3	48	59	—	92	99	99
6	39	48	—	80	93	100
12	13	26	—	65	86	99
4th	0	0	—	2	24	71
5th	0	0	—	0	24	75
9th	0	0	—	0	24	73
Numeral identification						
7	—	15	40	78	85	91
11	—	15	21	62	75	90
1	—	19	55	58	77	95
2nd	—	4	15	21	50	83
8th	—	15	33	28	55	89
10th	—	19	30	45	57	94

TABLE 5-4

Index- and Rote-Counting in 2- to 7-Year-Old Subjects (Percentages)

	Age group					
Item description	2	3	4	5	6	7
Index counting (objects)						
Number: 5	4	11	—	42	84	96
Number: 6	9	18	—	45	83	96
Quantity: 4	9	26	—	—	—	—
Index counting (position)						
Position: third	0	0	—	8	33	58
Position: second	0	0	—	33	63	82
Index counting (objects)—forced choice						
7	—	7	30	42	67	85
Index counting (position)—forced choice						
Fourth	—	0	18	40	82	95
Rote counting (cardinal)	(44) 4	(67) 22	—	(13) 82	(9) 90	(0) 100
Rote counting (ordinal)	(4) 0	0	—	(55) 2	(81) 10	(52) 46

identification among the younger children. Although identification at the 7-year-old level was inflated to some extent by chance identification, there was still a substantial percentage of correct identifications. Although the differences are small at age 3 between the ordinal and cardinal numeral data, the improvement in performance with cardinal numbers was rapid—it, however, lagged for ordinal numbers. Not until age 7 were they equal. The largest number, again, tended to be identified most poorly across ages; the inverse was true for the ordinal data. These somewhat inconsistent results may have been due to the late appearance of these items in the battery and manifested the effects of learning.

ROTE AND INDEX COUNTING

Number production was tested further with the counting of objects. The child was required to count objects (cardinal number) and also identify the relative position of a *stick* placed within a *row of sticks* (ordinal number). Number knowledge, in this instance, reflected the use of numbers (and number words) for indexing, that is, for identifying quantities and positions. The numbers used were small (*5, 6, second, third*). There was progression with age in the correct indexing of both quantity and position (Table 5-4). Cardinal number indexing was more difficult than (cardinal) numeral identification. Position indexing was not successful to any extent until kindergarten age (5 years), when there was a very clear difference in the ability to identify *sticks* in the *second* (33%) and *third* positions (8%). The relative difference remained into the seventh year.

The question again arises as to whether response differences were due to lack of lexical knowledge or to the inability to conceptualize certain aspects of number. The data show considerable variability in ordinal number performance that is not correspondingly true for cardinal number. These differences were not due solely to the differences between ordinal and cardinal number knowledge, however, as some ordinal terms appeared to be easier to deal with than some cardinal items. It would seem safe to say that, in general, the ordinal lags behind the achievement of cardinal number, but, once basic knowledge of the cardinal or ordinal principle is achieved, knowledge of particular lexical terms varies considerably. Whether the later emergence of correct ordinal performance is actually a problem in the understanding of the concept rather than in knowledge of the lexical terms is not conclusively determined, although the data suggest that the difficulty is conceptual because the early difficulty with the ordinal relation occurs both within and outside of the linguistic context.

In a series of investigations in which 6-year-old children were asked to identify 7 objects (*candles* on a cake, *dominoes*, etc. with various numbers) 58% to 93% of the children could do the task correctly (Brownell, 1941; Buckingham & MacLatchy, 1930; Grant, 1938; MacLatchy, 1931; Priore, 1957; Woody, 1930). The results tend to the higher end of the scale and approximate those of the present study (85%). Studies by Bjonerud (1960),

Grant (1938), Holmes (1963), and Harker (1960) dealt with the identification by 5- and 6-year olds of the first through *tenth* positions. In Bjonerud's study, 50% of the 5-year olds knew the *second* position, however only 20% could identify the symbol *second*. The other studies report 16% –66% of their subjects as capable of locating ordinal positions from *first* to *tenth*. In the present study, the mean percent of subjects of the same age locating *second, third* and *fourth* positions was 61%.

Rote counting ability was evident at an early age in the sample. Four percent of 2-year olds were able to count to at least *23,* and 44% were able to count to between *8* and *22* without error. The percent who could count to *23* increased rapidly so that by kindergarten 82% could do it. The counting of ordinal numbers was another matter, however. Very few 2- and 3-year-old children could count to between *fifth* and *twenty-second* without error, and none above that. At the 6-year-old-level, although 90% could count to *23,* only 10% could count to *twenty-third,* yet most children could count ordinally to at least *fifth.*

DEFINITIONS

The ability to verbally define number words was minimal in the 3-year-old group (Table 5-5). With each year this ability increased. By kindergarten age (5-years old), definitions were provided for each of the terms presented. The term *amount* which is used in many conservation studies was defined

TABLE 5-5

Number-Word Definitions Given by 2- to 7-Year-Old Subjects (Percentages)

Item description	2		3		4	5		6		7	
Number-word definitions											
Zero	0		0		—	15		57		86	
Amount	0	(9)	0	(4)	—	7	(13)	8	(54)	16	(59)
Dozen	0		0		—	3		6		54	
Begin	0		0		9	11		35		46	
Follow	—		—		—	2		2		12	
Below	—		4		6	3		21		41	
Number-word definition— forced choice											
Pair	—		41		46	60		65		80	
Triple	—		19		12	28		49		69	
Double	—		48		58	52		69		85	
Some	—		34		33	32		49		61	
Last	—		52		64	72		78		91	
Above	—		30		21	30		54		81	
Middle	—		52		61	70		71		88	

at some level of adequacy by only 20% of the 5-year olds and by 62% of the 6-year olds. When definitions were sought in a forced-choice context, slightly above-chance performance appeared for the 3-year-old subjects for *last* and *middle*. The term *some* was defined as *all* rather than *part* until the 7-year level when the *part* choice was above chance. This supports the interpretation that the response of *several* to *all* could be due to the later identification of *several* with *some*, although *some* is associated with *part*. *Some*, nevertheless, was the most poorly defined term for 7-year olds among the 6 terms given. Cardinal terms were not better defined than ordinal terms; if anything, the opposite was true although there was no consistency in this. The definitional difficulty with *some* suggests that considerable care should be taken in studies of part–whole relations made with pre-7-year-old children to ensure that they understand the desired meanings of this and related terms.

NUMBER ADDITION AND SERIATION

Subjects were tested in addition and subtraction of cardinal and ordinal numbers (Table 5-6). The youngest children were tested with the smaller numbers. A surprising proportion of the 2-year-old children could answer such questions as: "What is *2* and *3* equal to?" (13%); "If you had *4* marbles and gave away *2*, how many would you have?" (17%); "What

TABLE 5-6

Addition and Serial Ordering in 2- to 7-Year-Old Subjects (Percentages)

	Age group					
Item description	2	3	4	5	6	7
Addition and serial ordering						
6 + 5 = ?; revised: 2 + 3 = ? (*is equal to*)	13	11	—	13	33	82
12 − 4 = ?; revised: 4 − 2 = ?	17	11	—	8	34	53
11 ? 9; revised: 6 ? 4	13	26	—	37	54	84
First ? third	4	0	—	25	37	67
Fourth place + 1 = ?	4	4	—	13	48	81
Fifth place + = ? place; revised: second place + 2 = ? place	0	4	—	0	7	34
Addition and serial ordering (forced choice)						
1 + 1 = 3, 2 or 4? (*equal to*)	—	0	21	35	61	97
29 < 30? 29 > 30? or 29 = 30? (*less than, more than, equal*)	—	—	—	5	33	74
23 − 16 = 6, 7 or 8? (*take away*)	—	—	—	13	15	13
18th < 20th, 16th, or 8th? (*comes before*)	—	—	—	2	24	46
5 places < fifth, sixth, or fourth? (*before*)	—	4	15	17	32	24
fourteenth place + 8 = twenty-second, twenty-third or twenty-fourth?	—	—	—	13	22	45

number is less than *6* but more than *4?"* (13%). There was more difficulty in dealing with such questions as: "If there were *three* people in line in front of you, what position would you be in?" (4%). By 5 years of age, a fair number of subjects were able to answer the ordinal position questions to a greater extent than the addition–subtraction questions, although they tended to be about equal at the 6-year-old level.

When addition, subtraction, and ordinal position questions were asked in a multiple-choice format, performance was about the same as with the direct questions. To the question "Are there *5* places *before* the *fifth* place, *5* places *before* the *sixth* place, or *5* places *before* the *fourth* place?" 4% of the 3-year-olds answered correctly and the percentage correct at the 7-year-old level was no more than 42%. On the other hand, no child in the 3-year-old group answered the question: "Does *1 plus 1* equal *3, 2,* or *4?"* whereas 97% of the 7-year olds were correct and 61% of the 6-year olds were correct. The below-chance performance in the early grades indicates that children were probably responding to primacy or recency cues, i.e., to the first and last of the alternatives given them.

Brownell (1941) reports that in summing the integers *1* and *2,* 6-year-old subjects were, on the average 53% correct for a variety of tasks (compared with 61% of our sample). 30% of Brownell's subjects could handle subtraction facts employing the integers *1–5;* 15% of our 6-year olds could correctly respond to the *23–16* subtraction. In subtraction, 14% of Priore's 6-year-old subjects were correct (before instruction) in the *19 minus 2* subtraction, compared with 8% of our 5-year old subjects (38% of the 6-year olds) who were correct on a *12 minus 4* subtraction.

The reports from other studies (Buckingham & MacLatchy, 1930; MacLatchy, 1931, 1935) show smaller percentages of 6-year-olds subjects counting correctly (about 45%) than we report (90% able to count to *23* and beyond). This difference may be due to sample differences or to the changes in parental coaching practices between the 1930s and 1960s.

The importance of rote and index counting to mathematical and logical knowledge has been questioned by Piaget (1952), who points repeatedly to the limited utility of counting for logical thought development. More recently, there has been revived interest in counting as a measurement operation—particularly in its application as an algorithmic method in logical problem-solving and thinking (Galperin, 1966; Teplenkaya, 1966). It is necessary, however, to distinguish between learning the natural numbers as a form of serial learning, and the use of the natural number system, once learned, for indexing purposes in the counting of objects (Sicha, 1970). The latter plays a more significant role in dealing with the physical world, but the extent and nature of this role is not very well known.

Discussion

Evidence for the influence of the logic of the number system over the development of number-word knowledge (and use) was evident in our data from the general order of number-word acquisition. This acquisition order paralleled the general order of cognitive number development.

Some knowledge of number words was evident in 2- and 3-year-old children. This knowledge was manifest in their ability to rote-count cardinal numbers, as well as in their ability to identify and label number symbols. This type of performance represents a kind of prelogical knowledge that can be attained, at least in part, through the utilization of associative learning processes, although in a developmental system that is receptive to such learning.

The 3-year old appeared to have another kind of lexical knowledge as well that was reflected in his ability to respond to some relational terms, such as *in front of* which 30% of children at this age dealt with successfully. Although the 3-year-old child had some knowledge of comparative terms (*more, less, bigger*), the evidence is not clear as to whether the child understands the logical quantitative relations embodied in these terms. The terms themselves have meanings for adults which are both comparative and noncomparative. The same is apparently true for children. There is evidence that noncomparative uses of these relational terms are known before the comparative, although these noncomparative uses are quantitative nonetheless. We claim (Beilin, 1968) that the conception of *more* as 'addition to' is prior to knowledge of *more* as a comparative, as in "X is **more than** Y." The comparative, in turn, is known before *more* as a conserved comparative relation, that is, before it is conceived to be invariant in conditions in which inequalities appear to be equal. Bloom (1970) interprets the earlier noncomparative use of *more* to represent the meaning of "recurrence," a request for "another instance" in two-word constructions produced by the very young child. Weiner (1971) interprets her data as support for the latter rather than the former interpretation. The view of E. V. Clark (1971) is that the early use of the comparative *more* reflects an unmarked quantitative reference that later differentiates into the *more–less* distinction as the distinctive comparative attributes of the term come to be known. In Donaldson's conception, prior to complete differentiation, *less* has the attributes of *more*. Mehler and Bever (1967; Bever et al., 1968) are of the conviction that the 3-year old knows these relational terms in their comparative sense, and this makes possible the child's understanding of more complex numerical relations. Weiner's (1971, 1974) data do not support this interpretation either.

The evidence for what the 2- and 3-year old knows of the comparative relation is equivocal on the basis of the studies cited. The present study did not directly address itself to this issue, and provides little additional data for it. Although response to two comparative questions shows above-chance responding, the meaning of these data are difficult to interpret because there was insufficient variation in stimulus conditions to ensure that the knowledge of the comparative was not in fact psuedo knowledge. Nevertheless, it appears that even with extensive variation in stimulus conditions, response to comparative stimuli with very young children (2- to 3-year olds) is quite difficult to interpret (Weiner, 1971).

The 5-year-old children of our sample were able to respond with moderate success (60%) to tasks that required both appropriate cognition and language in the judgment of one-to-one correspondence of elements in sets. The 6-year-old subjects with equal success (64%) were able to respond to the language and tasks involved in the judgment of one-to-one correspondence of seriated sets. The 5- and 6-year-old children also had knowledge of relational terms of indeterminate reference, other than comparatives such as *size-place, after, before,* and *behind*. The abilities manifested by the 5- and 6-year-old children represent a preoperative logic of one-way mapping, as Piaget puts it, in which the child is capable of dealing with classification concepts as well as relational concepts, but these are limited in their application and fluency to one-way relations. They do not reflect two-way mappings in which a relation that is represented in one direction, for example, "X *in front of* Y" is understood at the same time as related to "Y is *behind* X," the inverse and reversible relation.

The age at which reversible relations become possible appears to be the age at which the majority of children studied manifested knowledge of the abstract class terms for *number* and *quantity*. This was evident in the 7-year-old child's knowledge of such terms as *amount, number, quantity,* and *position*. As the data of many studies show, most children at this age have acquired the cognitive schemes associated with the conservation of number and some of the operations necessary to an understanding of classification and relational logics.

The convergence or general synchrony between developments in the acquisition of lexical knowledge and those of cognitive development suggests, although it does not provide incontestable evidence for, the assertion that acquisition of the lexicon is under the progressive control of developing cognitive structures.

In the development of concrete logical operations, as reflected in conservation and the classification and relational logics, strong claims have been made by Bruner (Bruner, Olver, & Greenfield, 1966) to the effect that language plays a critical role in their acquisition, a view contested by most Piagetians. Although language presupposes certain underlying cognitive processes, Bruner contends that such properties of the cognitive system as those of hierarchy and transformation are first used and perfected within language and only gradually transferred to thinking in general. Although Bruner's views appear to be in accord with Piaget's conception of the development of the symbolic function and Vygotsky's view of the organizing role of language in respect to thought, he appears to place greater faith in the organizing role of language as symbolic behavior in the development of mental operations than is true for Piaget. Piaget is emphatic in denying to language more than the role of symbolically representing developed operational structures.

Bruner also claims that the acquisition of operative structures is a function of knowledge of relevent lexical terms. He (Bruner *et al.,* 1966, p. 204) observes that the child's understanding of the meaning of the terms *same* and *more* is different from that of the adult's. When the child hears these terms in a sentence during an experiment, "This beaker has *more* now than before and . . .," the significance of the perceived events is quite different for the child than the adult because each attributes different meanings to the lexical terms. Griffiths *et al.* (1967) make a similar observation. Bruner's and Sigel's observations have cogency for experiments conducted in a verbal context. They are not sufficient, however, to account for the results of experiments that are conducted nonverbally, (e.g., Braine, 1959; Gelman, 1969). Nor for Piaget's experiments, which demonstrate that although the child has "knowledge" of these very terms, his thinking is different from that of the older child. Although Bruner and Sigel's argument rests on the child's apparent language "deficiency," Piaget argues it is not language but cognition that defines the difference in their performance. Because lexical knowledge embodies the child's cognitive knowledge, the two are not fully separable. The linguistic argument is in a sense redundant, for if the basis for language is cognitive, to say that the child's understanding of terms is different from the adult's is to say at root that their cognitive systems are different.

Because abstract number terms were known in our sample at an age when operative levels of performance are generally evident suggests that learning the number lexicon is associated with developing cognitive structure, or that both language and operative structures have a common origin. Piagetian theory incorporates both possibilities. The earliest indications of language, which appear between 12 and 18 months, are concurrent with the manifestation of such nonlinguistic cognitive functions as "deferred imitation" and "symbolic imagery." Although these differ in kind, they have in common a "symbolic function"—that is, each is a form of symbolic representation. Language is probably the most sophisticated reflection of the symbolic function and has the greatest flexibility in representing ideas and characterizing the real world. In this view, linguistic representation presupposes a cognitive base that is composed of operative structures appropriate to the developmental history of the child. The data of this study are consistent with this view in that the progression in lexical knowledge acquired by the child paralleled the natural development of concrete operational thought. This was evident most clearly in the number-word associations.

We based this study on the assumption that the logic of the number system, which becomes progressively known to the child though his constructive response to experience, provides the base for learning the number lexicon. The young child has no conscious knowledge of the structure of the number system any more than he has conscious knowledge of the structure of his language. The structure of the lexicon, aside from knowledge of the specific words, thus has to be made evident by indirect means. The word-association data provided that evidence. It has been traditional to explain word associations in terms of associative bonding between stimulus and response. This interpretation has been superceded by a conception of word associations as reflecting more complex processes. One view is evident in a wide variety of studies showing that responses tend to occur within the same form class as the stimuli, and may be associated by virtue of similarity in any one of a variety of dimensions or properties. Some developmental data show that children at about the age of 7–8 tend to shift from heterogenous to paradigmatic responding, ostensibly, because the child learns the classes necessary to the categorization or clustering of responses (as suggested in the Brown and Berko [1960] study). Other studies (e.g., Lippman, 1971) show that such categorization rules are known to children as young as 3, long before the paradigmatic shift is usually observed. McNeill's (1966) thesis is that word associations are made according to lexical features, that is, according to the maximum number of semantic and grammatical features shared with the stimulus. McNeill's explanation of low paradigmatic responding is attributed to the child's lack of knowledge of the featural properties of words and not merely on the basis of associational bonds. Our data accords with this aspect of the thesis in showing that some types of word associations are not adequately explained by appeals to associations or associative bonding. It is unlikely that the children we studied had previously experienced the "setting conditions" or number stimuli under conditions of contiguity or reinforcement that could reasonably account for their implicit knowledge of the lexical distinctions between cardinality–ordinality, and determinacy–indeterminacy. These same data show further, however, that the structural features of the number language are not known simply by their linguistic characteristics, as is implicit in McNeill's claim. Word associations are not primarily a function of lexical features although this may be a by-product of the more significant effect. The associations are determined, instead, by a more abstract logical structure that defines the cognitive conception of number and organizes the lexical properties of number language. The data in this study indicate that knowledge of this structure increases with age. Some of this knowledge is available to the 3-year old; by age 7, 70% of the number-word associations show this kind of logical control.

The cardinal–ordinal lexical distinction is directly related to the development of number cognition; the determinate–indeterminate distinction is more associated with the properties of quantitative measurement. Piaget argues that knowledge of number comes when the child can coordinate the logic of classes (cardinality) with the logic of relations (ordinality). The *empirical* coordination of the two logics leads Piaget to argue that the *logical* properties of number require the inclusion of the concept of relative order as well as that of classification in the definition of number. This is contrary to the logicist's argument that follows Russell and Whitehead, in which number is defined in class or set terms (Benacerraf & Putman, 1964). Our data show a lag between the acquisition of certain features of cardinal and ordinal numbers that at first seems to contradict Piaget's empirical assertions. Counting ordinal numbers also lagged decidedly behind the counting of cardinal numbers, and the same was true for the identification of number symbols. Although these effects are clear, they do not really embarrass the Piaget conception because by the time the conceptualization of number is said to be achieved, at about the age of 6, children have both cardinal and ordinal counting and identification capacities fairly well established. A Piagetian could thus argue that the cardinal–ordinal lag in counting and identification are due to performance factors associated with such learning and do not affect the acquisition of number concepts, and that there is no lag by the time number conceptualization is acquired at 6- to 7-years old.

The conceptualization of number, as represented in such number operations as addition and ordering, would not be inhibited if communication involving these operations occurred in verbal form. The possibility that the logical operations of addition (in accord with the logic of classification) and those of ordering (in accord with the logic of relations) are achieved about the same time was evident in our data from the items responded to best in these categories. Addition and ordering relations showed parallel attainments at the 6- and 7-year-old levels.

Some complex language terms were acquired by children earlier than their ostensibly associated cognitive structures. If these number language elements in fact did precede the acquisition of the logical number operations, it would contradict the thesis that linguistic achievements are limited to concomitant or prior logical developments. To explain this apparent contradiction we invoke a notion we have employed previously to explain the acquisition of other types of language, prior to the natural acquisition of relevant logical operations. We have done this when linguistically represented solution rules were utilized by preoperational children as algorithms in solving conservation problems (Beilin, 1965). The same phenomenon was observed in the acquisition of pluralization rules through algorithmic instructional methods, even though the same children could not learn simple cardinal number concepts in a standard concept-learning task (Beilin & Kagan, 1969). Acquiring certain features of the number lexicon appears to fit the same pattern. The most striking example is in counting, which very early serves an algorithmic function, if only in object or positional indexing. The algorithmic function of counting elaborates considerably even when the logical aspects of number are not known to the child. Most children (and adults too) learn adding algorithms even though they never learn the logical principles basic to the addition of sets and numbers. It is long known that very young children learn to count by what appear to be rote methods, and it is sometimes thought because of this that the young child has significant mathematical facility. On this score, one of Piaget's achievements has been to demonstrate that number counting ensures little logical understanding of number. The implications of this, however, have been overdrawn by the Genevans to the point where the significance of counting in the cognitive development of the child is overlooked. There is increasing evidence from both American and Russian researchers (e.g., Galperin, 1966; Wohlwill, 1970) that counting operations can be used quite effectively as measurement algorithms to aid in the learning of such logical operations as conservation and classification. To generalize, mathematical language and the linguistic representation of logical and quasilogical rules may function very effectively as algorithmic devices. They may in fact be necessary to the development of both logical operations and linguistic structures. In regard to number language acquisition, however, the evidence suggests that most of the number lexicon is acquired not as algorithmic knowledge but directly under the control of the developing cognitive system.

In respect to the word-association data, we have emphasized the influence and potential control of the number system on the lexicon. These data, however, also show other semantic influences that make certain words associations more complex. Paradigmatic responses increased to the seventh year and probably beyond; however, there was also an increase in nonparadigmatic number associations. The forced-choice word-associations data suggest what occurred. The early association of *none* to the stimulus *all* shifted with age to both *none* and *several*. It shifted again for the older child, however, to *several*. Most developmental changes were due to a shift from nonparadigmatic to paradigmatic association, although the basis for this shift was apparently different. Here the shift was based on reference to another type of meaning. *Several*, as other data in the study show, was equated with the notion of *some*. *All*, denoting a positive quantity, and *some*, also denoting a positive quantity, were more closely associated in the mind of the 6- to 7-year old as quantities than the term *none*, which denoted the absence of quantity. Another semantic phenomenon which could have contributed to the association shift was a transition from antonym association to synonym. Thus, *all* and *some* may be closer in meaning in this sense than *all* and *none*. A more reasonable explanation possibly is that *some* (*several*) implies a part–whole relation. The association is thus made on the basis of a classification relation and thus paradigmatically. In any case, this atypical developmental pattern points to the possible effect of various types of word meaning upon number association, in addition to the implicit category structure that derives from the nature of number and quantitative measurement. An extensive literature on word-clustering in recall already shows this to be the case. In sum, the data from this study support the position that developing cognitive structure exercises a significant control over the functional aspects of number-lexical acquisition, although this control is not exclusive.

Experiment 2: Number Agreement[7]

Linguistic Theories of Agreement

Experiment (1) of this chapter dealt with the lexical representation of number and the cognitive correlates of lexical reference. This section is devoted to the place of number in syntax, in particular, to its role in number agreement in sentences. The function of agreement among sentence constituents in number as well as in case and gender is to ensure clarity in

[7] With the collaboration of Helen-Marie Natt. Valerie Jordan aided materially in the analysis of the data.

the meaning of a sentence. Without such agreement the listener–reader would find it difficult to establish the precise reference of a sentence such as *Tell him* (*them*) *to put on his* (*their*) *shoes* or *Tell him* (*them*) *to put on their* (*his*) *shoes*. The real-life context may be of little help to the hearer if all of *them* are shoeless.

Linguistic rules are required to deal with the many sentences in the language in which such ambiguities might arise. English and other natural languages embody such rules in their grammars, although languages differ in the ways they make number, case, and gender distinctions. Our concern in this section is to detail some of the agreement rules in English and various linguistic theories that account for them and then to report on how children acquire knowledge of agreement. In the course of this report we will pursue some issues that have been raised in other chapters.

Chomsky (1965) regards agreement rules as best characterized in terms of syntactic features. Some features, such as number, are in some instances inherent in the phrase marker or introduced by an agreement transformation. Other features are inherent in the lexical items themselves, and agreement is determined by the lexical entry or the position of lexical, insertion. Furthermore, features such as number that are inherent in nouns are assigned to verbs and adjectives only by transformation. It follows that agreement in the sentence is achieved through transformations to make the adjective and verb agree with the features of the noun, except in certain cases in which erasure and deletion transformation apply.

Another aspect of Chomsky's theory that bears upon the nature of agreement is the notion of indexing. Langendoen (1969) proposes that referential indices are assigned to nouns and noun phrases (the referential index of the first noun is denoted as 1, that of the next noun that refers to a different entity as 2). When a previously mentioned entity is referred to, it is assigned the same number as given in its original assignment. Thus nouns designating the same entities are assigned the same index. Coreferentiality defines the relationship between nouns with the same referential index. Thus, referential index offers a way of determining whether two or more successionally occurring nouns or noun phrases refer to the same thing.

Nouns, in addition to indicating the predication of such properties as human, male, and adult, are differentiated into individual and set indices, according to McCawley (1968b). Plural noun phrases refer to a set and the index of a plural noun phrase is said to behave like a set. McCawley holds that it must be possible to perform set-theoretical operations on indices and that syntactic rules must be able to make use of the results of such operations.[8] These notions are applicable to number agreement. McCawley points out that number agreement in its usual transformational formulation

---

[8] McCawley distinguishes between the use of *set* in English syntax and its use in mathematics. Although mathematical set theory admits of empty sets and one-member sets, only two or more members are considered to form a set in McCawley's usage. In this sense, an individual and one-member set is not distinguished and individuals are combined by the operation of union : $X_1 \cup X_2 = (X_1 X_2)$.

(e.g., Lees, 1963) states that a verb is marked as singular or plural depending on whether or not it is preceded by a plural morpheme, and also that plural number agreement is assigned when there is a conjoined subject (*Jack and Jill fetch a pail of water*), irrespective of whether there is a plural morpheme.

Both plural and conjoined noun forms are assigned a set index in contrast to an individual index because of the desire to have agreement occur with the "plurality of the whole subject" and not merely with the presence of the plural morpheme. The distinctions indicated in transformational descriptions (the above) are said to correspond closely to the individual-set distinction. It is thus the distinction between individual and set indices that determines number agreement rather than the presence or absence of a plural morpheme (although there are some exceptions as with *scissors* which takes a plural even though it is assigned an individual index).

The following unordered rules are proposed by McCawley for number agreement.

1. Mark a noun-phrase node (+ plural) if it has a set index and (− plural) otherwise.
2. Mark a noun-phrase node (+ plural) if it directly dominates a noun marked as belonging to the class *pluralia tantum* (e.g., *scissors*).
3. Mark a verb (+ plural) or (− plural) depending upon whether its subject is marked (+ plural) or (− plural).

The thrust of McCawley's proposal is to base agreement on *semantic* rather than syntactic considerations so that the semantic representation of the subject (the subject set or individual subject) is the source of agreement and not morphological indicators per se. Nor do the usual transformation rules pertain because the transformation feature must attach simultaneously to all verbs in a conjoined verb phrase rather than to a single verb; thus a compound subject simultaneously creates a conjoined verb phrase (*John and Bill are erudite*). Although Chomsky handles this by conjoining the underlying phrase markers through conjunction reduction, it cannot always be done as with *John and Bill are similar*. It thus requires that conjoined noun and verb phrases appear in the underlying structure.

Perlmutter (1972) identifies a number of difficulties in McCawley's account of agreement. One has to do with selectional restrictions for such verbs as *count* which McCawley says demand a plural object, *I counted the toys* but not *I counted the boy*, but it also takes grammatically singular objects such as *I counted the crowd*. McCawley represents the property of *crowd* by a set index which converts this into the feature (+ plural), and *crowd* should define general agreement on the verb.

Perlmutter writes that this is not the case for *The crowd was unruly—*The crowd were unruly*. Within McCawley's framework, says Perlmutter, a solution would be to mark collective nouns such as *crowd* as able to take a set or individual index. This, however, would be inconsistent with McCawley's claim that selectional restrictions are stated in terms of indices and other semantic properties of selectional restriction.

Perlmutter thus rejects McCawley's treatment of agreement in terms of set versus individual indices on the grounds that collective nouns (and also generic terms) behave like singulars in respect to agreement rules despite the fact that they denote sets. He argues instead that syntactic facts about collective nouns (and generic terms) account for the nature of the agreement between subjects and verb independently of the "semantic" fact that they denote sets.

According to Moravcsik's (1971) analysis of the traditional descriptions of grammatical classes, the English noun is characterized by agreement in gender, number, case, and definiteness, and the verb by agreement in person and number. Indirect articles and demonstrative pronouns are subject to number agreement—the third person pronoun agrees in gender, case and number. Relative pronouns and question pronouns agree in gender; indirect pronouns agree in number. Both the possessed and possessor show agreement as to gender, number, case, and definiteness.

Some agreement characteristics are said to be universal.

1. Every language considered by Moravcsik has at least a ternary person, a binary number, and a binary definiteness distinction in its pronouns.

2. Obligatory distinctions that apply to any grammatical class also imply the same distinctions for personal pronouns, anaphoric pronouns (that refer to an antecedent noun or NP), or deictic pronouns (that refers to a not previously mentioned person, object, or feature of a situation) such as those of person, number, definiteness, and gender.

3. The set of agreement features in a particular language, Moravcsik holds, is always included in the set of pronominal features. In no language, for example, may the noun and the verb agree with respect to *animacy*, and the personal, anaphoric, and deictic pronouns have no such distinction.

Moravicsik's own proposals for agreement rules assume coreferentiality and pronominalization and are consistent with those of Sanders (1967) whose theory predicts that verbs and anaphoric pronouns have exactly the same agreement features. From this it follows that (1) all agreeing terms should agree in pronominal features, (2) only pronominal features should show agreement, and also (3) all agreeing terms are coreferential.

Moravcsik makes a further distinction between *noun-phrase internal* agreement (involving agreement in the inflection of nouns, relative pronouns, possessives, articles, and numerals) and *noun-phrase external* agreement (involving agreement of nouns with anaphoric pronouns and verbs).

Upon examining a number of languages in respect to number agreement, she observes that there are three presumably universal number constructions that contrast with singular phrases, (*one man*). They are *pluralized noun phrases* (*men*), *numerated noun phrases* (*two men*) and *conjoined noun phrases* (*one man* and *another man*). Anaphoric pronominal reference to such noun phrases is always said to be plural, although for verb agreement the picture is not as consistent across languages. Aside from a few exceptions, verb agreement with the above noun phrases is also plural.

All noun phrases tend to be the same in regard to agreement, although a number of complications exist in the case of the conjoined noun phrase. Moravcsik nevertheless feels it is appropriate to generalize that noun phrases, whose underlying structure indicates at least one conjoining, take plural agreement in the anaphoric pronoun and verb. Going further, the essence of number agreement with respect to verbs and anaphoric pronouns rests on the plurality of the noun-phrase reference. (Plural agreement rests on underlying referent nonidentity within the noun phrase, and noun phrases with underlying referential identity or which lack referential marking, will not show plural agreement.)

The linguistic definition of plurality can take a number of forms. Thus the set of semantic features ([*Human*], [*Human, other*], [*X*], plural) would be lexicalized as *people*, whereas the set ([*Human*], [*Human, other*], [*X*] collective) would be lexicalized as *crowd*. The collective may take a singular predicate and noun in agreement, if it is considered as a unit. This gets around McCawley's difficulty by giving it an individual index because its reference is a unit.

In sum, linguistic theories concerning agreement fall into two classes. The generative transformational position interprets agreement rules on the basis of lexical marking and transformation rules. The other class of theories is based essentially on semantic grounds either in terms of identity of reference or to predication based on the singularity or plurality of object reference. Agreement in this class is based on semantic equivalence rather than on the syntactic equivalence that is typical of transformational theories. Both types of theory, with some exceptions, establish that the noun is the focus of number agreement.[9] The only exception to this appears to be Chafe (1970) who indicates that "the semantic choice resides in the Verb, which then determines the inflection of the Noun [p. 189]." A rather different view is expressed by Jespersen (1964) who writes that there is a general tendency in the development of languages to indicate number in nonsubstantive words. Consequently, he regards agreement of the verb with the surface structure subject as a phenomenon that affects neither the meaning nor logic of the sentence. Furthermore, pluralization denotes a quality of the noun itself and its referent; in verbs, plural refers to the plurality of the surface structure subject (noun and pronoun) rather than the action or state denoted by the verb.

Psycholinguistic Studies of Number Agreement

Until recently, few if any studies were addressed to the acquisition of agreement. The study by Keeney and Wolfe (1972) concerned knowledge of agreement between noun and verb in children 3–5 years of age. A number of linguistic and psychological arguments were summarized as to

[9] In tense agreement, however, the issue is more ambiguous and agreement is more likely with the verb than the subject noun.

why mastery of noun inflection should precede knowledge of verb inflection. (1) Numerosity is a component of the meaning of the noun and not of the verb. Although the meaning or referent of a noun is either singular or plural, the meaning of the verb embodies no such distinction. (2) Noun inflection appears more often than verb inflection in the experience of the child. The frequency difference is due, in part, to the relation between nouns and numerosity as nouns (at least count nouns) must always be inflected for number (with the exception of such nouns as *sheep*) yet verbs are inflected only in the third-person present tense.

Once noun inflection is acquired, the acquisition of verb inflection is retarded or inhibited because: (1) Verb inflection is informationally redundant, because the number of the sentence is signaled by the noun. (2) The regular rule for verb inflection is the converse of that for noun inflection (if the verb is inflected, the noun is not; if the noun is inflected, the verb is not, as in *The cat plays—The cats play*).

The irregular verb *be* is not subject to the direct influence of noun inflection, and it is suggested that the marking for irregular forms should become known before regular verbs as the data from Fraser *et al.* (1963) in fact do show.

Keeney and Wolfe's assumptions were based, in part, on the results of an earlier study (Keeney & Smith, 1971) on the comprehension of 4-year olds and imitation of sentences with nonsense words as subject nouns and both regularly inflected verbs and the irregular verb *be*. A high level of correct comprehension and imitation was found when subject nouns were inflected for number as in *snup—snups,* but not when uninflected as *snup—snup* (comparable to *sheep—sheep*). Children acted as though they did not understand regular verb inflection and could not take their number cue from it. Most correct responses were to the apparent number of the nonsense noun.

The two theses, that noun inflections are acquired prior to verb inflections, in agreeing and nonagreeing sentences, and that the irregular verb *to be* is acquired earlier than regular verbs were tested with three kinds of data (spontaneous speech, imitation, and comprehension) following the Fraser *et al.* model.

For subjects from age 3:0 to 4:11 (mean 4:0), only the data from the spontaneous speech samples and the imitations were significant. The remaining data from pictorial and verbal comprehension tasks showed only chance performance.

The spontaneous speech data showed that, for the sample as a whole, children produced many more grammatical (94%) than ungrammatical sentences in respect to subject—verb agreement when sentence subjects were both nouns and pronouns. Likewise, children made no errors with the irregular verb *to be*.

Subjects followed the rules of agreement in imitation. 81% of the grammatical sentences were imitated verbatim; ungrammatical sentences were correctly imitated 49% of the time; 93% of them were changed into grammatical sentences by alternating the noun and verb inflection.

Contrary to prediction, noun changes were no more frequent than verb changes. Overall, in fact, the subject noun was changed to agree with the verb rather than vice versa. The comprehension test data also showed no priority of noun over verb agreement.

The lack of performance differences in the pictorial and verbal tasks was in marked contrast with the results from an analogous pictorial technique used in a concept attainment task (Beilin & Kagan, 1969). In the latter task, subjects of approximately the same age showed 81% correct concept attainment of noun, verb, and possessive pluralization. The manner in which the Keeney and Wolfe task was presented apparently contributed to chance level performance. It is also possible that the imitation data in Keeney and Wolfe's study were affected by being collected after the child had considerable prior experience with plurals and grammatical and un-grammatical sentences.

The study by Shanon (1973) was more clear-cut in demonstrating the operation of agreement rules, at least in adults. The technique used was to present different, ungrammatical, Hebrew declarative sentences that varied in number, gender, and tense agreement. Agreement also varied between subject–verb, subject–adjective, and subject–relative pronoun. For tense, agreement was between verb and time adverb. Sentences also differed in the number of constituents involved in agreement violations as a way of varying complexity. The sentences were presented singly in three tasks: (1) the college undergraduate subjects were to interpret what the speaker intended to convey; (2) they were to change the presented sentences from the past tense to the future tense; (3) interrogative sentences were to be responded to in the affirmative. The results indicated that for number agreement, in all cases, the noun was kept intact and other sentence constituents were changed to agree with it. When noun and gender were ungrammatical, in all cases except one (the third-person plural of the future), the noun was kept intact. In the exceptional case, agreement was made with the verb. The inversion of verb–noun order did not affect the type of interpre-tation given. Shanon reports that simple sentences with the fewest constituent agreement changes were altered and interpreted principally in terms of syntactic rules. With more complex sentences, the interpretations given seemed to follow a least-effort principle, in which the least number of surface constituents were changed to make the sentences grammatical. In all, subjects appeared to follow syntactic, morphophonemic, semantic, pragmatic, and heuristic facts in processing ungrammatical sentences.

In a study with children 5- to 7-years old Huff (1972), following the Fraser et al. (1963) model, found that the subjects of sentences were "more prominent perceptually" than verbs and that modifiers were better number indicators to children than the plural morphemes (s). In this study, reversing subject–verb position did affect application of the agreement rules, contrary to the Shanon finding with adults. In reversed sentences, the subjects of the sentence became more salient than in the more familiar sentence order.

Dingwall and Tuniks (1973) were concerned with many issues in linguistic development, particularly as they are manifest in the acquisition of Russian as a first language. Although the investigation provides data on the development of number "concord and government," it also deals with verbal and prepositional government of cases, gender concord between modifiers and nouns and the past form of verbs, as well as person–number concord between nouns and verbs. The 28 subjects were between the ages of 1:8 and 8:0.

In a three-part experiment, the last part used collections of objects of the same size or color. The experimenter placed sets of from one to five objects in turn in the barn, and the child was asked, "How many objects went into the barn?" as a means of assessing knowledge of numeral–noun agreement. This is a complex matter in Russian. The cardinal number agrees with the noun it modifies: the numerals two through four govern the genitive singular in nouns; five and above, except for combinations with one through four as their last numeral, govern the genitive plural. The experiment indicated little improvement over the entire year span studied. The same was true of M. I. Popova's study after which it was modeled. An analysis of errors showed the children fell into three groups: (1) those who used the nominative with all numerals over one, (2) those who used the genitive singular, and (3) those who used the genitive plural. In addition, it was found that case marking in the plural lags considerably behind that in the singular for all ages.

The Dingwall and Tuniks study, considering the size of its sample (2 subjects at each age level spread over a range from 1:8 to 8:0), is mostly impressionistic. It suggests that Russian children have some knowledge of the organization of sentence constituents, however, there do not appear to be substantial changes in the child's knowledge of agreement over the age span not only in number but also in gender. This difficulty may be a function of the linguistic forms of Russian and the governing rule system or it may be due to the limited sample used to test this knowledge.

Overall, research on the acquisition and development of agreement rules is very limited. The data that are available indicate, in English, early mastery of number agreement in production and comprehension tasks, but apparently not in Russian. It appears that children as young as age 5 utilize the strategy of making other constituents agree with the noun. The effect of constituent order may affect children, it has no influence on adults' sentence processing.

The Number Agreement Study

The study we now report was concerned with the child's acquisition of the agreement rules between nouns, verbs, and number adverbs. We were interested not only in the child's ability to show his knowledge of agreement rules through comprehension and imitation procedures, but also the ability to judge the synonymity of grammatical and ungrammatical sentences that differed only in respect to agreement in number. The ability to judge grammatical sentences was tested both for equivalence in meaning and equivalence in phonemic features. Our interest generally was in the effects of syntactic constraints on the processing of sentences and other more cognitive-semantic considerations.

METHOD

Design

Understanding the rules of number agreement was tested through response to sentences that were grammatical in all respects including number agreement and to those that were ungrammatical because of nonagreement in number. Response to the grammatical and ungrammatical (agreed and non-agreed) sentences was tested in four tasks: *imitation, grammaticality judgment, synonymy judgment,* and *comprehension* through enactment.

The intent of the *imitation* task was to determine, first, if the information load represented by a sentence could be stored in memory. More important, the errors made in imitation were expected to provide a clue as to the nature of sentence processing and indicate the child's knowledge of number agreement.

The *grammaticality judgment* task tested the child's ability to judge agreed and non-agreed sentences as to their grammaticality. This was to provide further evidence of the child's knowledge of the agreement rule system, particularly through the corrections made of ungrammatical (and grammatical) sentences. On this task, the subject first identified whether a sentence was grammatical or not (i.e, sounded right or wrong), then identified the part that was ungrammatical, and, finally, corrected the sentence to make it grammatical.

The *synonymy judgment* task was designed to determine whether children perceived sentences as synonymous on the basis of equivalence in sound or equivalence in meaning. The child also indicated in what ways ungrammatical and grammatical sentences differed when he judged them to be different in meaning.

The *comprehension* task sought to establish the child's knowledge of agreement through his ability to act-out a sentence, which either did or did not agree in number.

Materials

There were two types of materials used: sentences and objects to which the sentences referred. Each sentence was composed of a subject and predicate. The subject consisted of an article (*a*) or adjective (*two*) plus a noun. The predicate consisted of a verb or a conjoined verb, and either an adverb or no adverb. The subjects and predicates were either plural or singular, and agreement between the subject and predicate defined its grammaticality. The nouns used were the names of animals (*monkey, lion, bear, tiger*), and their singular–plural denotation was made emphatic by the article *a* in the singular and the quantifying adjective *two* in the plural. There were three forms of verbs: (1) the uninflected form of the regular verbs *walk, run, jump, kick* that followed a plural subject, and the inflected form with the unvoiced /s/, and voiced /z/ endings that followed a singular subject (*walks, runs,* etc.); (2) the irregular verb represented by the copula (*be*) in the singular (*is*) and plural (*are*); and (3) the conjoined verb form *v + v*, with the same or different verbs that was designed to indicate repetition of the denoted action (pluralization of the action). The rationale for the use of the conjoined verb was to determine whether the pluralization of the verb would increase its salience in the sentence and influence the focus of agreement, to test in effect if arguments concerning the verb, such as Jespersen's (1964) that the verb carries no number value of its own, are in fact true. Number adverbs were included to emphasize the number in the verb. Four variations were included: (a) *no adverb*, (b) *once*, (c) *twice*, and (d) *all the time*.

Three lists of sentences were created. Each list for the imitation and grammaticality judgment task contained 14 sentences, half of which were grammatical, half ungrammatical. The three lists were created to allow some of the noun–verb–adverb combinations to be tested. Each list was given to a separate sample of subjects in a particular task. Each subject had all three tasks. For the synonymy task there were seven pairs of sentences in which a grammatical sentence was paired with an ungrammatical sentence, and two additional pairs in which both the sentences were grammatical or ungrammatical. The same variation and distribution of sentence constituents characterized the synonymy judgment sentences as did the grammaticality judgment and imitation sentences, except for the two additional sentences and one sentence in the synonymy list that differed. (The sentences in all three lists are to be found in Appendix C.) The reference objects for the nouns were toy animals (*bear, monkey, tiger,* and *lion*). The animals were approximately the same size.

Procedure

The tasks were administered in three individual sessions. One session each was given for the imitation (I), grammaticality judgment (G), and synonymy judgment (S) tasks. The order of administration was varied: (1) IGS, (2) GSI, and (3) SIG. The *enactment* procedure followed each of the other tasks (i.e., the subject enacted the sentences given in each of the other tasks).

1. In the imitation task the subject was told, "I am going to tell you some little stories. Listen carefully to what I say, and say it back to me just the way I say it. Listen carefully, and say what I say. Are you ready? Let's begin." The session was tape recorded and the experimenter wrote down incorrect responses.

2. In the grammaticality judgment task the subject was told, "I am

going to tell you some little stories. Listen carefully and tell me whether what I am saying sounds right or wrong to your ears." (This instruction was sometimes paraphrased as "Tell me if the story sounds right or wrong to your ears.") Are you ready? Listen carefully and tell me if I am saying the stories in the right way. Let's begin."

To determine what the subject thought was wrong with the sentence, the experimenter would then ask, "What part sounds wrong? Can you tell me what part sounds wrong? What is wrong with the way I am saying the sentence."

To correct the sentence the subject was asked, "Can you tell me how to make the sentence sound better. Tell me how to make the story sound better."

3. In the synonymy judgment task the experimenter said, "I am going to tell you two little stories. Listen carefully to what I say and tell me if the stories sound the same. Are you ready? Let's begin."

After the subject responded, the experimenter said, "Tell me, do the two stories mean the same thing? Do they mean something different?" The same procedure was followed for each sentence pair.

4. In the enactment procedure the subject was told, "Now we are going to play a game. See the animals here? Do you know their names? Tell me the names of the animals. Good." (If the subject did not know them, the experimenter named them and subject was asked to repeat the names. The subject was then initiated into the task with, "I am going to tell you what the animals do. Your job is to show me what the animals do. You must find the right animals and show me what it does. Sometimes, I will tell you about more than one animal. You must be careful to show me the right number of animals. Sometimes, I will tell you that the animal does more than one thing; you must be careful to show me the animal doing the right number of things. Do you understand? Good. Let's begin."

Two sample sentences were used in which the experimenter demonstrated the procedure. Those were followed by the test sentences.

Subjects

The subjects were 90 children from the nursery, kindergarten, and first- and second-grades of schools and camps in the New York City area. All spoke English as their native language, and none was judged by his teachers to have special language problems. The children were predominantly white middle-class as defined by neighbourhood residence. The few nonwhites in the sample spoke standard English and presented no language difficulties in their classes.

There were 18 subjects at each age level from 3- to 7-years old. The mean ages for each grade level were: 3:7, 4:6, 5:7, 6:4. The 90 subjects consisted of 42 boys and 48 girls. The youngest children (ages 3 and 4) were tested in a private, summer day-camp and in a private nursery school. The 5- to 7-year olds were tested in public elementary schools and private day camps.

TABLE 5-7

Mean Number of Correct Responses in Imitation, Grammaticality, and Synonymy Tasks by Age

Age	Grammaticality Judgments[a]			Imitation[a]			Synonymity Judgments				
							Different Pairs[a]			Same Pairs[b]	
	Gramatical sentences	Ungrammatical sentences	Total	Grammatical sentences	Ungrammatical sentences	Total	Sound different	Mean different	Total	Sound same	Mean same
3	4.11	3.06	3.58	3.61	1.61	2.61	2.89	3.11	3.00	1.17	1.00
4	4.78	2.00	3.39	6.06	3.78	4.92	3.11	2.83	2.97	1.56	1.30
5	5.44	3.00	4.22	5.94	3.78	4.86	3.56	3.11	3.33	1.56	1.44
6	6.33	3.72	5.03	6.56	5.33	5.94	4.33	3.11	3.72	1.94	2.00
7	6.39	6.11	6.25	6.72	5.39	6.06	6.72	4.78	5.75	2.00	1.94
Total	5.41	3.58	—	5.78	3.98	—	4.12	3.39	—	1.64	1.54

[a] Based on 7 pairs of grammatical and ungrammatical sentences. Correct response is *different*. Range 0–7; n = 18 per age.
[b] Based on 2 pairs of sentences. Correct response is *same*. Range 0–2; n = 18 per age.

TABLE 5-8

Data for Combined Imitation and Grammaticality Tasks (Mean Correct Responses) by Age

Age	Sentences[a]				Tasks[a]			
	Grammatical	Ungrammatical	F^b	p	Grammaticality	Imitation	F^b	p
3	7.72	4.67	8.53	$< .01$	7.17	5.22	6.12	$< .05$
4	10.83	5.78	20.53	$< .01$	6.78	9.83	23.62	$< .01$
5	11.39	6.78	19.23	$< .01$	8.44	9.72	3.58	N.S.
6	12.89	9.06	16.26	$< .01$	10.06	11.89	11.19	$< .01$
7	13.11	11.50	8.25	$< .01$	12.50	12.11	.46	N.S.
Total	11.19	7.56			8.99	9.76		

[a] Range of scores is from 0–14. Agreement totals are summed across imitation and grammaticality; grammaticality and imitation totals are summed across grammatical and ungrammatical sentences.

[b] These F values represent values from one-way repeated measures ANOVA of these means within each age group. The degree of freedom for each age level are (1,17). n of subjects at each age is 18.

RESULTS

Imitation

A four-way mixed analysis of variance was performed separately on the imitation, grammaticality judgment, and synonymy judgment data. For the imitation analysis, the between-subject variables were Age, Lists, and presentation order; the within-subject variable was Grammaticality (grammatical versus ungrammatical sentences) ($5 \times 3 \times 3 \times 2$). The scores for the imitation analysis were the number of correct imitations. Correct imitation required both subject and predicate constituents to be correct in respect to their number. The mean correct imitation scores based on pairs of sentences (7) are shown in Table 5-7, and those for all 14 sentences appear in Table 5-8 (the latter expressed in percentages appear in Table 5-9).

In the analysis of variance only the Age ($p < .01$) and Grammaticality ($p < .01$) main effects were significant. There appear to be, from an inspection of the means, two points at which a sizeable improvement in performance occurred, one point was between ages 3 and 4; the other was between ages 5 and 6. Individual comparison tests (Newman-Keuls) indicated the former difference was significant ($p < .01$), the latter not. The grammaticality effect was due to the fact that the grammatical sentences were easier to imitate than the ungrammatical ($p < .01$).

The break in performance between 3 and 4 and 5 and 6 is more clearly evident when the imitation of only matched pairs of grammatical and ungrammatical sentences is considered (i.e., the matched sentences were similar in all respects except number—*The tiger runs; the tiger run*). The percentage of correct responses (in Table 5-9) rose significantly between ages 3 and 4 and 5 and 6. At the same time, only at 3 years of age was there a substantial number of pairs in which subjects incorrectly imitated both the grammatical and ungrammatical sentence (41.3%). At other ages, if subjects were correct on both sentences of the pair, they were

TABLE 5-9

Imitation of Matched Sentences (Percentage of Responses)[a]

Age	Correct on both grammatical and ungrammatical	Correct on grammatical—incorrect on ungrammatical	Incorrect on grammatical—Correct on grammatical	Incorrect on both grammatical and ungrammatical
3	15.9	35.7	7.1	41.3
4	49.2	37.3	4.8	8.7
5	44.4	40.5	9.5	5.6
6	71.4	22.2	4.8	1.6
7	74.6	21.4	2.4	1.6

[a] Based on 126 pairs of matched sentences per age, 7 pair of stimuli for each 18 subjects.

most likely to be correct on the grammatical sentence and incorrect on the ungrammatical sentence. The difference between the imitation of grammmatical and ungrammatical sentences was large at every age level, with ungrammatical sentences more difficult to imitate. A significant fact that emerges from an analysis of errors in imitation is that subjects transformed ungrammatical sentences into grammatical sentences up to the age of 6. At age 6, they correctly imitated the ungrammatical sentences (i.e., they maintained their ungrammaticality).

Two general processes appeared to operate in imitation. Between the ages of 3 and 4, children appeared to master to a substantial degree the rules of number agreement. At the point when they acquired the rules, subjects were so bound by rules that they could not imitate the ungrammatical sentences, instead they transformed them into grammatical sentences. Only at age 6 were the ungrammatical sentences treated in an objective fashion and imitated without correction. The failure to imitate ungrammatical sentences was not due to the inability to imitate, however, because 86% of the grammatical sentences are imitated correctly by 4-year olds. It appears rather that a new process or set of processes began to operate at the 6-year old level that resulted in sentence objectification.

Grammaticality Judgment

The analysis of variance for grammaticality judgments employed the same mixed design and tested for age, lists, presentation order, and grammaticality judgment. Scores were based on the subject's correct judgments of the grammaticality or ungrammaticality of sentences. (Means for sentence pairs are indicated in Table 5-7 and for all 14 sentences in Table 5-8.) Age ($p < .01$), List ($p < .01$), and Grammaticality judgment ($p < .01$) main effects were significant, as well as the Presentation order × Grammaticality interaction ($p < .05$).

The age effect differed between ages 4 and 5, 5 and 6, and 6 and 7. All differences were significant ($p < .05$ for ages 4–6, $p < .01$ for ages 6–7). An inspection of the means and proportions correct indicates that performance remained fairly stable for the judgments of ungrammatical sentences up to the age of 7 when there was a sharp rise; at age 6, 53% of the responses were correct, which was at the chance level; at 7-years old it rose to 87% (Table 5-9). With grammatical sentences, performance rose from the third to fourth year (59% at age 3; 68% at age 4), and again in the fifth year (78%), and at the sixth year rose to a level at which 90% of the responses were correct (Table 5-9). Data for grammaticality judgments of matched pairs are indicated in Table 5-10.

Correct judgments for both sentences of the pair were low (11%) until about 5- and 6-years old (31–46%) when there was a substantial rise. The rise between 6 and 7 years of age was much more substantial however (80%). These data suggest a three-stage progression: (1) there is little or no knowledge of number agreement rules; (2) this is followed by a period in which the rules are apparently known to a fair extent (about 5- to 6-years old); finally, (3) the child's knowledge is complete at about age 7.

TABLE 5-10

Grammaticality Judgments of Matched Sentences (Percentage of Responses)[a]

Age	Correct on both grammatical and ungrammatical	Correct on grammatical—Incorrect on ungrammatical	Incorrect on grammatical—Correct on ungrammatical	Incorrect on both grammatical and ungrammatical
3	19.1	39.7	24.6	16.7
4	11.1	57.1	17.5	14.3
5	31.0	46.8	11.9	10.3
6	46.0	44.4	7.14	2.4
7	80.2	11.1	7.14	1.6

[a] Based on 126 pairs of matched sentences per age, 7 pair of stimuli for each of 18 subjects.

In general, the patterns for correct grammaticality judgment responses paralleled those for imitation, although correct imitation appeared at a somewhat earlier age (by a year at each of the proposed stages). In the grammaticality judgment task, subjects were asked whether a sentence was grammatical or not. If he judged a sentence ungrammatical, he was asked where it was incorrect and to make the correction. Table 5-11 indicates the sentence constituents that the subjects identified as requiring change to make the sentence grammatical. Some grammatical sentences were identified as ungrammatical, and some ungrammatical sentences were incorrectly changed so they remained ungrammatical. The majority of sentences that were identified for change, however, were the ungrammatical sentences that were changed correctly. The striking fact is that in each one of these conditions the sentence element that was changed to establish agreement was the verb.

Ungrammatical verb changes constituted 79% of all changes, whereas, only 5% of the responses were noun changes. The only other response category was the adverb, which was changed in conjunction with verb changes. Adverb changes, in fact, were always made in conjunction with a verb change in all conditions. Seventy-five percent of the verb changes were made independently of any other kind of change. When noun changes occurred in all conditions, they occurred with a verb or adverb change. The incorrect changes to ungrammatical sentences indicated the same distribution.

The changes that were made to grammatical sentences were somewhat different. Why subjects thought grammatical sentences were ungrammatical is not fully clear. Even though the predominant change was in the verb, there were a substantial number of changes in the nouns and articles, with fewer among the adverbs. The very fact that grammatical sentences were judged as ungrammatical indicates that the agreement rules were not fully known by this group of subjects.

TABLE 5-11

Sentence Constituents Identified for Change in Grammaticality Judgment Task by Age and Grammaticality Strategies (Percentages)[a]

Age	Grammatical sentences				Number (responses)
	Article	Noun	Verb	Adverb	
Incorrectly changed[b]					
3	12	38	38	12	8
4	9	9	73	9	11
5	13	13	61	13	15
6	11	11	78	0	9
7	0	0	100	0	1
Total	11	16	64	9	44
	Ungrammatical sentences				
Correctly changed[c]					
3	0	14	64	22	14
4	0	6	72	22	32
5	0	12	69	19	42
6	0	1	85	14	59
7	1	3	83	13	115
Total	0	5	79	16	262
Incorrectly changed[d]					
3	0	0	100	0	1
4	0	0	86	14	7
5	12	6	47	35	17
6	0	20	50	30	10
7	0	25	50	25	4
Total	4	10	56	28	39
Total ungrammatical	1	6	76	17	301

[a] As proportion of total responses for each age.
[b] Grammatical sentences the subject claims are ungrammatical, but subject's correction produces another incorrect sentence, e.g., *A monkey is running once* to *A monkey run once.*
[c] Ungrammatical sentences that are made grammatical.
[d] Ungrammatical sentences that when corrected remain ungrammatical, e.g., *A bear are kicking* to *A bear kicking.*

Note: The corrections indicated in this table are not independent, i.e., more than one correction may be made to a single sentence.

At each age from 3 to 7, the verb was the major constituent that was changed. Only when grammatical sentences were considered ungrammatical did nouns change to an equal degree as did verbs, but the number of responses was very small. Nevertheless some ungrammatical sentences also had noun changes (14% at age 3). At 6- to 7-years old, if grammatical sentences were judged to be ungrammatical there was a greater likelihood that the changes would be noun changes.

On the whole, one may conclude that the predominant strategy was to make the verb and adverb agree with the number of the noun. There was a secondary tendency to make the noun agree with the verbal element, but when such a change was made it was made together with a verb or adverb change. The strategy of changing the verb was the predominant one at an early age (3-years old) and remained so (through age 7), although as the number of corrections increased (from 14 to 115) the proportions that were verb changes increased as well (from 64 to 83%) and the proportions of other sentence constituent changes decreased. Again the transition from 6 to 7 years of age was the time when the greatest increase occurred in sentence correction (from 59 to 115), although no change occurred in the verb or noun strategy. Grammaticality judgments for grammatical sentences were superior to ungrammatical sentence judgments at all ages.

Individual comparisons indicate that the significant effect for lists was due to one list that was more difficult than the other two ($p < .05$). The effect was due to the appearance in one of the lists of ungrammatical sentences containing compound verbs (e.g., *jumps* and *jumps*) with and without adverbs. This construction was more difficult to judge as to its grammaticality than other forms. For example, the sentence *Two bears jumps and jumps* was difficult to judge correctly. This may have been due to the ambiguity of the relation between the subject and the compound verb. The child may have thought that *each* bear jumped, and so the singular inflection of the verb was appropriate for the noun even as expressed. Four of the sentences on this list were the most difficult to judge among all the lists.

The difference between the mean of this list and the others, although significant, did not appear to be of sufficient significance in other respects to warrant separate analysis of all the data by list. In addition, for the imitation and synonymy judgment tasks the list main effect was not significant. The lack of a presentation order effect in any of the analyses suggests that the Grammaticality×Order interaction was an idiosyncratic event.

Grammatical versus Ungrammatical Sentences

For a contrast of responses to grammatical and ungrammatical sentences, the imitation and grammatically data were combined. Grammatical sentences were more easily processed correctly than the ungrammatical sentences at all ages (and within all lists—see Table 5-8). The difference between the two sets of sentences was significant at each age ($p < .01$). Processing of grammatical sentences was near ceiling at age 7, it was not for ungrammatical sentences, which indicates that knowledge of agreement rules was not complete by age 7. Whether this was from lack of knowledge of the rule system or was a function of the processing procedure inherent in the tasks is not clear. If the agreement rules were known they should have applied equally well to the processing of grammatical and ungrammatical sentences, unless task-specific difficulties intervened.

Both the imitation and grammaticality judgments of grammatical sentences were consistently superior to the processing of ungrammatical sentences at each age level as seen in Figure 5-1. The changes in imita-

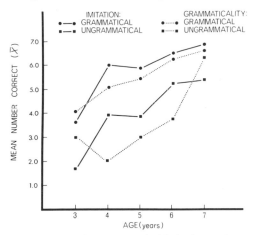

Fig. 5-1.   Correct grammatical and ungrammatical imitation and grammaticality response by age.

tion paralleled each other for each age, however, the grammaticality judgments for ungrammatical sentences became poorer from age 3 to 4 and then began to improve with a dramatic rise between ages 6 and 7.

Processing grammatical sentences in both imitation and grammatical judgment tasks was consistently superior to the processing of ungrammatical sentences, yet, it would appear that different processes were involved in the grammaticality judgments because knowledge of the agreement rules was common to both tasks. It is also evident from Figure 5-1 that at age 7, although imitation of ungrammatical sentences lagged behind, imitation of grammatical sentences and grammaticality judgments were near ceiling. The reason subjects were not fully able to imitate the ungrammatical sentences was due, as previously indicated, to their being bound to the rule system and their inability to treat the sentence in an objective fashion. The phenomenon is relative, however, because by age 7 a substantial proportion of all sentences were correctly imitated.

In considering the developmental changes for grammaticality judgment and imitation, it is evident (Fig. 5-1) that at ages 3 and 7 correct grammaticality judgment performance exceeded correct imitation performance (age 3 [$p < .01$]; age 7, *n.s.*) During the intervening years, imitation exceeds grammaticality (significantly at age 4 and 6 [$p < .01$]). At age 3, the inversion may have been due to the effect previously noted of the subject attempting to change ungrammatical to grammatical sentences. He was thus unable to do the task "properly." At age 7, with the subjects nearer the ceiling in performance, the difference could be attributed to chance.

The consistency of subject performance in the grammaticality judgment and imitation was assessed in a χ^2 analysis in which subjects who were correct on both the grammatical judgment task and the imitation task were compared with subjects who failed on both, as well as those who were correct on one task and not the other. The analysis with pooled age-groups shows a significant χ^2 for both the grammatical and ungrammatical sentences (Table 5-12). Many more subjects tended to be consistent in the

TABLE 5-12

Summary of X^2 Analyses

Success on grammatical and ungrammatical items across imitation and grammaticality tasks

	Grammatical items				Ungrammatical items		
	Grammaticality task				Grammaticality task		
Imitation	+	−		Imitation	+	−	
+	42	21	$\chi^2 = 5.64$	+	16	11	$\chi^2 = 10.059$
−	10	17	$p < .02$	−	14	49	$p < .01$
			$c = .24$				$c = .32$

Success on grammatical–ungrammatical sentences within imitation and grammaticality

	Imitation				Grammaticality		
	Grammatical				Grammatical		
Ungrammatical	+	−		Ungrammatical	+	−	
+	26	1	$\chi^2 = 10.97$	+	17	13	$\chi^2 = .005$
−	37	26	$p < .001$	−	36	24	N.S.
			$c = .33$				

Success on sound and meaning judgments on synonymy for 7 different pairs only, and for different–same pairs combined.

	Different pairs only				Same–different pairs		
	Sound diff.				Sound diff–same		
Mean different	+	−		Meaning	+	−	
+	25	1	$\chi^2 = 34.95$	+	26	0	$\chi^2 = 41.78$
−	16	48	$p < .001$	−	16	48	$p < .001$
			$c = .53$				$c = .56$

Note: *criterion for success:* subject's score must be 6 of 7 correct for imitation, grammaticality, and equivalence with different pairs, and 7 of 9 correct for equivalence with same–different pairs combined.

tasks than inconsistent, that is they were more likely to be correct or incorrect on both tasks than not. There was also a greater likelihood subjects would be correct on both tasks with grammatical sentences, and a greater likelihood they would be incorrect on both tasks with ungrammatical sentences. Furthermore, with grammatical sentences they were more likely to be correct in the imitation than the grammaticality task; for the ungrammatical sentences it made no difference. Coefficients of contingency (C) showed a higher relation between the two types of performance with the ungrammatical sentences than the grammatical (.32 versus .24).

An analysis of performance within the tasks themselves shows that, in the imitation task, subjects were much more likely to imitate a grammatical sentence correctly than an ungrammatical one, rather than the reverse (37 subjects to 1 [$p < .001$]). For grammatical judgments, the likelihood was reduced (the proportions change: 36 to 13 and the relation was not significant).

Synonymy Judgments

The synonymy judgment task data were subjected to the same mixed-type analysis of variance as the imitation and grammaticality judgment data. The scores used were the subject's judgments as to whether the two sentences read to him sounded the same (or different) and meant the same (or not). The analysis of variance was based only on the judgments for those sentence pairs that differed (i.e., one sentence was grammatical; the other ungrammatical).

The *same* sentence pairs in which two grammatical or two ungrammatical sentences were paired produced too limited variability (0–2 range) to justify an analysis of variance. Nevertheless, inspection of the means indicates that the same pairs were responded to at chance level at 3-years old in both types of judgment (sound and meaning). Ages 4 and 5 showed a substantial increase in correct responding and nearly perfect responding at age 6 and 7. The overall difference between "sound" and "meaning" judgments was significant ($p < .05$) with subjects more correct on judgment of same sound than same meaning, particularly at the younger ages.

In the analysis of variance of the different pairs, the between-subject effects were Age, List, and Presentation order. The within-subject effect was Synonymy judgment (sound versus meaning). The scores were correct synonymy judgments.

The main effects of Age ($p < .01$) and Synonymy judgment ($p < .01$) were significant. The Age × Synonymy judgment interaction was also significant ($p < .05$). An examination of the age means shows essentially chance performance from age 3 to 6. Only at age 7 was there a distinctive and significant ($p < .01$) improvement to a very high level of correct performance.

The difference between the judgment of synonymy on the basis of sound and on the basis of meaning differed overall across ages with the sound judgments proportionately more correct than the meaning judgments.

The Age × Synonymy judgment interaction was due to the lack of difference between sound and meaning judgments in the years 3 to 5, but significant differences in years 6 and 7 (both $p < .01$). There was a rise in correct synonymy judgments at age 6 for sound that was not evident for meaning. At age 7 when both synonymy responses improved significantly, the increase in correct, sound synonymy judgment was significantly greater than for meaning judgment.

The data for the *same* and *different* pairs are congruent in their developmental patterns, except that correct judgment was earlier for the same pairs, age 4 (than for different pairs ages 6 and 7).

The interrelation of sound and meaning judgment for the different pairs is indicated in Table 5-13. There were four possible interrelationships: judgments could be correct to both sound and meaning (+ +) or both incorrect (− −) or only one would be correct (+ −, − +). The distribution of these patterns with age parallels other data. The correct correlated responses (both correct) remained fairly stable up to age 7, at which point they improved dramatically. The inverse occurred for the double incorrect responses. At age 7 the only errors that appeared were in meaning judgments and not in sound. This finding is ambiguous in one respect, however. The ambiguity is associated with the difficulty in knowing whether the meaning of a sentence pair was different when it sounded different. A subject could very well believe that although one of the sentences was ungrammatical its *intended* meaning was the same as the grammatical one. In that case the subject's response would be in the category "sound different—mean same." In effect, it would be a "false negative" response.

The patterns in the data also suggest that up to 6 years of age children interpreted correspondence in sound to indicate correspondence in meaning, and noncorrespondence to indicate difference in meaning; thus, the young children, who misperceived the sound difference and called them the same sound, judged that they had the same meaning (47%–37% from 3- to 6-years old). Only at age 7, when the sound difference was clearly

TABLE 5-13

Synonymy Judgments to Sound and Meaning of Sentences that Differed (Percentage of Responses)[a]

Age	Sound same— Mean different (− +)	Sound same— Mean same (− −)	Sound different Mean different (+ +)	Sound different Mean same (+ −)	No response
3	11.9	47.6	33.3	7.0	(2)[b]
4	11.9	43.7	29.4	15.1	(10)
5	4.0	48.4	35.7	11.9	
6	.7	37.3	43.7	18.3	
7	0.0	2.4	65.9	31.7	

[a] Based on 126 possible responses per age group; 7 possible responses for each of 18 subjects.
[b] In number of responses.

differentiated, was there concomitantly a sharp rise in correct meaning judgments, and subjects were also able to maintain that although the sentences sounded different they could have the same meaning (although in this context they were incorrect).

With the data pooled for the age groups, consistency in the synonymy judgment task showed a similar pattern. There was a greater likelihood of consistency in being correct or incorrect on both tasks than being correct on one. When a subject was successful on one task, the likelihood was that he judged the sound equivalence correctly and meaning incorrectly. This was true for combined same and different sentence pairs and also when only the different pairs were considered. The correlation of both sound and meaning judgments was .53 with different pairs only, and .56 when same and different pairs were combined. It was thus more difficult for subjects to make a judgment of equivalence of meaning than it was to make a judgment of equivalence of sound.

In the synonymy judgment task, if a subject responded "different" to the sentences, he was asked to identify the constituent of the sentence that made them different. Three strategies characterized the responses: (1) irrelevant reference: subjects referred to facts that were irrelevant to either sentence—*because we have no ducks*, (2) single attribute reference: the subject referred to the constituents of only one sentence—*runs is different*, (3) comparative strategy: reference was made to both sentences in the pair and a comparison was made between them—*is and are, run and runs*. The distribution of the subjects' strategies by age (indicated in Table 5-14) is based on the strategy used most consistently by a child. The number of children at each age who were not consistent in strategy use was: age 3 (2), age 4 (2), age 5 (5), age 6 (1), and age 7 (1).

The comparative strategy was the most sophisticated: (1) the 3-year olds

TABLE 5-14

Synonymy Task: Dominant Responses Strategies by Age (in Percentage of Subjects)[a]

Age	Strategy		
	Irrelevant[b] reference	Single attribute[c] reference	Comparative[d] reference
3	22.2	5.5	0.0
4	11.1	27.7	11.1
5	0.0	55.5	16.6
6	0.0	50.0	22.2
7	0.0	38.8	55.5

[a] n of subjects at each age = 18.
[b] Irrelevant: reference to extrasentential facts.
[c] Single attribute: reference to constituents of one sentence only.
[d] Comparative: reference to both sentences.

made no use of it. (2) From 4- to 6-years old, a fair number of subjects employed the strategy (11–22%). (3) At age 7, there was a substantial rise in its use (55%). Single attribute development was curvilinear: (1) At three, very few subjects made use of it (5%). (2) Its use rose rapidly from 27% to 55% at 4 and 5 years old. (3) A decline set in slowly at first (age 6) but then more rapidly at age 7 (to 38%).

The inability of subjects, many of whom made correct equivalence judgments, to verbalize the fact that both sets of data entered into their descriptions can be accounted for in a number of ways. First is the child's limitations at description. Another is that the subject may have presumed that even if only one element was mentioned it would be understood by the hearer that a comparison was being made. A more likely possibility was that it was not until age 7 that a new strategy for looking at sentences emerged in which all of the information in the sentence was used and not simply part of it. The single-attribute subjects even at 7-years old may have been unable, in the Piagetian sense, to decenter, that is to treat the object in a way that involved the total examination of the constituents and compare one element relative to another. The comparative strategy, however, was a clear indication of decentering, and it was evident mainly at about age 7.

An indirect test of the effect of decentering was made in an analysis of the performance of one group of subjects who could be presumed to have reached the stage of sentence objectification compared with a group who had not. For this purpose, 6-year olds were selected who had *passed* the synonymy test (at least 6 of 7 pairs correct), and those of the same age who *failed* it (less than 6 correct). The 6-year-old group was selected because they were the only group who could provide both kinds of subjects in sufficient numbers. Table 5-15 indicates the correct imitation responses for the two groups. There was little difference in response to grammatical sentences; to the ungrammatical sentences and the sentence pairs, however,

TABLE 5-15

Performance of 6-Year-Old Synonymy Test Subjects (Pass versus Fail) on Imitation (Percentage of Correct Responses)

	Imitation		
	Grammatical[a] sentences	*Ungrammatical[a] sentences*	*Pairs of grammatical[b] and ungrammatical sentences*
Pass synonymy (n = 9)	96.8	82.5	80.9
Fail synonymy (n = 9)	90.4	69.8	61.9

[a] Based on 126 responses: 63 responses for those who passed and failed.
[b] Based on 126 pairs of grammatical and ungrammatical sentences.

TABLE 5-16

Performance of 6-Year-Old Synonymy Test Subjects (Pass versus Fail) on Grammaticality (Percentage of Correct Responses)

	Grammaticality		
	Grammatical[a] sentences	*Ungrammatical[a] sentences*	*Pairs of grammatical[b] and ungrammatical sentences*
Pass synonymy (n = 9)	87.3	82.5	71.4
Fail synonymy (n = 9)	93.6	23.8	14.0

[a] Based on 126 responses: 63 for those who pass and who fail.
[b] Based on 126 pairs of grammatical and ungrammatical sentences: 63 pairs for those who pass and fail.

there were differences in the proportions correct, with clear superiority for the synonymy judgment group who passed ($p < .05$). In the grammaticality task (Table 5-16) with the same subject breakdown, the pattern of differences was accentuated. There was essentially no difference in response to the grammatical sentences, but to the ungrammatical sentences the differences were large and significant ($p < .01$).

These findings indicate consistency in performance between the synonymy, imitation, and grammaticality judgment tasks. By the nature of the strategy data, one can infer that the differences in levels of performance were due to the inability to decenter and treat the sentence in an objective manner. The data also suggest that in imitation itself the subject deals with the sentence as a unit, relating its constituents to one another. The error data in imitation are consistent with this in that the 4- to 5-year old child's transformation of ungrammatical sentences to grammatical ones revealed that he was processing all the significant constituents relative to one another in the sentence. That he could do this in a single sentence and not between two sentences is further indication that the processing of a single sentence in this fashion reflected a one-way function and not the reversible function that comes at age 7 with operative thought.

Subject–Verb Enactment

The enactment task, in which the child was asked to act out the message in a sentence with appropriate toys, provided a further test of the child's ability to comprehend the meaning of the sentence. The experimenter made particular note of actions related to the sentence subject, principally for its singular or plural reference, and the predicate, also for its singular or plural reference. The combination of correct subject and predicate enactment was taken to indicate correct comprehension of the agreement

TABLE 5-17

Grammaticality Judgment and Imitation Task Responses as a Function of Number Adverb, Sentence Type, and Age (Percentages)[a]

Predicate +	Grammaticality						Imitation					
	3	4	5	6	7	Total	3	4	5	6	7	Total
Grammatical sentences												
No adverb:												
Singular	38	71	88	88	100	77	54	100	75	96	100	85
Plural	50	71	71	92	79	73	54	88	96	100	92	86
Total	44	71	79	90	90	75	54	94	85	98	96	85
Once												
Singular	67	78	78	100	94	83	67	83	83	94	100	86
Plural	67	75	92	100	92	85	67	92	100	92	100	90
Total	67	77	83	100	93	84	67	87	90	93	100	87
Twice												
Singular	67	50	75	83	83	72	25	83	67	83	92	70
Plural	83	67	83	92	92	83	50	92	83	92	83	80
Total	75	58	79	88	88	78	38	88	75	88	88	75
All the time												
Singular	58	42	75	75	83	67	42	83	83	92	100	80
Plural	67	83	58	92	92	78	42	58	92	100	100	77
Total	63	63	67	83	88	73	42	71	88	92	100	78
Total singular	55	64	80	88	92	76	50	89	77	92	98	82
Total plural	63	73	75	93	87	78	53	83	93	95	93	84
Total grammatical	59	68	78	90	90	77	52	87	85	94	96	83

[a] Percentages are based on n of correct responses per type of sentence divided by total n of responses for that type across items and forms for all subjects.

characteristics of the sentence (i.e., in respect to pluralization rules). Correct *ungrammatical* sentence enactment was expected to be a verbatim characterization of nonagreement in number between subject and predicate.

Sentence subject enactment was judged by whether the child picked up one or two objects. Predicate enactment was judged by whether the child carried out the action or actions indicated. Predicate plurality was represented principally by adverbial modifiers that indicated number.

In the following sentences, *The bear walks* and *A bear kicks*, the former indicates continuous action; in the latter, sentence action may be either a discrete singular event (a kick) or a series of such events. Definite, adverbial number indication was added to such sentences in order to make their reference unambiguous. It was expected, therefore, that enactment was likely to be unambiguous in such sentences as *A lion jumps once* and *Two lions walk twice*. With number modification introduced through a temporal adverb, it was expected that the child would demonstrate the

TABLE 5-17—*cont.*

Predicate +	Grammaticality						Imitation					
	3	4	5	6	7	Total	3	4	5	6	7	Total
Ungrammatical Sentences												
No adverb												
Singular	63	33	50	67	92	61	50	88	75	92	100	81
Plural	29	21	50	46	83	46	17	38	63	83	79	56
Total	46	27	50	56	88	53	33	63	69	88	90	68
Once												
Singular	28	17	39	50	94	46	28	56	50	89	78	60
Plural	42	33	42	67	75	52	0	42	25	33	67	33
Total	33	23	40	57	87	48	17	50	40	67	73	49
Twice												
Singular	58	33	58	42	100	58	17	58	50	83	75	57
Plural	25	25	17	33	100	43	8	50	33	67	67	45
Total	42	29	38	38	100	49	13	54	42	75	71	51
All the time												
Singular	58	67	50	75	92	68	42	58	67	75	75	63
Plural	50	8	25	42	58	37	0	25	42	58	50	35
Total	54	38	38	58	75	53	21	42	54	67	63	49
Total singular	52	35	48	59	94	58	36	68	62	86	85	68
Total plural	35	22	37	47	80	44	8	38	45	65	68	45
Total ungrammatical	44	29	43	53	87	51	23	54	54	76	77	57

purported action three or more times in such sentences as *A lion runs all the time* and *A monkey is kicking all the time.* When number was introduced into the sentence by repetition of the verb (in a compound verb), or in the combination of two different action verbs, it was expected that ambiguity would exist when the verb was repeated (*Two tigers jump and jump*) but not when two different verbs are combined (*Two lions jump and kick*).

Enactment data were sought after each sentence presented in the other tasks (except the synonymy judgment task). That is, after an imitation or grammaticality judgment, the subject was asked to enact the sentence he had just imitated or judged.

The enactment data for verbs and adverbs show then that

1. A sentence without a number adverbial relies, in part, for number reference on the nature of the verb, particularly on whether the verb is punctual or dural.

2. Compound verbs are interpreted as dual or multiple depending on whether the second verb is a repeat of the first verb or a new verb.

3. Number adverbials such as *once* or *twice* add number specification to the verb, but not unambiguously, because *twice* in some contexts suggests multiple actions and in other contexts singular or continuous action.

4. Number determination of the verb operates independently of the subject noun and is also independent of the verb form.

5. Comprehension of the verbal constituent of the sentence was unaffected by whether the sentence was grammatical or ungrammatical.

6. Comprehension of verbal number was achieved progressively over the age span from 3 to 7. When number was not indicated by a number adverbial, verb-number development was not progressive. When number was indicated by a number adverbial such as *once*, it was responded to correctly between ages 3 and 4, and if by the larger number (twice) then comprehended between ages 5 and 6. The *all the time* reference was comprehended at a very early age but more ambiguously interpreted with age as singularity and plurality began to qualify the child's response.

Effect of Number Adverbials on Imitation and Grammaticality Judgment

The effect of number adverbs on grammaticality judgments and imitation is indicated in Table 5-17. Adding number adverbials to grammatical sentences *improved* grammaticality judgments at the 3-year-old level but not after that. The presence of number adverbs appeared to improve imitation in some cases (*once*) at the 3-year level, but made it poorer for *twice* and *all the time*. With ungrammatical sentences, the addition of adverbs did not affect grammaticality judgments differently except in some instances, such as for *twice* when it was attached to sentences with plural subjects. In that case, correct judgment was reduced dramatically, relative to singular subjects (at 3-years old, 25% compared with 58%). With *once* the effect was just the opposite (28% with singular, 42% for plurals). This indicates that the function of the number adverb was known to the 3-year old and confusion resulted when the meaning of the term was not in agreement with the rest of the sentence. The real confusion created by these adverbs in ungrammatical sentences was not fully appreciated or comprehended until age 7, however, when a dramatic increase in correct response occurred. Confusion occurred in sentences such as *A boy jump once* (singular subject) and *Two boys jumps twice* (plural subject). In these cases, the adverb agrees with the noun in number but disagrees with the verb which it is supposed to modify. In *Two boys jumps once* and *A boy jump twice* in which the adverb is in agreement with the verb that it is expected to modify, correct response was far superior for judgments of grammaticality. It should be pointed out that the differences at the early ages were between levels of response that were *random*, indicating an equal choice (between two categories), and below-chance levels (when the child chose according to an incorrect hypothesis). It was not until the later ages that the chance responses become above-chance and the below-chance responses became chance responses. In the age transition, the relative positions remained the same.

The enactment data indicate that the difficulty experienced by the sub-jects was not due to lack of knowledge of the constituents themselves (their lexical meaning), but was due instead to the grammatical and cognitive relations between the constituents. Not even the 3-year olds had any difficulty with noun enactments in the singular or plural in ungrammatical sentences. Verb enactments were much more difficult for plurality, ostensibly because the verb and adverb were not unambiguously marked for number, although *once* was much more easily dealt with than *twice*. In fact, for the ungrammatical sentences with *twice*, performance was surprisingly poorer and became much poorer with age, at the same time that grammaticality judgments and imitation of the same sentences improved. This would indicate that the child was able to recover the number of the sentence even though the number indication of the verb was relatively ambiguous, and with some adverbs such as *twice* and *all the time* was very ambiguous. No comparable difficulty existed for the grammatical sentences, which were correctly judged at above-chance levels from the 3-year level on (except in the no-adverb condition). There is no difficulty even at age 3 in judging as grammatical such sentences as *A boy jumps once* or *Two boys jump once*.

In the imitation task, (Table 5-17) imitation of ungrammatical sentences did not follow the pattern for grammaticality judgments. With the *once* adverb, in fact, the pattern was reversed with the plural more difficult than the singular; for *twice* and the other adverbs, imitation paralleled gram-maticality judgment. This suggests that although imitation reflects the operation of some of the same grammatical processes as are involved in judgments of grammaticality, it involves other processes as well. These data also reinforce the observation that imitation was not under the control of linguistic rules alone, as was indicated by the difficulty in imitating ungram-matical sentences up to the age of 7; grammatical sentences were easily imitated at a much earlier age. Overall, the ungrammatical sentences were responded to more poorly than grammatical sentences in the grammaticality judgments and imitation tasks, but not in the enactment tasks.

Discussion

For all tasks the data show that knowledge of number agreement rules was achieved in a three-stage progression. At first, there was little or no knowledge of number agreement rules. It is not clear from our data, how-ever, at which ages this occurred because the youngest subjects (age 3) showed some evidence of knowledge of number-agreement rules. The first evidence of rule behavior was seen in the alteration of the verbal constituent in making ungrammatical sentences grammatical. The number of children who exhibited this characteristic at age 3 however was small. The more probable age for achieving the number agreement rules is 4-years old. In the the second stage, characteristic of the 4- to 5-year olds, successful performance was evident to a moderate if inconsistent extent. Many sub-jects at this stage were relying on one-attribute strategies in the analysis of sentences. At about 6 or 7 full knowledge of number agreement rules was achieved. This stage is characterized by the use of the comparative objectifying strategy, by which the child is able to compare sentence constituents and correct each relative to the other. The child is also able to treat the sentence objectively, that is, respond to a sentence without altering its structure in response to a command to imitate, for example.

In the second stage, in which the child acquires number agreement rules, there is the oft-noted tendency (e.g., Brown, 1973a) to overgeneralize. The child follows the rules compulsively and egocentrically as the imitation data show. The child is incapable, in fact, of imitating ungrammatical sentences during this period, insisting on transforming ungrammatical sentences into grammatical sentences according to the rules known to him. These findings point out the fact that the tendency to overgeneralize is part of an egocentric pattern that is given up only when the object (sentence) can be treated objectively.

Not until the 6-year level is the sentence treated as an object capable of having its parts examined and manipulated as a totality. It is then that the ungrammatical sentence is accepted for what it is—and the egocentric insistence on operating strictly by a known rule is given up. The emergence of these abilities at ages 6 and 7 was also manifest in the synonymy and grammaticality judgments. The same reflective function was seen in the synonymy judgments made of active and passive sentences (Chapter 3).

In sum, the reflective function (1) enables the child to deal with sentences as independent objects, (2) allows him to treat the sentence as a totality and at the same time contrast its constituents, (3) permits consideration of two or more elements in relation to one another within the same time-frame, modifying one in relation to the other, (4) become liberated from strict adherence to a rule or rule system, and (5) no longer operate on the strategy that equivalence in sound is equivalence in meaning.

These new achievements at age 6 and 7 are not attributable to the development of linguistic capacities as such. In the case of number agreement, it is apparent from the imitation and grammaticality data that learning the agreement rules takes place between ages 3 and 5, even if the rules are not applied consistently and ungrammatical sentences give the child trouble to at least the age of 6 and 7. These developments are not dependent on the acquisition of the rules, themselves, but on the ability to treat the sentence as an object in a manner analogous to the way all objects are treated, particularly when the objects are symbolic representations and not physical objects as such.

Grammatical sentences were those whose subjects and predicates agreed in number. The major difficulty in processing sentence constituents as the enactment data indicate appeared to be concentrated in the verbal constituent. There was no difficulty in enacting subject nouns of either ungrammatical or grammatical sentences. The difficulty of the verbal element was complicated by the fact that the rules for irregular verbs such as *be* (is, are) are learned later by children than those for regular verbs.

Nevertheless, the judgment of grammaticality was possible in spite of difficulty in dealing with the verbal element itself. The judgment of agreement based as it is on a relationship between noun and verbal elements appears to be, in part, independent of complete knowledge of the individual components. Although the child has difficulty with the verbal element, he nevertheless knows from a very early age (3 years old) that it is the dominant element to be altered in order to achieve agreement with the subject. These data then contradict those of Keeney and Wolf and are consistent with the data of Shanon and Huff. There was no developmental change in respect to this emphasis, except that the effect became more pronounced with age and the slight effect for other constituents to play a role dropped out. The role of the adverb in the sentence was to modify the verb; changes in the adverb always accompanied changes in the verb.

Our conclusion is that in order to apply the number agreement rules (i.e., the inverse inflection rules: if the noun has a plural inflection [/z/ or /s/], the verb is uninflected [no /z/ or /s/] and vice versa) two sets of facts (variation in the inflection of the noun and variation in the inflection of the verb) have to be placed in an inverse functional relation. To accomplish this requires the type of ability involved in operational thought, in which some form of logical multiplication must occur with the potential for logical reversibility and objectification. It is this capacity that becomes evident only at about 6- to 7-years old. To process grammatical sentences appears to require only single, one-way mappings when the need for analysis of both constituents in a two-way relation is not critical.

6

Connectives: Logical, Linguistic, and Psychological Theory

Harry Beilin and Barbara Lust

We now review the logical and linguistic theory of the connective, as well as the literature of its empirical study, as an introduction to an extensive developmental investigation that we report in Chapters 7 and 8. This analysis is designed to schematize the basic relations between cognitive, logical, and linguistic features of connectives, as these relations provided the rationale for the research.

Several theories propose that "logical form" defines the semantic base of language (Bierwisch, 1970; Keenan, 1972; G. Lakoff, 1970a; McCawley, 1968a, 1968b, 1971a, 1971b; Postal, 1971). The semantic base is proposed in some theories to replace syntactic deep structure, although the extent to which such generative semanticist theories represent a real difference from standard generative transformational theory is argued by Chomsky (1972) and J. J. Katz (1971). Standard transformational theory has also been interpreted to integrate with logical form J. J. (Katz, 1971).

The semantic base, at least in some of these views, is characterized very generally by the operations of symbolic logic. This point is significant because it suggests an approach to studying language–thought relations. If deep structure were indeed logically formed, it could provide the basis for formalizing the relations between language and cognition. The link with cognition could be made explicit in light of the parallel view that logical form defines many aspects of cognition. The latter view has been proposed, elaborated, and tested over a long period of time by Piaget. He comments in *Problème de Psycholinguistique* (Piaget, 1963a) that the nature of the relation between language and thought will be better defined when enough common points can be established between algebraic, logistic, and linguistic analysis of the mechanisms of thought. Some features of both generative semantic and generative transformational theory appear to provide the necessary linguistic development along these lines.

In a number of recent psycholinguistic investigations, much is made of the relevance of cognition to language (e.g., Bloom, 1970; Bloom, Hood & Lightbown, 1974; Slobin, 1971), but a definition of the *form* of cognition that has a bearing on the linguistic system is lacking in these discussions. Accordingly, theoretical and empirical specification of precise points of intersection between the linguistic system (formally described) and the cognitive system is also lacking; specification of aspects of a formal definition of language that are psychologically significant is itself lacking. Earlier psycholinguistic attempts to establish the psychological reality of linguistic structure by relating transformational histories to cognitive processes has been seriously questioned (as discussed in Chapters 2 and 3) on both theoretical and empirical grounds.

The view that the operations of logic are represented in certain linguistic operations long antedates current theories of logical form as basic to the grammar. Although little of this older view is preserved in contemporary discussions of the philosophy of language, one aspect is. The linguistic connectives, also termed *logical connectives—and, or, not,* are generally considered by logicians to map onto the logical operations $(\cdot)$, $(\vee)$, $(-)$ (Churchman, 1940; Copi, 1968; Quine, 1966). These operations denote statement *conjunction, disjunction,* and *negation* in a propositional calculus (Copi, 1968), and *set intersection, set union,* and *set complementation* in Boolean algebra (Barbut, 1967). An exact one-to-one mapping of these linguistic connectives (*and, or, not*) onto the logical system is denied by some logicians, linguists, and psychologists (Johnson-Laird, 1969; Staal, 1966; Strawson, 1952). However, the recent linguistic proposal that connectives are elements of the semantic base and are abstractly and systematically related to syntactic structures appears to improve the more general proposal of a mapping of connectives onto logical operations.

The hypothesized logic–language relation of the connectives remains, then, a fundamental though contested feature of modern logical theory (Quine, 1966) as well as an issue in linguistic theory. In light of the theoretical void in research on the relation between language and cognition, the connectives thus offer an ideal vehicle for an experimental analysis that may articulate logical, linguistic, and cognitive theory. For these reasons the study reported in Chapters 7 and 8 is concerned with the logical connectives.

The intent of the study was to investigate the empirical or psychological relations between the cognitive operations that underlie set union, intersection, complementation, and the comprehension of the theoretically correlated language connectives (*and, or, not*). A basic hypothesis of the study was that the capacity to deal with linguistic connectives develops concomitantly with the child's logical capacities, which are basically independent of language.

The study made the assumption that the linguistic properties of the connectives are defined by a grammar that provides the formal means for their analysis. Such formal description was considered necessary for the controlled manipulation of linguistic form in the experimental context which tests comprehension of the connectives.

Another assumption was that evaluation of the logical features of linguistic connectives does not deny the possible alogical or colloquial language use of these forms (Strawson, 1952), nor the possible qualifying effects of context upon their function (Grice, cited in J. J. Katz, 1972; Naess, 1972).

To provide an adequate basis for interpreting the data to be reported, we will review logical theories of the connective, psychological theories of the connective with particular emphasis on Piaget's theory, linguistic theories of the connective, and psycholinguistic studies of the connective.

Logical Theories of the Connective

The Connective in Logic

According to symbolic logic, connectives such as *and* and *or* (generally abbreviated as the conjunction and disjunction operators [·] and [∨] respectively) form compound statements out of simple statements. In line with the assumptions of a classical bivalent (2-value) logic, each simple statement is either true or false.[1] The truth value of the compound is "completely determined by the truth value of [its] components [Copi, 1968, p. 214]." By convention these are referred to as "truth-functional" compound statements. Given any two component simple statements, e.g., statement p and statement q, linked by a logical connective, there are, only four possible combinations to represent their truth and falsity: (1) p is true and q is true, (2) p is true and q is false, and (3) p is false and q is true, (4) p is false and q is false. Truth tables are devices used to detail such possibilities.

Each logical connective can be defined in terms of the four truth relations. Conjunction ($p·q$) of two simple statements is defined in the following truth table according to the four possible combinations of their truth and falsity:

p	q	$p·q$
T	T	T
T	F	F
F	T	F
F	F	F

[1] These definitions are provided here in the context of a two-value logic because most of Piaget's analyses concerning cognition are represented in these terms (see Piaget, 1967). Modern logical theory, however, includes modal logics (concerned with possibility and necessity) which are not two-valued. There is some work on the connectives within these theories of modal logic (e.g., Von Wright, 1966).

The set of possible truth-value combinations for true (T) and false (F) simple statements are in the left column; the right column describes the logical meaning of the connective in terms of these truth-value combinations. The conjunction thus is true if both of its conjuncts are true, but false otherwise.

Disjunction ($p \lor q$) is defined as follows:

p	q		$p \lor q$
T	T		T
T	F		T
F	T		T
F	F		F

Disjunction is true if *either* of the component statements (disjuncts), *or both*, is true. Only if both disjuncts are false is disjunction false. (The ambiguity in interpreting the disjunction connective will be discussed subsequently.)

Negation ($\bar{p}$) acts on a single statement to reverse its truth value.

p		$\bar{p}$
T		F
F		T

The negation of a true statement is false, and the negation of a false statement is true.

Truth functional compounds formed by logical connectives are formal constructions. Statements thus created are often considered "logical truths," and the entailments of such statements are often considered to be "analytic" [see Prior (1967) and Staal (1966) for discussion on this point].[2] Although Quine (1961) does not accept the analytic-syntactic distinction that has been so much a part of logical discourse since Kant, he does hold the connectives to be logical and the truth-functional statements that embody them to be "logical truths" [Quine, 1966]. In general, the connectives represent operations basic to rules of logical deduction.

By virtue of their logical character, the connectives ($\cdot$) ($\lor$) ($-$) have systematic relations with one another. Quine (1966, p. 24) holds that all truth-functional statement compositions can be paraphrased completely by conjunction and denial. (Thus [$\lor$] or disjunction could be interpreted as a derivative.) Within a logical system as well, a duality between conjunction and disjunction is noted (Quine, 1966, p. 53). Denial of conjunction leads to disjunction of negated terms; denial of disjunction leads to conjunction of negated terms.

---

[2] To oversimplify, analytic is used in the general sense of referring to the meaning of a statement as determined by the logical form of the statement. The truth of a synthetic statement is determined by reference beyond the logical form of the expression, i.e., by reference to the natural world.

The Logic of Natural Language Connectives

The logical nature of natural language connectives is questioned by modern logicians, particularly Strawson (1952). Strawson's (1952, p. 81) argument is that in ordinary writing and speech the connectives do not contribute to the truth conditions of sentences in the simple way they are pictured in truth tables. With connectives such as *and,* assertions that are considered true are not strung together at random; they are conjoined in a way that may confer upon them extralogical features at variance with the rules for ($\cdot$). One such feature conveyed by discourse is temporal order. In natural discourse, for example, when A and B represent separate propositions, it is often the case that $A \cdot B \neq B \cdot A$. It follows that *and* in natural language may be considered to have two meanings (Staal, 1968) (1) *and$_1$* is equivalent to the logical connective, i.e., there may be symmetrical equivalence between statements (A *and$_1$* $B \equiv B$ *and$_1$* A) (2) *and$_2$* designates the condition in which symmetry does not exist (A *and$_2$* $B \neq B$ *and$_2$* A). (For example, *She took arsenic and fell ill $\neq$ She fell ill and took arsenic.*) *And$_2$* according to Staal has the meaning of "and subsequently"or "and in consequence."   Chomsky (1965, p. 224 fn.), citing Grice, considers that the temporal order implied in *and* may be a feature of discourse and not part of the meaning of *and* (cf. Johnson–Laird [1969] for comments on temporal order in conjunction). Another alogical component of conjunctive meaning in language relates to iteration. Ziff (1972, p. 45) notes that *George ate: he ate and he ate and he ate and he ate* conveys the information that George ate a great deal, which the formal representation of this statement does not (formally $p \cdot p \cdot p \cdot p \cdot p \equiv p$).

Similar problems are found with the connective *or.* In natural language the truth of one disjunct may not be a sufficient condition for truth of a disjunction as it is in the truth table. With *Either we catch this bus or we shall have to walk all the way home,* if it turned out that the bus we caught was not the last one, we would say the man who made the statement had been wrong (Strawson, 1952, p. 90). Another problem is that the meaning of a disjunctive proposition may not convey the full meaning that may be given by the statement in context—a point made by Grice in his "theory of conversational implicature [J. J. Katz, 1972, p. 446]." The effect of discourse upon meaning is a broad issue that goes beyond that of disjunction and its ambiguities. There is, however, another issue of a logical nature concerning disjunction. This issue appears also in the natural language use of disjunction. It concerns the two types of disjunction readings characterized as inclusive and exclusive.

INCLUSIVE AND EXCLUSIVE DISJUNCTION

The description of disjunction given earlier was of inclusive disjunction (in this reading, *one or both of the disjuncts is true*). Although disjunction is often defined inclusively in logic (as in Boolean logic), another reading is possible (usually denoted as exclusive disjunction). In this case, disjunction means *either one of the disjuncts is true, but not both* (Copi, 1968).[3]

The natural language expression of disjunction *or* confounds the two meanings (Geis & Zwicky, 1971, p. 563), although the inclusive interpretation of *or* is considered by some to be the more common reading (Quine, 1966, p. 14). Moravcsik, on the other hand, who has studied the disjunction connective in about forty languages, assumes (as does Dik, 1968; R. Lakoff, 1971) that disjunction in natural languages is of the exclusive type; or else suggests Moravcsik (1970, p. 1), they are ambiguous as to whether they are inclusive or exclusive. Langendoen[4] suggests that in language use the inclusive reading for *or* may be a mistake for *and* (*This school accepts Germans or Americans*).

In logic, then, the inclusive reading is preferred, although truth-functional notation allows either reading to be unambiguously described. On the other hand, logicians consider the natural language connective *or* to be ambiguous. Certain linguists also hold this view, although other linguists consider the exclusive interpretation to be the preferred natural language reading of *or*. The ambiguity of *or* is another example of the ostensible disparity between the logical meaning and the linguistic meaning of the connective.

In summary,[5] the relation between linguistic and logical connectives is seen in two ways. In the first, emphasis is placed on the disparities between *parallel* linguistic and logical forms. In this sense, the three words (*and, or, not*) do not represent conjunction, disjunction, and negation exactly or unambiguously (Quine, 1960, p. 50). In the second, the interrelations between the logical and linguistic connectives are considered to exist in spite of some disparities. According to Strawson (1952), the parallel between the two systems is not "a simple mistake [p. 81]," and the logical form of the conjunction ($\cdot$), for example, may be considered to be an abstraction of the meaning of *and* (p. 82).

The primary issue reduces itself, in part at least, to the following question: "Whether some or all logical truths are perhaps presupposed in human language, and belong as such to the linguistic competence of every human being . . . [Staal, 1968, p. 81]," and, more specifically, whether there exists an "implicit presence of logical truths in the semantic structure of language [p. 88]." Staal, a philosopher, proposes that the study of the relation of logical truth "to the semantic systems of natural languages and

---

[3] Exclusive disjunction is sometimes denoted as $\bar{\vee}$ or W.

[4] Personal communication.

[5] The relation of the logical connective ($-$) to its natural language counterpart (not) will not be specifically addressed here. This connective reflects similar problems and issues, although there are a number of issues that are particular to negation. These are discussed in a series of papers in *Logique et Analyse* (1972, **57-58**). One relevant point made here is that there are two types of negation. One determines the exclusion of an affirmation, e.g., the exclusion of A given $\bar{A}$. The other determines the affirmation of a positive alternative, that is, the selection of some positive set of a universe, which is the complement of another set, e.g., $U - A = \bar{A}$. Psychological studies of negation usually concentrate on the latter form of negation, as does the study reported in the next chapter.

to possibily semantic universals could be a fruitful area of research [p. 85]." These comments articulate the fundamental assumptions of our study:

1. Logical truth is inherently related to the structure of natural language.
2. Analysis of the acquisition of language and logical truth is critical to the analysis of their relation.

A further assumption, which the Piagetian position makes explicit, appears implicit in Staal's statement, that logical truth itself has properties that are isomorphic with the structures and functions of cognition.

The view represented in the present study holds that logic and language are nonidentical. Although a relation is proposed to exist between language and logic, it is viewed as a complex relation based, in part, on the notion that logic has its origin in cognition and is not dependent upon language for its source. In turn, the logical character of some aspects of language has a relation to the logic of cognition but the relation is not that of identity. It is more likely to involve the intersection of two formal systems (language and logic or cognition).

Propositional and Class (Set) Logic for Connectives

Propositional and class logics represent two analogous ways of formalizing logical relations. As they both have a bearing upon the way logic is treated in psychological theory, we will discuss the relation between these approaches to logic.

Sentential or propositional logic is formally convertible to a logic of classes described by Boolean set theory.[6] The two systems have been characterized as having "the same abstract structure [Grize, 1967; also Mays, in Piaget, 1957, p. x]."

Set intersection ($\cap$) can be translated into propositional conjunction ($\cdot$); set union ($\cup$) into propositional disjunction ($\vee$); and set complementation ($\sim$) into propositional negation ($-$). (See Appendix D, Table 1 for definition of these operations). These translations to set theory follow upon the premise expressed by Boole (1958, p. 7) that logic deals with relations among things as well as relations among propositions as expressions of fact.

Disjunction and conjunction have particular relations with one another. Likewise in Boolean algebra the complement of intersection is union ($\overline{A \cap B} \equiv (\overline{A} \cup \overline{B})$) and the complement of union is intersection ($\overline{A \cup B} \equiv \overline{A} \cap \overline{B}$). These constitute the logical *laws of de Morgan*. The linguistic connectives then also map onto Boolean operations (Barbut, 1967). *And* is thus described by set intersection ($\cap$) as well as by propositional conjunction ($\cdot$), *or* by set union ($\cup$) as well as by disjunction ($\vee$), and negation by set complementation ($\sim$) as well as by negation ($-$).

[6] Set and class are used interchangeably here, although in some philosophic contexts the mathematical notion of set is differentiated from that of class; generally, however, the terms may be considered as equivalent (Mays, in Piaget, 1957, p. xi).

Boole (1958, p. 1) maintained that the operations of set theory characterize the fundamental laws of the operation of mind in the process of reasoning, with the caveat that "of course the laws must in both cases be determined independently; any formal agreement between them can only be established *a posteriori* by actual comparison [p. 6]." Boole's thesis was not greeted with general acceptance among philosophers although there has been a recent revival of interest in this view by generative semanticists (such as McCawley) and by psychologists (Grize, 1967; Hunt, Marin, & Stone, 1966; Piaget, 1957).[7]

Truth-Table Readings

If truth-function tables are used in defining the meaning of connectives, there are two possible interpretations that can be given to reading these tables. Different readings, as Reichenbach (1947) notes, yield different interpretations of connective meaning. For the *connective interpretation*, the truth table is read from "right to left." That is, read from the compound statement to the elementary propositions. In this interpretation, if the compound statement is true, one of its **T cases** is true. (A T case as reviewed above is any combination of elementary propositions to which a T is given according to the truth table for that particular compound.) For example, if (inclusive disjunction $A \lor B$) is true, then it is true that (1) *A is true and B is true* (line one of the truth table); (2) *A is true and B is false* (line two); or (3) *A is false and B is true* (line three). The compound statement establishes a *connection* between these T cases (if one T case does not occur, it is understood that another of the T cases will). In the example cited, an observed occurrence of one T case (*A is true and B is true*) can only confirm the compound statement $(A \lor B)$; it cannot totally verify it.

In the *adjunctive interpretation*, the truth table is read from "left to right," i.e., from the elementary proposition to the compound statement.[8] By this reading, if one of the T cases is true, the corresponding compound holds. In the case of $(A \lor B)$, for example, this compound is assumed to be true if only one of the T cases is found to be true. One T case then is held to verify, not merely confirm, the compound statement in this reading.

The definition of connectives, according to the adjunctive or connective interpretation, has been a matter of controversy. Reichenbach (1947) holds that the "exclusive *or*" is usually interpreted in the connective sense, *and*, in the adjunctive sense (p. 29), although there are no empirical data to decide the issue. For one, the connective reading is the formal reading of

---

[7] Piaget's conception of the "laws of thought" is broader than Boole's. Piaget's conception encompasses two kinds of knowledge: scientific and logicodeductive with formal relations between the two (Beth & Piaget, 1966; Piaget, 1957, p, 2).

[8] The *adjunctive interpretation*, to be more precise, is that "the truth tables are read in both directions," i.e., left to right *and* right to left (Reichenbach, 1947, p. 28). The manner in which it is presented above, however, suffices to indicate the difference between connective and adjunctive interpretations.

the truth table, based not on empirical observation but on "the structure of the formula [p. 40]." The adjunctive interpretation is considered by Reichenbach to be a "simplified concept [p. 30]."

The distinction between these interpretations needs to be borne in mind in the application of truth tables to empirical data because the significance of results may differ according to the interpretation applied.

We will now consider in greater detail Piaget's theory of logical development as it is concerned with the logical structure of thought and the cognitive origins of logic.

Cognition and Logic

Piaget's Theory

The operations of Boolean algebra and the propositional truth functions they underlie are descriptive of the structure of cognition in Piagetian theory. As Piaget states, "Formal logic, or logistics, is simply the axiomatics of states of equilibrium of thought, and the positive science corresponding to this axiomatics is none other than the psychology of thought [Piaget, 1950, p. 3]." Piaget (1957), however, distinguishes two types of logic, one formal, "the science of truth conditions," the other an "operational algebra with its procedures of calculation, its structures, etc." Although the two logics are correlative, it is the latter that is necessary "to disengage the logical structure of pyschological or mental 'facts' [p. 23]." Inhelder and Piaget (1964) emphasize that it is not the former logic (formal logic), but the latter calculus or algebra (symbolic logic) that they use in their analysis of psychological data.

Piaget's developmental analysis is designed to show that the formal "axiomatics" is behaviorally related, i.e., it characterizes actions and sets of actions and is, therefore, grounded in the "operational algebra." The formal aspects of logic, that is, the system coherence resulting in the truth-functional laws of deduction have developmental origins and therefore have psychological relevance.

Piaget's developmental thesis holds that "analytic coordinations derive genetically from synthetic coordinations [Apostel, Mays, Morf, & Piaget, 1957, p. 141]." Piaget (1957) declares, "The logic of classes is to be [logically] deduced from that of propositions, whilst from the genetic point of view propositional operations are derived from the logic of classes and relations [p. 24]." The significance of this stand is indicated by Grize (1967) who states that "to uphold as we do, the priority of the logic of classes over that of propositions is to refer to experience and to admit thus its value for logic [p. 145]." To admit the role of experience in the foundation of logical operations is, in turn, to posit the primacy of synthetic over analytic relations in the origin of knowledge. (Although in logical theory, "analytic" usually refers to statements, Apostel and Piaget use the term to characterize thought.)

The origins of analytic and synthetic relations are in the "operations" that describe the internalized and formal dimensions of the child's actions. Operations, usually referred to as logical operations, develop gradually from actions upon or transformations of reality. The operations that have a relationship to one another become organized into systems or *groups*. These groups have mathematical and logical parameters. Operations thus come to be defined by "reversible compositions and by the constitution of *structures d'ensemble* (structured wholes) that imply both invariants and a closed system of transformations [Piaget, 1968a, p. 202]." These attained cognitive structures define the stage of development in the child's thought as well as the logical power of that thought. The structures thus have psychological reality even though they are described by symbolic logic.

The more advanced structures of formal or propositional thought that are found only in older children and adults are characterized by the integration into a single system of the dual structures of a (complete) *lattice* and of a *group* (the mathematical four-group of Klein). Given a set of n bivalent elements (such as either physical objects or propositions), for example, the *lattice* represents the complete set of all possible combinations of these elements. Boolean algebra, which in contemporary mathematical treatment is subsumed under lattice theory (Mays, in Piaget, 1957, p. ix), takes as given the complete set of associations of bivalent propositions (isomorphic to those of the truth table—*TT, TF, FT, FF*, or AB, $\overline{A}B$, $A\overline{B}$, $\overline{AB}$) and generates the complete set of possible combinations by taking these $n \times n$. That is, it generates a complete set of 16 propositional operations. This set of operations is said to have a lattice structure in that (a) the set is partially ordered by the relation of inclusion, and (b) every subset of two elements has a greatest lower bound (that is, the greatest element included in both elements—called a "meet") and a least upper bound (that is, the smallest element that includes both elements—called a "join" by Piaget) [Mays, in Piaget, 1957].

The *group* represents a set of four transformations that can be defined on the lattice. The INRC group, as Piaget defines it, consists of the transformations that relate the members of the set of propositional associations to each other. Every propositional operation is said to have an inverse (N), $p \vee q/\overline{p}\cdot\overline{q}$, a reciprocal (R), $p \vee q \rightarrow \overline{p} \vee \overline{q}$, a correlate (C), $p \cdot q \rightarrow p \vee q$, and an identity operator (I), ± 0. These transformations have a systematic relationship to one another and are associative. Their interrelationships provide the internal coherence necessary to a formal deductive logic. The fact that these formal cognitive structures are attained only in adolescence suggests a long history of development of "more or less continuous transformations [Piaget, 1970, p. 34]."[9]

---

[9] The "continuity" indicated here is not to be underestimated although many who write about Piagetian theory do so. Piaget (1970) writes, "One never observes absolute commencements (discontinuities) in development and that which is new proceeds either from progressive differentiation or from gradual coordinations or from the two at once . . . [p. 34]."

Development of Logical Operations

The theoretical characterization of logic (cognitive) structure is confirmed in Piaget and Inhelder's extensive studies of the development of the child's thought. The articulation of the logical mathematical model with empirical data yields a theory of qualitatively differentiated stages in the development of logicomathematical thought.

The character of these stages will be briefly outlined (based on Piaget, 1970); these stages will be reinterpreted in terms of the specific logical operations relevant to the study reported in Chapters 7 and 8. The following characterization selectively focuses on the development of the truth-functional aspects of cognition; it does not detail the total range of cognitive functions and structures that develop during this era.

SENSORIMOTOR LEVEL (BIRTH—$1\frac{1}{2}$ TO 2-YEARS OLD)

Logicality as such results from the establishment of systematic coherence among actions. However, at the sensorimotor level there is no attempt at first to coordinate two or more actions among themselves. Subject and object are not clearly differentiated and the subject himself is not concerned with the "extension" of action schemes, as he is unable to evoke situations he does not actually perceive. The assimilation of schemes takes into account to some extent the properties of objects, "intension," but only at the moment they are perceived or by direct analogy with properties of an immediately prior situation. Certain formal parameters of action are, however, notable at this stage: recursion, reiteration, order, hierarchical inclusion (Piaget, 1970; H. Sinclair, 1971b).

PREOPERATIONAL LEVEL 1 (APPROXIMATELY $1\frac{1}{2}$ TO 4-YEARS OLD): PREFUNCTIONAL

This stage involves the attainment of language and other symbolic instruments as well as the attainment of initial cognitive invariance (i.e., object permanence). It is marked by the first clear differentiation between subject and object. Action becomes capable of being "interiorized" (and thus conceptualized, in a sense), and successive actions can be condensed or systematized in quasisimultaneous "totalities." The subject of an action (or its object) can be thought of with its durable properties (predicates or relations), and action itself can be conceptualized as a transformation between given or analogous terms. As a result, elementary inference becomes possible. Inference, however, is still closely related to immediate perceptions. For example, given some *round red* and *blue beads* (the *blue beads* are both *round* and *square*), the child at this level may identify two classes of the same extension (*All the round beads are red*), but he may refuse to admit that all the squares are *blue* because there are also *blues* that are round. The child still does not have the deductive apparatus permitting the regulation of part—whole relations, with the use of such terms as *all* and *some* (Piaget [1970] speaks of this stage as *preconceptual*). Thus, Piaget says, the child is often deceived by "the false absolutes inherent in purely predicative attributions [p. 25]." The object remains "halfway between the individual and the class. . . [p. 27]."

Logical predication and a limited concept of extension are the essential components of this stage. Establishment of the truth value of a statement or proposition (even a nonhypothetical proposition) does not occur at this stage as predication *per se* cannot be described as either true or false. Truth values may pertain to a given object, that is, truth or falsity may be related to the affirmation that an object satisfies the predicate (Grize, 1967, p. 149).

PREOPERATIONAL LEVEL 2 (APPROXIMATELY 4+ TO 6-YEARS OLD): CONSTITUENT FUNCTIONS

Internal coordination at this level is no longer simply between actions as in the prior level, but between "conceptualized actions." The semilogical elaboration of a cognitive "function" results. The "function" reflects the dependence between the variations of two terms that embody relational properties of objects. It is implied that the "terms" and "properties" of objects have cognitive "existence." That is, they are representations independent of actions per se. Action engenders the notion of property by way of predication, and a "function" results from the relation between two or more properties.

Development allows further dissociation of the individual object from the class. With sufficient advance in the recognition of logical *extension*, children in classification tasks now form "nonfigural" collections. Through trial and error the child is able to adjust his activity by taking account of feedback from previous actions. The child's thought at this level is "regulated" by this feedback; this differs from the internal control of *logical necessity* that appears in the following stage. Verification through feedback, as opposed to verification by deduction, is one example of the point made by Apostel *et al.* (1957) that early action coordination has a logico-mathematical character, but is synthetic rather than analytic.

The constituent functions of this stage are typically one-way mappings of relations, in addition to being ordinal and qualitative. That is, logical deduction is constrained by the fact that a relation is conceived as operating in one direction and cannot be reversed (A → B and not A ⇐ B). Piaget (1972) stresses that the logic of the constituent functions is a semilogic, in the precise sense of the term, i.e., there is a one-way operation but no inverse operation except for exceptional cases.[10]

---

[10] The Piagetian characterization of the level of constituent functions is less well-known in the English literature, and recent reports of it such as in the *Etude d' épistémologie Génétique* 1968, XXIII, exist only in French. A review of reports in this *Etude* by Piaget and by Grize on the notion of constituent functions is given in Appendix D—the notion is important for the analysis of the data to be reported.

CONCRETE OPERATIONS: LEVEL 1 (APPROXIMATELY 6+ TO 8-YEARS OLD)

The first structures that show system coherence, sufficient to allow certain logical, deductive operations, appear according to Piaget's data at about 7 years of age. The logicality of this structure derives primarily from the synchronization of a direct and an inverse operation (thus also generating an identity operation $\pm A = 0$). This integration results in the ability to reverse the compositions and decompositions of objects or elements and provides the child with the first intuitions of logical necessity. In respect to logical thought, this structure yields a limited class calculus. The invariances that are associated with conservation also are achieved at this time and provide the closure necessary for the logical system.

The trial and error (retroaction) of the prior stage becomes fused at this level with *anticipation*. Anticipation follows from the logical necessity that results from closure of a logical structure and from the attainment of the logical operations of this level. As already indicated, operations are attained when, through closure, interiorized actions become reversible transformations.

The logical structure of this stage, which results from the consolidation of the achievements of prior stages with new ones, is not the full *group* or *lattice* structure which characterizes the formal propositional logical system. Rather, this stage is characterized by a semilattice (i.e., the "meet' between classes of the same rank are all null, $A \times A = 0$, due to the fact that those concrete operations work on disjoint classes) and by a structured set of transformations (from the systematization of direct, inverse, and identity operations) that is termed a **groupement** (grouping). This groupement lacks the power of a group (INRC) because its power of associativity is limited by tautology $(A + A = A)$. (Thus, $A + [\overline{A} + \overline{B}] = [A + \overline{A}] + \overline{B}$, but $A + [A - A] \neq [A + A] - A$.) Nevertheless, the groupement does accomplish certain deductive functions. It works contiguously from class to class within the semilattice structure providing mainly successive class inclusions and partial complementations. Thus, for example, the complement of each class is formulated in relation to the class immediately above it $(A' = B - A, B' = C - B$, etc.) and inclusions are of an $A \supset B$ nature (in which $A + A' = B)$.

Within these constraints, the concrete operations provide class union (including class inclusion) and class complementation operations. Moreover, class intersection operations, which utilize two dimensions to achieve multiplicative relations and matrix classifications, are possible. In other words, for two events or properties, a and b, the child has a method of grouping which provides the elementary associations of the double-entry table, $ab, \bar{a}b, a\bar{b}, \bar{a}\bar{b}$. Inhelder and Piaget (1958) hold that this "most general concrete" grouping is "more general than the others in the sense that it contains them or they derive from it by successive specifications [p. 289]." A thorough analysis of the class calculus is found in Piaget and Inhelder (1967).

CONCRETE OPERATIONS LEVEL 2: (APPROXIMATELY 8- TO 10-YEARS OLD)

This stage is described as representing a "general equilibrium of concrete operations [Piaget, 1970, p. 46]." The operations described for the prior stage attain maximum extension and utility through generalization and equilibrium. For one, they are more spontaneously generated (as opposed to being induced by external events), and certain features of concrete logical thought (quantification of inclusion, intersection of nondisjoint classes (Piaget, 1970), certain aspects of complementation, as well as the generalized classification activity termed **vicariance** [Piaget & Inhelder, 1967]) became apparent at this stage. Vicariance is an operation of substitution—for a classification such as $A_1 + \bar{A}_1 = B$, another class A_2 can be substituted for class A_1; its complement $\bar{A}_2$ for A_1, resulting in $A_1 + \bar{A}_1 = \bar{A}_2 + A_2$, in which $A_2 \subset \bar{A}_1$ and $A_1 \subset \bar{A}_2$ (e.g., the French and the non-French = the Chinese and the non-Chinese [Piaget, 1957, p. 31]).

FORMAL OPERATIONS (APPROXIMATELY 11- TO 12-YEARS OLD)

This stage marks the attainment of complete lattice and group structures in logical thought. It is the stage in which the capacity for logical deduction is attained.

The essential change from the concrete class calculus is that the four basic associations formulated by the class calculus (the primitive units of the truth table) now themselves become elements or terms which are combined $n \times n$ to produce the 16 binary propositions of a two-valued propositional logic. Each association (AB, $\bar{A}B$, $A\bar{B}$, $\bar{A}\bar{B}$) can now be considered specifically in terms of its truth value independently of its content, and each association can be related systematically to the others. A "combinatorial" power that was lacking previously now appears. The generalized classification activity of vicariance now applied to product sets, resulting from the multiplication operation of the class calculus, yields a new structural integration that permits logical activity of much greater scope than could be achieved by the operations independently. The result is a qualitative difference in deductive thought, which no longer works from the "actual to the theoretical" but starts from "theory" to establish or verify the actual relations between things (Piaget, 1957). It proceeds, thus, from the possible to the actual and is primarily concerned with propositions (statements that have truth value) or hypotheses rather than with concrete references *per se* (Piaget, 1970).

Propositional Thought

The foregoing indicates the long developmental history that is necessary for the psychological achievement of the full structure of propositional logic and the deductive rigor involved in that logic. Two points regarding this development must be stressed:

1. "The essential characteristic of propositional logic is not that it is a verbal logic. First and foremost, it is a logic of all possible combinations whether those combinations arise in relation to experimental problems or purely verbal questions. Of course, combinations which go beyond simple regulation of data presuppose an inner verbal support; however, the real power of propositional logic lies not in this support, but rather in the combinatorial power which makes it possible for reality to be fed into the set of possible hypotheses compatible with the data [Inhelder & Piaget, 1958, p. 253]."

2. Although the formal combinatorial structure of adolescent and adult thought entails the use of propositions, it is also true that, during the concrete stages, reasoning also involves propositions (Inhelder & Piaget, 1958, p. 292). It is possible to obtain correct reasoning about simple propositions at the 7- to 8-year old level, provided that the propositions correspond to sufficiently concrete representations. Successful use of a proposition at this level results not from the way it is linked with other propositions but from its logical content, consisting of structures of classes and relations corresponding to actual objects, and from the concrete operation of decomposing and recomposing its content [p. 292]. When the proposition deals with possibility, and its composition and decomposition involve analyzing these possibilities, then one has to deal with the truth values of the combinations rather than with the objects; the more sophisticated structures of formal thought become necessary.[11, 12]

Linguistic Theories of the Connective

Before considering some data on the psychological relation between the logical connectives and the linguistic connectives, it is necessary to examine the place of the connective within linguistic theory.

Generative Transformational Theory

The type of sentence coordination provided by the connective has received slight but significant attention in contemporary linguistic theory. Chomsky (1964; Chomsky & Miller, 1963) has argued, for example, that phrase-structure grammars are unable to provide an adequate account of true coordinate forms and that only transformational theory offers the possibility of an adequate linguistic account of sentence coordination (Chomsky & Miller, 1963, p. 299). Nevertheless, some critics feel that

[11] The Piagetian account of the acquisition of truth-functional logic is fundamentally different from that of Quine (1960) in *Word and Object*, which is based on behavioristic laws of associational learning. See Chomsky (1969) on the difficulties with this view.

[12] It should be noted that Piaget is also concerned with the logic of relations (Inhelder & Piaget, 1964) that deals principally with the logical operations of seriation. These logical operations will not be treated in this report because they bear only indirectly on the logical operations of conjunction, disjunction, and complementation.

generative transformational theory has given the conjunction less attention than it deserves (Staal, 1966).

A theoretical shift occurred in Chomsky's description of conjunction between the 1957 and 1965 versions of his theory. In 1957, the phrase-structure rules generated no compound sentences. Conjunction coordination was achieved by a "generalized transformation,"[13] as were negatives, questions, etc. Conjoined sentences with conjunctions were thus grammatically derived through transformation. In *Aspects*, Chomsky (1965) proposed that compound sentences were generated by base rules through "generalized phrase-markers." Conjunction became an aspect of the base, given in deep structure, rather than defined as derived through transformation.

The *Aspects* rule for conjunction was given "roughly" as follows:

". . . if XZY and XZ'Y are two strings such that for some category A, Z is an A and Z' is an A, then we may form the string $X \frown Z \frown and \frown Z' \frown Y$ where $Z \frown and \frown Z'$ is an A [Chomsky, 1965, p. 212, fn. 9]." Although Chomsky does not specifically deal with the connective *or*, only with *and*, the rule can be assumed to be similar for it (see Gleitman, 1969). Moreover, the conjunction rule is applicable to *n* units, not only to two.

Several additional points should be made about this rule.

1. *Sentential conjunction.* In the Chomsky grammar, the deep structure form of conjunction is sentential conjunction, relating two or more complete sentences rather than constituent categories (for example, NPs). *Phrasal* conjunction (of nouns, verbs, etc.) is achieved by derivational reduction through a transformation called "conjunction reduction."[14] *Tessie and Max felt sad*, for example, derives by conjunction reduction from *Tessie felt sad* and *Max felt sad*.

Notably, in standard logic, $F(x) \wedge F(y)$ is a well-formed expression, whereas the reduced $F(x \wedge y)$ is not (Staal, 1966). It is this particular kind of contrast that in fact has been said by logicians to differentiate logical conjunction from linguistic (natural language) conjunction (Strawson, 1952, p. 79) because the occurrence of phrasal conjunction is noted in natural language.

Dik (1968, pp. 116–130) observes that the Chomsky proposal vis-à-vis the conjunction-reduction transformation is an "originally logical principle." Others, however, are more cautious as to whether the reduction principle is truly a logical principle or a linguistic one (Staal, 1966, p. 72).

2. *On conjunction reduction.* Although linguists accept the reduction postulate as a linguistic mechanism (Gleitman, 1969; Jacobs & Rosenbaum, 1968, etc.), there is disagreement as to whether conjunction reduction

[13] Generalized transformations were said to act on two or more structures at once, whereas singulary transformations were to act on single structures.

[14] The conjunction reduction transformation is generally defined (Langendoen, 1969) as one that ". . . operates on conjoined sentences so as to delete repeated occurrences of the same constituents and to rearrange the resulting constituent structure appropriately [p. 149]."

provides an adequate explanation of all or some natural language cases (Dik, 1968; Dougherty, 1970, 1971; McCawley, 1968a; G. Lakoff & Peters, 1969; C. S. Smith, 1969). Arguments against the reduction postulate are usually based on the premise that the semantic information of the conjoined product is not equivalent to the sum of the semantic information in each of the simple conjoined sentences. Often the product form introduces ambiguity or additional meaning. Gleitman (1969, pp. 88, 100) shows, for example, that *John and Mary carried baskets* can be related to several sets of base sentences: *John was carrying a basket and Mary was carrying a basket* and *John was carrying baskets and Mary was carrying baskets*.

Because the study to be reported was concerned with the linguistic correlates of logical conjunction, it was particularly addressed to sentential conjunction and took as valid the grammatical reduction rule in the expression of this conjunction, even though it is evident that within linguistic theory the reduction rule has some unresolved difficulties. Sentential forms of conjunction and disjunction, which were considered to be linguistically equivalent to the logical forms (to the logical form $F[x] \wedge F[y]$ rather than the form $F[x \wedge y]$), were utilized. The Stockwell *et al.* 1973 grammar, which embodies the reduction transformation, was used in preference to theories of phrasal conjunction as the basic descriptive instrument for the linguistic expression of conjunction.

Before proceeding to a description of the Stockwell grammar for conjunction, it would be instructive to consider recent developments in generative semantic theory in respect to some of the linguistic issues we have just discussed.

Generative Semantics

The Lakoff–McCawley–Postal theories of generative semantics imply that the formation rules of conjunction in symbolic logic would correspond to the basic rules governing the manner in which linguistic categories are conjoined. Neither McCawley nor Lakoff, however, explicitly discuss the implications for a theory of conjunction which follow from their proposals, although they do provide data which ostensibly deny the validity of the reduction hypothesis as well as the notion of sentential conjunction that resides in the base of the grammar. Both authors, however, assert the existence of logical parameters of conjunction in language that would permit or assume sentential conjunction in the base. The logical parameters of linguistic conjunction are seen in McCawley's (1968a) formalization of the "respectively transformation."

According to McCawley, Postal points out that the McCawley (1968a) description of the respectively transformation subsumes "much of what has been regarded as a syntactic transformation of conjunction [p. 166]." The significance of Postal's observation and McCawley's agreement with it is that conjunction reduction is no longer considered a purely syntactic transformation in which the transformation is defined as mapping from one phrase marker to another phrase marker, in the Chomskyan sense, but an operation performed directly on logical form. Chomsky considers this proposal as simply a notational variation on the standard theory (Chomsky, 1971, p. 193).

An Integrated Theory of Conjunction: Stockwell

The Stockwell, Schachter, and Partee (1968, 1973) characterization of a grammar for coordinating conjunction (and disjunction) is unique as a systematic attempt to describe natural language conjunction. Stockwell *et al.* address the issue of whether there is a deep structure relationship between sentential conjunction and other conjoined structures, i.e., to the question of conjunction reduction. They hold that derived conjunction rather than phrasal conjunction underlies the conjunction of nonsentences, and that a single process defines all derived conjunction. Thus they hold sentential conjunction to be the basic type. Their description of conjunc-tion reduction or "derived conjunction" involves both "structure building" and reduction (i.e., deletion).

The operation of conjunction derivation is said to depend on *schemata*. Schemata differ from ordinary transformation rules in two ways: (1) by their "structure building powers" as in conjunction, for example, they "not only add new nodes but build whole new trees to replace old ones"; (2) they involve variables in the structure indices of structures upon which they perform, thus "abbreviating in one statement a large (possibly infinite) number of transformation rules [Stockwell *et al.*, 1968, p. 25]."

In the conjunction derivation two schemata are critical, "a derived conjunction schema," and a "node relabeling schema." The second is obligatory when the first has been optionally applied. Other rules and schemata, then, apply to yield the finally derived form.

1. *Derived conjunction schema.* This device provides for the insertion, over a set of conjoined single-constituents, of a node of the same type as the individual members of the set (Stockwell *et al.*, 1968, p. 537). In the derivation of (a) from (b), (a) *John and Mary sang* and (b) *John sang and Mary sang*, a new NP node has been inserted over *John and Mary*.

2. *A node relabeling* schema is then applied to this structure converting it to:

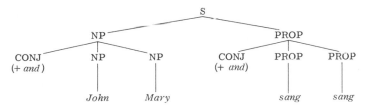

3. An *identical-conjunct* collapsing schema is then applied acting (in

the example above) on the PROP set of totally identical conjuncts to replace it with a single member of the set, yielding:

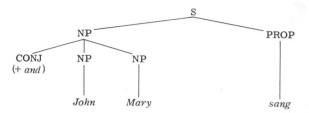

4. A *set marking* operation then applies to the constructed NP node establishing the node feature of plural number; this would be apparent in surface structure if it were necessary, for example, to mark plural agreement of the verb as in converting *John sings and Mary sings* to *John and Mary sing*.

5. An optional quantifier *"both" insertion schema* may apply:

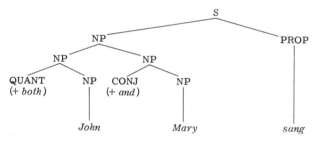

The same basic schemata are generally applicable to the disjunction *or*, with some substitutions and alterations (Stockwell *et al.*, 1968, p. 398).

The complete set of rules and schema applicable to conjunctions (Stockwell *et al.*, 1968, p. 355) are the following: they are arranged in order of application; the rules that have been used in the design of the sentences in the study to be reported subsequently are *italicized*; those applicable to both conjunction *and* and disjunction *or* sentences are indicated by an asterisk—(a) *derived conjunction,** (b) *node relabeling,** (c) *identical-conjunct collapsing,** (d) *set marking,** (e) *conjunction spreading*, (f) "respectively" insertion, (g) plural collapsing, (h) "respectively" → "respective" and "respectively" deletion, (i) "both" *insertion*, (j) "either" *insertion,** (k) "all" insertion, (l) "each" insertion, (m) quantifier movement, (n) *initial conjunction deletion,** (o) medial conjunction deletion.

In sum, the Stockwell *et al.* grammar of derived conjunction provides for the building of new linguistic structures resulting from the fusion of two or more conjoined (or disjoined) sentences. The resulting sentence reflects the application of schemata for segmentation and set organization of like constituents to achieve appropriate phrasal conjunctions; it also reflects the use of appropriate collapsing and deletion processes for redundant elements and the introduction of appropriate features (e.g., + *plural*) on newly created nodes.

The Stockwell *et al.* proposal for negation regards the question of the deep structure position of the negative to be open (Stockwell *et al.*, 1968, p. 290), and the relation of negation to the *and* and *or* conjunctions to contain many unexplored problems (Stockwell *et al.*, 1968, p. 269). In the study to be reported subsequently, we have used negation of a nominal in one or both conjuncts of a conjoined sentence (e.g., *the dolls which are not girls*).[15] Although we assume the basic specification of negation to exist at a deep structure level of the grammar, it is recognized that the exact facts of this description are unclear.

Linguistic Conjunction and Disjunction in the Present Study

Three types of linguistic conjunction (*and*) and disjunction (*or*) sentences were considered for this study. They are exemplified by the following: (1) *Give me the dolls which are boys* **and** *give me the dolls which are girls* (2) *Give me the dolls which are boys* **and** *the dolls which are girls* (3) *Give me* **both** *the dolls which are boys* **and** *the dolls which are girls*. The three linguistic forms represented by these sentences are (1) non-derived conjoined sentence form, (2) a derived conjunction form (wherein appropriate obligatory devices of node relabeling, identical conjunct collapsing, etc. can be assumed to have applied in addition to the primary conjunction derivation schema), and (3) a form in which quantification by *both* (in conjunction) or *either* (in disjunction) has applied to a derived sentence. Schematized tree structures for these sentences are as follows, approximating the Stockwell *et al.* model:

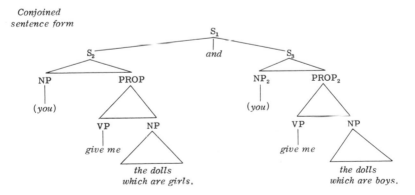

Conjoined sentence form

15 The relative clause has been used in these sentences to facilitate expression of the negative. An overt negation plus an attributive (e.g., *Not boy dolls*) is not grammatical; *Dolls which are not boys* is. Langendoen (personal communication) indicates that the linguistic reasons for this are not clear.

*Quantified derived
sentence form*

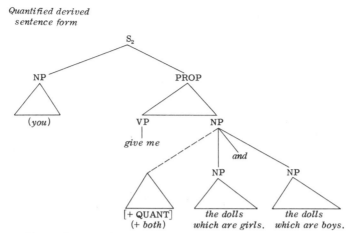

Transformation and Meaning Change

The above derivations have been constrained so that transformation would involve no obvious meaning change. As some linguists suggest, however, derivation in some cases appears either to create ambiguity or to introduce meaning change. For example: (1) *Give me the blocks which are red and give me the blocks which are square*; (2) *Give me the blocks which are red and the blocks which are square*; (3) *Give me the blocks which are red and square*. Sentence (2) derived from (1) maintains the meaning of (1), but the ostensibly derived form of (3) introduces both ambiguity and change of meaning. Sentences (1) and 2 request the *union* of two separate sets (the set of *red blocks* and the set of *square blocks*). Sentence 3 requests a single set, characterized by the *intersection* of *red and square* at once. When (3) is put into preposed adjectival form, (4) *Give me the red and square blocks*, the sentence is ambiguous; it may be given the union reading or the intersection reading.

Summary of Linguistic Issues

The facts and theoretical views set forth in regard to the linguistic status of the connectives suggest that conjunction, disjunction, and negation are linguistic primitives initiated in the base levels of linguistic representation, whether conceived in the form of semantic representation (or logical form), or in the form of deep syntactic structure. These connectives play an integral role in the rules of the grammar.

Conjunction reduction, the principal grammatical transformation involved in the linguistic expression of conjunction and disjunction appears to respect the logical form of conjunction and disjunction. This argues for the view that logical form may provide in a substantial way for the linguistic character of the connective. If this logical form is, in turn, a fundamental feature of cognition, as Piagetian theory suggests it is, this would lend support to the thesis that cognitive processses significantly influence the nature of linguistic rule systems rather than the reverse.

Psycholinguistic Studies of the Connective

Empirical study of the relation between linguistic connective comprehension (*and, or, not*) and the comprehension of the conceptually related, logical set operations (intersection, union, complementation) similar to the one reported in Chapters 7 and 8 has been very limited, although the need for such study has been noted, as in Suppes and Feldman (1971, p. 304).

Feldman (1968) undertook a study of this type by testing the comprehension of logical union (as measured by the Piagetian inclusion task) and the comprehension of linguistic negation with subjects 3.3–7.9 years of age. Feldman's interpretation of Piagetian theory was admittedly tentative, and the linguistic and cognitive dimensions were not clearly differentiated theoretically. Her results are perhaps best described as equivocal.

Piaget (1928) assessed the quality of interpropositional relations in children's speech, and Inhelder and Piaget (1958) in later work with adolescents formalized their analyses with regard to truth-functional logic. Inhelder and Piaget concluded that linguistic analyses were quite limited in what they could offer to an understanding of cognition including that of the truth-functional logic. They felt that language was not the primary key to understanding thought, including logical thought, As they put it,

> It is fruitless to look for an exclusively verbal or linguistic criterion for truth-functional logic . . . rather only certain expressions are conclusive indices. . . . But in the majority of cases language remains implicit and the subject does not disentangle the details of his inferences. Moreover, the details of verbal expression vary between subjects and sometimes even from moment to moment for a single subject. All in all, the subjects' language expresses their thoughts only in a rough way [Inhelder & Piaget, 1958, p. 279].

Recent psychological work that utilizes linguistic analyses as an index to logical thought (Bynum, Thomas, & Weitz, 1972; Weitz, Bynum, Thomas, & Steger, 1973) is limited for these reasons.

A study by Jones (1972), which reports on the formal operational thought of adolescent boys (11- to 13-years old) and its relation to their verbal repertoire, in particular to their use of "tentative" statements in speech (supposition, condition, disjunction), further documents the limitation of linguistic evidence as the sole index of cognitive ability. Children with high ability and high IQs were reported to use more tentative statements in the description of pictures than did boys of equal IQ but of low verbal ability. However, there was no difference between the groups in their performance on formal operational (Piagetian) tasks. Unfortunately, the connectives used in this study were not precisely defined, and there was no test of connective comprehension so that an adequate assessment of the subject's linguistic knowledge of the tentative components of speech was not available.

One can see from this list that the number of studies that relate logical and linguistic connectives is quite limited, both in scope and in precision. A larger number of studies are concerned, however, with the comprehension of language connectives per se. A series of studies in the concept attainment literature is also addressed to logical conjunction, disjunction, and negation. A few studies are addressed to the more general problem of the analyticity of language forms.

In a number of the concept attainment investigations, as well as in some linguistic connective studies, truth-functional logic is assumed to be involved psychologically in concept and connective processing. That is, truth-table relations are considered as algorithmic subroutines in information-processing systems.

An outline of these different sets of studies is briefly summarized next, with emphasis on the developmental studies.

Analyticity as Psychological Reality

As suggested above, **analyticity** generally refers to the determinability of the truth of a sentence from evidence internal to the form of the sentence. Both J. J. Katz (1967) and Quine (1967) suggest that this notion is meaningful to the degree that it can be given a firm "empirical basis" (although J. J. Katz [1972, p. 252] specifies that this empirical basis can only support a formal definition by semantic theory—it cannot replace it).

J. J. Katz (1967) suggests that an appropriate paradigm for testing the notion of analyticity would be to ask speakers to make intuitive judgments about analytic sentences. He suggests a sorting task wherein subjects are asked to classify sentences into several piles (analytic, synthetic, contradictory) after having seen example sentences of each type. To the degree that the prediction by semantic theory of certain sentences as analytic coincides with the classification behavior of speakers, the notion of analyticity is given empirical reality.

Steinberg (1970a, 1970b) applied the paradigm suggested by Katz (using analytic sentences in which subject and predicate were redundant (*The husband is a man*) and concluded that "the results strongly support the validity of the semantic categories." Apostel *et al.* (1957) used a similar paradigm with several different and more complex types of analytic statements. They presented subjects with sentences generally considered analytic, synthetic, or intermediate between the two (problematic), but did not model sorting-behavior. Subjects were asked to (1) spontaneously classify, (2) to spontaneously reclassify, (3) to dichotomize, and then (4) to seriate classes of sentences. Following this, they were asked to classify according to verbal definitions of analytic and synthetic classes. Results of this experiment regarding the empirical reality of the analytic–synthetic distinction are probably best described as ambiguous.

J. J. Katz (1972) has recently extended the theoretical definition of analyticity. Analytic statements, he suggests, are determined by analysis of the propositions expressed by sentences, rather than of the sentences themselves. By Katz's definition, in analytic sentences (in which the sentences are "determinate" and thus make a statement) the assertion of the proposition involves no more information than is already contained in the presupposition of the sentence. The analytic sentence is thus necessarily true, "secured against falsehood." This extended semantic theory suggests possibilities for further empirical analysis of the notion, although such work has not yet been undertaken (to our knowledge).

Natural Language Connectives

The comprehension of conjunction, disjunction (both inclusive and exclusive), and negation was investigated by Suppes and Feldman (1971) in children from 4 years, 5 months to 6 years, 7 months of age. Commands for block-sorting were expressed in connective sentences. The conjunct classes were semantically intersecting (e.g., *red* and *square*). Although *idiom* was varied in the commands, this variation was not formally defined in linguistic terms. The connectives, moreover, did not map in a one-to-one fashion onto the logical form of sentences (e.g., *and* was not necessary to a conjunction item, nor *or* to a disjunction item). The reason for this was apparently the desire of the authors to be faithful to the actual logical nature of the set responses required by the command. One could alternatively choose to be faithful to linguistic form (as was done in our own study). Each approach has its assets and limitations.

Regression analysis determined the factors in comprehension difficulty. The connectives were shown to account for a large part of the variance in sentence comprehension. Idiom and negativity were also found to be significant in affecting difficulty. The conclusions offered were tentative, however, in light of limited linguistic analysis, lack of explicit cognitive correlations, and limited developmental data.

A Japanese study by Nitta and Nagano (1966) also concerned the comprehension of conjunction, disjunction, and negation. Five age groups (from kindergarten through junior high) were administered paper and pencil tests that called for response to connective commands by circling sets of elements. Conjunct classes were intersecting (e.g., *birds* and *black*). disjoint (e.g., *birds* and *flowers*), or inclusive (e.g., *flowers* and *daisies*), and the elements were pictures, letters, or Venn diagrams. A complete set of conjunctive, disjunctive, and univariate forms were tested (A, $\bar{A}$, B, $\bar{B}$, $A \cdot B$, $A \cdot \bar{B}$, etc.) Japanese has two kinds of connectives for disjunction (*ka* is 'selective,' allowing either an inclusive or exclusive reading, but when at least one object is intended; *to* is 'cumulative,' favoring an inclusive meaning when all appropriate elements are intended). Both types were tested.

The developmental data indicate that disjunction develops later than conjunction, assertion, and negation. Even the youngest children understood A and $\bar{A}$ type forms. Intersection ($A \cdot B$) was difficult for the youngest children but improved in the older subjects. Union ($A \vee B$) was difficult even for older children. Cumulative disjunction was found to be easier than selective disjunction. Error analysis indicated that subjects interpret disjunction as conjunction. Fewer subjects interpreted conjunction as disjunction.

Neimark and Slotnick (1970) replicated part of the Nitta and Nagano study with English-speaking third- through ninth-graders and adults. They used picture and verbal forms for intersecting conjuncts. The conjunction *and* was used for all conjunction forms, and *or–or both* and *either–or* for the two types of disjunctions. For Neimark and Slotnick as for Nitta and Nagano, an inclusive disjunction response was always considered a correct response to disjunction. Subjects, with some exceptions, did better on the *either–or* form of disjunction. Neimark and Slotnik's findings in general confirm those of the Japanese study although they indicate that Japanese children appear to have earlier comprehension of Japanese connectives than do American children of English connectives. This difference could, however, be due to the greater ambiguity of the English connectives. *And* and *or* must carry a variety of connective meanings, for which Japanese has different connectives. Thus, greater success by the Japanese children could have been due to the fact that Japanese commands were less ambiguous.

Hatano (1973), again with Japanese subjects (fourth- and sixth-grade and junior college), investigated the child's understanding of conjunction when the conjunct classes were disjoint or intersecting, and, when conjoining, created meaningful classes of two mutually exclusive classes (*flowers—tulips* and *dandelions*). Hatano found that change in conjunct relations from intersecting to disjoint (mutually exclusive) altered the relative success of conjunction and disjunction forms ($A \cdot B$ and $A \vee B$). This was contrary to the previously found asymmetry between them in which conjunction is usually easier.

A study by Paris (1973) attempted to assess the validity of a truth-table cognitive model for the comprehension of natural language connectives. It involved the analysis of conjunction (with the connectives *and*, *both–and*, *but*), a negative form called conjunction (*neither–nor*), disjunction (*or*, *either–or*), conditional (*if–then*), and biconditional (*if and only if–then*) in children of the second, fifth, eighth, and eleventh grades and college adults. Although Paris claims that the data lead to the rejection of the truth-functional model, his conjunction and disjunction data nevertheless do not contradict it because Paris (1973) found a developmental pattern towards "separation of the components [of compound propositions] and independent evaluation of their truth value [p. 288]," though the conditional and biconditional data might be so interpreted. The data additionally support a developmental differentiation of disjunction from conjunction and a developmental preference for exclusive over inclusive readings for disjunction. Although semantic relations between conjuncts are said by Paris to be important in determining connective meaning, this was not systematically studied in the experiment. Shine and Walsh (1971), who assessed comprehension of four logical connectives (*and, or, if, only if*) and their negations in children of grades 2, 4, 6, and 8, concluded that their data might be in accord with a truth-table model.

Several other studies deal with the development of interpropositional connectivity (Piaget, 1928; Vygotsky, 1962, p. 105; Werner & Kaplan, 1963). Piaget notes that it is characteristic of the child's speech up to the age of 7–8 for statements to be "juxtaposed" without explicit relation between propositions. Werner and Kaplan have a similar theory of child speech wherein speech progresses from "paratactic" connection between propositions (in which connection is not articulate and is assumedly carried by the context) to "hypotactic" connection (in which a connective morpheme carries an articulated and differentiated relation between propositions).

In summary, the above studies as well as others that are generally consistent with them are concerned with the comprehension of the connective in a linguistic context. They do not explicitly evaluate the connective's cognitive correlates, although in some cases the relevance of a truth-table cognitive structure is examined. The logicality of connective comprehension is generally accepted (Suppes & Feldman, 1971) although it is denied by at least one source (Paris, 1973). None of these studies, however, involved a comprehensive empirical analysis of the relations among connectives, just as no comprehensive theoretical statement exists on the relation between (cognitive) logicality and linguistic connectivity. The connective expressions used varied from study to study, and they varied between oral and written tasks. Developmental evidence, sufficient to define changes in the nature of connective comprehensive over an extended age span, is not available.

Conjunction and Disjunction as Cognitive Concepts

An extensive literature deals with the attainment of conjunction and disjunction concepts through rule and attribute learning (Bourne, 1970). In these studies, concepts are treated as abstractions induced from stimuli with no necessary involvement of language connectives per se.

A hierarchy of difficulty among univariate and bivariate concepts (Neisser & Weene, 1962) suggests a psychological differentiation among concepts that has no precise parallel in the formal logical relations among them. Disjunction, for example, is more difficult than conjunction, as it is in linguistic connective studies. The varying degrees of difficulty experienced in processing different connective concepts are explained by such factors as the role of positive and negative information in connective meaning and the size of relevant sets (Battig & Bourne, 1961; Bourne, 1970, 1972; Bourne & Guy, 1968; Conant & Trabasso, 1964; Hovland & Weiss, 1953; Hunt & Hovland, 1960).

A related group of studies concerns itself with formal decision tree models for the simultaneous description of the logical and psychological realities of concept processing. The work of Trabasso et al. (1971) is an example. Hunt et al. (1966; Hunt, 1962) theory similarly defines relations between decision tree models of concept processing by a truth-tabular logic and the intensional and extensional aspects of connectives. Haygood and Bourne (1965), in turn, propose that subjects process stimuli in rule-learning tasks by classifying them according to truth-table categories, suggesting again the psychological validity of logical structures in which the truth-table acts as a cognitive algorithm in the processing of particular logical concepts. The most extensive analysis consistent with this view, as already indicated, is that of Piaget (Inhelder & Piaget, 1958; Piaget & Inhelder, 1967) in studies of the truth-functional and propositional logical systems and their relations to the classification capacities of children. Other developmental studies of concept processing treat some of the same issues (Bourne & O'Banion, 1971; DiVesta & Walls, 1969; King, 1966; King & Holt, 1970; Snow & Rabinovitch, 1969; and others). The work of Furth (1971; Furth & Youniss, 1965; Furth, Youniss, and Ross, 1970), Youniss, Furth, and Ross (1971), and Youniss and Furth (1964, 1967) is concerned with the symbolic treatment of connective concepts, although not with language connectives as such.

These studies indicate a widely held view that concept processing, whether conceived of from a Piagetian, information-processing or concept-learning perspective, involves the operation of a truth-functional logic as part of the cognitive apparatus available to the adult, or to the child at least in certain stages in his development.

Individual Connective Concepts

LOGICAL AND LINGUISTIC DISJUNCTION

As indicated, disjunction was found to be more difficult to process psychologically than conjunction (Bruner, Goodnow, & Austin, 1956; and others). This asymmetry has been taken as evidence of a difference between formal logic, which defines no asymmetry, and logical thought, which displays it (e.g., Papert, 1963). Anisfeld (1968), however, argues that the source of the psychological asymmetry is an experimental artifact; others have also commented that the conjunction–disjunction difference is spurious (Bar-Hillel & Eifermann, 1970; Eifermann & Steinitz, 1971).

In regard to the inclusive–exclusive disjunction distinction, the role that propositional content can play in determining which interpretation is employed is suggested by Naess (1962). A study by Ghobar (cited in Piaget, 1963b) also at Geneva, showed that younger children (about age 7) can be trained to attain the exclusive disjunction concept through a nonverbal manipulation procedure. Piaget comments that although the possibility of training children at this age on an operation that is not "natural" to them may be successful, the acquisition of such an operation as an isolated state is not equivalent to its later acquisition when the operation is part of the system of 16 binary operations in a combinational structure informed by the INRC group of transformations.

Neimark (1970) demonstrates that the disjunction *or* (when inclusive disjunction is intended) is difficult for even high school subjects. She reports data showing gradual improvement in performance on a paper and pencil test from ninth to twelfth grades (approximately 14- to 17-years old).

The fact that syntactic considerations, in addition to semantic considerations affect performance with disjunction, is indicated by a study with adults (Langendoen, 1970). The subjects who had to determine number (and gender) assignment in making the verb agree with its disjunction subject had considerable difficulty in deciding whether to make the assignment to the disjunctive node or to one of the disjuncts. Paris (1973) in a study with children (previously cited) found that quantification of the *or* connective by *either* increased exclusive interpretations of disjunction.

LOGICAL AND LINGUISTIC CONJUNCTION

The two conceptions of the connective *and*, symmetric (reversible), and asymmetric (ordered) were analyzed in a study by Fillenbaum (1971). Adult subjects were found to be sensitive to the semantic properties of verbs that govern the temporal relations between clauses, with the mode of entry to memory for the temporally ordered *and* differing from that for symmetric *and*. Permutation of clause order resulted in false recognition more frequently for symmetric *and* sentences. A study by E. W. Katz and Brent (1968) considered the effect of a match between linguistic conjunct order and situation order in sentences with *and*. Subjects (grades 1, 6, and college) showed a developmental preference for matching linguistic and context orders. Another study intended to define those aspects of linguistic connectives (including *and*) which differentiate them from logical connectives (Fillenbaum & Rapoport, 1971). The subject's expectations and his anticipatory assumptions (he knew either *A* or *B* to be true) were found to differentiate responses to combinatorial and contrastive connectives.

LOGICAL AND LINGUISTIC NEGATION

Negative sentences, in general, are more difficult to process than affirmative sentences (Wason, 1959, 1961). Similar results have been found with children (Donaldson, 1970; Feldman, 1968; Gaer, 1969; Slobin, 1966; and others). Because this result again differs from what one would expect from solely logical considerations or from transformational theory considerations, it has led to a wide-ranging investigation of the psychological properties of negation, including the effects of negation on the verification of truth values. Wason (1972) and Apostel (1972) review the psychological literature in respect to these issues and discuss the semantic and logical factors that enter into the processing of negative sentences. A review of the literature on negation may also be found in Feldman's (1968) dissertation.

LOGICAL AND LINGUISTIC IMPLICATION

The implication, or conditional (*if–then*), is perhaps the most studied of the connectives. Although implication was not the subject of study in our investigation, the issues nonetheless are common to those of the other connectives; namely, they concern (1) the nature of the relation between the linguistic connective and its formal logical correlate, (2) the relation of the connective to a truth-functional logic, and (3) the characterization of developmental change in connective meaning.

Research with adult subjects (Wason, 1968, 1970, Wason & Johnson-Laird, 1969; and others) generally suggests a nontruth-functional interpretation of the linguistic conditional or implicative connective. Work with children (Hill, 1961; Matalon, 1962; Peel, 1967; Roberge & Paulus, 1971; etc.) is in accord with this generalization, which suggests, in general, that truth tables "schematize a property of implication and do not define it (as they are classically defined in logic) [Papert, in Piaget, 1963a, p. 32]."

In a recent paper Taplin, Staudenmayer, and Taddonio (1974) apply a truth-table analysis to determine change with age in children's interpretation of the conditional connective. Bourne (1972) in commenting on the significance of this study suggests that most of the data support a hypothesis of developmental change in logical interpretation but that some of the data show no such developmental change—only difference. As Bourne states, Taplin's experiment does not enable one to make a decision between the alternative interpretations (Bourne, 1972, p. 31). Bourne and his associates are also concerned with other aspects of comprehension of the conditional and biconditional (*if and only if*) (Bourne, 1972). Finally, O'Brien and others in a series of papers (O'Brien, 1972; O'Brien & Shapiro, 1968; O'Brien, Shapiro, & Reali, 1972) confirm the noncongruence between a full truth-functional logic and the linguistic connective. Shapiro and O'Brien (1973) have developed the notion of "quasichild logics" whereby children at various ages are predicted to function with distinct although limited sets of logical processes in connective comprehension.

Children's Knowledge of Connectives

Data on the onset of connective comprehension in early language development is not available, although limited data exist as by-products of general developmental analyses.

Regarding conjunction, Brown (1970, 1973a) reports that during primary language development in Stages I–III (MLU = 1.5–3.5) children produce single sentences or fragments exclusively. Only at Stage IV (MLU = 3.5) are sentences conjoined.[16] Although Brown (1973a) asserts that ". . . constructional and semantic knowledge is fairly uniform at a given MLU [p. 100]." he offers no precise correlation of conjunction structures with the child's mean length of utterance.

The *and* conjunction does not occur in any single word utterances of Bloom's subjects' (Bloom, 1970). Bloom suggests, however, that in early 2 + word speech, some N + N constructions without connectives may actually evidence conjunctive semantic relations (that is, they may be

[16] Age does not map onto MLU regularly. The age range for Stage IV is from about 22 to 36 months (Brown's subject, Eve, reached this point at 22 months; Adam at 35 months, and Sarah at 36 months).

asyndetic conjunctions).[17] A study by H. Sinclair and Bronckart (1972) shows that young children given NNV and VVN compounds impose conjunctive meanings on these forms in some conditions. Menyuk (1971) has suggested that sentential conjunction may precede conjunction reduction in free speech developmentally, as have Slobin and Welsh (1973).

Regarding the negation connective (*no*), there is evidence that it does occur at the single-word stage of language production (Bloom, 1970). Semantic aspects of negation in development are discussed by Bloom (1970), Greenfield, Smith and Laufer (1972), McNeill (1970), and Slobin (1971).

In sum, relatively little attention has been given to connective comprehension and/or production at the age of speech onset or to the logical and linguistic processes involved in early connective development.

CONJUNCTION AS A COGNITIVE AND LINGUISTIC UNIVERSAL

The connective may provide material for the analysis of universal aspects of both cognition and language to the degree that these are determinable.

Work by Cole, Gay, and Glick (1968) on concept acquisition (conjunction, disjunction, and negation) by Kpelle (African) and American adults and children suggests that the Kpelle learned the conjunction and disjunction concepts to an equal extent, although conjunction was learned more easily than disjunction by the American subjects. This suggested to the authors a possible linguistic influence on concept acquisition because Kpelle has several connectives to express disjunction. Later work by Cole, Gay, Glick, and Sharp (1971) attributed the result to limitations in commonly employed methodology. These authors stress the degree to which cultural context and the structure of experimentation interact to complicate the assessment of logical concepts cross-culturally.

A more recent study (Cibrowski & Cole, 1972) in which the truth-tabular concept acquisition model was applied to the study of conjunction and disjunction with both Kpelle and American (child and adult) subjects indicated "very faint evidence of partitioning of instances into (truth-tabular) subclasses" and "poor verbalization" about rules by the Kpelle (p. 784). When memory aids were supplied to the Kpelle subjects, however, acquisition of these concepts was equal or superior to that of the American subjects. Additional data showed that the oft-reported conjunction–disjunction differences has cross-cultural generality.

Data from cross-cultural acquisition studies may suggest cross-cultural generality in the acquisition and use of logical and linguistic connectives.

---

[17] Moravcsik (1970) had studied the occurrence of asyndetic constructions (which omit the connective in a compound construction) across languages. They are noted to occur in English and several other languages, mostly in question constructions and idiosyncratic contexts such as number names (e.g., four-hundred twenty).

However, to date, such studies have not specifically studied the acquisition of conjunction. The data are thus too meager to establish those features of logical and linguistic processing that are universal.

SUMMARY OF PSYCHOLINGUISTIC STUDIES

This rather sketchy review of psycholinguistic and cognitive literature on the connective[18] both as a linguistic and cognitive phenomenon su ggests several conclusions:

1. Psycholinguistic research has barely addressed the issue of the precise correlation of the interpropositional operations of conjunction, disjunction, and negation in natural language with their theoretically related cognitive operations.

2. Experimental variation of the linguistic form of connective expression is rarely found in research on the connective.

3. The relevance of truth-tabular logic to linguistic connective comprehension and logical connective comprehension has been proposed by Piagetian, information-processing, and concept-learning theories.

4. The fact that both language and logical connective comprehension undergo qualitative change with age has been recognized, although there exists no comprehensive study of the development of language connective comprehension comparable to that which is available for the development of truth-functional logic. Likewise, no comprehensive study of the specific relation between linguistic and logical (cognitive) development in respect to the connective is available.

5. Data are particularly meager in respect to the period of onset of connective comprehension and production.

6. Cross-cultural data concerning the universality of language–logic relations, particularly for the connective, are also very limited.

7. Finally, the lack of comprehensive assessment of the connective from cognitive and linguistic points of view is probably due to the lack of theoretical proposals for definition of the nature of this relationship. The review of logical and linguistic theory above was intended to schematize basic aspects of these relations. In light of these considerations, the study reported in Chapters 7 and 8 was undertaken. It presents and discusses experimental data that bear on most of these issues.

---

[18] Earlier work on the connective is reviewed by McCarthy (1954). Studies in syllogistic reasoning also have a bearing on the study of the connective (e.g., Henle, 1962) as do studies on intrapropositional logicality (e.g., Johnson-Laird, 1968b). However, as these studies do not bear centrally on the particular issues dealt with here, they have not been discussed above.

7

A Study of the Development of Logical and Linguistic Connectives: Linguistic Data

Harry Beilin and Barbara Lust

Our intent in this study was to examine the relation between the logical connectives in language and their cognitive correlates. The study assumed that a formal relationship mediated through logical representation exists between the child's cognition and his linguistic knowledge. It was also assumed that this relationship would be most readily exposed in a developmental study. We propose, consistent with Piagetian theory, that knowledge of truth-functional logic develops through the attainment of logical set operations (as discussed in Chapter 6). The concomitant achievement of linguistic connective comprehension and knowledge of logical set operations would be evidence of a fundamental logic–language relation. More specifically, comprehension of the set operations of intersection, union, and complementation may relate psychologically to linguistic comprehension of connectives *and*, *or*, and *not*. The set of univariate $(A, \overline{A})$ and bivariate forms $(A \cdot B, A \cdot \overline{B}, \overline{A} \cdot \overline{B}, A \vee B, A \vee \overline{B}, \overline{A} \vee \overline{B})$, which is generated by the composition of assertion, negation, and connection, provided a model for the linguistic materials of the study. The propositional connectives of conjunction ($\cdot$) and disjunction ($\vee$) were represented linguistically by the connectives *and* and *or* respectively. The negation operator ($-$) was represented linguistically by the morpheme *not*. The linguistic connectives were used to connect sentences that were either affirmative or negative according to the logical form.

The univariate logical forms A (assertion) and $\overline{A}$ (negation) were assumed to represent the primary or atomic elements involved in compound forms, such as the bivariate connectives. They represent, independently, the propositional assertion of truth $(T = A)$ and falsity $(F = \overline{A})$. They also provide the primary components of the truth-tabular structure—the organized set of associations between these two operations (TT, FT, TF, FF) defines the truth table. If development of the truth-tabular structure underlies connective development as we hypothesize, it may also be predicted that the comprehension of these atomic elements should be attained prior to or concurrent with the development of knowledge of connectivity.

In general, the negation operation represents the logical inverse of the assertion operation. In Piagetian theory, the integration of an inverse operation with an assertion operation defines the logical aspects of a cognitive operation. The synchronous and primary development of A and $\overline{A}$ would suggest achievement of the underlying logical apparatus necessary for propositional connective comprehension.

In sum, a developmental model was employed for examining the epistemological and psychological issues concerned with the role of logic in both cognition and language.

Method

Two sets of tasks were used in the study, one linguistic and the other cognitive. Order of presentation was counterbalanced.

The *linguistic* tasks, which assessed comprehension of the intersection union, and complementation connectives (*and*, *or*, and *not* respectively) when used linguistically as intersentential connectives, required subjects to sort a reference set.[1] Variations in the linguistic form of sentences was used in relation to this reference set to test for the effects of conjunction reduction on connective comprehension. These linguistic variations, as discussed in Chapter 6, were conjoined sentences, derived conjunction and quantified conjunction. Negation effects were assessed through single conjunct negation and double conjunct negation. The *cognitive* tasks, based on Piagetian methodology, assessed the ability to perform the correlative classification operations of class (multiplication) intersection, class (addition) union, and class complementation. Both cognitive and linguistic tasks relied on the same reference set of materials (a four-class set of *dolls* in which the classes = *girls*, *boys*, *monkeys*, *bears* with two subclasses in each, *big* and *little*).

Linguistic Tasks

LINGUISTIC BATTERY (1)

This group consisted of 48 items. Thirty-six of these were composed of six basic logical connective forms created by the multiplication of asser-

---

[1] It should be pointed out again (see Chapter 6) that in this study the design of the linguistic items for conjunction and disjunction (or intersection and union) was defined with respect to the interpropositional connectives (*and* or *or*). This decision was based on the desire to hold linguistic form of interpropositional connection constant in order to evaluate its correlation with the cognitive set operations.

tion and negation ($A \cdot B$, $A \cdot \overline{B}$, $\overline{A} \cdot \overline{B}$, $A \vee B$, $A \vee \overline{B}$, $\overline{A} \vee \overline{B}$) in each of three specified linguistic forms (conjoined, derived, and quantified derived). Each combination was replicated once. The 12 remaining items consisted of four single-conjunct forms (A), four simple negation forms ($\overline{A}$), and replications of each of two distributive connective forms ($\overline{A} \vee \overline{B}$), ($\overline{A} \cdot \overline{B}$). Although two observations per cell limit the range of scores and yields small variance for an ANOVA design, this scale has been shown to be sufficient for the statistic (Hsu & Feldt, 1969). The total set of logical forms was randomized with the constraint that the first item was to be a simple (nonconnective) form.

Each of the propositional conjuncts consisted of a class predication. For example, in one conjunct a subject would be asked "Give me the *dolls* which are *girls*;" in the other conjunct he would be asked, "Give me the *dolls* which are *boys*." The conjoined form ($A \cdot B$) would be, "Give me the *dolls* which are girls and give me the *dolls* which are *boys*."

Connectives always applied to homogeneous classes (*boys and girls* or *monkeys and bears*) and not to heterogeneous classes (*monkeys and boys*) or to bidimensional or intersecting classes (*boys and big*). Connected classes were thus always unidimensional or disjoint (*boys and girls*).

The above methodological constraints maintain logical symmetry in conjunction. Thus, "Give me the *dolls* which are *boys and* give me the *dolls* which are *girls*" is equivalent to "Give me the *dolls* which are *girls and* give me the *dolls* which are *boys*." Temporal order and other alogical functions, which might otherwise interact with connective comprehension, are precluded.

Each of the class compounds (*monkeys and bears* and *boys and girls*) and its reversed order form was randomly and equally distributed among the connective types. The replication of each connective type contained the alternative compound. Conjunction and disjunction forms were also matched in lexical components.

The linguistic transformations which were applied to the six basic connective forms all maintained the connective's intersentential function. A **conjoined sentence** form consisted of the conjunction or disjunction of two complete sentences, "Give me the *dolls* which are *boys* **and** give me the *dolls* which are *girls*." The **derived form** consisted of a reduction of the conjoined form by conjunction derivation and deletion "Give me the *dolls* which are *boys* **and** the *dolls* which are *girls*." In creating the transformationally derived form, deletion was restricted in order to maintain the interpropositional status of the connective and in order not to change the meaning of the form by creating a phrasal conjunction, "Give me the *dolls* which are *boys* and *girls*." The final linguistic form **quantified—derived** created by transformation inserted a quantifier in the derived form (*both* in the conjunction sentences, *either* in the disjunction sentences—"Give me *both* the *dolls* which are *boys and* the *dolls* which are *girls*").

The full set of logical forms and their description in terms of the four-class reference set, *boys, girls, monkeys, bears*, is shown in Table 7-1.

TABLE 7-1

Description of Logical Forms and Their Linguistic Translation

Symbolic designation	Name	Description of positive instance given a four-class universe $(ABCD)$ [a]	Linguistic Form	Example [b]
Definition				
A	Assertion	A alone must be present. B, C, and D must not be present.		Give me the dolls which are girls
$\overline{A}$	Negation	A must not be present. B, C, and D must be present.	not	Give me the dolls which are *not* girls
Intersection				
$A \cdot B$	Conjunction	Both A and B must be present. C and D must not be present.	and	Give me the dolls which are girls *and* give me the dolls which are boys.
$A \cdot \overline{B}$	Exclusion	A must be present and B not present. C and D must be present also.	and/not	Give me the dolls which are girls *and* give me the dolls which are *not* boys.
$\overline{A} \cdot \overline{B}$	Conjunctive absence	A and B must both be absent. C and D must be present.	not/and/not	Give me the dolls which are *not* girls and give me the dolls which are *not* boys.
Union				
$A \vee B$	Disjunction	1. Exclusive interpretation: A may be present, B, C and D must be absent; or B may be present, A, C, and D must be absent. 2. Inclusive interpretation: (A or B or) A *and* B are present. C and D must be absent. [c]	or	Give me the dolls which are girls *or* give me the dolls which are boys.

$A \vee \overline{B}$	Disjunction with exclusion	1. Exclusive interpretation: A must be present. B, C, and D must be absent.[d] 2. Inclusive interpretation: A, C, and D must be present. B must be absent.	or/not	Give me the dolls which are girls *or* give me the dolls which are *not* boys.
$\overline{A} \vee \overline{B}$	Disjunctive absence	1. Exclusive interpretation: A is absent and B, C, and D are present. Or, B is absent and A, C, and D are present. 2. Inclusive interpretation: C and D are present. Both A and B are absent.	not/or/not	Give me the dolls which are *not* girls *or* give me the dolls which are *not* boys.

DeMorgan's Rules

$\overline{(A \cdot B)}$	Conjunction complementation	Equivalent to $\overline{A} \vee \overline{B}$ (ambiguous—see text. C and D considered correct resolution.)	not (——and——)	Give me the dolls which are *not* (girls and boys).
$\overline{(A \vee B)}$	Disjunction complementation	Equivalent to $\overline{A} \cdot \overline{B}$	not (——or——)	Give me the dolls which are *not* (girls or boys.)

[a] The four classes of the universe set were: *girls, boys, monkeys, bears*. Each class consisted of two subclasses (*big* and *little*). Each subclass consisted of three exemplars.
[b] All intersection and union-type connectives were actually presented in three linguistic forms (conjoined sentences, derived conjunctions, and quantified-derived conjunctions). The representation above is the basic *conjoined sentence* form, from which the other two are transformational derivatives.
[c] Only the *A and B* response differentiates the inclusive interpretation from the exclusive interpretation empirically.
[d] See discussion in text regarding difficulties with this form.

LINGUISTIC BATTERY 2

This group for 2- and 3-year olds consisted of 18 items. With the negation factor omitted, this battery provided a set of two connectives ($A \cdot B, A \vee B$), which were linguistically varied in the same three forms (conjoined sentences, derived, and quantified derived). In addition, simple assertion (A) and negation ($\overline{A}$) forms were included. Each specification was repeated once. In contrast to the 4- to 10-year-old battery, in the 2- to 3-year-old battery the relative clause was omitted from the single conjunct expression. (For example, subjects were asked, "Give me the *girls*" rather than "Give me the *dolls* which are *girls*.") In addition, two forms of negation were assessed: (1) a relative clause form identical to Battery 1, "Give me the *dolls* which are *not* girls," and (2) a denial form, "Do *not* give me the *girls*."

The battery for 2- and 3-year-old subjects followed the counterbalancing procedures of the 7- to 10-year-old battery. In addition, two different randomized forms of this battery were prepared. Half the children received form A, half form B.

Six school-attending 3-year olds were administered another battery identical to the linguistic 2- to 3-year -old battery, but including 4 replications of each item rather than 2, thus totaling 36 items. This variation was included to increase the reliability of the battery. The variation proved not to be significant.

Finally, linguistic battery *1* was administered to adults in order to provide reference data in respect to their comprehension of the same linguistic connectives. These adult subjects were not tested on cognition tasks.

TOY MATERIALS

These materials were used with the linguistic and cognitive batteries. They consisted of 24 *dolls*. Each *doll* varied in two dimensions of two values: size and sex (or species). The total reference set was composed of two subsets (*people* and *animals*) each of which consisted of two classes: *boys* and *girls* in the *people* set and *monkeys* and *bears* in the *animal* set.

The total set thus consisted of four classes or eight subclasses (species or sex size) across a binary (genus) subset division. Each specification was represented by three exemplars giving a total of 24 elements, with 12 elements in each subset and three in each subclass.

The *boy* and *girl dolls* composing the classes of the base set were identical in size (*big* $11\frac{1}{2}$ in, *little* 6 in.) Dolls were uniformly dressed in simple clothing made for the experiment. Sex differentiation was indicated by clothing. Clothing texture and color were held constant across sex. *Animal dolls* were identical to each other within class and similar to the *people* set in size (*big*, $7\frac{1}{2}$ in, *little*, 4 in); *animal* classes were similar to each other in color. Proportionality of *big* to *little* sizes in each subset was approximately equal (.52 *people*, .53 *animals*).

PROCEDURE

Children were pretested to ensure that they were familiar with the vocabulary identifying each of the classes in the reference set (*girls, boys, monkeys, bears*), and were trained to proper identification, if necessary.

Each subject was tested individually by the same experimenter. A second experimenter who acted as recorder (*R*) was occasionally present. For the language tasks, the experimenter held a receptor basket tray and administered 48 *commands* for various subsets of *dolls*. Subjects were told: "I am going to ask you to give me some of the *dolls*. You try to give me just the ones I say, okay? Put just the *dolls* I say in the basket." They were told that some of the items were *easy* and some *tricky* in order to encourage subjects' differentiation among items. The commands followed in the prescribed form, "Give me the . . ." Emphasis was placed on the connective. The command was administered once at the beginning, and once at the completion of the item—the latter in the form "Did you give me the . . .?" In addition, commands were repeated once or more during the child's response if (1) the child requested repetition, and if (2) the experimenter judged that the subject was losing attention or memory of the item. This was intended to ensure that memory was not a factor in the child's response.

The presentation of the total battery of 48 items was divided into several sessions according to the age and individual needs of the child. The mean number of sessions for linguistic testing for the 8- to 10-year-old group was .9; for the 6- to 7-year-old group 1.9; for the 4- to 5-year olds, 3.4; and for the 2- to 3-year olds, 2.9. The mean for the 6 school-attending 3-year olds who had the longer battery of 36 items was 4.0. The mean for the home 2- and 3-year olds who had a shorter battery of 18 items was 2.3 sessions.

Cognitive Tasks

DESIGN

A series of Piagetian tasks designed to test the classification operations of intersection, *logical multiplication*, union, *logical addition*, and complementation, *logical complementation*, (hereafter referred to as ×, +, − respectively) were administered in a single order. These included: (1) a spontaneous classification task, assumed to be representative of an integration of the (×, +, −) operations, (2) two matrix tasks, assumed to be representative of logical multiplication (×): one was a 4-class matrix construction task and the other a Piagetian matrix task (also with 4 classes) calling for insertion of a missing element from an established matrix (matrix abstraction), (3) an inclusion task, assumed to be representative of logical addition (+), and (4) a complementation task, termed by Piaget the *espèce unique* or singular class task, said to be representative of logical complementation (−). As discussed in Chapter 6 in terms of Piagetian theory, which is based on Boolean set theory, logical multiplication (matrix tasks) is represented by class *intersection*; logical addition (inclusion task) is represented by class *union*; and logical complementation (singular class task) is represented by class *complementation*.[2]

Vicariance, a complex logical activity requiring the integration of complementation and additive classification processes ($-$ $+$) was also tested with a Piagetian-type methodology. In addition, adjunction of identical and foreign elements and dichotomy was also tested. These latter two are referred to as "functions" for the purposes of this study. (They are opposed to the "operations" of $\times$, $+$, $-$.)

The vicariance and function tasks were added to the study because the attainment of vicariance has been found in cognitive development to correlate with passage from class set operations to propositional operations (Piaget, 1957). The functions were included to assess some of the components (subprocesses) of logical classification operations.

MATERIALS

The same materials as in linguistic testing were used. The cognitive tasks are defined and interpreted with reference to the employed materials in Appendix D.

The cognitive battery was divided into three parts: Part (A) consisted of the *spontaneous classification task* that was intended to provide data on class compositional processes. One (base) set of the two-set universe from the linguistic tasks was used here. The combination of two dimensions (two values) permitted four classifications (AB, $A\bar{B}$. $\bar{A}B$, $\bar{A}\bar{B}$) in this set. Part (B) consisted of a series of "provoked" classification activities designed to isolate specific classificatory operations and functions. The operations included complementation and vicariance. Classification functions included dichotomization and adjunction of identical and foreign elements. Testing was repeated with both base and extended set sizes. The extended set was the two-set universe used in the linguistic tasks. Multiplicative classification (matrix construction) was requested on the base set. Part (C) consisted of tasks designed to assess logical multiplication and logical addition. These were the matrix (abstraction) and inclusion tasks respectively. The latter tasks provided data that, combined with the data of the preceding parts of the battery, yielded a set of converging measures on operations central to the study.

For the preschool 2- and 3-year olds, the cognitive testing design was repeated, except that Part (C), the matrix (abstraction) and inclusion tasks, was omitted.

APPARATUS

The classification tasks were conducted with a raised 3-dimensional structure that could be placed on the floor.[3] It consisted of an opaque, plastic, open box 24 in $\times$ 24 in $\times$ 2$\frac{3}{4}$ in) that allowed partitioning by both

[2] The concrete logical operations defined by Piaget with which this study deals are described as acting primarily on disjoint classes.

[3] The apparatus was built by Edward Blackstock.

dichotomy (2 cell) and matrix (4 cell) divisions of the classification surface. The size of each matrix cell allowed placement of three elements of each subclass.

The apparatus also allowed insertion in each matrix cell of a blue plastic plaque, in the center of which was fastened a single subclass exemplar. Arrangements of these plaques in the various matrix positions, with one position blank, were used to reproduce the Piagetian matrix (abstraction) task.

PROCEDURE

After the initial, spontaneous classification task was performed on the base set (Part A), this set was reduced in size to one subclass. It was then gradually increased in a regulated order (Part B). Adjunction functions were tested at various points of this extension, and dichotomy and vicariance operations were tested at each full-class extension. Once the full-set size had been reached on the base set, the matrix construction operation was requested. Extension to full-set size (extended set of two subsets) was then begun. The order of extension and testing duplicated that on the base set during this process. Matrix (abstraction) and inclusion tasks were administered at the end (Part C).

Table 7-2 summarizes Piagetian stages for each of the major cognitive operations. These stage definitions have been adapted from Piaget and Inhelder (1967) to meet the empirical specifications and the theoretical focus of this study.

In general, the cognitive (Piagetian) tasks were administered by the techniques used in Geneva.[4] The clinical method usually employed has been modified in several ways, however. In particular, these adaptations restrict the experimenter's verbal statements in task administration. (1) All connectives (*and, or, not*) were eliminated from commands. (Usually the command could be reformulated in two separate sentences.) This was an issue in particular in the inclusion task (which asks, for example, "Are there more a *or* more A?"), and in the matrix command (which normally calls for the intersection connective *and*—"Fix these so that this goes with this *and* with this at the same time."). This constraint was held to be essential to ensure that the use of linguistic connectives did not confound the cognitive testing. (2) The experimental commands were designed to include the minimum amount of verbalization necessary to convey the command. (3) Although repetition of requests for a response was designed at several points in order to maintain an essential aspect of Piagetian testing methodology, maximum numbers of repeated requests for performance were set. In order to maintain another essential feature of Piagetian methodology, however, no time limits were imposed on the cognitive battery. Protocols recorded the continuity of child behavior as well as any dialogue between subject and experimenter.

As in linguistic testing, cognitive testing was carried out in several

[4] The experimenter was Barbara Lust who studied at the University of Geneva.

TABLE 7-2

Levels of Cognitive Development for Each of Five Basic Logical Classificatory Operations[a,b,c]

Cognitive level	Classification — Logical addition, multiplication, and complementation (Spontaneous classification)	Class union — Logical addition (Inclusion)	Class intersection — Logical multiplication (Matrix abstract)	Class intersection — Logical multiplication (Matrix constructed)	Class complementation — Logical complementation (Singular class)	Vicariant classification — Logical addition (Vicariance)
Sensorimotor	1 Assimilation to action schemes. Piling-processes disregarding reference to precise elements.	0 General incapacity for the task.	0 Incapacity for the task.	1 Piling processes usually using one matrix cell only.		
Elementary	2 Limited temporal and/or spatial orders of elements that are not integrated.	0 Deny class membership, i.e., $x \in X$	1 Approach matrix by placement of odd element, random choice, or response set.	2 Do not achieve four-class construction. Pairs, couples or other alogical procedures.	1 No class complementation with singular element and none even with plural elements. Neglect singular element, treating it in its likeness to others.	1 Children may or may not have achieved an original dichotomous classification, but do not succeed a reclassification by vicariance either by anticipation or by E's disassembling of the standing classification.
Figural	3 Organization achieved spatially rather than by subclasses.		2 Solution of matrix by element identity.	3 Achieve four-class construction in each matrix cell. No intersection of classes.		

	Constituent functions	Operational
Assert class membership, but without logical class inclusion mechanism, $A \subset B$. 1 Fail extensive quantification of the predicate. 2 Succeed extensive quantification of the predicate.	Demonstrate logical class inclusion mechanism ($A \subset B \Rightarrow A = B - \bar{A}$) in addition to class membership 3 Fail extensive quantification of the predicate. 4 Succeed extensive quantification of the predicate.
4 Some achievement of apparently logical classes or subclasses. However, construction is by trial and error rather than by anticipation, and may not be complete.	5 Achievement of complete logical classification of the universe set by anticipatory procedures.
3 Solution of matrix correct by intersection on at least two of four forms. However, justification and/or stability are lacking. 4 At least two correct element choices with proper justification. 5 Solution by identity on diagonal but with proper justification. 6 At least three correct element choices. Justification and/or stability lacking.	7 Solution of matrix consistently correct by intersection with justification and stability of response.
4 Succeed four-class matrix construction with class intersection. However, lack justification and/or stability.	5 Succeed four-class matrix construction with class intersection and with justification and stability.
2 Class complementation established not with singular element, but with plural elements.	3 Class complementation established with singular element.
2 After having achieved an original dichotomous classification, Ss do not anticipate vicariance but achieve it by trial and error after Es disassembling the previous classification.	3 Anticipation of vicariance posibility: $A/\bar{A} = B/\bar{B}$ (given AB, $A\bar{B}$, $\bar{A}B$, $\bar{A}\bar{B}$).

[a] Numbers refer to cognitive level scores.

[b] Stages are described by Piaget and Inhelder (1967). They have been slightly modified here to meet empirical specifications of the tasks in this study; abstractions have been made from full cognitive level specifications to meet the theoretical focus of this study.

[c] Each of five operations (classification, union, intersection, complementation, and vicariance) is specified in its heading by the logical grouping to which it pertains (logical addition, logical multiplication, logical complementation, inclusion, etc.) on lines 1, 2, and 3 of the heading respectively.

227

sessions according to the age and individual needs of the child. The mean number of sessions for cognitive testing for ages 8–10 was 1.0; for 6- to 7-year olds, 1.5; for 4- to 5-year olds, 2.0; and for 2- to 3-year olds, 2.0. For the six school-attending 3-year olds who were also given matrix (abstract) and inclusion tasks, the mean number of sessions was 2.8; for the preschool 2- and 3-year olds who had the abbreviated battery, the mean number of cognitive sessions was 1.6.

The mean number of test sessions, including both cognitive and linguistic tasks, was 2.0 for the 8- to 10-year olds; 3.5 for the 6- to 7-year olds; 5.5 for the 4- to 5-year olds; and 5.1 for the 2- to 3-year olds. The mean for six school-attending 3-year olds was 6.8 and for the preschool 2- and 3-year olds was 4.0.

Linguistic and cognitive testing procedures for the older children were followed as much as possible in the testing of preschoolers. The 2-year olds and the youngest 3-year olds were tested in their homes with their mothers present or nearby. A carpeted floor-surface of a living room or the child's playroom was chosen for testing. Sessions lasted according to the child's individual needs and interests. However, due to the complexities of testing children of this young age, there were several procedural adaptations. The first session included a preliminary period devoted to allowing the child to become acquainted with the experimenter (the experimenter often played some of the child's games). This allowed the experimenter to obtain speech samples (see the section "Supplementary Tasks"). Mothers were usually present during this session and the speech samples include mother–child exchange. A pretesting session followed. During linguistic testing, an attempt was made to obtain a response to each of the 18 items. In cases in which no response was given due to inattention or distraction on the child's part, the experimenter would attempt to repeat the item at another time. In cases in which it was not possible to elicit response to an item, after several such repetitions, it was scored as a nonresponse and entered into the miscellaneous error category. Sessions were often interrupted by the experimenter so that the experimenter and subject could play "another game" (of the child's), after which they would return to the experimenter's game. This procedure was adopted to ensure sustained attention to the test tasks. All items were attempted for each child at least once.

The permissible response categories for linguistic items were extended for the 2- to 3-year-old children. When children simply referred to one, two, or more exemplars by simply touching them, or pointing to them, or by giving them directly to the experimenter rather than by placing them in the basket, these responses were recorded and scored.

Simpler classification commands were given to this age group. Subjects were first asked, "Can you fix these dolls up?" (a simple command used by Ricciuti, 1965) followed by the same commands that were given to older subjects, "Put together all those dolls that go together. Make order with the dolls." Second and third requests for reclassification were not given to these subjects.

Subjects of this age were generally nonresponsive to requests for vicariance, "Can you do it another way?" Although this question was sometimes asked of the 2- to 3-year-old children, it was not repeated and the child was not pressed to respond.

Data Analysis

In addition to the ANOVAS performed on the linguistic task data, analyses of the cognitive data produced a cognitive level score for each of the subjects for each task. The relation between linguistic and cognitive data was assessed by both contingency and correlational analyses. Correlational analyses consisted of bivariate correlations between the specified components of each dimension, and a canonical correlation between sets of scores on the cognitive and linguistic dimensions.

Because the 2- to 3-year olds were administered connective sentences in a slightly different linguistic form from the 4- to 10-year olds, as specified above, most linguistic analyses were performed separately on the 2- to 3-year-old data.

Supplementary Tasks (2- and 3-Year-Old Sample)

SPEECH SAMPLE

Speech samples were collected from each child in the youngest age group to determine his natural-language developmental level.

IMITATION

A randomized list of eight items consisted of one item of each of the three linguistic forms applied to the two logical forms $A \cdot B$ and $A \vee B$ (six items) as well as one item of each negation form (relative clause and denial) of the linguistic test. Two lists were composed. One list used the *monkey–bear* lexical conjuncts; the other the *girl–boy* lexical conjuncts. Each child received at least one list. Imitation data were obtained on the last day of testing after all other data were collected. Imitations were taped as were the speech samples. The conditions for obtaining these samples generally followed those of Slobin (1967).

Subjects

Sixty-four children between 2 and 10 years of age in four age-groups of 16 subjects each were studied. In addition, 16 adults were tested on the linguistic battery alone. All children, except for 10 preschoolers (from 2 to 3 years of age), attended a private elementary school in Greenwich, Connecticut. Six of the preschoolers were from the Greenwich–Stamford area surrounding the school; the remaining 4 were from New York City. Eight of the 10 preschoolers' parent-pairs had a college background;

six of these families included at least 1 parent who had pursued graduate study. The *2-to 3-year-old age group* (8 at each age level) ranged in age from 2.2.23 (years, months, days) to 3.9.26 with a mean age of 3.1 (years, months—age at date of initial testing).

The *4- to 5-year-old group* (nine 4-year olds; seven 5-year olds) of school children ranged in age from 4.4.7 to 5.10.19 (mean 5.0). The *6- to 7-year-old group* (8 in each level) in the middle-school age ranged from 6.1.4 to 7.7.12 (mean of 6.11). The *8- to 10-year-old group* (5, 6, and 5 at each year) of the upper-school age ranged in age from 8.3.15 to 10.10.23 (mean age 9.6).

Half of the subjects in each group were male, half female except for the 4- to 5-year-old group which consisted of 9 females and 7 males. A total of 33 females and 31 males was tested.

All subjects were white, monolingual children. No child with a specific language disability was included in the sample. Teacher judgment was used as the basis for this sorting. To check on the accuracy of their judgments, for the oldest group the profiles of scores on SAT word meaning, paragraph meaning, and arithmetic comprehension were inspected for their deviation from the norms (SAT–Otis IQ Conversion Table norms). Only one child showed a profile with a negative deviation for a language task (paragraph meaning or word meaning) with a positive correlation on the mathematics task. This near-perfect concordance of teacher judgment with objective test measures was taken to indicate the adequacy of teacher judgment as the basis for subject selection. (Teachers had judged the one exceptional child to be average in classroom language performance.)

The mean IQ of the oldest subject group (8- to 10-years old) was 120.2. The mean IQ of the 6- to 7-year olds was 114.2 (based in general on the Otis test). IQ scores were not available for the younger children. The group of 16 adult subjects was recruited from psychology departments at the Graduate Center of the City University. Their average age was 24.6 years. An equal number of males and females were tested.

Testing Order Effects

The order of administering cognitive and linguistic tests was counterbalanced within each group. To evaluate the order effect, two-way analyses of variance on age and order factors were performed on both linguistic and cognitive data. On the *linguistic battery* the effect of Order was not significant. There was, however, a significant interaction with Age ($p < .05$). At 4- to 5-years old, those who had language testing first were significantly better on the language test ($p < .01$). The only significant effect of order was at this age. In order to locate the effects of order, ANOVAS were performed on each of the connectives at the 4–5 age group. The order effect was found to be significant for ($A \cdot B, \overline{A} \cdot \overline{B}, A \vee B$—all at $< .05$ level but not for $A \cdot \overline{B}, A \vee \overline{B}, \overline{A} \vee \overline{B}$). One can conclude that the effect of order per se on language performance was not significant for the 4- to 10-year olds, although an unexplained effect was shown in the performance of the 4- to

5-year-old subjects on three connectives of the language battery. An ANOVA performed on the 2- and 3-year-old linguistic data showed no effects of order.

For the *cognitive data*, comparable ANOVAS were performed to evaluate the effect of age and order on each of the basic cognitive operations: spontaneous classification, inclusion, matrix (abstraction), matrix (construction), and complementation (pooled estimate of base and extended set operations), as well as on vicariance and connective functions.

For the basic cognitive tests, no order effect was found on basic operations at any age. However, comprehension of vicariance by 6- to 7-year olds was significantly improved by prior language testing experience. Limited effects were also found on cognitive functions. Because of the limited nature of these order effects, subsequent analyses combined these data. The significance of these findings is discussed later.

OTHER EFFECTS

It was also possible that response to connective items would be affected by their position within the test series of linguistic Battery *1* (4- to 10-year olds). This possibility was greater with younger subjects by virtue of the rather long testing periods over which the battery was administered. If this were the case, there might be spurious differences between responses to the first item of a form and the later repetition of it. Analyses indicated that differential responding to connectives was not significantly confounded by item order or length.

Boys and girls were not significantly different on the linguistic test as shown by analysis of variance on children's total linguistic scores. This was true for both 2–3 and 4–10 age groups. The data for boys and girls were therefore pooled.

Possible differences in the comprehension of connectives due to the nature of the *lexical* classes forming the conjuncts of the connectives was tested. It is possible that children might succeed more easily within conjunction or disjunction of *monkey–bear* pairs or *girl–boy* pairs. Tests for independent proportions were not significant over age or for any particular age group. Comparison of pairs within each bivariate logical form at each age and over all ages confirmed that there were no significant differences within any particular form. Some limited differences were found with single conjunct forms (A and $\overline{A}$) which will be discussed subsequently.

Reliability of Cognitive Scoring

Cognitive testing was scored by one experimenter. Reliability of the scoring was assessed with another rater in the application of Piagetian stage categories to the spontaneous classification task. The spontaneous classification task was taken as an index of the reliability of the scoring of the entire cognitive battery because spontaneous classification was the most general task of the battery and, thus, was probably most susceptible to variation in scoring. A 14-stage scale was composed for the evaluation of classification behavior. The second rater, a psychology graduate student familiar with Piagetian theory, but unfamiliar with this study, was trained to apply the stage criteria. In 64 subjects' protocols, there were 7 scoring discrepancies between the two raters. All discrepancies were one step on the scale ($r = .99$). Interrater reliability was thus satisfactory.

Results—Linguistic

The results of the study are presented in three parts:
(1) *linguistic comprehension*, (2) *cognitive comprehension*, and (3) *relations between linguistic and cognitive comprehension*.

1. Analyses of linguistic comprehension included analyses of variance (ANOVAS) on the six linguistic bivariate connectives ($A \cdot B$, $A \cdot \bar{B}$, $\bar{A} \cdot \bar{B}$, $A \vee B$, $A \vee \bar{B}$, $\bar{A} \vee \bar{B}$), and independently on the two univariate base forms A and $\bar{A}$. ANOVA was also used to investigate the relation of the distributive connectives ($\overline{A \cdot B}$) and ($\overline{A \vee B}$) to the base forms A and $\bar{A}$. The analyses were intended to determine the effects of age, logical form, and interrelations among logical forms upon comprehension.

2. Structural relations among the forms were assessed by constructing comprehension hierarchies at each age and measuring association among these hierarchies. Developmental profiles were evaluated to establish **clusters** (forms that developed concurrently). The existence of such clusters was considered to be evidence of inherent structural relations among the forms in the linguistic system.

3. The nature of errors made in response to linguistic commands was assessed in order to gain an indication of the quality of children's prelogical or semilogical comprehension at different ages. In particular, responses were not only required to refer to the correct classes required by connective comprehension (intension) but also to give all exemplars of each of the classes (extension).

4. Separate analyses established Piagetian cognitive levels for each subject on each task of the set of cognitive operations and functions (classification, union, intersection, complementation, vicariance, dichotomy and element adjunction).

5. The two sets of data (linguistic and cognitive) were then statistically interrelated to establish developmental precedence and to assess the structural and functional relations between these two domains.

Linguistic Comprehension (ANOVA I)

Responses were judged correct if the subjects carried out the sorting commands of the various linguistic statements. A correct response was considered an indication of the child's comprehension of the compound statement and of the connective function it embodied.

For the purposes of this study, correct disjunction response was an

TABLE 7-3

Mean Number of Correct Responses at Each Age Group under All Conditions of ANOVA 1

	A.B				A ∨ B			
Age group	A.B	A.$\bar{B}$	$\bar{A}$.$\bar{B}$	Total A.B	A ∨ B	A ∨ $\bar{B}$	$\bar{A}$ ∨ $\bar{B}$	Total A ∨ B
4–5								
Conjoined sentences	1.25	0.13	0.88	0.75	0.75	0.63	0.00	0.46
Derived sentences quantified	1.00	0.06	1.00	0.69	0.75	0.63	0.00	0.46
Derived sentences	1.25	0.13	0.81	0.73	0.44	0.56	0.00	0.33
6–7								
Conjoined sentences	1.63	0.75	1.44	1.27	1.00	1.00	0.06	0.69
Derived sentences	1.63	0.63	1.56	1.27	1.19	0.94	0.00	0.71
Quantified derived sentences	1.69	0.69	1.44	1.27	1.06	1.19	0.00	0.75
8–10								
Conjoined sentences	2.00	1.38	1.88	1.75	1.94	1.50	0.81	1.42
Derived sentences	2.00	1.56	1.94	1.83	2.00	1.00	0.38	1.13
Quantified derived sentences	1.94	1.50	2.00	1.81	2.00	1.56	0.56	1.38
4–10								
Conjoined sentences	1.63	0.75	1.40	1.26	1.23	1.04	0.29	0.85
Derived sentences	1.54	0.75	1.50	1.26	1.31	0.85	0.13	0.76
Quantified derived sentences	1.63	0.77	1.42	1.27	1.17	1.10	0.19	0.82

exclusive disjunction response. Thus, for example, to be correct, subjects asked for A or B and had to give A or give B, but **not both** A and B.

Means for each age group of the six connective types ($A \cdot B$, $A \cdot \bar{B}$, $\bar{A} \cdot \bar{B}$, $A \vee B$, $A \vee \bar{B}$, $\bar{A} \vee \bar{B}$) and the three sentence forms (conjoined, derived, quantified derived) are given in Table 7-3.

The ANOVA was based on a four-factor design ($2 \times 3 \times 3 \times 3$) with repeated measures on the first 3 factors. The factors were *connective* type (*and–or*), *negation* (no negation, single conjunct-negation and double conjunct-negation), *linguistic form* (conjoined, derived, quantified derived), and *age* (ages 4–5, 6–7, and 8–10).

MAIN EFFECTS

Each of the main effects was significant except Linguistic form. (Age: $p < .001$; Connective: $p < .001$; Negation: $p < .001$; Linguistic form: *n.s.*). Comparison of means (by Newman-Keuls procedures, Winer, 1972) indicated that the differences between age groups were significant ($< .01$). Children showed increasing success in connective comprehension with increasing age (χs $= .57, .99, 1.55$).

The significant effects of connective type indicated disjunction forms to be generally more difficult than conjunction form ($p < .001$).

The order of difficulty of negation was no negation, single negation, double negation, with the last the most difficult (Table 7-4). Performance for the no negation forms was significantly greater ($p < .01$)than for single negation forms and double negation forms. The difference between single negation and double negation was not significant, indicating that the main effect was based on the addition of negation to the connective form. The double use of the negative operator in the sentence was not critical to the effect.

Although the effect of linguistic form was not significant, it did create subtle effects by differential interaction with connective type at different ages and with different levels of negation.

INTERACTIONS

Connective × Negation

A significant Connective × Negation interaction ($p < .001$) is illustrated in Figure 7-1. (The figure represents the interaction of connective × negation × linguistic form, which will be discussed later.) ANOVAS on simple effects showed that negation had a significant effect on both *and* and *or* ($p < .001$ in each case). As can be seen in Figure 7-1, the significant interaction reflected different patterns of difficulty created by the integration of negation with each of the two connectives. With *and*, mean performance was highest for no negation ($A \cdot B$), lower for the double negation form, and lowest for single negation ($A \cdot \bar{B}$). The differences between no negation ($A \cdot B$) and single negation ($A \cdot \bar{B}$), and between double negation ($\bar{A} \cdot \bar{B}$) and single negation ($A \cdot \bar{B}$), were significant ($p < .01$). However, the difference between double negation ($\bar{A} \cdot \bar{B}$) and no negation ($A \cdot B$) was not significant.

TABLE 7-4

Mean Number of Correct Responses at Three Levels of Negation[a]

	Age group	No negation	Single negation	Double negation
	4–5	0.91	0.35	0.45
	6–7	1.37	0.87	0.75
	8–10	1.98	1.42	1.26
Total				
	(4–10)	1.42	0.88	0.82

[a] Summed over both connective forms (*and* and *or*).

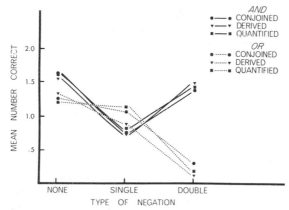

Fig. 7-1. Negation responses as a function of type of negation and linguistic form for conjunction and disjunction.

With *or*, the negative caused a continuous although not a linear decrease in comprehension with each negation operator added, as Figure 7-1 shows. The no-negation form $(A \lor B)$ was significantly less difficult than either single $(A \lor \bar{B})$ $(p < .05)$ or double $(\bar{A} \lor \bar{B})$ $(p < .01)$ negation of disjunction forms.

As Figure 7-1 indicates, *and* was significantly easier than *or* at two levels of negation, namely, no negation and double negation $(p < .01)$. Conversely, *or* with single negation $(A \lor \bar{B})$ was significantly easier than *and* with single negation $(A \cdot \bar{B})$ $(p < .05)$.

Age × Connective × Negation

A significant Age × Connective × Negation interaction $(p < .05)$ is shown in Figure 7-2. This figure indicates that although the Connective ×

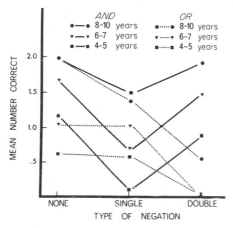

Fig. 7-2. Negation responses as a function of type of negation and age for conjunction and disjunction.

Negation interaction was evident at each age, and although the form of this interaction remained generally constant at both the 4–5 and 6–7 age levels, a qualitative shift in the form of the interaction occurred at the 8–10 age level.

With the *and* connective, no negation was significantly easier than single negation ($p < .05$ at ages 8–10; $p < .01$ at ages 4–5 and 6–7), and single negation was significantly more difficult than double negation ($A \cdot \bar{B} < \bar{A} \cdot \bar{B}$) ($p < .05$ at ages 8–10; $p < .01$ at ages 4–5 and 6–7). At no age, however, did no negation differ significantly from double negation. With the *or* connective at 4–5 and 6–7 years of age, both no negation and single negation were significantly easier than double negation ($p < .01$), although they did not differ significantly from each other. In contrast, with the oldest children (8– to 10-years old), each negation form of disjunction differed significantly from the other ($p < .01$) with successful comprehension decreasing as negation complexity increased.

Comparing connectives *and* and *or*, the age breakdown indicated the following: (1) with no negation, *and* was significantly easier ($A \cdot B < A \vee B$) than *or* at ages 4–5 ($< .05$) and at ages 6–7 ($< .01$), but not at the 8- to 10-year old level; (2) with single negation, *and* was significantly more difficult than *or* ($A \cdot \bar{B} > A \vee \bar{B}$) only with ages 4–5 ($p < .05$); differences between $A \cdot \bar{B}$ and $A \vee \bar{B}$ gradually narrowed over age; (3) with double negation, *and* was significantly ($p < .01$) less difficult than *or* at each age ($\bar{A} \cdot \bar{B} < \bar{A} \vee \bar{B}$).

Connective × Negation × Linguistic Form

The significant Connective × Negation × Linguistic form interaction ($p < .01$) showed (Fig. 7-1) that in addition to age, Linguistic form was a significant factor in the comprehension of some connective-negation compounds. Comparing the Connective × Negation interaction and the Connective × Negation × Linguistic form interaction shows that the linguistic form of the expressions of the connective *or* ($A \vee B$, $A \vee \bar{B}$, $\bar{A} \vee \bar{B}$), in particular, differentiated the profile of *or* comprehension.

These effects were quite specific, however, to the particular form of the connective, i.e., to its negation. Two forms ($A \vee \bar{B}$, $\bar{A} \vee \bar{B}$) were most affected by linguistic transformation (see the following section).

Age × Connective × Linguistic Form

The significant Age × Connective × Linguistic form interaction ($p < .01$) indicated that the influence of linguistic form on the connectives *and* and *or* (summed across all negation types) was not uniform at each age or for each connective (Fig. 7-3).

As suggested above, it was specifically *or* on which linguistic form had its effects. *And* connectives as a group appeared relatively unaffected by

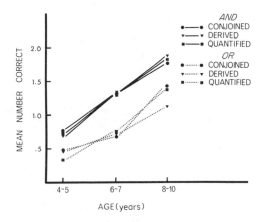

Fig. 7–3. Conjunction and disjunction response by age and linguistic form.

linguistic form at all ages. Tests of simple effects revealed that the Connective × Linguistic form interaction was significant only at ages 8–10 ($p < .01$) in respect to the *or* connective.

The nonuniformity of the effects of linguistic form on disjunction (*or*) is shown by the following (Fig 7-4). At ages 4–5, the conjoined and derived sentences were easier than the quantified form (*either*) of $A \vee B$; at ages 6–7, all of the linguistic forms were comparable; at ages 8–10, for $A \vee \bar{B}$ and $\bar{A} \vee B$ the derived form was considerably more difficult than the conjoined and quantified forms. With development, the quantified form of disjunction went from significantly more difficult to significantly less difficult yet the derived form was significantly more difficult than the other forms at the older age level.

Comparing *and* and *or* in each linguistic form at each age revealed that,

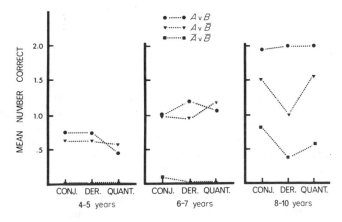

Fig. 7–4. Disjunction response by linguistic form for 3 age groups.

with the exception of 4- to 5-year olds in the derived sentence form, *and* connectives as a group were significantly easier than *or* connectives. At 4- to 5-years old, in the derived form, *and* and *or* connectives did not differ significantly.

In summary, the significant Age × Connective × Linguistic form interaction was primarily due to the differentiated performance in *or* connective comprehension created by different linguistic forms at particular ages. In particular the effects were most notable in 8- to 10-year olds.

SUMMARY OF ANOVA I

The results of ANOVA I on the linguistic comprehension of children from 4 to 10 years of age suggests that connective comprehension was affected by age, connective type (*and* and *or*), and negation. The connectives as a group developed over the full 4- to 10-year period; disjunction was more difficult than conjunction, although negation as well as linguistic form could modify this relation.

Negation affected connectives differently. In general, connective comprehension was not significantly affected by the linguistic form of the expression, although at certain ages, linguistic form did affect specific connective forms (connective *or* with negation). These effects of linguistic form were most notable at ages 8–10.

Linguistic Connectives: Comprehension of 2- to 3-Year Olds (ANOVA II)

The data for 2- and 3-year-old children were analyzed separately from the 4- to 10-year olds because the younger subjects did not receive all of the logical forms. They did not receive connectives with negation, although they did receive the negative single conjunct form ($\overline{A}$), as well as A and the bivariate connectives $A \cdot B$ and $A \vee B$. The means for each age group are presented in Table 7-5. ANOVA II was the same as ANOVA I, except for the omission of negation as a main effect. Similar to the results of ANOVA I on older children, the effect of Connective type was significant ($p < .001$) while Linguistic form was not. Age, however, was not significant, and none of the interactions was significant.

Even at ages 2–3 a differentiation between the *and* connective and the *or* disjunction was evident. Disjunction comprehension only appeared for the first time at 3-years old, and at that only minimally. Some comprehension of *and* was evident at age 2.

An inspection of the individual means (Table 7-5) suggests that linguistic form had some effects on connective comprehension, as did age although the effects were not statistically significant. Because a priori theoretical considerations render these differences important, individual comparisons (Winer, 1972, p. 551) were made of certain specific pairs of means to further analyze these effects. (The zero variance in several of these conditions prohibited several statistical comparisons.) Differentiation of con-

TABLE 7-5

Mean Number of Correct Conjunction and Disjunction Responses by LInguistic Form for 2- and 3-Year Olds

Age and sentence type	A.B	A v B
2-year olds		
Conjoined sentences	0.38	0.00
Derived sentences	0.25	0.00
Quantified derived sentences	0.00	0.00
Total	0.21	0.00
3-year olds		
Conjoined sentences	0.75	0.25
Derived sentences	0.75	0.25
Quantified derived sentences	0.75	0.13
Total	0.75	0.21
Total: 2- and 3-year olds	0.48	0.10

nectives by linguistic form at each age is seen in Figure 7-5. The quantified form with *and* (i.e., *both*) at the 2-year-old level and the quantified form with *or* (i.e., *either*) at the 3-year-old level reduced connective comprehension. The difference between conjoined and quantified forms of *or* at the 3-year-old level was, however, not significant. The quantified derived form of *and* was more difficult than the conjoined sentence form for 2-year olds, although the derived form was not. All linguistic forms of *and* were processed similarly by the 3-year olds (Table 7-4).

A test of the difference between means of *and* (over all linguistic forms) between 2 and 3 years was significant ($p < .05$) suggesting that the comprehension of *and* significantly increases from ages 2 to 3. As suggested

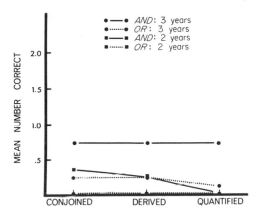

Fig. 7–5.   Conjunction and disjunction response by linguistic form for 2- and 3-year olds.

above, however, the increase, in success with *or* from ages 2 to 3 years was minor.

The differences between the comprehension of 2- and 3-year olds on the quantified forms of *and* was large (not testable) as was the difference between their performance on the derived linguistic forms of *and* ($p < .05$). The difference between their performance on the conjoined sentence form of *and* was not significant. Thus an age effect (increase in success from ages 2 to 3) was more evident in the linguistically transformed *and* forms.

In summary then, the 2- to 3-year-old data confirm the differences between conjunction and disjunction found with older (4- to 10-year olds) children, with conjunction significantly easier than disjunction. Comprehension of conjunction ($A \cdot B$) appeared earlier developmentally than disjunction ($A \vee B$) with some evidence of success at the 2-year-old level; the latter appeared at 3-years old. As with older children, linguistic form was not a significant effect.

Base Forms A and $\overline{A}$

The above analyses dealt with comprehension of the six bivariate connectives administered to 4- through 10-year olds, two of which were also administered to 2- through 3-year olds.

We are now concerned with the comprehension of the *univariate* forms A ("Give me the *dolls* which are *girls*") and $\overline{A}$ ("Give me the *dolls* which are not *girls*"). The first of these analyses was intended to determine the relationship of these univariate forms to each other.

COMPREHENSION OF A AND $\overline{A}$ BY 4- THROUGH 10-YEAR OLDS

The means for each age group are shown in Table 7-6. An ANOVA based on correct comprehension responses showed both age and logical form

TABLE 7-6

Mean Number of Correct Responses on A and $\overline{A}$

		$\overline{A}$	
Age	A	$\overline{A}_{(w)}$	$\overline{A}_{(n+w)}$
2-year olds	0.00	0.00	0.00
3-year olds	0.63	0.00	0.25
2- to 3-year olds (Total[a])	0.21	0.00	0.13
4- to 5-year olds	2.06	0.69	2.13
6- to 7-year olds	3.19	1.88	2.81
8- to 10-year olds	3.94	2.63	3.75
4- to 10-year olds (Total[b])	3.06	1.73	2.90

[a] Range for 2- to 3-year olds = 2.
[b] Range for 4- to 10-year olds = 4.

to be significant (Age: $p < .001$; Logical form, A versus $\bar{A}$: $p < .001$). Comparison of individual means revealed that change in the comprehension of these connective forms from ages 4 5 to 6–7 was significant ($p < .05$), but increase from ages 6–7 to 8–10 was not. Overall change from 4- to 10-years old was significant ($p < .01$). The difference between A and $\bar{A}$ (with A superior) was statistically significant at each age.

COMPREHENSION OF A AND $\bar{A}$ BY 2- TO 3-YEAR OLDS

Comprehension by 2- and 3-year olds of single conjunct forms (A and $\bar{A}$) is shown in Table 7-6. ANOVA was not possible because of zero variance in major cells in the design. Two-year olds showed no success on either A or $\bar{A}$). $\bar{A}$ was, in addition, not succeeded by any 3-year old. An interaction effect was indicated by the data: while the A form underwent change from 2 to 3 years of age, the $\bar{A}$ form remained at zero across these ages.

In summary, 3-year olds showed a higher performance on A than on $\bar{A}$; 2-year olds had no success on either type sentence. Comprehension of A made its first appearance at age 3; $\bar{A}$ was not initially understood until ages 4–5.

These findings appear to disconfirm the theorized equal developmental priority of A and $\bar{A}$ as base logical forms underlying the development of linguistic connectives. In general, the developmental priority of A argues against the (cognitive) logicality of primitive propositional forms because, as suggested above, it has been held (by Piaget) that the concurrent inverse operator is a necessary condition for logicality in cognitive structure. It should be considered though that the inability to succeed in the $\bar{A}$ task, as defined in this study, does not signify the young child's total inability to comprehend negation.

Negation

Two modes of logical negation are developmentally differentiated, according to Piagetian theory. A "wide" mode (hereafter referred to as $\bar{A}_w$) in which $\bar{A} = U - A$ results from gradual closure of the full cognitive lattice structure and culminates in the formal structure of adolescent cognition. A "narrow" mode, on the other hand (hereafter referred to as $\bar{A}_n$), in which $\bar{A} =$ the nearest class neighbor of A in U, may appear in a limited prelattice cognitive structure. The analyses reported above were concerned with the wide type of negation response only.

Inspection of types of response in children's comprehension of negation (Table 7-7) shows the *wide* type of response gradually increases with age (0% at 2- to 3-years old; 17.2% at 4- to 5-years old; 46.9% at 6- to 7-years old; 65.6% at 8- to 10-years old). The *narrow* type response, on the other hand, increases (6.3% at ages 2–3; 35.9% at ages 4–5) but then decreases (23.4% at ages 6–7; 28.1% at ages 8–10). Correct wide-responding reached 50% (of responses) only at age 7, and remained at this level to age 10 when near-complete (90%) response occurred.

TABLE 7-7

Distribution of Wide, Narrow, and Combined Wide and Narrow Responses on $\bar{A}$[a] (Percentages)

Age group	$\bar{A}$		
	Wide	*Narrow*	*Combined wide + narrow*
2–3 years old	0	6	6
4–5 years old	17	36	53
6–7 years old	47	23	70
8–10 years old	66	28	94

[a] Based on four items per subject for ages 4–10; two items per subject for ages 2–3. Percentages are based on the total number of items.

For the 2- to 3-year olds, all "correct" negation responses (in which correct includes either narrow or wide-responding) were narrow. At 4- to 5-years old, 67.6% of the correct negation responses were narrow and 32.4% were wide. By ages 6–7, 66.7% of these negation responses were in the wide mode. There was a clear shift, then, from narrow to wide - mode comprehension of negation from 4- to 5- and 6- to 7-years old.

Tests for dependent means were performed on the differences between wide and narrow responses at each of the four age levels and across ages. Only at the 8–10 age level was the difference between wide and narrow type responses significant ($p < .05$). The effect across all ages was not significant. The replacement of narrow by wide responding was thus gradual, culminating only at ages 8–10.

In order to consider the relation of early comprehension of negation ($\bar{A}$) to the comprehension of assertion (A), the above ANOVA analyses were repeated, accepting as correct, those negation responses of both the narrow and the wide type.

RELATION OF FORM A TO $\bar{A}$ (NARROW AND WIDE RESPONSE TYPES)

In the new analysis of A and $\bar{A}$ on children 4- to 10-years old, when both wide and narrow negation responses were considered as correct, Age was again significant ($p < .001$). Again, comparison among means revealed that change from ages 4–5 to 6–7 was significant ($p < .05$), but from ages 6–7 to 8–10 it was not. Overall change was again significant ($p < .01$). When A and $\bar{A}$ were analyzed separately only overall change from ages 4–10 was significant for each. In this analysis, form (A versus $\bar{A}$) did not yield a significant effect.

Results for the 2- to 3-year olds were analogous to those for 4- to 10-year-old children. Age again appeared to affect comprehension. Three-year olds did better on both forms than the 2-year olds. Two-year-old performance was zero on both forms. Two-year olds thus demonstrated no comprehension of $\overline{A}$ either in a wide or a narrow sense on these tasks just as they did not demonstrate comprehension of A. Three-year olds, however, showed initial although slight comprehension of both A ($\overline{X} = .63$) and $\overline{A}_{nw}$ ($\overline{X} = .25$). Comprehension of A was slightly superior to $\overline{A}_{nw}$, although the difference was not significant.

Therefore, with 2- to 3-year olds as with 4- to 10-year olds, A and $\overline{A}$ did not differ significantly from each other when a narrow response was considered as correct. For the older as well as younger subjects, this was at variance with the significant difference between these forms when only a wide response to negation was taken as correct.

It follows then that comprehension of A, and a qualified comprehension of $\overline{A}$, developed synchronously. This synchrony had its onset at age 3. Major development of these forms occurred before 6- to 7-years old. This synchrony suggests that the logical features of propositional connective comprehension begin with these base logical forms at a very early age.

Relation of Distributive Connectives to Base Logical Forms A and $\overline{A}$

A pooled score for distributive connectives was composed by summation across the two items of each distributive form ($\overline{A \cdot B}$ and $\overline{A \vee B}$), yielding a range of scores from 0 to 4.[5] When the single conjunct forms A and $\overline{A}_w$ were compared to the distributive forms in an ANOVA for children from ages 4 to 10, both Age ($p < .001$) and Logical form (A, $\overline{A}_w$, $\overline{A \cdot B}$, $\overline{A \vee B}$) were significant ($p < .001$) as in the A and $\overline{A}$ analyses. When means were compared, it was found that significant change occurred between ages 4–5 and 6–7 ($\overline{X} = 1.8$ and $\overline{X} = 2.9$ respectively—$p < .01$), as well as between ages 6–7 and 8–10 ($\overline{X} = 2.9$ and $\overline{X} = 3.8$, respectively—$p < .05$), differing from the A and $\overline{A}$ analyses. In addition, not only did A and $\overline{A}_w$ differ significantly from each other, but the distributive forms also differed significantly from $\overline{A}_w$ ($p < .01$). The distributive forms did not differ significantly, however, from A.

In a second ANOVA relating distributive forms to A and $\overline{A}_{nw}$ (in which both wide and narrow negation responses were taken as correct for A), Age was again significant ($p < .001$); Logical form was not. Not only did A and $\overline{A}_{nw}$ not differ significantly from each other but neither did the distributive connectives differ significantly from either of these. When comparisons were made between specific age level data, it was found that here too the increase in comprehension from ages 6–7 to 8–10 was significant ($p < .05$), in addition to the change from ages 4–5 to 6–7 ($p < .01$).

The distributive connectives, then, cluster developmentally with the base forms, A and $\overline{A}_{nw}$. Growth in comprehension of this set of forms continued to 8–10 years of age.

---

[5] For these analyses $\overline{A \cdot B}$ was considered correct when it was interpreted as $\overline{A \vee B}$, which was the most common response to these forms.

Connective Clusters

Having separately considered *univariate* forms and *bivariate* connectives (as well as distributive connectives), we now compare these and analyze the full set for its structural characteristics. One hypothesis of this study was that the primitive single conjuncts, assertion (A) and negation ($\overline{A}$) integrate to form the foundation for the acquisition of the basic association between conjuncts ($A \cdot B$). A close developmental relation between ($A \cdot B$) and the ($+$) and ($-$) (or T and F) functions as represented by A and $\overline{A}$, would argue for a semilogical basis for the association $A \cdot B$, its structure being relevant to the later logical structure of a truth-tabular matrix.

As suggested in Chapter 6, some logicians consider A and $\overline{A}$ and conjunction ($A \cdot B$) to be an epistemologically basic set of logical operations. Establishing developmental primacy of the set (A, $\overline{A}$, and $A \cdot B$) would argue that this basic group of operations has psychological as well as epistemological validity.

Figure 7-6 graphs the developmental curves for the six bivariate connectives and two univariate forms. (Curves for both types of negation response are shown.) The developmental curves (defined by the percentages of correct responses at each level for each logical form) indicate three clusters of connectives. Clusters are defined by similarity in height and slope of developmental growth curves; they thus suggest developmental synchrony.

The linguistic connective forms can be examined to see if their comprehension appears (1) prior to age of cognitive attainment of concrete logical operations, i.e., approximately ages 6–7, (2) concurrent with the onset of these operations, or (3) concurrent with closure of concrete logical operations and with onset of formal or propositional logical operations, i.e., approximately ages 8–10 .

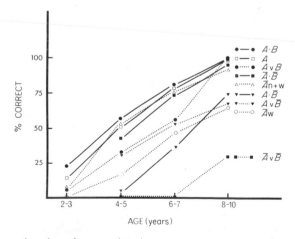

Fig. 7–6.   Comprehension of connectives by age.

CLUSTER 1: THE BASE SET (A, $\overline{A}_{nw}$, AND $A \cdot B$)

1. The curves indicating the development of comprehension of A (single conjunct assertion and $\overline{A}_{nw}$ (negation) show similar developmental trends with an intersection of the two (A and $\overline{A}_{nw}$) at ages 4–5. This was the age level at which simple conjunction ($A \cdot B$) attained the 50% success level. As the curves confirm, the near-parallel cluster of A and $A \cdot B$ forms and the closely parallel development of $\overline{A}_{nw}$ continues over the total age-span studied.

2. Two additional connective forms (tested only with children from ages 4–10) can be added to this cluster as behaving homogeneously with the base set. The pair ($\overline{A \vee B}$ and $\overline{A \cdot B}$) (i.e., the distributives, disjunction complementation, and conjunction complementation; they are not shown in Figure 7-6) approaching the 50% success level in the 4- to 5-year-old group, and equal the base set forms at close to 100% at ages 8–10. The near 50% achievement at ages 4–5 and the attainment of ceiling near 100% at ages 8–10 serve as defining criteria for Cluster 1.

CLUSTER 2: CONCRETE-OPERATIONAL LEVEL CONNECTIVES ($A \vee B$, $A \vee \overline{B}$, $\overline{A}$ [WIDE], $A \cdot \overline{B}$)

This set of connectives reaches a 50% success level only at about ages 6–7, and by ages 8–10 most of the connectives in this group (except for $A \vee \overline{B}$) have attained a near 70% level of success. These success levels serve as defining criteria for Cluster 2. $A \vee \overline{B}$ differs from the others in this cluster by attaining a near 100% group success level at ages 8–10, thus merging with Cluster 1 at this point. $A \cdot B$ differs from the cluster by a below 50% success level at ages 6–7. However, this low level of success at ages 6–7 on $A \cdot \overline{B}$ was due to the onset of comprehension of this form at only 7 years of age (in the 6- 7-year-old range); at age 7, percentage of success surpassed 50% (60.4%).

Two subparts can be distinguished in Cluster 2. (1) The two disjunctive forms ($A \vee B$ and $A \vee \overline{B}$) developed synchronously from ages 4–5 to 6–7. (At 8–10, however, the $A \vee B$ form approached 100%: $A \vee \overline{B}$ showed less attainment. The development of $A \vee \overline{B}$ will be discussed subsequently.) (2) On the other hand, $\overline{A}_w$ and $A \cdot \overline{B}$ appeared to bear a particular relation to each other; $A \cdot \overline{B}$ comprehension increased at a growth rate similar to that of $\overline{A}_w$ until ages 6–7 (judged from parallel slopes of lines, which then converged at ages 8–10).

CLUSTER 3: FORMAL LEVEL CONNECTIVE: $\overline{A} \vee \overline{B}$

Finally, comprehension of $\overline{A} \vee \overline{B}$ was marked by very late developmental onset, being nearly zero at ages 4–5 and 6–7 and only 29.2% at the 8- to 10-year-old level; growth in comprehension only started for this form at 9-years old (44.4%).

Interrelations Among Connectives

Figure 7-7 shows some changes in the patterns of relations among connectives at the 8–10 age level. Except for those shifts among 8- to 10-year olds, the developmental curves for the connectives remain fairly constant relative to each other across development, with continued improvement in comprehension for each connective and the maintenance of the clusters through development. Although $A \vee B$ and $A \cdot \overline{B}$ change their relative position at the 8- to 10-year-old level, the general picture suggests a structure which is remarkably consistent through development.

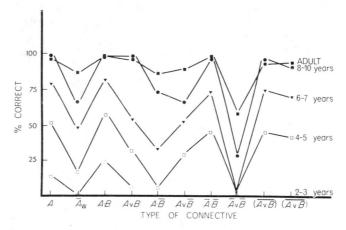

Fig. 7–7. Comprehension of connectives by adults and children.

LINGUISTIC CONNECTIVES

Rank-Order Hierarchies

The consistent relational structure among connectives is confirmed by the rank-order hierarchies of connectives at each of the three age levels. Comprehension, measured by percentage of correct responses, was used to rank the six bivariate connectives at each age level (see Table 7-8). The rank-order correlation (Spearman R) between the 4–5 and 6–7 age groups is $R = 1.0$ (perfect), and between the 6–7 (or 4–5) and 8–10 age groups is .84 ($p < .05$).

A measure of association between several rankings, Kendall's *coefficient of concordance* $W = .87$, ($p < .05$) confirmed the interrelations among the three hierarchies (Siegel, 1956). When rank orders of all ten connective forms (including the single conjunct and distributive forms) were correlated across age levels, correlations were still highly significant. The rank order correlation between 4- and 5- and 6- and 7-year olds was again 1.0; between 6–7 and 8–10 it was .90; and between ages 4–5 and 8–10, .81 (all $p < .01$). Kendall's coefficient of concordance across all three sets of ten connectives yielded $W = .755$ ($p < .02$).

TABLE 7-8

Rank Order of Connectives by Age Group (Percentage of Correct Responses)

Adult		Ages 8–10		Ages 6–7		Ages 4–5		Ages 2–3	
$A \cdot B$	99	$A \cdot B$	99	$A \cdot B$	82	$A \cdot B$	58	$A \cdot B$	24
$\overline{A} \cdot \overline{B}$	99	$A \vee B$	99	A	80	A	52	A	16
$\overline{A \cdot B}$	97	A	98	$\overline{A \vee B}$	75	$\overline{A \vee B}$	47	$A \vee B$	5
A	95	$\overline{A} \cdot \overline{B}$	97	$\overline{A} \cdot \overline{B}$	74	$\overline{A} \cdot \overline{B}$	45	$\overline{A}_w$	0
$A \vee B$	95	$\overline{A \vee B}$	97	$\overline{A \cdot B}$	72	$\overline{A \cdot B}$	41		
$\overline{A \vee B}$	94	$\overline{A \cdot B}$	94	$A \vee B$	54	$A \vee B$	32		
$A \vee \overline{B}$	90	$A \cdot \overline{B}$	74	$A \vee \overline{B}$	52	$A \vee \overline{B}$	30		
$\overline{A}_w$	88	$A \vee \overline{B}$	68	$\overline{A}_w$	47	$\overline{A}_w$	17		
$A \cdot \overline{B}$	87	$\overline{A}_w$	66	$A \cdot \overline{B}$	34	$A \cdot \overline{B}$	5		
$\overline{A} \vee \overline{B}$	59	$\overline{A} \vee \overline{B}$	29	$\overline{A} \vee \overline{B}$	1	$\overline{A} \vee \overline{B}$	0		

Finally, when only the four forms on which the 2- to 3-year olds were tested are considered (Table 7-8), only the ranking 8- to 10-year olds did not correlate perfectly with other age rankings on this basic set. (A perfect correlation was necessary for a $p < .05$ level of significance here.) The Kendall measure of association across all four age hierarchies was $S = 67.5$, $p < .01$. The comprehension hierarchy for the connectives was thus fairly constant across ages (2- to 10-years old). Only at age 8–10 did some changes in the order structure appear.

DISTRIBUTIVE CONNECTIVES

The structural interrelationships inherent in the linguistic connectives was also evident in the relation of the distributive connectives to the other forms. The distributive connectives ($\overline{A \vee B}$ and $\overline{A \cdot B}$) are logical equivalents to $\overline{A} \cdot \overline{B}$ and $\overline{A} \vee \overline{B}$, respectively, by the laws of deMorgan as described in Chapter 6. It should follow, then, that each distributive form would develop in close synchrony with its logical counterpart: ($\overline{A \vee B}$–$\overline{A} \cdot \overline{B}$) and ($\overline{A \cdot B}$–$\overline{A} \vee \overline{B}$). This finding would lend further support to the thesis that development is structured by the logical nature of a connective and not by the linguistic form of its expression.

Logical Equivalents ($\overline{A \vee B}$–$\overline{A} \cdot \overline{B}$)

These two forms develop in close synchrony. When the percentages of children who consistently succeed on these forms (at least all but one correct) are computed, the developmental progressions are almost identical. Contingency tables showing relations between subject's comprehension of $\overline{A} \cdot \overline{B}$ and $\overline{A \vee B}$ also show, at each age, and across ages, this close relation. These findings provide strong evidence for the existence of a logical structure underlying language connective comprehension.

Although these forms ($\overline{A} \cdot \overline{B}$ and $\overline{A \vee B}$) are not similar in surface form, their formal logical relation of equivalence (by distributivity) appears to provide the source of their synchrony in development.

Logical Equivalents ($\overline{A \cdot B} - \overline{A} \vee \overline{B}$)

It is difficult to evaluate the development of these two forms due to the ambiguity of the $\overline{A \cdot B}$ form as it was used in this study. For a subject to offer a *logical* response to the latter form it was necessary for him to assert its *ambiguity* (recognition of ambiguity response) or to give an $\overline{A} \vee \overline{B}$ response. It was also possible to give an intuitive or semilogical response which would entail interpreting this form as identical to $\overline{A} \vee \overline{B}$ and thus as equivalent logically to $\overline{A} \cdot \overline{B}$ (*resolution of ambiguity* response).

If the $\overline{A \cdot B}$ connective is scored correct when a resolution of ambiguity response is given, as it was for the analyses reported above, then the two distributive connectives $\overline{A \cdot B}$ and $\overline{A} \vee \overline{B}$ develop in close synchrony. Further evidence that the $\overline{A \cdot B}$ form is treated by subjects as $\overline{A \cdot B} = \overline{A} \vee \overline{B}$ $= \overline{A} \cdot \overline{B}$ comes from its close developmental synchrony with $\overline{A} \cdot \overline{B}$.

If recognition of ambiguity is considered the only correct response to the $\overline{A \cdot B}$ distributive form, then a closer synchrony appears with development of $\overline{A} \vee \overline{B}$ because recognition of ambiguity of $\overline{A \cdot B}$ is zero before ages 8–10 and initial development of $\overline{A} \vee \overline{B}$ starts at this age. (Adult data lend some support to this thesis and will be discussed later.)

A last point should be made in respect to the distributive forms. The first equivalent pair to develop is clearly the $\overline{A \vee B} = \overline{A} \cdot \overline{B}$ pair. The $\overline{A} \vee \overline{B}$ = (recognition of ambiguity $\overline{A \cdot B}$) pair is very late in development. This general differentiation between pairs suggest that is is not the linguistic connective per se (*and* or *or*) that determines primacy in development, but the logical structure underlying the connective. Thus the distributive form with the connective *or* ($\overline{A \vee B}$) develops very early; a fact explained by the premise that its logical structure is defined by $\overline{A} \cdot \overline{B}$, a conjunctive logical structure which develops early.

CONNECTIVE HIERARCHIES

Strong concordance among connective sets has been shown to hold across ages with some shift in the rankings occurring at ages 8–10. However, the previous analyses (Spearman's R and Kendall's W), do not expose certain properties of the connectives which have been treated in prior research. They also do not inspect relations between individual connective pairs.

For these purposes, a technique used by Neisser and Weene (1962) to measure connective hierarchies in adult concept comprehension was adapted for this study and applied to the 4- to 10-year-old data. Neisser and Weene propose "three degrees of hierarchical depth" in the set of ten connectives they analyzed. Negation, conjunction and disjunction were assumed to be basic operations in forming connectives in their system.

Their first level consisted of univariate connectives, A and $\overline{A}$; the second level consisted of a set of six bivariate connectives, such as $A \cdot B$, $A \vee B$. The third level contained two more complex forms based on the disjunction of certain conjunctive pairs. They interpreted their data as supporting a hierarchy in "concept attainment."

The connectives of the present study, contained a univariate pair analogous to that of Neisser and Weene: A and $\overline{A}$. Because our data show that a *narrow* interpretation of negation may be primitive, although a *wide* interpretation of negation is not, the *narrow* negation type was taken as part of the basic univariate set. All the bivariate connective forms were of Neisser and Weene's second-level type. No level identical to Neisser and Weene's third level was available in this study. On the basis of our own findings of relative difficulty, $\overline{A} \vee \overline{B}$ was treated as a third level.

Performance on one logical form as compared to another is indicated in Table 7-9 for the 4- to 10-year-old subjects. The data show the number of children with complete success on one form as opposed to incomplete (or no) success on another. As in the Neisser and Weene analysis, these figures indicate proportions of subjects who found one form easier than the other. The subjects who either succeeded or failed both forms are omitted from the analyses. The null hypothesis is that the logical forms are equally difficult and the proportions differ from one-half only by chance. A two-tailed binomial test was used as a test of significance. The Neisser and Weene convention of designating interlevel comparisons by a heavy line is followed. The comparisons that fall above and to the left of the line predict the lower-level logical form to be easier.

As can be seen from Table 7-9, the data show comprehension of connectives to be strongly hierarchical. The "hierarchical" depth was more complex than found in adults by Neisser and Weene. In the set of eight forms there were three general levels. Seventeen of the 19-interlevel comparisons were statistically significant. However, two of 9 intralevel comparisons were also significant. In general, a primary and tertiary level could be differentiated, with a secondary level somewhat more complex, perhaps consisting of one or more sublevels in light of the fact that $A \vee \overline{B}$ and $A \cdot \overline{B}$ were significantly more difficult than $A \vee B$.

There is no reason to suppose that this hierarchical structure is homogeneous at each of the three age levels pooled here: ages 4–5, 6–7, and 8–10. Reapplication of the above analyses to each of the age levels suggested that the hierarchical structure developed only gradually from ages 4–10. The 4- to 5-year olds cannot be differentiated by levels. Only three comparisons were significant here ($p < .05$), with the form $\overline{A} \cdot \overline{B}$ appearing as significantly easier than three of the five other bivariate connectives. In general, the consistency of processing logical forms was striking at this age. Subjects did not perform with consistent success on one connective set and consistent failure on another.

At ages 6–7 the connective set differentiates into two levels. The A, $\overline{A}_{nw}$, $A \cdot B$, and $\overline{A} \cdot \overline{B}$ set was significantly easier than the other four forms; 12 of the 16 interlevel comparisons were significant. None of the intralevel

TABLE 7-9

Proportion of Children for Whom One Logical Form Was Easier Than Another: Ages 4–10 (n = 48)[a]

	Level 3	Level 2			Level 1		
	$\bar{A} \vee \bar{B}$	$A \cdot \bar{B}$	$A \vee \bar{B}$	$A \vee B$	$\bar{A} \cdot \bar{B}$	$A \cdot B$	$\bar{A}_{nw}$
A	30/30***	19/20***	24/24***	12/14*	9/15	3/7	7/10
$\bar{A}_{n+w}$	26/26***	15/16***	21/22***	9/12	8/17	4/13	
$A \cdot B$	31/31***	20/21***	25/25***	12/13**	6/8		
$\bar{A} \cdot \bar{B}$	27/27***	18/21**	22/24***	12/16			
$A \vee B$	20/20***	9/10*	16/18**				
$A \vee \bar{B}$	6/6*	5/16					
$A \cdot \bar{B}$	12/12***						

[a] Numerators show number of subjects who succeed item of row while failing item of column. Denominators show number of subjects who perform differentially on the two forms. Success means all items correct. Comparisons between two different levels are above and left of the line.
* $p < .05$.
** $p < .01$.
*** $p < .001$.

comparisons was significant, suggesting consistency within logical level at this age level.

The data for ages 8–10 show further differentiation into three levels—the $\bar{A} \vee \bar{B}$ form is in a third level and $A \vee B$ shifts to Level 1. The $A \vee B$ and $A \cdot B$ forms define Level 2. At this age, 14 of the 17 interlevel comparisons were significant.

The above analyses are based on subject's performance dichotomized as completely correct or not for each logical form. For the bivariate connectives this concerned six items per logical form (two items each for three different linguistic forms). In the case of the single conjunct forms this concerned four items for each logical form. It is possible that the homogeneity among forms in the youngest children was due to the stringency of this requirement as fewer children at the youngest ages succeeded on a form completely (for all items). To assess this possibility a more sensitive analysis was undertaken of the six bivariate connectives.

The connective forms themselves were matched for success for each of the three linguistic modes in which they were expressed and then the results of the three comparisons were summed. There was a total n of 48 comparisons per each age group (16 subjects × 3 linguistic forms) and an n of 144 over all three groups.

TABLE 7-10

Proportion of Responses on Which One Connective Was Easier Than Another (with New Criterion) Ages 4–10

	$\bar{A} \vee \bar{B}$	$A \cdot \bar{B}$	$A \vee \bar{B}$	$A \vee B$	$\bar{A} \cdot \bar{B}$
$A \cdot B$	101/101***	64/65***	58/61***	34/38***	18/22*
$\bar{A} \cdot \bar{B}$	87/87***	52/55***	52/63***	29/42*	
$A \vee B$	71/71***	37/41***	39/53**		
$A \vee \bar{B}$	50/54***	32/56			
$A \cdot \bar{B}$	40/42***				

* $p < .05$.
** $p < .01$.
*** $p < .001$.

With the new criterion (Table 7-10), the six bivariate forms are even more highly hierarchically ordered over the 4–10 age span. Five "levels" can be defined on this basis for the 6 connectives. Only $A \vee \bar{B}$ and $A \cdot \bar{B}$ did not differ significantly from each other in the hierarchy. All other comparisons were significant.

In an age analysis, development was seen to be marked by progression from greater differentiation among the connectives to a three-level hierarchy. At the 4–5 age level, 11 of the 15 comparisons were significant. $A \cdot \bar{B}$ and $\bar{A} \vee \bar{B}$ were not differentiated and neither were $A \cdot B$ and $\bar{A} \cdot \bar{B}$. The remaining connectives reflected a loose step-wise progression between forms. The progression was loose because several immediate comparisons were not significant ($A \vee B / A \vee \bar{B}$; $\bar{A} \cdot \bar{B} / A \vee B$). At the 6–7 age level a four-level structure was apparent: (1) $\bar{A} \cdot \bar{B}$, $A \cdot B$; (2) $A \vee B$; (3) $A \vee \bar{B}$, $A \cdot \bar{B}$; and (4) $\bar{A} \vee \bar{B}$. Again, designation of levels was loose. At the 8–10 age level, the same structure found in the subject analysis appeared. Three levels were defined: (1) $A \vee B$, $\bar{A} \cdot \bar{B}$, $A \cdot B$; (2) $A \cdot \bar{B}$, $A \vee \bar{B}$; and (3) $\bar{A} \vee \bar{B}$.

Thus in contradistinction to the findings of Neisser and Weene, the subject analysis shows that the first level in a hierarchy of logical connectives includes not only the primal univariate forms A and $\bar{A}_{nw}$ but also the bivariate $A \cdot B$ and $\bar{A} \cdot \bar{B}$ forms (at ages 6–7 and in the overall analysis from ages 4–10). Furthermore, at 8- to 10-years old, an additional bivariate form is added to this level, $A \vee B$. Also, $\bar{A} \vee \bar{B}$ separates out from Neisser and Weene's second level as a distinct third-level form (8- to 10-years old and in the overall analysis).

When the six bivariate connectives were analyzed alone in terms of item correctness rather than consistent subject correctness, the developmental trend to a three-degree hierarchical depth was again evident. However, the trend was reversed. Instead of passage from global homogeneity to gradual differentiation of leveled subsets of connectives, development progressed from differentiation among connectives to a gradual integration in which three levels were defined.

In summary, young subjects (4- to 5-years old) did not perform with consistent success on one set of forms as opposed to another. As their comprehension of the connectives developed (6- to 7-years old) their performance differentiated so that two subsets were formed, one superior $(A, \bar{A}_{nw}, A \cdot B, \bar{A} \cdot \bar{B})$ and one inferior $(A \vee B, A \vee \bar{B}, A \cdot \bar{B}, \bar{A} \vee \bar{B})$. Finally, at 8- to 10-years old, three degrees of hierarchy could be differentiated: (1) $A, \bar{A}_{nw}, A \cdot B, \bar{A} \cdot \bar{B}, A \vee B$; (2) $A \vee \bar{B}, A \cdot \bar{B}$; (3) $\bar{A} \vee \bar{B}$. When item success was used as the criterion, comprehension of connectives by children was seen to be as strongly (almost totally) hierarchical. Only gradually were levels formed through the clustering of connective forms.

The item and subject analyses merged at the 8- to 10-year-old level. Only at this age did differentiation among connective forms reflect consistent subject performance.

RELATION OF NEGATION TO OTHER CONNECTIVES

Because the negation type used in establishing the hierarchies was the $\bar{A}_{nw}$ type, no assessment has been given of the relation of a full comprehension of negation $(\bar{A}_w)$ to the other connectives. Table 7-11 shows proportion of precedence in each pair-wise comparison using the same method employed in the above analysis. As the data indicate, two con-

TABLE 7-11

Proportion of Subjects Who Find Negation ($\bar{A}_w$) Easier Than Each Connective[a,b]

	Age groups			
	Ages 4–10	Ages 4–5	Ages 6–7	Ages 8–10
$A \cdot B$	2/23 − ***	1/6 −	1/8 −	0/9 − **
$A \cdot \bar{B}$	5/10	1/1	2/3	2/6 −
$\bar{A} \cdot \bar{B}$	4/23 − **	1/7 −	3/8 −	0/8 − **
$A \vee B$	4/16 −	1/2	3/5	0/9 − **
$A \vee \bar{B}$	12/18	1/2	5/6	6/10
$\bar{A} \vee \bar{B}$	12/12***	1/1	5/5	6/6*

[a] Fractions are based on denominators representing total number of children who performed differentially on the two forms of the pair. Numerators show number of subjects who succeed A_w while failing item of rows.

[b] Where fractions are in the opposite direction, i.e., show superiority of the connective over negation, a minus sign is shown after the fraction.

* $p < .05$.
** $p < .01$.
*** $p < .001$.

nectives take precedence over $\overline{A}_w$: $A \cdot B$ $(p < .001)$ and $\overline{A} \cdot \overline{B}$ $(p < .01)$. $\overline{A}_w$ takes precedence over the $\overline{A} \vee \overline{B}$ connective $(p < .001)$, the third level connective, according to the hierarchies established above.

These results suggest that connective $\overline{A}_w$ would best fit into a level two-set in the three-level hierarchy proposed for the 4- to 10-year olds above. The three connective comprehension levels, then, are: (1) A, $\overline{A}_{nw}$, $A \cdot B$, $\overline{A} \cdot \overline{B}$; (2) $A \vee \overline{B}$, $A \cdot \overline{B}$ $\overline{A}_w$; and (3) $\overline{A} \vee \overline{B}$.

Comprehension of the Disjunction Connective 'Or': Inclusive versus Exclusive Disjunction

As suggested in Chapter 6, the general nature of disjunction comprehension is an independent theoretical issue supplementing the major issues of this study. Its inclusive or exclusive interpretation in natural language is a linguistic and psychological issue that may or may not be independent of the logical issues surrounding this connective (see Chapter 6).

As the data above indicated (ANOVA I), exclusive disjunction was significantly more difficult than conjunction under most conditions; its comprehension appeared at the second or putatively concrete operational level in the connective hierarchy. The evidence that defines its psychological character as inclusive or exclusive will now be analyzed.

$A \vee B$

As can be seen from Figure 7-8, an "inclusive-both" disjunction reading (on which subjects offer both x and y disjunctions to commands embodying the disjunction or, e.g., x **or** y) at first increased and then sharply declined from ages 2–3 to 8–10 (19%, 21%, 25%, 1% for each of the four age

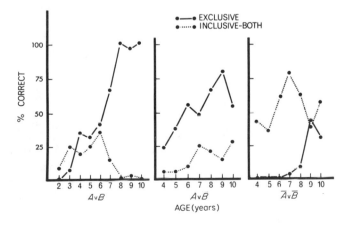

Fig. 7–8.   Comprehension of exclusive and inclusive-both disjunction by age.

groups: percentages refer to proportions of responses). Z tests show the final decline to be significant ($p < .01$). At the same time, as the above analyses show, the exclusive disjunction reading (in which subjects gave only one of the two disjuncts) increased gradually to 54.2% at the 6- to 7-year-old level and 99.0% at the age level of 8–10, thus eventually replacing inclusive type responses.

The developmental trend thus shows considerable regularity in pro- gression towards exclusive disjunction with the most distinct growth occur- ring between 6 and 7 years of age. Not until age 7 was a 50% level of exclusive type-responding surpassed (66.7%).

A logical definition of **inclusive** disjunction is composed of the judg- ment that *either one or the other or both* of the disjuncts is a possible response. An inclusive reading implies the subject's realization that three responses are possible. The choice of two disjuncts is therefore not necessarily a logically inclusive disjunction reading, but it is also necessarily not an exclusive reading (which consists of choosing only one disjunct but not both). Furthermore, because the children were not questioned as to whether they thought another response was possible, none of the res- ponses can be judged absolutely as either exclusive or inclusive.

The purpose of this part of the study, however, was to determine what the "natural" reading was for the disjunction *or* and to assess the possible developmental aspects of this reading. It may be assumed that the child's first response is a significant index of the nature of the subject's comprehen- sion.

The responses show that one particular interpretation was preferred at each age, with the exception of the 4- to 5-year olds who split between an *exclusive* reading (32.3%) and an *inclusive-both* reading in which subjects give both disjuncts [20.8%]).

That younger children were not simply hearing the connective *or* as *and*, and thus giving a conjunction response, is suggested both by the fact that emphasis was placed by the experimenter on the connective in announcing the item and by subjects' spontaneous verbal comments to the items. The 4- to 5-year old subjects indicated that they thought that *both* disjuncts could be given and, when only one was given, it was a deviation from giving both. For example, one child (4 years, 10 months) articulated this while giving a consistent inclusive response, **Both** *together I give*. This suggests developmental priority of the inclusive-both type reading.

At 6- to 7-years old, some of the same type of spontaneous verbal com- ment persisted. However, other comments appeared which suggested that the inclusive reading was developing. It now appeared to consist of three possibilities including the exclusive choice. Such responses included the questions asked of the experimenter by different subjects: *Either one?* (6 years, 4 months); *One of them or both?* (6 years, 6 months); and the comment *Let me see which one I give . That's all unless you want to have these* (the other class) (6 years, 7 months).

At the 8- to 10-year stage, not only did behavioral responses to $A \vee B$

shift dramatically, but verbal comments did too. There were no more *both* comments. Instead subjects often made a verbal announcement of the disjunct of their choice: *The x* (*The boys,*); *The dolls which are x*; *I might as well give you the x this time*, etc. Other subjects made pronouncements articulating the choice possibility: *Any one I pick?* (10 years, 4 months); *Whichever one?* (10 years, 10 months); *Either?* (9 years, 9 months).

Inspection of the 2- to 3-year-old responses suggests that some sense of a disjunction choice exists even at this age. However, the behavioural inclusive-both response is strikingly predominant.

At the 2- to 3-year level a common finding was the child's announced choice of a disjunct, followed by an inclusive-both response. After these subjects first announced the choice of a disjunct, e.g., *I'll give you boys*, they often then gave elements from both disjuncts (as well as others). Moreover, several subjects responded in ways that suggested that their verbalization had little relation to their response. For example (3 years 8 months), *I'll put the bears in*, then *Monkeys too I'll put*, resulting in a total set inclusive-type response.

In conclusion, these results suggest that an intuitive or semi-logical inclusive-both type response is the first interpretation of *or* given by subjects; after this an exclusive response becomes possible, and is then preferred. If the fully logical inclusive reading encompasses the possibility for exclusivity, then the fully logical inclusive reading for disjunction must await the development of exclusivity; and according to our data must appear late developmentally. Genevan data appear to be consistent with this (Sinclair, personal communication).

The data also support the view that inclusive disjunction as a *logical* entity has a bearing on the linguistic meaning of *or*. This would not be obvious from a superficial inspection of the 8- to 10-year-old (or adult) data alone, which are most exclusive, but it is evident from the developmental data, both of subject's responses and their verbal comments.

CHOICE OF DISJUNCT

Children show no preference for either the first or second disjunct at any age in making an exclusive disjunction response. Percentages of first and second disjunct choices are nearly 50–50 at each age level.

It can be concluded that children at all ages choose randomly from between the two disjuncts. This evidence supports the suggestion that response to the connective *or* is at least partially logical, i.e., the two separate variable class referents (*x* and *y*) are given equal value. Disjunctive choice is not interrupted by parametric constraints such as memory in these cases.

$A \vee \bar{B}$

Analysis of responses to the other two disjunction forms confirms the general pattern in the above data: exclusive responses increased sharply with age. Inclusive responses increased at first, then decreased. Specific developmental patterns differed, however, with each connective (Fig. 7-8).

For $A \vee \bar{B}$, exclusive responses increased in linear fashion attaining a 50% level at ages 6–7 as with $A \vee B$. Similarly, there was a small percentage of exclusive responses at ages 4–5 (30.2%) as there was with $A \vee B$ (32.3%). However: (1) with $A \vee \bar{B}$ inclusive-both responses did not decline completely (19.8%) at 8- to 10-years old as they did for $A \vee B$ (1% ($p < .01$); (2) in addition, the increase in exclusive responses was less sharp after 6- to 7-years old (67.7% of 8- to 10-year-olds' responses for $A \vee \bar{B}$ versus 99.0% of 8- to 10-year-olds' responses for $A \vee B$, $p < .01$).

On the whole, the exclusive response to $A \vee \bar{B}$ increased regularly to age 6, then increased irregularly between ages 7 and 10. There were slightly but nonsignificant differences between "exclusive" responding to $A \vee B$ and to $A \vee \bar{B}$ (over all ages).

For the $A \vee B$ form, sustaining an exclusive disjunction reading presented some problems in interpretation. Because $\bar{B}$ must include A, the second disjunct choice ($\bar{B}$) cannot be chosen by exclusive disjunction procedures as in the $A \vee B$ form. If it were chosen, then the response would be identical to an inclusive-both disjunction response. The only ostensible exclusive response is choice of A, the first (and the positive) conjunct. Logically, because A does represent $\bar{B}$, at least partially, it is also not fully exclusive; thus, a purely exclusive response is not possible on this form. However, for the purposes of our analysis, A was considered an exclusive-type response. An inclusive response was defined as a response in which both A and other ($\bar{B}$) classes were given.

The greater success achieved on this connective than on $A \vee B$ at ages 5 and 6 suggests that at these ages, when the exclusivity scheme was developing, the scheme could be forced in response to *or* by the negative nature of one of the conjuncts. Subjects might understand that a choice was possible and that they could take this alternative as a means of avoiding the negative, (whereas with $A \vee B$, subjects often seemed to sense the possibility for exclusive choice, but took a *both* alternative). A choice of *both* conjuncts with $A \vee \bar{B}$, however, would require dealing with the negative. The choice of A is not necessarily a true, exclusive disjunction choice, because it may be based on an avoidance of one of the disjuncts, rather than a choice between two variables considered as equivalent referents.

At age 7, when the logical structure for exclusive disjunction is achieved, as suggested by analysis of the $A \vee B$ form, children begin to appreciate the possibility of a $\bar{B}$ alternative and to seek other ways of handling the full form with other than the mere first-conjunct A response (apparent inclusive-both type-responding on this form increased to 25% at age 7).

In general, these results are in accord with the pattern of development of exclusive responding to the *or* connective, and in a more complicated fashion support the speculation that an inclusive reading is implicit in the definition of this conjunction. Moreover, they support the speculation that some intuitive type of exclusivity notion of *or* may exist at an early age.

Comprehension of this connective, however, can be forced by the context, i.e., the presence of a negative as one of the disjuncts.

$\bar{A} \vee \bar{B}$

Exclusive responding to the double negative disjunction form began late developmentally (Figure 7-8). The trend towards the exclusive reading, which reached a 50% level on the other disjunction forms at ages 6–7, awaited the 8- to 10-year-old level before becoming evident (29.2%) for $\bar{A} \vee \bar{B}$. Inclusive-both responding increased until age 7 (Figure 7-8) and then began declining. At age 7, the first expression of correct, exclusive $\bar{A} \vee \bar{B}$ responding appeared (2.1%) concurrent with this decrease. Inclusive responses increased significantly from ages 4–5 to 6–7 and then decreased significantly at ages 8–10 ($p < .01$ in both cases).

For the $\bar{A} \vee \bar{B}$ form, then, the general pattern of inclusive–exclusive response relations was analogous to that of the other disjunction forms, although its onset was considerably delayed. Inclusive responding generally increased to the point where exclusive responding began; then it declined, as it was gradually replaced by exclusive responding.

Intension–Extension Differences in Comprehension

Children's responses to linguistic items were scored correct if they demonstrated both correct intension and correct extension. That is, subjects were required to refer both to the correct classes and subclasses involved in the connected form (intension) and also to give every exemplar in each of these classes (extension). A supplementary analysis assessed responses that demonstrated correct intension alone. Correct intension was considered a sufficient demonstration of general (semilogical) comprehension of the connective or logical form. For example, if subjects chose *two dolls* (one from each of the subclasses) for each conjunct of the conjunction $A \cdot B$, three instead of the *six dolls* for each conjunct that complete the subclasses (three exemplars per subclass), the subject was considered to have demonstrated some sense of the meaning of the connective *and*, although the meaning was not extensionally quantified. The lack of complete extension could be due to carelessness errors or to more basic classification errors. The mean percentage of success (over all logical forms and connectives) for intension responses ran consistently higher than for the *intension + extension* responses at each age level, with convergence at ages 8–10. Differences, however, were not large. The general form of development of intension alone was, in most cases, parallel to the development of intension and extension responses, although slightly in advance.

COMPREHENSION OF *A* (INTENSION AND EXTENSION) VERSUS COMPREHENSION OF *A·B* (INTENSION)

The close association of the comprehension of the $A \cdot B$ conjunction to the comprehension of the single conjunct form A has already been discussed. The comprehension of *and* ($A \cdot B$) by correct intension alone may be a fundamental type of connective comprehension, and sufficient to the demonstration of basic connectivity by conjunction. It would be of interest to consider the nature of this primitive type of connective comprehension. First, it is necessary to inquire if comprehension of the connective *and* ($\cdot$), using the intensional criterion was preceded by the intension and extension comprehension of A, or whether the mere comprehension of A by intension alone was sufficient. If full comprehension including extension of A was a necessary developmental precedent of $A \cdot B$, then connectivity by ($\cdot$) could be assumed to require the prior synthesis of connective components of conjuncts. This would imply that component classes must be fully composed by intension and extension before connectivity could function. These classes, then, would function as atomic components in connective comprehension. If, on the other hand, comprehension by intension of A were sufficient to the onset of intensional comprehension of $A \cdot B$, then intensional *connectivity* by ($\cdot$) would appear not to require prior full class composition of the atomic elements.

There are then two views of connective development. One, an **atomic** view, considers that connectivity ($\cdot$) in $A \cdot B$ requires prior and separate development of the connected components A and B. Only after complete knowledge of the components has been achieved does their integration take place. The other, **synthetic** view, considers the construction of components to be concurrent with and integrally related to the development of the coordination of the components.

For this analysis, subjects' correct intension scores were calculated for each of the forms (A and $A \cdot B$) regardless of whether responses were successful in extension or not. The correlation of comprehension of A by intension with the intensional comprehension of $A \cdot B$ was .82 ($p < .01$); whereas the correlation of comprehension of A by intension and extension with intensional comprehension of $A \cdot B$ was .67 ($p < .01$). The difference between these correlations is significant ($p < .02$). Full synthesis of class construction (e.g., of a single conjunct form, A) by extension as well as intension appears not to have been necessary for the onset of intensional connective comprehension.

Similarly, full comprehension of $A \cdot B$ by intension + extension correlated significantly more highly ($p < .01$) with comprehension of A by intension + extension ($r = .82$, $p < .01$) than with comprehension of A by intension alone ($r = .63$, $p < .01$). This suggests that as subjects improved in A comprehension through the quantification of extension, they did so concurrently with $A \cdot B$.

CONCLUSIONS REGARDING INTENSION–EXTENSION

Several general conclusions follow the results of these analyses of intensional versus extensional comprehension of linguistic connectives. First, one notes a close correspondence between comprehension by intension and comprehension by extension, despite a slight precedence of comprehension by intension alone. A slight predominance of comprehension by intension in classificatory tasks has been noted by Piaget (1968b) as common to constituent–functional cognitive processes. The general close integration of intension and extension, however, is in accord with Piagetian theory (Inhelder & Piaget, 1964), and the final integration of the two capacities at age 8 for these data corresponds to their findings for classification data.

The criterion for correct intension adopted in this study was a strict one: subjects had to sample from each subclass involved in the conjunct class referent (s). Intension was thus not simply predication of a property or properties but predication of a property across difference. Intensional comprehension, for example, *Give me the girls* (A), required giving at least (both) one *little* girl and one *big* girl. In a sense, then, there was a quantitative aspect to this intension which may explain its developmental similarity to full extensional comprehension.

The data suggest, at any rate, that, in responses to linguistic commands, comprehension by intension when defined as establishment of a class property that is invariant over subclass differences, develops intimately with the capacity to comprehend this class property by the full quantification of extension over all elements of all subclasses. The high correlation between these two aspects of comprehension was relatively constant across logical forms, whether univariate or bivariate.

Response Errors to Bivariate Forms

Analysis of the type of errors subjects made in response to linguistic connectives provides information on the type of cognitive process being used in approaching the logical form of each statement. Age changes in error types suggest that these processes are related to the child's developing cognitive structures.

The error data for the three conjunction forms permit certain generalizations about the nature of conjunction comprehension at early ages.

There is some evidence from the $A \cdot B$ response data that comprehension of ($\cdot$) conjunction, prior to the age of ages 8–10 was in terms of a successive or juxtapositional type of class composition: in the $A \cdot B$ form, by the design of this study, proposition = class composition, with disjoint classes. Therefore, ($\cdot$) to act correctly can function as a succession operator rather than as an intersection operator.

As an intersection operator, ($\cdot$) would lead to class and proposition multiplication. With $A \cdot \bar{B}$, propositional multiplication *is* required in order that a correct response is produced. This requirement is based on the fact that the conjunct $\bar{B}$ includes A, as well as other classes (C and D). The construction of the $\bar{B}$ conjunct would have to integrate with the operation of ($\cdot$) as a conjunction operator; the conjunction operator, in turn, would operate on both the positive conjunct A and the negative conjunct $\bar{B}$.

Correct responding by a majority of subjects on the $A \cdot \bar{B}$ form was evident only at ages 8–10. Success appeared to depend on prior attainment of correct negation construction; this age was also the first at which the majority of $\bar{A}$ responses were correct. Even when subjects had begun to give *wide* negation responses to $\bar{B}$ alone (e.g., at ages 6–7), however, they do not do so as much for $A \cdot \bar{B}$ until 8- to 10-years old. Subjects' errors to $A \cdot \bar{B}$ give some indication of the nature of conjunction comprehension. Prior to the development of $\bar{B}$ as an independent conjunct and even persisting after a wide-negation schema's availability (at 6- to 7-years old level), one type of error appears to conflate the two conjunct predicates in $A \cdot \bar{B}$ so they are viewed as mapped onto a single reference so that the negation is canceled, i.e., subjects give just A. The ($\cdot$) may thus serve as a redundancy operator based on the matching of two successive conjuncts. There is apparent simultaneity of conjunct comprehension involved in this error, but it is based on conjunct identity rather than on the logical multiplication of conjuncts considered as independent. The result is not logical simultaneity, but association in a manner similar to that which may yield $A \cdot B$ responses. Prior to its full comprehension, ($\cdot$) in the $A \cdot \bar{B}$ connective, may simply juxtapose an assertion (A) and a denial ($\bar{B}$).

With $\bar{A} \cdot \bar{B}$, as with $A \cdot \bar{B}$ errors, associational simultaneity but not logical simultaneity appears characteristic of conjunction comprehension. Logical simultaneity would produce the intuition of a "problem" in dealing with the $\bar{A} \cdot \bar{B}$ form (because $\bar{A} \supset B$ and $\bar{B} \supset A$). Again, the independent propositions ($\bar{A} = B \cdot C \cdot D$) and ($\bar{B} = A \cdot C \cdot D$) are not considered simultaneously, but the predicates $\bar{A}$ and $\bar{B}$ are. $\bar{A} \cdot \bar{B}$, in this sense, is the reciprocal of $A \cdot B$. It signifies successive subtraction of classes rather than successive addition of classes. Each form divides the total universe in half; one requests the positive set, $A \cdot B$, the other requests its complement, $C \cdot D$. Developmentally, the comprehension of a complementary universe subset defined by two classes ($\bar{A} \cdot \bar{B} \equiv C \cdot D$) was found to be almost synchronous with development of a positive universe subset composed of two positive classes ($A \cdot B$).

When *proposition = class*, as in this study, propositional connection is equivalent to class connection. Inspection of the $A \cdot B$ data suggests that such class association was achieved by many of the 4- to 5-year-old subjects. The exception was the case in which the class was negated. In this case, proposition no longer equals class, but a set of classes (e.g., $\bar{A} = B \cdot C \cdot D$). Simultaneous consideration of sets of classes may be considered equivalent to propositional thought. The $A \cdot \bar{B}$ form may thus have been developmentally late because the acquisition of propositional operations was late. The $\bar{A} \cdot \bar{B}$ form was an exception in being developmentally early, but, as was seen, correct responses to this form could be achieved by associative predication alone. Error analyses then appear to suggest that conjunction meaning seems to develop during the period from ages 2-10 passing from an associative juxtapositional operator to an interpropositional operator.

Analysis of errors, as either inclusive or exclusive, on the disjunction connectives supports the general developmental pattern indicated by the correct response data. During the period from ages 2–10, the exclusive reading became the dominant interpretation of natural language *or*. This held for all disjunctive forms: $A \vee B$, $A \vee \bar{B}$, $\bar{A} \vee \bar{B}$. Prior to this, errors were heterogeneous (inclusive–exclusive) for $A \vee B$, appeared to favor exclusive-type responding for $A \vee \bar{B}$, and favored inclusive responses for $\bar{A} \vee \bar{B}$. In particular for $A \vee B$, alternation between inclusive-both and exclusive-type responding to *or* was primary developmentally and was followed by consistently correct exclusive responding.

THE RELATION OF CONJUNCTION TO DISJUNCTION

Distributions of subjects' responses (correct and incorrect) for conjunction and disjunction forms are compared in Table 7-12–7-14 showing matched connective pairs (1) $A \cdot B$ and $A \vee B$, (2) $A \cdot \bar{B}$ and $A \vee \bar{B}$, (3) $\bar{A} \cdot \bar{B}$ and $\bar{A} \vee \bar{B}$. Differentiation between conjunction and disjunction appeared with age. The $A \cdot B – A \vee B$ distributions are similar at 2- to 3-years old, although not exactly so. Differentiation in performance appeared at 4- to 5-years old, and was complete by ages 8–10. For $A \cdot \bar{B} – A \vee \bar{B}$, 4- to 5-year-old responses were similar for both forms. Differentiation was first apparent at 6- to 7-years old and increased at ages 8–10. For $\bar{A} \cdot \bar{B} – \bar{A} \vee \bar{B}$, similar distributions are found at ages 4–5, with differentiation apparent at ages 6–7 and marked at 8–10. For all forms, combined age data showed conjunctive responses to be made more often to conjunction forms than

TABLE 7-12

Distribution of Response Types to $A \cdot B$ and $A \vee B$ (Percentage of Responses)[a,b]

Age group	Connective	Response types[c]			
		$A \cdot B$ or $\frac{1}{n}(A \cdot B)$	$A \vee B$ or $\frac{1}{n}(A \vee B)$	ABCD	Other
2–3	$A \cdot B$	53	19	22	6
	$A \vee B$	32	30	20	18
4–5	$A \cdot B$	94	3	3	0
	$A \vee B$	42	56	2	0
6–7	$A \cdot B$	98	1	1	0
	$A \vee B$	31	67	0	2
8–10	$A \cdot B$	100	0	0	0
	$A \vee B$	1	99	0	0
Total					
2–10	$A \cdot B$	86	6	7	2
	$A \vee B$	27	63	6	5

[a] $n = 16$ in each group.
[b] Six items (three linguistic forms) tested each connective at each age.
[c] The $1/n$ notation refers to a partial selection of elements from a class. This holds for tables 7-13 and 7-14 as well.

TABLE 7-13

Distribution of Response Types to $A \cdot \bar{B}$ and $A \vee \bar{B}$ (Percentage of Responses)

		$(A \cdot \bar{B})$	(A)		$(\bar{B})$		
Age group	Connective	$A \cdot C \cdot D$ or $\frac{1}{n}(A \cdot C \cdot D)$	A or $\frac{1}{n}A$	$C \cdot D$ or $\frac{1}{n}(C \cdot D)$	$C \vee D$ or $\frac{1}{n}(C \vee D)$	$A \cdot (C \vee D)$ or $\frac{1}{n}(A \cdot (C \vee D))$	Other
4–5	$A \cdot \bar{B}$	14	59	10	3	5	8
	$A \vee \bar{B}$	12	51	12	10	1	14
6–7	$A \cdot \bar{B}$	40	52	1	1	5	1
	$A \vee \bar{B}$	19	70	7	2	2	0
8–10	$A \cdot \bar{B}$	76	20	2	0	0	2
	$A \vee \bar{B}$	21	68	10	0	0	1
Total 4–10	$A \cdot \bar{B}$	43	44	5	1	4	4
	$A \vee \bar{B}$	17	63	10	4	1	5

Response types

TABLE 7-14

Distribution of Response Types to $\bar{A} \cdot \bar{B}$ and $\bar{A} \vee \bar{B}$ (Percentage of Responses)

								Response types		
Age group	Connective	$A \vee B$ or $\frac{1}{n}$ ($A \vee B$)	$A \cdot B$ or $\frac{1}{n}$ ($A \cdot B$)	$C \cdot D$ or $\frac{1}{n}$ ($C \cdot D$)	$C \vee D$ or $\frac{1}{n}$ ($C \vee D$)	$(A \cdot C \cdot D) \vee (B \cdot C \cdot D)$ or $\frac{1}{n}$	All	Nothing	Other
4–5	$\bar{A} \cdot \bar{B}$	1	0	70	23	0	0	5	1
	$\bar{A} \vee \bar{B}$	3	1	65	23	2	2	3	1
6–7	$\bar{A} \cdot \bar{B}$	0	0	92	6	2	0	0	2
	$\bar{A} \vee \bar{B}$	5	4	80	8	1	0	1	0
8–10	$\bar{A} \cdot \bar{B}$	0	0	91	2	1	0	0	6
	$\bar{A} \vee \bar{B}$	10	0	51	6	30	1	0	1
4–10	$\bar{A} \cdot \bar{B}$	0	0	84	10	1	0	2	2
	$\bar{A} \vee \bar{B}$	6	2	65	13	11	1	1	1

to disjunction forms, and disjunctive responses were made more often to disjunction forms than to conjunction forms.

It was reported earlier that younger subjects' responses to disjunctive connectives were often of the inclusive-both type. This type of response is behaviorally identical to a conjunctive response and appears as such in the above analyses. The data, however, fit an *inclusive disjunction model* as much as they fit a *conjunction model*. When it appears that young subjects, ages, 2–3 and 4–5, were not differentiating between conjunction and disjunction, we propose that subjects may in fact differentiate between them but treat the disjunction inclusively. However, this proposal is based on theoretical adequacy. The data themselves do not differentiate distinctly between these explanations. Close inspection of errors to $A \lor B$, as above for example, however, does suggest that subjects are hearing *or* and responding to it as distinct from *and*.

Elicited Imitation and Spontaneous Connective Production by 2- and 3-Year Olds

The natural language of the 16 youngest subjects in this study who ranged in age from 2 to 3 (mean age: 3 years, 1 month) was assessed in order to determine (1) their developmental language level and (2) the extent of their spontaneous use of connectives. This language level assessment was considered necessary due to large age variation at the earliest stages of language development (e.g., Bloom, 1970), and the fact that subjects of these young ages often respond ambiguously to structured tests of language comprehension (e.g., McNeill, 1970). The data were obtained to support those elicited in structured tasks, thus augmenting the description of connectives in the young child's language.

To these ends, speech samples were obtained from all subjects in the 2- to 3-year-old group ($n = 16$). Thirteen of these subjects were also administered an imitation task based on the conjunction, disjunction, and negation items used in the language comprehension testing reported above.

SPEECH SAMPLES

The durations of the speech samples for the 2-year olds ranged from 13 to 45 min ($\overline{X}$ duration was 24.4 min); for the 3-year olds these durations ranged from 5 to 30 min ($\overline{X}$ duration 13.5 min). Speech samples were transcribed from tape by the experimenter; a second experimenter verified the typed transcript. The measures calculated for the speech samples included each subject's upper bound (UB), i.e., length of longest utterance, and $\overline{X}$ length of utterance (MLU). Although MLU is not considered by all to be a highly significant measure of language development, its use was considered necessary in this study to establish comparability with other studies. The Slobin (1967) *Field Manual* criteria (which are based on Brown's criteria) were used for the calculation of MLU.[6] Other evaluations were made in view of this study's particular attention to conjunction; in particular, the proportions of connectives (*and*, *or*, *not*, as well as *but*) used by each subject in his or her speech. Proportions were computed relative to the total number of words and relative to the total number of utterances in each subject's sample.

Table 7-15 summarizes these data for the 16 subjects. MLU for the 2-year olds ranged from 2.6 to 4.5 ($\overline{X}$ 3.23). MLU for the 3-year-old subjects ranged from 3.94 to 6.84 ($\overline{X}$ 4.98). As would be expected, the increase from 2- to 3-years old was significant ($p < .001$). The 2- and 3-year olds fell within Brown's (1970) language Stages III–V and beyond. $\overline{X}$ MLU for both groups combined was 4.1.

The upper bound for the 2-year olds ranged from 6 to 21 morphemes; for the 3-year olds from 8 to 18 morphemes. The $\overline{X}$ UB for 2-year olds was 9.12 (median 8.0); for 3-year olds it was 13.5 (median 13.01). (The increase from 2 to 3 years was not significant.)

When the use of connectives (*and*, *or*, *not*, *but*) in spontaneous speech was analyzed, 2-year olds used a total of 110 connectives, which was 3.2% of the total number number of words used, and 10.5% of the total number of their utterances. Three-year olds used a total of 174 connectives, which was 6.8% of the total number of words used and 32.2% of the total number of utterances. Two-year olds thus used approximately I connective in every 10 utterances; 3-year olds used 1 in every 3 utterances. This increase was significant ($p < .001$). For 3-year olds, 44% of connectives usage was the conjunct *and*; 47% was a negation connective (*no* or *not*); no child used the disjunction connective *or* even once. For the 2-year olds, 42% of the connectives used was the conjunction *and*; 55% was the negation operators; again, no child used the disjunction connective *or*. Several children used the connective *but* (which is said by some logicians to represent *and–not*). The use of *but* occurred mainly at age 3, (9% of connective usage at age 3, only 1% at age 2). For both 2- and 3-year olds, *and* usage was about equal to negation operator usage. When connective usage is measured as proportion of words and utterances, the same pattern, holds. *And* and *not* type connectives accounted for 4 and 5% of utterances, respectively, at the 2-year-old level and 14% and 15% of utterances, respectively, for the 3-year olds. (Each increase with age was significant $p < .001$.)

The *percentage of utterance* index is more significant than *percentage of words*, developmentally, because on all measures there was very little difference between 2- and 3-year olds in connective use as percentages of words.

---

[6] When mean length of utterance (MLU) for a sample is computed, according to Slobin (1967), MLU calculations should be made on the basis of at least 100 utterances. The speech samples of our eight 2-year olds approximated that number; however, the 3-year-old samples often included fewer utterances. As most of the 3-year olds had advanced speech development, speech sample analyses seemed less essential in these cases and were obtained simply to provide a general index of language level.

TABLE 7-15

Summary Statistics from Speech Samples of Sixteen 2- and 3-Year Olds

Subject	Age (months—days)	Duration of speech sample (min)	Total— utterances	Total— words	Mean utterance length	Upper bound
2-year olds						
1	28–5	23	132	391	2.96	7
2	31–6	15	123	417	3.39	7
3	30–16	24	99	302	3.05	6
4	32–20	13	76	225	2.96	9
5	34–17	23	183	832	4.54	21
6	28–14	31	169	593	3.50	9
7	26–23	21	178	468	2.62	7
8	27–24	45	91	255	2.80	7
Total 2-year olds	29–27	24.37	1051	3483	3.23	9.12
3-year olds						
1	46–4	12	49	220	4.48	14
2	47–23	5	26	125	4.80	14
3	43–7	20	80	409	5.11	17
4	43–17	9	44	240	5.45	15
5	46–27	5	46	229	4.97	11
6	47–1	8	46	315	6.84	18
7	35–22	30	133	525	3.94	8
8	37–8	19	116	493	4.25	11
Total 3-year olds	43–3	13.50	540	2556	4.98	13.50
Total 2- and 3-year olds	36–15	18.93	1591	6039	4.10	11.31

Four subjects (2-year-olds ranging in age from 2 years, 2 months, 23 days to 2 years, 6 months, 16 days) did not use *and* even once in their speech sample. Three of these subjects had MLUs of below 3.0 (2.62–2.96), and the fourth had an MLU of 3.05 (late III and early IV stages according to Brown's scale). These data appear to confirm Brown's (1973b) conclusion that, in Stages I to III of his scale, subjects are working mainly with simple sentences. Two of these subjects, however, used a negation operator in their speech.

Finally, several forms of negation were evident in the child's speech: *no, not,* and the inflected *don't* or *doesn't.* At the 2-year-old level, most negation connective usage was a *no* operator (54%); 43% was the inflected *n't* type; only 3% was a full *not* negation. At 3-year old, however, most negation was the inflected type (52%) and *no* and *not* were used equally (24% each). The developmental order of negative lexical expression was: *no, n't* inflection, *and not.* (The latter *not* form was used in the experimental connective study and was very difficult for these subjects.)

In summary, the 2-year olds studied here showed the onset of *and*

TABLE 7-15—*cont.*

	And			But			Not		Or	Total Connectives		
n	% Words	% Utterances	n	% Words	% Utterances	n	% Words	% Utterances	n	n	% Words	% Utterances
0	0	0	0	0	0	8	2	6	0	8	2	6
3	0	2	0	0	0	7	1	5	0	10	2	8
0	0	0	0	0	0	0	0	0	0	0	0	0
5	2	6	0	0	0	1	0	1	0	6	3	8
17	2	9	0	0	0	17	2	9	0	34	4	19
24	4	14	1	0	0	16	2	9	0	41	7	24
0	0	0	0	0	0	11	2	6	0	11	2	6
0	0	0	0	0	0	0	0	0	0	0	0	0
49	1	4	1	0	0	60	1	5	0	110	32	11
4	1	8	0	0	0	6	2	12	0	10	5	20
2	1	7	0	0	0	8	6	23	0	10	8	38
11	2	13	0	0	0	12	2	15	0	23	6	29
11	4	25	1	0	0	11	4	25	0	23	10	52
4	1	8	7	2	15	10	4	21	0	21	9	46
17	5	36	1	0	2	4	1	8	0	22	7	48
17	3	12	3	0	2	17	3	12	0	37	7	28
11	2	9	3	0	2	14	2	12	0	28	6	24
77	3	14	15	0	2	82	3	15	0	174	7	32
126	2	7	16	0	1	142	2	8	0	284	5	18

conjunction usage. Most subjects at both ages 2 and 3 were found to make some use of negation. Total connective use (conjunction and negation) increased significantly as the percentage of utterances from 2- to 3-years old. Two-year olds used about 1 connective in every 10 utterances; 3-year olds about 1 in every 3. Both 2- and 3-year olds used the connective *and* and a negation operator about equally. The form of the negation operator changed in natural speech production over this age span from the *no* operator to the *not* operator by way of an inflected form of negation of the verb. Connection with *but* occurred for the first time primarily at age 3. No child of either age 2 or 3 used the connective *or* even once.

RELATION OF PRODUCTION TO COMPREHENSION OF CONNECTIVES

Connective production in normal speech described above was correlated with connective comprehension in comprehension tasks of the connective study. Performance of 2- and 3-year olds on $A \cdot B$ and $A \vee B$ items in conjoined sentences, derived, and quantified-derived linguistic forms, as well as performance on A and $\overline{A}$ forms, were correlated with speech sample variables: mean length of utterance, length of upper bound, conjunction *and* usage, and negation usage (as proportion of number of words and as proportion of number of utterances).

In general, the results show that the indices of productive language development (MLU, UB) did not correlate with the subject's performance on specific language comprehension tasks, but other measures of connectives in the child's speech often did. Conjunction production did correlate with comprehension of the quantified conjunction *both–and* form ($r = .54$; $p < .05$).

An unexpected finding was the correlation of conjunction *and* speech usage with disjunction *or* connective comprehension ($r = .57$; $p < .05$). Although children did not use *or* in their speech at this age, their speech production of the *and* connective appeared to parallel the development of their comprehension of *or* connectivity.

IMITATION

Thirteen 2- to 3-year -old subjects (ages 2 years, 3 months, I day to 3 years, 11 months, 2 days on the date of the imitation task; $\overline{X}$ age 2 years, 11 months) were administered at least one randomized set of eight imitation items that consisted of one example of each of the linguistic forms (conjoined, derived, and quantified derived) of each of the two connectives ($A \cdot B$, *and* and $A \vee B$ *or*), and 1 example of 2 forms of negation ($\overline{A}$) (a relative clause form and a denial form). These sentences had been used to test comprehension in the connective study. Thus, each item or its type had been heard at least twice prior to imitation. Each set of eight imitation sentences used one pair of homogeneous classes as conjuncts (e.g., *girls and boys* or *monkeys and bears*). When possible, the experimenter also administered additional imitation items from the second set and replications of items. The $\overline{X}$ number of items administered to 2-year olds was 11.1; to 3-year olds, 15.0; and to the group as a whole 12.6. Imitation responses were tape recorded and transcribed by the experimenter, and transcriptions were verified by a second experimenter.

The number of conjunction and disjunction sentences administered to 2- and 3-year olds and the proportions imitated correctly appear in Table 7-16. A total of 126 sentences was administered to the 2- to 3-year-old group: 68 to the 2-year-olds and 58 to the 3-year olds. In general, items were very difficult for the 2- and 3-year-old subjects; only 7% of 126 connectives items were imitated correctly. Moreover, all of the correct imitations were achieved by the 3-year olds; 16% of the items were imitated correctly by the 3-year olds. Success was nearly equal on conjunction and disjunction items (16% and 15% respectively).

Subjects refused to imitate 16% of the items. All refusals were by 2-year olds; (29% of items); and more refusals were to disjunction items than to conjunction items (38%–23% respectively). A refusal may be considered an indication of subjects' inability to process a sentence form. All of the subjects who refused to imitate some or all connective forms did imitate a one-conjunct form (e.g., *Give me the girls*). A connective feature of the linguistic form thus appeared to be critical to the refusal to imitate.

The first possible basis for explaining the poor imitations of the young subjects on these forms is the morpheme length of the utterances. The *conjoined sentences* form, the longest of these connectives, totaled nine morphemes. In light of the MLUs of these subjects (3.23 for the 2-year olds and 5.09 for the 3-year olds), it might be considered that subjects failed because the sentences taxed their processing capacities and not because they failed any structural features of the connective sentences. As already noted, however, the upper bounds of these subjects ranged from 6–21 morphemes (6 to 21 for 2-year olds, 8 to 18 for 3-year olds); a quantity of conjunction and negation usage (although not disjunction) was evident in their speech. Moreover, Clay (1971) cites Menyuk's (1969) conclusion that for subjects as young as age 3, "length was not critical for successful repetition within the bounds of 2–9 word sentences [p. 11]." This view is supported further by our finding that UB and MLU did not correlate with connective imitation. It can be concluded then that poor imitation performance in these sentences was due to the presence of connectives and their correlative structure, as well as to the processing constraints which exist at this age.

That processing constraints may be involved in these imitation results is suggested by the fact that subjects responded differentially to connectives expressed in the three linguistic forms: conjoined, derived, and quantified derived sentences. Most correct responses were to conjunction or disjunction expressed in the derived linguistic form (i.e., after deletion which had the effect of producing a shorter sentence, seven morphemes); 33% of derived connective sentences were correct at the 3-year old level; only 5% of conjoined sentence forms; and 11% of the quantified derived sentences were correct. Two-year-olds' refusal to imitate, however, was not affected by linguistic form.

Negation showed similar results. Two-year olds did not imitate negation items correctly, neither the relative clause form nor the more simple denial form. Three-year olds, however, imitated the denial form rather well (43%), but not the relative clause form. Moreover, the 2-year-olds' refusal to imitate differed for the two forms of negation; 50% of the relative clause negation items were refused; only 9% of the denial items were refused.

CONNECTIVE MORPHEME IMITATION AND BINARY CONJUNCT IMITATION: CONJUNCTION AND DISJUNCTION

Imitation responses were analyzed to determine the proportions of (1) correct imitation of *connective morphemes*, i.e., the words *and*, *or* and (2) correct associative *sense* of the connected sentence by correct repetition of both conjuncts (or disjuncts) of the sentence, with or without correct repetition of the connective morpheme. (We will designate the latter as *binary conjunct associativity*.) If the connective morpheme carries

TABLE 7-16

Correct Responses and Type of Imitation Errors by Type of Connective and Age Group (Percentages)

Type of connective and age group	Distribution of items			Error type[b]					
					Binary conjunct		Single conjunct	Linguistic form	
	n given	% not responded	% correct responses[a]	Connective morpheme error	Reversal	Substitution	Substitution	Elaboration[c]	Reduction[d]
A · B									
2-year olds (N = 8; n = 30)	39	23	0	57	13	17	10	0	92
3-year olds (N = 5; n = 32)	32	0	16	41	16	6	22	6	56
Total *A · B*									
2-year olds (N = 13; n = 62)	71	13	7	48	15	11	16	3	72
A v B									
2-year olds (N = 8; n = 18)	29	38	0	61	28	11	0	0	100
3-year olds (N = 5; n = 26)	26	0	15	42	0	8	23	5	83

Total $A \vee B$									
2- + 3-year olds ($N = 13$; $n = 44$)	55	20	7	50	11	9	14	3	90
$A \cdot B + A \vee B$									
2-year olds ($N = 8$; $n = 48$)	68	29	0	58	19	15	6	0	94
3-year olds ($N = 5$; $n = 58$)	58	0	16	41	9	7	22	6	64
Total $A \cdot B + A \vee B$									
2- + 3-year olds ($N = 13$; $n = 106$)	126	16	7	49	13	10	15	3	77

Note: N = number of subjects; n = number of items responded to.
[a] Percentage of items administered.
[b] Percentages based on number of type of error divided by number of items responded to.
[c] Proportion of number of items in derived or quantified-derived linguistic form.
[d] Proportion of number of items in conjoined sentence form.

an associative meaning, we would then predict that production of connective *sense*, denoted by binary conjunct associativity, would be developmentally simultaneous with utterance of the connective morpheme. To the degree that this associative meaning is independent of the connective morpheme, however, it is possible that comprehension of associativity would be prior to comprehension of the connective morpheme. The imitation task is one way to approach such a difference.

For this analysis, only the subject's first responses to administered items were considered because there appeared to be no significant differences in first response items and the full set of administered items. There were 30 of these items for 3-year olds ($n = 5 \times 6$ connective forms) and 48 items for 2-year olds ($n = 8 \times 6$ connective forms), or a total of 78 items for the whole group. For this analysis, scoring was performed independently for (1) connective morpheme imitation and for (2) binary conjunct associativity (Table 7-17).

The results showed that correct binary conjunct associativity (repeating the two conjunct classes together, with or without the correct connective between them and with or without correct order) develops in advance of correct connective morpheme imitation for both *and* sentences and *or* sentences. It appears that, generally, young children who were able to imitate the logical connective morpheme *and* and *or* were also able to maintain conjunct (or disjunct) associativity essential to the meaning of this connective. Seventy-nine percent of correct *and* imitations showed correct conjunct associativity; 93% of correct *or* imitations showed correct disjunct associativity. A subject could maintain associativity without necessarily imitating the connective correctly, however; 63% of responses showing correct conjunct associativity accompanied correct connective morpheme imitation and 68% of correct disjunct associativity responses accompanied correct morpheme imitation.

Although the above is not a contingency analysis, a contingency relationship is supported by the correlation between connective-morpheme imitation scores and binary-conjunct associativity scores. Conjunction connective-morpheme imitation and conjunct associativity correlated ($r = .63$, $p < .05$); disjunction connective-morpheme imitation and disjunction associativity correlated ($r = .50$, $p < .05$, $n = 13$).[7]

In general, imitation data showed both conjunct associativity and connective-morpheme imitation to be succeeded relatively well by 3-year olds; at least two-thirds of their responses were successful in both cases. Binary conjunct associativity was almost complete for *and* at age 3 (93%), and somewhat lower for *or* sentences (74%). Associativity was in advance of connective morpheme imitation, particularly for *and* sentences. Imitation of the connective morpheme *or* was still inferior to *and* at this

---

[7] Connective morpheme imitation scores (0, 1, 2) and conjunct associativity imitation scores (0, 1, 2) on first responses were summed within conjunction and disjunction forms to yield morpheme imitation and conjunct associativity scores. See Footnote b in Table 7-17 for scoring criteria.

TABLE 7-17

Distribution of Connective Morpheme and Binary-Conjunct Associativity Responses on Conjunction and Disjunction Imitation by Age Group (Percentages)[a,b]

Age	Score	Connective morpheme		Binary conjunct associativity	
		and	or	and	or
2-year olds					
(n = 8)	2	33	21	42	46
		(53)	(39)	(67)	(85)
	1	13	8	16	8
		(20)	(15)	(27)	(15)
	0	54	71	42	46
		(27)	(46)	(6)	(0)
3-year olds					
(n = 5)	2	73	67	93	74
	1	7	0	7	13
	0	20	33	0	13
2- to 3-year olds					
(n = 13)	2	49	39	61	56
		(64)	(54)	(80)	(79)
	1	10	5	13	10
		(13)	(7)	(17)	(14)
	0	41	56	26	34
		(23)	(39)	(3)	(7)

[a] Percentages in parentheses are based on number of attempted imitation responses, excluding nonresponses. Only first responses are considered in this analysis.

[b] Scoring criteria (*Imitation of connective morpheme*) : 2 = correct imitation, 1 = imitation unclear, or phonetic filler, 0 = omission, or replacement by another connective. (*Binary conjunct associativity*) : 2 = repeats both conjuncts, 1 = repeats only one conjunct, 0 = repeats neither conjunct correctly.

Note: Each subject received three linguistic forms of each connective. Total number of items thus equals 15 for each connective in the group of 3-year olds, and a total number of 24 for each connective in the group of 2-year olds. Figures in parentheses represent proportions of only attempted responses (excluding nonresponses), i.e., of 15 and 13 items for conjunction and disjunction items respectively for the 2-year olds.

age (67% and 74% respectively), but the difference was less than at age 2, and sizeable proportions of both types were correct. Two-year olds showed poor performance on both connective morpheme imitation and associativity with associativity in advance of morpheme imitation. The above analyses included nonresponses (which occurred with 2-year olds) in the total number of items considered. (These were given a zero score.)

CONNECTIVE MORPHEME IMITATION AND CLASS-REFERENCE IMITATION: NEGATION

Similar analyses were performed on subjects' responses to negation items (in both relative clause and denial form). Subjects, as previously

TABLE 7-18

Distribution of Connective Morpheme and Class Reference Responses on Imitation of Relative Clause and Denial Negation, by Age Group (Percentages)[a]

| Age | Score | Relative clause negation | | Negation by denial | |
		Connective morpheme	Class reference	Connective morpheme	Class reference
2-year olds	2	25 (67)	25 (67)	50 (57)	63 (72)
	1	0 (0)	12 (33)	25 (29)	12 (14)
	0	75 (33)	63 (0)	25 (14)	25 (14)
3-year olds	2	100	60	80	80
	1	0	0	0	0
	0	0	40	20	20
2- to 3-year olds	2	54 (88)	38 (63)	62 (66)	69 (75)
	1	0 (0)	8 (12)	15 (17)	8 (8)
	0	46 (12)	54 (25)	23 (17)	23 (17)

[a] Percentages in parentheses are based on total number of items attempted, excluding nonresponses. Only first responses are considered in this analysis.

indicated, were more willing to imitate the denial forms of negation than the relative clause forms, especially in the 2-year-old group. There were thus very few relative clause forms of negation by 2-year olds available for analysis. Imitation of the negative connective morpheme in the relative clause form occurred in only 25% of all responses (including nonattempts) at age 2 as did correct class reference (Table 7-18).

Subjects who correctly imitated the negation connective were also correctly imitating the class reference. At age 2, *not* connective morpheme imitation was succeeded by all subjects, with class reference less so.

IMITATION ERRORS

Several types of imitation error were observed: (1) errors in the connective morpheme, (2) errors in the binary conjuncts, (3) errors by maintaining only a single conjunct of the binary form, (4) errors in the linguistic form of the connected sentence (i.e., pertaining to the specified derivation of conjunction reduction), and (5) miscellaneous errors.

The considerable extent to which subjects manipulated the sentence forms is most evident from these errors (Table 7-16). Most 2-year olds (94% of responses) when administered a compound sentence (either conjunction or disjunction) in conjoined sentence form, eliminated the redundant verb elements in their imitation and thus often "reduced" the full form to a form more closely resembling a "derived" form. For example, when asked to imitate *Give me the girls* and *give me the boys*, subjects often produced *Give me the girls* and (the) *boys* or some variant thereof. (Miscellaneous errors occurred on a large percentage, 59% of items.) No 2-year old elaborated a derived sentence to full-conjoined sentence form. Sixty-four percent of responses to the conjoined form by 3-year olds were reduced to the derived form; 6% of the responses of 3-year olds to derived forms did, however, show an elaboration to full-conjoined sentences.

No other error occurred with such frequency as the reduction error, although a large proportion (58%) of 2-year-old responses erred on the connective morpheme. Connective morpheme errors persisted, although to a lesser extent, at the 3-year-old level (41% of responses). Most connective errors for both 2- and 3-year olds were connective omissions. Two-year olds erred on the quantifier in 94% of imitations of quantified sentences, 3-year olds on 61%. Most errors were quantifier omissions. More errors appear on the disjunction quantifier (*either*) than on the conjunction quantifier (*both*).

It might be speculated on the basis of the errors made by 2-and 3-year olds that early imitation responses (at age 2) in particular to connective forms maintained the binary class association of the connected conjuncts with or without the connective morpheme per se, and with or without quantifiers. Analyses of connective morpheme imitation and binary conjunct associativity reported above confirm this.

At age 3, these errors continued but there was indication that subjects were able to hold linguistic form (in the case of conjoined sentences) constant to a greater extent and to repeat the connective morpheme more accurately. These new developments may explain the larger percentage of single conjunct errors (when subjects repeat only one conjunct) at this age (22%, an increase over the 6% of the 2-year olds). In the attempt to hold constant the full and complete linguistic form of conjuncts, subjects who did not succeed at this time may have demonstrated the single conjunct-type error.

The changes from ages 2 to 3 in the child's treatment of the connected sentence may represent a change in the child's comprehension of the connective. At age 2, the child's conception of logical connectivity appeared to be one of primitive associativity based on conjunct (class) juxtaposition, without the maintenance of the elements of the compound as independent wholes. At 3-years old, the increase in single conjunct-type responses and the decrease in reduction-type errors suggests that elements in the connected form began to be treated to a certain extent as independent units. It follows that the meaning of the connective was differentiating, by signifying a connection of differentiated elements rather than the previous *connective + elements*, indicative of a primitive syncretic whole created by conjunct juxtaposition.

NEGATIVE SENTENCE: IMITATION ERRORS

Negative sentences, as already indicated, especially in relative clause form were particularly difficult for 2- and 3-year olds. Errors on the *not* connective morpheme for the relative clause form were mainly omission

TABLE 7-19

Intercorrelations between Speech Production and Imitation Responses for 2- and 3-Year Olds (n = 13)

	Imitation					
Speech measures	Conjunction associativity	Conjunction morpheme and	Disjunction associativity	Disjunction morpheme or	Conjunction and disjunction total associativity	Conjunction and disjunction (total morphemes)
MLU	.50	.50	.38	.55*	.47	.54
UB	.12	.27	.07	.30	.11	.29
Conjunction						
% Words	.57*	.70**	.35	.75**	.49	.75**
Conjunction						
% Utterances	.55*	.61*	.38	.73**	.50	.69**
Negation						
% Words	.64*	.31	.22	.25	.46	.29
Negation						
% Utterances	.64*	.39	.30	.42	.50	.42
Connective total (conjunction and negation)						
% Words	.77**	.71**	.44	.70**	.64*	.73**
% Utterances	.68**	.61*	.41	.69**	.58*	.67*

* $p = .05$.
** $p < .01$.

errors (83% of these errors); for the denial form, errors were mainly substitution errors with *no* or *don't* inserted in place of *not* (71% of these errors). The errors confirm the greater difficulty of relative clause negation than denial noted above.

Two out of the three 2-year-old children who tried to imitate the relative clause form did not make a connective morpheme error, but instead reduced the whole sentence to *Not the x*, e.g., *Not the bears*. This implies a capacity to abstract the semantic element in the negative morpheme and negated class from a complex sentence. Two-year-old responses to the denial forms were similar; here the *give me* predicate was often preserved in addition to the negation morpheme and the class referents. This preservation of the essential semantic, i.e., logical, meaning of the sentence in the case of negation was similar to the abstraction evident in conjunct juxtaposition in the imitation of disjunctive and conjunctive sentences.

MORPHEME UNIT ANALYSIS

In another analysis, each morpheme was treated as an equivalent unit and the errors for each unit were summed. It was found that the proportions of error were not markedly higher at the initial or terminal ends of sentences

TABLE 7-19—*cont.*

| | | | | Relative clause + denial | | Conjunction, disjunction relative clause total | |
| | | | | Reference | Morpheme | Associative conjunct reference | Morpheme |
Relative clause negation reference	Relative clause negation morpheme	Denial reference	Denial morpheme				
.50	.54	.24	.42	.50	.66*	.50	.61*
.18	.13	.41	.56*	.37	.45	.13	.30
.21	.24	−.09	.44	.09	·45	.46	.74**
.42	.40	.10	.41	.35	.56*	.51	.72**
.40	.54	.10	.29	.34	.59*	.47	.37
.48	.59*	.18	.38	.44	.68**	.52	.50
.39	.49	−.03	.44	.25	.64*	.62*	.77**
.50	.55*	.14	.45	.43	.69**	.60*	.73**

(serial position effect) as an information-processing model might predict. Instead, errors were distributed more or less equally throughout the sentence (an imitation result similarly found by Clay, 1971). There was some evidence, however, that, at age 3 errors tended to the right most, i.e., the second-conjunct terminal elements. Thus, there may have been some change in processing from ages 2 to 3. However, the highest proportions of error usually included the connective morpheme, and in the case of quantified derived forms, the connective quantifier (*both–either*). Thus the structural aspects of sentence processing were more critical to the interpretation of error than serial position effects.

CORRELATION OF IMITATION AND PRODUCTION

As with conjunction and disjunction imitation scores (see Footnote 7 for scoring), subjects' scores on both types of negation were summed across negation types to give a total negation-imitation score. Connective scores and negation scores (by relative clause) were further summed to produce a total connective-imitation score.

The correlations between the speech production measures and imitation scores appear in Table 7-19. (A minimum correlation of .55 was necessary for a significance level of $p < .05$, and .68 for $p < .01$ with an n of 13.) Summary statistics related to these correlations appear in Table 7-20.

TABLE 7-20

Summary Statistics on Connective Morpheme and Conjunct Associativity (or Reference) on Connective and Negation Imitation Items, Across 2- and 3- Year Olds

	Connective morpheme			Conjunct associativity/reference		
	Mean score	SD	Range	Mean score	SD	Range
Connectives[a]						
Conjunction imitation	3.23	2.52	0–6	4.00	2.31	0–6
Disjunction imitation	2.46	2.57	0–6	3.69	2.25	0–6
Conjunction and disjunction: total score	5.69	4.94	0–12	7.69	4.31	0–12
Negation[b]						
Relative clause imitation	1.08	1.04	0–2	.85	.99	0–2
Denial imitation	1.38	.87	0–2	1.46	.88	0–2
Relative clause + denial imitations (negation total)	2.46	1.39	0–4	2.31	1.44	0–4

[a] Connection and disjunction: based on 39 items for the group; 3 per subject; scores ranging from 0–2.
[b] Negation: based on 13 items for the group; 1 per subject; scores ranging from 0–2.

Several of the speech-imitation correlations were significant. The general language measures MLU and UB did not correlate with connective imitation (*and* and *or* morpheme imitation or conjunct associativity) except in one instance. On the other hand, production of connectives in speech correlated with the ability to imitate sentences employing these connectives. Although no production of disjunction *or* was noted in the children's speech, *and* conjunction use correlated with the ability to imitate *or*. Both conjunction associativity imitation and conjunction *and* morpheme imitation correlated with *and* production, and *not* imitation correlated with negation production.

RELATION OF CONNECTIVE PRODUCTION IN SPONTANEOUS SPEECH TO COGNITIVE TASK PERFORMANCE

The principal cognitive measures available on 2- and 3-year-old subjects were: classification score, complementation and (constructed) matrix scores, and dichotomy scores. Classification correlated significantly with conjunction usage (as a proportion of utterances, $r = .57$, $p < .05$) in natural speech. It did not correlate significantly with negation production or with the language development indices, MLU and UB. On the other hand, the (constructed) matrix scores correlated significantly with MLU ($r = .50$, $p < .05$), with negation usage (as proportion of utterances, $r = .52$, $p < .05$), and with connective usage (as a proportion of utterances, $r = .50$, $p < .05$). Of all the cognitive measures, only the (constructed) matrix correlated significantly with age. As the speech production measures correlated with age as usual, the significant matrix-speech correlations are less interesting than the conjunction-classification correlation, neither of which correlated significantly with age. However, given the theorized relation of logical multiplication to the language connectives that was confirmed in our other data analyses, the correlations of speech measures with the matrix scores are theoretically significant. It will be reported later that classification also correlated significantly with conjunction ($A \cdot B$) comprehension (in the section in Chap 8.on language–cognition relationships). The finding that classification scores correlated significantly with both $A \cdot B$ (*and*) comprehension, and with *and* production, although these did not correlate significantly with each other, (except in the quantified derived form, *both–and*), is informative. One might speculate that the underlying cognitive structures are related to both language comprehension and language production despite the partial independence of the language systems (comprehension and production).

RELATION OF CONNECTIVE IMITATION TO COGNITION

The child's ability to imitate conjunction, disjunction, and negation did not correlate with classification ability, as both connective use and comprehension did to some extent. However, performance on the (constructed) matrix task, which correlated significantly with connective production, also correlated with total connective-morpheme imitation (*and*, *or*, and *not*) ($r = .55$, $p < .05$). It correlated with *and* morpheme imitation in particular ($r = .58$, $p < .05$), but with none of the other connectives considered separately. (Again, connective morpheme imitation also correlated with age.) Disjunction associativity imitation correlated significantly with complementation ($r = .59$, $p < .05$). However, no other imitation–cognition relationship was significant.

In summary, despite the small *n* on which the data are based, the evidence of a network of significant speech, production-language comprehension-cognitive classification relations for conjunction, which did not include imitation, is itself significant. It may indicate that imitation is less subject to cognitive control than either the production or comprehension of connectives. Nonetheless, considering the sample size, we approach these conclusions as suggestive and tentative.

SUMMARY AND DISCUSSION

The natural speech samples for 2- and 3-year-old subjects indicated: (1) The asymmetry between the comprehension of conjunction and disjunction evident in tests of the comprehension of older children and adults. No 2- to 3-year-old child used *or* even once in 5.05 hr of speech time. (2) A preconjunction period of natural speech may exist (confirming Brown, 1970). Four out of eight 2-year olds in this study (MLU 2.62–3.05) did not use *and* in the entire sample of their natural speech production. (3) Negation appeared early in child speech relative to other connectives. Two of the four subjects who demonstrated no use of *and* did use a negation operator. The lexical form of negation appeared to change within the 2- to 3-year period (cf. Bloom, 1970; Greenfield *et al.*, 1972). No analysis was made of the syntactic aspects of negation in the speech samples. (4) In general, the 2- to 3-year period is important for connective development in child speech. Subjects in this period go from the use of 1 logical connective (*and–or–not*) in 10 utterances to 1 in 3 utterances, a significant increase.

Children's early imitation of connective sentences indicated the following: (1) Conjunct and disjunct associativity (preservation of both conjuncts or disjuncts) generally preceded correct connective morpheme imitation. (2) The predominance of an apparent reduction operation in the imitations of connective sentences by 2- and 3-year olds provided further evidence that the essential nature of conjunction for 2- to 3-year olds was binary conjunct associativity. The connective morpheme articulated the meaning or sense implicit in the associativity previously expressed by juxtaposition. (3) There was significantly greater delay in the ability to imitate the disjunction connective *or* than to imitate conjunction connective *and*. Thus, the asymmetry between conjunction and disjunction was also evident in imitation, as well as in connective speech production. At the same time, however, proportions of sentences correctly imitated did not differ between conjunction and disjunction. (4) There was a significant increase from ages 2 to 3 in both aspects of connective sentence imitation: morpheme imitation and conjunct associativity. Quantification was a late feature of connective sentence imitation as very few children even at age 3 were successful at this aspect of sentence imitation.(That quantification of disjunction was inferior to quantification of conjunction, again confirmed an asymmetry between conjunction and disjunction.) The production of connectives in natural speech correlated with aspects of connective imitation and confirmed prior reports of a correlation between spontaneous speech and imitation (McNeill, 1970). The ostensible advance of imitation over natural speech production with regard to the connective morpheme (e.g., some children imitated *or* and did not use *or* in speech) also confirmed a previously reported finding. However, these data also offer evidence that specific structural elements of natural speech production correlate with specific structural elements in imitation, e.g., imitation of *or* connective correlated with natural language production of conjunction by *and*, as did imitation of *and* connective morpheme and associativity.

Cognitive classification correlated with speech production as well as with conjunction comprehension, but not with conjunction imitation. Conjunction imitation, however, correlated with conjunction comprehension as well as with conjunction in speech production. This suggests a language–cognition model which distances imitation from cognition, as follows:

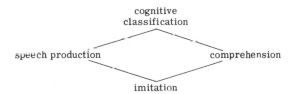

Several points can be made regarding the nature of language at the 2- to 3-year-old level. The evidence for early conjunction production in child speech (67% of attempted imitations at age 2, or 42% of administered items, show conjunct associativity; 33% of administered imitations at age 2, or 53% of attempted imitations, show correct connective morpheme *and* imitations) suggests that conjunction (by both juxtaposition and morpheme occurrence) is within the child's language repertoire at a very early age. The evidence for earlier ability for associativity than connective morpheme production suggests that the 'meaning' of conjunction was achieved earlier than the "lexical representation" of conjunction.

Whether the comprehension of conjunction by juxtaposition is concurrent with the onset of language was not answered by this research. As was seen, half of the youngest subjects (2-years old) did not use *and* in natural speech; in addition, most of these did not imitate *and*. This suggests a period of language use that does not include the connective morpheme.

The reported results bear on the sentential or phrasal nature of conjunction in deep structure (reviewed in Chapter 6). Reduction of conjoined sentences by 2- to 3-year olds could be interpreted to indicate that phrasal conjunction is developmentally prior to sentential conjunction in production.

This conclusion is not valid, however. It does not follow that because subjects *produce* phrasal conjunction forms that sentential conjunction is not basic to their *comprehension*, because they need to be able to comprehend conjoined sentences in order to reduce them appropriately in their imitations. Given the same data, it is possible to accept an alternative explanation that conjunction reduction, in which full-conjoined sentence forms are reduced to phrasal conjunction, is an obligatory transformation that subjects are able to apply from the time they are first capable of conjunction. The available data do not permit an adequate test of these two explanations.

Adult Comprehension of Connectives

Sixteen adult graduate students ($\overline{X}$ age, 24.6) were administered the same test of linguistic comprehension as given to the forty-eight, 4- to 10-year olds. This was to provide data for subjects who ostensibly would have reached the most advanced level of cognitive functioning. In addition, it was considered important to determine whether structural relations among connectives changes from ages 8–10 to adulthood.

As some connective forms had not indicated ceiling performance in the 8- to 10-year-old group, we wished to determine whether this was reached in a more sophisticated group. The most marked "deficits" were for the $\overline{A} \vee \overline{B}$ form, which showed only 30% correct responses in the 8- to 10-year-old group. $\overline{A}$ yielded 90% success only at the 10-year-old level (in the 8- to 10-year range) and $A \vee \overline{B}$ showed a somewhat irregular course of development.

Adults' performance was near ceiling (85% of responses or over) for all linguistic connectives but one (Table 7-21). Only 59.4% of responses were correct for $\overline{A} \vee \overline{B}$; most errors were of an inclusive disjunction type. However, additional analysis showed that 75% of the adult sample gave a correct (exclusive disjunction) response to this form at least once, whereas only 56% of the 8- to 10-year -old sample had done so. This suggests that, although adults had the capacity to comprehend this form in an exclusive disjunction manner, they considered an inclusive response a legitimate alternative. The form was thus considered ambiguous by adults. This was confirmed by a significant item-order effect from the first to the second item of $\overline{A} \vee \overline{B}$ ($p < .05$). (Several subjects, in fact, volunteered the comment that they were "changing their minds" on how this form was best responded to on its second occurrence.)

There was also evidence for other disjunction forms from subjects' verbal comments that an inclusive response was considered "possible," although the exclusive response was behaviorly clearly preferred in these cases. Regarding the $A \vee \overline{B}$ form, for which a somewhat artificial criterion

TABLE 7-21

Mean Number of Correct Responses for Adults on Comprehension of Connectives

	$A \cdot B$				$A \vee B$			
	$A \cdot B$	$A \cdot \bar{B}$	$\bar{A} \cdot \bar{B}$	Total	$A \vee B$	$A \vee \bar{B}$	$\bar{A} \vee \bar{B}$	Total
Conjoined	2.00	1.81	2.00	1.94	1.88	1.69	1.44	1.67
Derived	2.00	1.75	2.00	1.92	1.81	1.75	1.13	1.56
Quantified	1.94	1.63	1.94	1.83	2.00	1.94	1.06	1.67
Total for each connective	1.98	1.73	1.98	1.90	1.90	1.79	1.21	1.63

for a correct exclusive response had been adopted in the child data, it is interesting that the great majority (89.6%) of adult responses were of this kind.

Regarding negation $\bar{A}$, although 87.5% of adult responses were of the (correct) wide-negation type, the remaining responses were of the narrow-negation type; subjects ostensibly considered this an acceptable alternative response.

These data show that the completed logical structures of both negation and disjunction allow alternative-processing strategies. The fact remains, however, that prior to approximately age 7 (the period of concrete operational thought) subjects did not demonstrate capacity for wide negation. Narrow-negation responding was apparently not an alternative for the younger subjects but a necessity in the given situation. A similar situation holds for $\bar{A} \vee B$ at the 9–10 age level (when concrete operative structures are achieving completion and there is onset of formal operations), in which subjects demonstrated the capacity for an exclusive disjunction response.

RELATIONS BETWEEN CONNECTIVES

When the adult data are inspected, equivalent comprehension success is evident for some connectives. At the same time, when these data are compared with those of children, the rank hierarchy of success in adults does not deviate to a major degree from the hierarchy at younger ages (see Table 7-8). When association among the rank hierarchies of all 10 forms was assessed across the four age groups, Kendall's $W = .88$, $p < .001$; average Spearman $r = .85$, $p < .01$. The consistency of rank hierarchies of connective comprehension thus persists into adulthood.

INTENSION–EXTENSION

There was only a minimal difference between correct intension and correct extension in connective comprehension for adults ($\bar{X}\%$ differences $= 2\%$). This is consistent with the 8- to 10-year-old data.

ANOVA ON 6 BIVARIATE CONNECTIVES

An ANOVA analogous to that applied to the 4- to 10-year-olds' comprehension data was applied to the adult data. The age factor was omitted, providing a 3 factor (Connective type × Negation × Linguistic form) $2 \times 3 \times 3$ analysis with repeated measures on all factors. The analysis was intended to show whether the main effects and interactions in connective comprehension that were noted for children also persisted in adults. Despite the fact that the means on most connective forms were near ceiling, results showed similar effects to those for children. As with the child data, significant main effects of Connective type $(p < .01)$, and Negation $(p < .05)$ were found. As in the children's data, Linguistic form was not significant.

The only significant two-way interaction, as in the child data, was the Connective × Negation interaction $(p < .05)$. Finally, the three-way interaction, Connective × Negation × Linguistic form, was significant for adults $(p < .01)$ as with the child data. Similar factors were involved in causing the adult two-way interaction; in particular, negation did not have the same effect on *or* as on *and*. In the three-way interaction, linguistic form differentiated connective comprehension to a greater degree among the adults. This is interesting because the 8- to 10-year-old data showed increased linguistic form differences relative to the younger children. Again, the greatest effect of linguistic form was on the comprehension of disjunction connectives.

For adults as for 8–10 year olds, quantification aided comprehension of $A \vee B$ and $A \vee \bar{B}$ disjunction forms. With the disjunction form $\bar{A} \vee \bar{B}$, however, the nontransformed conjoined sentence form aided comprehension. It may be that quantification by *either* served to accentuate the exclusive rather than inclusive response to disjunction, once the capability for exclusive disjunction had been achieved (at ages 8–10 and adult levels). Thus both $A \vee B$ and $A \vee \bar{B}$ were improved by quantification. The $\bar{A} \vee \bar{B}$ disjunction form, because of its cognitive difficulty, may be less adaptable to linguistic transformation.

In general, then, structural interrelations among connectives persisted into adulthood. The evidence points to competence in adults for the comprehension of connectives that were difficult for 8- to 10-year olds (e.g., $\bar{A} \vee \bar{B}$). The 4- to 10-year-old data that showed the effects of linguistic transformation mainly in the older children (ages 8–10) were confirmed by similar effects in adults. The effects of linguistic transformation were limited to the disjunction connectives and were mainly due to the quantification of disjunction by *either*.

Finally, 14.6% of adult responses to $\bar{A} \cdot B$ indicated recognition of the ambiguity in this connective; 21.9% of adult responses recognized the ambiguity of $\overline{A \cdot B}$. The data indicate that adults, to an even greater extent than older children, recognize the ambiguity of those connective forms, but the proportions are still not very large. Instead, subjects, for the most part, tend to resolve logical connective ambiguity by alternative intuitive interpretations.

8

A Study of the Development of Logical and Linguistic Connectives: Cognitive Data and Summary

Harry Beilin and Barbara Lust

As stated in Chapter 6, language connectives (*and, or, not*) were hypothesized to correlate theoretically with the logical operations of intersection, union, and complementation. Thus, one of the major purposes of this study was to investigate a possible psychological relation between the linguistic connectives and logical operations. This chapter will report on the logical abilities of the subjects whose linguistic comprehension has been assessed (see Chapter 7) and inspect the correlation between their linguistic and cognitive comprehension. Description of the developmental levels of cognitive knowledge which underlie the specified logical operations (as measured by cognitive tasks) appears in Table 7-1.

Results—Cognitive Development

Operational Cognition

Table 8-1 shows the percentage of subjects at each age level who attained operational performance in the logic tasks: spontaneous classification, logical intersection (matrix abstract), logical union (inclusion task), logical complementation task, and logical vicariance. As discussed in Chapter 6, the understanding of the operational levels of these tasks implies the existence of cognitive groupings (logical structures that have psychological reality according to Piagetian theory). This structure permits anticipatory and deductive behaviour in respect to the logical relations between classes. The primary characteristic of operational level performance is the

TABLE 8-1

Percentage of Subjects Operational on Cognitive Tasks[a]

Age group	Spontaneous classification $(+, \times, -)$	Intersection $(\times)$ (logical multiplication)		Union $(+)$ (logical addition)	Logical complementation[b] $(-)$	Logical vicariance[b]
		Matrix abstract	Matrix constructed			
2–3	0	0[c]	0	0[c]	13	0
4–5	19	19	13	19	13	0
6–7	63	44	38	56	31	31
8–10	81	94	81	94	63	69

[a] See Table 7-1 for definition of operational performance.

[b] These tasks were measured on two set sizes, base set and extended set. Percentages here represent operational success on at least one of these set sizes.

[c] Only school-age 3-year olds tested on these tasks ($n = 6$).

reversibility feature of the grouping structure; it signals the attainment of operational logic and thus the basic capacity for logical deduction.

Most concrete logical operations were attained by 50% of the group at 6- to 7-years of age; near 100% group success was attained at ages 8–10. This is in accord with predictions from Piagetian developmental theory. Logical complementation and logical vicariance were distinct in that they reached the 50% success level at age 7, and the 100% level was not fully attained by ages 8–10. The greater difficulty of these tasks is also in accord with Piagetian predictions.

A second logical intersection test was administered to obtain additional data on the intersection process. This was the (constructed) matrix task. When operational level success on this task is compared with that on the (abstract) matrix task, the developmental data are seen to be very close. Table 8-1 shows the age distribution of these data. A logical intersection score was thus derived for each subject by a pooled estimate of his performance on both intersection tasks. This logical intersection score was used in several language—cognition analyses that follow.

Constituent Functions

As indicated in Chapter 6 and Appendix D, constituent functions are the cognitive precursors of operations; they involve one-way mappings, they are not anticipatory and are often achieved by trial and error. Piaget defines them as semilogical.

The proportions of subjects at each age who achieve at least constituent-function comprehension as the minimum are shown in Table 8-2. By 4- to 5-years of age, a large proportion of subjects (approximately 75%) achieved at least a constituent function level on most classification tasks. Functional vicariance appeared later, with 50% group success at 6- to 7-years, while functional spontaneous classification was achieved earlier (56% at ages 2–3).

Cognitive Functions: Dichotomy and Adjunction

Two subprocesses in the comprehension of classification were investigated: dichotomy and adjunction (Table 8-3).

DICHOTOMY

Dichotomy is the division of a set according to the binary values of one of its major dimensions. For example, given the set AB, AB', $A'B$, $A'B'$, two dichotomies are possible: $A–A'$, $B–B'$.

Eight dichotomies were possible over the full course of cognitive testing. The first two concerned a simple one-class dichotomy. That is, given the class of *girls*, subjects were required to dichotomize the class into two subclasses: *big girls* and *little girls* (of three exemplars each). The remaining

TABLE 8-2

Percentage of Subjects Attaining at Least the Level of Constituent Functions on Cognitive Tasks[a] (n = 16 at Each Age Level)

Age group	Spontaneous classification (+, ×, −)	Intersection (×) (logical multiplication)		Union (+) (logical addition)[b]	Logical complementation[c] (−)	Logical vicariance[c]
		Matrix abstract	Matrix constructed			
2–3	56	0[d]	0	83[e]	38	0
4–5	88	63	69	81	75	38
6–7	100	88	94	75	100	50
8–10	100	100	88	100	100	81

[a] See Table 7-2 for definition of constituent functional level performance.

[b] Because all children were constituent functional on this task, percentages here include subjects who succeeded quantification questions a and c at least (type A < B). Subjects who succeeded the operational level are also included in these percentages.

[c] Based on pooled estimate of performance on two set sizes, base and extended (success included success on at least one set size).

[d] Based on attainment of figural level response (see Table 7-2).

[e] n = 6 here; 2-year olds and at-home 3-year olds were not tested on these tasks.

TABLE TABLE 8-3

Percentage of Subjects Attaining Set Dichotomy and Adjunction Functions, and Mean Number of Dichotomies

		Adjunction of elements[b]	
Age group	Set dichotomy[a]	Identical elements	Foreign elements
2–3	25 (.31)[c]	31	13
4–5	94 (1.94)	88	19
6–7	100 (3.5)	88	25
8–10	100 (4.75)	94	75

[a] At least one full set dichotomy succeeded of the six possible: *boys/girls, big/little; bears/people, big/little; animals/people, big/little*.

[b] Subjects succeeded in at least four of the six cases in which they were required to adjoin an additional element to a previous classification.

[c] Mean number of correct dichotomies.

dichotomies consisted of: (*big* and *little*) *girls* and *boys*, and (*girls and boys*); (*big* and *little*) *animals* and *people*, and (*animals and people*) in which *animals — bears;* (*big and little*) *animals* and *people*, and (*animals and people*) in which *animals= monkeys* and *bears.*

The $\bar{X}$ dichotomies achieved by each age group over the six full-set dichotomies appears in Table 8-3. First success (at least one correct) on full-set dichotomy was achieved at ages 4–5 (actually at age 4); near complete success occurred only at ages 8–10 (actually at age 10). Simple one-class dichotomy was first successful at age 3.

ADJUNCTION

In order to score correct on the adjunction items, subjects had to have chosen the appropriate subclass to which the adjoined element belonged (e.g., to correctly adjoin *one little girl*, a subject had to add this element to a classification of *three little girls*). If the *three little girls* had previously been displaced (not classified as a unit), no correct adjunction could be achieved. In a sense, these adjunction items then tested "class or subclass maintenance" rather than the simple identity function of putting like with like.

The same constraint held for the adjunction of foreign elements. If the foreign element was an exemplar of a new subclass (e.g., *one big boy* when the subject had previously handled only *big* and *little girls* and *little boys*), the subject would have had to correctly classify the relevant value of either dimension (*big* or *boy*) in order to be scored correct for this adjunction function. Two- to 3-year olds began to succeed on these items and success remained high with age. The data for the foregoing cognitive operations and functions is summarized in Table 8-4.

TABLE 8-4

Summary Statistics on Cognitive Operations[a] and Functions from 4- to 10-Years Old (n = 48)

	Range	Mean	SD
Spontaneous classification	3–5	4.50	0.58
Inclusion	1–4	2.69	1.36
Matrix abstract	1–7	5.33	2.08
Matrix constructed	2–5	3.90	1.15
Multiplication[b] pooled	3–7	5.52	1.46
Complementation[c] pooled	1–5	2.98	1.12
Vicariance[c] pooled	1–5	2.52	1.74
Dichotomy[d]	0–6	3.40	1.91
Adjunction[e]			
Identical elements	0–6	4.96	1.44
Foreign elements	0–4	2.73	1.23

[a] Scores are cognitive level scores.
[b] Scores are based on performance on both matrix abstract and matrix constructed tasks.
[c] Scores are based on performance on both base and extended sets.
[d] Scores are sums of number of dichotomies achieved on the full set.
[e] Scores are number of correct, achieved adjunction functions.

Correlations Among Cognitive Tasks

All cognitive tasks (+, ×, −) correlated (.25–.90) significantly with each other, except for complementation with spontaneous classification (4- to 10-year-old sample, n = 48). Among the functions, dichotomy (number of dichotomies successfully achieved) correlated significantly with all operations and with the adjunction functions. The adjunction functions (number of adjunctions successfully achieved) correlated significantly with both complementation and vicariance among the operations (Table 8-5). Adjunction of foreign elements also correlated significantly with inclusion and the (abstract) matrix task.

When χ^2 was computed for each cognitive task interrelation in order to determine the contingency relations among tasks, and when the proportions of precedence of one operation over another were calculated for each pair (with the same method used previously in determining linguistic hierarchies see Chapter 7, section "Connective Hierarchies"), three levels of cognitive processing appeared (Table 8-6): (1) cognitive functions (dichotomy and adjunction); (2) basic cognitive operations (classification, inclusion and the matrices); and (3) higher-order cognitive operations (complementation and vicariance).

Complementation, however, did not clearly fit a Level 3 profile. Although it appeared later than operational performance on the other basic tasks (classification, inclusion, matrices), the precedence proportions of complementation over these were not all significant.

TABLE 8-5

Correlation Matrix for Cognitive Tasks (Operations and Functions) 4–10-Year Olds (n = 48)[a,b]

| | Operations | | | | | | Functions | | |
	Inclusion	Matrix (abstract)	Complementation (pooled)	Classification	Vicariance (pooled)	Matrix (constructed)	Dichotomy	Adjunction Identical	Adjunction Foreign
Operations									
Matrix (abstract)	.47**								
Complementation	.39**	.28*							
Classification	.34**	.58**	.15						
Vicariance	.59**	.46**	(.57**)	.47**					
Matrix (constructed)	.41**	.47**	.43**	.49**	.61**				
Functions									
Dichotomy	.60**	.43**	(.71**)	.41**	(.90**)	.70**			
Adjunction									
Identical	.05	.06	.41**	.03	.46**	.33*	.45**		
Foreign	.25*	.28*	.58**	.22	.65**	.33*	.65**	.72**	—

All scores are cognitive level scores.
Figures in parentheses are based on dependent measures, e.g., in order to achieve vicariance, subjects first had to have achieved a dichotomy.
* p < .05.
** p < .01.

TABLE 8-6

Proportions of Children (Ages 2-10)[a] for Whom One Cognitive Operation or Function Was Easier than Another for All Pairs of Cognitive Tasks[b]

| | Level 3 | | Level 2 | | | | Level 1 |
| | | | Matrix | | | | |
	Vicariance	Complementation	Constructed	Abstract	Inclusion	Classification	Dichotomy
Identity	30/30***	35/35***	34/35***	23/25***	22/25***	30/33***	8/13
Dichotomy	35/35***	32/32***	30/30***	25/26***	23/24***	26/27***	
Classification	11/12**	14/21	8/11	5/9	6/13		
Inclusion	12/13**	14/18*	10/14	7/12			
Matrix							
Abstract	11/13*	13/18	7/10				
Constructed	6/10	9/16					
Complementation	6/9						

[a] n = 64 (ages 2–10) for identity, dichotomy, classification, matrix constructed, complementation. and vicariance tasks. n = 54 (ages 3–10) for inclusion and matrix abstract tasks.

[b] Numerators show number of subjects who succeed item of row while failing item of column. Denominators show total number of subjects who perform differentially on the two tasks.

* $p < .05$.
** $p < .01$.
*** $p < .001$, two-tailed tests

In general, these analyses show that the basic operations $(+, \times, -)$ relate to a single operatory kernel as suggested by Piagetian theory, with vicariance acting as a higher-order expression of these operations. Complementation $(-)$ as measured by the singular class task, differed from the other basic operations to a certain extent by being somewhat more difficult. The hierarchical order in cognitive logical capacities suggested by these developmental patterns enters into later analyses of language–cognition relationships; the cognitive hierarchies are compared with the linguistic hierarchies reported above.

Summary of Cognitive Development

The above report of the findings on the development of cognitive logical abilities allows several generalizations. The preoperational child could establish simple predication $(x = a)$ and simple class membership of a predicated element $(a \in A)$ (adjunction). Even the youngest subjects (ages 2–3) often constructed one "class," e.g., *three little girls*, (constituent-function spontaneous classification) and most 4- to 5-year olds could construct two to four "classes" (i.e., more advanced constituent-function classification) on the given universe set. Simple adjunction functions which maintain primitive class unity were also in the young child's repertoire. These "classes," however, were the products of one-way functions; they were not anticipatory, and neither additive nor multiplicative relations were established between them. In a technical sense, class had the meaning of collection for these young subjects.

The preoperational child could differentiate subclasses into A and A' by a direct one-way function (within certain simple limits); the 3-year old could do this when $A = AB$ and $A' = A'B$; the 4- to 5-year olds began to be able to do this when $A = AB + AB'$ and $A' = A'B + A'B'$. But the preoperational child could not establish more complex relations between these classes (as in class inclusion, comparing them while holding the higher class constant as an abstract reference, that is, part-to-whole). As a consequence, he could not recognize that $A = B - A'$ when performing complex relations between A and A' or between A and B. A single class (e.g., B) did not exist as an abstract entity for these subjects.

In particular, children from 2- to 5-years of age could not establish systematic relations between classes that were themselves associations (e.g., AB versus AB' versus $A'B$ versus $A'B'$). Failure of the younger children to reach operational performance on the matrix tasks demonstrated this.

Older children, however, beginning at about 6- to 7-years old could relate subclasses A and A' to a higher-order class B. At this age, class began to take on the status of an abstraction. Class union operations (inclusions) were achieved, and classes were considered as associations of dimensions, which could be entered into the logical matrix or double entry table and of which all the dimensional interrelations among these associations could be plotted. Class intersection operations (matrix) were attained at this time.

Finally, only the oldest children (performance-perfect at age 10) could operate on an abstract system of classes (created either by logical union or logical intersection) by anticipating alternative classifications—(vicariance). For the younger, concrete operational subjects, a logical system was to a certain extent dependent on the concrete nature of its components. Only at the beginning of the formal logical stage did the logical system allow interactions among operations.

When this study was undertaken, these developments in cognitive capacity were expected to be directly related to and possibly responsible for developments in acquisition of connective comprehension in language. The following sections assess the interrelations among the differentiated components of the linguistic and cognitive systems.

Results—Relations between Cognitive and Linguistic Performance

The relations between linguistically expressed logical connectives and cognitive logical operations were measured in several ways. These analyses will be presented in their order of generality, from the most general to the most specific. They include comparisons of comprehension data for both linguistic and cognitive tasks, correlations between components of the linguistic and cognitive dimensions and analyses of comprehension of components of the linguistic dimension at each cognitive level. The final analyses consider the effects of *age* on cognitive explanations for linguistic functioning.

Developmental Synchrony of Linguistic and Cognitive Comprehension

The developmental data for both cognitive and linguistic tasks provided the basis for testing the specific hypothesized relations between intersection–conjunction, union–disjunction, and complementation–negation.

TABLE 8-7

Percentage of Subjects Demonstrating Consistent Success on Linguistic Connectives[a] **(n = 16 in Each Age Group)**

Age group	A[b]	$\overline{A}_w$[b]	$A \cdot B$	$A \vee B$	$A \cdot \overline{B}$	$A \vee \overline{B}$	$\overline{A} \cdot \overline{B}$	$\overline{A} \vee \overline{B}$	$\overline{A \vee B}$[c]	$\overline{A \cdot B}$[c]
2–3	6[c]	0[c]	13	0	—	—	Not tested	—	—	—
4–5	50	13	56	25	0	19	38	0	31	25
6–7	75	38	75	44	25	31	69	0	69	63
8–10	100	56	100	100	75	38	94	13	94	88

[a] Based on six items (two per each of three linguistic forms). Criterion of consistent success: at least five of six correct.
[b] Based on four items. Criterion: at least three of four correct.
[c] Based on two items. Criterion: two of two correct.

The general relations between dimensions were first defined by inspecting the proportions of subjects in each age group who achieved operational performance in the cognitive tasks (Table 8-1) and the proportions of subjects in the same groups who achieved consistent success on linguistic connectives (Table 8-7). (Consistent linguistic success was defined as success in all items but one.) If larger proportions of subjects at each age showed cognitive comprehension than connective comprehension, this would be taken as general evidence of cognitive precedence over language at these ages; if not, then either concomitant development or linguistic precedence was possible.

CONJUNCTION–INTERSECTION

Logical intersection was proposed (see Chapter 6) as the cognitive analogue of the *and* conjunction ($\cdot$) in language. The development of operational intersection and comprehension of the conjunction forms ($A \cdot B$, $A \cdot \bar{B}$, $\bar{A} \cdot \bar{B}$) is shown in Figure 8-1. (The data for this figure are shown in Table 8-7.) $A \cdot \bar{B}$ differs from the others in this set in showing prior achievement of the cognitive operation. Development of logical intersection is congruent with development of linguistic ($A \cdot \bar{B}$) comprehension and precedes it at each age. Comprehension of the linguistic connectives $A \cdot B$ and $\bar{A} \cdot \bar{B}$, however, develops at rates different from the cognitive operation, and precedes it at each age except at 8–10, when linguistic and cognitive comprehension intersect.

DISJUNCTION–UNION

Logical union (addition) was proposed as the cognitive correlate of the disjunction connective *or* ($\vee$) The development of operational union and

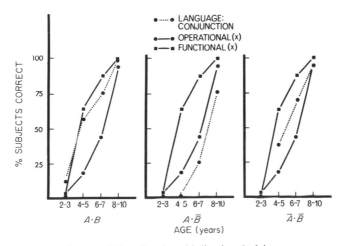

Fig. 8–1. $A.B$, operational and functional multiplication ($\times$) by age.

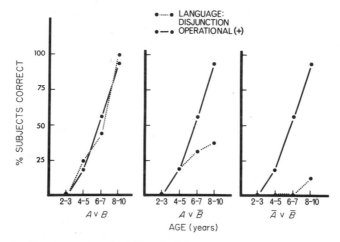

Fig. 8–2. $A \vee B$ and operational addition ($+$) by age.

disjunction ($A \vee B$, $A \vee \bar{B}$, $\bar{A} \vee \bar{B}$) is graphed in Figure 8-2. In contrast to the conjunctive set, each of the disjunction connectives shows a cognitive precedence or concordance relation. For $A \vee B$, the relation is marked by near concordance. For $A \vee \bar{B}$, there is overlap between the language form and operational union from ages 2–3 to 4–5; thereafter, cognitive precedence appears (partially due perhaps to the depressed developmental curve of the $A \vee \bar{B}$ form). In the case of $\bar{A} \vee \bar{B}$, operational union was succeeded by a majority of the 6- to 7-year-old group before the onset of linguistic comprehension.

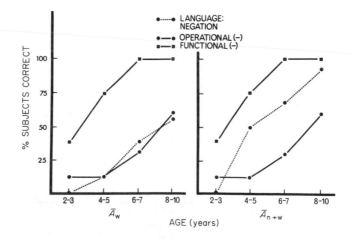

Fig. 8–3. Language negation and operational and functional complementation ($-$) by age.

NEGATION–COMPLEMENTATION

Logical complementation was proposed to be related to linguistic negation *not* (−). The complementation–negation relationships indicated in Figure 8-3 show that operational complementation and linguistic negation developed in close synchrony.

CONSTITUENT–FUNCTIONS

Using the criterion of operational performance did not yield a high degree of correlation between logical intersection and the conjunction forms, $A \cdot B$ and $\overline{A} \cdot \overline{B}$. Thus, the data were re-analyzed with the criterion of at least attainment of constituent functional comprehension of logical intersection. This level of performance when compared with that of linguistic comprehension (Figure 8-1) shows the two linguistic forms to relate much more closely to constituent functional intersection than was evident with operational performance. Developmental curves approximate each other much more closely in shape, and cognitive precedence is indicated particularly for the $\overline{A} \cdot \overline{B}$ form. The precedence of cognitive function relative to the $A \cdot \overline{B}$ form, on the other hand, was greatly increased, although the curves no longer approximate each other in shape.

With the new criterion, negation ($\overline{A}$ wide), when related to constituent functional performance at least on complementation (Fig. 8-3), showed cognitive precedence to a clear, constant, and large extent.

DISJUNCTIVE ABSENCE–VICARIANCE

The $\overline{A} \vee \overline{B}$ form was preceded by the logical union operation. The integration of negation with each disjunct of the disjunction connective suggests that a higher-order operation similar in nature to cognitive vicariance may be required for its comprehension because, as suggested, vicariance integrates union with a general complementation operation. Vicariance developed at a much faster rate than $\overline{A} \vee \overline{B}$ (Fig. 8-4), which showed sharp linear growth with its onset delayed, relative to the onset of cognitive growth. The relation of functional vicariance to $\overline{A} \vee \overline{B}$ (Fig. 8-4) shows that the onset of $\overline{A} \vee \overline{B}$ comprehension was delayed until functional vicariance was achieved by at least 50% of the 6- to 7-year-old group.

BASE CONNECTIVES—SPONTANEOUS CLASSIFICATION

Finally, classification was described as a general activity calling for addition, multiplication, and complementation operations. It was possible that this general cognitive capacity would relate more closely to elementary connectives than would the more differentiated cognitive processes which isolate specific operations. As can be seen, operational classification was preceded by linguistic comprehension of A and $A \cdot B$ (Fig. 8-5), although

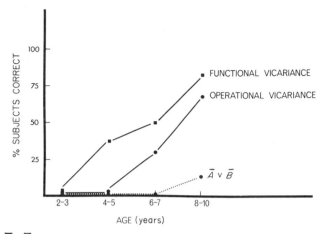

Fig. 8–4. $\overline{A} \vee \overline{B}$, operational and functional vicariance by age.

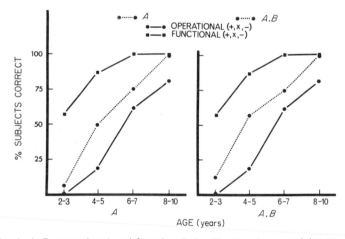

Fig. 8–5. $A, A \cdot B$, operational and functional classification $(+, \times, -)$ by age.

functional level classification preceded both A and $A \cdot B$ comprehension (Fig. 8-5), and at ages 2–3 it was synchronous with it. (The minimum criterion for functional classification was the subject's specification of at least one subclass.)

Again, for the basic connective $\overline{A}$ (narrow and wide) in which a narrow interpretation of negation was also considered correct, functional classification showed constant cognitive precedence (Fig. 8-5), although operational classification did not (Fig. 8-6). When complementation is compared to this form (Fig. 8-3) it is again the constituent functional level which shows developmental precedence over linguistic comprehension. In both cases (functional classification $\overline{A}$ and functional complementation $\overline{A}$), the shape of the cognitive and linguistic developmental curves is similar and converges at ages 8–10.

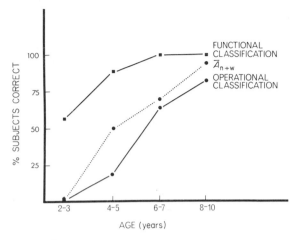

Fig. 8–6. $\overline{A}_{n+w}$, operational and functional classification by age.

SUMMARY OF DEVELOPMENTAL PARALLELS

In general, comparisons of the development of linguistic and cognitive performance showed that comprehension of many linguistic connectives (negation $\overline{A}$; disjunctions $A \vee B$, $A \vee \overline{B}$, $\overline{A} \vee B$; conjunction with exclusion $A \cdot \overline{B}$) appeared to develop later than, or concurrently with, operational level performance in theoretically related cognitive tasks. For the basic forms (A, $\overline{A}_{nw}$) and the two simple connectives $A \cdot B$ and $\overline{A} \cdot \overline{B}$, linguistic comprehension appeared later than, or concurrently with, the constituent–functional level of cognitive performance.

These cognition–language comparisons, however, provide only a general notion of developmental relations between language and logic. These relations were examined further by correlational and contingency analyses, based on a within-subject consistency criterion.

Canonical Correlation

Canonical correlation was applied to the data because of its power to measure the interrelatedness of two sets of variables in two different conceptual domains with concurrent measures for each subject (Cooley & Lohnes, 1971). In this study, the set of language connectives (*and, or, not*) and the set of theoretically related logical processes (intersection, union, complementation) provided the relevant domains. Because this statistic is still relatively uncommon, some descriptive comments will be made. The statistic improves upon a matrix of correlations by estimating the underlying unity of sets of variables. It thus reduces the number of individual correlations, advancing interpretability of the relations inherent in the data. As Cooley and Lohnes (1971) state, "To try to think about all these correlations simultaneously is very difficult if one is trying to generalize about the extent and nature of interrelationships of the domains [p. 168]." The canonical correlation analyzes the structure of relationships across domains of measurement similar to the manner in which factor analysis analyzes the structure of relationships within a domain.

The canonical model, in general, selects linear functions that have maximum covariances between domains, each subject to the constraint of orthogonality. It assesses the extent to which individuals "occupy the same relative positions in one measurement space as they do in the other [p. 169]." The model defines a value, Rc, canonical correlation, which is the maximum correlation that can be obtained by the selection of linear functions from the two sets. It also defines canonical factors; these are the factors of the two sets that have the highest correlations across domains. The model also allows assessment of those elements in the reference sets that contribute most heavily to the maximum correlation.

The model also provides for the derivation of a measure of "redundancy" between the two sets, that is, of the amount of "overlap" between the two sets involved in the Rc. This redundancy is defined both in terms of the variance in the factor of one set (the left side) given the other set (right set), and for the variance in the (right set) factor given the left set. This measure is important because the Rc is a measure of overlap not between the two sets but between two canonical variates that may or may not be important in their own batteries (Cooley & Lohnes, 1971).

A series of canonical factors and their appropriate Rc are derived in the same way. Each is necessarily orthogonal (uncorrelated with the first pair of components). The significance of each canonical r can be tested by a conversion to X^2 (Cooley & Lohnes, 1971, p. 175).

Cognition and language data provided the two domains relevant to the canonical r. The measures chosen to represent the cognitive domain included the basic logical processes: logical intersection (multiplication), logical union (addition), logical complementation (negation), and a general classification assessment integrating these operations (spontaneous classification). The linguistic domain consisted of the six connectives, three conjunction forms $A \cdot B$, $A \cdot \bar{B}$, $\bar{A} \cdot \bar{B}$ and three disjunction forms $A \vee B$ $A \vee \bar{B}$, $\bar{A} \vee \bar{B}$.

According to the basic thesis of this study, the two domains (connectives and logical processes) should be significantly related. Therefore, at least one Rc should be significant. According to the logical theory of the connectives, however, it might be predicted that specific relations would hold between the domains. Each connective might be expected to relate particularly to its theoretical correlate. If the two relations (conjunction–intersection and disjunction–union) were psychologically equivalent, it would follow that the structure of the canonical r should show equal weightings on conjunction and disjunction and on intersection and union operations in each set. Moreover, at least two Rc should be significant as intersection–conjunction and union–disjunction relations would be orthogonal.

On the other hand, if the relations between domains were multiplex, e.g., one cognitive operation explains some or all of connective performance, then only one Rc should be significant and the structure of the relation would indicate the relevant asymmetry. If asymmetry were structurally evident in the linguistic domain (e.g., if the one cognitive operation related to some but not all linguistic operations equally), it would argue for non-homogeneity in the nature of connective forms, certain ones being more closely related to cognitive processes than others.

The largest canonical r was .79 ($\chi^2 = 58.22$, $p = .0002$). The cognitive domain of logical set processes was thus correlated with the linguistic domain of logical connectives; at least one dimension of linguistic connectives was significantly related to a corresponding dimension of cognitive processes. The next highest correlation was not significant, $r = .50$ ($\chi^2 = 18.13$, $p = .26$).

The first canonical variates were primarily functions of $A \vee B$ (disjunction) and logical intersection (abstract matrix) in the linguistic and cognitive batteries respectively. The factor structure of the relations between linguistic and cognitive domains, which indicates the correlations of the elements in the sets with the maximally correlated components, shows (Table 8-8) that $A \vee B$ (disjunction) is a primary component of the linguistic set correlating with the created factor ($r = .87$). Supplementarily, $\bar{A} \cdot \bar{B}$ (conjunction plus double negation) and $A \cdot \bar{B}$ (conjunction plus single negation) emerge as components of this correlation ($r = .62$ and .61 respectively). On the other hand, $A \cdot B$, $A \vee \bar{B}$, and $\bar{A} \vee \bar{B}$ are the least involved linguistic components in the correlation between the two domains.

In the cognitive set, logical multiplication is the principal component of the interrelation between the linguistic and cognitive domains ($r = .93$).

TABLE 8-8

Interdomain Structure of Linguistic Connectives and Cognitive Operations: Structure Coefficients for the First Canonical Correlation (n = 48, Ages 4–10)

Linguistic connective Factor 1 ($Rc = .79$)		Cognitive operation Factor 1 ($Rc = .79$)	
$A \cdot B$ (and)	.45	Classification $(+, \times, -)$	.40
$A \cdot \bar{B}$ (and/not)	.61	Logical union (inclusion	
$\bar{A} \cdot \bar{B}$ (not/and/not)	.62	task) $(+)$	.60
$A \vee B$ (or)	.87	Logical intersection	
$A \vee \bar{B}$ (or/not)	.43	(matrix task) $(\times)$	.93
$\bar{A} \vee \bar{B}$ (not/or/not)	.48	Logical complementa-	.54
		tion $(-)$	
Factor redundancy	.22	Factor redundancy	.26
Total redundancy	.27	Total redundancy	.33

As a secondary component, logical union ($r = .60$) enters this relationship, followed by logical complementation ($r = .54$). Classification is least involved in the significant canonical correlation. In the cognitive domain, then, logical intersection emerges as the single most important element in the correlation with language connective comprehension.

The redundancy measures show that the amount of total overlap between the domains is not high. The redundancy of the linguistic connectives given the cognitive operations is only .27. Similarly, the redundancy of the cognitive operations given the linguistic connectives is .33. The redundancy of the linguistic connectives given the logical processes contained in just the first (significant) factor is .22; the redundancy of the logical processes given the connectives in the first factor is .26. Thus, each domain, cognitive and linguistic, has an independent residual that is not involved in the relation between the two sets, i.e., in the canonical structure. At the same time, however, this first factor extracts 35% of the variance from the linguistic set and 42% of the variance from the cognitive set. This amount is considered sufficient to support the conclusion of interrelatedness of the sets.

The structure of the relations between cognitive groupings and linguistic connective domains then appears to be strong ($Rc = .79$, $p = .0002$), but specific (based on low redundancy measures). Logical intersection and linguistic disjunction ($A \vee B$) appear to be the primary foci of interrelations of the two domains.

Product–moment correlations previously reported also showed high correlations between intersection (particularly abstract matrix) and connectives, particularly disjunction. The two analyses thus complement each other.

Contingency Relations between Connective Comprehension and Logical Operations

The results of the above correlational analyses suggest a significant relation of specific cognitive processes to the comprehension of language connectives. The results indicate, further, that these relations were strongest for the disjunction connective *or* and logical intersection. To obtain further information on the nature of these cognitive–language relationships, a series of contingency analyses were undertaken in which concurrence of subject achievement on the connectives and the cognitive tasks was tested.

Subjects were classified for their achievement on each linguistic connective in relation to their achievement on each of the cognitive functions and operations. As described above, the cognitive tasks included: (1) *cognitive operations*: spontaneous classification, logical intersection (as measured by the matrix abstract and matrix constructed tasks), logical union as measured by the inclusion task, complementation and vicariance; (2) *cognitive functions*, adjunction of elements and dichotomy.

The criterion for connective achievement was success on at least all but one of the items administered. Criterion for success on cognitive operations was attainment of the *operational* level. For complementation and vicariance operations, which had been treated on two set sizes, a pooled estimate was used, and the criterion for success in each case was attainment of the operational level on at least one set size. For dichotomy, subjects were scored positively on the cognitive dimension if they achieved at least one full-set dichotomy. On the adjunction function, subjects were scored positively on the cognitive dimension if they succeeded in at least four of the six adjunctions of identical element items.

Cognition–language contingency analyses were performed at each of four age-levels (2–3, 4–5, 6–7, 8–10) and over all ages (2–10, $n = 64$). When 2- to 3-year olds were not tested on cognitive or language items, they were omitted from these analyses ($n = 48$ or 54).

PRECEDENCE OF COGNITION OVER LANGUAGE PERFORMANCE

Proportions of subjects (over all ages) who succeeded in a cognitive operation but did not succeed in comprehending a language form were computed. To calculate these proportions for each cognition–language pair, the number of subjects who succeeded in the cognitive operation but failed language comprehension was taken as a proportion of the total number of subjects who performed differentially on the two tasks, i.e., subjects who passed or failed both tasks were omitted from consideration. (This is the same method used in establishing linguistic hierarchies, see above.) Thus only the $(+ -)$ and $(- |)$ groups were used for the computation. The binomial test (one-tailed) was applied to the fractions. The null hypothesis was that cognitive performance would not be in significant advancement over linguistic performance. Significant fractions above one-half were interpreted as evidence of cognitive precedence.

The fractions reveal three levels of relationship (Table 8-9) corresponding to the linguistic hierarchy which was found above to exist in the data. Fractions above and to the right of the black line designate inter-domain comparisons in which there is cognitive precedence; 33 of these 39 fractions were significant.

For the earliest developing language forms (A, $A \cdot B$, $\overline{A} \cdot \overline{B}$, and $\overline{A}_{nw}$), achievement of cognitive functions (adjunction and dichotomy) preceded linguistic comprehension. For the more complex connectives, ($A \vee \overline{B}$, $\overline{A}$ wide, $A \cdot \overline{B}$) the basic cognitive operations (classification, matrices, intersection, union, inclusion, complementation), as well as the cognitive functions, were achieved prior to linguistic comprehension (60% of these fractions were significant). Finally, vicariance, a more complex operation in the Piagetian system was achieved before the most complex connective, $\overline{A} \vee \overline{B}$, as were all other operations and functions. The connective $A \vee B$ (disjunction) was an exception to these levels in that its attainment was concurrent with the attainment of the basic logical operations. This finding will be discussed subsequently.

TABLE 8-9

Cognitive Functions and Operations: Precedence of Cognition Over Language Connectives[a,b,c]

	A	$\bar{A}_{n\&w}$	A·B	$\bar{A}\cdot\bar{B}$	A∨B	A∨$\bar{B}$	$\bar{A}(w)$	A·$\bar{B}$	$\bar{A}\vee\bar{B}$
Functions									
Identity	20/23***	23/26***	20/25**	14/17**	29/31***	30/31***	40/43***	28/29***	41/41***
Dichotomy	15/16***	17/17***	13/14***	15/15***	24/24***	33/33***	34/34***	31/31***	45/45***
Operations									
Classification (+, ×, −)	—	—	—	—	—	15/18**	15/21*	13/16**	24/24***
Matrix (constructed) (×)	—	—	—	—	—	13/19	11/18	9/13	19/19***
Matrix (abstract) (×)	—	—	—	—	—	14/17**	14/20[d]	11/13**	23/23***
Inclusion (+)	—	—	—	—	—	17/21**	16/22*	12/13**	25/25***
Complementation (pooled)(−)	—	—	—	—	—	12/21	10/18	8/15	15/15***
Vicariance (pooled)	—	—	—	—	—	10/18	—	—	14/14***

Note: Proportions show number of subjects who succeed cognitive process of the row, while failing language comprehension of the column. Denominators show number of subjects who perform differentially on the two.

[a] Criteria for *cognitive* attainment: identity—at least 4 of 6 items; dichotomy—at least one full set size dichotomy; classification, matrix, inclusion—operational category; complementation and vicariance—operational on at least one set size. Criterion for *language* attainment: success on all but one item.

[b] $n = 48$, except in cases of A, $\bar{A}$, $A \cdot B$, $A \vee B$ in which 2- and 3-year data were available, ($n = 64$). On these forms, inclusion and matrix abstract ($n = 54$) because only 6 of the youngest children were administered these tasks.

[c] Fractions which do not show cognitive dominance are noted by (−).

[d] $p = .058$.

* $p < .05$.

** $p < .01$.

*** $p < .001$. (one-tailed).

It is also evident that whereas the cognitive functions preceded the achievement of the A, $\overline{A}_{nw}$, $A \cdot B$, $\overline{A} \cdot \overline{B}$, and $A \vee B$ connectives, once the connectives were achieved these in turn preceded or were concomitant with the achievement of the cognitive *operations*. Later analyses will show that the achievement of the cognitive preoperational level of constituent functions related to the attainment of these language forms.

We originally proposed that linguistic connectives were related to cognitive processes through developing operativity. Additional analyses were undertaken to determine how the set of simpler connectives considered here were related to the cognitive processes that develop prior to cognitive operations. The following section reports these relations.

Contingency Relations between Connectives and Constituent Functions

As discussed in Chapter 6, in Piagetian theory cognitive operations result from the closure of logical structure. Cognitive structures make it possible for a one-way cognitive process to realize its logical inversion synchronously, and thus achieve operational status. Such structures, including their subcomponents and subprocesses, are elaborated in gradual, constructive development. Piaget has spoken of the cognitive achievements that precede operational structures as constituent functions.

We propose that the development of certain elementary language forms would be contingent upon the prior or concomitant development of these constituent functions. To test this hypothesis, success of subjects on the simple connectives was related to success on the cognitive tasks, defined as attainment of the constituent function level at least. $A \vee B$ was included in this analysis because it had shown concordance rather than precedence in comparison with operational cognition.

PRECEDENCE OF CONSTITUENT FUNCTIONS OVER LANGUAGE

The data for this analysis (Table 8-10) were calculated in the same manner as in the comparable, cognitive operational analyses. Only functional vicariance did not consistently yield fractions in the expected direction to show cognitive achievement prior to linguistic achievement. For the remaining constituent functions, only 4 of 25 comparisons were not significant, although even these were in the expected direction (above one-half). A and $A \cdot B$ were not significantly preceded by matrix functions although they were significantly preceded by all other cognitive functions (classification, union, and complementation), except vicariance.

CONTINGENCY ANALYSES BY AGE

Contingency analyses show precedence of constituent functions (except for vicariance functions) over elementary language forms at ages 4–5, with continued cognitive precedence or concordance at ages 6–7. At

TABLE 8-10

Cognitive Constituent Functions: Precedence of Cognition Over Language[a,b,c]

	A	$\overline{A}$ (narrow + wide)	$A \cdot B$	$\overline{A} \cdot \overline{B}$	$A \vee B$
Classification	18/18***	22/23***	16/16***	14/14***	28/28***
Matrix (abstract)	8/12	8/10[d]	7/12	9/10**	14/15***
Matrix (constructed)	11/17	13/18*	8/13	11/14*	19/23***
Inclusion	13/16**	16/20**	10/12*	11/13**	22/25***
Complementation (pooled)	15/17***	17/18***	13/15**	12/12***	23/23***
Vicariance (pooled)	—	—	—	—	—

[a] Criteria for cognitive attainment: at least constituent function level score (except in the case of matrix constructed in which criterion is at least figurative score). Criterion for language attainment is success on all but 1 item at least.

[b] $n = 48$ in all cases except $A, \overline{A}$, $A \cdot B$, $A \vee B$. Here, when 2- and 3-year old data were available, $n = 64$ in all cases except inclusion and matrix abstract ($n = 54$). (Only 6 of the youngest children were administered these tasks.)

[c] Fractions are tested for deviation from $\frac{1}{2}$ by binomial test (one-tailed). Fractions which do not show cognitive dominance by surpassing $\frac{1}{2}$ are designated by (−).

[d] $p = .055$.

* $p < .05$.
** $p < .01$.
*** $p < .001$.

ages 6–7 and finally at 8–10, of course, subjects indicated comprehension of both cognitive and language tasks.

For $A \cdot B$ and A, functional intersection shows precedence over A at both ages 4–5 and 6–7, although not significantly so (Table 8–10). For $A \cdot B$ similarly, (abstract) matrix functions were concordant with language comprehension at 2- to 3- and 4- to 5-years old and took precedence at ages 6–7; (constructed) matrix was in concordance at 2- to 3-years old and took precedence at both 4- to 5- and 6- to 7-years old.

All cognitive constituent functions developed prior to comprehension of the $A \vee B$ form (as noted before, cognitive operations developed in concordance with the $A \vee B$ form). Constituent functional comprehension of vicariance was also achieved before $A \vee B$ at ages 4–5 and then was in concordance with it at ages 6–7.

Vicariance constituent functions are preceded by comprehension of A, $A \cdot B$, and $\overline{A}_{nw}$ at ages 4–5 and 6–7; but are in concordance with comprehension of $\overline{A} \cdot \overline{B}$ and the distributive connectives at ages 4–5.

SUMMARY OF LANGUAGE–COGNITION CONTINGENCY RELATIONS

Comprehension of the elementary set of connectives and basic forms (A, $A \cdot B$, $\overline{A} \cdot \overline{B}$, $\overline{A}_{nw}$, and distributive connectives) were found to be significantly preceded, developmentally, by the cognitive functions of adjunction of identical elements and dichotomy, and by the constituent functions of basic cognitive processes of union, intersection, and complementation, although they, in turn, preceded attainment of the operational level of cognitive processes. Comprehension of several of the elementary connectives also preceded understanding of both constituent-functional and operational vicariance.

The more complex connectives ($\overline{A}_w$, $A \cdot \overline{B}$, and $A \vee \overline{B}$) were found to be generally preceded by operational comprehension of cognitive processes as well as by the cognitive functions. Cognitive complementation and vicariance were often achieved in concordance with these linguistic forms. Constituent-functional complementation and vicariance, however, significantly preceded them.

Comprehension of $A \vee B$ was found to be preceded by adjunction of identical elements and dichotomy functions and to develop in concordance with most of the basic cognitive operations and with constituent-functional vicariance. Constituent-functional forms of other cognitive classificatory processes significantly preceded comprehension of the $A \vee B$ connective. The most complex connective, $\overline{A} \vee \overline{B}$, was significantly preceded in development by all cognitive processes including operational vicariance and complementation. Most subjects showed full language and cognitive attainment by ages 8–10.

Connective Comprehension as a Function of Cognitive Level

The foregoing analyses imply a developmental interaction between the subject's cognitive level and the hierarchical levels of connective comprehension. Cognitive level is defined by the stages in the progressive attainment of operativity in the performance of logical tasks. The following analysis examined specifically the relation of the subject's cognitive level to his comprehension of connectives.

The canonical correlation data already pointed to the critical role of logical multiplication (intersection) in connective comprehension. For this reason, logical multiplication was taken as the criterion measure for indicating the child's level of cognitive development in the analysis that follows. Children were grouped by cognitive level on a 4-level scale based on their performance on both constructed and abstract matrix tasks. Level 1 represents premultiplication, or prefunctional comprehension of logical intersection. Level 2 represents constituent-function comprehension (at best, on at least one task). Level 3 represents operational performance on one task only, and Level 4 represents operational performance on both tasks. The cognitive level scale, ranging from sensorimotor to stable, operational multiplication comprehension, provides an alternative to classification by age and in our view (as well as that that of Sinclair & Ferreiro, 1970) should be a better predictor of linguistic success than age. The percentages of subjects in each age group for each of the combined cognitive levels appears in Table 8-11. The proportion of success on linguistic connectives at each of the cognitive levels is shown in Table 8-12.

TABLE 8-11

Percentage of Subjects at Each (Cognitive) Level of Logical Multiplication by Age Group

	Age				$\bar{X}$ age
Cognitive level	3	4–5	6–7	8–10	(years and months)
1 ($n = 12$)[a] premultiplication (sensorimotor, elementary, or figurative)	50	42	8	0	4,5
2 ($n = 15$) constituent functions (on at least 1 task)	0	47	47	6	6,0
3 ($n = 9$) operational (on one task)	0	33	45	22	6,9
4 ($n = 18$) operational (on both tasks)	0	6	22	72	8,10

[a] When the 3-year olds ($n = 6$) are omitted from this sample (in order to conduct analyses on connectives on which these children were not tested), the mean age of this group becomes 5, 1 ; ($n = 6$).

TABLE 8-12

Correct Responses on Linguistic Connectives by Cognitive Level on Logical Multiplication (in Percentages)[a,b]

Cognitive level	$A \cdot B$	$A \cdot \bar{B}$	$\bar{A} \cdot \bar{B}$	$A \vee B$	$A \vee \bar{B}$	$\bar{A} \vee \bar{B}$	A	$\bar{A}_w$	$\bar{A}_{nw}$
1 ($n = 12$) prefunctional	39[c]	3[c]	17[c]	15	42[c]	0[c]	40	8	23
2 ($n = 15$) constituent functions	72	28	66	32	26	0	62	37	65
3 ($n = 9$) Operational on 1 task only	72	24	74	67	56	15	72	42	58
4 ($n = 18$) Operational on both tasks	100	65	94	96	70	19	100	58	97

[a] Cognitive level is a pooled estimate of performance on two logical multiplication tasks (matrix abstract) and (matrix constructed).
[b] Number of linguistic items = 6 per S for bivariate connectives and 4 items per S for univariate connectives.
[c] $n = 6$ (3-year olds were not tested on these linguistic forms).

To assess the change in linguistic comprehension as a function of cognitive level, tests of independent proportions compared increase in percentages of correct connective responses at each cognitive level. Passage from Levels 1 to 2 (prefunctional to constituent functions) and from Levels 3 to 4 (operational-one task, operational-two tasks) showed major periods of growth in comprehension of connectives and base forms (A, $\overline{A}_{nw}$).

The results suggest that, for most of the connectives and base forms (with exceptions of $A \vee \overline{B}$ and $\overline{A} \vee \overline{B}$), constituent functions are associated with either onset of connective development or major improvement in achievement.

These results relate to the linguistic *clusters* discussed previously. For Cluster 1, connectives and basic forms (A, $\overline{A}_{nw}$, $A \cdot B$, $\overline{A} \cdot \overline{B}$), passage from Level 1 to 2 (prefunctional to functional) was associated with the major advance in linguistic comprehension. A high proportion of success in these forms was associated with the achievement of Level 2 (constituent functions).

For Cluster 2 forms ($A \vee B$, $\overline{A}_w$, $A \cdot \overline{B}$), passage from Levels 1 to 2 was related to the transition from a very low level of success to improved (but still low) success; for these forms, the constituent function level was associated with the initiation of successful performance.

Passage from Levels 3 to 4 was associated with an increase in comprehension (to the 100% level) for Cluster 1 connectives. For Cluster 2 type connectives ($A \cdot \overline{B}$, $A \vee B$), transition from Level 3 to 4 led to significant improvement in comprehension (although not to the 100% level). ($\overline{A}_w$, of the 2 Cluster, was an exception in not increasing significantly from 3 to 4.)

These results suggest that, for simple connectives and basic forms ($A \cdot B$, A, $\overline{A}_{nw}$, $\overline{A} \cdot \overline{B}$), constituent functions may be a necessary cognitive prerequisite for significant growth in comprehension. Operational achievement (passage from Level 3 to 4) appeared to stabilize linguistic comprehension of these connectives. The latter finding is significant because early comprehension (at least 50% of the group) of these first connectives might suggest that they were achieved prior to cognitive operations and were therefore independent of them. The cognitive level analysis shows on the contrary that (1) these connectives were related to cognitive processes, but to cognitive constituent functions rather than cognitive operations; (2) the intrinsic relation of cognitive function to operation was seen further in the fact that the rise to an operational level resulted in significant achievement in comprehension of these linguistic items.

For the disjunction forms, $A \vee B$ and $A \vee \overline{B}$, transition from constituent-functional to operational cognition (Level 2 to 3) was significant. This distinguishes these forms from the "easier" set of forms, $A \cdot B$, $\overline{A} \cdot \overline{B}$, $\overline{A}_{nw}$, A, and from the more difficult $\overline{A} \vee \overline{B}$. Disjunction was thus more directly related to operational level achievement.

Passage from Level 3 (operational on one task) to Level 4 (operational on two tasks) was also significant for these connectives, suggesting that full operational attainment was necessary to the comprehension of these forms. In fact, every cognitive level advance showed a significant advance in the comprehension of $A \vee B$.

The $A \cdot \overline{B}$ and $\overline{A}_w$ forms behaved differently from the other forms. With regard to cognitive level, $\overline{A}_w$ was achieved more gradually although constituent functions significantly aided the onset of growth. Level 4 was necessary for attaining 50% group success. $A \cdot \overline{B}$, which also showed significant improvement in passage to Level 2, also required full, operational level achivement (Level 4) for increased comprehension.

$\overline{A} \vee B$ was not significantly differentiated by cognitive level in this analysis. This was due to its late onset, which occurred at Level 3. It may be speculated that the concrete operational groupings were necessary to the onset of comprehension of $\overline{A} \vee \overline{B}$, although they were not sufficient for its full achievement.

For $A \vee \overline{B}$, success decreased rather than improved at Level 2. This finding confirms the interpretation that the response considered "correct" for this form was not *necessarily* a logical response. The increase in comprehension of $A \vee \overline{B}$ from Level 2 to 3 was significant ($p < .001$). This significant increase with the onset of operations suggests that this response may *also* be operationally or logically deduced.

Connective Comprehension as a Function of Age

As in our studies of the development of the comprehension and production of the passive (Chapter 3), one may ask whether the child's age or his cognitive level is a better predictor of linguistic achievement.

AGE CORRELATION WITH COGNITIVE LEVEL

The four-step cognitive level scheme does not exactly parallel the age levels (see Table 8-11). The correlation of the four levels with age was $r = .78, p < .01$ ($n = 54$). Approximately 60% of the variance of the cognitive levels is thus accounted for by age.

Because the concept of "age" is psychologically vacuous, however, only specification of the processes of psychological change associated with age can make this concept meaningful. The following analysis supports the conclusion that cognitive structure is the major component of age change that is relevant to linguistic (i.e., connective) comprehension. The fact that change in cognitive structure is partially redundant with age change explains why age appears predictive of change in linguistic performance.

COGNITIVE LEVEL DIFFERENCES WITH AGE

For this analysis, language comprehension data from children of approximately the same age but differentiated by cognitive level were inspected.

Five 4- to 5-year olds, $\overline{X}$ age 58.8 months, who showed cognitive multiplication performance at the figurative level or below (Level 1) were compared with seven 4- to 5-year-olds, $\overline{X}$ age 57.9, who were constituent functional on one or both tasks (Level 2). (The difference between the mean ages was not significant.) Table 8-13 shows success on language connectives by the two groups. Comprehension of $A \cdot B$ in the constituent-function group was significantly advanced $p(< .05)$ over that in the figurative group at this 4–5 age, as was comprehension of $\overline{A} \cdot \overline{B}$ ($p < .01$). These connectives appeared early in development, the age analysis having shown them to appear preoperationally. This cognitive level analysis makes the important point that the onset of constituent functions at 4- to 5-years old accounts for the onset of these connectives. This analysis confirms what the age analysis suggested: constituent functions rather than cognitive operations are required for the development of these early connective forms.

TABLE 8-13

Correct Responses on Linguistic Connectives at Two Cognitive Levels of Logical Multiplication for 4- and 5-Year Olds (in Percentages)

Cognitive level	$A \cdot B$	$A \cdot \overline{B}$	$\overline{A} \cdot \overline{B}$	$A \vee B$	$A \vee \overline{B}$	$\overline{A} \vee \overline{B}$	A	$\overline{A}_w$	$\overline{A}_n$
Figurative or below ($\overline{X}$ age = 58.8) ($Ss = 5$)[a]	40	3	17	20	27	0	40	20	40
Constituent functions[b] ($\overline{X}$ age = 57.9) ($Ss = 7$)[c]	62	10	48	26	12	0	50	25	57
Z test of proportion differences	1.83*	—	2.71**	—	—	—	—	—	—

[a] Total number of items = 30.
[b] Constituent functions on one or both tasks.
[c] Total number of items = 42.
* $p < .05$.
** $p < .01$ by one-tailed test; — = not significant. Only significant Zs are reported.

At the 6–7 age level, two groups of subjects of equivalent age were also classed by cognitive level and tested for differentiation of language comprehension. Seven of these subjects, $\overline{X}$ age 82.3 months, showed constituent-function cognition; eight subjects, $\overline{X}$ age 84.9 months, showed operational cognition. (The difference between the mean ages was not significant.)

Significant increases in comprehension success by the operational children were found for $A \vee B$ ($p < .001$), $A \vee \overline{B}$ ($p < .01$), and A ($p < .05$) [Table 8-14]. As suggested above, the delayed appearance of $A \vee B$ at the 6–7 age level suggested that cognitive operations were necessary to its

TABLE 8-14

Correct Responses on Linguistic Connectives at Two Cognitive Levels of Logical Multiplication for 6- and 7-Year Olds (*in Percentages*)

Cognitive level	$A \cdot B$	$A \cdot \overline{B}$	$\overline{A} \cdot \overline{B}$	$A \vee B$	$A \vee \overline{B}$	$\overline{A} \vee \overline{B}$	A	$\overline{A}_w$	$\overline{A}_{n\&w}$
Constituent functions[a] ($\overline{X}$ age = 82.3) ($n = 7$)[b]	79	45	79	14	36	0	68	43	68
Operational[c] ($\overline{X}$ age = 84.9) ($n = 8$)[d]	83	29	77	75	63	2	88	56	78
Z test of proportion differences	—	—	—	5.76***	2.53**	—	1.84*	—	—

[a] Constituent functions on one or both.
[b] Total number of items for each form = 42.
[c] Operational on one or both.
[d] Total number of items for each form = 48.
* $p < .05$.
** $p < .001$ by one-tailed test; — = not significant. Only significant Zs are reported.

development. The present analysis confirms that view and eliminates the confounding of age from the cognitive effect. $A \vee \overline{B}$ was observed to develop in close synchrony with $A \vee B$, although it has been suggested that this form might be treated inconsistently by subjects. The present analysis suggests that the close developmental synchrony of $A \vee \overline{B}$ with $A \vee B$ was due to their similar relation to cognitive operations at 6- to 7-years old.

These analyses, although limited by small numbers of subjects, confirm the conclusions of the more general, cognitive level analyses that did not partial-out the effects of age; they also confirm that developing cognitive structure rather than age, per se, is the major determinant in the achievement of connective comprehension.

Discussion

The question and issues that were basic to the design of this research may be summarized as follows:

1. Are natural language connectives related to the operations of logic? The theories of Quine and Strawson (see Chapter 6) epitomize the extremes of the controversy that bear upon this issue.

2. Given the assumptions of Piagetian theory, the prior question may be reformulated as: Is the comprehension of natural language connectives related to the processes of cognition? This reformulation is based on the

assumed relation in Piagetian theory between cognition and the operations of logic.

3. Is there autonomy or interdependence of language and cognition with regard to the connectives? If the relation is characterized by dependence what is the direction of the dependence?

4. Assuming a logical basis for linguistic connectives use, are natural language connectives analytic or adjunctive? This problem, old to philosophical inquiry, is reiterated by Reichenbach (1947), cf. Chap. 6.

5. Does linguistic form affect connective comprehension? A subsidiary question, perhaps more basic, concerns the place of the connective in linguistic structure, i.e., language as formally described by a grammar. The deeper the level of the connective in the grammar, the more profound the relation of language to cognition is likely to be, in respect to the connective.

6. Are linguistic connectives progressively achieved in development? Staal (1966) asks this question because of its bearing on epistemological issues.

Developmental data do in fact provide information in respect to these questions.

Language Connectives and Their Relation to Logical (Cognitive) Operations

PARALLEL DEVELOPMENTS

The data of this study show that the full period required for the development of concrete operations (i.e., particularly the class logic that precedes the development of propositional logic in Piagetian theory) is required for the comprehension of the full set of logical connectives ($A \cdot B$, $A \cdot \bar{B}$, $\bar{A} \cdot \bar{B}$, $A \vee B$, $A \vee \bar{B}$, $\bar{A} \vee \bar{B}$). The linguistic comprehension data for children from ages 4–10 (ANOVA I) suggested that connective comprehension improved at least up to the 8- to 10-year-old level, with significant changes in performance at each age level. Only at the end of this period, toward 10 years of age, did the comprehension of the final connective in this set ($\bar{A} \vee \bar{B}$) begin. Most forms reached full understanding at age 10. Moreover, as the cognitive level analysis showed, even forms that were understood by children at primary cognitive levels (e.g., $A \cdot B$) improved significantly as the child made the transition to the final level of concrete operations, the highest operational level assessed. A general correlation between the connective and the properties of logical *class operations* was thus indicated by the data.

CORRELATED DEVELOPMENT

The correlation between the development of concrete operations and the development of language connective comprehension was further supported by the fact that the last stage in the development of concrete operations at 8- to 10-years old correlated with structural changes in connective comprehension at that time. Not only was (1) the most difficult connective $\bar{A} \vee \bar{B}$ first understood at that age, but (2) there was a shift in the structure of interrelations among connectives that until that age level had remained relatively constant. This was shown both by the hierarchy concordance analyses and by ANOVA I. In the latter analysis a qualitative shift was found in the *Connective* × *Negation* interaction at 8- to 10-years old, which was due mainly to the equalization in comprehension difficulty between conjunction and disjunction for the *no* negation ($A \cdot B$–$A \vee B$) and *single* negation ($A \cdot \bar{B}$–$A \vee \bar{B}$) forms. Moreover, (3) linguistic form had an effect on connective comprehension at 8- to 10-years old, but not prior to that.

CONSISTENCY IN HIERARCHICAL STRUCTURE

The relative consistency in the hierarchical structure of connective comprehension across age groups (until the 8- to 10-year-old shift noted above) shows that the connectives have an ordered relation to each other and implies the existence of an inherent structure among connective forms. The structure is probably best described in logical terms. The basis of connective comprehension may thus be structured by the logical system.

MAPPING OF LANGUAGE CONNECTIVES AND LOGICAL SET OPERATIONS

The canonical correlation provides further support for the theoretical issues addressed here. The fact that the cognitive and linguistic domains were found to be highly and significantly related by this statistic validates the general thesis that cognitive groupings, the psychological structures underlying cognitive performance, map onto the basic linguistic connectives. This finding supports the contention that the propositional language connectives are at least in some respect "logical connectives."

The structures of this mapping is equally important. Structural coefficients showed that the interrelation between the linguistic and cognitive domains was not bivariate. That is, it did not consist of independent correlations between the theoretical counterparts of conjunction-intersection and disjunction-union. Instead, it showed a multiplex relation with the major cognitive influence by logical intersection (multiplication) and the major linguistic influence by disjunction ($A \vee B$). Negated conjunction ($A \cdot \bar{B}$, $\bar{A} \cdot \bar{B}$) also contributed to the relation between the domains.

The absence of independent zero-order correlations between intersection-conjunction and union-disjunction suggests the psychological reality of a *single operatory kernel* in cognition, which consists of the basic group of set or class operations (intersection, union, complementation). Logical multiplication, however, is a grouping "more general than the others in the sense that it contains them or that they derive from it by successive specifications [Inhelder & Piaget, 1958, p. 389]." This grouping provides the cognitive logical base for the double-entry table that represents the logical associations between two dimensions based on the systematic organization of truth and falsehood: $A \cdot B$, $A \cdot \overline{B}$, $\overline{A} \cdot B$, $\overline{A} \cdot \overline{B}$. The set of elementary associations, ordered in truth-table form, provides a formal logical structure by which connectives are described and defined as logical forms. In general, the truth-table structure determines a logical form's "analytic" status (Staal, 1966). The higher correlation of connectives with this cognitive structure, intersection, ($r = .93$ in the interdomain structure) confirms a relation of truth-functional logic to connective comprehension.

Linguistic disjunction ($A \vee B$) may be considered an "analytic" connective (cf. B. Russell, 1940) in that there are no empirical facts to which its meaning can be directly related. Its meaning is structural, and the truth table serves as its structural definition. The heavy involvement of $A \vee B$ in the canonical correlation ($r = .87$) suggests that the analytic or structural property provides a principal component of the relation between linguistic connectives and cognitive (logical) operations. The fact that negated conjunction forms also participate in the language–logic correlation confirms our original speculation that negation taps the logical power of the conjunction *and*. The integration of conjunction with negation is a further and necessary component of the truth-table structure.

The low correlation of the cognitive factor with $A \cdot B$ confirmed the semilogical quality of the association in certain referential and linguistic contexts. Similarly, the low correlation with $A \vee \overline{B}$ confirmed the judgment that this linguistic disjunction could be solved by means of semilogical processes. The low factor weighting for $\overline{A} \vee \overline{B}$ suggests that the concrete operations were not related most specifically to its achievement, particularly as there was little comprehension of this connective until the end of the age-range studied (onset of formal logical operations)—all of the other connectives had been achieved by the end of the concrete operational period. This would suggest that propositional logic (formal thought) rather than class logic may be more specifically related to this connective.

In contrast to logical multiplication, ($r = .93$) classification had the lowest correlation with the canonical factor ($r = .40$). This may follow from the fact that classification does not measure a particular logical operation such as logical multiplication but the behavioral integration of addition, complementation, and multiplication. It may be a general activity that is less closely related to discrete cognitive operations.

Notably, low redundancy measures between the connective and logical sets suggest that both linguistic and cognitive systems are characterized by a certain degree of autonomy, specifically a linguistic connective truth-functional logic relation may be most highly reflected in an analytic, connective-logical multiplication relation. It should be kept in mind that the canonical correlation was based on data that ranged over a considerable developmental period and, in addition, assumed an underlying additivity and continuity in the data. The underlying relations may, in fact, be non-additive and discontinuous as is assumed in a number of stage theories [see Beilin (1971a) for a discussion of this issue].

Several other analyses confirmed the major findings of the canonical correlation analysis.

1. Product-moment correlations confirmed (a) the high correlation between connective comprehension and logical multiplication (particularly the abstract matrix task), and (b) suggested that concrete operations (intersection, union, and complementation) were not significantly differentiated in their relations with the connectives *and*, *or* and *not* respectively.

2. The developmental patterns of connective comprehension generally paralleled those of cognitive comprehension over the age range tested.

MAPPING OF SPECIFIC CONNECTIVES AND LOGICAL SET OPERATIONS

Children 4- to 5-years old in large measure comprehended the conjunction $A \cdot B$ when the statements represented a juxtaposition of propositions (proposition = class) and the classes were disjoint (i.e., no intersection response was requested of the subject). It was at this age also that comprehension of A (assertion), and primitive (narrow) comprehension of $\overline{A}$ (negation) were attained. The fact that both assertion (A) and negation ($\overline{A}_{nw}$) forms developed concurrently with the first connective ($A \cdot B$) indicates the basic "logical" (albeit semilogical) quality (i.e., concerning truth-value relations) of this first association ($A \cdot B$).[1]

Characterization of the essentially logical nature of the linguistic connectives at this age level was also supported by the fact that the distributive logical connective ($\overline{A \vee B}$) and its logical counterpart $\overline{A} \cdot \overline{B}$ were also comprehended by 4- to 5-year olds, alhough less than the $A \cdot B$ A, $\overline{A}_{nw}$ forms. The $\overline{A} \cdot \overline{B}$ form, which is the reciprocal of the $A \cdot B$ form, also required a two-class composition performed on the universe set. Given $ABCD$, the subject had to compose CD. These two classes were complementary, however, and not primary classes as in the case of $A \cdot B$. The fact that the 4- to 5-year old began to comprehend $\overline{A} \cdot \overline{B}$ soon after he comprehended $A \cdot B$ suggested that the young child can integrate negation with the juxtaposition relation of $A \cdot B$. Moreover, the 4- to 5-year-olds' comprehension of the logically equivalent $\overline{A \vee B}$ form suggests that negation also distributed over the connective as a whole for them, e.g., not (*boys* or *girls*).

For $\overline{A} \cdot \overline{B}$, however, negation appeared as juxtaposed denials. The child did not treat each negation conjunct as a separate complement set (e.g., $\overline{A} = B \cdot C \cdot D$) but as juxtaposed classes as in ($A \cdot B$). Again, although essentially logical processes seemed to characterize the connectives that were comprehended at 4- to 5-years old, this logicality was limited.

---

[1] Quine (1966) and other logicians suggest that affirmation (A), conjunction ($\cdot$) and negation ($-$) comprise a set of basic operators, upon which all other logical connective relations are based.

Connectivity is perhaps best characterized as juxtapositional at this age level.

Only subsequently, toward 6- to 7-years old, were connectives understood that were not interpretable as juxtapositional one-way mappings from proposition to reference. The more advanced connective included (1) negation $(\overline{A}_w)$, in which a wide universe response was comprehended; (2) disjunction *or* $(A \vee B)$; (3) disjunction and negation $(A \vee \overline{B})$; (4) $A \cdot \overline{B}$, negated conjunction; and (5) $\overline{A} \vee \overline{B}$, in which disjunction operates on negative disjuncts. In general, the more complex connectives included negation, disjunction, and conjunction with single conjunct negation. Negation and disjunction are both more "analytic" in that their meaning is not described by empirical reference. Disjunction (in the exclusive disjunction reading) implies a subject's simultaneous (abstract) consideration of two disjuncts as the possible behavioral reference and the choice of one of the disjuncts as response.[2] Mapping from class to connective response is thus not direct. Negation also implies reference to a complement set that has no single defining property (see "Cognitive Priorities in the Development of Negation," p. 318). It would thus be theoretically justified for the comprehension of these forms to be attained only after the full set of truth-functional associations, accomplished through logical multiplication, had been attained psychologically. This, in fact, is what the data suggest.

By the nature of its integration with negation, the $A \cdot \overline{B}$ connective could not be interpreted as a direct mapping of class to proposition. It follows that the $(\cdot)$ connective has a logical power in this form that it does not necessarily have in the simple $A \cdot B$ form. To comprehend $A \cdot \overline{B}$ it is necessary to comprehend $\overline{B}$ as an independent proposition that refers to a complement set (A, C, D) that includes conjunct A but does not totally reduce to it. The connective $(\cdot)$ must connect the conjunct A to this $\overline{B}$ conjunct, that is, it achieves the intersection of class A with the set A, C, D. Younger subjects (younger than 7-years old) mainly tried to reduce the second $(\overline{B})$ proposition to the first, holding that $A = \overline{B}$ and giving A as sufficient to both conjuncts, i.e., $A = A \cdot \overline{B}$. The connective in this pre-7-year-old solution again reflected a kind of juxtaposition whereby the conjuncts were conflated or one was reduced to the other. Conjuncts were not treated as independent propositions and connectivity was not articulate. One implication that follows from this is that although the simple conjunction of classes $(A \cdot B)$ is achieved early (towards 4- to 5-years old as already discussed) it appears that only at later ages may the connective *and* enter into more complex logical relations, such as the conjunction of a positive with a negative conjunct in which the two conjuncts are intersecting sets, e.g., $A \cdot \overline{B}$.

The connective $\overline{A} \vee \overline{B}$, which was the most difficult connective in the 4- to 10-year-old range, calls for yet more abstract connective activity. Disjunction $(\vee)$, per se, requires holding two disjuncts as reference and

---

[2] Reference is considered *abstract* because the subject does not actually construct the two classes but considers them as *possible*.

choosing only one. In the $\overline{A} \vee \overline{B}$ disjunction, however, neither disjunct is affirmative and there is no direct reference to a concrete class, as each disjunct refers to a complement set $(\overline{A} = B, C, D; \overline{B} = A, C, D)$. Moreover, the two disjuncts are partially contradictory, i.e., the assertion of one implies the denial of another, $\overline{A} = B$ and $\overline{B} = A$. An exclusive disjunction response implies that choice of one disjunct is the partial denial of the other. Comprehension of $\overline{A} \vee \overline{B}$, in fact, appears to require vicariance of the universe set; each disjunct implying an alternative classification. Only the 8- to 10-year-old group was able to show any success with this connective. Notably, this is the age at which closure of the concrete operational structure is achieved just prior to the development of formal truth-functional or propositional logic in the Piagetian system. The vicariance operation is a characteristic property of this operational transition, as the data above suggest.

DEVELOPMENTAL PRIORITY OF COGNITIVE PROCESSES

The contingency and cognitive level analyses confirmed an intricate set of interrelations between the developing language and developing cognitive systems. Discrete cognitive functions (dichotomy and adjunction of identical elements) and the constituent-functions of intersection, union, and complementation developmentally preceded or coincided with comprehension of the earliest connectives forms $(A, \overline{A}_{nw}, A \cdot B, \overline{A} \cdot \overline{B})$. As indicated, these linguistic forms could be comprehended by simple juxtapositional processes.

The attainment of (concrete) operational logic, which suggests the capacity for the earliest logical deduction, appears necessary for the comprehension of more complex connectives, as these connectives are not interpreted by juxtapositional processes alone. Achievement of concrete logical operations is thus necessary for disjunction comprehension $(A \vee B, A \vee \overline{B})$. In addition, the attainment of operational logical capacity was necessary for the comprehension of $A \cdot \overline{B}$ and $\overline{A} \vee \overline{B}$, which, as indicated, were understood only with full attainment of concrete operations.

COGNITIVE PRIORITIES IN THE DEVELOPMENT OF NEGATION

Moreover, the comprehension of single attribute negation (in which the subject was required to operate on a four-class universe, $U - A = \overline{A}$, and a wide or total-complement set response was considered correct) developed as a clearly postoperational pheomenon. First success on this form occurred at age 6 (34.4%), and a sharp increase in the percentage of correct response occurred at 7-years old (59.4%). Near-perfect success (90%) came only at 10 years of age. The growth pattern for negation approximated a step-like curve with success awaiting the attainment of concrete logical operations at 6- to 7-years old and attaining ceiling at age 10.

Cognitive precedence data, relative to $\overline{A}_w$, suggested that development of the basic cognitive operations either had to precede or accompany the comprehension of the language connective $\overline{A}_w$. The clear dependence of the comprehension of negation on the child's cognitive operations is particularly significant because negation was found to be an important factor in connective difficulty (ANOVA I; Suppes & Feldman, 1971).[3] These results are in general accord with the findings of Feldman (1968) that negation was difficult for children in the 4- to 6-year-old range. However, as Table 8-15 shows, Feldman found a more gradual age development with 6- and 7-year olds performing about equally to 5-year olds. The results of the present study, as well as those of Feldman, however, are not in accord with Inhelder and Piaget's (1964) data, although a similar sorting task was used, nor with the data of Nitta and Nagano (1966), or of Neimark and Slotnick (1970) [see Table 8-15]. The latter used a different type of task (paper and pencil) as well as a smaller reference set (8 items, compared with 12 or 18 items in Feldman, 18 items in Piaget and Inhelder, and 24 items in the present study). The Nitta, Neimark, and Piaget studies found high percentages of comprehension of single attribute negation by 4- to 5-year olds. The success of the Nitta and Nagano and Neimark and Slotnick subjects may be explained by the difference in tasks and the small reference sets; the success of Piaget's subjects is more difficult to explain, and may be due to the testing methods used in Geneva.

In the present study, the most frequent error to $\overline{A}$ was selecting a single class from the complement set in which the class was homogeneous with the negated class (called "narrow negation"). For example, when asked, "*Not girls*," subjects gave *boys* rather than *monkeys* or *bears*. This was also found by Feldman (1972). The most common error she observed, a "perserverative response," was one in which subjects gave "one of the disjoint subsets of the requested complementary set, which has one of the attributes in the same dimension as the requested set [p. 10]." The subjects appeared not to complete the transformation $\overline{A} = U - A$, but to effect this transformation only to the extent that the complement class bore some similarity to the negated class. As Feldman also holds, this amounted to a failure to realize that a complement set was not necessarily characterized by any particular affirmative property common to the whole set.

The reason the current study showed even more of this error, and why developmental curves mapped more clearly onto concrete operational development is probably related to the nature of the universe set. The universe set here consisted of two perceptually (and conceptually) distinct subsets of a genus specification: *people* (*boys*, *girls*) × *animals* (*bears*, *monkeys*). If one of the factors in negation difficulty was the composition of the complement set by union of its subsets, then it would

---

[3] Also, the recent study by Bourne and O'Banion (1971) found the conditional to be more difficult than conjunction or disjunction, although Neisser and Weene had found all three of these concepts to be equivalent. Bourne and O'Bannion (1971, p. 532) consider the conditional $x \rightarrow y$ to be equivalent to the disjunction and negation form $\overline{x} \vee y$, and suggest that negation may be involved as a factor in connective difficulty.

TABLE 8-15

Comprehension of Single Attribute Negation in Several Developmental Studies[a,b]

Source:	Nitta and Nagano[c]		Hatano[d]		Neimark and Slotnick[e]		Feldman[f]	Piaget and Inhelder[g]		Beilin and Lust[h]
Language:	Japanese		Japanese		American English		American English	Swiss French		American English
	A	B	A	B	A	B		A	B	
Age (grade)										
4–5 (kindergarten)	64	58					(3-years old) 21	80	100	17
	(86)	(76)					(4-years old) 44			
6–7 (second-grade)	66	64			(58)	(85)	(5-years old) 51	64	70	47
(third-grade)	(66)	(57)					(6-years old) 57	95	100	
8–10 (fourth-grade)	90	92	96	96			(7-years old) 60	100	100	66
	(92)	(86)	(92)	(94)						
Adult					(79)	(100)				87
					(100)	(100)				

[a] Nitta and Nagano (1966), Hatano (1973), Neimark and Slotnick (1970), Feldman (1968), Piaget and Inhelder (1967), Beilin and Lust.

[b] Percentages of correct responses except for Piaget and Inhelder which is percent of subjects. (Negation refers to disjoint classes except when percentages are in parentheses, referring to intersecting classes.)

[c] Data extracted from the Japanese report of this study with the aid of Tasuko Kaneda. Set (pictorial) : (birds, flowers) × (black, white) × (big, little) = eight elements, one element per condition. $\bar{A}$ = not birds; $\bar{B}$ = not flowers (disjoint) = not black (intersecting).

[d] Data kindly conveyed by Hatano (personal communication, 1973). Set = same as Nitta and Nagano (Footnote c above) for intersecting classes. For disjoint classes set = mutually exclusive classes : (tulips, dandelions, birds) × (black, white) = eight elements, one per condition. (One black tulip and one white dandelion appear again in little size.) $\bar{A}$ and $\bar{B}$ = same as Nitta and Nagano for intersecting classes. $\bar{A}$ = tulip; $\bar{B}$ = dandelion for disjoint classes.

[e] Duplication of Nitta and Nagano for intersecting classes.

[f] Set (blocks) = (green, black, red) × (circle, star, square) × 2 elements each = 18 elements.

[g] Set (blocks) = (square, triangle, circle) × (big, small) × (red, white, blue) = 18 elements with one exemplar per condition.

[h] Present study. See text.

follow that complementation difficulty would be increased in cases in which there was greater perceptual and/or conceptual disparity among the subsets of the complement, making their union more difficult. The subjects in the present experiment when asked, "Not girls" had to operate on the universe set $(U - A = \overline{A})$ to give the total complement of [(boys) and (bears and monkeys)]. Many young subjects were capable of giving one class from this complement, i.e., B (boys), when B was the homogeneous class relative to A; but did not give C and D also.

It appears, then, that cognitive operations were necessary to the comprehension of negation when comprehension included overcoming the perceptual factors associated with the constituents of the complement set. Feldman did experimentally vary heterogeneity of complement set and found no differences in performance. Her heterogeneous complement set, however, consisted of single blocks in each of 12 different specifications of shape × color, and thus did not have the perceptual unity of subsets which this study did.

Other evidence of the effect of perceptual factors in negation comes from the finding that the nature of the negated set (*people* or *animals*) influenced correct negation-responding in this study. Subjects from 4- to 10-years old were more likely to give a wide-type negation response to a negation from the *animal* set than from the *people* set. The fact that this effect was still significant for 8- to 10-year olds suggests that this factor was still viable after concrete operational thought was fully attained.

The data of this study are consistent with Piagetian claims that the nature of negation comprehension changes with the development of a cognitive lattice structure. The secondary class or nearest neighbor of a negated class (narrow response) may result from an incomplete lattice structure; the wide negation response would require a more developed lattice structure.

INCLUSIVE-BOTH RESPONSE TO DISJUNCTION

The early development of the inclusive-both response to disjunction *or*, and the concordance of the development of an exclusive *or* interpretation in concordance with the development of concrete operations, both confirm the relation of logical thought to the comprehension of linguistic disjunction. This relation is further confirmed by the fact that conjunction and disjunction connectives $(A \cdot B, A \vee B; A \cdot \overline{B}, A \vee \overline{B})$ were equal in difficulty at the 8- to 10-year-old level when the logical system (truth-functional logic) was basically attained. On logical grounds alone there should be no difference between conjunction and disjunction comprehension.

DISTRIBUTIVE CONNECTIVE $(\overline{A \vee B})$ AND $\overline{A} \cdot \overline{B}$

The near-perfect developmental correlation between the distributive connective $\overline{A \vee B}$ and its logical equivalent $\overline{A} \cdot \overline{B}$ offers seemingly clear confirmation that the interrelations among connectives are determined by their logical equivalence rather than by their linguistic form. In sum, various aspects of developmental evidence from this study firmly support the view that the development of logical thought has a direct and supporting relation to the development of linguistic connective comprehension.

Autonomy or Dependency between Linguistic and Logical Systems

A

The cognitive and linguistic tasks requested theoretically related set operations on the same universe. In the cognitive tasks, the operations consisted of classification activities that required minimal verbal involvement. In the linguistic tasks, the operations were linguistically defined and responses represented comprehension of linguistic expressions of these logical operations. The design of the study, using as it did these two correlated sets of tasks, could very reasonably have induced order effects as, in fact did the second passive study reported in Chapter 3. Children performing on the cognitive tasks after having been exposed to 48 linguistic items had considerable experience with the relevant sets and the connectives between them. Similarly, performance on the linguistic task could be expected to have been affected by prior exposure to the "cognitive" manipulations. The lack of an order effect on the basic, concrete cognitive operations suggests independence between the linguistic and cognitive systems at this level.

The lack of significant order effect on the dichotomy operation, combined with a significant effect on the vicariance operation, which consisted of a mobile "shifting" from one dichotomy to another, is intriguing in light of the Piagetian position that propositional relations "become closely interconnected to speech" in a way not available to concrete operations. Vicariance reflects closure of a system of concrete operations and the onset of formal or propositional operations. In this study, at age 9, vicariance showed 66.7% success; at age 10, it showed 100% success. (This is the age of onset of formal thought.) This finding also supports Piaget's notion that language is an instrument of cognitive "mobility", rather than an instrument of actual cognitive operations.

The effect of testing order on cognitive *functions* (adjunction of foreign and identical elements) is more difficult to interpret. These one-way, non-reversible or nonoperational cognitive activities consist of single element predication and the ability to unite these predications with elements of identical predications. The cognitive ability tested is a simple one-way addition. It may be that the 48-item linguistic experience facilitates predication by providing verbal labels or some form of algorithm for the processing of single elements. The fact that the order effect occurred on both identical and "foreign" elements suggests that algorithms may generalize across slight physical differences (e.g., *big boy* versus *little boy*). On the other hand, the fact that language experience has no effect on classification performance indicates the Piagetian proposal that classification is not based on identity or other element adjunction functions but implies cognitive structure.

The additional fact that, for adjunction of identical elements, the effect of order was not significant at the 4- to 5-year-old levels or 2- to 3-year-old levels, while it was effective for older groups, suggests that operational classification had to have been achieved before language could affect cognitive subprocesses or functions. The significant order effect for adjunction of foreign elements only at the 8- to 10-year-old level indicates that this might be an even higher-order function requiring further construction of operative classification structures before language can have a significant effect on subprocesses. This finding of partial system autonomy confirmed the finding of low redundancy by canonical correlation, reported above.

B

In general, item order did not significantly affect connective comprehension. This finding also confirms the consistency of connective comprehension, and contradicts what has come to be called the "familiarity hypothesis of rule differences." Bourne (1972, with Taplin) suggests that to support this hypothesis one must find that "through a program of extensive practice at identifying the different concept types, differences in difficulty between concepts disappear [p. 3]." The familiarity hypothesis implies that linguistic practice should affect the comprehension of connectives. The lack of such an effect supports autonomy between the linguistic and cognitive systems. The limited effects of item order that were found qualify this generalization. Specific item-order effects were found for two forms: (1) the most difficult disjunction form, $\bar{A} \vee \bar{B}$, and (2) negation, $\bar{A}_w$. Both effects were significant only for the 8- to 10-year-old group. The $\bar{A} \vee \bar{B}$ effect (from first to second item) was also significant in adult testing. This may be explained by the fact that both disjunction and negation forms are logically ambiguous. For disjunction, either an inclusive reading or an exclusive reading was possible, and for negation, either a wide or a narrow negation response was possible. Developmental cognitive theory would predict that only at the 8- to 10-year-old level and in adulthood were cognitive structures sufficiently developed so that two logical readings could in fact be made. The data indicate that only at these older ages did order effects occur. It would appear, then, that such "experimental" order effects interact particularly with logically ambiguous forms. In conclusion, although the data suggest an integration between the linguistic and cognitive systems on psychological as well as formal grounds, a certain degree of autonomy between these systems nevertheless exists.

Linguistic Connectives as Analytic or Adjunctive

As suggested in Chapter 6, analytic or formal connective meaning depends on reference to the full truth-tabular set of associations (*TT, TF, FT, FF*). A pattern of truth and falsity of these associations defines the formal meaning of each connective. As stated in Chapter 6, Reichenbach

(1947) notes, however, that adjunctive readings of the truth tables are also possible. In this sense, the truth of one of the associations, (e.g., $TT = T$) may imply the truth of the connective (e.g., $A \cdot B$).

Reichenbach raised the question as to which interpretation should be favored on logical as well as psychological grounds. We too question which is favored psychologically and whether developmental evidence favors adjunctive readings over connective readings or the reverse. According to the Piagetian view the ability to utilize the full set of truth-table associations is achieved only with the development of concrete operations and logical multiplication, at approximately 7 years of age. Logical multiplication permits the generation of $2^2 = 4$ possible intersections of a set of two bivalent factors, whether the factors are events, properties, or propositions, and yields the multiplicative associations of these factors: $x \cdot y$, $x \cdot \bar{y}$, $\bar{x} \cdot y$, $\bar{x} \cdot \bar{y}$. Even at 7-years old, when the full set of combinations becomes available, they are still partially synthetic according to Piagetian theory. That is, they are constructions of reality and do not function as abstract units related to one another on the basis of their truth value. The latter system of relations, which is basic to truth-functional logic, is only attained psychologically toward 11+ years old with the construction of "formal operational logic."

The cognitive theory predicts, then, that truth-tabular logic is first available to children at the first operational level, toward age 7, but, even then, truth-functional relations must apply directly to "concrete" reality. Truth-tabular logic is thus achieved in progressive fashion over the age span from childhood to adolescence. Only at the "formal" operational level would a "connective" reading of truth tables be therefore possible.

A

It is significant that the first two connectives to appear, $A \cdot B$ and $\bar{A} \cdot \bar{B}$, can be described as either analytic or adjunctive (in Reichenbach's sense). In other words, they can be characterized as connectives in a formal sense or as mere associations. $A \cdot B$, for example, can be identified by its truth-tabular pattern or by one particular adjunction of that truth table (noted by the arrow below):

		$A \cdot B$
→	*TT*	*T*
	TF	*F*
	FT	*F*
	FF	*F*

Similarly, $\bar{A} \cdot \bar{B}$ can be described by its tabular pattern or by one particular adjunctive association.

		$\bar{A} \cdot \bar{B}$
	TT	*F*
	TF	*F*
	FT	*F*
→	*FF*	*T*

The truth-tabular patterns of these two connectives are symmetrical. Each is a "simple form" in that it calls for a single truth judgment; all other associations of the table are treated as false. The two connectives are differentiated only by a reversal of the T or F value of the two homogeneous adjunctions (TT and FF). Each connective asserts the truth of the adjunctive association to which it corresponds, e.g., $A \cdot B \equiv TT$, $\overline{A} \cdot \overline{B} \equiv FF$.

In structure, $A \cdot B$ and $\overline{A} \cdot \overline{B}$ are related by their symmetry. In function, they are simple, that is they assert only one truth statement, to the one adjunction to which they are identical in form. In principal, they confound adjunction of conjuncts (e.g., TT) with the truth-tabular pattern which gives them formal connective status.

Both forms were comprehended by about 50% of the subjects at the 4- to 5-year-old level. They thus anticipate operational achievement of logical structures, according to Piagetian norms, at the same time that they synchronize in achievement with (cognitive) constituent functions. Form $\overline{A} \cdot \overline{B}$ was slightly delayed in relation to $A \cdot B$. This may have been due to the effect of the negative value of the conjuncts.

The next two connectives ($A \vee B$ and $A \vee \overline{B}$) were also achieved almost concurrently. Again, $A \vee \overline{B}$ was slightly delayed. These might be considered specifically "analytic" connectives in that they are not equivalent to any one of the four adjunctions which compose a truth table but require a statement of interrelations among adjunctions (i.e., the truth table itself) for their description. Each includes two truth statements and the connective is described by the relation of the two. No one adjunction is sufficient to define the connective. These two connectives are also symmetrical:

	$A \vee B$	$A \vee \overline{B}$
TT	F	T
TF	T	F
FT	T	F
FF	F	T

The nature of the symmetry between these two forms differs, however, Symmetry consists not in a reversal of positions of truth judgment, as in the $A \cdot B - \overline{A} \cdot \overline{B}$ comparison, but in a precise reversal of each and every truth judgment (to the four associations). What is true becomes false, what is false becomes true; the pattern otherwise remains the same.

An additional source of complexity in these forms involves the nature of the truth judgments required by the disjunction $A \vee B$. These judgments are no longer made to homogeneous adjunction (TT or FF) but must be made to heterogeneous adjunctions (TF and FT) and only to these. (In the case of exclusive disjunction, TT and FF are both judged false by the table.) For $A \vee \overline{B}$, all individual truth judgments are inherent in the structure of the first two connectives ($A \cdot B$ and $\overline{A} \cdot \overline{B}$), so that only the pattern is new. As this form appears in development only slightly after disjunction ($A \vee B$), it is possible that, psychologically, making truth-judgments to both TT and FF, as this form demands, requires the prior ability to make truth judgments of the heterogeneous adjunctions, as the disjunction form ($A \vee B$)

demands. $A \vee B$ and $A \vee \overline{B}$ forms were comprehended at the 50% level at ages 6–7, although consistent success followed later. Comprehension of these connectives coincided with the attainment of concrete operations.

The next form that appeared, $A \cdot \overline{B}$, called for a truth judgment of only one of the heterogeneous adjunctions and a concurrent false judgment of the other. As with the disjunction ($A \vee B$), it called for concurrent false judgments of each of the other (homogeneous) adjunctions. The $A \cdot \overline{B}$ form reached 50% correct performance at the 8- to 10-year-old level. It thus awaited full achievement of concrete operations and onset of formal operations.

This form, again, called for only one truth judgment in its truth-table pattern. If all adjunctions were in fact cognitively equivalent, then the truth-value judgment in this case should have been equivalent to that of $A \cdot B$ and $\overline{A} \cdot \overline{B}$, as these too required only one truth judgment. The developmental delay of $A \cdot \overline{B}$ suggests that the truth judgments inherent in its structure are not equivalent, and that the nature of the adjunction on the basis of which a "true" judgment is made, as well as the truth-table pattern itself, are factors in connective difficulty. Moreover, the number of "true" judgments within the table did not seem to be the sole factor in connective difficulty nor did the mere equivalence of connective to adjunction, as $A \cdot \overline{B}$ is equivalent to the adjunction TF for which its truth table gives a "true" judgment.

The connective $\overline{A} \vee \overline{B}$ in turn is marked by "true" judgments to each of the complex adjunctions (TF, FT) and by "false" judgments to both TT and FF. The truth table is then identical in structure to $A \vee B$, simple exclusive disjunction. For $\overline{A} \vee \overline{B}$, however, the truth-table structure must operate on negative disjuncts rather than on affirmative disjuncts. The late development of the $\overline{A} \vee \overline{B}$ form suggests that the truth value of the connective disjuncts did interact with truth-tabular structure in creating both cognitive complexity and psychological difficulty.

In summary, then, the analysis of the truth-tabular structure of connectives suggests this structure to be relevant to connective comprehension. Structural complexity also appears to affect the chronology of developmental achievement; several features of the data support this conclusion:

1. Forms which were achieved concurrently tended to be alike in truth-tabular form, i.e., symmetrical, ($A \cdot B - \overline{A} \cdot \overline{B}$; $A \vee B - A \vee \overline{B}$).
2. The equivalence of the connective to the adjunction on which the truth table makes a "true" judgment appears to give developmental priority to the connective when the *adjunction* $= TT$ ($A \cdot B$) or *FF* ($\overline{A} \cdot \overline{B}$), but not when the adjunction is *complex* $= TF$ ($A \cdot \overline{B}$).
3. The form of the truth table interacted with the affirmative or negative value of the connective's conjuncts. Negative value was associated with developmental delay in comprehension of a form. This was dramatically shown in the case when the truth-tabular structure was complex ($\overline{A} \vee \overline{B}$), and less so when the structure was simple ($\overline{A} \cdot \overline{B}$).

B

Bourne (e.g., 1972) proposes that truth tables function algorithmically in rule-learning tasks in which primary bidimensional rules are involved, e.g., conjunction, disjunction. Rule learning tasks, he claims, "are directly soluble by coding the stimulus patterns into xy (or TT), x$\bar{y}$ (or TF), $\bar{x}$y (FT) and $\bar{x}\bar{y}$ (or FF) classes using the given attributes x and y, and then applying the truth-table principle." Subjects appear to accomplish this coding by acquiring "an intuitive strategy having all the features of the truth-table [Bourne, 1972, p. 2]."

Whether or not the truth-table functions algorithmically in some or all concept acquisition and/or language connective comprehension tasks, as Bourne claims, is an issue not identical to the thesis of this study. Rather, the data of this study support a more general relation between truth-functional logic and language connectives. Developmental analyses suggest that truth-functional logic must be attained by the child at least in concrete operational form before certain connectives are comprehended ($A \vee B$, $A \cdot \bar{B}, \bar{A} \vee \bar{B}, \bar{A}_w$). This suggests that the cognitive structure or *groupement*, which provides for logical multiplication and allows the achievement of the truth-table set of associations, is necessary to the comprehension of interpropositional relations. Cognitive structure is not identical to truth-table structure, however. Rather, the truth table is perhaps best defined in relation to the distinction between competence and performance. The data of this study support the thesis that the cognitive capacities basic to truth-functional logic define at least part of the competence of the child who comprehends natural language connectives. How this competence is invoked in an experimental or natural situation is a performance problem. It is possible, for example, that, in some abstract situations, a truth-table algorithm may be necessary, when in more concrete situations, it may not be. The thesis of this study and the Bourne thesis are interrelated, however, in that prior to the attainment of concrete operations, a truth-tabular algorithm would not be available to the child to aid him in performance.

C

In general, if linguistic connectives map onto cognitive operations in the way proposed in this study, then gradually evolving analyticity of the cognitive system (Apostel *et al.*, 1957) would be paralleled by gradual development of analyticity in linguistic connectivity; the data suggest this may be so.

D

The evidence that correct intension and extension in connective comprehension develop in close rapport provides further evidence that the development of linguistic connectives is rooted in the synthetic, constructive processes of developing cognition rather than in the intensional processes of language. The fact that the intension–extension difference in connective comprehension decreases to near zero, precisely at the point of full achievement of concrete operations (i.e., at the 8- to 10-year-old level), further confirms this proposal.

Linguistic Form and Comprehension of Logical Connectives

The effect of linguistic form on connective comprehension was evaluated, varying linguistic form through conjunction reduction and through quantification of the reduction by *both* or *either*. Assuming that transformations do not change meaning, it would thus be possible to manipulate conjunction form without changing its logical meaning. Such formal manipulation proved particularly difficult and the requirement to maintain meaning constant allowed only limited scope to the conjunction deletion processes. The data showed that this controlled conjunction reduction did not have a consistently significant effect across connectives, negation forms, and ages.

The nonsignificant effect of linguistic form (in ANOVA I) for 4- to 10-year olds indicated that the comprehension of logical form was not affected by linguistic transformation. This finding could be interpreted as confirming that a certain amount of autonomy exists between the linguistic and logical systems. It also implies that the comprehension of linguistic form of connectives is closely bound to comprehension of the logical form itself. The 2- to 3-year-old imitation data that indicated early ability to derive conjunction forms by reduction or deletion from the time the general "sense" of binary conjunct associativity was comprehended, further supports this speculation.

There was, however, some evidence of the effect of linguistic form on connective comprehension. The major effects were the following:

1. The linguistic quantification of reduced conjunction was difficult for children prior to the development of full comprehension of the logical connective form. Quantification of *and* ($A \cdot B$) by *both* was significantly more difficult for 2- to 3-year olds than other linguistic forms, but not for 4- to 5-year olds. A 50% level of success with *and* ($A \cdot B$) was only attained at the 4- to 5-year-old level. Quantification of *or* ($A \vee B$) by *either* was significantly more difficult than nonquantified forms for 4- to 5-year olds, but not for 6- to 7-year olds. A 50% success level for *or* ($A \vee B$) was only achieved by the 6- to 7-year olds. It would appear that quantification required an understanding of the logical aspects of connective usage, and the concurrent development of concrete operational thought in the case of disjunction, and constituent-function cognition in case of conjunction. With conjunction, quantification by *both* may have served to emphasize the binary or double conjunct nature of the form rather than the primitive syncretic or undifferentiated unity of the form. With *or*, quantification by *either* may have served to emphasize not its binary nature, but the exclusivity of disjunction (see below).

2. There appeared to be a qualitative change in the relation of linguistic form to the comprehension of logical connectives at the 8- to 10-year-old level (*cf.* significant Connective × Negation × Linguistic form and Age × Connective × Linguistic form interactions of ANOVA I). The qualitative change was evident in the significant effect of quantification on comprehension of the connective *or* at the 8- to 10-year-old level.[4] Transformation by quantification plus deletion increased comprehension of the connective *or* at this age. Consistent with the design of this study, this signified that quantification by *either* increased an exclusive reading for the *or* connective. (Paris [1973] found a similar effect for *either*.)

That this effect occurred only at the 8- to 10-year-old level is significant. The 8- to 10-year-old level, as discussed above, represents the full achievement of concrete operations and the onset of (formal) propositional thought. From a cognitive viewpoint, it appears that only at ages 8–10 was the ambiguity of disjunction fully comprehended, i.e., only at this time were the inclusive and exclusive interpretations available as alternative readings for this form. An exclusive response only became available at ages 6–7. Thus the *either* transformation may have acted specifically to resolve the cognitive ambiguity inherent in disjunction by provoking the exclusive interpretation; before ages 8–10, the *either* operator did not have this effect on *or* forms. At ages 8–10, the effect was found only for the more complex *or* forms ($A \vee \bar{B}$ and $\bar{A} \vee \bar{B}$); with the simple *or* form ($A \vee B$), exclusivity was the favored response and almost all subjects give it for all linguistic forms. It would appear that only with the more complex *or* forms did the inclusivity–exclusivity choice create ambiguity at ages 8–10. The simple conjoined sentence form of the disjunction had an effect equivalent to the quantified form in encouraging an exclusive reading. By contrast, the simple derived form favored the inclusive interpretation and thus reduced success in comprehension.

The above findings also have linguistic implications. They suggest that linguistic "schemas," as are involved in conjunction reduction with sentences (or propositions), have qualitatively different effects at the level of achieving propositional logic. The fact that a propositional transformation of linguistic form interacted with connective comprehension only at an age when (formal) propositional thought began to be attained, suggests that the connective here assumed the role of a propositional operator. (As reviewed above, the developmental data point to a qualitative shift in the nature of connective operations at ages 8–10, when full achievement of concrete operations was attained.)

3. The data, including the imitation data for 2- to 3-year olds did not provide clear support for a theory of connective comprehension based on

---

[4] It is interesting that Staal (1966) in his discussion of the analyticity of logical truth in language says: "It may also be noted that the semantic analysis of *or* may not be so straightforward as that of *and* and may even require the general doctrine that transformations do not change meaning, to be adapted in some way [p. 72]."

the primacy of the nontransformed *conjoined sentence* form. Subjects of the youngest age tested (2 years) showed only a nonsignificant increase in comprehension of the conjoined sentence form over the derived sentence forms, although the comprehension task was on the whole very difficult for subjects of this age. The same lack of differentiation in comprehension was found for older children (4- to 10-years old), except for the specific effects on disjunction noted above at ages 8–10.

Complementary to the comprehension task, the imitation data for 2- to 3-year olds provide evidence of a primacy of the derived conjunction form in production. Most attempted imitations by 2- and 3-year olds reduced conjoined sentences to the derived form. This result differs from Slobin and Welsh's (1973) finding that a 2-year old, given derived conjunction forms to imitate, often elaborated their structure to the fully conjoined form. It should be noted, regarding the difference between Slobin's and our results, that imitation does not involve a one-to-one mapping of its mechanisms onto comprehension. In the present study, when subjects reduced full sentences in imitation, they apparently comprehended the sentences they were reducing.

In conclusion, the most likely explanation of the derivation phenomenon in young children appears to be that, from the time they comprehend a fully conjoined sentence form, they have control of a reduction transformation for conjunction. This reduction transformation respects both structure and meaning in that only redundant elements are deleted and meaning is preserved. In addition, if binary conjunct associativity is considered primarily a logical phenomenon, and if asyndetic conjunction is considered an expression of such associativity, then the primacy of logical form over linguistic form is again confirmed by these data.

In general, the above points concerning the interaction of logical and linguistic form in the comprehension of connectives suggest the primacy of logical structure over linguistic form, when linguistic form is varied through the reduction transformation. The data also indicate the effects of cognitive development, particularly at ages 8–10.

Linguistic Connective Development

The evidence suggests that development of connective comprehension is characterized by (1) gradual improvement, with 100% achievement of comprehension on most connectives only at the oldest age and the highest cognitive level; (2) qualitative change in the ability to comprehend connectives with the more logically powerful connectives, $A \vee B$, $A \cdot \bar{B}$, $\bar{A}_w$, $\bar{A} \vee \bar{B}$, $A \vee \bar{B}$, achieved later in development (3) progressive change in the structural interrelationships among connectives. The connective hierarchy analyses show no within-subject hierarchy at ages 4–5, only minimal hierarchization at 6- to 7-years old (into an inferior and superior group), and a three-level hierarchy at ages 8–10. The connective hierarchy of 4- to 10-year olds differed from the Neisser and Weene adult hierarchy in that only two levels characterized the latter's performance on these connectives; and (4) Finally, there was evidence that the meaning of certain, early attained connectives changed with development. To the young child, $\overline{A}$ signified primarily *narrow* negation; to the older child, *wide* negation. The young child gave $A \vee B$ an *inclusive-both* reading (as they did other disjunctions); the older child gave them an exclusive interpretation.

Developmental changes in meaning appeared to be directly related to the development of cognitive processes. Several stages are evident in this development:

1. Children of ages 4–5, whose cognitive development is at the stage of "constituent functions," apply juxtapositional processes to connective interpretation. These interpretations reflect one-way class-proposition mappings. Through the application of these interpretations, subjects: (a) begin to understand A and $A \cdot B$, (b) solve $A \cdot \overline{B}$ by a process whereby $A = \overline{B}$, (c) begin to understand $\overline{A} \cdot \overline{B}$; (d) solve $A \vee B$ by an inclusive-both reading (i.e., give $A \cdot B$ both), (e) solve $A \vee \overline{B}$ by a primitive exclusive-type response resulting from avoidance of the negative; (f) do not understand $\overline{A} \vee \overline{B}$, although they begin to solve this form by inclusive-both reading; and (g) apply a narrow-negation interpretation to $\overline{A}$.

2. Children of ages 6–7, who for the most part are concrete operational, begin to apply truth-functional-like processing to connectives. They (a) become more successful in the comprehension of A and $A \cdot B$, (b) begin (at age 7) to comprehend $A \cdot \overline{B}$, (c) significantly improve in the correct exclusive reading to $A \vee B$, and $A \vee \overline{B}$, (d) still do not understand $\overline{A} \vee \overline{B}$, largely solving it by inclusive-both reading, and (e) begin to give a wide-negation interpretation to $\overline{A}$.

3. Children of age 8–10, who are fully concrete operational and have a partial capacity for formal operational thinking, make significant improvements in the comprehension of basic connectives. They show complete comprehension of (a) A and $A \cdot B$, (b) for the first time show considerable success on $A \cdot \overline{B}$, (c) significantly improve in $\overline{A} \cdot \overline{B}$, (d) show complete exclusive responding for $A \vee B$, (e) appear to recognize logical difficulties in interpreting $A \vee \overline{B}$, (f) first begin to correctly comprehend $\overline{A} \vee \overline{B}$, and (g) increase $\overline{A}$ wide-negation comprehension.

In summary, developmental changes in connective comprehension appear to be both qualitative and quantitative. The full use of the truth table, i.e., the structural set of true and false associations of the truth table, is only achieved at about 7 years of age, and the higher-order use of these truth-tabular associations is achieved after age 10. Before 7 years of age or so, a semilogic consisting of one-way operations characterizes the child's thought. These semioperations or *functions* are constituents of later, logical structures. Connective comprehension may thus be viewed as progressing from associative to analytic processing.

There is finally the question of how these developmental data compare with other developmental studies of connective comprehension. The question has already been addressed with regard to negation; we now consider the conjunction and disjunction forms. As noted in Chapter 6, no other study directly comparable in its design to the present study has been reported. (1) Linguistic form has not previously been controlled, except for the idiom specifications of Suppes and Feldman (1971). (2) Several studies were of the paper and pencil type (Neimark & Slotnick, 1970; Nitta & Nagano, 1966) in distinction to the orally administered sorting-task of this study. When a sorting task had been individually administered (Suppes & Feldman, 1971), other discrepancies exist. Comparisons with these studies are limited by these differences. (3) Several studies use intersecting classes as conjuncts, and as noted in Chapter 6, Hatano (1973) proposes that this has a significant effect upon performance in some cases.

Suppes and Feldman (1971) assessed connective comprehension in 4- to 6-year olds with a sorting task similar to the one used in the current study. They, however, (1) did not map the connective morpheme onto conceptual categories but interpreted the connective in terms of its semantic or referential meaning. As a consequence, several of their items that used the *and* connective were classified as *disjunctive*.[5] (2) In addition, they used intersecting classes (shape × color) which distinguished that study from this one.

The data on 4- to 5-year olds of the current study are compared with selected data from Suppes and Feldman (1971) in Tables 8-16 and 8-17. Suppes and Feldman report data from two experiments. The second used a somewhat younger age sample. Conjunction with *and* $(A \cdot B)$ was succeeded more highly in the present study than in Suppes and Feldman. This was probably due to the increase in difficulty in this form when intersecting classes are involved. Disjunction with *or* $(A \vee B)$, when an exclusive disjunction was intended), conjunction with *not* $(A \cdot \bar{B})$, and disjunction *or* with *not* $(A \vee \bar{B})$ were succeeded similarly in both studies. Suppes and Feldman further found in their error analyses with $A \cap \bar{B}$ $(\equiv A \cdot \bar{B}$, in this study) commands that the most common error was "giving the intersection of one set with only a part of the complementary set." This accords with the most common error with this logical form in this study (i.e., young Ss gave the A conjunct as response). As Suppes and Feldman comment, it is not clear from this error whether the difficulty is in the intersection operation, or the complementation operation. Data from this study would suggest that both processes cause difficulty at young ages.

---

[5] For example, *Give me the red things and the square things* was categorized by Suppes and Feldman as a disjunctive form $(A \cup B)$ as it requests not only the intersection between A and B but the complete union of both classes. Accordingly Suppes and Feldman are working with the $\cap$ and $\cup$ notation, which applies to classes, as opposed to the $(\cdot)$ and $(\vee)$ notation, which refers to propositions as used in this study. The two notations are convertible as are the class and propositional dimensions, $\cap \equiv \cdot$ and $\cup \equiv \vee$.

TABLE 8-16
Comprehension of Conjunction ($A \cdot B$, $A \cdot \bar{B}$, $\bar{A} \cdot \bar{B}$) in Several Developmental Studies[a][b]

Source:	Nitta and Nagano[c]	Hatano[d]	Neimark and Slotnick[e]	Suppes and Feldman[f]	Beilin and Lust
Language:	Japanese	Japanese	American English	American English	American English
$A \cdot B$					
4–5 (kindergarten)	22			(14) (42)	58
6–7 (second grade)	5			(33) (42)	82
(third grade)			(35)		
8–10 (fourth grade)	33	20	(50)		99
(sixth grade)	63	31			
Adult			(93)		99
$A \cdot \bar{B}$					
4–5 (kindergarten)	58			(0) (34)	5
6–7 (second grade)	52			(5) (56)	34
(third grade)			(38)		
8–10 (fourth grade)	47	42	(67)		74
(sixth grade)	67	51			
Adult			(97)		86
$\bar{A} \cdot \bar{B}$					
4–5 (kindergarten)	81				45
6–7 (second grade)	82				63
(third grade)			(54)		
8–10 (fourth grade)	92	96	(67)		97
(sixth grade)	94	98			
Adult			(93)		99

[a] Nitta and Nagano (1966), Hatano (1973), Neimark and Slotnick (1970), Suppes and Feldman (1971), Beilin and Lust.

[b] Percentages of correct responses. A and B refer to disjoint classes except when percentages are in parentheses—here A and B refer to intersecting classes.

[c] Data extracted from Japanese report of this study with the aid of Tatsuko Kaneda. Set = same as specified in Table 8-15.

[d] Set (for mutually exclusive classes) is as specified in Table 8-15.

[e] Set is as specified in Table 8-15.

[f] Set consisted of blocks of (3 shapes) × (3 colors) × (3 sizes) × (2 exemplars in each class) = 18 elements. In order to attain comparability to Beilin and Lust data, Suppes and Feldman (1971) commands using the connective *and* are tabled here regardless of their referential meaning. Suppes and Feldman ran two experiments, one consisting of subjects, 4.6–6.0, and the other, 4.5–6.7. Data are reported in this vertical order. For each experiment, data are reported for two differently worded commands: For $A \cdot B$, first percentages are for Suppes and Feldman statements of the type "Give me the *black* things and the *square* things" and second percentages are for statements of the type "Give me the things that are *red* and *square*." For $A \cdot \bar{B}$, first percentages are for Suppes and Feldman commands of the type "Give me the *round* things and the not *green* things" and second for "Give me the things that are *stars* and not *black*."

TABLE 8-17

Comprehension of Disjunction (A v B, A v B̄, Ā v B̄) in Several Developmental Studies[a,b]

	Inclusive reading correct					Exclusive reading correct	
	Nitta and Nagano[c]		Hatano[d]	Neimark and Slotnick[e]		Suppes and Feldman[f]	Beilin and Lust[g]
	to	ka		(or or both)	(either-or)	or	(or-either-or)
A v B							
4–5 (kindergarten)	85	49				(34)	32
6–7 (second grade)	82	63				(68)	54
(third grade)							
8–10 (fourth grade)	88	67	42	(15)	(12)		99
(sixth grade)	94	86	75	(8)	(29)		95
Adult				(97)	(97)		95
A v B̄							
4–5 (kindergarten)	22	19					30
6–7 (second grade)	30	21				(21)*	52
(third grade)							
8–10 (fourth grade)	51	41	32	(4)	(4)		68
(sixth grade)	65	41	24	(0)	(0)		
Adult				(66)	(79)		90
Ā v B̄							
4–5 (kindergarten)	0	2					0
6–7 (second grade)	0	0					1
(third grade)							
8–10 (fourth grade)	0	0	0	(0)	(0)		29
(sixth grade)	2	6	0				
Adult				(59)	(59)		59

[a] Nitta and Nagano (21966), Hatano (1973), Neimark and Slotnick (1970), Suppes and Feldman (1971), Beilin and Lust.

[b] In percentage of correct responses. A and B refer to disjoint classes except when percentages are in parentheses (A and B refer to intersecting classes).

[c] The Japanese connectives ka and to are ambiguous, as is the English, or. However, to has a preferred inclusive reading; ka a preferred exclusive reading. Set (pictorial) = same as in Table 8-15.

[d] Set (pictorial) = same as specified (for mutually exclusive classes) in Table 8-15.

[e] Set (pictorial) = same as specified in Table 8-15.

[f] See specification of age groups in Table 8-15.

[g] The response percent starred for A v B̄ stands for percentage of choice of the first disjunct (A); this is the response scored correct in Beilin and Lust.

Nitta and Nagano (1966) tested 679 children from kindergarten through eighth grade, and Neimark and Slotnick (1970) tested 455 children from third through ninth grades as well as 58 adults on a 16-item paper and pencil test. Two different verbal expressions for disjunction were used in both cases. These data need to be interpreted with care since three different Japanese connective forms were employed for the four conjunctions $(A \cdot B, \overline{A} \cdot B, A \cdot \overline{B}, \overline{A} \cdot \overline{B})$, and two disjunction connectives ka and to had exclusive and inclusive connotations, respectively; the Neimark and Slotnick or—both and either—or idioms had inclusive and exclusive connotations respectively.

Tables 8-16 and 8-17 also compare selected aspects of the Nitta and Nagano and Neimark and Slotnick data with those of the present study. For $A \cdot B$, the Japanese subjects showed greater success at early ages than our subjects. Neimark and Slotnick subjects show much less success than either of the above. It seems that the use of intersecting classes in $A \cdot B$ makes this form more difficult (as in Nitta and Nagano and Neimark and Slotnick); although the simplicity of the reference set should increase its ease (only two items were black and birds for example, in Nitta and Nagano and Neimark and Slotnick also). For $A \cdot \overline{B}$, Nitta and Nagano and Neimark and Slotnick forms requested an intersect operation Things which are birds and are not black, which is intuitively simpler than the operation required in our study;[6] and succeeded earlier (before ages 8–10) in these other studies. All studies show earlier attainment of the $\overline{A} \cdot \overline{B}$ form, with delay again in the Neimark and Slotnick subjects. In general, the Japanese data show the earliest success on these conjunction forms. It is not clear whether these results are due to the nature of Japanese connectives, per se, or to the effects of Japanese education. High levels of achievement were evident by 8- to 10-years old in all three studies.

For all studies, success at the younger ages was less for the disjunction forms than that for conjunction forms, even though Nitta and Nagano, and Neimark and Slotnick scored an inclusive disjunction response as correct $(A, B,$ or both A and $B)$; Beilin and Lust scored only an exclusive response as correct $(A$ or $B,$ but not both). The Japanese study showed first success on $A \vee B$ at 8- to 10-years old. Neimark and Slotnick found this only at adult age (cf. also Neimark, 1970). Beilin and Lust found first significant success on $A \vee B$ at ages 6–7. Task differences, inclusive—exclusive response differences, disjunct class differences, and the effect of the Japanese connective probably interact to explain these differences. $A \vee \overline{B}$ was succeeded less than $A \vee B. \overline{A} \vee \overline{B}$ was a very difficult form in Beilin and Lust, Nitta and Nagano, and Neimark and Slotnick studies, with substantial success only at the adult ages.

[6] A similar problem arises here as with the Suppes and Feldman study, due partially to these studies' use of intersecting classes and due partially to the Beilin and Lust control of linguistic form. For $A \cdot \overline{B}$, N–N, and N–S items request only the intersect of A and $\overline{B}$. Beilin and Lust request the complete union of both sets including the intersect. The Beilin and Lust $A . \overline{B}$ item is thus closer to the disjunctive $A \vee \overline{B}$ item of N–N and N–S.

Given the firm developmental trend towards exclusive disjunction which was found in our current study, it might be inferred that subjects made this type of error in the Nitta and Nagano and Neimark and Slotnick studies, thus explaining the low success for disjunction. Neimark and Slotnick did not present data showing choice of first or second disjuncts in disjunction items; however, their error analyses suggest that the response of giving just one class was rare at all ages for pictorial forms, and somewhat more common but still infrequent with verbal forms. When Nitta and Nagano data are examined for disjoint classes, it is evident that the exclusive type error was very rare for $A \vee B$ and $\overline{A} \vee \overline{B}$ forms, but more frequent for single negation forms ($A \vee \overline{B}$, $\overline{A} \vee B$). This amounts to a tendency to avoid the negative disjunct by taking advantage of the ambiguity allowed by the disjunction connective. This finding accords with those of the current study for the $A \vee \overline{B}$ form.

In conclusion, task differences, irregularity of linguistic form, inconsistency in the meaning of logical forms due to differences in reference set and to differences in semantic relations between conjunct and disjunct classes, as well as inconsistency in treatment of the connective morphemes, make cross-study comparisons very difficult. In general, conjunction appears less difficult than disjunction, especially at younger ages; comprehension of both conjunction and disjunction increases with age to about ages 8–10 for conjunction forms, to adult age for disjunction forms. Comprehension of A is early.

Summary

This study was based on a formal truth-functional interpretation of the connectives. Its intent was to establish the relationship of the linguistic connectives to cognition by way of the truth-functional logic that is basic to cognitive development, according to Piagetian theory.

The data show that truth-functional logic develops with age in accord with Piagetian theory. Development of linguistic connective comprehension (*and*, *or*, and *not*) was found to closely relate to the development of the comprehension of theoretically related truth-functional logical processes (intersection, union, and complementation). These cognitive processes did not map in one-to-one fashion onto comprehension of *and*, *or*, and *not* respectively, however. Rather, a cognitive operatory kernel, which concurrently permitted logical deduction and the comprehension of connectives, was indicated. The connectives related developmentally most highly to intersection (or logical multiplication). We propose this to be the consequence of the *general* nature of this operational structure and to its direct relation to the structure of the truth table.

The linguistic form in which logical connectives were embodied was not a major factor in connective comprehension. No support was found for sentential conjunction as developmentally antecedent to phrasal conjunction, or *vice versa*. This finding is interpreted as support for the *logical* nature of the linguistic connective. Partially autonomous linguistic and cognitive processes are theorized to be relevant to the *logical form* of linguistic deep structure. A relation between natural language connectives and logical connectives by virtue of the intersection of their separate formal systems is proposed, rather than identity between them.[7]

---

[7] Lust, B. On the notion "logical form" : The intersection of formal systems. Unpublished manuscript, Developmental Psychology Program, City University of New York, 1971.

9

The Cognitive Basis of
Language Development

The results of the studies reported in the preceding chapters are best interpreted in a broader context, in which the findings of investigations conducted on younger and older subjects for related linguistic issues are considered.

Prelinguistic Vocalization

Linguistic behavior begins with the vocal activity of the neonate. Upon its arrival and for the period thereafter, the infant's vocalizations are clearly interpretable on some occasions; on others they are not. Interpreting the meaning of very early patterns is difficult because, if their intent is to convey messages, the code to these utterances is only partially known. The primary function of these early emissions is generally considered to be the communication of affective states associated with the child's physiological needs and body comfort. Cries of discomfort and the signs of pleasure seem clearly discernable, but these same sounds also accompany response to novel and other stimuli and so their significance is difficult to ascertain.

Contrary to earlier views, the infant is much engaged in activity other than eating and sleeping. He is actively engaged, in fact, in a visual, auditory, and tactual encounter with his environment, collecting information and organizing his perceptions (Kessen, Haith, & Salapatek, 1970). The earliest perceptual and response systems available to the infant appear in large measure biologically determined. That is, simple response systems such as innately given reflexes provide the foundation for the constructed action systems that develop later. In like manner, the infant of two months is apparently endowed with the biological capacity to make such fundamental phonemic feature discriminations as between /p/ and /b/ (Eimas, Siqueland, Jusczyk, & Vigorito, 1971; Moffitt, 1971). To these, more complex feature discriminations are added and integrated as the infant matures.

Lewis (1936), upon reviewing the research literature on infant vocalizations published to that time, concluded that there was general agreement in the view that the differentiation of vocalization with age was increasingly associated with internal affective and conative states. Recent research on infant vocalization (Wolff, 1969), based on the use of more sophisticated methods (i.e., spectographic analyses), delineates a basic cry, an angry cry, a pain cry, gastromic discomfort, and frustration cries. "Faking cries," in addition, reflect more than just affective state or reflexive response; they appear to have a conative function, that is, they are an indication of the child exercising his will (Dore, 1973).

In the period from birth to about a year and a half the child improves sufficiently in auditory discrimination to be able to respond differentially to the patterning of sounds as well as to individual sounds. The first evidence of differentiation between intonation patterns comes at about 8 months (Kaplan, 1969). Lewis (1936) also claimed that the infant expresses his internal states or attitudes by utterances that become more and more like "intonation patterns," and that they are able to imitate their parents' patterns at 8 months. Response to adults' speech is said at first to be principally to these intonation patterns, with the use of words for reference following the association of intonation with specific situations.

The critical question in the research into prelinguistic nonsegmented vocalization (i.e., before first words) is what it is that infant vocalizations are meant to express. There appears to be, according to Dore (1973, p. 44), general agreement on these points;

1. Vocalizations are not random, undifferentiated, or unexpressive.
2. Vocalizations are "fairly reliable" indicators of affective and conative states.
3. Before the infant develops the segmented phonemic system, some prosodic features of his language are already in evidence.
4. Near the end of the first year the infants' vocalizations begin to express his "intentions".

The use of vocalization for the purpose of expressing *intention*, that is for indicating what he wishes, and possibly more, suggests that the child of one year has cognitive structures and processes already developed in addition to the conative and affective states that define his motivational system.

The principal evidence of the nature of the cognitive structures that develop in the period from birth to 1 and $1\frac{1}{2}$ years comes from Piaget.

Prelinguistic Cognitive Development

The period from birth to about $1\frac{1}{2}$ years, according to Piaget, marks the era of sensorimotor development that culminates in the achievement of practical or sensorimotor intelligence. The primary elements in this development are focused in the child's actions by virtue of which progressively more complex coordinations are made between perceived events and the physical response to them. These coordinations are embodied in *schemas* that define the consistencies in the infant's response to environmental events. These action schemas are "coordinated systems of movements and perceptions, which constitute any elementary behavior capable of being repeated and applied to new structures, e.g., grasping, moving, shaking an object [Piaget, 1962, p. 274]." The sensory schemas of seeing, hearing, and touching are thus coordinated at first with the motor schemas of sucking, clutching, pushing, etc. These simple schemas are elaborated into those in which the child's actions are designed to make interesting events last and ultimately leads to a differentiation between means and ends.

In the period of prelinguistic sensorimotor development there are a number of singular accomplishments that have a profound bearing on the later development of linguistic structure and behavior.

1

The period from birth to about the end of the first year marks the era in which the child's self becomes differentiated from the world, that is, from everything which is not the self. This differentiation occurs while the infant is in a constant transaction with his immediate environment. Only gradually, while acting on the world, does the child learn of the diversity of its features and at the same time learn of the diversity of his own action possibilities. Although objects appear at first to have no permanence, the conception of object permanence becomes the first conceptual invariant in the child's cognitive repertoire. It also marks the clear differentiation of the child himself from the world of objects. Out of this differentiation come three major classes, the *self* (the agent of action), *objects* (the objects of action), and the *action relation* between them. The differentiation of self from other persons, which becomes more pronounced with development, signals the need for communication. This need is made even more acute as the added mobility of the child reduces direct physical contact with others, such as his parents (Sinclair 1971b). The earliest forms of vocal activity thus serve to communicate the affective and conative states of the child; later forms serve cognitive and other functions.

2

The actions of the child, comprised of various (hierarchic) levels of action schemas, are endowed with structural properties, which although quite rudimentary are nevertheless continuous with the more formal logical and mathematical properties that define the child's behavior at a later period. In the sensorimotor period these structures are evident in the reversible actions of the child when he displaces objects (including himself) and even through detours is able to return them to their original locations. These reversible actions identify the first "group-like" structures of spatial displacement and are dependent upon the prior development of the concept of object permanence (Sinclair, 1971b). These group-like structures encompass many behaviors that by the end of the sensorimotor period may be said to reflect true intelligence. They display intentionality, an understanding of (albeit primitive) causal relations, and the practical experimentation with objects. This intelligence, however, is directed to problem solving in the immediate present, and is associated primarily with interest in directly perceived objects.

3

In the period from 2 to 4 months, the child is able to imitate sounds in what Piaget (1962) calls "vocal contagion" (the voices of others stimulate the child's own voice), mutual imitation (as the experimenter imitates the child, there is a redoubled effort to imitate the experimenter), and sporadic imitation (of a known sound). At this stage, however, there is no imitation of what is new; sounds that are imitated are those that are clearly in the child's repertoire, and, when apparently novel imitations occur, Piaget is at pains to demonstrate that these are pseudo imitations. In the stage that follows, systematic imitation of sounds already in his phonation appears. The aim of imitation at this point is to make the sounds that are interesting continue, in very much the same way that he makes interesting sights and actions last.

While in this period, the child is responding to *signals* that are linked to immediate action; in the later periods (8–12 months), response is more to mobile signs that Piaget calls *indices*. These give rise to anticipations and reconstructions that go beyond immediate perception (Piaget, 1962, p. 19). Imitations that are made in this period show, in effect, the application of familiar tools to situations which are new. (The child will, by analogy for example, imitate the opening and closing of the experimenter's eyes by opening and closing of his mouth and hands.)

The period that follows (12–18 months) is characterized by the imitation of new models, whereas before (up to age 8 months) the child's imitations were simple, rigid, and uncoordinated. The beginning of new imitation at 12 months is associated with the onset of the mobile coordination of new schemas. When active experimentation becomes the mode, it generalizes to the imitation of new models of all kinds.

The last stage of the sensorimotor period (about 16 months to 2 years) shows the further development of imitation in so-called deferred imitation (imitation at a later time of observed actions of the model), which Piaget (1962, p. 68) considers to imply the internal representation of the perceived event, in fact, as a symbolic representation of the event.

Imitation in the sensorimotor period thus progresses from signal response to the symbolic representation of an external event. Sensorimotor imitation takes place in the presence of the model; representational imitation, which follows it, is deferred imitation and is based on the mental *image* of the model. In this way imitation serves in the development of sensorimotor intelligence and is also an active component of the process of schema coordination and structuring.

4

The sensorimotor period marks the emergence of the semiotic function. Its origins are in the earliest sign-activities of the 2 to 4 month period wherein the infant responds to associative "signals" as conditioned associations (i.e., conditioned stimuli function as signals). These sign responses are augmented by the system of indices. Whereas the "signal" is firmly embedded in the schema that coordinates (associates) a particular stimulus with a particular response, the index is a *mobile* sign in that it is *detached* from the action made in response to a stimulus event. A sound, for example, may index a particular visually perceived event to a child and give meaning to it that it would not otherwise have. Thereafter, the sound may play little or no role at all in his response to the event (if it were a signal, it would have to persist in its association with the event).

Signals and indices have the limitation of evoking actions only in the presence of objects. With the development of representation, as in representative imitation, objects not actually present can be evoked by "signifiers" that recall them to mind. "Representation is thus the union of a 'signifier' that allows of recall, with a 'signified' supplied by thought [Piaget, 1962, p. 273]."

In the sensorimotor period, indices and signals serve as signifiers and reflect an aspect of the object or the action schema. When the signs that evoke actions include *symbols*, that is the mental *images* that stand in the place of the absent objects, then it may be said that the child has developed the symbolic function. In representative imitation (or deferred imitation), which develops at the end of the sensorimotor period, an internal image establishes the connection between the absent external model and the later imitation of the model.

Verbal representation is a new and different kind of representation in that it is conceptual, and symbolic representation which precedes it makes its development possible. It is also Piaget's view that imitation, helped by images, constitutes the essential system that serves the function of "personal" symbolism, but it also makes possible the acquisition of language, which is viewed as a (nonpersonal) system of conventional and arbitrary signs. Only gradually does one function merge into the other (the personal and conventional) through the mediation of the perceptual, representational functions of language.

In terms of its relevance for later-developing language, then, certain consistent properties of action schemas are developed in the sensorimotor period, recursion, reiteration, order, and hierarchical inclusion (Piaget, 1970; Sinclair, 1971b). With the advent of the semiotic function at the end of the sensorimotor period, with its true (linguistic) signs and symbols, there emerges the accompanying ability to solve problems without actually carrying out an action. This ability implies mental representation that encompasses the recognition of past actions and the anticipation of future action (Sinclair, 1971b).

Single-Word Utterances

The meaning and function of the child's first words has been the subject of some controversy. The difficulty in assessing its function is principally in establishing its cognitive role on one hand and its linguistic role on the other. Piaget, in distinguishing the functions of the concept, the word and the image (Piaget & Inhelder, 1971), characterizes the *image* as a symbolic entity that through schematization designates the entity it represents. The function of the *concept* (relation, class, etc.) is to comprehend and interpret some deductive reasoning by way of causal explanation. The concept, in effect, abstracts the constituent characteristics of that which it expresses and places them in relation to other terms that do the same. The *words* used in association with these concepts are verbal signs, and, although they have their own characteristics and laws, they add nothing to the conceptual relations themselves. They "merely designate conceptual articulations [Piaget & Inhelder, 1971, p. 382]." The *word*, then, has more than one function, i.e., it is cognitive and has particular linguistic properties, but its associated *concept* is exclusively cognitive.

Consistent with the notion that words designate conceptual relations, Piaget asserts that the child's first words function as "holophrases," in the sense that they are predications, that is, they assert or affirm something. This conception underlies his characterization of holophrases as "expressing a possible action" and "action judgment [Sinclair, 1971a, p. 208]." De Laguna (1927) appears to have had a similar conception in interpreting first words as signifying the object and its properties together with the actions with which it is associated. She also points out that to interpret the meaning of these holophrases adequately one must examine the context in which the word is spoken and thus see what the child is doing to fully appreciate its significance (de Laguna, 1927, pp. 90–91).

This notion of predication has been conflated with the grammatical representation of predication embodied in the sentence predicate. This is why McNeill attributes to de Laguna the view that the holophrastic word is the comment, which together with its extralinguistic context, the topic of the comment, serves as a "rudimentary kind of proposition and thus amounts to a full sentence conceptually [McNeill, 1970, p. 22; cf., Brown, 1973a, on this point]."

The recent desire to make the holophrase into a rudimentary sentence construction has to be seen in its historical context as an effort to place Chomskyan syntactic structure into the (innate) competence of the child. If such abstract structures (as S) were to exist in the competence of the child, they would have to be manifest in some, albeit primitive, form in the first utterances; in the recent era of generative transformational   linguistics they were so interpreted. It is a different matter, however, to interpret the holophrase as predication, rather than as a primitive, predicate form. To see the holophrase as prediction is to see it as a part of the continuity of cognitive development, whereas as a predicate it would be the initial form of syntactic construction. As a syntactic form, the holophrase would require a subject or its equivalent to justify its role in a sentence, however primitive. Thus, although there may be considerable justification in questioning the holophrase as a syntactic predicate, there is also considerable justification in accepting the holophrase as indicating cognitive predication.

Bloom (1974) defines two groups of first words: one group includes substantive words with the quality of strong *word-image* representation. These make reference to specific objects or persons (*birds*, for example, refers to those in a particular mobile). The second group includes function words that "extend across classes of object and events." These words reflect the child's recognition of behaviors that different objects share (e.g., saying *gone* as a comment on the disappearance of objects). It is Bloom's contention that the reason children say one word at a time (Bloom, 1973) is that they lack a linguistic code for representing information through semantic–syntactic relations between words (Bloom, 1974). Children in, effect, develop conceptual representations of regularly occuring events and they tag on whatever words conveniently code such conceptual notions. She argues further, based on an analysis of the production and understanding of early speech, that there are not sufficiently clear-cut data available to indicate what the child knows of the structure needed for understanding sentences. In any case, Bloom does not consider single-word utterances as sentences.

Brown (1973a), in assessing the evidence for considering first words as "sentences" and as expressing "semantic intentions" more complex than they seem to express, reports that all observers agree that single-word utterances vary in prosodic features so that they appear to be declarative, interrogative, or emphatic. Some investigators report that prosodic patterns do not seem to be used consistently for semantic contrast, while others do report such contrastive use. Brown considers, however, that the evidence does not justify considering holophrases as "sentences."

Research on one-word utterances is, on the whole, relatively meagre. Nonetheless, their prosodic features and the content and function of these words indicate an attempt on the part of the child to represent his already developed conception of the world. This conception, however, is limited to objects (persons and things) and the actions carried out on them. This knowledge, even though concrete, nevertheless embodies many properties of a physical nature. The first words that represent this knowledge are conceptual, or more precisely preconceptual, in these senses: they embody pre-class characteristics, that is, they lack extension to other objects of the same kind, and they embody relations that show limited attribution of the same action property across individual words (Bloom's function words). These first words, which are more identified with preconcepts than true concepts, nevertheless reflect a general predication and referential function that some identify as "semantic intention" (Slobin, 1971), although the term "intention" appears to be relatively vague in this context. (Whether it is meant as the determination to act in a certain way as by design, or as referring to having a concept or notion, is not clear.)

Two and Three-Word Utterances

Early linguistic development occurs by one-word accretions. The child is first in a one-word period that lasts for about 3 months to a year. It has its onset at about the twelfth month and thus lasts up to about 24 months of age. The period of two-word utterances spans the period from approximately 24–36 months, and is then followed by the period of three-word utterances. After this point, increases in length are not by one-word additions.

Pivot Grammars and Telegraphic Speech

Two-word utterances have the semblance of syntactic structure if for no other reason than changes in word order are possible. Since word order is a significant feature of the surface structure of sentences, it holds the possibility of indicating knowledge of sentence (i.e., syntactic) structure. The impetus for seeking structure in two-word utterances was undoubtedly affected by Chomsky's claims concerning competence and his purported views of the creative nature of language production, namely, that with knowledge of a limited set of syntactic rules the speaker is able to generate an infinite number of discrete sentences. Two proposals were offered to account for the seeming regularities in two-word utterances: (1) the characterization of such speech as *telegraphic* by Brown (Brown & Fraser, 1963; Brown & Bellugi, 1964), and (2) the *pivot grammars* of Braine (1963) and W. Miller and Ervin (1964).

The pivot grammar has received the lion's share of attention because it suggests, first, that two-word combinations are systematic and follow well-defined rules, and secondly, because these rules of construction appear to be generative in a manner consistent with the claims of the generative transformational linguistics, although Braine's views were definitely not in accord with those of transformational theory.

The claims of the pivot grammars are detailed by Bowerman (1973) Brown (1973a), and Bloom (1970) as follows:

1. In two-word utterances, there are two classes of words: pivots (P) and an open class (O).
2. Pivot words have the properties of (a) high frequency, (b) fixed position, (c) they combine with any word not in its class, and (d) they do not occur in isolation, or in combination with each other.
3. Open class words can (a) occur in either initial or final position, (b) occur in isolation or in combination with any pivot or with each

other, and (c) be subdivided further on the basis of their distribution in use.

4. The pivot grammar permits the following combinations based on 2 and 3 above: $P+O$, $O+P_2$, $O+O$, and O.
5. The pivot grammar does *not* permit: P, P_1+P_2, or P_2+P_1.
6. The claims made for the pivot grammar include the claim for universality, that is, the pivot-open dichotomy should exist in all languages.
7. It is also claimed that this grammar fully represents the child's linguistic knowledge at the two-word stage.

What Bloom (1970), Bowerman (1973), and Brown's (1973a) research makes abundantly clear is that on no score do the claims for pivot grammar hold up well, although some children's two-word utterances do exhibit pivot grammar properties (Bloom, 1970; Bowerman, 1973).

The data from all three studies, and others, show that:

1. Pivot words do occur in isolation.
2. Pivot words do occur in combination with one another.
3. Distributional evidence indicates that more than two word-classes exist in the two-utterances of children, i.e., the pivot grammar does not fully represent all the data in the childs' grammar.
4. The $O+O$ rule is inadequate because it fails to differentiate structural meanings such as the genitive, locative and agent–action that appears in two-word utterances. The pivot grammar thus does not capture all the meanings conveyed by two-word utterances.
5. The pivot-open distinction is not characteristic of other (non English) languages studied (Bowerman, 1973; and others). Instead, children use the dominant word orders in their respective languages to express subject–verb–object (or agent–action–object–acted upon); possession–object possessed, and object location–location relations. Pivot grammars, on the other hand, simply represent these relations as $O+O$, N–V–, N–N, V–N.

The characterization of early speech as "telegraphic" by Brown was based on the analogy between the way adults speak and the way they represent that speech in telegrams, i.e., by omitting redundant or otherwise unnecessary words while still preserving the essential message. Brown reported the existence of two classes: *contentives* (nouns, verbs, and adjectives that in the main involve reference to persons, objects, actions, and qualities), and *functors* that provide grammatical structure with the ability to modulate the meanings of the contentives (these include inflections, auxiliary verbs, prepositions and conjunctions). The former class has many members, the latter few, and thus the pivot- (with few members) open class (with many) distinction is paralleled to some extent.

Brown (1973a, p. 88) now believes that the conception of telegraphic speech as earlier defined has not been borne out by the evidence, and that if it has any validity at all, it is in some fairly restricted sense. The functor-contentive distinction is said to fall down in not fully expressing the basic semantic relations that exercise control over speech in Stage 1 (that includes two-word utterances).

Thus, the two main attempts to characterize two-word utterances on the basis of primitive grammatical rules, embodying the distinction between two constituent classes bound by certain selectional restrictions, appears to have failed, and there is agreement as to why they failed, namely, in focusing largely on the linguistic (i.e., syntactic) properties of language while disregarding the cognitive (or semantic) basis for language acquisition.

Two- and Three-Word Utterances from a Cognitive and Semantic Point of View

A slight digression is in order here to deal with the distinction between cognition and semantics. Both terms refer to meaning. The former term refers to the processes and structures by which meaning is known, represented, and created. Meaning, in a cognitive sense, appears in different contexts: in affectivity, motivation, play, action, imagery, and language. When it appears in language it is usually denoted as semantic and is known, represented, and created in the context of the processes and structures of language (in the lexion and in syntax). In some theories (e.g., generative transformational) it is said to reside in the so-called semantic component. The confinement of meaning interpretation to a particular component now appears to be quite arbitrary. Except for some purely structural or arbitrary properties of language, almost all its structures and functions affect or influence meaning. It also appears that the distinction between semantic and cognitive is designed to differentiate only the linguistic context from other contexts—to identify as semantic those (cognitive) aspects of meaning that exist in language. Linguistic meaning may or may not be different from other kinds of meaning. It has already been pointed out if an adequate definition or theory of meaning were available it would be possible to more adequately differentiate between cognition and semantics. For the present, however, it appears necessary to establish links between the cognitive (or semantic) aspects of language and comparable and noncomparable domains outside of language. The early attempt of generative transformational linguists to keep the logical foundation of syntax independent of considerations of meaning quickly failed. The parallel attempts of some psycholinguists to account for language acquisition by writing descriptive grammars (such as the pivot grammar) devoid of reference to meaning also failed. This pursuit has been superceded by efforts directed to an examination of the role of semantics and cognition in language acquisition and development.

We have already detailed the Piagetian claims concerning the cognitive basis of early language acquisition, which for the most part are general, descriptive, and programmatic. More recent research by Genevans and others has fleshed out, to some extent, the bare-bones of the earlier

Piagetian characterization of language acquisition. The influence of the Piagetian position is seen in the studies of Bloom, Brown, Slobin and others.

Bloom's Studies

Bloom's (1970) study of language acquisition has the virtue of indicating the limitations of pivot grammar and at the same time proposes an alternative account of early language development that is an amalgam of assumptions from generative transformational theory and Piagetian theory. Her study parallels the method used in a number of other, naturalistic longitudinal studies (e.g., Brown, 1973a), in which the verbal productions of three children were recorded over a period of time and their contents analyzed for the purpose of writing a grammar that would be descriptive of the child's linguistic rule system. Her method, however, differs from most other investigations conducted during the era of generative transformational influence, in that note was made of the context in which the child's verbal statements were made, including the child's own actions. Bloom's approach was consistent with de Laguna's (1927) assertions concerning the context-related meaning of children's early language and the more recent Russian efforts that stress that the meaning of the young child's utterances becomes clear only when the situation in which speech occurs is taken into account (Elkonin, 1971). Bloom's (1970) conclusions and findings were as follows:

1. The child's speech is very much tied to its situational context and to the child's behavior. It is only by neglecting these facts that other investigators have come to largely incorrect conclusions concerning the grammar that describes child's language (e.g., pivot grammars). She says, "The extent to which children's speech is stimulus-bound mitigates against the assumption of true linguistic creativity [p. 233]." In other words, an ideal language processor, operating solely by abstract syntactic rules, does not exist in early childhood.

2. Basic grammatical relations were not present in her subjects' grammar from the beginning. For all her subjects, the predicate relation of verb–object (V–O) was fully in evidence, although the grammatical relation subject-verb (S–V) did not exist in the earliest sentences of Gia and Eric. The subject–object (S–O) relation was learned by Gia first, and Eric learned the verb–object (V–O) first. Both, later learned the subject–verb (S–V) relation, although this structure was least used by all three subjects. By the end of the study period the subject–predicate relation was judged to be fully in evidence for only two of the subjects and was only beginning for a third (Eric), although the children were at about the same age level. Bloom (1970) notes that, if the early two-word utterances of children had expressed all possible combinations of subject–verb–object, it could be assumed that the children had knowledge of those basic grammatical relations from the beginning, but it was not so. The fact that achievement

of these syntactic structures was progressive shows that its development depended on the prior development of those "cognitive organizations of experience that are coded by language [p. 228]."

3. The child's utterances, taken together with the context in which they were produced, provided the basis for assigning a semantic function (i.e., interpretation) to a partial syntactic structure or construction. The concepts that define the meanings intended by the subject's utterances (such as *more milk*) were the following: *existence, nonexistence, recurrence*, and for negation there are the added semantic categories of *nonexistence, rejection* and *denial*.

4. Although the specification of semantic functions for syntactic structures distinguishes Bloom's contribution, her analysis of the child's language also includes the writing of a generative transformational-type grammar, with specification of constituent phrase structure, lexical feature rules, and transformation rules. In respect to transformations, Bloom proposes that only positing the existence of a "reduction transformation" in her subjects' grammars permits an adequate account of the child's linguistic output. She points out that (a) Kathryn (in Stage 1) learned subject–verb–object order (from evidence of the "productive" occurrence of subject–verb, verb–object, and subject–object strings); (b) this order is important for the meaning of sentences; and (c) although all the major constituents were learned, there were apparently constraints on putting them into a single utterance, indicating that the underlying structure that one can assume accounts for surface structure sentences is more complex than the surface forms themselves. Only a "reduction transformation" then, could account for the difference between the richer underlying structure and the surface forms. Bloom (1970) assumes that the reduction transformation deletes category constituents. Thus, Kathryn was able to say *Mommy pull* and *Pull hat*, and Bloom infers that *Mommy hat* was possible, although not actually uttered, as Kathryn had said *Mommy sick* [p. 73].

Bloom holds that reduction occurs as a result of something more than a production limitation on sentence length. It is said to be due to a cognitive limitation on handling structural complexity. The number of syntactic operations or the complexity of grammatical relations increases cognitive "weight" of the sentence. Reduced "sentences" reflect an inability to carry a full sentence load.

5. Bloom cites negation as indicating how prior cognitive development underlies the emergence of different syntactic structures. Different semantic categories of negation were expressed by her subjects without, at the same time, learning the appropriate linguistic structures for expressing them. As Slobin (1971) and Piaget (1962) also point out, when the child acquires a new conception (such as *rejection* and then *denial* in respect to negation), he uses a previously learned linguistic structure, which had been used to express an earlier conception (i.e., nonexistence), to now express his new conception. Our data (and those of Sinclair, as well) similarly show in the early production of the passive, that an older form

(an active sentence) is first used by the child to express the meaning of the passive, but, as we will point out later, the old forms are reconstructed and integrated in new ways to achieve their new purpose even before the appropriate and completely new forms are acquired.

6. Children showed evidence of knowing both substantive and relational aspects of language. They had learned substantive forms with inherent meaning (e.g., *mommy*), and also the semantic relations that hold between substantive forms—those that introduce differences in grammatical meaning—i.e., *mommy* as subject (*Mommy push*), as object (*Push mommy*), as possession (*Mommy's shoe*), and as possessed (*My mommy*). Thus the grammatical meaning of substantive words changed as they were arranged with other words in a sentence.

7. There were individual differences in the strategies used in acquiring linguistic structures. Eric's grammar was pivotal; Kathryn's and Gia's categorial. These strategies were not, however, mutually exclusive.

8. There were instances in which the child's language was more mature than the underlying cognitive function (e.g., the use of negation and the temporal adverbs, *today*, *tomorrow*). There were also other examples of out-of-phase matching of linguistic and semantic elements, e.g., over-generalization of inflections. Thus growth of linguistic expression and cognitive development did not necessarily proceed hand-in-hand. (Such structures in Piaget's terminology would be pseudo structures, or pre-structures, and we have referred to these as linguistic algorithms [Beilin & Kagan, 1969]).

Brown's Studies

The period of two-word and three-word utterances is placed by Roger Brown (1973a, 1973b) in the first two stages in language development. Stage 1 is labeled to indicate the development of *semantic roles and syntactic relations.* It is followed by Stage 2, *grammatical morphemes and modulation of meaning.* These stages are not "true stages" in Piaget's sense, because, says Brown, they do not represent qualitative changes in organization but are named either to characterize the major development of a particular process or to denote an extensive or elaborated set of procedures.

Characterization of the development of Stage 1 reflects an acceptance of the position of Bloom and others that these early utterances are designed to communicate intentions or meanings. Brown proposes a set of such meanings that are said to be embodied in the child's utterances. The set includes Bloom's categories as well as a supplementary list.

1. *Nomination.* This is Bloom's "existence "category, and Braine's "ostensive sentences." It is associated with utterances of the form *introducer + x.* It includes the subcategories of pure nomination (that involve naming), and demonstrative and entity relations (that include the use of demonstrative forms *this–that* and *here–there,* which occur when the referent is present).

2. *Recurrence.* Bloom's category. In this construction the subject either comments on (declarative) or requests (imperative) recurrence of an object or event. It may mean: (a) reappearance, (b) appearance of a new instance, or (c) additional quantity.
3. *Nonexistence.* In the referential context the object is not present. Whether the child considers the object to be truly nonexistent is left open. For Bloom, the developmental expression of negation starts with nonexistence, then rejection, and finally, denial.
4. *Agent and action.* From Fillmore and Chafe. Constructions in which an animate or inanimate source instigates some action.
5. *Action and object.* Fillmore and Chafe. Constructions in which the patient undergoes a change of state.
6. *Agent and object.* A semantic relation that exists where there is a (syntactic) juxtaposition of subject and object (e.g., *boy—ball*).
7. *Action or location.* Utterances that represent place or locus of action.
8. *Entity and locative.* Utterances that locate an object in space.
9. *Possessor and Possession.* The semantic relation of possession.
10. *Entity attribute.* Characterization of the attributes of an object.
11. *Demonstrative and entity.* The semantic relation already defined under nomination.

This set of operations and relations is said to describe all of the meanings expressed in his Stage 1 subjects' utterances. Brown leaves open the question as to whether this is the full range possible.[1]

Brown (1973b) also accepts the Piagetian thesis that there are cognitive prerequisites for early language development. He posits, on the basis of Piaget's characterization of sensorimotor development, that *nomination* and *recurrence* presume the ability to recognize objects and actions. *Nonexistence* presumes the ability to anticipate objects and actions, and the enduring nature of objects.

> The productive, freely combinatorial, use of agent, action, and object construction would seem, minimally, to presume the ability to distinguish an action from the object of the action and the self from other persons and objects [p. 200].

Brown (1973b) sums up these developments and adds an interpretation of them:

> I think that the first sentences express the construction of reality which is the terminal achievement of the sensori-motor intelligence. What has been acquired on the plane of motor intelligence (the permanence of form and substance of

[1] Schaerlaekens (1973) also relying on a contextual semantic interpretation of two-word utterances concludes that two-word utterances have a grammar (and are thus sentences) that express nine different semantic relations. Three of them are expressed by all six of her Dutch subjects, the relation of **fixed allocative** (expressing possession or destination), **coincidence** (expressing place, association, or identification), and **affirmation–negation** (expressing approval or disapproval).

immediate objects) and the structure of immediate space and times does not need to be formed all over again on the plane of representation. Representation starts with just those meanings that are available to it, propositions about action schemas involving agents and objects, assertions of nonexistence, recurrence, location and so on [p. 200].

As Piagetian as this view may seem, it differs from it in two respects. First, it contradicts the Piagetian assertion that the child at the level of representation re-forms (in the process of reflective abstraction) what he acquired on the level of sensorimotor intelligence. It differs also from Piaget's position that reconstruction at the level of representation also occurs as some form of action, in fact, as a form of internalized action.

In essence, Piaget's position is that, at the level of representation (even linguistic representation), schematic relations have to be constructed. The alternative view is that language is a special form of representation in which reconstruction through action is not necessary. We will discuss this issue later as it is important for both language acquisition and cognition, but it should be clear at this point that, although Brown accepts certain aspects of the Piagetian view, he does not incorporate some of its fundamental assumptions.

Brown's analysis of Stage 2 development is based on the appearance of 14 grammatical morphemes (e.g., plurals, tenses, prepositions) in his subjects' speech. The criterion used for assuming knowledge of a grammatical morpheme was that it appeared in three successive samples of the child's speech (6 hr of transcription) 90% of the time, and appeared in obligatory contexts, that is, it appeared grammatically where it should have appeared. What was found was that the developmental order of morpheme appearance was "amazingly" constant although the rate of development varied widely. Before full appearance of the morpheme was reached, production seemed to be governed by variable rules, whereas, for adults, production was governed by categorical rules. According to Brown, the reason grammatical morphemes enter into the child's grammar as late as they do (i.e., Stage 2) is because their function is to modulate meanings and not create or represent them; they thus cannot be acquired before content words or before the rules of order and combination are acquired. Brown concludes that the primary determinant of the developmental order of morpheme acquisition is the complexity of semantic and grammatical elements that enter into sentence production.

Bowerman's Study

Bowerman's (1973) study provides a critical analysis of pivot grammar, transformational grammar, and case grammar as applied to the speech production of Finnish, English, Samoan, and Luo children. She found that none of these grammars was fully adequate to decribe speech production. Pivot grammar was found to be least adequate; transformational and case grammars were found to have some features that appear essential to a description of the child's Stage 1 speech. In early Stage 1 speech (MLU1. 3–1.5 morphemes), the most productive two-word utterances had the form: subject–verb, verb–object, modifier–noun, noun–locative, demonstrative pronoun–noun, subject–object. When three-word utterances appeared in early Stage 1, they were in S–V–O, and also S–V–locative and V–O locative forms.

In late Stage 1 speech, transformational operations for embedding and conjoining were lacking, as were obligatory functions such as inflections, conjunctions, prepositions, articles, and copulas. However, virtually all children had learned the word orders of their language. Bowerman concludes that transformational theory is appropriate in some ways for describing the child's linguistic output, but in others it is difficult to justify. She questions the appropriateness of the subject–predicate distinction for Stage 1 speech which is used by both Chomsky and Bloom. She further feels that the relative frequencies of various constituents in actual production give little justification to a constituent structure analysis of utterances; nor does it seem appropriate to posit an understanding of hierarchic organization of constituents by the child in order to explain his production of two and three-word utterances. Instead, she feels that children learn constituent structures gradually as their grammars develop.

The notion of "subject" as grammatical concept, too, appears more abstract than is needed to adequately represent the grammatical elements in early utterances. For one, the transformations that are a necessary accompaniment of the syntactic subject are absent in children's speech. Instead sentence subjects are almost always (semantic) agents, or instigators of action. Only with development are various notions dealt with consistently in similar ways and only then is the syntactic abstraction of subject achieved.

Case grammar is said to more adequately represent the semantic functions of early speech than alternative linguistic theories. Case grammar also avoids assumptions about the subject and constituent structure that is critical to the transformational view. It is inadequate, however, in that some semantic categories find no case representation. Also critical, is the fact that the modality–proposition distinction of case grammar is absent in child speech.

Bowerman concludes that the child bases his first utterances on semantic concepts. As he begins to recognize the regularities in the way different semantic concepts are dealt with, his knowledge is gradually organized into more abstract syntactic concepts. The optimal grammar, then, has to be capable of operating on both semantic and syntactic levels.

Menyuk's Studies

Menyuk (1969), on the basis of language data collected from children in the age range from 2- to 7-years old, proposes that the earliest (one-word) utterances are produced from the base structure rules with only two elements, an "intonation-marker," for questions, imperatives, and declarative sentences, and the category "topic", which may belong to any class, such as N, V, Prep, Adj, and Adv. Topics are said to have semantic properties. At a later stage (the two-word stage), modifiers are introduced so that the functional relation is one of topic and modifier. At the next stage, the T element, which previously was only an intonation marker, becomes expanded to some morpheme (NP, *no, now, what, where*) and conjoined to a base structure string, which itself contains NP and VP elements. Out of this development comes the subject–predicate relationship and the delineation of classes.

The active change in linguistic structures that first occurs is dependent upon changes in the child's underlying psychological mechanisms, such as his memory capacity. At the start of language development, the child begins with component rules and structures. These contain a limited set of semantic properties and an incomplete set of transformation rules that place a natural limit on the childs' linguistic output. From 4- to 9-years old there is (1) expansion of base structure nodes (i.e., branches) through increases in (lexical) class membership, (2) increasing knowledge of selectional restrictions and co-occurrence rules for the lexicon, and (3) an increased repertoire of transformation rules, with the application of the syntactic operations of addition, deletion, substitution, and permutation (Menyuk, 1969, p. 150).

Menyuk (1969) also holds that the sensorimotor actions that co-occur with the child's first utterances indicate a topic–modifier relation, which can also be characterized as a subject–predicate relation if omissions are postulated to exist at some other level. Thus, as the child begins to make observations of the world about him, the subject–predicate distinction appears (p. 32). The very early use of demonstrative determiners (*this*) is taken as further evidence that language at this stage is used, in the Piagetian sense, as an expression of overt acts rather than as a referential system (i.e., the terms are not used as labels).

Limitations on language acquisition are not ascribed to limitations in memory capacity for sentence or morpheme length, but to capacity limitations in processing basic and elaborated syntactic structures, which require increasing differentiation and a larger number of rules for their generation (Menyuk, 1969, p. 39).

Lastly, the word-order rule for early utterances is S + V, with the position of O optional, so that such sentences as OSV may be produced. However, there were no SOV constructions in her sample.

Menyuk's position, then, is that the first productions of children are determined by a transformational generative type of linguistic system of which the child possesses incomplete and limited knowledge. His knowledge of base structure rules and transformation and phonological rules are differentiated and elaborated with age as the child's capacity for retaining sentence rules develops. His early utterances show the subject–predicate distinction, if one takes the extralinguistic context into account.

Sinclair's Studies

In a study by Sinclair and Bronckart (1972), 68 French-speaking children between the ages of 2 years, 10 months and 7 years were asked to guess the meaning of deviant three-word utterances that resembled the spontaneous utterances of very young children. The test word-combinations consisted of two nouns and a verb, or one noun and two verbs (the verb could be transitive or intransitive). The two nouns plus one transitive verb combinations could be reversible (*Boy pushes girl*) or nonreversible (*Boy opens box*). The three-word combinations were presented in the six possible word orders.

There were three developmental steps in the kinds of responses made by subjects. The two earliest solutions were "intransitive response" (e.g., *He pushes*) and "x-agent responses" (the child himself acting on the two Ns), which had the common property of consisting of two parts only: a person name and action, or an action word and the name of the person on whom the action was performed. Word order played little or no part in determining the child's response.

In the second stage, the word groupings were considered as consisting of three parts: agent, action, and patient. First, emphasis was on the agent–action bond with closeness to the verb determining what was agent, and the remaining noun taken as patient. Concurrently, or shortly thereafter, the verb–object link was established. Verb order was not critical, and the noun nearest the verb was taken as the patient of the action and the remaining noun was the agent.

In the third stage, proximity lost its significance and the first noun in NNV and VNN strings was taken as agent and the second as patient, irrespective of the position of the verb, in SVO, SOV, and VSO patterns.

Sinclair postulates that the SVO order of French, active declarative sentences is built up from the earliest two-word utterances to the simplest sentences, in both comprehension and production, on the basis of the understanding of three rules. The first rule is: an utterance has two parts that (1) can be a description of a state, object, or person. It can describe a property (*truck broke*), possession (*Mommy cup*), location (*Birdie there*) and so on, very much in the manner of Bloom's (1970) categories, or (2) it can be the expression of an action on an object or person (e.g., *Hit ball, Coat off*). In these cases, focus on the topic determines its location in the utterance.

The second rule or set of rules pertains to utterances describing actions performed on objects. The rule or rules state(s) that an utterance may consist of three parts. The key is the action–word (the verb) and its semantic properties. In accord with the syntactic and semantic properties of the verbs, one of two rules is to be followed; (1) an agent–action link is established, whatever is left is the patient, or (2) establish a patient–action link, whatever is left is agent. Topicalization determines the ordering.

A third set of rules is based on the conception that a sentence consists of two parts, a subject and a predicate. Both parts may be composed of subjects. The ordering rule is SVO and topicalization follows transformational rules.

Two- and three-word productions are not seen as truncated copies of adult sentences. Although imitation is to some extent involved in their construction, they are achievements based on active constructions created from knowledge of a set of linguistic rules. These rules are for the most part known by the age of 5 (range, 2- to 6-years old) and appear to have been acquired in Piaget's period of semilogical thought, i.e., they do not require the development of operative thought (which is acquired from age 6 onwards). These linguistic developments are based on two Piagetian postulates (Sinclair-de-Zwart, 1973) : (1) Very general cognitive structures, composed of systems of actions, are established during the first two years of life. These systems constitute the basis for many different types of cognitive structure, as much for the construction of linguistic structure as for logicomathematical knowledge and knowledge of the physical world. Linguistic structures may be another manifestation of a very general, in fact, universal cognitive system that underlies such concepts as causality and time, and that can take different representational forms (Piaget, in Ferriero, 1971, preface). (2) Higher level knowledge involves a reconstruction of already acquired concepts and patterns and thus shows a formation process isomorphic to that by which earlier knowledge was acquired (Sinclair-de-Zwart, 1973, p. 24).

Summary of Two- and Three-Word Constructions

The various investigations into the comprehension and production of two-word and three-word utterances just considered converge on a number of common conclusions, notwithstanding important differences among the findings and theoretical interpretations of the individual studies.

1. Two-word utterances represent to most investigators a two-part syntactic construction that serves a variety of semantic or cognitive functions. The basic data providing information, concerning the semantic function of these utterances, were obtained from the content of the child's speech and the natural context in which speech occurred, i.e., from the actions that accompanied the child's speech, or the verbal antecedents of what was said (see Bloom, 1970; Brown, 1973b; Bowerman, 1973; Menyuk, 1964), as well as from experiments in which linguistic and context conditions were systematically varied (see Sinclair & Bronckart, 1972; Menyuk, 1969).

The varied descriptions of the semantic functions of language at the stage of the two-word utterance reduce to attempts on the part of the child to describe or make assertions about *actions* and *states* of the physical world he directly perceives or of which he retains some memory. The *states* are those of possession, location, having attributes, existence (conceived as object permanence), nonexistence (conceived as object permanence with object not present), etc. *Actions* that are represented at this stage are principally physical actions, although actions words, in effect, are subcategories of *process* words. *State* and *process* are distinguished (J. J. Katz, 1972) by the fact that a *state* is a "condition of something (be it person, place, thing or whatever) at a given time or during a given time interval, while a *process* is a thing or transition from one state to another over a given time interval [p. 303]." Although states and processes are usually expressed by verbs, they are also expressed by nouns and adjectives. The attempt to express relations pertaining to states and processes dominates the early utterances of children. In early utterances, state and process are associated with objects and persons. Objects are either agent or patient entities associated with state and process terms, and are usually action terms, or attributive entities associated with process or stative terms. Examples of the former are *Daddy hit* and *Hit Daddy*; examples of the latter are *Mommy's cup* and *Doll broke*.

Thus when the child attempts to represent the characteristics of objects or persons he perceives, or the actions he or others perform, he does so in two-word utterances with the minimum of syntax (as *N–N, N–V, V–N*, but rarely as *V–V*). The emphasis at this stage is on state–process characterizations, which reflect the two sides of an action-oriented linguistic and extralinguistic universe. The relation of state to process is a dynamic relation of change or arrested change, with objects and persons oriented to one another and to the subject himself in some kind of meaningful relationship.

There are two questions concerning two-word utterances. One is whether the words that enter into two-word utterances fully represent the child's conceptions of reality. Most investigators hold that (a) two-word utterances reflect the child's *functional* cognitions, which Bloom and Brown's functional semantic categories denote, but also (b) the richness of the child's cognition is not fully captured linguistically. That is, one must assume on the basis of the extralinguistic context, and the child's own actions, that much is left out of his linguistic representations. *Mommy cup*, which is semantically equivalent to *The cup that belongs to Mommy*, or *The cup that Mommy has*, etc. is an example. Reconstructing the child's knowledge of the world and his cognitive capacities from his two-word utterances yields a much more restricted version of his cognitive capacities than is indicated by Piaget's characterization of those capacities based on the child's actions during the same period. Although this may be a function of the restricted sample of two-word utterances that have been obtained and analyzed to date, it is more likely that two-word utterances by their limited nature are unable to represent the richness and power of the cognitive structures already instated in the child.

The second question involves the syntactic function of the constituents of the two-word utterances. Greater differences of opinion presently exist concerning the syntactic function of two-word utterances than concerning their semantic function. The generative transformational interpretation, which Bloom favors, is that base structure is necessary for the generation of two-word utterances with the base made up of such constituents as enter into subjects and predicates. Although some children sample from the base, so that S–O constructions appear in their speech first, others appear to sample differently so that S–V constructions appear first. By the end of the two-word utterance stage, most children have all the grammatical constituents of the base in their productions. Bloom argues that only a "reduction transformation" can adequately account for the nature of two-word utterances considering the nature of the base. Menyuk's view is that the child starts with incomplete constituent structure and an incomplete set of transformation rules; these becomes progressively more complete with development.

Brown and Bowerman, on the other hand, argue that two-word combinations cannot be interpreted as subject–predicate relations because such an assumption would require more consistent use of the words in the child's lexicon as class terms than is actually found; at the two-word stage the necessary consistencies and variations that would make a word or set of words "subjects" do not appear in the child's speech.

Sinclair appears also to believe that two-word utterances mainly reflect functional semantic categories; in three-word utterances there emerges the agent–action–patient relation, as well as the subject–verb–object relation. Earlier three-word utterance order is controlled by temporal topicalization rules (as are the two-word utterances), which only later are superceded by transformational rules associated with the subject–predicate distinction.

Thus the weight of present opinion seems to be that the earliest utterances that have syntactic form (i.e., two-word) lack subject–predicate differentiation, in its syntactic sense, although a parallel distinction may appear in the cognition of the child. Although generative transformational grammar appears to distinguish many of the features of later three-word utterances (such as constituent structure, some transformational rules and the abstract subject–predicate distinction), the earlier three-word utterances appear to have an intermediate status in which *agent–process* (or *state*)–*patient* distinctions have developed (on a level less abstract that the subject–predicate distinction, as Bowerman points out), as well as rules of combination and order. Prior to that, the elements of two–word utterances have primitive rules of combination associated with them that are closely related to the semantic functions they represent.

2. As indicated earlier, Brown holds that what had been acquired on the plane of motor intelligence in the sensorimotor period does not need to be formed again on the plane of representation. Representation starts with just those meanings that were available to it. If this were construed as an assertion that no new meanings are created in language that are not already in sensorimotor cognition, it would appear to be true. If it were construed, however, as maintaining that new constructions generated in language are isomorphic with sensorimotor structures and need not be constructed again as they were on the level of action, it would represent a view at variance with Piaget's, whose position is that such reconstructions are necessary. The action base of the sensorimotor period, by means of which thought

structures are created, is paralleled in the constructive processes of language. Aside from the constructive process itself, the principal focus of early utterances is on action, particularly when one considers the context in which the utterance occurs. Thus, the early two- and three-word constructions have the verb (either expressed or implied) as their central element and those other constituents that represent state and process. If anything, the evidence from various studies, including Brown's would seem to support the Piagetian thesis that language is a constructive process, and construction on the level of linguistic representation repeats, in a general sense, the constructive process of the sensorimotor period.

It is also the case that early language construction occurs over a relatively long period of time.[2] Two-word constructions may extend over a period of 6 months, and three-word constructions may undergo qualitative change over a period of a year, although considerable addition, differentiation, and integration of constructions occurs within this   period. Nevertheless, the power   represented   by these linguistic constructions far outweighs the intellectual force of nonlinguistic structures.

At the same time, as both Bloom and Sinclair note, the child acquires linguistic structures (characterized as pseudostructure or prestructures) that often outdistance the underlying cognitive capacity of the child. Although some of these may be pseudostructures, it may also be that, in natural language acquisition, not all linguistic structures are, in fact, constructed by the child. Some complete linguistic structures may be assimilated by the child quite readily through modeling and similar procedures. These structure may become functional (in whole or part) in the way an algorithmic subroutine functions in an information-processing system. Such routines may on occasion be out of phase with the available cognitive system, in which case they may be kept as place holders until the appropriate cognitive structures develop and articulate with them. If not appropriately integrated into the cognitive system, they may be lost to memory and would have to be constructed or reconstructed at a later time. It has been demonstrated (Beilin 1965; Beilin & Kagan, 1969) that children can acquire such linguistic algorithms even through training so that they are successful in problem solving, concept learning, and linguistic comprehension. These were experimental demonstrations, however, and only little is known of how similar language structures function algorithmically in natural language acquisition.

---

[2] According to Schaerlaekens (1973) and others, after the appearance of the first two-word utterances, there is a period of about 5 months in which no change in (grammatical) rules occurs. Then the expansion of two-word utterances into three-word utterances is signalled in different ways. First, the two-word utterance has a third word "juxtaposed" to it, e.g., *drinks tea/milk*. Second, two-word constructions may be topicalized, so that a subject or object is repeated before or after the two-word utterance and separated from it by a short pause, shorter than the normal pause between two utterances (or sentences), e.g., *butter take/butter butter*. Third, the two-word utterance is coordinated with another two-word utterance, e.g., *yes carrot/yes gone*.

The Sentence

At the point at which the child is able to understand and produce sentences it becomes possible to ask what underlying, linguistic rule system exercises control over the sentences produced. It is clear from what has already been said that, prior to full sentence construction, a great deal of the child's linguistic output is in the service of the child's cognition. There comes a point, however, when regularity and order define the relations among linguistic units and these appear to result from processes that do not exist in the surface structure of the sentence strings themselves. This is so even for three-word utterances, and it has been observed by Bowerman and Bloom that for many of the child's earliest utterances the only adequate account for the regularities among them is a Chomskyan type of generative transformational grammar. As the earlier one-, two- and three-word utterances are under considerable cognitive control, it is unlikely that such control abruptly ends as the linguistic rule system becomes dominant in language production. The question then becomes one of knowing in what ways cognitive structures and processes function in respect to language and how linguistic rules themselves are structured and function.

The Reality of Deep Structure

Both linguists and psychologists recognize that the surface structure of a sentence does not necessarily represent its meaning unambiguously. It has become a generally accepted thesis that the rule system from which sentences are generated to express such meaning exists at a level other than the surface itself. If it is the case that cognitive structures and rule systems also exist at a *deep* level (or at least other than the surface level), then the possibility exists that surface structure utterances are influenced by two deep-level phenomena, linguistic and cognitive. It may be, of course, that defining two deep structures is really looking at two sides of the same coin; that one kind of deep structure (the linguistic) subsumes the other. This position is held by some, but it is made dubious by the evidence of a prelinguistic period of cognition in which thought is devoid of linguistic representation. Some adult cognition is undoubtedly nonlinguistic as well, as is evident in *geometric* and related imagery.

The generative semanticist solution of considering the deep level to be semantic or to embody "logical form," is nevertheless a linguistic conception, and, although some draw parallels between logical systems and language, there is no specified dependence or association with cognitive processes or structures. Part of the difficulty may be that in discussions of the relation between logic and language it is not always realized that "logic" is a *product* of thought and is not a characterization of the thought process itself. Although those like Piaget claim that formal logical systems *do* define cognitive development, this claim is based on empirical studies of the thought processes themselves. Most other claims concerning the relation between logic and language, however, are based on the assumption that logical theory as such provides a "window into the mind," without attempting to establish the connection between such models or metaphors and the empirical facts about thought. Although language production or comprehension can be considered one such set of empirical data, formal linguistic theories do not represent such data but only another formal logical system. What is needed then is clearer specification of the relation between cognitive processes, which may be defined by logical theory, and the logical properties of language. The logical theory that may explain or describe empirical facts concerning language may of course do the same for nonlinguistic cognition.

Suppes (1974) also proposes that logic and language are intimately related. The *theory of models* in logic, "which is really the semantic theory of formal languages," is said to apply to natural language. Some elementary examples from child language are provided to illustrate the potential utility of applying logical models to linguistic data. Illustrations are provided to show that semantic tree structures are logical in nature and equivalent to formal logical relations. The sentence *Bring me some more candles* is said to be equivalent in logical status to *Add 5 and 7*. The proposal implies that the structure that underlies natural languages sentences is a logical structure that looks very much like the structure of logic itself. In this case, it is modal logic that is held to apply most appropriately to language. Suppes' proposal is very much akin to Lakoff's (in press), who views modal logic as "giving promise of making considerable strides in extending logic to cope with natural language phenomena. . . ." In both interpretations, an isomorphism is established between logical structures and surface structures through their representation as phrase structure trees. Lakoff, however, attempts to differentiate logical structure from deep structure, at least in its Chomskyan sense. His view in essence is that "the basic claim of generative semantics . . . is that the rules of grammar for a language are not separable from the rules that relate logical forms and surface forms." In contrast to the views of most logicians he does not consider the rules of (natural language) syntax to be independent of logical structure, "nor even independent of the modal-theoretic interpretation of such structures." It is held further that natural logic characterizes all rational thought that can be carried out in a natural language. It thus provides insight into the nature of conceptual structure. These proposals appear to do for language what Piaget proposes for thought. Both language and thought are said to be defined by logical structure, to which logical models may be applied. The Piagetian view in respect to language, however, is that the models of logic and cognition do not apply directly, that language appears to have properties of its own that are at least partially independent of logical and other cognitive systems (in Ferriero, 1971, preface). Our data support this view. The conception of the relationship between cognition, logic, and language that seems most consistent with the data is one that posits an abstract cognitive system of structures whose basic relations and functions are realized in systems of thought (logical and otherwise) and in language, each system with properties independent of the other. The fundamental relations, then, between these systems are not direct but are mediated through a common abstract system of relations and structures. Although it would be premature to assert what form such an abstract system would take, it can be indicated as to how the relations between language and cognition manifest themselves empirically.

Relations between Linguistic and Cognitive Processes

THE LEXICON

The lexicon of each language contains a vast store of information, for its function is to enable a speaker to make reference to every conceivable state of the natural world, and even more broadly, to every conceivable state. To the extent that knowledge itself is amenable to organization, so is the lexicon because the lexicon is in at least two senses a form of knowledge. First, the words themselves represent certain parts of speech and have various functions in the grammar. This may be said to represent a type of linguistic knowledge. Secondly, the information inherent in the word reflects knowledge of the real world. Such knowledge is extralinguistic knowledge and it is acquired as knowledge of the world is acquired, and not necessarily as linguistic knowledge is acquired. Evidence from the number language study (Chapter 5) shows that, at least in that segment of the lexicon which may be prototypic of many other portions of it, knowledge of its terms is acquired gradually, and, more significantly, it is acquired in a progression that is in accord with the nature of the child's developing conception of number. It thus appears that the logic of the number system exercises control over the development of number-word knowledge.

The developmental progression is from an associational knowledge of number symbols and rote counting, together with some knowledge of relational terms (but not in a relational sense) at ages 2–3, to knowledge at 5-years old of the language appropriate to the one-to-one correspondence of sets and indeterminate number reference. Up to this point, number-word knowledge is acquired concomitant with the development of cognitive structures and functions characterized by one-way mappings (i.e., non-reversible relations). At 6- to 7-years old, abstract number terms become known concurrent with the achievement of operational thought.

Two developmental processes appear to be at work in the acquisition of the lexicon. First, the lexicon becomes progressively differentiated, in that new meanings are added to available terms, and new terms are added with new meanings. The similarities and differences between and among all terms at the same time become more apparent. Secondly, the lexicon becomes more integrated in that meanings embodied in both old and new terms are related to one another in new ways. The number-lexicon organization that results is manifest in the differentiation between cardinal and ordinal terms and in the simultaneous differentiation between determinate and indeterminate reference. These two dimensions of number concepts and quantitative measurement organize the child's implicit and explicit knowledge of number language so that even 7-year olds were able to respond to number terms in what appeared to be organized response patterns.

As the logic of the number system defines the underlying structure of the number lexicon, so do the logical relations of time and space structure the time lexicon. The time lexicon, as the number lexicon, is acquired progressively (see Chapter 4) so that time words related to motion and velocity (speed words) are acquired quite early (4-years old), while terms of order and duration are acquired later.

The subjective lexicon, that is, the child's knowledge of the lexicon, is thus organized and derives its meaning from the more general cognitive systems that structure the child's knowledge of the world. In the case of both number and time, this knowledge is only partly physical knowledge. Its principal component is logicomathematical knowledge that involves the application of logical operations to the abstract relations that exist between represented forms of physical knowledge. Acquiring both physical and logicomathematical knowledge requires an extended period of development and this is reflected in the acquisition of lexical knowledge in these domains. Although children of the ages of 2 and 3 have a vocabulary of some scope, which increases at a very rapid rate, the development of particular systems of terms within the total set is under the control of the knowledge of their related conceptual systems. If terms are acquired "earlier" than their related cognitive systems, the terms may lack meaning and are usually used in inappropriate ways; they also lack the system properties associated with the appropriate cognition.

SYNTAX

How cognitive processes affect syntactic structure is more difficult to assess, if for no other reason than syntactic structure includes more than one linguistic phenomenon, i.e., it embodies phrase structure rules, transformation rules, lexical insertion rules, and so on. Our data concern some of these structures.

1

The passive transformation involves a set of rules associated first with changes in word order so that the noun in the second position (in an N_1–V–N_2 sentence), which functions as the grammatical object, is transposed to the first position to serve as the grammatical subject, although its semantic function, that of serving as patient relative to the agent, remains the same. In turn, the noun that serves as grammatical subject is transposed to the vacated second position; its semantic function as agent remains the same. The second rule change involves the verb. From the active declarative form it is changed to the *is* **verb** *by* or *got* **verb** *by* form. The cognitive processes necessary to acquire knowledge of these rules, appear to be those involved in operational reversibility.

The data of the study of the passive (Experiment 1, Chapter 3) show that for both comprehension and production a child who demonstrates a low level of reversibility performance is also characterized by poor language performance; a high reversibility level is accompanied by superior comprehension and production. This concurrence is to some extent independent of age. Not only is the relationship evident in the extent of correct comprehension and production of passive sentences, but the syntactic structure of passive sentence production is related to the child's reversibility level. Generally, primitive passive-attempting responses are made by low-reversibility-level subjects, and fully correct passives are produced by children with high reversibility levels. Again, development of the passive construction is more related to the child's reversibility level than to his age.

Further, judgment of the synonymy of active and passive sentences is related to reversibility level, at least when a verbal judgment of synonymy has to be made; in a task in which synonymy is indicated through picture selection, performance is poor even at the second grade.

Although the data in this study show a consistent relationship between the child's reversibility level and his comprehension and production of the passive, the evidence does not point to a perfect one-to-one cognitive-linguistic mapping, because being at a low reversibility level did not necessarily preclude a subject from demonstrating adequate linguistic performance, nor did a high reversibility level ensure adequate linguistic performance. A *direct* relation between cognitive and linguistic processes in respect to knowledge of voice, therefore, cannot be maintained, although there is good evidence for an indirect relationship. The lack of direct empirical relationship therefore does not bear out the ostensible, formal (logical) similarity between the reversibility features of the passive transformation rules and cognitive reversibility.

2

In respect to time syntax, a similar relationship between reversibility and syntactic structure was posited in the Weil study (Chapter 4). The formal relation between time reversibility, implicit in the tenses, and cognitive reversibility was expected to be reflected in the child's knowledge of both. The expected relation did not manifest itself for the simple tenses (past, present, and future), although the complex tenses (progressive, perfect) did manifest more of a contingent relationship between tense knowledge and reversibility. One possibility as to why more of a relationship between tense knowledge and reversibility did not appear for the single tenses is that knowledge of these could have been achieved as one-way relations considering the manner in which they were tested in Weil's experiment. In the Cromer and Ferreiro studies, when more of a contingent relation between reversibility and time relations was found, the knowledge expected of the subject may have embodied more of the two-way reversibility operation.

With time conjunctions (*before–after*), a reversibility operation was more implicit in the test, particularly when sentence order was noncongruent with event order, with the result that comprehension was shown to be more related to the subject's reversibility level, although there were significant exceptions in the Weil experiment to this generalization.

One may say then that the evidence speaks in favor of a relation between time reversibility and time operativity in respect to time syntax, taking the Ferreiro, Cromer, and Weil studies together. There were sufficient exceptions, however, to say, as with the passive transformation, that cognitive structures for time do not map directly onto linguistic structures. In essence the properties of both cognitive and linguistic systems are sufficiently different to exclude a direct mapping.

3

Our expectation was that the "logical" connectives as well as the time connectives would manifest a contingent relation with the development of operational thought. Here too our expectation was borne out (Chapters 7 and 8) although again the mapping of the cognitive forms onto linguistic forms was not direct. The evidence indicated:

a. Knowledge of most linguistic connectives studied ($\bar{A}$, $A \vee B$, $A \vee \bar{B}$ $\bar{A} \vee \bar{B}, A \cdot \bar{B}$) was manifest later than, or at the same time, as the achievement of operational level performance in related cognitive tasks.

b. Knowledge of the basic forms A and $\bar{A}_n$; $A \cdot B$ and $\bar{A} \cdot \bar{B}$ connective comprehension appeared later than or concurrently with achievement of the constituent-function level of cognition.

c. The bivariate and distributive connectives correlated most consistently with performance in the logical intersection tasks. This relationship was made manifest by both the Pearson and canonical correlation analyses.

d. Looked at in another way, the cognitive functions of adjunction and dichotomy and the constituent functions of union, intersection and complementation were known to children prior to or concurrent with their knowledge of the earliest language forms: $A, A \cdot B, \bar{A} \cdot \bar{B}, \bar{A}_n$.

The basic cognitive operations of classification, intersection, union, and complementation were known before the comprehension of disjunction or concurrent with it. In turn, vicariance as well as all other cognitive processes were achieved before knowledge of the most complex connective studied, $\bar{A} \vee \bar{B}$.

e. The logical connective study showed that developing cognitive structure rather than age was the major determinant of connective comprehension. The apparent reason for this is that the various logical connectives share a common structure, as was evident from the data on the development of the hierarchical structure of connectives. The hierarchial structure is best described as logical and it maps onto the cognitive groupings. (This was best shown in the canonical correlations.) The statistical mapping showed that the most general influence in this relation was logical intersection on the cognitive side and disjunction on the linguistic side. What is further confirmed by these correlations is the relation of truth-functional logic on the cognitive side to linguistic connective comprehension.

Nevertheless, in this context as for the passive transformation, the tenses and the time conjunctions, the mappings of cognitive onto linguistic processes are not complete. There are, in fact, a number of indications of autonomy between the systems. The lack of testing order effects upon comprehension, for example, and the nonsufficiency of cognitive level for linguistic knowledge and vice versa lend support to the idea that at least part of each system is independent of the other.

Despite this caveat, however, the partially autonomous linguistic and cognitive systems appear to integrate at an abstract logical level which may be said to inform both linguistic and cognitive structure. Thus, natural language and logical connectives are not characterized by identity but by a relation of intersection of their formal properties. This may be said to be true not only in respect to the logical connectives, but to the syntactic structures of time and the passive transformation, and possibly to the totality of the linguistic and cognitive systems. Thus, it may be reasonable to infer from these data that if there is a level of linguistic deep structure it maps onto a deep level of cognitive structure. How much this mapping represents a two-way interaction is not fully evident. That is, whether cognition is affected by linguistic form to the same extent that language is affected by logical (cognitive) form is not known, although it would appear that at some ages and in some conditions the mapping may be bidirectional; at other ages and in other conditions the mapping is more likely to be uni-directional. We will consider this issue next.

The Mapping of Cognition onto Language: One-Way or Two-Way

In the (Weil) time language study (Chapter 5), a time-concept training experiment was conducted to bring subjects to the criterion level of per-formance on the concepts of *more* or *less* time. The subjects who lacked the concepts were trained through a series of procedures which included motor simulation and verbal rule instruction. The "sufficiency" of language for cognitive functioning was thus given a test. Only 20% of the first- and second-graders profited from the language training, whereas almost all ninth- to eleventh-graders did. It was also shown that younger, trainable subjects used conceptual strategies similar to those used by younger, nontrainable subjects, which suggests that the ability of subjects to acquire the time concepts was a function of the cognitive processes available to them. The limited effectiveness of verbal training on subjects lacking in an available cognitive operational structure is consistent with our earlier studies (Beilin, & Franklin, 1962; Beilin & Gillman, 1967; Beilin & Kagan, 1969). At the same time, the very fact that verbal training could affect subject's performance (as demonstrated in Beilin [1965] and substantiated by others—see Beilin [1971b]) indicated that language can play a role in cognitive development. The critical question, however, is what occurs when conceptual learning takes place through linguistic intervention. Is an operational structure or system instated by virtue of linguistic training? From the Piagetian view, it usually is not. On our view, learning a linguistic structure in an experimental context, introduces an algorithm that functions as a cognitive processing routine. It ordinarily has limited applicability to the concrete elements to which it is applied in training. It can also act as a place holder until the appropriate cognitive structures can build round it or integrate with it, in which case it may acquire greater generality. This same phenomenon has been observed in natural language development, as we have indicated earlier in this chapter. Our knowledge of this phenomenon applies to subjects at the concrete operational level and below and to tasks that are appropriate for that level. At a later age, when children reach the level of formal operational thought, a completely different set of conditions may apply; in fact, our expectation would be that verbal rule instruction would have considerable cognitive generality as the linguistic and cognitive systems approach a closer formal relationship.

Nonetheless, the role of language structure in cognitive functioning has been little explored particularly in the early years. Knowledge of the number series (1, 2, 3 . . .), for example, which is acquired very early through associative processes, appears from observation to be used by young children for indexing purposes (i.e., for ordering and enumerating objects) before a more conceptual knowledge of number is acquired. In its algorithmic and indexing functions, language may have a more significant role in the formation of thought than Piaget, for example, would allow, even though language may still not be the principal determinant of thought, as Bruner (Bruner et al., 1966) and Vygotosky (1962) propose. Thus, although it appears that language acquisition may not be a sufficient condition for thought in respect to most cognitive functions, it may play a role in significant ways that are, at present, little understood. The Piagetian view, relative to the one-way relation between cognition and language, should not become a bar to discovering the ways in which a two-way relation exists.

One may thus conclude that the mapping of cognitive structures onto linguistic structures at an early age appears to be primarily a one-way mapping, i.e., from the cognitive to the linguistic, although as we have pointed out, not fully so. To a lesser extent, language may affect the development of cognitive structure so that a reverse mapping exists as well. This relationship probably becomes more of a full two-way mapping when language can be used as a propositional or modal logical system in its full sense, and the child is capable of formal logical thinking. This concurrence is not likely, in most instances, before the ages of about 10–12.

Language Acquisition as a Constructive Process

As the data of the various studies reported in this volume show, language acquisition is gradual and takes place over a relatively long period of time. Some linguistic processes and structures are acquired early and others relatively late. The fact that language acquisition proceeds gradually does not in itself indicate that language acquisition occurs by means of constructive processes. It could just as readily indicate, for one, that the developmental process is the result of forces acting solely external to the person. This view is usually favored by behaviorists and some neobehaviorists. Another possibility is that the acquisition of new linguistic forms results from the operation of a maturational process, an unfolding of structures that by the nature of the species has already been preprogrammed to develop in the appropriate circumstances. This appears to be a possibility that Chomsky (1968) favors. To establish that language acquisition and development is a constructive process requires evidence that different linguistic components are actively composed into new units that differ qualitatively from their constituents. The data from each of our studies shows this to be the case. Imitation data in the number agreement study (Chapter 5), for example, indicate a developmental progression from lack of agreement-rule knowledge to the attainment of such knowledge at about ages 3–4, although accompanying this transition is rule-boundedness and egocentrism. A later transformation takes place at age 6 or 7, when rule knowledge is associated with an objectification of the sentence so that it becomes possible for the child to imitate sentences even if they are ungrammatical. The imitation of passive sentences (Chapter 3) also showed a three-stage progression. Likewise, the imitation of connectives showed a stepwise progression with differences between 2- and 3-year-old's performance. Although 2-year-olds were poor in both conjunct associativity and connective morpheme imitation, there was substantial improvement at age 3 in conjunct associativity although it was less evident for morpheme imitation.

There were many instances in the comprehension data of stepwise qualitative differences in performance that suggest transitions in development from one type of linguistic processing to another. Two- to three-year-old's responses to complementary sets (in the logical connective study), for example, showed that they were not structured by intensional reference to the nearest neighbor of the negated class but to the simple juxtaposition of classes, i.e., to $B \vee C \vee D$. At ages 4–5, however, attention to set extension became evident, and, at ages 6–7, both narrow and wide interpretations of the negated class A appeared as alternatives. Although at ages 8–10 the same alternation appeared in the responses of subjects, most responses were of the wide type.

There were a number of other instances in the data that suggest the constructive nature of the acquisition processes, but probably the clearest evidence comes from the child's production of the passive (Chapter 3). There appeared three stages in the construction of the passive (four, if one counts the period in which no response to a command for the passive was made). In the first stage, the child barely attempted to produce a passive sentence. He used active sentences in an attempt to preserve the meaning of the perceived action relation. The nature of the constituents used in his sentences indicated that the child implicitly recognized that the agent of the action could not be in the grammatical subject position and that the elements in the sentence could not be in event or temporal order. The first attempts at construction of the passive, as the child apparently did not have adequate linguistic resources available to him, depended on the use of linguistic devices that were in his repertoire. Because his task was to establish the causal relation between the first and second nouns, the lack of word-order rules and the passivizing rules for verbs led to the failure to represent the meaning intended adequately, but his attempt at least reflected that the child knew that the critical relation was one between agent and patient, and probably also between subject and object. The next stage was one in which the child had greater linguistic resources for approximating a passive construction. In these instances he composed two active sentences into a single construction. For this he employed word-order devices, putting the patient in the first sentence and the agent in the second, thus approximating the word order of the passive. The casual relation between the two was approximated by "semantic" means more than by syntactic forms, and the meaning of the action relation between agent and patient was thus communicated by way of the active sentences used. The final stage was one in which the word-order transposing device was articulated with the proper verb form to permit the coordination of the logical relation with the grammatical relation. The process of achieving the passive construction was thus progressive, with some parts of the process of construction achieved earlier than others. There were intermediate stages in which a level of integration was achieved with partial forms that could serve, even if inadequately, to represent the child's conception of the events he wished to represent. The experimental production task, which has been found so useful in the Piagetian-type of linguistic research thus shows, in a kind of slow motion, the processes that are at work in linguistic construction. One has to infer, of course, that similar processes are at work in normal development. Natural conditions do not always command response in the way the experimental tasks do, and, thus, one does not see the constructive process in so obvious a fashion.

The extent to which language acquisition is defined by this type of constructive process is not clear then. It may be that some aspects of language acquisition are acquired quite differently and in the construction of sentences and other units of discourse that other processes such as imitation and modeling play a role. In addition, looked at in the totality and across different language groups, consistency and regularity in the order of acquisition of linguistic structure would suggest some form of genetic (i.e., innate) control over the acquisition process. Of this very little is known. For the present, however, an understanding of the processes that lead to developmental change would seem in greater need of explication.

Developmental Order in Language Acquisition

In practically every area of research reported in this volume there is a developmental progression in the acquisition of the linguistic components of the particular systems studied. This was so for the passive, the number lexicon, number agreement, the time lexicon, and time syntax, as well as for the linguistic connective. These findings are in accord with other reports of developmental progressions in language acquisition (e.g., Brown, 1973b). The explanation of developmental order differs, however, among investigators.

One explanation (as discussed in Chapter 2) is that developmental order is a function of derivational complexity. The development of the passive relative to the negative transformation, for example, is explained in this way. As a number of studies have shown, though, derivational complexity offers an inadequate explanation of developmental order as well as of sentence comprehension. Another possibility is that information-processing complexity accounts for developmental order very much as it is said to account for relative-sentence processing difficulty. Still another explanation is that developmental differences are due to differences in the semantic characteristics of sentences. It appears to us that each of these explanations reflects a part of the truth. There is no reason to believe that language development as complex as it is can be accounted for by a single process. However, some processes may be more critical or significant for development than others. This differentiation is usually highlighted by the effects of different task demands. This fact is suggested over and over again by the great variation in results from study to study bearing upon the same linguistic phenomenon, with only slight variation in task requirements. When Olson and Filby (1972), for example, claim that pictures in a comprehension task are easier for younger children to process, whereas sentences are easier for older children, this is true in only certain contexts. When active–passive sentence pairs, for example, are processed for their synonymity, Olson's generalization does not hold, although if the sentence pairs involve simple subject–object reversal without passivization, it does hold (as indicated in Chapter 3). One must assume then that sentence comprehension, and the processes associated with language development generally, are affected by a complex of factors that include conditions external to the individual as well as internal.

What appears in most of our studies as the single most critical element in sentence processing and in the development of linguistic knowledge is the extraction and representation of meaning. In the cited examples concerning the synonymity judgments of sentences, the findings (Experiment 2, Chapter 3) indicate that full storage of sentence constituents (as for Sachs, 1967) is not necessary in order to make correct judgments. "Meanings" are instead stored, and, in the context of a synonymity task, meanings are compared and contrasted. It would appear then that information-processing models may be more adequately constructed on the basis of comparing meanings than on the matching of sentence constituents, whether as surface structures or deep structures.

It further appears that the significant aspect of meaning that enters into sentence processing is logical meaning, represented by the logical relationship between agents and patients on one level (the surface level), and between inherent logicomathematical systems on another level (a deeper level). The number lexicon, the time lexicon, the tenses, and the logical linguistic connectives all attest to the logical system properties that enter into linguistic processing and language development.

We propose, then, that logical meaning exercises critical constraint on the development of at least a substantial portion of linguistic knowledge; it is a type of meaning that derives from the logical structures and processes that are inherent in nonlinguistic cognitive functioning. This does not deny that the linguistic system does not have system properties unique unto itself that also affect sentence generation and processing; but the development of knowledge of this system is bound to be constrained by the properties of the child's cognitive capacities which are defined by logicomathematical and other structures.

Developmental Objectification of the Sentence: Intuition and the Reflective Function

The development of linguistic knowledge undergoes a striking change at about 6–7 years of age. Although the child from about $2\frac{1}{2}$ to 7-years old acquires a formidable repertoire of linguistic rules, enough in fact to have led earlier psycholinguists to claim that the child learned all the essentials of syntax by the age of 4 or 5, a significant capacity is still absent—the ability to treat the sentence objectively, that is, to treat it as an object capable of direct manipulation. This phenomenon bears upon the problem of consciousness in language and the nature of intuitions into the grammar. It is evident that without consciousness of what he or she is doing, the child is able to generate language according to a rather complex rule system, which to this date defies wholly adequate description. We know, in part by the errors he makes in speech, and more from corrections he makes of such errors, that the child produces sentences and discourse creatively from such rules. Even more is known from the "grammars" that describe the child's linguistic output. Whether the child can be said to have intuitions into his grammar, as an adult can be said to possess, so that a sentence can be judged grammatical or ungrammatical, is not known. Gleitman and Shipley (quoted in Brown, 1973b) studied three very young children (2-years old) for their judgments of grammaticality (characterizing imperative sentences with correct and incorrect word orders as "good" or "silly"). This was a means of obtaining some indication of children's intuitions into the grammar. They found that the 2-year olds were able to make a "substantial" number of "good" responses to correct sentences, but there was also a high proportion of such responses to incorrect word-order sentences (as Brown and de Villiers and de Villiers point out). When de Villiers and de Villiers (1972) adapted the Gleitman and Shipley method and used it with 8 children who varied in MLU from 2.87 to 4.67, they found that judgments of "wrong" to incorrect sentences did not go over 50% until MLU 4.16 was reached (after Brown's Stage 5). Active correction of incorrect word order was made only by the most advanced subjects with MLU 4.67. Brown suggests the possibility that "children do not have a given syntactic feature on the level of judgment and correction until long after they have it in the level of spontaneous speech and discriminating response [1973b, p. 163]." Our data show, consistent with this, that it is long after knowledge of a syntactic form appears that the ability to make synonymity judgments between active and passive sentences appears, and this is at the age of about 6–7. The evidence shows (Experiments 1 and 2, Chapter 3) that passive sentences were comprehended at least one or two years before the age when children were able to judge that an active sentence and its passive transform are equivalent in meaning. We will discuss the question of synonymity later, here we wish simply to indicate that the ability to make judgments of sentences is dependent upon the ability to deal with the sentence in an objective fashion and it depends on the development of the "reflective function."

The developing objectification of sentences was also evident in the data of our number agreement study (Chapter 5). In imitation, as we have already indicated, many children up to the age of 6 were unable to imitate un-grammatical sentences without transforming them into grammatical sentences. Only at 6-years old could they imitate ungrammatical sentences as they were. This result was not due to difficulty in imitation, per se, because, as the passive and logical connective studies show, even 3-year olds were able to imitate very well. The difficulty appeared instead to be associated with the egocentric rule-boundedness of the preoperational child. This state was paralleled by the child's inability to make correct judgments of the grammaticality of ungrammatical sentences (in respect to the nonagreement in number of relevant sentence constituents). Only at age 7 were children able to go above a chance level in making correct judgments (87%). Although judgments of grammatical and ungrammatical sentences were easier to make (68% at age 4), when matched pairs of grammatical and ungrammatical sentences were analyzed, it was not until age 7 that correct judgments exceeded a chance level. The processes involved in sentence objectification and the reflective function are seen also in the nature of the strategies subjects used in making synonymity judgments of sentences that differed from each other in grammaticality, that is, when one was grammatical and the other ungrammatical. Again for these judgments, only at age 7 was there a level of correct performance above chance. When the children reported their basis for making synonymity judgments, the most advanced strategy involved a comparison between the constituents of the two sentences, and this was found in substantial numbers (55%) only in the 7-year-old subjects (the 4-to 6-year old group reported only 11–12%). This "comparative strategy" reflects the operation of a decentering process, and it may be assumed that one of the components of the reflective function that enables the sentence to be treated in an objective fashion, which is also a feature of operativity and reversibility, is the ability to decenter. In fact, when subjects were asked to make synonymity judgments of nonreversible sentences, they were able to do this at an earlier age than when reversible sentences were involved (Sack, 1973).

This provides further evidence that the comparative strategy requires the ability to decenter because the reversible and nonreversible sentences differed in the reversibility operations required. It also indicates that non-reversible sentences require a type of processing to extract their meaning that is available to the preoperational child. Reversible sentences, however, present a more complex form from which it is more difficult to extract meaning, at least for the purpose of making judgments of synonymy.

The reflective function, then, develops at about the sixth to seventh year and enables the child to deal with sentences as independent objects, either as a totality or as composed of a number of constituents. Two or more of these constituents can be manipulated within the same time frame, modifying one in relation to the other. The child is concomitantly liberated from an egocentric and rigid adherence to a linguistic rule system.

Thus, if intuition into the grammaticality of sentences is based on a judgmental criterion, the evidence at this point is very meager as to the ability of children to have such intuitions prior to about age 5–7. Nor are children younger than about age 6 or 7 able to make judgments of the synonymity of sentences. If intuition were based on another criterion, such as the ability to correct incorrect sentences lexically and syntactically, one could say that children were capable of such "intuitions," at least on an implicit, nonconscious level. If an "intuition" criterion were based on the ability to recognize sentences on the basis of their equivalence in meaning, then one might say that young children had such intuitions, as it was evident from Experiment 2, Chapter 3 that children could make such judgments. However, such criteria would be based on a notion of "intuition" into the grammar that departs radically from a phenomenological "intuition" that is at least partly conscious. It appears, then, that in a complete sense the process of linguistic intuition has at least two components: an unconscious process of comparing meaning and testing grammatical acceptability according to known rules, and a conscious process that is at least partially under the control of the reflective function. The latter component is the later in development.

Synonymity

Chomsky (1957) claimed that synonymity, that is, the equivalence in meaning of sentences, could not be the basis for constructing a grammar; that the similarities among sentences had to be defined in structural rather than semantic terms. Even the 1965 version that introduced the semantic component into the base did not alter the fundamental view concerning synonymity, although, in the case of active and passive sentences, J. J. Katz and Postal (1964) were willing to recognize that they could be synonymous, although their interpretation was made on syntactic grounds. Although the "extended standard theory" recognizes that some of the meaning of the passive sentence can be determined by its surface structure, there nevertheless appears to be no basic change in the theory in respect to synonymity.

In the study in which we were concerned with the psychological judgments of the synonymity of active and passive sentences, it was recognized that in some sense an active and passive sentence could differ in meaning, but that in other senses most passives could act as adequate paraphrases and be considered as logically equivalent to their corresponding activities. It was nevertheless found in Experiment 1 (Chapter 3) that linguistic judgments of sentence synonymy (equivalence in meaning) was achieved only at the second-grade level (7-years old), which was also true for the subject—object reversal sentences (without passivization). When a picture equivalent task was used as a criterion measure, response to the subject—object reversal sentences was near-perfect at kindergarten, although active—passive pair judgments never went above chance even in the second grade. Experiment 2 verified the synonymy effect in linguistic judgment, that is, the lag between knowledge of the passive itself and the meaning equivalence of active—passive sentence pairs. It also showed, as we have already pointed out, younger children could indicate in recognition (and also recall) tasks that actives and passives had the same meaning to them.

All these facts suggest that the judgment of synonymity does not occur at the surface structure level. In fact, the evidence of Experiment 2 (Chapter 3) shows that word order and verb changes in surface structure interfered with both sentence comprehension and judgment. Thus, the equivalence of sentences was judged at a meaning level and was not bound up in sentence (i.e., syntactic) form. In addition, it was shown that the synonymy of sentences with lexical synonyms was understood at nursery school level (Sack, 1973). Thus, the principal deterrents to making meaning equivalence judgments were (1) the nature of the syntactic form in which meaning was represented, which required some type of reprocessing to extract its meaning, and (2) the judgmental process itself, which as we have indicated, is possessed only when the child has developed the reflective function.

Thus, it is evident that surface structure is not processed directly by children in making synonymy judgments, in fact it may interfere with them. Likewise, it seems that accounting for synonymity solely in terms of deep syntactic structure is not sufficient either. As in all the phenomena we have studied, it would appear that, at the *deep* level, both syntactic rules and cognitive processes are involved in affecting the way in which sentences are processed.

Appendix A

Passive Study—Experiment 1

1.

The experimenter presents *two dolls, Mark* and *Susan.*

The experimenter says: *Here are two dolls that we call Mark and Susan. Do you know which one is Mark and which one is Susan? Take the dolls and show me: Mark pushes Susan. Now show me with the dolls what* **Susan pushes Mark** *would look like. Very good. What would* **Mark is pushed by Susan** *look like? Now show me* **Susan is pushed by Mark***.*

2

The experimenter says: *Show me what* **Mark washes the car** *would look like with the toys here. Show me what* **The car washes Mark** *would look like. Does that mean anything? Show me what* **The car is washed by Mark** *would look like. Does that mean anything?*

3

The experimenter presents a *truck* and a *car.*

The experimenter says: *Show me* **The truck is bumped by the car***. Show me* **The truck bumps the car***. Show me now* **The car bumps the truck***. Now show me* **The car is bumped by the truck***.*

4

The experimenter presents pictures illustrating *Mark hits Susan* and *Susan hits Mark.*

The experimenter says: *Here are some pictures about Mark and Susan. First, can you say* **Mark hits Susan**? *Let me hear you say that. Now point to the picture that shows us* **Mark hits Susan***. Can you say* **Susan is hit by Mark**? *Say it out loud. Now point to the picture that shows us* **Susan is hit by Mark***. Can you say* **Susan hits Mark**? *Let me hear you say that. Point to the picture that shows* **Susan hits Mark***. Now say* **Mark is hit by Susan***. Very good. Show me which picture is* **Mark is hit by Susan***.*

5

The experimenter presents four pictures that illustrate the set *Susan gives the book to Mark.*

The experimenter says: *Say these two sentences out loud:* **Susan gives the book to Mark. Mark is given the book by Susan***. Now pick out the pictures that show what you just said. Listen to these sentences again:* **Susan gives the book to Mark. Mark is given the book by Susan***. Do they* **mean** *the same thing or do they mean something different? Very good. Now say these two sentences aloud:* **Susan is given the book by Mark; Susan gives the book to Mark***. Now pick out the pictures that show what you just said. Listen to them again:* **Susan is given the book by Mark. Susan gives the book to Mark***. Are they different or the same?*

6

The experimenter presents two pictures of *Mark washes the car.*

The experimenter says: *Let me hear you say* **Mark washes the car***. Point to the picture that shows* **Mark washes the car***. Which picture shows* **The car washes Mark**? *Which picture shows* **The car is washed by Mark**?

7

The experimenter presents the four pictures that illustrate the set *Mark hits Susan.*

The experimenter says: *Say these two sentences aloud:* **Mark hits Susan. Susan hits Mark.** *Which pictures show what you just said? Listen again:* **Mark hits Susan. Susan hits Mark.** *Are they the same or different? Now say these two sentences:* **Susan is hit by Mark. Mark hits Susan.** *Pick out the pictures that show what you just said. Listen again:* **Susan is hit by Mark. Mark hits Susan.** *Are they different or the same?*

8

The experimenter presents the first two pictures that illustrate the set *Susan gives the book to Mark.*

The experimenter says: *Let me hear you say* **Susan is given the book by Mark.** *Pick out the picture that shows this. Now can you say* **Susan gives the book to Mark?** *Pick out the picture that shows* **Susan gives the book to Mark.** *Now say* **Mark gives the book to Susan.** *Could you pick out the picture that shows* **Mark gives the book to Susan?** *Let me hear you say* **Mark is given the book by Susan.** *Pick out the picture that shows* **Mark is given the book by Susan.**

9

The experimenter presents the dolls *Mark* and *Susan.*

The experimenter says: *Here are Mark and Susan again. Now say these two sentences out loud:* **Mark pushes Susan; Susan is pushed by Mark.** *Show me how what you just said would look like with these toys. Listen to these sentences again:* **Mark pushes Susan; Susan is pushed by Mark.** *Do these two sentences mean two different things or do they mean the same thing?*

The experimenter acts out with dolls: *Mark pushes Susan.*

The experimenter says: *Tell me what is happening but start your sentence with* **Susan.**

The experimenter acts out with dolls: *Susan pushes Mark.*

The experimenter says: *Tell me what is happening now, but start your sentence with* **Mark.**

10

The experimenter acts out: *The truck bumps the car.*

The experimenter says: *Tell me what is happening but start your story with* **The car**.

The experimenter acts out: *The car bumps the truck.*

The experimenter says: *Tell me what is happening but start your story with* **The truck**. *Very good. Now say these two sentences out loud:* **The truck bumps the car. The car is bumped by the truck.** *Show me how what you just said would look like with these toys. Listen to these sentences again:* **The truck bumps the car. The car is bumped by the truck.** *Do these sentences mean two different things or do they mean the same thing?*

Appendix B

Number Language Instrument[1]

Introduction

The experimenter says: *We are going to play some games. Sometimes I will show you some things and ask you questions about them and sometimes I will just ask you questions. Please don't touch any of the things I show you. This is just a game and if you're not sure of an answer, guess. Are you ready to begin?*

Preliminary Explanation: Items 1–3.

1. The experimenter shows the subject a *pig* and a *bird*. The experimenter asks:
   a. *Is the animal here the same kind of animal as the animal here?* If answer is *NO*, the experimenter continues with Number 2.
   b. If answer is *YES*, the experimenter says: *Wrong, this one is a pig and this one is a bird.*

2. The experimenter shows *two horses*. The experimenter asks:
   a. *Is the animal here the same kind of animal as the animal here?* If answer is *YES*, the experimenter continues with Number 3.
   b. If answer is *NO*, the experimenter says: *Wrong, they are both horses, even though they are not the same color.*

---

[1] The NLI was prepared in two forms, the main instrument indicated here and a revision for 2- to 4-year olds. The revised form either deleted items kindergartners were unable to answer or revised them to make their contents easier for younger children to process.

379

3. The experimenter shows *two cows.* The experimenter asks:
    a. *Is the animal here the same kind of animal as the animal here ?* If answer is *YES,* the experimenter continues with Number 4.
    b. If answer is *NO,* the experimenter says: *Wrong, they are both cows, even though this one's head is up and this one's head is down.*
4. a. The experimenter shows *four red sticks* and says: *Look at these sticks.* The experimenter places a group of *four green sticks* behind a group of *four red sticks* and says: *Now look at these sticks. Are these sticks here* (the experimenter points to *four red sticks*) *the same as these sticks here* (the experimenter points to *four green sticks*) *in any way?*
    b. If response is *YES,* the experimenter asks: *In what way are the sticks here the same as the sticks here?*
    c. If the subject gives irrelevant or wrong answer to 4b, the experimenter prods by asking: *Are they the same in any other way?*
    d. Regardless of the subject's response to 4a, the experimenter replaces the *four red sticks* with the *six red sticks* and asks: *Are these sticks here* (the experimenter points to *six red sticks*) *the same as these sticks here* (the experimenter points to *four green sticks*) *in any way?*
    e. If response is *YES,* the experimenter asks: *In what way are the sticks here the same as the sticks here?*
    f. If the response is any other than **equal in number,** the experimenter asks: *Are they the same in any other way?*
5. The experimenter presents a set of *trains* in correct order and says: *This is the way the trains should look.* The experimenter adds set of *trains* with *engine* out of order and asks:
    a. *Is there anything wrong here?*
    b. If answer is *YES,* the experimenter asks: *What is wrong?*
    c. If irrelevant answer is given, the experimenter asks: *Is there anything else wrong?*
6. a. The experimenter shows *two* sets of *four green sticks* which are in random array. The experimenter asks: *Is the number of sticks here* (the experimenter points to one set) *the same as the number of sticks here* (the experimenter points to other set)?
    b. The experimenter replaces one of the sets of *four sticks* (set A) with set of *five sticks.* The experimenter asks: *Is the number of sticks here the same as the number of sticks here?* (The experimenter points.)
7. a. The experimenter shows *three ordered houses* with the backs of the *houses* facing the subject. The experimenter asks: *Are these houses in size place?*
    b. The experimenter adds *house* out of order (smallest house in third position). The experimenter asks: *Are these houses in size place?*
8. The experimenter shows *four houses* in order from small to large with

four colored sticks in order, placed in correspondence in front of the houses. The experimenter asks:

  a. *Is the order of the houses the same as the order of the sticks?*

  b. The experimenter adds *black stick* in correct order (between *blue* and *red sticks*—intermediate size and therefore lack of correspondence). The experimenter asks: *Is the order of the houses the same as the order of the sticks?*

  c. The experimenter adds *purple stick* in wrong order (between *yellow* and *green sticks*). The experimenter asks: *Is the order of the houses the same as the order of the sticks?*

9. The experimenter shows *seven assorted shapes* and *nine assorted objects*. The experimenter asks: *Is the quantity of things here* (the experimenter points to *shapes*) *the same as the quantity of things here* (the experimenter points to *objects*)?

  a. The subject responds. The experimenter asks: *How do you know?*

  b. The experimenter replaces *nine objects* with *seven objects*. The experimenter asks (while pointing): *Is the quantity of things here the same as the quantity of things here?*

  b1. The experimenter asks: *How do you know?*

10. The experimenter shows *four colored sticks* that were used previously in Question 8 (*blue, red, yellow, green*). The experimenter says: *Point to the red stick. Point to the blue stick. Point to the yellow stick. Point to the green stick.* If the subject makes any errors, the experimenter corrects on color naming.

  a. The experimenter points to the left and asks: *Starting from here, is the red stick before or after the blue stick?*

  b. The experimenter points to the left and asks: *Starting from here, is the yellow stick behind or in front of the green stick?*

11. a. The experimenter shows *five blue sticks* in front of *five green rectangles*. The experimenter asks: *Is the amount of things here* (the experimenter points to blue sticks) *the same as the amount of things here* (the experimenter points to green rectangles)?

  b. The experimenter replaces *five blue sticks* with *six blue sticks*. The experimenter asks: *Is the amount of things here* (the experimenter points to blue sticks) *the same as the amount of things here* (the experimenter points to green rectangles)?

12, 13, 14. The experimenter says: *When you hear a word, sometimes it makes you think of another word. If you hear cat, you might think of milk or purr or dog or black, almost anything.*

  x. *What does cat make you think of?*

  y. *What does eat make you think of?* (If the subject responds to *cat* or *eat* with a multi-word answer, the experimenter says: *say the first* **word** *that it makes you think of. Only say* **one** *word.*)*What does* _____ *make you think of?*

  12a. *less*   13a. *none*   14w. *fewer*

12b. *eleventh*	13b. *two*	14x. *any*
12c. *position*	13c. *billion*	14y. *several*
12d. *seventy-second*	13d. *amount*	14z. *fewest*
12e. *next*	13e. *fourteen*	
12f. *first*	13f. *number*	

15, 16, The experimenter says: *I am going to say a word to you. Sometimes a word makes you think of a lot of other words that seem like it. If you hear the word chair you might think of seat, bench, stool.*

    x. *What does the word night make you think of? Say as many words that seem like it as you can. What does the word _____ make you think of?* (The experimenter gives the subject 15 sec for each.)

15a. *seven*	16a. *ninety-ninth*
15b. *all*	16b. *more*
15c. *fifty*	16c. *fortieth*
15d. *hundred*	16d. *eighth*

17, 18, 19. The experimenter says: *Now we are going to play another game.*

    x. *Which word goes better with brother: sister or father?* Repeat until understood, if necessary. The experimenter asks: *Which word goes better with_____:_____ or _____?*

17a. third: ninth–bird	18a. single: double–bubble	19a. end: number–next
17b. fourth: sixth–path	18b. all: several–none	19b. pair: series–amount
17c. first: time–tenth	18c. two: arms–five	19c. twelve: eighty–sixteenth
17d. primary: second-ary–library	18d. twenty: dirty–sixth	19d. fifteenth: third–eleven
17e. eighteenth: sweet–second	18e. twelve: eleven–o'clock	19e. nineteenth: book–seven
	18f. two: eight–blue	19f. ten: marbles–seventeenth
		19x. most: toys–least
		19y. many: children–few

20a. The experimenter shows the subject a *3*. The experimenter asks: *What do we call this?* If the subject says, **A number,** the experimenter asks: *What number?*

  b. The experimenter shows the subject a *6*. The experimenter asks: *What do we call this?* If the subject says, **A number,** the experimenter asks: *What number?*

  c. The experimenter shows the subject a *12*. The experimenter asks: *What do we call this?* If the subject says, **A number**, the experimenter asks: *What number?*

21a. The experimenter shows the subject a *4th*. The experimenter asks:

What do we call this ? If the subject says, **A number,** the experimenter asks: *What number ?*

  b. The experimenter shows the subject a *5th.* The experimenter asks: *What do we call this ?* If the subject says, **A number,** the experimenter asks: *What number ?*

  c. The experimenter shows the subject a *9th.* The experimenter asks: *What do we call this ?* If the subject says, **A number,** the experimenter asks: *What number ?*

22, 23. The experimenter says: *Sometimes a word stands for another word or means almost the same thing. For example, large means big. What does _____ mean ?*

22a. *zero*	23a. *begin*
22b. *amount*	23b. *follow*
22c. *dozen*	23c. *below*

24, 25. The experimenter shows *twelve cards* with number symbols on them. (Arranged as follows: *2, 11, 11th, 1, 10th, 8, 2nd, 8th, 10, 1st, 7, 7th*). The experimenter says:

  24a. *Point to the card with only the number 7 on it.*
  24b. *Point to the card with only the number 11 on it.*
    c. *Point to the card with only the number 1 on it.*
  25a. *Point to the card that has 2nd on it.*
    b. *Point to the card that has 8th on it.*
    c. *Point to the card that has 10th on it.*

26, 27. The experimenter says: *Sometimes a word stands for another word or means almost the same thing. For example, as I said before, large means big. Does _____ mean _____ or _____ ?*

26a. *pair: three–two*	27a. *last: tall–end*
26b. *triple: three–four*	27b. *above: on top of–next to*
26c. *double: trouble–twice*	27c. *middle: midget–center*
26x. *some: part–all*	

28. The experimenter shows five objects (*yellow doughnut, small house, red disc, orange circle, small blue cup*). The experimenter asks:

  a. *What is the number of things on the card ?*
  b. The experimenter adds *large blue cup.* The experimenter asks: *What is the number of things on the card ?*

29. The experimenter shows *twelve* differently *colored sticks* of same size in a row with *purple stick* on the subject's left.

  a. The experimenter points to *3rd (yellow) stick* and asks (while indicating beginning): *Starting from here, what position is this ?* If the subject gives irrelevant answer, prod by asking: *Is it the first one ?* (If the subject says no, the experimenter asks: *Which one is it ?*)

  b. The experimenter points to *2nd (black) stick* and asks (while indicating beginning): *Starting from here, what position is this ?* If the subject gives irrelevant answer, prod by asking: *Is it the first one ?* (If the subject says no, the experimenter asks: (*Which one is it ?*)

30. The experimenter shows *seven red sticks* and *nine green sticks* arranged in a row with *two red sticks* to the subject's left. The experimenter points to *first red stick* and asks:
  x. *What color is this stick?* (If the subject gives wrong answer, the experimenter corrects).
  y. The experimenter points to *first green stick* and asks: *What color is this stick?* (If the subject gives wrong answer, the experimenter corrects).
  a. *Is the number of red sticks, six, seven, or eight?*
31. The experimenter shows *five* different *colored sticks* (*green, yellow, purple red, blue*) with *green stick* at the subject's left. The experimenter points to *first (green) stick* and asks: *Starting from here, is the red stick in the third, fourth, or fifth place?*
32, 33, 34, 35.   The experimenter asks:
  32a. *What is six and five equal to?*
  32b. *If you had 12 marbles and gave away 4, how many would you have?*
  32c. *What number is less than 11 but more than 9?*
  33a. *What position comes after the first one but before the third?*
  33b. *If there were four children on line in front of you, which place would you be in?*
  33c. *If you were in the fifth place in a line, and you moved back seven more places, which place would you be in?*
  34a. *Does 1 plus 1 equal 3, 2, or 4?*
  34b. *Is 29 less than 30, more than 30, or equal to 30?*
  34c. *Does 23 take away 16 equal 6, 7, or 8?*
  35a. *Does the eighteenth place in a line come before the twentieth, before the sixteenth, or before the eighth place?*
  35b. *Are there five places before the fifth one, five places before the sixth one, or five places before the fourth one in a line?*
  35c. *If you were on the fourteenth step on a staircase and you went up eight more, would you then be on the twenty-second, twenty-third, or twenty-fourth step?*
36. The experimenter says: *I am going to ask you to count for a while. I'll tell you when to stop. Go ahead.*
   The experimenter stops the subject after 23 by saying: *That's fine.*
37a. The experimenter says: *What comes after first?*
37b. If the subject says *second*, the experimenter says: *Please continue counting like that.* The experimenter stops the subject after twenty third by saying: *That's fine.*

Appendix C

Number Agreement
Study–Sentence Lists

List 1

Grammatical and Ungrammatical*

1. *A bear is kicking.*
2. **A bear are kicking.*
3. *Two monkeys are jumping twice.*
4. **A monkey jump and jump.*
5. **Two monkeys is jumping twice.*
6. *A monkey is kicking all the time.*
7. *A bear is walking twice.*
8. **Two tigers is running once.*
9. **A monkey are kicking all the time.*
10. *A lion runs all the time.*
11. *A monkey jumps and jumps.*
12. *Two tigers are running once.*
13. **A lion run all the time.*
14. **A bear are walking twice.*

Equivalence Pairs

1. **Two tigers is running once.*
   Two tigers are running once.
2. *A lion runs all the time.*
   **A lion run all the time.*
3. *A monkey jumps and jumps.*
   **A monkey jump and jump.*

385

4. *Two monkeys is jumping twice.*
   Two monkeys are jumping twice.
5. *A monkey is kicking all the time.*
   **A monkey are kicking all the time.*
6. *A bear is walking twice.*
   A bear is walking twice.
7. **A bear are kicking.*
   A bear is kicking.
8. **A lion are jumping twice.*
   A lion is jumping twice.
9. *Two tigers jump.*
   Two tigers jump.

List 2

*Grammatical and Ungrammatical**

1. *Two lions walk twice.*
2. **Two lions walks twice.*
3. *Two tigers run all the time.*
4. **Two lions sleeps and kicks.*
5. **Two tigers runs all the time.*
6. *A tiger kicks and kicks twice.*
7. *Two bears jump and jump.*
8. **A monkey are running once.*
9. **A tiger kick and kick twice.*
10. *A lion jumps once.*
11. *Two lions sleep and kick.*
12. **A lion jump once.*
13. *A monkey is running once.*
14. **Two bears jumps and jumps.*

Equivalence Pairs

1. *A monkey is running once.*
   **A monkey are running once.*
2. *A lion jumps once.*
   **A lion jump once.*
3. **Two lions sleeps and kicks.*
   Two lions sleep and kick.
4. *Two tigers run all the time.*
   **Two tigers runs all the time.*
5. *A tiger kicks and kicks twice.*
   **A tiger kick and kick twice.*
6. *A bear is walking twice.*
   A bear is walking twice.

7. *Two bears jump and jump.*
   *Two bears jumps and jumps.
8. **Two lions walks twice.*
   Two lions walk twice.
9. *Two tigers run.*
   Two tigers run.

List 3

Grammatical and Ungrammatical*

1. *A lion walks.*
2. **A lion walk.*
3. *Two tigers walk.*
4. **Two monkeys is walking.*
5. **Two tigers walks.*
6. *A tiger is running.*
6. *A tiger is running.*
7. *Two bears are kicking all the time.*
8. **A monkey run once.*
9. **A tiger are running.*
10. *Two tigers jump once.*
11. *Two monkeys are walking.*
12. *A monkey runs once.*
13. **Two tigers jumps once.*
14. **Two bears is kicking all the time.*

Equivalence Pairs

1. **A monkey run once.*
   A monkey runs once.
2. *Two bears are kicking all the time.*
   *Two bears is kicking all the time.
3. *Two monkeys are walking.*
   *Two monkey is walking.
4. **Two tigers walks.*
   Two tigers walk.
5. *A tiger is running.*
   *A tiger are running.
6. *A bear jumps.*
   A bear jumps.
7. **Two bears is kicking all the time.*
   Two bears are kicking all the time.
8. **A lion walk.*
   A lion walks.
9. *Two tigers run.*
   Two tiger run.

Appendix D–1

Connective Study

TABLE 1

Basic Boolean Operations Between Classes[a]

Class operation		Propositional counterpart
Intersection	A and B are two parts of C, their intersection, denoted as $\cap$, is the part common to A and B. These elements are *all* the elements common to A and B. Intersection is usually translated *and*.	$A \cdot B$
Union	Denoted as $\cup$, it is the part of E constituted by all the elements belonging either to A or to B or to both (inclusive reading)—including all those which belong at once to both of these parts, i.e., the intersection $A \cap B$). In the case of disjoint classes (as shown here) the intersection is null. Union is usually translated *or*.	$A \vee B$
Complementation	By this operation, for each part of the universe C, one can associate its complement, i.e., A' as the complement of A. Complementation may be translated *not*.	$\bar{A}$

[a] From Barbut (1967).

The above operations are marked by a basic duality, i.e., every expression written with the symbol $\cap$ or $\cup$ has its dual by the exchange of $\cup$ and $\cap$ (or *and* and *or*). This duality results from the operation of complementation.

N. B. In the appendices we follow the convention of using pirmes for *not*, whereas in the text overbars are used. They are interchangeable.

Appendix D-2

Cognitive Functions—Defined

Adjunction Functions

Element adjunction functions were tested both with identical elements and with foreign (nonidentical) elements. For example, having classified *big* and *little girls*, the subject is given another *little girl* for further classification (*adjunction of identical element*), or for example, having classified *girls* and *little boys*, the subject is given *one big boy* to classify (*adjunction of foreign element*). Adjunction functions were scored as correct if the element was added to the proper subclass (in the case of identical elements) or to one of the dimensional classes to which it was relevant (in the case of foreign elements, in the above example, the *big boy* element could have been correctly added to either a class of *big* [*girl*] *dolls* or to the class of *boy* [*little*] *dolls*). Notably, these scoring criteria for functions insist that some base of classification activity exist before they can be correct. If no appropriate subclasses have been maintained previously by subjects no adjunction function can be considered correct. In a sense, then, these adjunction tasks are **class maintenance** tasks, testing classification subprocesses (i.e., these are not simply *identity* functions in a stimulus-matching sense).

Dichotomy

Dichotomy operations tested were of two sorts. The first tested a simple (A and $A' = B$) dichotomy with three elements in each subclass (of *big* and *little girls*). Here the subject was scored correct if he or she clustered elements of each subclass together or if, when a partitioned space was presented, he or she used the partition to divide the two subclasses.

The second sort of dichotomy operation was a full set dichotomy which was requested throughout the battery at each major set extension. Six such dichotomies were possible (e.g., *big/little, girls/boys; big/little, people/animals* [= *bears*] *; big/little, people/animals* [= *bears* and *monkeys*]). For correct attainment of this dichotomy it was necessary that it be achieved on the basis of the total set (dichotomies achieved before complete set element adjunction, for example were not considered correct). Classification responses during testing, then, were inspected at all points at which the subject was working with the proper set size in order to determine dichotomy achievement. Notably, however, processes by which these dichotomies were achieved were not taken into acount by scoring procedures adopted. Thus, for example, some dichotomies may have been achieved by maintenance of a standing dichotomy over plural element adjunctions others by total set rearrangement after set removal.

Appendix D-3

Constituent Functions—Defined

The cognitive level termed **constituent functions** defines the logic of preoperatory structures (Piaget, 1968a, p. 231). Piaget differentiates these constituting functions, *"fonctions constituantes,"* from constituted functions, *"fonctions constituees,"* which are formed later by the gradual qualification of constituting functions and their integration with operations. According to Piaget, "We call 'constituted' the innumerable differentiated functions which elaborate in interaction with operations. Their most general character is due to passage from qualitative co-properties resulting from elementary "applications" to operationally quantifiable covariations, then to variations of variations, etc. [Piaget, 1968a, p. 223]." Constituent functions appear genetically earlier than operations (when operations are defined in the Piagetian sense) (Piaget, 1968a, p. 202), and in fact represent "the formative matrix of future operatory structures [Piaget, 1968a, p. 217]."

Whereas operations suppose a differentiation between intension and extension and a quantification of classificatory extension, functions are mainly intensional and qualitative. Although the function informs structure and is therefore "logical" in nature (p. 231), the function is dominated by order rather than by relation. It consists in the establishment of an oriented one-way, *"unovique à droite"* and dependent correspondence between properties of objects (e.g., $x = f(y)$ where "x is the same color as y" and where determination of the color of x is dependent upon prior determination of the color of y), and is thus not reversible.

Piaget graphs function as a many-to-one correspondence:

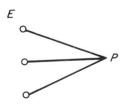

(where *E* and *F* are sets; notably set and element are confounded in *F*). A one-to-many inverse correspondence is represented by operational structure, however:

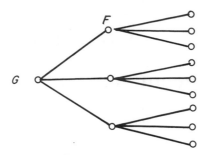

In order to attain this latter process, "It is necessary that a subject can pass indifferently from one sense of orientation to the other in the system of these co-univocal correspondences (one to many or many to one) [Piaget, 1968b, p. 219]." The reversibility involved here allows for an inclusion system, basic to hierarchical classification, and thus to quantification of class extension.

According to Piaget, functions arise naturally from action schemes which are viewed as producing oriented assimilation of objects and thus as primitive types of "applications." Application is here considered in the mathematical sense; "An application is a correspondence which to each element *x* of a set *A* (called departure set of the application) associates one and only one element of a set *B* (called arrival set of the application) [Barbut, 1967]." Constituent functions then are defined by Piaget as "the very dependencies common to schemes of action [p. 203]." Specifically they characterize "The links introduced or noticed between the objects to which the action scheme is applied [p. 206]."

The formative mechanisms that produce functions are defined by both Piaget (1968a) and Grize (1967) as a set of elementary coordinators that are common to action and to a formal combinatory logic, but limited by nonreversibility here. These mechanisms would include: W—a repeator, I—an identifier, C—a permuter which works by either substitution or permutation, B—an associator.

Piaget (1968a) is careful to explain that these formative mechanisms have both physical and cognitive correlates: "When the subject admits a physical or objective dependency $y = f'(x)$ (where $f' =$ physical function) he must begin by using and 'applying' a mental or cognitive dependency $y = f(x)$ of which the significance is that to know or determine *y* it is necessary first to know *x* [p. 213]."

Grize (1967) holds that there is a direct passage from function to operatory inclusion of classes. Piaget (1968, p. 217) supports this theoretically and an experiment by Schmid-Kitzikis (cited in Piaget, 1968a) exemplifies this passage empirically. Grize notes two modes of classification: one by local constructions, or direct union of individual elements; the other by subdivision of the initial set in classes and subclasses. Piaget (1968a, p. 220) comments that this theoretical division is relative to the instruments of construction: the individual unions are relative to one-way applications (i.e., functions) and the subvidisions to reversible operations of inclusion. There are two levels here, continues Piaget, one preoperatory, the other operatory. Note, says Piaget, that "in his spontaneous classifications, the child himself passes in a general fashion from the first approach to the second, the latter being imposed later by the development of operatory structures which surpass constituent functions by generalizing co-univocal correspondences in the two senses of these relations [p. 220]." (See preceding diagrams.)

It should be noted finally, however, that the formal logical character of function and compositions of functions is described by Grize (1967) and supported by Piaget (1968a) as a logical category structure. Although Piaget makes some comments on the distinction between this logical structure and that of the Boolean algebra-defined grouping (p. 222) which related to operational class logic, these formal relations (category logic—algebra of Boole) are relatively unelaborated.

Grize holds, with the general support of Piaget, that functions appear to express the constructive aspect of classification (see p. 181). Piaget adds, "It is possible also—and that would permit explanation of precocious success on certain tasks—that the structuring functions are, at a given moment of genesis, a type of concrete substitute, acted, of the combinatory future [Piaget, 1968a, p. 196]." (Translations from Piaget, 1968a in this section are by Barbara Lust).

In defining and isolating cognitive functions, then, this study isolates operative mechanisms developmentally antecedent to fully structured operations. Early classification activity,showing subjects' establishment of identical coproperties among two or more elements by the mechanisms of I-identifier and B-associator, are interpreted in this study as functional classifications. They characterize a constituent functional stage in the development of classification processes and they have been evaluated in isolation as functions per se. Constituent functional levels have been specified for each cognitive process in general accord with Piagetian theory: intersection, union, complementation, vicariance. The above remarks must be applied to the interpretation of these levels.

Appendix D–4

Cognitive Operations and Tasks—Defined

Logical Union (Logical Addition)

A class B may consist of subclasses A and A' in which A and A' are disjoint and A' is thus the complement of A under B. A and A' are extensional parts which must be related by the operation of inclusion to the whole B. This operation, however, requires that the S is able to hold B constant conceptually while dissociating its parts: he must not identify B with its extension A and A' as young children do.

Thus says Piaget, young children, when asked the question "All the A, are they B?" (e. g., *All the white beads, are they wooden*"), will not translate the concept of this B to its extension A and A', thus realizing "All the A are some B." In other words, they are not capable of performing the logical inversion operation, $A = B - A'$. The reason for this difficulty is that "A, once separated from B (in act or thought), the whole B no longer exists as visible collection, but solely as abstract class, and the relation between the subclass A and this class perceptively dissociated but abstractly invariant independently of the dissociation [Piaget & Inhelder, 1967, p. 67]." must be achieved. The essence of logical inclusion then is to "constitute precisely a joining (of classes) in extension and not simply a differentiation in intension [Piaget & Inhelder, 1967, p. 108]."

Young children, given the full class B, may be able to differentiate it into two subclasses (or collections actually), A and A', yet not being able to perform the inverse operation $B = A - A'$, which is necessary to this inclusion question. In the preoperational situation A and A' are differentiated but not hierarchized with regard to B. Subjects' responses to the inclusion task in this study are analyzed with regard to subjects' ability to perform the logical inversion operation necessitated by logical inclusion. Other tasks assessed subjects' ability to create the more primitive differentiation $A + A' = B$ (see Dichotomy in Appendix D-2).

Inclusion Task

.The child is presented with a display of the $B = A + A'$ set. Here $B = girls$, $A = big$ (*girls*), $A' = little$ (*girls*). A series of questions test the subjects' conceptualization of the hierarchical classificatory structure of the full class B.

1. Class membership ($a \in A$): this tests the child's ability to apply a given predicate, e.g., *girl*, to a single element. This is essentially class **intension**.

2. Logical inclusion: Subjects, by this question, are asked to dissociate parts A and A' from the whole B cognitively and, while holding the class B constant as a cognitive reference, compare it to one of its parts, e.g., A. For example, subjects would be asked to judge which is bigger—the class of all the *girl dolls* or the class of all the *big dolls*.

3. Four questions are used to judge subjects' quantification of the class predicate, or articulation of the extensional qualities of classes. Two are of the type A < B, asking if all the elements of a part A show characteristics of the whole B (correct response is "Yes"); two are of the type $B > A$, asking if all the elements of a whole B present the characteristics of the part A (correct response is "No").

Class Intersection (Logical Multiplication)

Given: a set of elements differentiated by two dimensions of two values each (*boys* and *girls, big* and *little*) which can be exhaustively divided into two classes, A and A' according to either dimension. Thus $B_1 = A_1 + A_1' \rightarrow$ *girls and boys*, and $B_2 = A_2 + A_2' \rightarrow big$ and *little*. B is in each case the (additive) union of the two classes A and A'. "The multiplicative classification then will consist in classing the elements at the same time according to the additive classification B_1, and according to the additive classification B_2, which will produce four distinct classes [Piaget & Inhelder, 1967, p. 153]": $B_1 \times B_2 = A_1A_2 + A_1A_2' + A_1'A_2 + A_1'A_2' = B_1B_2$.

The matrix or double entry table is the symbolic means of representing these four multiplicative classes in such a way as to maintain the spatial relations of the additive subclasses in integration with multiplicative relations:

	A_1	A_1'
A_2		
A_2'		

Logical multiplication is seen thus to be logically more complex than addition because multiplication, as seen above, implies addition, although the subject achieves a mastery of these two classificatory operations relatively synchronically "for reasons of internal operatory coherence. [Piaget & Inhelder, 1967, p. 153]."

Matrix (Abstract) Task

For this task, a partial matrix set-up of these four multiplication classes is established for the child. An exemplar from three of the four multiplicative cells is placed for the child (leaving the bottom-right cell empty). The subject must complete the matrix by choice of an exemplar to fill the missing cell. Notably this requires abstraction of the dimensions (or classes) relevant to both axes and the choice of an exemplar that satisfies both dimensions at once. It is the simultaneity of this binary reference that characterizes the multiplicative aspect of this operation (*biunivocal* correspondence of classes).

Matrix (Constructed) Task

This task, a spontaneous or constructive-type multiplicative classification adapted from Piagetian procedures (Piaget & Inhelder, 1967, p. 168), calls for the construction of four classes in a matrix form (an open box partitioned to four cells), in intersecting order prescribed by the double entry table structure. Subjects are presented with a randomized four-class universe created by the multiplication of two 2-valued dimensions as above (size × sex) with three exemplars in each class. This is formally identical to the set in the matrix (abstraction) task, but here full extension is involved rather than a single exemplar. (This set is identical to that used in the spontaneous classification task, and to that used in linguistic tasks except for the omission of the animals subset.)

This matrix (constructed) task calls for the subject's complete classification of the set into the four appropriate classes, necessitating the subject's establishment of relevant classificatory criteria, as well as the arrangement of these classes, in order, showing intersection in the partitioned cells. As in the matrix (abstraction) task, justification and stability are requested in order to assure that an intersection order has been applied neither by chance nor by perceptual mechanism alone.

Class Complementation: Simple Set

Assessment of complementation was by a specific complementation operation, called by Piaget **espèce unique** or **singular class**. The child, having achieved some classification (or merely structuration) of one set of elements (*big/little* [*girls*]), is given a single new element which shares a criterion (*little*) with the former elements but also represents a new criterion (*boy*). The child then has the option of merely adding this new element to his previous classification (as another little element), thus recognizing its positive quality, or of recognizing that a reclassification is necessary with regard to this new element, thus recognizing its negative or complementary property (*boy*). In the latter case, he must treat this single exemplar as *standing for* or in itself constituting a class, thus giving the *girls/boy* reclassification by shifting *big* and *little girls* to the same side of the dichotomy partition (i.e., *girls/boy*).

In this cognitive battery, if the child first added the *doll* to his standing classification, he was then asked if he could do it another way. If he succeeded on either of these items, he then was scored as *operational*. Constituent functional levels of this operation are defined by the child's necessitating plural elements, thus figurative support, in order to achieve the complementation operation (in this case to give the *girls/boys* classification). In this battery the child was first offered two more *little boys*, and asked again for another way of classifying; then *one big boy*; then *two* more *big boys*. He was then asked if all these could be reclassified. After this, the experimenter removed and re-randomized all dolls, re-requesting reclassification. If the subject discontinued his previous classification by giving the relevant *boys/girls* classification at any point in this series of items he was scored as *constituent functions* in his comprehension of complementation. If the child never succeeded in reclassifying the elements according to a positive set, *girls*, versus the complementary set, *boys*, even with pluralization of the class *boys*, he was scored as *pre-complementation*.

Logical Complementation: Complex Set

The complementation operation is identical in this extended set case to the simple complementation operation above (i.e., the operation itself is not more complex). The set upon which the operation must work is wider in scope however. Thus in this case the child's base classification is (*big/little*, *boys/girls*). He is then given a *big bear*, i.e, one element from an *animals* set complementary to the above *people* set. The procedure, then, is the same as that in the *simple* situation. The child is given *two* more *big bears* and asked for "another way", if necessary—*one little bear* and then *two little bears* and asked for another way. Finally, the experimenter removed all and re-requested classification.

Testing then continued with addition of another negative subset, the *monkeys*, in the same gradual way. (First, *one big monkey*; *two* more *big monkeys*; *three little monkeys*. The child was then asked to reclassify and then the experimenter removed all dolls and requested classification.) Thus on complex complementation, the subject was given another class and another set of items on which to succeed the *animals/people* complementation. At the completion of this testing the subject was handling the full set used in linguistic testing, and the number of classes and of elements was equivalent in both sets (*animals/people*).

Vicariance: Simple Set

Given a full multiplicative set characterized by two 2-valued dimensions (AB, AB', $A'B$, $A'B'$) two dichotomous classifications are possible: (1) $A/A' \to AB$, $AB'/A'B$, $A'B'$, and (2) $B/B' \to AB$, $A'B/AB'$, $A'B'$. To demonstrate vicariance, subjects must, on the basis of one accurate dichotomy, provide another dichotomy. For example, they move from full classification of the given set by (*boys/girls*) to a new classification by (*big/little*). *Previcariance*—subjects may (or may not) achieve a first dichotomous classification, but they do not reclassify either by anticipation or after trial and error. *Functional vicariance*—children do not succeed by anticipation. They do succeed when the experimenter removes all dolls, thus removing the child's previous structure and allowing him by trial and error to begin again. The child is here asked to "Do it another way" and is faced with a new classification task. *Operational vicariance*—children anticipate vicariance. Here, while the child's previous classification remains standing, the experimenter asks, "Can you fix them another way?" The child himself decomposes and recomposes with regard to an anticipatory scheme for the alternate classification.

Vicariance: Complex Set

Given an extended set characterized by two subsets of two 2-valued dimensions (AB, AB', $A'B$, $A'B'$) and ($A''B$, $A''B'$, $A'''B$, $A'''B'$), in which A and A' define a *people* class and A'' and A''' define an *animals* class, the subjects may generate the following two dichotomous classifications: (1) $A,A'/A''A'''$, and (2) B/B'—in which B and B' represent the size dimension (*big/little*) as in the simple set.

Formally, the vicariance operation here is the same as that required for the simple set. The scope of the set upon which the operation must be performed is larger however, and the $A,A'/A''A'''$ dichotomy (or *animals/people* dichotomy) is a more general classification than the A/A' (or *boys/girls*) dichotomy required for the simple set.

References

Amidon, A., & Carey, P. Why five-year-olds cannot understand before and after. *Journal of Verbal Learning and Verbal Behavior*, 1972, **11**, 417–423.

Anderson, B. The short-term retention of active and passive sentences. Unpublished doctoral dissertation, Johns Hopkins University, 1963. Cited by H. H. Clark, Some structural properties of simple active and passive sentences. *Journal of Verbal Learning and Verbal Behavior*, 1965, **4**, 365–370.

Anisfeld, M. Disjunctive concepts. *Journal of General Psychology*, 1968, **78**, 223–228.

Anisfeld, M., & Klenbort, I. On the function of structural paraphrase: The view from the passive voice. *Psychological Bulletin*, 1973, **79**, 117–126.

Apostel, L. The relation between negation in linguistics, logic and psychology. A provisional conclusion. *Logique et Analyse*, 1972, **57/58**, 333–401.

Apostel, L., Mays, W., Morf, A., & Piaget, J. *Études d'épistémologie génétique*. Vol. IV. *Les liasons analytiques et synthétiques dans les comportements du sujet*. Paris: Presses Universitaires de France, 1957.

Ayer, A. J. *Language, truth and logic*. (2nd ed.) Hormonsworth, Eng.: Pelican Books, 1946.

Bandura, A. Vicarious processes: A case of no-trial learning. In L. Berkowitz (Ed.), *Advances in experimental social psychology*. Vol. 2. New York: Academic Press, 1965.

Barbut, M. *Mathematiques des sciences humaines*. Paris: Presses Universitaires de France, 1967.

Bar-Hillel, Y., & Eifermann, R. R. Who is afraid of disjunctive concepts? *Foundations of Language*, 1970, **6**, 463–472.

Battig, W. F., & Bourne, L. E., Jr. Concept identifications as a function of intra- and inter-dimensional variability. *Journal of Experimental Psychology*, 1961, **61**, 329–333.

Beilin, H. Perceptual-cognitive conflict in the development of an invariant area concept. *Journal of Experimental Child Psychology*, 1964, **1**, 208–226.

Beilin, H. Learning and operational convergence in logical thought development. *Journal of Experimental Child Psychology*, 1965, **2**, 317–339.

Beilin, H. Cognitive capacities of young children: A replication. *Science*, 1968, **162**, 920–921.

Beilin, H. Developmental stages and developmental processes. In D. R. Ross, M. P. Ford, & G. B. Flamer (Eds.), *Measurement and Piaget*. New York: McGraw-Hill, 1971, Pp. 172–188. (a)

Beilin, H. The training and acquisition of logical operations. In M. F. Rosskopf, L. P Steffe, & S. Taback (Eds.), *Piagetian cognitive-development research and mathematical education*. Washington, D. C.: National Council of Teachers of Mathematics, 1971. Pp. 81–124. (b)

Beilin, H. Development of the number lexicon in young children. Presented at the Developmental Psycholinguistics Conference, State University of New York at Buffalo, New York, 1971. (c)

Beilin, H. Development of the number lexicon in young children. In F. J. Monks, W. W. Hartup, & J. de Wit (Eds.), *Determinants of behavioral development*. New York: Academic Press, 1972.

Beilin, H., & Franklin, I. C. Logical operations in area and length measurement: age and training effects. *Child Development*, 1962, **33**, 607–618.

Beilin, H., & Gillman, I. S. Number language and number reversal learning. *Journal of Experimental Child Psychology*, 1967, **5**, 263–277.

Beilin, H., & Kagan, J. Pluralization rules and the conceptualization of number. *Developmental Psychology*, 1969, **1**, 697–706.

Beilin, H., & Spontak, G. Active-passive transformations and operational reversibility. Paper presented at the biennial meeting of the Society for Research in Child Development, Santa Monica, Calif., March 1969.

Benacerraf, P., & Putnam, H. (Eds.) *Philosophy of mathematics: Selected readings*. Englewood Cliffs, N. J.: Prentice-Hall, 1964.

Berko, J. The child's learning of English morphology. *Word*, 1958, **14**, 150–177.

Beth, E. W., & Piaget, J. *Mathematical epistemology and psychology*. Dordrecht, Neth.: Reidel Publ., 1966.

Bever, T. G. The cognitive basis for linguistic structures. In J. R. Hayes (Ed.), *Cognition and the development of language*. New York: Wiley, 1970. Pp. 279–362.

Bever, T. G., Mehler, J., & Epstein, J. What children do in spite of what they know. *Science*, 1968, **162**, 921–924.

Bierwisch, M. Semantics. In J. Lyons (Ed.), *New horizons in linguistics*. London, Eng.: Penguin Books, 1970, Pp. 166–184.

Bjonerud, C. E. Arithmetic concepts possessed by the pre-school child. *Arithmetic Teacher*, 1960, **7**, 347–350.

Bloom, L. *Language development: Form and function in emerging grammars*. Cambridge, Mass.: MIT Press, 1970.

Bloom, L. *One word at a time: The use of single-word utterances before syntax*. The Hague: Mouton, 1973.

Bloom, L. Talking, understanding and thinking. In R. Schiefelbusch & L. Lloyd (Eds.) *Language perspective—acquisition, retardation, and intervention*. Baltimore: University Park Press, 1974.

Bloom, L., Hood, L., & Lightbown, P. Imitation in language development. If, when and why. *Cognitive Psychology*, 1974, **6**, 380–420.

Boole, G. *An investigation of the laws of thought*. New York: Dover, 1958. (Original edition: 1854.)

Bourne, L. E., Jr. *Human conceptual behavior*. Boston: Allyn & Bacon, 1966.

Bourne, L. E., Jr. Knowing and using concepts. *Psychological Review*, 1970, **77**, 546–556.

Bourne, L. E., Jr. Learning, development and application of logico-conceptual skills.

Program on Concept Learning, Report No. 28, Institute for the Study of Intellectual Behavior, University of Colorado, 1972.

Bourne, L. E., Jr. & Guy, D. E. Learning conceptual rules. II : The role of positive and negative instances. *Journal of Experimental Psychology*, 1968, **77**, 488–494.

Bourne, L. E., Jr., & O'Banion, K. Conceptual rule learning and chronological age. *Developmental Psychology*, 1971, **5**, 525–534.

Bowerman, H. *Early syntactic development*. London & New York : Cambridge University Press, 1973.

Braine, M. D. S. The ontogeny of certain logical operations : Piaget's formulation examined by non-verbal methods. *Psychological Monographs*, 1959, **73** (5, Whole No. 475).

Braine, M. D. S. On learning the grammatical order of words. *Psychological Review*, 1963, **70**, 323–348.

Brown, R. *Psycholinguistics*. New York : Free Press, 1970.

Brown, R. Development of the first language in the human species. *American Psychologist*, 1973, **28**, 97–106. (a)

Brown, R. *A first language: The early stages*. Cambridge, Mass.: Harvard University Press, 1973. (b)

Brown, R., & Bellugi, U. Three processes in the child's acquisition of syntax. *Harvard Educational Review*, 1964, **34**, 133–151.

Brown, R., & Berko, J. Word association and the acquisition of grammar. *Child Development*, 1960, **31**, 1–14.

Brown, R., & Fraser, C. The acquisition of syntax. In C. N. Cofer & B. S. Musgrave (Eds.), *Verbal behavior and learning: Problems and processes*. New York : McGraw-Hill, 1963.

Brown, R., & Hanlon, C. Derivational complexity and order of acquisition in child speech. In J. R. Hayes (Ed.), *Cognition and the development of language*. New York : Wiley. 1970.

Brownell, W. A. Arithmetic in grades I and II. *Duke University Research Studies in Education*, 1941, No. 6.

Bruner, J. S., Goodnow, J. J., & Austin, G. A. *A study of thinking*. New York : Wiley, 1956.

Bruner, J. S., Olver, R. R., & Greenfield, P. M. (Eds.) *Studies in cognitive growth*. New York : Wiley, 1966.

Buckingham, B. R., & MacLatchy, J. H. Number abilities of children when they enter grade one. *Yearbook of the National Society for the Study of Education*, 1930, **29**, 473–524.

Buswell, G. T., & John, L. The vocabulary of arithmetic. *Supplementary Educational Monographs*, 1931, No. 38.

Bynum, T. W., Thomas, J. A., & Weitz, L. J. Truth-functional logic in formal operational thinking : Inhelder and Piaget's evidence. *Developmental Psychology*, 1972, **7**, 129–132.

Caprez, G., Sinclair, H., & Studer, B. Entwicklung der passivform im Schweizer-deutschen. *Archives de Psychologie*, 1971, **41** (161), 23–52.

Carroll, J. B. (Ed.) *Language, thought and reality: Selected writings of Benjamin L. Whorf*. Cambridge, Mass.: MIT Press, 1956.

Carroll, J. B. Process and content in psycholinguistics. In R. Glaser (Ed.), *Current trends in the description and analysis of behavior*. Pittsburgh : Pittsburgh University Press, 1958, Pp. 175–200.

Caws, P. The functions of definition in science. *Philosophy of Science*, 1959, **26**, 201–228.

Chafe, W. L. *Meaning and the structure of language*. Chicago : University of Chicago Press, 1970.

Chase, W. G., & Clark, H. H. Mental operations in the comparison of sentences and pictures. In L. Gregg (Ed.), *Cognition in learning and memory*. New York: Wiley, 1972, Pp. 205–251.

Chomsky, C. *The acquisition of syntax in children from 5 to 10*. Cambridge, Mass.: MIT Press, 1969.

Chomsky, N. *Syntactic structures*. The Hague: Mouton, 1957.

Chomsky, N. Review of B. F. Skinner, *Verbal behavior. Language*, 1959, **35**, 26–58.

Chomsky, N. On the notion "rule of grammar." In J. A. Fodor & J. J. Katz (Eds.), *The structure of language*. Englewood Cliffs, N. J.: Prentice-Hall, 1964.

Chomsky, N. *Aspects of the theory of syntax*. Cambridge, Mass.: MIT Press, 1965.

Chomsky, N. The formal nature of language. In E. H. Lenneberg, *Biological foundations of language*. New York: Wiley, 1967, Pp. 397–442.

Chomsky, N. *Language and mind*. New York: Harcourt, 1968.

Chomsky, N. Deep structure, surface structure, and semantic interpretation. In D. D. Steinberg & L. A. Jakobovits (Eds.), *Semantics: An interdisciplinary reader in philosophy, linguistics and psychology*. London & New York: Cambridge University Press, 1971, Pp. 183–216.

Chomsky, N. *Studies on semantics in generative grammar*. The Hague: Mouton, 1972.

Chomsky, N., & Miller, G. A. Introduction to the formal analysis of natural languages. In R. D. Luce, R. R. Bush, & E. Galanter (Eds.), *Handbook of mathematical psychology*. Vol. II. New York: Wiley, 1963, Pp. 269–321.

Churchman, C. W. *Elements of logic and formal science*. New York: Lippincott, 1940.

Cibrowski, T., & Cole, M. A cross-cultural study of conjunctive and disjunctive concept learning. *Child Development*, 1972, **43**, 774–789.

Clark, E. V. How young children describe events in time. In G. B. Flores D'Arcais & W. J. M. Levelt (Eds.), *Advances in psycholinguistics*. New York: American Elsevier, 1970, Pp. 275–284.

Clark, E. V. On the acquisition of the meaning of *before* and *after. Journal of Verbal Learning and Verbal Behavior*, 1971, **10**, 266–275.

Clark, H. H. Some structural properties of simple active and passive sentences. *Journal of Verbal Learning and Verbal Behavior*, 1965, **4**, 365–370.

Clark, H. H. Comprehending comparatives. In G. B. Flores D'Arcais & W. J. M. Levelt (Eds.), *Advances in psycholinguistics*. New York: American Elsevier, 1970, Pp. 294–306. (a)

Clark, H. H. The primitive nature of children's relational concepts. In J. R. Hayes (Ed.), *Cognition and the development of language*. New York: Wiley, 1970, Pp. 269–278. (b)

Clark, H. H. Semantics and comprehension. In T. A. Seboek (Ed.), *Current trends in linguistics*. Vol. 12: *Linguistics and adjacent arts and sciences*. The Hague: Mouton, 1973.

Clark, H. H., & Chase, W. G. On the process of comparing sentences against pictures. *Cognitive Psychology*, 1972, **3**, 472–517.

Clay, M. M. Sentence repetition: Elicited imitation of a controlled set of syntactic structures by four language groups. *Monographs of the Society for Research in Child Development*, 1971, **36** (3, Whole No. 143).

Cole, M., Gay, J., & Glick, J. A. Some experimental studies of Kpelle quantitative behavior. *Psychonomic Monograph Supplements*, 1968, **2** (10, Whole No. 26).

Cole, M., Gay, J., Glick, J. A., & Sharp, D. W. *The cultural context of learning and thinking*. New York: Basic Books, 1971.

Conant, M. B., & Trabasso, T. Conjunctive and disjunctive concept formation under equal-information conditions. *Journal of Experimental Psychology*, 1964, **67**, 250–255.

Cooley, W. W., & Lohnes, P. R. *Multivariate procedures for the behavioral sciences.* (2nd ed.) New York: Wiley, 1971.

Copi, I. M. *Introduction to logic.* (3rd ed.) London: Macmillan, 1968.

Cromer, R. F. The development of temporal reference during the acqusition of language. Unpublished doctoral dissertation, Harvard University, 1968.

Cromer, R. F. The development of the ability to decenter in time. *British Journal of Psychology,* 1971, **62**, 353–365.

Dantzig, T. *Number, the language of science.* New York: Macmillan, 1954.

de Groot, A. W. Subject-predicate analysis. *Lingua,* 1957, **6**, 309–310.

de Laguna, G. *Speech: Its function and development.* New Haven, Conn.: Yale University Press, 1927.

de Villiers, P. A., & de Villiers, J. G. Early judgements of semantic and syntactic acceptibility by children. *Journal of Psycholinguistic Research,* 1972, **1**, 299–310.

Dik, S. C. *Coordination.* Amsterdam: North-Holland Publ., 1968.

Dingwall, W. O. (Ed.) *A survey of linguistic science.* College Park, Md.: Linguistics Program, University of Maryland, 1971.

Dingwall, W. O., & Tuniks, G. Government and concord in Russian: A study in developmental psycholinguistics. In B. Kachru, R. B. Rees, Y. Malkiel, & S. Saporta (Eds.), *Issues in linguistics: Papers in honor of Henry and Renee Kahane.* Urbana, Ill.: University of Illinois Press, 1973.

DiVesta, F. J., & Walls, R. T. Rule and attribute identification in children's attainment of disjunctive and conjunctive concepts. *Journal of Experimental Psychology,* 1969, **80**, 498–504.

Donaldson, M. Developmental aspects of performance with negatives. In G. B. Flores D'Arcais & W. J. M. Levelt (Eds.), *Advances in psycholinguistics.* New York: American Elsevier, 1970, Pp, 397–410.

Donaldson, M., & Balfour, G. Less is more: A study of language comprehension in children. *British Journal of Psychology,* 1968, **59**, 461–471.

Dore, J. The development of speech acts. Unpublished doctoral dissertation, City University of New York, 1973.

Dougherty, R. C. A grammar of coordinate conjoined structures, I. *Language,* 1970, **46**, 850–898.

Dougherty, R. C. A grammar of coordinate conjoined structures, II. *Language,* 1971, **47**, 298–339.

Eifermann, R. A., & Steinitz, R. A comparison of conjunctive and disjunctive concept identification. *Journal of General Psychology,* 1971, **85**, 29–37.

Eimas, P. D., Siqueland, E. R., Jusczyk, P., & Vigorito, J. Speech perception in infants. *Science,* 1971, **171**, 303–306.

Elkonin, D. B. Development of speech. In A. V. Zaporozhets & D. B. Elkonin (Eds.), *The psychology of preschool children.* Cambridge, Mass.: MIT Press, 1971. Pp. 111–185. (Original Russian version: 1964.)

Feldman, S. S. *Children's understanding of negation as a logical operation in a classification task.* (Doctoral dissertation, Stanford University) Ann Arbor, Mich.: University Microfilms, 1968. No. 69–219.

Feldman, S. S. Children's understanding of negation as a logical operation. *Genetic Psychology Monographs,* 1972, **85**, 3–49.

Ferreiro, E. *Les relations temporelles dans le language de l'enfant.* Geneva: Librairie Droz, 1971.

Ferreiro, E., & Sinclair, H. Temporal relations in language. *International Journal of Psychology,* 1971, **6**, 39–47.

Fillenbaum, S. On coping with ordered and unordered conjunctive sentences. *Journal of Experimental Psychology*, 1971, **87**, 93–98.

Fillenbaum, S., & Rapoport, A. *Structures in the subjective lexicon*. New York : Academic Press, 1971.

Fillmore, C. J. The case for case. In E. Bach & R. T. Harms (Eds.), *Universals in linguistic theory*. New York : Holt, 1968, Pp. 1–88. (a)

Fillmore, C. J. Types of lexical information. In D. D. Steinberg & L. A. Jakobovits (Eds.). *Semantics: An inderdisciplinary reader in philosophy, linguistics and psychology*. London & New York : Cambridge University Press, 1971, Pp. 370–392.

Fodor, J. A., & Garrett, M. Some reflections on competence and performance. In J. Lyons & R. J. Wales (Eds.), *Psycholinguistic papers*. Edinburgh : Edinburgh University Press, 1966, Pp. 135–179.

Fodor, J. A., & Garrett, M. Some syntactic determinants of sentential complexity. *Perception & Psychophysics*, 1967, **2**(7), 289–296.

Fraser, C., Bellugi, U., & Brown, R. Control of grammar in imitation, comprehension and production. *Journal of Verbal Learning and Verbal Behavior*, 1963, **2**, 121–135.

Furth, H. G. Linguistic deficiency and thinking : Research with deaf subjects 1964–9. *Psychological Bulletin*, 1971, **76**, 58–72.

Furth, H. G., & Youniss, J. The influence of language and experience on discovery and use of logical symbols. *British Journal of Psychology*, 1965, **56**, 381–390.

Furth, H. G., Youniss, J., & Ross, B. M. Children's utilization of logical symbols : an interpretation of conceptual behavior based on Piagetian theory. *Developmental Psychology*, 1970, **3**, 36–57.

Gaer, E. P. Children's understanding and production of sentences. *Journal of Verbal Learning and Verbal Behavior*, 1969, **8**, 289–294.

Galperin, P. Y. A. A method, facts and theories in the psychology of mental action and concept formation. In Symposium 24, Concept formation and "inner action." *International Congress of Psychology, 18th, Moscow*, 1966, 48–59.

Garrett, M., & Fodor, J. A. Psychological theories and linguistic constructs. In T. R. Dixon & D. L. Horton (Eds.), *Verbal behavior and general behavior theory*. Englewood Cliffs, N. J., : Prentice-Hall, 1968, Pp. 451–477.

Geis, M. L., & Zwicky, A. M. On invited inferences. *Linguistic Inquiry*, 1971, **2**, 561–566.

Gelman, R. Conservation acquisition : A problem of learning to attend to relevant attributes. *Journal of Experimental Child Psychology*, 1969, **7**, 67–87.

Gleitman, L. R. Coordinating conjunctions in English. In D. A. Reibel & S. A. Schane (Eds.), *Modern studies in English*. Englewood Cliffs, N. J. : Prentice-Hall, 1969, Pp. 80–112.

Goldman-Eisler, F., & Cohen, M. Is N, P, and PN difficulty a valid criterion of transformational operations? *Journal of Verbal Learning and Verbal Behavior*, 1970, **9**, 161–166.

Goodman, N. *Languages of art: An approach to a theory of symbols*. New York : Bobbs-Merrill, 1968.

Gough, P. B. Grammatical transformations and speed of understanding. *Journal of Verbal Learning and Verbal Behavior*, 1965, **4**, 107–111.

Gough, P. B. The verification of sentences : The effects of delay of evidence and sentence length. *Journal of Verbal Learning and Verbal Behavior*, 1966, **5**, 492–496.

Grant, A. An analysis of the number knowledge of first-grade pupils according to levels of intelligence. *Journal of Experimental Education*, 1938, **7**, 63–66.

Greenfield, P. M., Smith, J. H., & Laufer, B. Communication and the beginnings of language : The development of semantic structure in one-word speech and beyond. Unpublished manuscript, Harvard University, 1972.

Griffiths, J. A., Shantz, C. A., & Sigel, I. E. A methodological problem in conservation studies: The use of relational terms. *Child Development*, 1967, **38**, 841–848.

Grize, J.-B. Historique, logique des classes et des propositions. Logiques des predicats. Logiques modales. In J. Piaget (Ed.), *Logique and connaissance scientifique*. Paris: Editions Gallimard, 1967, Pp. 135–289.

Gumenik, W. E., & Dolinsky, R. Connotative meaning of sentence subjects as a function of verb and object meaning under different grammatical transformations. *Journal of Verbal Learning and Verbal Behavior*, 1969, **8**, 653–657.

Harker, W. H. Children's number concepts: Ordination and cardination. Unpublished master's thesis, Queens University, Kingston, Canada, 1960.

Harris, R. *Synonymy and linguistic analysis*. Oxford: Blackwell, 1973.

Hatano, G. Understanding and the use of logical connectives. Paper presented at the biennial meeting of the Society for Research in Child Development, Philadelphia, March 1973.

Haygood, R. C., & Bourne, L. E., Jr. Attribute- and rule-learning aspects of conceptual behavior. *Psychological Review*, 1965, **72**, 175–195.

Hayhurst, H. Some errors of young children in producing passive sentences. *Journal of Verbal Learning and Verbal Behavior*, 1967, **6**, 634–639.

Henle, M. On the relation between logic and thinking. *Psychological Review*, 1962, **69**, 366–378.

Herriot, P. The comprehension of time in young children. *Child Development*, 1969, **40**, 103–110.

Hill, S. A. *A study of the logical abilities of children*. (Doctoral dissertation, Stanford University) Ann Arbor, Mich.: University Microfilms, 1961. No. 61–1229.

Holmes, E. E. What do first-grade children know about number? *Elementary School Journal*, 1963, **63**, 397–403.

Hornby, P. A. Surface structure and topic-comment distinction: A developmental study. *Child Development*, 1971, **42**, 1975–1988.

Hornby, P. A., & Hass, W. A. Use of contrastive stress by preschool children. *Journal of Speech and Hearing Research*, 1970, **3**, 395–399.

Hornby, P. A., Hass, W. A., & Feldman, C. A. A developmental analysis of the "psychological" subject and predicate of the sentence. *Language and Speech*, 1970, **13**, 182–193.

Hovland, C. I., & Weiss, W. Transmission of information concerning concepts through positive and negative instances. *Journal of Experimental Psychology*, 1953, **45**, 175–182.

Howe, E. S. Passive transformation, cognitive imbalance, and evaluative meaning. *Journal of Verbal Learning and Verbal Behavior*, 1970, **9**, 171–175.

Hsu, T. C., & Feldt, L. S. The effect of limitations on the number of criterion score values on the significance level of the F-test. *American Educational Research Journal*, 1969, **6**, 515–527.

Huff, R. L. Resolution of subject number and verb number in sentence comprehension by children aged five to seven. *Dissertation Abstracts International*, 1972, **33**(4), 1795B–1796B.

Hunt, E. B. *Concept learning: An information processing problem*. New York: Wiley, 1962.

Hunt, E. B., & Hovland, C. I. Order of consideration of different types of concepts. *Journal of Experimental Psychology*, 1960, **59**, 220–225.

Hunt, E. B., Marin, J., & Stone, P. J. *Experiments in induction*. New York: Academic Press, 1966.

Huttenlocher, J., Eisenberg, K., & Strauss, S. Comprehension: Relation between perceived actor and logical subject. *Journal of Verbal Learning and Verbal Behavior*, 1968, **7**, 527–530.

Inhelder, B., & Piaget, J. *The growth of logical thinking from childhood to adolescence.* New York: Basic Books, 1958.

Inhelder, B., & Piaget, J. *The early growth of logic in the child.* London: Routledge & Kegan Paul, 1964. (Original French edition: 1959.)

Jacobs, R. A., & Rosenbaum, P. S. *English transformational grammar.* Boston: Ginn (Blaisdell), 1968.

Jespersen, O. *The philosophy of grammar.* London: Allen & Unwin, 1924.

Jespersen, O. *Essentials of English grammar.* University, Ala.: University of Alabama Press, 1964. (Original edition: 1933.)

Johnson, M. G. Syntactic position and rated meaning. *Journal of Verbal Learning and Verbal Behaviour*, 1967, **6**, 240–246.

Johnson-Laird, P. M. The choice of the passive voice in a communicative task. *British Journal of Psychology*, 1968, **59**, 7–15 .(a)

Johnson-Laird, P. M. The interpretation of the passive voice. *Quarterly Journal of Experimental Psychology*, 1968, **20**, 69–73. (b)

Johnson-Laird, P. M. "&." *Journal of Linguistics*, 1969, **6**, 111–114.

Jones, P. A. Formal operational reasoning and the rise of tentative statements. *Cognitive Psychology*, 1972, **3**, 467–471.

Joos, M. *The English verb: Form and meaning.* Madison, Wis.: University of Wisconsin Press, 1964.

Kaplan, E. I. The role of intonation in the acquisition of language. Doctoral dissertation, Cornell University, 1969.

Katz, E. W., & Brent, S. B. Understanding connectives. *Journal of Verbal Learning and Verbal Behavior*, 1968, **7**, 501–509.

Katz, J. J. Some remarks on Quine on analyticity. *Journal of Philosophy*, 1967, **64**, 36–52.

Katz, J. J. Generative semantics is interpretative semantics. *Linguistic Inquiry*, 1971, **2**, 313–331.

Katz, J. J. *Semantic theory.* New York: Harper, 1972.

Katz, J. J., & Postal, P. M. *An integrated theory of linguistic descriptions.* Cambridge, Mass., MIT Press, 1964.

Keenan, E. L. On semantically based grammar. *Linguistic Inquiry*, 1972, **3**, 413–461.

Keeney, T. J., & Smith, N. D. Young children's imitation and comprehension of sentential singularity and plurality. *Language and Speech*, 1971, **14**, 372–383.

Keeney, T. J., & Wolfe, J. The acquisition of agreement in English. *Journal of Verbal Learning and Verbal Behavior*, 1972, **11**, 698–705.

Kemp, J. *The philosophy of Kant.* London & New York: Oxford University Press, 1968.

Kessen, W., Haith, M. M., & Salapatek, P. H. Infancy. In P. H. Mussen (Ed.), *Carmichael's manual of child psychology.* (3rd ed.) Vol. I. New York: Wiley, 1970, Pp. 287–446.

King, W. L. Learning and utilization of conjunctive and disjunctive classification rules: A developmental study. *Journal of Experimental Child Psychology*, 1966, **4**, 217–231.

King, W. L., & Holt, J. R. Conjunctive and disjunctive rule learning as a function of age and forced verbalization. *Journal of Experimental Child Psychology*, 1970, **10**, 100–111.

Lakoff, G. Linguistics and natural logic. *Synthese*, 1970, **22**, 151–271. (a)

Lakoff, G. Repartee, or a reply to "negation, conjunction and quantifiers." *Foundations of Language*, 1970, **6**, 389–422. (b)

Lakoff, G. On generative semantics. In D. D. Steinberg & L. A. Jakobovitz (Eds.), *Semantics: An interdisciplinary reader in philosophy, linguistics and psychology.*

London & New York: Cambridge University Press, 1971, Pp. 232–296.

Lakoff, G., & Peters, S. Phrasal conjunction and symmetric predicates. In D. A. Reibel & S. A. Schane (Eds.), *Modern studies in English*. Englewood Cliffs, N. J.: Prentice-Hall, 1969, Pp. 113–142.

Lakoff, R. If's, and's, and but's about conjunctions. In C. J. Fillmore & D. T. Langendoen (Eds.), *Studies in linguistic semantics*. New York: Holt, 1971, Pp. 115–149.

Langendoen, D. T. *The study of syntax*. New York: Holt, 1969.

Langendoen, D. T. *Essentials of English grammar*. New York: Holt, 1970.

Lees, R. B. *The grammar of English nominalizations*. The Hague: Mouton, 1963.

Lenneberg, E. H. Of language knowledge, apes and brains. *Journal of Psycholinguistic Research*, 1971, **1**, 1–29.

Lewis, M. M. Infant speech, a study of the beginnings of language. New York: Harcourt, 1936.

Lippman, M. Z. Correlates of contrast word associations: Developmental trends. *Journal of Verbal Learning and Verbal Behavior*, 1971, **10**, 392–399.

Lovell, K., & Dixon, E. M. The growth of the control of grammar in imitation, comprehension and production. *Journal of Child Psychology and Psychiatry*, 1967, **8**, 31–39.

Lovell, K., & Slater, A. The growth of the concept of time: A comparative study. *Journal of Child Psychology and Psychiatry*, 1960, **1**, 179–190.

Lust, B. On the notion "logical form": The intersection of formal systems. Unpublished manuscript, Developmental Psychology Program, City University of New York, 1971.

Lyons, J. *Introduction to theoretical linguistics*. London & New York: Cambridge University Press, 1968.

MacDonald, R. R. Prepositions of time in English. *Languages and Linguistics Working Papers*, 1972, No. 4, 94–110.

MacLatchy, J. H. A phase of first grade readiness. *Educational Research Bulletin*, 1931, **10**, 377–380.

MacLatchy, J. H. Number abilities of first-grade children. *Childhood Education*, 1935, **11**, 344–347.

Matalon, B. Etude genetique de l'implication. *Etudes d'empistemologie genetique*. Vol. XVI. *Implication, formalisation et logique naturelle*. Paris: Presses Universitaires de France, 1962. Pp. 69–95.

McCarthy, D. Language development in children. In L. Carmichael (Ed.), *Manual of child psychology*. (2nd ed.) New York: Wiley, 1954, Pp. 492–630.

McCawley, J. D. Concerning the base component of a transformational grammar. *Foundations of Language*, 1968, **4**, 243–269. (a)

McCawley, J. D. The role of semantics in a grammar. In E. Bach & R. I. Harms (Eds.), *Universals in linguistic theory*. New York: Holt, 1968, Pp. 125–169. (b)

McCawley, J. D. Interpretative semantics meets Frankenstein. *Foundations of Language*, 1971, **7**, 285–296. (a)

McCawley, J. D. Where do noun phrases come from? In D. D. Steinberg & L. A. Jakobovitz (Eds.), *Semantics: An interdisciplinary reader in philosophy, linguistics and psychology*. London & New York: Cambridge University Press, 1971, Pp. 217–231. (b)

McMahon, E. Grammatical analysis as part of understanding. Unpublished doctoral dissertation, Harvard University, 1963. Cited by J. A. Fodor & M. Garrett, Some reflections on competence and performance. In J. Lyons & R. J. Wales (Eds.), *Psycholinguistic papers*. Edinburgh: Edinburgh University Press, 1966, Pp. 135–179.

McNeill, D. A study of word association. *Journal of Verbal Learning and Verbal Behavior*, 1966, **5**, 548–557.

McNeill, D. *The acquisition of language: The study of developmental psycholinguistics.* New York: Harper, 1970.

Mehler, J. Some effects of grammatical transformations on the recall of English sentences. *Journal of Verbal Learning and Verbal Behavior,* 1963, **2**, 346–351.

Mehler, J., & Bever, T. G. Cognitive capacities of very young children. *Science,* 1967, **158**, 141–142.

Menninger, K. W. *Number words and number symbols: A cultural history of numbers.* Cambridge, Mass.: MIT Press, 1969. (English translation: Revised German edition, 1958.)

Menyuk, P. *Sentences children use.* Cambridge, Mass.: MIT Press, 1969.

Menyuk, P. *The acquisition and development of language.* Englewood Cliffs, N. J.. Prentice-Hall, 1971.

Miller, G. A. Some psychological studies of grammar. *American Psychologist,* 1962, **17**, 748–762.

Miller, G. A., & Chomsky, N. Finitary models of language users. In R. D. Luce, R. R. Bush, & E. Galanter (Eds.), *Handbook of mathematical psychology.* Vol. 2. New York: Wiley, 1963, Pp. 419–491.

Miller, G. A., & McKean, K. A chromometric study of some relations between sentences. *Quarterly Journal of Experimental Psychology,* 1964, **16**, 297–308.

Miller, W., & Ervin, S. The development of grammar in child language. *Monographs of the Society for Research in Child Development,* 1964, **29**, 9–34.

Moffitt, A. R. Consonant cue perception by twenty- to twenty-four-week-old infants. *Child Development,* 1971, **42**, 717–731.

Moravcsik, E. A. On disjunctive connectives. Paper presented at the meeting of the Linguistic Society of America, Washington, D. C., December 1970.

Moravcsik, E. A. Working Papers on Language Universals, No. 5, Language Universals Project, Committee on Linguistics, Stanford University, May 1971.

Morris, V. A., Rankine, F. C., & Reber, A. S. Sentence comprehension, grammatical transformations and response availability. *Journal of Verbal Learning and Verbal Behavior,* 1967, **7**, 1113–1115.

Naess, A. L'emploi de la disjonction chez les adolescents. In E. A. Beth, J. B. Grize, R. Martin, B. Matalon, A. Naess, & J. Piaget. *Etudes d'épistémologie génétique.* Vol. XVI. *Implication, formalisation et logique naturelle.* Paris: Presses Universitaires de France, 1962. Pp. 151–164.

Neimark, E. D. Development of comprehension of logical connectives: understanding of "or." *Psychonomic Science,* 1970, **21**, 217–219.

Neimark, E. D., & Slotnick, N. S. Development of the understanding of logical connectives. *Journal of Educational Psychology,* 1970, **61**, 451–460.

Neisser, U., & Weene, P. Hierarchies in concept attainment. *Journal of Experimental Psychology,* 1962, **64**, 640–645.

Nitta, N., & Nagano, S. Basic logical operations and their verbal expressions. *Research Bulletin of the National Institute for Educational Research, Tokyo,* 1966, No. 7.

Novinski, L. S. Recognition memory in children for semantic versus syntactic information. Unpublished doctoral dissertation, University of California, Berkeley, 1968.

O'Brien, T. C. Logical thinking in adolescents. *Educational Studies in Mathematics,* 1972, **4**, 401–428.

O'Brien, T. C., & Shapiro, B. J. The development of logical thinking in children. *American Educational Research Journal,* 1968, **5**, 531–542.

O'Brien, T. C., Shapiro, B. J., & Reali, N. C. Logical thinking-language and context. *Educational Studies in Mathematics,* 1971, **4**, 201–219.

Olson, D. R. Language use for communicating, instructing and thinking. Paper prepared for C.O.B.R.E. Workshop on Language Comprehension and the Acquisition of Knowledge, Rougemont, N. C., March 1971.

Olson, D. R., & Filby, N. On the comprehension of active and passive sentences. *Cognitive Psychology*, 1972, **3**, 361–381.

Omar, M. K. The acquisition of Egyptian Arabic as a native language. Unpublished doctoral dissertation, Georgetown University, 1970.

Palermo, D. S. More about less: A study of language comprehension. *Journal of Verbal Learning and Verbal Behavior*, 1973, **12**, 211–221.

Palermo, D. S., & Molfese, D. L. Language acquisition from age five onward. *Psychological Bulletin*, 1972, **78**, 409–428.

Papert, S. Sur la logique piagetienne. In J. Piaget (Ed.), *Etudes d'épistémologie génétique*. Vol. XV. *La filiation des structures*. Paris: Presses Universitaires de France, 1963. Pp. 107–129.

Paris, S. G. Comprehension of language connectives and propositional logical relationships. *Journal of Experimental Child Psychology*. 1973, **16**, 278–291.

Peel, E. A. A method for investigating children's understanding of certain logical connectives used in binary propositional thinking. *British Journal of Mathematical and Statistical Psychology*, 1967, **20**, 81–92.

Perlmutter, D. M. A note on syntactic and semantic number in English. *Linguistic Inquiry*, 1972, **3**, 243–246.

Piaget, J. *Judgment and reasoning in the child*. London: Routledge & Kegan Paul, 1928.

Piaget, J. *Psychology of intelligence*. London: Routledge & Kegan Paul, 1950. (Original French edition: 1947.)

Piaget, J. *The child's conception of number*. London: Routledge & Kegan Paul, 1952. (Original French edition: 1941.)

Piaget, J. *Logic and psychology*. New York: Basic Books, 1957. (University of Manchester Press edition: 1953.)

Piaget, J. *Play, dreams and imitation in childhood*. New York: Norton, 1962. (Original edition: La formation du symbole, 1946.)

Piaget, J. Le langage et les opérations intellectuelles. In J. de Ajuriaguerra, F. Bresson, P. Fraisse, B. Inhelder, P. Oléron, & J. Piaget, *Problèmes de psycho-linguistique*. Paris: Presses Universitaires de France, 1963, Pp. 51–72. (a)

Piaget, J. Les travaux de l'anée 1959–60 et le cinquieme symposium (27 Juin—2 Juillet 1960) du Centre International d'Epistemologie Genetique. In P. Gréco, B. Inhelder, B. Matalon, & J. Piaget, *Études d'épistémologie génétique*. Vol. XVII. *La formation des raisonnements récurrentiels*. Paris: Presses Universitaires de France, 1963 Pp. 3–46. (b)

Piaget, J. Epistémologie de la logique. In J. Piaget (Ed.), *Logique et connaissance scientifique*. Paris: Editions Gallimard, 1967, Pp. 375–399.

Piaget, J. Conclusions generales. In J. Piaget, J.-B. Grize, A. Szeminska, & Vinh Bang, *Études d'épistémologie génétique*. Vol. XXIII. *Épistémologie et psychologie de la fonction*. Paris: Presses Universitaires de France, 1968, Pp. 198–235. (a)

Piaget, J. Explanation in psychology and psychophysiological parallelism. In J. Piaget, P. Fraisse, & M. Reuchlin, *Experimental psychology: Its scope and method*. I. *History and method*. New York: Basic Books, 1968, Pp. 153–192. (Orig. French edition: 1963.) (b)

Piaget, J. Quantification, conservation, and nativism. *Science*, 1968, **162**, 976–981. (c)

Piaget, J. *The child's conception of time*. London: Routledge & Kegan Paul, 1969. (Original French edition: 1927.)

Piaget, J. *L'épistemologie génétique*. Paris: Presses Universitaires de France, 1970.

Piaget, J. *Essai de logique opératoire*. Paris: Dunod, 1972. (Original edition: 1949.)

Piaget, J., & Inhelder, B. *Genèse des structures logiques elementaires*. Neuchatel: Delachaux et Niestle, 1967.

Piaget, J., & Inhelder, B. *Mental imagery in the child*. London: Routledge & Kegan Paul, 1971. (Original French edition: 1966.)

Popova, M. I. Grammatical elements of language in the speech of preschool children. In C. A. Ferguson & D. I. Slobin (Eds.), *Studies of child language development*. New York: Holt, 1973, Pp. 269–280.

Postal, P. M. On the surface verb "remind." In C. J. Fillmore & D. T. Langendoen (Eds.), *Studies in linguistic semantics*. New York: Holt, 1971.

Prentice, J. L. Response strength of single words as an influence in sentence behavior. *Journal of Verbal Learning and Verbal Behavior*, 1966, **5**, 429–433.

Prior, A. N. The runabout inference-ticket. In P. F. Strawson (Ed.), *Philosophical logic*. London & New York: Oxford University Press, 1967, Pp. 129–131.

Priore, A. Achievement by pupils entering the first grade. *Arithmetic Teacher*, 1957, **4**, 55–60.

Quine, W. V. O. *Word and object*. Cambridge, Mass.: MIT Press, 1960.

Quine, W. V. O. *From a logical point of view: 9 logico-philosophical essays*. Cambridge, Mass.: Harvard University Press, 1961.

Quine, W. V. O. *Elementary logic*. (rev. ed.) Cambridge, Mass.: Harvard University Press, 1966.

Quine, W. V. O. On a suggestion of Katz. *Journal of Philosophy*, 1967, **64**, 52–54.

Quine, W. V. O. *Methods of logic*. New York: Holt, Rinehart & Winston, 1972.

Reichenbach, H. *Elements of symbolic logic*. New York: Macmillan, 1947.

Ricciuti, H. N. Object grouping and selective ordering behavior in infants 12 to 24 months old. *Merrill-Palmer Quarterly*, 1965, **11**, 129–148.

Roberge, J. J., & Paulus, D. H. Developmental patterns for children's class and conditional reasoning abilities. *Developmental Psychology*, 1971, **4**, 191–200.

Russell, B. *An inquiry into meaning and truth*. London: Allen & Unwin, 1940. (Reprinted: 1966.)

Russell, N. M. Arithmetical concepts of children. *Journal of Educational Research*, 1936, **29**, 647–663.

Sachs, J. S. Recognition memory for syntactic and semantic concepts of connected discourse. *Perception & Psychophysics*, 1967, **2**(9), 437–442.

Sack, H. G. Semantic factors in children's judgments of active-passive synonymy. Unpublished doctoral dissertation, University of Maryland, 1973.

Sack, H. G., & Beilin, H. Meaning equivalence of active-passive and subject–object first cleft sentences. Presented at the Developmental Psycholinguistics Conference, State University of New York at Buffalo, New York, 1971.

Sanders, G. A. Some general grammatical processes in English. Unpublished doctoral dissertation, University of Indiana, 1967. (Mimeo.: University of Indiana Linguistics Club, 1968.)

Savin, H., & Perchonock, E. Grammatical structure and the immediate recall of English sentences. *Journal of Verbal Learning and Verbal Behavior*, 1965, **4**, 348–353. Cited by M. Garrett & J. A. Fodor, Psychological theories and linguistic constructs. In T. R. Dixon & D. L. Horton (Eds.), *Verbal behavior and general behavior theory*. Englewood Cliffs, N. J.: Prentice-Hall, 1968, Pp. 451–477.

Schaerlaekens, A. M. *The two-word sentence in child language development*. The Hague: Mouton, 1973.

Shanon, B. Interpretation of ungrammatical sentences. *Journal of Verbal Learning and Verbal Behavior*, 1973, **12**, 389–400.

Shapiro, B. J., & O'Brien, T. C. Quasi-child logics. *Educational Studies in Mathematics*, 1973, **5**, 181–184.

Shine, D., & Walsh, J. F. Developmental trends in the use of logical connectives. *Psychonomic Science*, 1971, **23**, 171–172.

Sicha, J. F. Counting and the natural numbers. *Philosophy of Science*, 1970, **37**, 405–416.

Sigel, S. *Nonparametric statistics for the behavioral sciences*. New York: McGraw-Hill, 1956.

Sinclair, A., Sinclair, H., & de Marcellus, O. Young children's comprehension and production of passive sentences. *Archives de Psychologie*, 1971, **41**(161), 1–22.

Sinclair-de-Zwart, H. Developmental psycholinguistics. In D. Elkind & J. H. Flavell (Eds.), *Studies in cognitive development: Essays in honor of Jean Piaget*. London & New York: Oxford University Press: 1969, Pp. 315–376.

Sinclair, H. Piaget's theory and language acquisition. In M. F. Rosskopf, L. P. Steffe, & S. Taback (Eds.), *Piagetian cognitive-development research and mathematical education*. Washington, D. C.: National Council of Teachers of Mathematics, 1971, Pp. 203–214. (a)

Sinclair, H. Sensorimotor action patterns as a condition for the acquisition of syntax. In R. Huxley & E. Ingram (Eds.), *Language acquisition: Models and methods*. New York: Academic Press, 1971, Pp. 121–135. (b)

Sinclair-de-Zwart, H. Language acquisition and cognitive development. In T. E. Moore (Ed.), *Cognitive development and the acquisition of language*. New York: Academic Press, 1973, Pp. 9–26.

Sinclair, H., & Bronckart, J. P. S.V.O. A linguistic universal? A study in developmental psycholinguistics. *Journal of Experimental Child Psychology*, 1972, **14**, 329–348.

Sinclair, H., & Ferriero, E. Comprehension, production et repetition des phrases au mode passif. *Archives de Psychologie*, 1970, **40**(160), 1–42.

Slobin, D. I. Grammatical transformations and sentence comprehension in childhood and adulthood. *Journal of Verbal Learning and Verbal Behavior*, 1966, **5**, 219–227.

Slobin, D. I. (Ed.) *A field manual for cross-cultural study of the acquisition of communicative competence*. Berkeley, Calif.: University of California, 1967.

Slobin, D. I. Imitation and grammatical development in children. In N. S. Endler, L. R. Boulter, & H. Osser (Eds.), *Contemporary issues in developmental psychology*. New York: Holt, 1968, Pp. 437–443. (a)

Slobin, D. I. Recall of full and truncated passives in connected discourse. *Journal of Verbal Learning and Verbal Behavior*, 1968, **7**, 876–881. (b)

Slobin, D. I. Developmental psycholinguistics. In W. O. Dingwall (Ed.), *A survey of linguistic science*. College Park, Md.: Linguistics Program, University of Maryland, 1971, Pp. 298–400.

Slobin, D. I., & Welsh, C. A. Elicited imitation as a research tool in developmental psycholinguistics. In C. A. Ferguson & D. I. Slobin (Eds.), *Studies in child language development*. New York: Holt, 1973, Pp. 485–497.

Smith, C. S. Ambiguous sentences with *and*. In D. A. Reibel & S. A. Schane (Eds.), *Modern studies in English*. Englewood Cliffs, N. J.: Prentice-Hall, 1969.

Smith, C. S. Paraphrase and performance. *Recherches Linguistique*, 1972, **1**, 35–45. (Publication of Universitee' de Paris-Vincennes, Department de Linguistique.)

Smith, C. S. Children's judging and production of paraphrases. Unpublished manuscript, University of Texas at Austin, 1973.

Smith, K. H., Coriell, A. S., & McMahon, L. E. The role of active and passive voice in answering questions. Unpublished manuscript, Bell Laboratories, 1971.

Smith, K. H., & McMahon, L. E. Understanding order information in sentences: Some recent work at Bell Laboratories. In G. B. Flores D'Arcais & W. J. M. Levelt (Eds.), *Advances in psycholinguistics*. New York: American Elsevier, 1970, Pp. 253–274.

Snow, C. E., & Rabinovitch, M. S. Conjunctive and disjunctive thinking in children. *Journal of Experimental Child Psychology*, 1969, **7**, 1–9.

Staal, J. F. Analyticity. *Foundations of Language*, 1966, **2**, 67–93.

Staal, J. F. "And." *Journal of Linguistics*, 1968, **4**, 79–81.

Steinberg, D. D. Analyticity, amphigory, and the semantic interpretation of sentences. *Journal of Verbal Learning and Verbal Behavior*, 1970, **9**, 37–51. (a)

Steinberg, D. D. Negation, analyticity, amphigory and the semantic interpretation of sentences. *Journal of Experimental Psychology*, 1970, **84**, 417–423. (b)

Sternberg, S. Memory-scanning : Mental processes revealed by reaction-time experiments. *American Scientist*, 1969, **57**, 421–457.

Stockwell, R. P., Schachter, P., & Partee, B. H. Integration of transformational theories of syntax. Command Systems Division, Electronic Systems Division, Air Force Systems Command, United States Air Force, L. G. Hanscom Field, Bedford, Mass., 1968.

Stockwell, R. P., Schachter, P., & Partee, B. H. *The major syntactic structures of English*. New York : Holt, 1973.

Strawson, P. F. *Introduction to logical theory*. London : Methuen, 1952.

Suppes, P. The semantics of children's language. *American Psychologist*, 1974, **29**, 103–114.

Suppes, P., & Feldman, S. S. Young children's comprehension of logical connectives. *Journal of Experimental Child Psychology*, 1971, **12**, 304–317.

Svartvik, J. *On voice in the English verb*. The Hague : Mouton, 1966.

Tannenbaum, P. H., & Williams, F. Generation of active and passive sentences as a function of subject or object focus. *Journal of Verbal Learning and Verbal Behavior*, 1968, **7**, 246–250. (a)

Tannenbaum, P. H., & Williams, F. Prompted word replacement in active and passive sentences. *Language and Speech*, 1968, **11**, 220–229. (b)

Taplin, J. E., Staudenmayer, H., & Taddonio, J. L. Developmental changes in conditional reasoning : Linguistic or logical. *Journal of Experimental Child Psychology*, 1974, **17**, 360–373.

Teplenkaya, K. M. The formation of logical structures in 6–7 year-old children. In Symposium 24, Concept formation and "inner action." *International Congress of Psychology, 18th, Moscow*, 1966, 115–120.

Trabasso, T. Mental operations in language comprehension. In R. O. Freedle & J. B. Carroll (Eds.) *Language comprehension and the acquisition of knowledge*. Washington, D. C. : Winston/Wiley, 1972, Pp. 113–137.

Trabasso, T., Rollins, H., & Shaughnessy, E. Storage and verification stages in processing concepts. *Cognitive Psychology*, 1971, **2**, 239–289.

Turner, E. A., & Rommetveit, R. The acquisition of sentence voice and reversibility. *Child Development*, 1967, **38**, 649–660. (a)

Turner, E. A., & Rommetveit, R. Experimental manipulation of the production of active and passive voice in children. *Language and Speech*, 1967, **10**, 169–180. (b)

Turner, E. A., & Rommetveit, R. Focus of attention in recall of active and passive sentences. *Journal of Verbal Learning and Verbal Behavior*, 1968, **7**, 543–548.

van Katwijk, A. A grammar of Dutch number names. *Foundations of Language*, 1965, **1**, 51–58.

Von Wright, G. H. And then. *Commentationes Physico-Mathematical*, 1966, **32**, 1–11.

Vygotsky, L. S. *Thought and language*. Cambridge, Mass. : MIT Press, 1962. (Original edition : 1934).

Wason, P. C. The processing of positive and negative information. *Quarterly Journal of Experimental Psychology*, 1959, **11**, 92–107.

Wason, P. C. Response to affirmative and negative binary statements. *British Journal of Psychology*, 1961, **52**, 133–142.

Wason, P. C. Reasoning about a rule. *Quarterly Journal of Experimental Psychology*, 1968, **20**, 273–281.

Wason, P. C. Psychological aspects of inference. In G. B. Flores D'Arcais & W. J. M. Levelt (Eds.), *Advances in psycholinguistics*. New York: American Elsevier, 1970, Pp. 344–346.

Wason, P. C. In real life negatives are false. *Logique et Analyse*, 1972, **57/58**, 17–38.

Wason, P. C., & Johnson-Laird, P. M. Proving a disjunctive rule. *Quarterly Journal of Experimental Psychology*, 1969, **21**, 14–20.

Wason, P. C., & Jones, S. Negatives: Denotation and connotation. *British Journal of Psychology*, 1963, **54**, 299–307.

Weil, J. The relationship between time conceptualization and time language in young children. Unpublished doctoral dissertation, City University of New York, 1970.

Weiner, S. L. On the development of *more* and *less*, Unpublished doctoral dissertation, Columbia University, 1971.

Weiner, S. L. On the development of *more* and *less*. *Journal of Experimental Child Psychology*, 1974, **17**, 271–287.

Weitz, L. J., Bynum, T. W., Thomas, J. A., & Steger, J. A. Piaget's system of sixteen binary operations: an empirical investigation. *Journal of Genetic Psychology*, 1973, **123**, 279–284.

Werner, H., & Kaplan, B. *Symbol formation*. New York: Wiley, 1963.

Weyl, H. *Philosophy of mathematics and natural science*. Princeton, N. J.: Princeton University Press, 1949. (Atheneum paperback edition: 1963.)

Winer, B. J. *Statistical principles in experimental design*. (2nd ed.) New York: McGraw-Hill, 1972.

Wohlwill, J. F. The place of structured experience in early cognitive development. *Interchange*, 1970, **1**(2), 13–27.

Wolff, P. H. The natural history of crying and other vocalizations in early infancy. In B. Foss (Ed.), *Determinants of infant behavior*. Vol. IV. London: Methuen, 1969.

Woody, C. The arithmetic background of young children. *Journal of Educational Research*, 1931, **25**, 188–201.

Wright, P. Transformations and the understanding of sentences. *Language and Speech*, 1969, **12**, 156–166.

Wright, P. Some observations on how people answer questions about sentences. *Journal of Verbal Learning and Verbal Behavior*, 1972, **11**, 188–195.

Youniss, J., & Furth, H. G. Attainment and transfer of logical connectives in children. *Journal of Educational Psychology*, 1964, **55**, 357–361.

Youniss, J., & Furth, H. G. Learning of logical connectives by adolescents with single and multiple instances. *Journal of Educational Psychology*, 1967, **58**, 222–230.

Youniss, J., Furth, H. G., & Ross, B. M. Logical symbol use in deaf and hearing children and adolescents. *Developmental Psychology*, 1971, **5**, 511–517.

Ziff, P. *Understanding understanding*. Ithaca, N. Y.: Cornell University Press, 1972.

Zimilies, H. The development of conservation and differentiation of number. *Monographs of the Society for Research in Child Development*, 1966, **31**(6), Whole No. 108.

Subject Index